Treasury of the True Dharma Eye

Dōgen's *Shōbōgenzō*

Treasury of the True Dharma Eye
Dōgen's *Shōbōgenzō*

Volume IV

The Seventy-five-Chapter Compilation

Part 4

Chapters 46–60

An annotated translation
by the Sōtō Zen Text Project

Sōtōshū Shūmuchō
Tokyo

University of Hawai'i Press
Honolulu

© 2023 by Sōtōshū Shūmuchō
The Administrative Headquarters of Sōtō Zen Buddhism
All rights reserved.
Printed in China
Treasury of the True Dharma Eye: Dōgen's *Shōbōgenzō*
Volume IV: The Seventy-five-Chapter Compilation, Part 4, Chapters 46–60
Published in Japan by Sōtōshū Shūmuchō, Tokyo
ISBN: 978-4-911061-00-8
Published for the rest of the world by University of Hawai'i Press, Honolulu

Library of Congress Cataloging-in-Publication Data

Names: Dōgen, 1200–1253, author. | Sōtō Zen Text Project, translator.

Title: Treasury of the true dharma eye : Dōgen's Shōbōgenzō / an annotated translation by the Sōtō Zen Text Project.

Other titles: Shōbō genzō. English

Description: Honolulu : University of Hawai'i Press, [2024] | Published in Japan by Sōtōshū Shūmuchō, 2023. | Includes bibliographical references and index. | Contents: v. 4. The seventy-five-chapter compilation, part 4, chapters 46–60

Identifiers: LCCN 2024004760 (print) | LCCN 2024004761 (ebook) | ISBN 9780824899172 (v. 1 ; paperback) | ISBN 9780824899189 (v. 2 ; paperback) | ISBN 9780824899196 (v. 3 ; paperback) | ISBN 9780824899202 (v. 4 ; paperback) | ISBN 9780824899219 (v. 5 ; paperback) | ISBN 9780824899226 (v. 6 ; paperback) | ISBN 9780824899233 (v. 7 ; paperback) | ISBN 9780824899240 (v. 8 ; paperback) | ISBN 9780824899257 (paperback) | ISBN 9798880700264 (v. 1 ; pdf) | ISBN 9798880700271 (v. 2 ; pdf) | ISBN 9798880700288 (v. 3 ; pdf) | ISBN 9798880700295 (v. 4 ; pdf) | ISBN 9798880700301 (v. 5 ; pdf) | ISBN 9798880700318 (v. 6 ; pdf) | ISBN 9798880700325 (v. 7 ; pdf) | ISBN 9798880700332 (v. 8 ; pdf)

Subjects: LCSH: Sōtōshū—Doctrines—Early works to 1800.

Classification: LCC BQ9449.D653 E5 2024 (print) | LCC BQ9449.D653 (ebook) | DDC 294.3/85—dc23/eng/20240318

LC record available at https://lccn.loc.gov/2024004760
LC ebook record available at https://lccn.loc.gov/2024004761

Cover art: Eihei Dōgen Zenji Gyōjōzu scroll, courtesy of Rev. Ōtani Tetsuo
Cover design by Urs App

University of Hawai'i Press books are printed on acid-free paper and meet the guidelines for permanence and durability of the Council on Library Resources. Printer-ready copy has been provided by Sōtōshū Shūmuchō

Contents

Volume IV

The Seventy-five-Chapter Compilation

Part 4

Conventions iii
Abbreviations v
46. The Insentient Preach the Dharma *Mujō seppō* 無情説法 1
47. Sūtras of the Buddhas *Bukkyō* 佛經 27
48. Dharma Nature *Hosshō* 法性 55
49. Dhāraṇī *Darani* 陀羅尼 67
50. Washing the Face *Senmen* 洗面 83
51. Face-to-Face Conferral *Menju* 面授 111
52. Buddhas and Ancestors *Busso* 佛祖 135
53. Plum Blossoms *Baika* 梅華 145
54. Washing and Purifying *Senjō* 洗淨 169
55. The Ten Directions *Jippō* 十方 193
56. Seeing Buddha *Kenbutsu* 見佛 213
57. Extensive Study *Henzan* 遍參 249
58. The Eye *Ganzei* 眼睛 271
59. Everyday Matters *Kajō* 家常 285
60. The Thirty-seven Factors of Bodhi *Sanjūshichi hon bodai bunpō* 三十七品菩提分法 299

Conventions

This publication is an annotated translation, in seven volumes, of one hundred three texts of Dōgen's Japanese *Shōbōgenzō*, plus an additional volume containing an introduction, supplementary notes, appendices, and list of works cited. The translation is based on the edition of the *Shōbōgenzō* published in Kawamura Kōdō 河村孝道, ed., *Dōgen zenji zenshū* 道元禅師全集, vols. 1-2 (Tokyo: Shunjūsha, 1991, 1993), cited herein as DZZ.1 and DZZ.2; volume and page numbers of this edition are noted in braces at the corresponding locations in the translation.

The Japanese text accompanying the translation here follows the punctuation and *kanazukai* of the Kawamura edition; for ease of reference to premodern sources, Kawamura's modern Japanese kanji have been replaced with traditional forms. Also, for ease of reference, the sections into which the texts of the Kawamura edition are divided have been assigned numbers in square brackets by the translators. The translation of Kawamura's longer sections is sometimes broken into separate paragraphs, and transitions to new topics between sections are sometimes marked by a string of asterisks.

Though primarily written in Japanese, the *Shōbōgenzō* includes many passages of Chinese, ranging from long quotations of texts to short phrases inserted into the Japanese sentences. Since this inclusion of Chinese is a prominent linguistic feature of the original texts, the translation seeks to indicate such passages by the use of oblique font. The reader is warned that, given the ubiquity in the Japanese language of expressions adopted from Chinese, the identification of the shorter phrases as Chinese, rather than Japanese, is often rather arbitrary.

Much of the *Shōbōgenzō* is devoted to comment on material in other texts. The translation uses quotation marks to indicate terms and passages on which Dōgen is commenting. Here, again, the reader is warned that the distinction between use and mention can often be difficult to draw.

Sanskrit, Chinese, and Japanese terms appearing in the *Oxford English Dictionary* (3rd edition) are considered to have been adopted into English; other such terms are treated as foreign words and rendered in italics. Romanization of all such terms, whether treated as foreign or English, is given with diacritics.

With some exceptions, Chinese transliterations of Sanskrit terms are rendered as romanized Sanskrit. Indic proper nouns, whether transliterated or translated in the Chinese, are rendered as their presumed originals where possible; the reader is warned that some such reconstructions are unattested and speculative.

The proper noun "Zen" is used in reference to (a) the tradition that Dōgen calls the "buddhas and ancestors," and (b) the Japanese instantiation of that tradition; the Chinese name "Chan" is used in reference to the Chinese instantiation of the tradition.

Romanized readings of the Japanese text given in the notes follow wherever possible the ruby in Kawamura's text; readings not provided by Kawamura are based on *Zengaku daijiten* 禅学大辞典 (1978) and/or Katō Shūkō 加藤宗厚, *Shōbōgenzō yōgo sakuin* 正法眼藏用語索引 (1962).

Citations of T (*Taishō shinshū daizōkyō* 大正新脩大藏經) are from the *SAT Daizōkyō Text Database* (https://21dzk.l.u-tokyo.ac.jp/SAT). Citations of ZZ (*Dainihon zokuzōkyō* 大日本續藏經) are from the *CBETA Hanwen dazangjing* 漢文大藏經 (http://tripitaka.cbeta.org). Citations of KR are from *Kanripo* 漢リポ *Kanseki Repository* (https://www.kanripo.org).

The Kawamura edition provides colophons from several sources, some following the relevant chapter, some in the head notes of the chapter, some in the collation notes (*honbun kōi* 本文校異) for that chapter in the end matter of DZZ.1 and DZZ.2. For the convenience of the reader, this translation collects these colophons (and occasionally others omitted by Kawamura) at the end of each chapter. Colophons without attribution are assumed to have been written by Dōgen.

Abbreviations

C   Chinese language

DZZ   *Dōgen zenji zenshū* 道元禅師全集, Kagamishima Genryū 鏡島元隆 et al., compilers. 7 vols. Tokyo: Shunjūsha, 1988–1993.

ESST   *Eihei Shōbōgenzō shūsho taisei* 永平正法眼藏蒐書大成, Kawamura Kōdō 河村孝道, ed. 27 vols. Tokyo: Taishūkan Shoten, 1974-1982.

J   Japanese language

KR   Kanseki Repository (Kanseki Ripo 漢籍リポ). Online: https://www.kanripo.org

M   *Dai kanwa jiten* 大漢和辞典, Morohashi Tetsuji 諸橋轍次, ed. 13 vols. (plus 2-vol. supplement). Tokyo: Taishūkan Shoten, 1955-1960.

S   Sanskrit

SCZ   *Shōbōgenzō chūkai zensho* 正法眼藏註解全書, Jinbo Nyoten 神保如天 and Andō Bun'ei 安藤文英, eds. 11 vols. Reprint Tokyo: Nihon Bussho Kankōkai, 1956-1957.

SZ   *Sōtōshū zensho* 曹洞宗全書. 20 vols. Tokyo: Kōmeisha, 1929-1938.

T   *Taishō shinshū daizōkyō* 大正新脩大藏經, Takakusu Junjirō 高楠順次郎 and Watanabe Kaikyoku 渡邊海旭, eds. 100 vols. Tokyo: Daizōkyōkai, 1924–1935.

ZT   *Zengaku taikei* 禪學大系. 8 vols. Tokyo: Kokusho Kankōkai, 1952 (orig. publ. 1910-11).

ZTS   *Zengaku tenseki sōkan* 禅学典籍叢刊, Yanagida Seizan 柳田聖山 and Shiina Kōyū 椎名宏雄, eds. 12 vols. Kyoto: Rinsen Shoten, 1999-2001.

ZZ   *Dainihon zokuzōkyō* 大日本續藏經. 150 vols. Kyoto: Bussho Kankōkai, 1905-1912.

TREASURY OF THE TRUE DHARMA EYE

NUMBER 46

The Insentient Preach the Dharma
Mujō seppō
無情説法

The Insentient Preach the Dharma

Mujō seppō

INTRODUCTION

This chapter was composed in the autumn of 1243, at Kippōji, the monastery in Echizen Province where Dōgen taught following his move from the capital in the summer of that year. It occurs as number 46 in both the seventy-five- and sixty-chapter compilations of the *Shōbōgenzō* and as number 53 in the Honzan edition.

The title theme of the essay is best known in Zen literature from the teachings of the eighth-century figure Nanyang Huizhong 南陽慧忠, a disciple of the Sixth Ancestor and the subject of a number of famous koans. Dōgen offers here commentary on a conversation on the theme between Huizhong and an unidentified monk, as well as on a very similar conversation between the ninth-century master Dongshan Liangjie 洞山良价 and his teacher Yunyan Tansheng 雲巖曇晟.

It was not uncommon in Dōgen's day for Japanese Buddhists to imagine that the natural world, including inanimate objects, was somehow expressing Buddhist truths. Indeed, in his celebrated "Mountains and Waters Sūtra" ("Sansui kyō" 山水經) and other chapters of the *Shōbōgenzō*, Dōgen himself often seems to affirm such a view. Yet, in this essay, he warns us not to confuse the preaching of the dharma with "the rustling branches of the forests," and not to think that the insentient are simply the "grasses and trees, tiles and pebbles" of our natural world. Rather, as he emphasizes in his opening remarks, we should understand the insentient preaching the dharma as the fundamental activity of the buddhas and ancestors, the "realized kōan" (*genjō kōan* 見成公案) handed down in the lineage of Zen.

正法眼藏第四十六

Treasury of the True Dharma Eye
Number 46

無情説法

The Insentient Preach the Dharma

[46:1] {2:2}

説法於説法するは、佛祖附嘱於佛祖の見成公案なり。この説法は法説なり。有情にあらず、無情にあらず、有爲にあらず、無爲にあらず、有爲・無爲の因縁にあらず、從縁起の法にあらず。しかあれども、鳥道に不行なり、佛衆に爲與す。大道十成するとき、説法十成す、法藏附嘱するとき、説法附嘱す。拈華のとき、拈説法あり、傳衣のとき、傳説法あり。このゆえに、諸佛諸祖、おなじく威音王以前より、説法に奉觀しきたり、諸佛以前より、説法に本行しきたれるなり。説法は、佛祖の理しきたるとのみ參學することなかれ、佛祖は、説法に理せられきたるなり。この説法、わづかに八萬四千門の法藴を開演するのみにあらず、無量無邊門の説法藴あり。先佛の説法を後佛は説法す、と參學することなかれ。先佛きたりて後佛なるにあらざるがごとく、説法も、先説法を後説法とするにはあらず。このゆえに、

Preaching the dharma in preaching the dharma is the realized kōan that the buddhas and ancestors bequeath to the buddhas and ancestors.[1] This "preaching the dharma" is the dharma preaching. It is not sentient, not insentient; it is not constructed, not unconstructed; it is not the causes and conditions of the constructed or the unconstructed; it is not a dharma

---

1 **Preaching the dharma in preaching the dharma** (*seppō o seppō suru* 説法於説法する): A tentative translation of an odd locution, in mixed Chinese and Japanese syntax, that can be variously interpreted. This rendering treats the particle *o* 於 (Chinese *yu*) as a locative marker (Japanese *ni okite*), suggesting a sense "to preach the dharma where (or while) the dharma is being preached"; it could also be read as an accusative (Japanese *o*), which would yield "preaching the dharma of [i.e., regarding] the preaching of dharma." Though probably less likely here, the particle could also be taken as a dative marker — paralleling its use in the immediately following clause — and the phrase parsed "preaching the dharma to preachers of the dharma."

the realized kōan that the buddhas and ancestors bequeath to the buddhas and ancestors (*busso fuzoku o busso no genjō kōan* 佛祖附嘱於佛祖の見成公案): Or "the realized kōan of the buddhas and ancestors bequeathing to the buddhas and ancestors." The expression "realized kōan" here translates *genjō kōan* 見成公案 (more often written 現成公案), one of Dōgen's favorite expressions and the title of one of the most celebrated chapters of the *Shōbōgenzō*. See Supplementary Notes, s.v. "Realized kōan."

arising from conditions.[2] Nevertheless, it is not following the path of the bird: it is for the buddha assembly.[3]

When the great way is complete, preaching the dharma is complete; when the treasury of the dharma is bequeathed, preaching the dharma is bequeathed.[4] When the flower is taken up, preaching the dharma is taken up; when the robe is transmitted, preaching the dharma is transmitted.[5]

---

2 **It is not sentient, not insentient** (*ujō ni arazu, mujō ni arazu* 有情にあらず、無情にあらず): The term "sentient," or "sentient being," typically refers to the "living," or "animate," beings (*shujō* 衆生; S. *sattva*) subject to rebirth in the five (or six) states of saṃsāra; in contrast to (a) inanimate objects, both vegetable and mineral (*mujō* 無情; "the insentient"), and (b) the "sages" (*shō* 聖), or transcendent buddhas and advanced bodhisattvas.

constructed (*ui* 有爲); **unconstructed** (*mui* 無爲): Taking these terms in the common Buddhist sense of *saṃskṛta* ("compounded," "produced [by causes and conditions]") and *asaṃskṛta* ("uncompounded," "unproduced") respectively. They can also be (and often are here) taken in the sense, regularly found in Zen literature, of "intentional" and "unintentional" respectively.

the causes and conditions of the constructed or the unconstructed (*ui mui no innen* 有爲・無爲の因縁): A somewhat obscure phrase, probably meaning something like "subject to, or causally connected with, either the constructed or unconstructed."

a dharma arising from conditions (*jū engi no hō* 從縁起の法): I.e., a teaching reflecting dependent origination; possibly alluding to a line in the *Lotus Sūtra* (*Miaofa lianhua jing* 妙法蓮華經, T.262.9:9b8-9):

諸佛兩足尊、知法常無性、佛種從緣起、是故説一乘。
The buddhas, most honored among the two-legged,
Knowing that the dharmas are always without nature,
And that the seeds of buddhahood sprout from conditions,
Therefore teach the one vehicle.

3 **not following the path of the bird** (*chōdō ni fugyō* 鳥道に不行): Likely meaning that preaching the dharma is not merely the free expression of liberation that leaves no traces. (See, e.g., *Shōbōgenzō keiteki* 正法眼藏啓迪 3:510.) "The path of the bird" (*chōdō* 鳥道) is a well-known expression of the Tang-dynasty master Dongshan Liangjie 洞山良价 (807-869), often invoked by Dōgen; see Supplementary Notes, s.v. "Dongshan's three roads."

for the buddha assembly (*busshu ni iyo su* 佛衆に爲與す): The predicate *iyo su* 爲與す does not occur elsewhere in the *Shōbōgenzō*; it is taken here as "to provide for the sake of." The term *busshu* 佛衆, while regularly used in reference to an assembly of buddhas, here more likely indicates the followers of the buddhas.

4 **treasury of the dharma** (*hōzō* 法藏): Typically, denoting the Buddhist scriptures, especially the sūtras; here, perhaps, more broadly, the Buddhist teachings.

5 **When the flower is taken up** (*nenge no toki* 拈華のとき); **when the robe is transmitted** (*den'e no toki* 傳衣のとき): Allusion to the transmission of Zen. The former phrase recalls the famous legend of Buddha Śākyamuni's holding up a flower to transmit "the treasury of the true dharma eye" to the First Ancestor, Mahākāśyapa; see Supplementary Notes, s.v. "Hold up a flower." The latter phrase may invoke the tradition that Śākyamuni also gave his robe to Mahākāśyapa; but it is more often treated as an allusion

46. The Insentient Preach the Dharma *Mujō seppō* 無情説法

Therefore, the buddhas and ancestors, from before King Majestic Voice, have all been paying their respects to preaching the dharma; from before the buddhas, they have all been originally practicing preaching the dharma.[6]

Do not study this only as meaning that preaching the dharma has been governed by the buddhas and ancestors: the buddhas and ancestors have been governed by preaching the dharma. This preaching the dharma does not only expound merely the aggregate of eighty-four thousand dharmas; there is a preaching of the aggregate of incalculable, limitless dharmas.[7] Do not study this to mean that later buddhas preach the dharma of the dharma preaching of prior buddhas: just as prior buddhas have not come to be later buddhas, so with preaching the dharma, the prior dharma preaching is not made the later dharma preaching.

Therefore,

[46:2] {2:3}
釋迦牟尼佛道、如三世諸佛説法之儀式、我今亦如是説無分別法.

Buddha Śākyamuni said,
In the manner that the buddhas
Of the three times preach the dharma,
I also now preach
The dharma without distinctions.[8]

---

to the legend that the Fifth Ancestor in China, Hongren 弘忍, bequeathed the robe of Bodhidharma to Huineng 慧能 as a symbol of the latter's status as Sixth Ancestor.

6 **before King Majestic Voice** (*Ion'ō izen* 威音王以前): A common expression, occurring often in Dōgen's writing and other Zen texts, used to suggest the primordial past or a state prior to any differentiation; see Supplementary Notes, s.v. "Before King Majestic Voice."

originally practicing (*hongyō* 本行): Likely reflecting a passage in the *Lotus Sūtra* (*Miaofa lianhua jing* 妙法蓮華經, T.262.9:42c22-23) cited in several places in the *Shōbōgenzō*:

諸善男子、我本行菩薩道所成壽命、今猶未盡、復倍上數。
Good sons, the lifespan attained by my original practice of the bodhisattva path is even now still not exhausted; it is twice the above number.

7 **aggregate of eighty-four thousand dharmas** (*hachiman shisen mon no hōun* 八萬四千門の法藴): A standard expression for the enormous number of teachings by the Buddha; the "aggregate of dharmas" (S. *dharma-skandha*) is virtually synonymous with the "treasury of the dharma" (*hōzō* 法藏) mentioned above.

8 **Buddha Śākyamuni** (*Shakamuni butsu* 釋迦牟尼佛): Quoting a passage from the "Upāya-kauśalya" chapter of the *Lotus Sūtra* (*Miaofa lianhua jing* 妙法蓮華經, T.262.9:10a22-23).

[46:3]

しかあればすなはち、諸佛の、說法を使用するがごとく、諸佛は、說法を使用するなり。諸佛の、說法を正傳するがごとく、諸佛は、說法を正傳するによりて、古佛より七佛に正傳し、七佛よりいまに正傳して、無情說法あり。この無情說法に、諸佛あり、諸祖あるなり。我今說法は、正傳にあらざる新條、と學することなかれ。古來、正傳は舊窠の鬼窟、と證することなかれ。

Thus, just as the buddhas employ preaching the dharma, so the buddhas employ preaching the dharma. Just as the buddhas directly transmit preaching the dharma, so the buddhas directly transmit preaching the dharma; and thus there is the insentient preaching the dharma, directly transmitted from the old buddhas to the seven buddhas, directly transmitted from the seven buddhas to the present.[9] In this "insentient preaching the dharma," there are the buddhas, there are the ancestors. Do not study that "I now preach the dharma" means new items not directly transmitted; do not attest that what is directly transmitted from ancient times is a ghost cave of old dens.[10]

* * * * *

[46:4]

大唐國西京光宅寺大證國師、因僧問、無情還解說法否。國師云、常說熾然、說無間歇。僧曰、某甲爲甚麼不聞。國師曰、汝自不聞、不可妨他聞者也。僧曰、未審、什麼人得聞。國師曰、諸聖得聞。僧曰、和尚還聞否。國師曰、我不聞。僧曰、和尚既不聞、爭知無情解說法。國師曰、賴我不聞、我若聞則齊於諸聖、汝即不聞我說法。僧曰、恁麼則衆生無分也。國師曰、我爲衆生說、不爲諸聖說。僧曰、衆生聞後如何。國師曰、即非衆生。

---

9 **from the old buddhas to the seven buddhas** (*kobutsu yori shichi butsu ni* 古佛より七佛に): Or "from the old buddha to the seven buddhas." "The seven buddhas" refers to what are often called "the seven buddhas of the past" (*kako shichi butsu* 過去七佛): i.e., Śākyamuni and the six buddhas (the names of which vary according to the source) said to have preceded him; see Supplementary Notes, s.v. "Seven buddhas." The term "old buddha" (*kobutsu* 古佛) is used in Zen texts to refer both to these seven buddhas and as an honorific for certain esteemed Zen masters; here, it no doubt indicates the buddhas of prior kalpas, such as Buddha Bhīṣmagarjitasvararāja mentioned above. See Supplementary Notes, s.v. "Old buddha."

10 **"I now preach the dharma"** (*ga kon seppō* 我今說法): Dōgen is here borrowing the words of Śākyamuni quoted just above.

ghost cave of old dens (*kyūka no kikutsu* 舊窠の鬼窟): A mixing of two common metaphors. "Old den" (or "nest," or "burrow"; *kyūka* 舊窠) is regularly used in Zen literature for old or habitual ways of thinking, "tired" concepts or clichés. "Ghost (or 'phantom') cave" (*kikutsu* 鬼窟) is used in reference to the dark confines of intellectual nihilism or contemplative oblivion; see Supplementary Notes, s.v. "Ghost cave." Here, presumably, mere dogma.

46. The Insentient Preach the Dharma *Mujō seppō* 無情説法

National Teacher Dazheng of the Guangzhai Monastery in the Western Capital of the Land of the Great Tang was once asked by a monk, "Can the insentient preach the dharma?"[11]

The National Teacher said, "They're constantly preaching with ardor; they preach without pause."

The monk said, "Why can't I hear it?"

The National Teacher said, "That you can't hear it doesn't prevent others from hearing it."

The monk said, "I don't understand. Who can hear it?"

The National Teacher said, "The sages can hear it."[12]

The monk said, "Can the Reverend hear it?"

The National Teacher said, "I can't hear it."

The monk said, "If the Reverend can't hear it, how does he know that the insentient preach the dharma?"

The National Teacher said, "Fortunately, I don't hear it. If I heard it, I would equal the sages, and you wouldn't hear me preaching the dharma."

The monk said, "In this case, living beings have no part in this."[13]

The National Teacher said, "I preach for living beings; I don't preach for sages."

The monk said, "After the living beings hear it, how are they?"

The National Teacher said, "They're not living beings."

---

11 **National Teacher Dazheng of the Guangzhai Monastery in the Western Capital of the Land of the Great Tang** (*Daitō koku Saikyō Kōtakuji Daishō kokushi* 大唐國西京光宅寺大證國師): I.e., Nanyang Huizhong 南陽慧忠 (d. 775), disciple of the Sixth Ancestor and the subject of a number of famous kōans. "The Western Capital" (*Saikyō* 西京) refers to Chang'an, site of the Guangzhaisi 光宅寺 where Huizhong resided. The exact source of Dōgen's version of Huizhong's conversation on the insentient preaching the dharma has not been identified; a similar passage occurs in a longer discussion on the topic at *Jingde chuandeng lu* 景德傳燈錄 (T.2076.51:438a9-25).

12 **"sages"** (*shoshō* 諸聖): I.e., advanced spiritual adepts. In technical Buddhist usage, the "nobles" (S. *ārya*), or those well established on the "noble path" (*shōdō* 聖道; S. *ārya-mārga*), as opposed to the "commoners" (*bonbu* 凡夫; S. *pṛthagjana*), or ordinary folk.

13 **"living beings have no part in this"** (*shujō mubun* 衆生無分): I.e., living beings are not in a position to hear the preaching. The term "living beings" (*shujō* 衆生; S. *sattva*) is synonymous with "the sentient" (*ujō* 有情); here, used in contrast to "the sages."

[46:5] {2:4}
無情説法を參學せん初心・晩學、この國師の因縁を直須勤學すべし。

Beginners and latecomers who would study "*the insentient preach the dharma*" should study with diligence this episode of the National Teacher.

[46:6]
常説熾然、説無間歇とあり。常は、諸時の一分時なり。説無間歇は、説すでに現出するがごときは、さだめて無間歇なり。無情説法の儀、かならずしも有情のごとくにあらんずる、と參學すべからず、有情の音聲、および有情説法の儀のごとくなるべきがゆえに。

"*They're constantly preaching with ardor; they preach without pause.*" "Constantly" is one time among all times.[14] "*They preach without pause*": preaching that is certainly appearing is definitely "without pause." We should not study that the manner in which *the insentient preach the dharma* must necessarily be like that of the sentient because it ought to be like the voices of the sentient and the manner in which the sentient preach the dharma.[15]

[46:7]
有情界の音聲をうばふて、無情界の音聲に擬するは、佛道にあらず。無情説法、かならずしも聲塵なるべからず、たとへば、有情の説法、それ聲塵にあらざるがごとくなり。しばらく、いかなるか有情、いかなるか無情、と問自問他、功夫參學すべし。

To snatch away the voices of the sentient realm and liken them to the voices of the insentient realm is not the way of the buddhas. *The insentient preaching the dharma* is not necessarily sound, just as preaching the dharma by the sentient is not sound. We should make concentrated effort and study this a while, asking ourselves, asking others, what is "the sentient," "what is the insentient"?

---

14 **one time among all times** (*shoji no ichibunji* 諸時の一分時): A tentative translation of an ambiguous phrase, which might be understood "each moment of all times," suggesting perhaps that each time somehow incorporates or expresses all times.

15 **because it ought to be like the voices of the sentient and the manner in which the sentient preach the dharma** (*ujō no onjō, oyobi ujō seppō no gi no gotoku naru beki ga yue ni* 有情の音聲、および有情説法の儀のごとくなるべきがゆえに): The translation here follows Kawamura's punctuation of this phrase, which takes it as modifying the preceding clause. The passage could be, and in some other editions is, parsed such that the phrase modifies the following sentence (in the section below) — a reading that would yield, "[Thinking that] because it ought to be like the voices of the sentient and the manner in which the sentient preach the dharma, to snatch away the voices of the sentient realm and liken them to the voices of the insentient realm is not the way of the buddhas."

[46:8]
しかあれば、無情説法の儀、いかにかあるらんと、審細に留心參學すべきなり。愚人おもはくは、樹林の鳴條する、葉華の開落するを、無情説法と認ずるは、學佛法の漢にあらず。もししかあらば、たれか無情説法をしらざらん、たれか無情説法をきかざらん。しばらく廻光すべし、無情界には、草木・樹林ありやなしや、無情界は有情界にまじはれりやいなや。しかあるを、草木・瓦礫を認じて無情とするは、不遍學なり、無情を認じて草木・瓦礫とするは、不參飽なり。たとひいま、人間の所見の草木等を認じて無情に擬せんとすとも、草木等も凡慮のはかるところにあらず。ゆえいかんとなれば、天上・人間の樹林、はるかに殊異あり、中國・邊地の所生、ひとしきにあらず、海裏・山間の草木、みな不同なり。いはんや空におふる樹木あり、雲におふる樹木あり。風火等のなかに所生長の百草萬樹、おほよそ有情と學しつべきあり、無情と認ぜられざるあり、草木の人畜のごとくなるあり、有情・無情いまだあきらめざるなり。いはんや仙家の樹石・華果・湯水等、みるに疑著およばずとも、説著せんに、かたからんや。ただわづかに神州一國の草木をみ、日本一州の草木を慣習して、萬方・盡界もかくのごとくあるべし、と擬議・商量することなかれ。

Thus, we should carefully take heed and study in what manner it is that *the insentient preach the dharma*. One who considers, as the foolish think, that the rustling branches of the forests, the opening and falling of leaves and flowers, are the insentient preaching the dharma — this is not a person who studies the buddha dharma. If this were the case, who could not know the preaching of the insentient, who could not hear the preaching of the insentient? We should reflect a while.[16] In the realm of the insentient, are there grasses, trees, and forests? Is the realm of the insentient mixed into the realm of the sentient? Still, those who consider grasses and trees, tiles and pebbles as the insentient have not studied extensively; those who consider the insentient as grasses and trees, tiles and pebbles have not studied their fill.

Even if, for now, we were to accept the plants seen by humans and treat them as the insentient, grasses and trees are also not what is fathomed by common thinking. Why? There is a vast difference between the forests of the heavens and those among humans; what grows in central countries and marginal lands is not the same; the grasses and trees in the ocean and in the mountains are all dissimilar.[17] Not to mention that there are forests growing in the sky, forests growing in the clouds. Of the hundred grasses and myriad trees that grow in wind, fire, and the rest, there are in general

---

16 **We should reflect** (*ekō su beshi* 廻光すべし): An unusual usage not appearing elsewhere in Dōgen's writing. The term *ekō* typically occurs in the fixed phrase *ekō henshō* 回光返照, "turn the light around and shine it back [on oneself]"; see Supplementary Notes, s.v. "Turn the light around and shine it back."

17 **central countries and marginal lands** (*chūgoku henchi* 中國・邊地): Likely referring to places at the center and borders respectively of our continent of Jambudvīpa. See Supplementary Notes, s.v. "Four Continents."

those that should be studied as sentient, those that are not recognized as insentient.[18] There are grasses and trees that are like humans and beasts; whether they are sentient or insentient is not clear.[19] Not to mention the trees and rocks, flowers and fruits, hot and cold waters of the transcendents — though when we see them we have no doubts, when we would explain them, is it not difficult?[20] Seeing merely the grasses and trees of the one Land of Shenzhou, being familiar with the grasses and trees of the one region of Nihon, do not consider or deliberate that the myriad quarters and all the worlds must be like them.[21]

[46:9] {2:5}
國師道、諸聖得聞。いはく、無情説法の會下には、諸聖立地聽するなり。諸聖と無情と、聞を現成し、説を現成せしむ。無情、すでに諸聖のために説法す、聖なりや、凡なりや。あるひは、無情説法の儀をあきらめをはりなば、諸聖の所聞かくのごとくあり、と體達すべし。すでに體達することをえては、聖者の境界をはかりしるべし。さらに、超凡越聖の通霄路の行履を參學すべし。

"The National Teacher said, 'The sages can hear it.'" This says that, in the community where the insentient preach the dharma, *the sages stand and listen*.[22] The sages and the insentient manifest hearing, manifest

---

18 **wind, fire, and the rest** (*fū ka tō* 風火等): Likely here an abbreviation for the four elements of Buddhist cosmology: earth, water, fire, and wind; see Supplementary Notes, s.v. "Four elements and five aggregates."

19 **whether they are sentient or insentient is not clear** (*ujō mujō imada akiramezaru nari* 有情・無情いまだあきらめざるなり): The translation follows Kawamura's punctuation here, treating this as a dependent clause modifying the preceding "plants"; it could also be read as a separate sentence: "The [categories of] sentient and insentient are not clear."

20 **the transcendents** (*senke* 仙家): Likely a reference to the hermit sages (*sennin* 仙人) of Daoist lore, known for their thaumaturgic powers, in whose mountain haunts one can expect uncanny occurrences.

when we would explain them, is it not difficult? (*setchaku sen ni, katakaran ya* 説著せんに、かたからんや): The translation here follows those editions that read *katakarazaran ya* かたからざらんや.

21 **the one Land of Shenzhou** (*Shinshū ikkoku* 神州一國): I.e., the country of China. The term *shinshū* 神州 (literally "divine region") is sometimes thought to reflect *shendan* 神丹, a transliteration of *Cīnasthāna*, a Sanskrit name for China. The term is also used in Japanese in reference to Japan, where it is understood as "the region of the *kami*."

the myriad quarters and all the worlds (*manpō jinkai* 萬方・盡界): The translation follows Kawamura's punctuation; the phrase might also be read, "all the worlds in the myriad quarters."

22 **the sages stand and listen** (*shoshō ritchi chō* 諸聖立地聽): I.e., attend respectfully to the preaching, as at the formal dharma talk of a Zen master. This expression seems to be a variant of the more common "the buddhas of the three times stand and listen" (*sanze shobutsu ritchi chō* 三世諸佛立地聽), best known from the words of Xuansha

46. The Insentient Preach the Dharma *Mujō seppō* 無情説法   11

preaching. Since the insentient preach the dharma for the sages, are they sages or are they commoners? Again, if we have finished clarifying the manner in which *the insentient preach the dharma*, we should personally realize that what the sages hear exists like this.[23] Having gained personal realization, we should gauge the realm of the sages.[24] Further, we should study the conduct on the road through the clouds that *transcends the commoner and surpasses the sage*.[25]

[46:10] {2:6}

國師いはく、我不聞。この道も、容易會なり、と擬することなかれ。超凡越聖にして不聞なりや、擘破凡聖窠窟のゆえに不聞なりや。恁麼功夫して、道取を現成せしむべし。

"The National Teacher said, '*I don't hear it.*'" Do not consider that these words are easy to understand. Does he "not hear it" having *transcended the commoner and surpassed the sage*? Or does he not hear it because he *breaks down the dens and caves of "commoner and sage"*? Working at it in this way, we should actualize his words.

Shibei 玄沙師備 (835-908) that Dōgen discusses in his "Shōbōgenzō gyōbutsu iigi" 正法眼藏行佛威儀.

23 personally realize (*taitatsu* 體達): There are two lines of interpretation of the term *tai* 體 in this compound expression found throughout Buddhist literature and Dōgen's writings: (a) "bodily," "physically"; "personally" (as taken here); or (b) "substance," or "essence" (which would yield here something like "realize, or penetrate, to the essence").

what the sages hear exists like this (*shoshō no shomon kakunogotoku ari* 諸聖の所聞かくのごとくあり): The pronoun "this" here lacks any obvious antecedent. Could be taken to mean "what the hearing of the sages is like," but the sense may be simply that the sages do in fact hear the preaching of the insentient.

24 should gauge the realm of the sages (*shōja no kyōkai o hakarishiru beshi* 聖者の境界をはかりしるべし): I.e., "should (or will) determine the experience of the sage." While the term *kyōkai* 境界 is often used in a general sense for "realm," or "sphere," given our context, it may carry here its more technical Buddhist usage as "sensory field" or "object of cognition." The suffix *beshi* here may be taken either as conjecture ("will likely," "may be expected to") or as imperative ("ought to").

25 road through the clouds (*tsūshōro* 通霄路): A tentative translation for a fixed expression, found in Song-dynasty Chan texts, indicating a "higher" way, beyond the standard understandings of Buddhist practice. The term *shō* 霄, translated here as "clouds," can also refer to, and is probably most often interpreted here as, the "heavens," or "firmament," as well as the "night." The term occurs elsewhere in the *Shōbōgenzō* only in "Dōtoku" 道得 (DZZ.1:376), probably in the sense "celestial passage."

transcends the commoner and surpasses the sage (*chōbon osshō* 超凡越聖): I.e., to go beyond the stages of the Buddhist spiritual path; a common expression in Zen literature.

[46:11]
國師いはく、賴我不聞、我若聞、齊於諸聖。この舉示、これ一道兩道にあらず。賴我は、凡聖にあらず、賴我は、佛祖なるべきか。佛祖は、超凡越聖するゆえに、諸聖の所聞には一齊ならざるべし。

"The National Teacher said, 'Fortunately, I don't hear it. If I heard it, I would equal the sages.'" This presentation is not one word or two words.[26] "Fortunately I" is not commoner or sage; should "fortunately I" be a buddha and ancestor?[27] Because the buddhas and ancestors transcend the commoner and surpass the sage, [what they hear] should not be equal to what the sages hear.

[46:12]
國師道の汝即不聞我説法の理道を修理して、諸佛・諸聖の菩提を料理すべきなり。その宗旨は、いはゆる、無情説法、諸聖得聞、國師説法、這僧得聞なり。この理道を、參學功夫の日深月久とすべし。しばらく國師に問著すべし、衆生聞後はとはず、衆生正當聞説法時如何。

Dealing with the reasoning of the National Teacher's words, "*you wouldn't hear me preaching the dharma,*" we should manage the bodhi of the buddhas and the sages.[28] Its essential point is that, when the insentient preach the dharma, the sages can hear it; when the National Teacher preaches the dharma, this monk can hear it. On this reasoning, we should take long days and months of study and concentrated effort.[29] For now, we should question the National Teacher: "I'm not asking about 'after

---

26 **This presentation** (*kono koji* この舉示): The term *koji* (also written 舉似), "to take up and present [a topic]," is used in reference especially to a comment on a Zen case. Though here likely a reference to the National Teacher's words, it could also be read in reference to Dōgen's comment: i.e., "the comment on this [saying]."

not one word or two words (*ichidō ryōdō ni arazu* 一道兩道にあらず): Perhaps meaning "not simply a few [ordinary] words."

27 **"Fortunately I"** (*raiga* 賴我): Dōgen has here created a neologism from the first two words of the National Teacher's remark; presumably to be understood as "the fortunate person [who does not hear]."

28 **Dealing with the reasoning ... we should manage** (*ridō o shuri shite* 理道を修理して... *ryōri su beki nari* 料理すべきなり): A tentative translation of a passage likely meaning something like, "We should master the meaning [of the National Teacher's words] and handle [the bodhi of the buddhas and sages]." The translation fails to capture the play with the graph *ri* 理 ("reason") in this sentence. The terms *ridō* 理道 and *shuri* 修理 are not common in Dōgen's writing: the former might be parsed here as "reasoned words"; the latter, normally "to repair, "to put in order," may have the sense here of "to train," "to practice." The term *ryōri* 料理 appears elsewhere in the *Shōbōgenzō* ("Jippō" 十方, DZZ.2:97) in the sense "to have control over, or mastery of [a topic]"; it could also be rendered "to reckon," "to estimate," or "to consider."

29 **long days and months** (*nisshin gekkyū* 日深月久): Literally, "a depth of days and length of months," a fixed expression for the extended passage of time; not common in Buddhist texts nor occurring elsewhere in Dōgen's writings.

46. The Insentient Preach the Dharma *Mujō seppō* 無情説法   13

living beings hear it'; *how about at the very moment that living beings hear the preaching of the dharma?*"

* * * * *

[46:13]

高祖洞山悟本大師、參曩祖雲巖大和尚、問云、無情説法什麼人得聞。雲巖曩祖曰、無情説法、無情得聞。高祖曰、和尚聞否。曩祖曰、我若聞、汝即不得聞吾説法也。高祖曰、若恁麼即某甲不聞和尚説法也。曩祖曰、我説汝尚不聞、何況無情説法也。高祖乃述偈呈曩祖。曰、也太奇、也太奇、無情説法不思議、若將耳聽終難會、眼處聞聲方得知。

The Eminent Ancestor, Great Master Wuben of Dongshan, when studying with the Ancient Ancestor, Most Reverend Yunyan, asked him, "When the insentient preach the dharma, who can hear it?"[30]

Yunyen, the Ancient Ancestor, said, "When the insentient preach the dharma, the insentient can hear it."

The Eminent Ancestor said, "Does the Reverend hear it?"

The Ancient Ancestor said, "If I heard it, you couldn't hear my preaching the dharma."

The Eminent Ancestor said, "In that case, I don't hear the Reverend preaching the dharma."

The Ancient Ancestor said, "Even when I preach, you still don't hear. How much less when the insentient preach the dharma."

The Eminent Ancestor then expressed a *gāthā* presented to the Ancient Ancestor:

> How strange! How strange!
> The insentient preaching the dharma is inconceivable.
> If we use the ear to hear it, it's hard in the end to understand;
> Only when the eye hears the voices do we know it.[31]

---

30   **The Eminent Ancestor, Great Master Wuben of Dongshan** (*kōso Tōzan Gohon daishi* 高祖洞山悟本大師): "Great Master Wuben" (*Gohon daishi* 悟本大師) is the posthumous title conferred on Dongshan Liangjie 洞山良价; "Eminent Ancestor" (*kōso* 高祖) is an honorific recognizing Dongshan as founder of the Caodong (Sōtō) lineage. "Ancient Ancestor, Most Reverend Yunyan" (*nōso Ungan daioshō* 曩祖雲巖大和尚) refers to Dongshan's master, Yunyan Tansheng 雲巖曇晟 (782-841), disciple of Yaoshan Weiyan 藥山惟儼 (751-834). Their conversation also appears in Dōgen's *shinji Shōbōgenzō* 眞字正法眼藏 (DZZ.5:204, case 148), as well as in his *Eihei kōroku* 永平廣錄 (DZZ.4:40, 4:316). While generally following the version of this episode found in the *Jingde chuandeng lu* 景德傳燈錄 (T.2076.51:321b27-c11), Dōgen's rendition of Dongshan's verse diverges in favor of a slightly expanded treatment of the story seen in Dahui's 大慧 *Zhengfayanzang* 正法眼藏 (ZZ.118:76b17-a6).

31   **the eye** (*genshō* 眼處): The "eye," of course, can serve as a metaphor for wisdom; but, here, no doubt, for the sake of the seven-glyph line, Dongshan uses the Buddhist

[46:14] {2:7}

いま高祖道の無情説法什麼人得聞の道理、よく一生多生の功夫を審細にすべし。いはゆるこの問著、さらに道著の功徳を具すべし。この道著の、皮肉骨髓あり、以心傳心のみにあらず、以心傳心は、初心晩學の辦肯なり、衣を擧して正傳し、法を拈じて正傳する關棙子あり。いまの人、いかでか三秋四月の功夫に究竟することあらん。高祖、かつて大證道の無情説法諸聖得聞の宗旨を見聞せりといへども、いま、さらに無情説法什麼人得聞の問著あり。これ肯大證道なりとやせん、不肯大證道なりとやせん、問著なりとやせん、道著なりとやせん。もし總不肯大證、爭得恁麼道、もし總肯大證、爭解恁麼道なり。

The meaning of these words of the Eminent Master, "*When the insentient preach the dharma, who can hear it?*" we should examine in detail through an entire life and many lives of concentrated effort. This question he asks should additionally be endowed with the virtue of a statement.[32] This statement has the skin, flesh, bones, and marrow; it is not only *transmitting the mind by the mind*. "*Transmitting the mind by the mind*" is something confirmed by the beginner and latecomer.[33] There is a pivotal point directly transmitted by taking up the robe, directly transmitted by holding up the dharma.[34] How could people today fulfill it in three or four autumns of work.[35] The Eminent Ancestor, though he had previously heard the essential point of Dazheng's words, "*when the insentient preach the dharma, the sages can hear it*," goes on here to have the question, "*when the insentient preach the dharma, who can hear it?*" Do we take this as *affirming Dazheng's words*, or take it as *not affirming Dazheng's words*? Do we take it as a question, or take it as a statement?

---

technical term for the visual sense sphere (S. *cakṣurāyatana*), defined as the eye organ and its object. Dōgen will play with the element *sho* 處 ("place"; i.e., "sense sphere") in his comments below. See Supplementary Notes, s.v. "Eye."

32 **should additionally be endowed with the virtue of a statement** (*sara ni dōchaku no kudoku o gu su beshi* さらに道著の功徳を具すべし): I.e., the interrogative, "who can hear it?" (*jūmo nin toku mon* 什麼人得聞) could be taken in a declarative sense: "'Who' can hear it"; a play on the interrogative not uncommon in Dōgen's writings.

33 **something confirmed by the beginner and latecomer** (*shoshin bangaku no benkō* 初心晩學の辦肯): I.e., the lesser understanding of those not yet mature in Buddhist training; see Supplementary Notes, s.v. "Beginner's mind."

34 **taking up the robe** (*e o koshite* 衣を擧して); **holding up the dharma** (*hō o nenjite* 法を拈じて): Here likely reflecting Bodhidharma's "skin, flesh, bones, and marrow" mentioned just above and alluding to Bodhidharma's saying to his successor, Huike, that he was bestowing on him the true dharma and his *kāṣāya*.

35 **three or four autumns** (*sanshū shigetsu* 三秋四月): Literally, "three autumns, four moons"; likely a variation on *sanshi shūgetsu* 三四秋月 ("three or four autumn moons"). Some would take *shū* 秋 here as "month" and read this as "three or four months." The expression seems not to be a common one and does not occur elsewhere in Dōgen's writings.

If he is not affirming Dazheng at all, how could he talk this way? If *he is completely affirming Dazheng, how could he talk this way?*

[46:15]
曩祖雲巖曰、無情説法、無情得聞。この血脈を正傳して、身心脱落の參學あるべし。いはゆる無情説法、無情得聞は、諸佛説法、諸佛得聞の性相なるべし。無情説法を聽取せん衆會、たとひ有情・無情なりとも、たとひ凡夫・賢聖なりとも、これ無情なるべし。この性相によりて、古今の眞僞を批判すべきなり。たとひ西天より將來すとも、正傳まことの祖師にあらざらんは、もちいるべからず。たとひ千萬年より習學すること聯綿なりとも、嫡嫡相承にあらずば、嗣續しがたし。いま、正傳すでに東土に通達せり、眞僞の通塞、わきまへやすからん。たとひ衆生説法、衆生得聞の道取を聽取しても、諸佛諸祖の骨髓を稟受しつべし。雲巖曩祖の道を聞取し、大證國師の道を聽取して、まさに與奪せば、諸聖得聞の道取する諸聖は、無情なるべし、無情得聞と道取する無情は、諸聖なるべし。無情所説無情なり、無情説法即無情なるがゆえに。しかあればすなはち、無情説法なり、説法無情なり。

The Ancient Ancestor Yunyan said, "*When the insentient preach the dharma, the insentient can hear it.*" There should be a study of body and mind sloughed off that directly transmits this vital artery.[36] This "*when the insentient preach the dharma, the insentient can hear it*" must be the nature and marks of "*when the buddhas preach the dharma, the buddhas can hear it.*"[37] The community that would listen to the insentient preaching the dharma — whether they be sentient or insentient, whether they be common people or worthies and sages — must be insentient. On the basis of this nature and marks, we should judge the genuine and spurious in past and present.

Even if brought from Sindh in the West, if it is not by a true ancestral master of authentic transmission, it is of no use. Even for one whose training has been continuous for a thousand myriad years, if it is not what is inherited by successor after successor, it is difficult to succeed to it. Now, the authentic transmission has penetrated to the Land of the East, and it ought to be easy to distinguish the passage and blockage

---

36　**a study of body and mind sloughed off that directly transmits this vital artery** (*kono kechimyaku o shōden shite, shinjin datsuraku no sangaku* この血脈を正傳して、身心脱落の參學): Probably meaning something like, "a study that is liberated (or liberates us) through inheritance of this teaching." The term *meimyaku* 命脈 ("vital artery") occurs often in the *Shōbōgenzō*, in the senses both of the "lifeblood" and the "bloodline" (especially of the lineage of the buddhas and ancestors). "Body and mind sloughed off" (*shinjin datsuraku* 身心脱落) is one of Dōgen's favorite expressions for spiritual liberation; see Supplementary Notes.

37　**must be the nature and marks of** (*no shōsō naru beshi* の性相なるべし): I.e., "must be the same as"; "nature and marks" (*shōsō* 性相) is a standard expression in Buddhist writing for the essence (S. *svabhāva*) of a thing, and its defining characteristics, or attributes (S. *lakṣana*).

of the genuine and spurious. Even listening to the words, "*when living beings preach the dharma, living beings can hear it,*" we should surely accept them as the bones and marrow of the buddhas and the ancestors. In hearing the words of the Ancient Ancestor Yunyan, in listening to the words of the National Teacher Dazheng, when we truly appraise them, the sages referred to in "*the sages can hear it*" must be insentient; and the insentient referred to in "*the insentient can hear it*" must be sages. *What is preached by the insentient is insentient*; for *the insentient preaching the dharma is itself insentient*. Therefore, it is *the insentient preach the dharma*, and *preaching the dharma is the insentient*.

[46:16] {2:8}

高祖道の若恁麼、則某甲不聞和尚説法也。いまきくところの若恁麼は、無情説法、無情得聞の宗旨を擧拈するなり。無情説法、無情得聞の道理によりて、某甲不聞和尚説法也なり。高祖、このとき、無情説法の席末を接するのみにあらず、爲無情説法の志氣あらはれて、衝天するなり。ただ無情説法を體達するのみにあらず、無情説法の聞・不聞を體究せり。すすみて有情説法の説・不説、已説・今説・當説にも體達せしなり。さらに、聞・不聞の説法の、これは有情なり、これは無情なる道理を、あきらめをはりぬ。

The Eminent Ancestor said, "*In that case, I don't hear the Reverend preaching the dharma.*" The "in that case" we hear here is taking up the essential point of "when the insentient preach the dharma, the insentient can hear it": based on the principle that, "*when the insentient preach the dharma, the insentient can hear it,*" it is, "*I don't hear the Reverend preaching the dharma.*"[38] At this point, the Eminent Ancestor is not merely taking a rear seat for *the insentient preaching the dharma*; his aspiration to *preach the dharma for the insentient* manifests itself and assaults the heavens.[39] He does not simply personally realize "*the insentient preach the dharma*"; he has personally investigated the hearing and the not hearing of *the insentient preaching the dharma*. He has gone on personally to realize the *preaching and not preaching, the past preaching, present preaching, and future preaching* of the *sentient preaching the dharma*. And he has further completed clarification of the principle that the heard and unheard preaching of the dharma is sentient and is insentient.

38　**The "in that case" we hear here** (*ima kiku tokoro no nyaku inmo* いまきくところの若恁麼): Note that Dōgen's interpretation of Dongshan's "in that case" ignores the more obvious antecedent of Yunyan's immediately preceding statement, "If I heard it, you could not hear my preaching the dharma."

39　**rear seat** (*sekimatsu* 席末): I.e., a back seat in the assembly [listening to the insentient preach].

assaults the heavens (*shōten* 衝天): A fixed phrase for vaulting ambition or high aspiration; occurs several times in Dōgen's writings.

46. The Insentient Preach the Dharma *Mujō seppō* 無情説法

[46:17]

おほよそ聞法は、ただ耳根・耳識の境界のみにあらず、父母未生已前、威音以前、乃至盡未來際、無盡未來際にいたるまでの擧力・擧心・擧體・擧道をもて聞法するなり、身先心後の聞法あるなり。これらの聞法、ともに得益あり。心識に緣ぜざれば聞法の益あらず、といふことなかれ。心滅身沒のもの、聞法得益すべし、無心無身のもの、聞法得益すべし。諸佛諸祖、かならずかくのごとくの時節を經歷して、作佛し、成祖するなり。法力の、身心を接する、凡慮いかにしてか覺知しつくさん。身心の際限、みづからあきらめつくすことえざるなり。聞法功德の、身心の田地に下種する、くつる時節あらず。つひに生長、ときとともにして、果成必然なるものなり。

In general, hearing the dharma is not merely the object of the ear organ and ear consciousness: *from before your father and mother were born, from before Majestic Voice, to the limit of the future, to a limitless future,* we hear the dharma with our entire strength, entire mind, entire body, entire way; there is hearing the dharma before the body and after the mind.[40] All of these ways of hearing the dharma have their benefits. Do not say that there is no benefit in hearing the dharma when it does not register in consciousness.[41] Those with mind extinguished and body extinct should benefit from hearing the dharma; those with no mind and no body should benefit from hearing the dharma.[42] The buddhas and

---

40 **before your father and mother were born** (*bumo mishō izen* 父母未生已前): Also read *fubo mishō izen*. Also sometimes interpreted "before your father and mother gave birth." A famous expression in Zen literature suggesting what one is before one's identity as a person, what one really is before one can be identified; often associated with "one's original face" (*honrai menmoku* 本來面目). See Supplementary Notes, s.v. "Before your father and mother were born."

before Majestic Voice (*ion izen* 威音以前): See above, Note 6.

to the limit of the future, to a limitless future (*naishi jin miraisai, mujin miraisai* 乃至盡未來際、無盡未來際): "Limit of the future" is a common Buddhist term for the extreme limit of time, to which Dōgen here adds his own variant.

entire strength, entire mind, entire body, entire way (*koriki koshin kotai kodō* 擧力・擧心・擧體・擧道): Following the usual reading of *ko* 擧 ("to raise") here as "all," "whole," etc.; but the passage could be read, "taking up our strength, taking up our minds, taking up our bodies, taking up the way (or the words)."

before the body and after the mind (*shin sen shin go* 身先心後): An unusual expression, not occurring elsewhere in the *Shōbōgenzō*, suggesting "beyond body and mind" (or "before and after this body and mind"); variation on "before the body, after the body" (*shin sen shin go* 身先身後) — i.e., what precedes and follows a given lifetime.

41 **when it does not register in consciousness** (*shinshiki ni en zezareba* 心識に緣ぜざれば): Literally, "when it does not serve as the object of a mental consciousness."

42 **mind extinguished and body extinct** (*shin metsu shin motsu* 心滅身没); **no mind and no body** (*mushin mushin* 無心無身): Two unusual expressions, not occurring elsewhere in the *Shōbōgenzō*. While they may of course be read simply as states of unconsciousness, they may also suggest advanced spiritual states in which body and mind

ancestors always become buddhas and become ancestors by passing through such times.[43] The power of the dharma to touch the body and mind — how could common thinking fully perceive it? The limits of the body and mind cannot be fully clarified. The merit of hearing the dharma plants a seed in the field of body and mind that will never decay; eventually it will sprout and grow, and with time, will inevitably bear fruit.

[46:18] {2:9}
愚人おもはくは、たとひ聞法おこたらずとも、解路に進歩なく、記持に不敢ならんは、その益あるべからず、人天の身心を擧して、博記多聞ならん、これ至要なるべし、即座に忘記し、退席に茫然とあらん、なにの益かあらん、とおもひ、なにの學功かあらん、といふは、正師にあはず、その人をみざるゆえなり。正傳の面授あらざるを、正師にあらず、とはいふ。佛佛正傳しきたれるは、正師なり。愚人のいふ、心識に記持せられて、しばらくわすれざるに、聞法の功、いささか心識にも蓋心・蓋識する時節なり。この正當恁麼時は、蓋身・蓋身先・蓋心・蓋心先・蓋心後・蓋因・縁・報・業・相・性・體・力、蓋佛・蓋祖、蓋自・他、蓋皮・肉・骨・髄等の功徳あり。蓋言・説、蓋坐・臥等の功徳現きたれる成して、彌淪・彌天なるなり。

The foolish think that, even if we do not neglect to hear the dharma, without advancement on the road of understanding and no claim to a good memory, there will be no benefit in it.[44] Taking up the body and mind of humans and devas, to be one of extensive memory and much learning — this is the most essential. To forget on the spot and be at a loss once we depart — what benefit, they think, is there in that? What merit of learning, they say, is there in that? This is because they have not met a true master, because they have not seen that person.[45] One who lacks face-to-face conferral of the direct transmission is said not to be a true master. One who has received the direct transmission of buddha after buddha is a true master. When, as the foolish say, it is remembered in consciousness and not forgotten for a while, this is the time when

---

have been sloughed off. The term *shinmetsu* 心滅, translated here "mind extinguished," is commonly used for the cessation of a thought; "no mind" (*mushin* 無心) appears regularly as a spiritual virtue in Zen texts.

43   **passing through such times** (*kaku no gotoku no jisetsu o kyōryaku shite* かくのごとくの時節を經歴して): The antecedent of "such" here is unclear; perhaps such occasions of hearing the dharma.

44   **without advancement on the road of understanding and no claim to a good memory** (*gero ni shinpo naku, kiji ni fukan naran* 解路に進歩なく、記持に不敢ならん): The term *gero* 解路 ("road of understanding") is taken as "reasoning," "rational understanding"; *fukan* 不敢 (here, "claim to") is the colloquial "not at all," a polite response to a compliment.

45   **that person** (*sono hito* その人): An expression occurring several times in the *Shōbōgenzō* in the sense "a real person," "a person with real understanding."

the merit of hearing the dharma slightly covers the mind and covers the consciousness. At this very time, there is the merit that *covers the body, covers before the body, covers the mind, covers before the mind, covers after the mind; covers cause, conditions, recompense, deed, attribute, nature, substance, and power; covers the buddhas, and covers the ancestors, covers the self and the other, covers the skin, flesh, bones, and marrow.*[46] A virtue appears that *covers words and speech, covers sitting and reclining,* everywhere throughout the heavens.[47]

[46:19]
まことにかくのごとくある聞法の功德、たやすくしるべきにあらざれども、佛祖の大會に會して、皮肉骨髓を參究せん、説法の功力、ひかざる時節あらず、聞法の法力、かうぶらしめざるところあるべからず。かくのごとくして時節劫波を頓・漸ならしめて、結果の現成をみるなり。かの多聞博記も、あながちになげすつべきにあらざれども、その一隅をのみ要機とするにはあらざるなり。參學、これをしるべし、高祖、これを體達せしなり。

Although truly merit such as this in hearing the dharma is not easily known, when we join the great assembly of the buddhas and ancestors and investigate the skin, flesh, bones, and marrow, there is no time when the efficacy of preaching of the dharma does not lead us; there is no place in which we are not blessed by the dharma power of hearing the dharma. In this way, making the times and kalpas sudden or gradual, we see the realization of the results.[48] It is not that we should necessarily cast aside much learning and extensive memory; but we are not to take that one corner alone as the essential function. Students should know this. The Eminent Ancestor has personally realized this.

[46:20] {2:10}
曩祖道、我説法汝尚不聞、何況無情説法也。これは、高祖、たちまちに證上になほ證契を證しもてゆく現成を、曩祖、ちなみに開襟して、父祖の骨髓を印證するなり。

The Ancient Ancestor said, "*Even when I preach the dharma, you still don't hear it. How much less when the insentient preach the dharma.*" Here, given that the Eminent Ancestor has immediately verified the verification of the accord even beyond his verification, the Ancient Ances-

---

46　**cause, conditions, recompense, deed, attribute, nature, substance, and power** (*in en hō gō sō shō tai riki* 因・縁・報・業・相・性・體・力): From the list of the so-called "ten types of suchness" (*jū nyoze* 十如是) given in the *Lotus Sūtra* (*Miaofa lianhua jing* 妙法蓮華經, T.262.9:5c12-13).

47　**everywhere throughout the heavens** (*mirin miten* 彌淪・彌天): Combining two common expressions for universal pervasion. *Mirin* 彌淪 ("everywhere") is more often written 彌綸.

48　**making the times and kalpas sudden or gradual** (*jisetsu kōha o tonzen narashimete* 時節劫波を頓・漸ならしめて): I.e., either immediately or after æons.

tor opens his collar and seals and verifies the bones and marrow of the forefathers.[49]

[46:21]
なんぢなほ我説に不聞なり。これ凡流の然にあらず。無情説法たとひ萬端なりとも、爲慮あるべからず、と證明するなり。このときの嗣續、まことに秘要なり。凡聖の境界、たやすくおよびうかがふべきにあらず。

"You do not hear even my preaching."[50] Here, it is not that he is like the common types. He is attesting that, while *the insentient preaching the dharma* is of myriad sorts, he should give no thought to it.[51] The succession at this time is truly the secret essence.[52] In the realms of the common person and sage, one cannot easily reach it or hear of it.

[46:22]
高祖、ときに偈を理して雲巖曇祖に呈するにいはく、無情説法不思議は、也太奇、也太奇なり。しかあれば、無情および無情説法、ともに思議すべきことかたし。いはくの無情、なにものなりとかせん。凡・聖にあらず、情と無情にあらずと參學すべし。凡・聖、情・無情は、説・不説ともに思議の境界およびぬべし。いま不思議にして太奇なり、また太奇ならん。凡夫・賢聖の智慧・心識およぶべからず、天衆・人間の籌量にかかはるにあらざるべし。

The Eminent Ancestor then expressed a gāthā and presented it to the Ancient Ancestor Yunyan, saying that "*the inconceivability of the insentient preaching the dharma*" is "*How strange! How strange!*" Therefore, both the insentient and *the insentient preaching the dharma* are difficult to conceive. How are we to take this "insentient"? We should study that it is neither commoner nor sage, is neither sentient nor insentient. Whether commoner or sage, sentient or insentient, both their preaching and not preaching must belong to the realm of the conceivable. Here, it is "incon-

---

49 **given that the Eminent Ancestor has immediately verified the verification of the accord even beyond his verification** (*kōso, tachimachi ni shōjō ni nao shōkai o shōshi moteyuku genjō o* 高祖、たちまちに證上になほ證契を證しもてゆく現成を): An attempt to capture something of Dōgen's variations on the term *shō* 證 ("to verify"). "Verification of the accord" translates *shōkai* 證契 (elsewhere rendered "verify and accord"), an expression for spiritual realization, occurring several times in Dōgen's writings, that suggests the confirmation of a matching of minds between teacher and student.

opens his collar (*kaikin shite* 開襟して): An idiom, rather like the English "bare one's soul," for expression of one's true feelings.

50 **"You do not hear even my preaching"** (*nanji nao gasetsu ni fumon nari* なんぢなほ我説に不聞なり): Dōgen here rephrases Yuyan's remark in Japanese.

51 **he should give no thought to it** (*iryo aru bekarazu* 爲慮あるべからず): The term *iryo* 爲慮 typically means "to be concerned about," "to worry about"; but here the sense may be "conceptual thinking."

52 **secret essence** (*hiyō* 秘要): A term that, while common enough in Buddhist texts, does not occur elsewhere in the *Shōbōgenzō*.

ceivable"; it is "how strange!" and again, "how strange!" The wisdom and consciousness of the common people or the worthies and sages cannot reach it; it does not have to do with the calculations of devas or humans.

[46:23]
若將耳聽終難會は、たとひ天耳なりとも、たとひ彌界・彌時の法耳なりとも、將耳聽を擬するには、終難會なり。壁上耳・棒頭耳ありとも、無情説法を會すべからず、聲塵にあらざるがゆゑに。若將耳聽はなきにあらず、百千劫の功夫をつひやすとも、終難會なり。すでに聲色のほかの一道の威儀なり、凡聖のほとりの窠窟にあらず。

"*If we use the ear to hear it, it's hard in the end to understand*" means that, whether it be the deva ear or the dharma ear that fills the world and fills time, if we think to "*use the ear to hear it,*" "*it's hard in the end to understand.*"[53] Even if there are ears on walls or ears on staffs, they will not understand *the insentient preaching the dharma*; for it is not sound.[54] It is not that there is no "*if we use the ear to hear it,*" but even though we spend the concentrated efforts of a hundred thousand kalpas, "*it's hard in the end to understand.*"[55] Since it is the deportment of the one way beyond sound and form, it is not the dens and caves in the vicinity of the common person or sage.[56]

---

53 **deva ear** (*tenni* 天耳): Paranormal hearing; S. *divya-śrotra*, one of the standard five or six paranormal powers of the advanced contemplative; see Supplementary Notes, s.v. "Spiritual powers."

dharma ear (*hōni* 法耳): An unusual expression, no doubt intended to parallel the common "dharma eye" (*hōgen* 法眼) possessed by the advanced bodhisattva, as seen in "Shōbōgenzō mitsugo" 正法眼藏密語.

54 **ears on walls** (*hekijō ni* 壁上耳): Perhaps a play on the expression "the mouth hung on the wall" (*kō ka heki jō* 口挂壁上) — i.e., putting away the mouth and no longer using it to speak.

ears on staffs (*bōtō ni* 棒頭耳): Perhaps a play on the common expression "the staff has eyes" (*bōtō u gen* 棒頭有眼), meaning the master's staff knows when and where to strike. See Supplementary Notes, s.v. "Staff."

55 **It is not that there is no "if we use our ears to hear it"** (*nyaku shō ni chō wa naki ni arazu* 若將耳聽はなきにあらず): Probably meaning, "While we may use the ears to hear it." The odd English reflects Dōgen's retention of the conditional conjunction "if" (*nyaku* 若) from the verse.

56 **deportment of the one way beyond sound and form** (*shōshiki no hoka no ichidō no iigi* 聲色のほかの一道の威儀): No doubt reflecting a line in a verse by Xiangyan Zhixian 香嚴智閑 (d. 898) recorded in the *shinji Shōbōgenzō* 眞字正法眼藏 (DZZ.5:134, case 17) and invoked elsewhere in Dōgen's writings:

處處無蹤跡、聲色外威儀。
No traces wherever I go;
Deportment beyond sound and form.

See Supplementary Notes, s.v. "Deportment."

dens and caves (*kakutsu* 窠窟): See above, section 10.

[46:24] {2:11}
眼處聞聲方得知。この道取を、箇箇おもはくは、いま人眼の所見する草木華鳥の往來を、眼處の聞聲といふならん、とおもふ。この見處は、さらにあやまりぬ、またく佛法にあらず、佛法は、かくのごとくいふ道理なし。

"*Only when the eye hears the voices do we know it.*" This saying, people think must mean that the comings and goings of grass, trees, flowers, and birds seen by the human eye are "the eye hearing the voices." This viewpoint is completely mistaken, not the buddha dharma at all. The buddha dharma has no reasoning like this.

[46:25]
高祖道の眼處聞聲の參學するには、聞無情說法聲のところ、これ眼處なり、現無情說法聲のところ、これ眼處なり。眼處、さらにひろく參究すべし。眼處の聞聲は、耳處の聞聲にひとしかるべきがゆえに、眼處の聞聲は、耳處の聞聲にひとしからざるなり。眼處に耳根あり、と參學すべからず、眼即耳、と參學すべからず、眼裏聲現、と參學すべからず。

In studying "*the eye hears the voices*" said by the Eminent Ancestor, where we *hear the voices of the insentient preaching the dharma*, this is "the eye"; where we *manifest the voices of the insentient preaching the dharma*, this is "the eye."[57] We should investigate "the eye" still more broadly. Since the eye hearing the voices should be the same as the ear hearing the voices, the eye hearing the voices is not the same as the ear hearing the voices.[58] We should not study it to mean there is an ear organ in the eye; we should not study it to mean that the eye is the ear; we should not study it to mean that the voices occur within the eyes.

[46:26]
古云、盡十方界是沙門一隻眼。

Of old it was said, "*All the worlds in the ten directions are the single eye of the śramaṇa.*"[59]

---

57 **where we hear the voices of the insentient preaching the dharma, this is "the eye"** (*mon mujō seppō shō no tokoro, kore gensho nari* 聞無情說法聲のところ、これ眼處なり): In his use here of *tokoro* ところ ("the place where"), Dōgen seems to be playing with the element *sho* 處 ("place"; S. *āyatana*) in Dongshan's "eye" (*gensho* 眼處); similarly, *mutatis mutandis*, in the next clause. See Supplementary Notes, s.v. "Eye."

58 **Since the eye hearing the voices should be the same as the ear hearing the voices, the eye hearing the voices is not the same as the ear hearing the voices** (*gensho no monshō wa, nisho no monshō ni hitoshikaru beki ga yue ni, gensho no monshō wa, nisho no monshō ni hitoshikarazaru nari* 眼處の聞聲は、耳處の聞聲にひとしかるべきがゆえに、眼處の聞聲は、耳處の聞聲にひとしからざるなり): The odd logic of this sentence seems to be explained by Dōgen's remarks following it: i.e., the eye and ear are the same in that they have their distinct functions and, therefore, are not the same.

59 **"All the worlds in the ten directions are the single eye of the *śramaṇa*"** (*jin jippō kai ze shamon isseki gen* 盡十方界是沙門一隻眼): Also read *isseki gan*. Words, attribut-

[46:27]
この眼處に聞聲せば、高祖道の眼處聞聲ならん、と擬議商量すべからず。たとひ古人道の盡十方界一隻眼の道を學すとも、盡十方はこれ一隻眼なり。さらに千手頭眼あり、千正法眼あり、千耳眼あり、千舌頭眼あり、千心頭眼あり、千通心眼あり、千通身眼あり、千棒頭眼あり、千身先眼あり、千心先眼あり、千死中活眼あり、千活中活眼あり、千自眼あり、千他眼あり、千眼頭眼あり、千參學眼あり、千豎眼あり、千横眼あり。

We should not consider and deliberate that, if our eye hears the voices, it is the "*eye hears the voices*" said by the Eminent Ancestor. Although we study the words said by the ancient, that "*all the worlds in the ten directions are the single eye*," all the ten directions are themselves "the single eye." Moreover, there are a thousand hand eyes, a thousand true dharma eyes, a thousand ear eyes, a thousand tongue eyes, a thousand mind eyes, a thousand eyes throughout the mind, a thousand eyes throughout the body, a thousand staff eyes, a thousand eyes before the body, a thousand eyes before the mind, a thousand eyes of death within death, a thousand eyes of life within life, a thousand eyes of self, a thousand eyes of other, a thousand eyes of eyes, a thousand eyes of study, a thousand vertical eyes, a thousand horizontal eyes.⁶⁰

[46:28] {2:12}
しかあれば、盡眼を盡界と學すとも、なほ眼處に體究あらず、ただ、聞無情説法を眼處に參究せんことを急務すべし。いま高祖道の宗旨は、耳處は無情説法に難會なり、眼處は聞聲す。さらに通身處の聞聲あり、遍身處の聞聲あり。たとひ眼處聞聲を體究せずとも、無情説法、無情得聞を體達すべし、脱落すべし。この道理つたはれるゆゑに、

Thus, though we study all eyes as "all the worlds," we still lack personal investigation of "the eye." We should make it our urgent business to investigate *hearing the insentient preach the dharma* with "the eye."⁶¹ The Eminent Ancestor's essential point here is that for the ear it is "hard

---

ed to the ninth-century Chan figure Changsha Jingcen 長沙景岑 (dates unknown); see Supplementary Notes, s.v. "All the worlds in the ten directions are the single eye of the śramaṇa."

60 **a thousand hand eyes** (*senjutō gen* 千手頭眼): No doubt an allusion to Bodhisattva Avalokiteśvara of a thousand arms and a thousand eyes (*senju sengen Kannon* 千手千眼觀音), who is depicted with an eye in the palm of each hand. The topic is the subject of a conversation between Yunyan Tansheng 雲巖曇晟 and fellow disciple Daowu Yuanzhi 道吾圓智 (769-835) that is recorded in the *shinji Shōbōgenzō* 眞字正法眼藏 (DZZ.5:182, case 105) and discussed in the "Shōbōgenzō Kannon" 正法眼藏觀音; see Supplementary Notes, s.v. "His body throughout is hands and eyes."

a thousand staff eyes (*sen bōtō gen* 千棒頭眼): See above, Note 54.

61 **investigate hearing the insentient preach the dharma with "the eye"** (*mon mujō seppō o gensho ni sankyū sen* 聞無情説法を眼處に參究せん): The adverbial phrase "with the eye" (*gensho ni* 眼處に) here could modify either "investigate" or "hearing."

to understand" *the insentient preaching the dharma*; the eye hears the voices. Going further, there is "the body throughout" hearing the voices; there is "the body everywhere" hearing the voices.[62] Though we have not personally investigated "*the eye hears the voices*," we should personally realize, and should cast off, "*when the insentient preach the dharma, the insentient can hear it.*" Because this principle has been transmitted,

[46:29]
先師天童古佛道、胡蘆藤種纒胡蘆。

My former master, the Old Buddha of Tiantong said, "The bottle gourd vine entwines the bottle gourd."[63]

[46:30]
これ曩祖正眼のつたはれ、骨髄のつたはれる説法無情なり。一切説法無情なる道理によりて、無情説法なり、いはゆる典故なり。無情は爲無情説法なり。喚什麽作無情、しるべし、聽無情説法者是なり。喚什麽作説法、しるべし、不知吾無情者是なり。

This is *the insentient that preach the dharma* transmitting the true eye, transmitting the bones and marrow, of the Ancient Ancestor.[64] On the principle that *all preaching the dharma is insentient*, it is "*the insentient preach the dharma*"; this represents the standard case.[65] The insentient preach the dharma for the sake of the insentient. What should we call the insentient?[66] We should know: *it is the one who hears the insentient preaching the dharma*. What should we call preaching the dharma? We should know: it is *the one who does not know it is insentient*.

---

62 **"the body throughout"** (*tsūshin sho* 通身處); **"the body everywhere"** (*henshin sho* 遍身處): Terms reflecting the dialogue on the thousand eyes and arms of Avalokiteśvara alluded to in the preceding section; see above, Note 60. The English "body" here loses Dōgen's playful replacement of *shin* 身 in the original dialogue with *shinsho* 身處 ("tactile sense field"; S. *kāyātana*), in keeping with Dongshan's *gensho* 眼處 ("sense of vision"); see above, Note 31.

63 **Old Buddha of Tiantong** (*Tendō kobutsu* 天童古佛): I.e., Dōgen's teacher Tiantong Rujing 天童如淨 (1162-1227). See Supplementary Notes, s.v. "The bottle gourd vine entwines the bottle gourd." Dōgen often cites or alludes to this saying in the *Shōbōgenzō*.

64 **This is the insentient that preach the dharma transmitting the true eye, transmitting the bones and marrow, of the Ancient Ancestor** (*kore Nōso shōgen no tsutaware, kotsuzui no tsutawareru seppō mujō nari* これ曩祖正眼のつたはれ、骨髄のつたはれる説法無情なり): I.e., Rujing's intertwining vines are the essence of the insentient preaching Yunyan's Buddhism.

65 **this represents the standard case** (*iwayuru tenko nari* いはゆる典故なり): Likely meaning that the Ancient Ancestor's words, "the insentient preach the dharma," represent "the *locus classicus*" or "the governing precedent" of this teaching.

66 **What should we call the insentient?** (*kan jūmo sa mujō* 喚什麽作無情): Here and in the following three sentences, Dōgen shifts to a mixed Chinese-Japanese syntax.

46. The Insentient Preach the Dharma *Mujō seppō* 無情説法

* * * * *

[46:31]

舒州投子山慈濟大師＜嗣翠微無學禪師、諱大同。明覺云、投子古佛。＞因僧問、如何是無情説法。師曰、莫惡口。

> Great Master Ciji of Mount Touzi, from Shuzhou (Succeeded Chan Master Wuxue of Cuiwei; named Datong.[67] Of whom Mingzue said, "Touzi is an old buddha"), was once asked by a monk, "What is the insentient preaching the dharma?"
>
> The Master said, "Don't be foul mouthed."

[46:32] {2:13}

いまこの投子の道取するところ、まさしくこれ古佛の法謨なり、祖宗の治象なり。無情説法ならびに説法無情等、おほよそ莫惡口なり。しるべし、無情説法は、佛祖の總章これなり。臨濟・德山のともがらしるべからず、ひとり佛祖なるのみ參究す。

What Touzi says here is truly the dharma plan of the old buddhas, the edict of the ancestors.[68] *The preaching of the dharma by the insentient, the insentient that preach the dharma*, and the like, are, in sum, "*Don't be foul mouthed.*" We should know, "*the insentient preaching the dharma*" is the head office of the buddhas and ancestors.[69] The confederates of Linji and Deshan cannot understand it; only those who are buddhas and ancestors investigate it.[70]

正法眼藏無情説法第四十六
Treasury of the True Dharma Eye
The Insentient Preach the Dharma
Number 46

---

67 **Great Master Ciji of Mount Touzi, from Shuzhou** (*Joshū Tōsuzan Jisai daishi* 舒州投子山慈濟大師): (The parenthetical remarks following are in the original.) Ciji 慈濟 is the posthumous name granted to Datong 大同 (819-914), who received dharma-transmission from Cuiwei Wuxue 翠微無學, a monk in the lineage of Qingyuan Xingsi 青原行思. This conversation can be found at *Liandeng huiyao* 聯燈會要, ZZ.136:777a1.

68 **dharma plan of the old buddhas** (*kobutsu no hōmo* 古佛の法謨): The unusual term *hōmo* 法謨 suggests a "master plan for the buddha dharma."

69 **head office of the buddhas and ancestors** (*busso no sōshō* 佛祖の總章): From the Zongzhang 總章, the administrative office in the Chinese imperial palace.

70 **Linji and Deshan** (*Rinzai Tokusan* 臨濟・德山): I.e., Linji Yixuan 臨濟義玄 (d. 866) and Deshan Xuanjian 德山宣鑑 (780-865). One of several slights in the *Shōbōgenzō* of these two famous masters.

[Ryūmonji MS:]

爾時寛元元年癸卯十月二日、在越州吉田縣吉峰寺示衆
Presented to the assembly at Kippō Monastery, Yoshida District, Esshū; second day, tenth month of the junior water year of the rabbit, the first year of Kangen [November 15, 1243][71]

[Tōunji MS:]

同癸卯十月十五日、書寫之。懷奘
Copied this the fifteenth day, tenth month of the junior water year of the rabbit [28 November 1243]. Ejō

于時文明十二庚子春王正月朔日、於于越州吉田郡志比吉祥山永平寺承陽庵、比丘光周書之
In the Jōyō Hermitage, Eihei Monastery, Mount Kichijō, Shihi, Yoshida District, Esshū; on the first day of the first month, the King of Spring, senior metal year of the rat, the twelfth year of Bunmei [11 February 1480], Bhikṣu Kōshū copied this[72]

---

71 The Tōunji 洞雲寺 MS shares an identical colophon.

72 **Jōyō Hermitage** (*Jōyōan* 承陽庵): Dōgen's memorial shrine at Eiheiji 永平寺, from his posthumous title Great Master Jōyō (*Jōyō daishi* 承陽大師).

King of Spring (*shun'ō* 春王): The first lunar month.

Bhikṣu Kōshū (*biku Kōshū* 光周): Fifteenth abbot of Eiheiji (1434–1492?).

TREASURY OF THE TRUE DHARMA EYE

NUMBER 47

Sūtras of the Buddhas

Bukkyō

佛經

Sūtras of the Buddhas

Bukkyō

INTRODUCTION

This essay was composed at Kippōji in the ninth lunar month of 1243. It represents number 47 in the seventy-five-chapter *Shōbōgenzō* and number 52 in the Honzan edition; it is not included in the sixty-chapter compilation but is found as number 4 of fascicle 3 in the twenty-eight-text collection.

The essay concerns the centrality of the sūtras in the Zen tradition. In this, it is directed against those that would see the tradition as "a separate transmission outside the teachings" (*kyōge betsuden* 教外別傳), "not dependent on words and letters" (*furyū monji* 不立文字). In the first part of his essay, Dōgen argues that the sūtras and Zen masters convey the same teachings, that the activities of the Zen master are the enactment of the sūtras, that indeed, when properly understood, the sūtras are "all the worlds in the ten directions."

The remainder of the essay is devoted to a sharp criticism of recent developments in Chan in the Song dynasty: for example, the view that we should abandon study and simply empty our minds; the practice of using stock lines of the Chan masters as the standards for training; or the view that the three traditions of Confucianism, Daoism, and Buddhism are ultimately one. In the course of this criticism, Dōgen dismisses the famous Tang-dynasty figure Linji Yixuan 臨濟義玄 while praising his own teacher, Tiantong Rujing 天童如淨; he ends with a warning against the assumption that foreign monks and imperial teachers are necessarily accomplished in Buddhism.

In its themes and its strongly polemical tone, this essay has similarities with three other *Shōbōgenzō* chapters — "Butsudō" 佛道, "Shohō jissō" 諸法實相, and "Mitsugo" 密語 — that date from the ninth month of 1243 and represent Dōgen's first thoughts after abandoning his mission in the imperial capital and moving his community to the isolated region of Echizen.

正法眼藏第四十七
Treasury of the True Dharma Eye
Number 47

佛經
Sūtras of the Buddhas

[47:1] {2:14}
このなかに、教菩薩法あり、教諸佛法あり。おなじくこれ大道の調度なり。調度、ぬしにしたがふ、ぬし、調度をつかふ。これによりて、西天東地の佛祖、かならず或從知識、或從經卷の正當恁麼時、おのおの發意・修行・證果、かつて間隙あらざるものなり。發意も經卷・知識により、修行も經卷・知識による、證果も經卷・知識に一親なり。機先句後、おなじく經卷・知識に同參なり。機中句裏、おなじく經卷・知識に同參なり。

Among these, there is the "*dharma taught to the bodhisattvas*"; there is the *dharma taught to the buddhas*.[1] They are both implements of the great way. The implements fit their owners; the owners use the implements. Due to this, at the very time that each of the buddhas and ancestors of Sindh in the West and the Land of the East, *whether from a wise friend, whether from a sūtra scroll*, brings forth the thought [of bodhi], practices, and verifies the fruit, there has never been any gap.[2] Bringing forth

---

1 **Among these** (*kono naka ni* このなかに): In the absence of any antecedent, the surprising pronoun at the head of the essay must refer to the "sūtras" of the title (though some would read this expression in the sense "here").

"dharma taught to the bodhisattvas" (*kyō bosatsu hō* 教菩薩法): Recalling the introduction to the *Lotus Sūtra* (*Miaofa lianhua jing* 妙法蓮華經, T.262.9:2b7-9):

爾時世尊、四衆圍遶、供養恭敬尊重讚歎、爲諸菩薩説大乘經、名無量義、教菩薩法、佛所護念。

At that time, the World-Honored One, surrounded by the fourfold congregation, favored with offerings, honored and revered, preached a sūtra of the great vehicle for the bodhisattvas entitled *Immeasurable Meaning*, a dharma taught to the bodhisattvas, that the buddhas bear in mind.

The following "dharma taught to the buddhas" (*kyō shobutsu hō* 教諸佛法) is Dōgen's variation on the sūtra phrase.

2 **whether from a wise friend, whether from a sūtra scroll** (*waku jū chishiki, waku jū kyōkan* 或從知識、或從經卷): A fixed phrase, in Chinese syntax, that occurs often in Dōgen's writings; see Supplementary Notes.

there has never been any gap (*katsute kangeki arazaru mono nari* かつて間隙あらざるものなり): Exactly what "gap" is being denied here is not entirely obvious; perhaps, the gaps in the sequence of the bodhisattva's initial aspiration for bodhi, practice on the

the thought depends on sūtra scrolls and wise friends; practice depends on sūtra scrolls and wise friends; verifying the fruit is wholly intimate with sūtra scrolls and wise friends. *Before the function and after the words* are both studying together with sūtra scrolls and wise friends; *in the function and within the words* are both studying together with sūtra scrolls and wise friends.[3]

[47:2]
知識は、かならず經卷を通利す。通利す、といふは、經卷を國土とし、經卷を身心とす、經卷を爲他の施設とせり、經卷を坐臥・經行とせり、經卷を父母とし、經卷を兒孫とせり、經卷を行解とせるがゆえに、これ知識の、經卷を參究せるなり。知識の洗面・喫茶、これ古經なり。經卷の、知識を出生するといふは、黄檗の六十拄杖、よく兒孫を生長せしめ、黄梅の打三杖、よく傳衣・付法せしむるのみにあらず、桃華をみて悟道し、竹響をききて悟道する、および見明星悟道、みなこれ經卷の、知識を生長せしむるなり。あるいは、まなこをえて經卷をうる皮袋・拳頭あり、あるいは、經卷をえてまなこをうる木杓・漆桶あり。

Wise friends are always well versed in the sūtra scrolls. "Well versed" means they take the sūtra scrolls as the land; they take the sūtra scrolls as their bodies and minds; they take the sūtra scrolls as provisionally established for the sake of others; they take the sūtra scrolls as sitting, reclining, and walking; they take the sūtra scrolls as their father and mother; they take the sūtra scrolls as their descendants; they take the sūtra scrolls as practice and understanding. It is for this reason that wise friends investigate the sūtra scrolls. Wise friends' washing their faces and taking tea — these are the old sūtras.[4] That the sūtra scrolls give birth to wise friends means not only Huangbo's sixty blows nurturing his descendants, and Huangmei's three strikes transmitting the robe and bequeathing the dharma, but also seeing the peach blossoms and awakening to the way, hearing the sound of the bamboo and awakening to the way, seeing the dawn star and awakening to the way: these are all the

---

path, and final awakening, though, given what follows in this section, one might also imagine the gap between the "wise friend" and the "sūtra scroll" as spiritual resources throughout this sequence.

3 **Before the function and after the words** (*kisen kugo* 機先句後): Variation on the more common *shōzen kugo* 聲前句後 ("before the voice and after the words"), suggesting what is before and after anything exists or happens; in the context here, it may be that the unusual phrase is meant to invoke the "function" of the wise friends and the "words" of the sūtras.

4 **Wise friends' washing their faces and taking tea** (*chishiki no senmen kissa* 知識の洗面・喫茶): Possibly an allusion to the story of Weishan Lingyu 潙山靈祐 (771-853) washing his face and taking tea with Xiangyan Zhixian 香嚴智閑 (d. 898) and Yangshan Huiji 仰山慧寂 (803-887) (see, e.g., *Jingde chuandeng lu* 景德傳燈錄, T.2076.51:265c16-21; *shinji Shōbōgenzō* 眞字正法眼藏, DZZ.5:158, case 61). Dōgen discusses the story in his "Shōbōgenzō jinzū" 正法眼藏神通.

sūtra scrolls growing wise friends.[5] There are skin bags and fists who get sūtra scrolls by getting eyes; there are wooden ladles and lacquer buckets that get eyes by getting sūtra scrolls.[6]

[47:3] {2:15}
いはゆる經卷は、盡十方界これなり。經卷にあらざる時處なし。勝義諦の文字をもちい、世俗諦の文字をもちい、あるいは天上の文字をもちい、あるいは人間の文字をもちい、あるいは畜生道の文字をもちい、あるいは修羅道の文字をもちい、あるいは百草の文字をもちい、あるいは萬木の文字をもちいる。このゆえに、盡十方界に森森として羅列せる長・短・方・圓・青・黃・赤・白、しかしながら經卷の文字なり、經卷の表面なり。これを大道の調度とし、佛家の經卷とせり。

"Sūtra scrolls" are all the worlds in the ten directions. There is no time or place that is not a sūtra scroll. They use the script of ultimate truth; they use the script of conventional truth. Or they use the script of the heavens above, or they use the script of humans, or they use the script of the path of the beasts, or they use the script of the path of the *asuras*, or they use the script of the hundred grasses, or they use the

---

5 **Huangbo's sixty blows** (*Ōbaku no rokujū shujō* 黃檗の六十拄杖): Allusion to the tradition that Huangbo Xiyun 黃檗希運 beat his student Linji Yixuan 臨濟義玄 (d. 866) sixty times (see, e.g., *Biyan lu* 碧巖錄, T.2003.48:222b19-21); re-introduced below, section 18.

Huangmei's three strikes (*Ōbai no da sanjō* 黃梅の打三杖): Allusion to the story that, when the future Sixth Ancestor, Huineng 慧能, was husking rice at the Fifth Ancestor's monastery at Huangmei 黃梅, the latter signaled his acknowledgment of the former by striking the mortar three times, after which he transmitted the dharma and gave him the ancestral robe of Bodhidharma; see, e.g., *Tiansheng guangdeng lu* 天聖廣燈錄, ZZ.135:645a9-11. Dōgen tells a version of the story in his "Shōbōgenzō inmo" 正法眼藏恁麼.

seeing the peach blossoms (*tōke o mite* 桃華をみて): Allusion to the story that Lingyun Zhiqin 靈雲志勤 awakened to the way upon viewing peach trees in bloom; see Supplementary Notes, s.v. "Peach blossoms." Dōgen includes the story in his *shinji Shōbōgenzō* 眞字正法眼藏 (DZZ.5:206, case 155) and recounts the episode in his "Shōbōgenzō keisei sanshoku" 正法眼藏溪聲山色.

hearing the sound of the bamboo (*chikukyō o kikite* 竹響をききて): Allusion to the story that Xiangyan Zhixian 香嚴智閑 gained an understanding upon hearing a bit of debris strike a bamboo stalk; see Supplementary Notes, s.v. "A painted cake can't satisfy hunger." Dōgen includes the story in his *shinji Shōbōgenzō* 眞字正法眼藏 (DZZ.5:206, case 155) and recounts the episode in his "Shōbōgenzō keisei sanshoku" 正法眼藏溪聲山色.

seeing the dawn star and awakening to the way (*ken myōjō godō* 見明星悟道): Allusion to the tradition that Buddha Śākyamuni was awakened upon seeing the planet Venus. See, e.g., *Xiuxing benji jing* 修行本記經, T.184.3:471c29.

6 **skin bags and fists** (*hitai kentō* 皮袋・拳頭); **wooden ladles and lacquer buckets** (*mokushaku shittsū* 木杓・漆桶): Common ironic references to Zen masters; see Supplementary Notes, s.v. "Bag of skin," "Fist," and "Lacquer bucket."

script of the myriad trees. For this reason, the long and short, the square and round, the blue, yellow, red, and white, densely arrayed throughout all the worlds in the ten directions, are all the script of the sūtra scrolls, the surfaces of the sūtra scrolls. These, we take as the implements of the great way, we take as the sūtra scrolls of the house of the buddhas.

[47:4]

この經卷、よく蓋時に流布し、蓋國に流通す。教人の門をひらきて、盡地の人家をすてず、教物の門をひらきて、盡地の物類をすくふ。教諸佛し、教菩薩するに、盡地・盡界なるなり。開方便門し、開住位門して、一箇半箇をすてず、示眞實相するなり。この正恁麼時、あるいは諸佛、あるいは菩薩の慮知念覺と無慮知念覺と、みづからおのおの強爲にあらざれども、この經卷をうるを、各面の大期とせり。

These sūtra scrolls spread through all times and circulate through all lands. Opening the gate that teaches humans, they do not forsake any human of all the earth; opening the gate that teaches things, they save the beings of all the earth. When they teach the buddhas and teach the bodhisattvas, it is all the earth and all the realms. "Opening the gate of expedient means," opening the gate of abiding in position, without forsaking one or a half, they "reveal the true real mark."[7] At this very moment, whether the buddhas or the bodhisattvas, in their thinking and perceiving, and in their not thinking and perceiving, though not their own deliberate demand, have, each of them, made getting this sūtra scroll their great aspiration.[8]

[47:5]

必得是經のときは、古今にあらず、古今は得經の時節なるがゆえに。盡十方界の、目前に現前せるは、これ得是經なり。この經を讀誦通利するに、佛智・自然智・無師智、こころよりさきに現成し、身よりさきに現成す。このとき、新條の特地、とあやしむことなし。この經の、われらに受持讀誦せらるるは、經の、われらを攝取するなり。文先句外、向下節上の消息、すみやかに散華貫華なり。

---

[7] **"Opening the gate of expedient means"** (*kai hōben mon* 開方便門); **"opening the gate of abiding in position"** (*kai jūi mon* 開住位門); **they "reveal the true real mark"** (*ji shin jissō* 示眞實相): Allusions to lines in the *Lotus Sūtra*. The first and third phrases occur in a sentence at *Miaofa lianhua jing* 妙法蓮華經, T.262.9:31c16-17:

此經開方便門、示眞實相。

This sūtra opens the gate of expedient means and reveals the true real mark.

The second phrase is Dōgen's play on the first, alluding to a line he often cites. See Supplementary Notes, s.v. "Dharmas abide in their dharma positions."

[8] **At this very moment** (*kono shō inmo ji* この正恁麼時): This convoluted sentence might be paraphrased, "When the sūtras reveal the real mark, the buddhas and bodhisattvas all greatly anticipate obtaining the sūtras, whether or not they are consciously aware of and intentionally trying for this."

47. Sūtras of the Buddhas *Bukkyō* 佛經   33

The time in which they "*surely get this sūtra*" is not past or present; for past and present are the time they get the sūtra.⁹ The manifesting before their eyes of all the worlds in the ten directions — this is "getting this sūtra." When they "read, recite, and are well versed in" this sūtra, "buddha wisdom, natural wisdom, untaught wisdom" are realized before the mind, are realized before the body.¹⁰ At that time they do not doubt it as a new, special state. When these sūtras are received and kept, read and recited by us, the sūtras gather us in. The circumstances *before the writing and beyond the words, going beneath and above the sections*, are immediately scattered flowers and strung flowers.¹¹

---

9   **The time in which they "surely get this sūtra"** (*hitsu toku ze kyō no toki* 必得是經のとき): Again, an allusion to the *Lotus Sūtra* (*Miaofa lianhua jing* 妙法蓮華經, T.262.9:61a21-22):

善男子善女人、如是成就四法、於如來滅後、必得是經。

If good sons and good daughters achieve four dharmas in this way, after the extinction of the Tathāgata, they will surely get this sūtra.

for past and present are the time they get the sūtra (*kokon wa toku kyō no jisetsu naru ga yue ni* 古今は得經の時節なるがゆえに): Perhaps, the seemingly nonsensical logic here can be understood as something like, "Getting the sūtra is not something that happens at a time in history; for all of history is the time of getting the sūtra." The translation follows Kawamura's punctuation, but it is also possible to read this phrase with the following sentence, thus yielding something like, "Because all of history is the time of getting the sūtra, everything that appears in the present is getting the sūtra."

10   **When they "read, recite, and are well versed in" this sūtra** (*kono kyō o dokuju tsūri suru ni* この經を讀誦通利するに): Perhaps another allusion to the *Lotus Sūtra* (*Miaofa lianhua jing* 妙法蓮華經, T.262.9:58b10-12):

世尊、若善男子善女人、有能受持法華經者、若讀誦通利、若書寫經卷、得幾所福。

[Bodhisattva Medicine King asked,] "World-Honored One, if there are good sons and good daughters who receive and keep the *Lotus Sūtra*, who read, recite, and are well versed in it, who copy the sūtra scrolls, how much merit will they get?"

"buddha wisdom, natural wisdom, untaught wisdom" (*butchi jinenchi mushichi* 佛智・自然智・無師智): Again, reflecting the *Lotus Sūtra* (*Miaofa lianhua jing* 妙法蓮華經, T.262.9:13b24-28):

若有衆生。從佛世尊聞法信受。勤修精進。求一切智佛智自然智無師智如來知見力無所畏。憨愍安樂無量衆生。利益天人度脱一切。是名大乘。

If there are beings who, hearing the dharma from a buddha, a World-Honored One, believe it, diligently practice it, and make efforts, seeking universal wisdom, natural wisdom, untaught wisdom, the knowledge, powers, and fearlessness of the tathāgata, mercifully thinking on and providing joy to incalculable beings, benefiting devas and humans and delivering them all, these are called the Great Vehicle.

11   **going beneath and above the sections** (*kōge setsujō* 向下節上): A tentative translation of an obscure phrase not encountered elsewhere in Dōgen's writing; perhaps meaning both implicit ("beneath" the text) and explict ("above" the sections of text).

scattered flowers and strung flowers (*sange kange* 散華貫華): Perhaps meaning that the various teachings all come together. Likely reflecting the simile of a sūtra as a thread

[47:6] {2:16}

この經を、すなはち法となづく。これに八萬四千の説法蘊あり、この經のなかに、成等正覺の諸佛なる文字あり、現住世間の諸佛なる文字あり、入般涅槃の諸佛なる文字あり。如來・如去、ともに經中の文字なり、法上の法文なり。拈華瞬目、微笑破顔、すなはち七佛正傳の古經なり。腰雪斷臂、禮拜得髓、まさしく師資相承の古經なり。つひにすなはち傳法・附衣する、これすなはち廣文全卷を附屬せしむる時節至なり。みたび臼をうち、みたび箕の米をひる、經の經を出手せしめ、經の經に正嗣するなり。

These sūtras are called the dharma. In them, there is the preaching of the eighty-four-thousandfold aggregate of dharmas; within these sūtras, there is script that is the buddhas who have attained perfect awakening; there is script that is buddhas presently abiding in the world; there is script that is buddhas passed into *parinirvāṇa*.[12] The thus-come ones and the thus-gone ones are both the script in these sūtras, the script of the dharma on the dharma.[13] *Holding up a flower and blinking the eyes, breaking into a smile*, are an old sūtra directly transmitted by the seven buddhas.[14] Hip-deep in snow and cutting off an arm, making a bow and getting the marrow, are an old sūtra inherited from master to disciple.[15] Eventually, the transmission of the dharma and the bestowal of the robe

---

that prevents the teachings from scattering, as a garland keeps flowers from scattering in the wind. See, e.g., *Shanjianlü piposha* 善見律毘婆沙, T.1462.24:676a29-b3.

12 **script that is the buddhas who have attained perfect awakening** (*jō tōshōgaku no shobutsu naru monji* 成等正覺の諸佛なる文字): I.e., the sūtra texts are the dharma body of the buddhas. The term *monji* 文字 ("script"; also read *moji*) can refer either to the content of the texts or to the glyphs with which they are written.

13 **The thus-come ones and the thus-gone ones** (*nyorai nyoko* 如來・如去): Two interpretations of the Sanskrit epithet for buddhas, *tathāgata*, read either as *tathā-āgata* ("come thus") or *tathā-gata* ("gone thus").

the script of the dharma on the dharma (*hōjō no hōmon* 法上の法文): The exact sense is uncertain; perhaps meaning that the text of the dharma inscribes the dharma in the sūtras.

14 **Holding up a flower and blinking the eyes, breaking into a smile** (*nenge shunmoku, mishō hagan* 拈華瞬目、微笑破顔): Allusion to the famous first transmission of Zen, on Vulture Peak, when Buddha Śākyamuni held up a flower, and Mahākāśyapa smiled. The expression *mishō hagan* 微笑破顔 ("breaking into a smile") is normally written in reverse order: *hagan mishō* 破顔微笑. See Supplementary Notes, s.v. "Holding up a flower and blinking the eyes."

15 **Hip-deep in snow and cutting off an arm, making a bow and getting the marrow** (*yōsetsu danpi, raihai tokuzui* 腰雪斷臂、禮拜得髓): Allusion to two incidents in the transmission from Bodhidharma to the second Chinese ancestor, Huike 慧可: the former phrase refers to the legend that Huike stood through a snowy night, waiting for Bodhidharma to acknowledge him, and then finally cut off his own arm as an offering (see Supplementary Notes, s.v. "Cut off an arm"); the latter phrase recalls the scene in which Huike expressed his understanding of Bodhidharma's teaching by bowing silently, and Bodhidharma said, "You've gotten my marrow" (see Supplementary Notes, s.v. "Skin, flesh, bones, and marrow").

47. Sūtras of the Buddhas Bukkyō 佛經

— this was the arrival of the time when all the scrolls of the vast writings are entrusted; striking the mortar three times, sifting the rice three times, are a sūtra holding out a sūtra, a sūtra directly succeeding a sūtra.[16]

[47:7]
しかのみにあらず、是什麼物恁麼來、これ教諸佛の千經なり、教菩薩の萬經なり。説似一物即不中、よく八萬蘊をとき、十二部をとく。いはんや拳頭・脚跟、拄杖・拂子、すなはち古經・新經なり、有經・空經なり。在衆辦道、功夫坐禪、もとより頭正也佛經なり、尾正也佛經なり。菩提葉に經し、虛空面に經す。

Not only this, but *what thing is it that comes like this?* — this is the thousand sūtras taught to the buddhas, the myriad sūtras taught to the bodhisattvas; *to say it's like any thing wouldn't hit it* preaches the eighty-thousandfold aggregate, preaches the twelvefold division.[17] Not to mention that *the fist and heel, the staff and whisk,* are old sūtras and new sūtras, sūtras of being and sūtras of emptiness.[18] *Pursuing the way in the assembly and making concentrated effort in seated meditation* are fundamentally *a sūtra of the buddhas true from the head,* are *a sūtra of*

---

16 **the transmission of the dharma and the bestowal of the robe** (*denbō fue* 傳法・付衣); **striking the mortar three times, sifting the rice three times** (*mitabi usu o uchi, mitabi mi no kome o hiru* みたび臼をうち、みたび箕の米をひる): References to the transmission from the Fifth Ancestor to Huineng; see above, Note 5. Dōgen's version of the story (see, e.g., "Shōbōgenzō inmo" 正法眼藏恁麼) is unusual in having Huineng respond to the Ancestor's three strikes by sifting the rice in his winnow three times.

17 **"what thing is it that comes like this?"** (*ze jūmo butsu inmo rai* 是什麼物恁麼來); **to say it's like any thing wouldn't hit it** (*setsu ji ichimotsu soku fuchū* 説似一物即不中): Reference to a conversation, much quoted by Dōgen, between the Sixth Ancestor and Nanyue Huairang 南嶽懷讓. The first sentence is the Ancestor's question; the second, is Huairang's response. See Supplementary Notes, s.v. "What thing is it that comes like this?"

eighty-thousandfold aggregate (*hachiman un* 八萬蘊); **the twelvefold division** (*jūni bu* 十二部): I.e., the entire body of sūtras. The former phrase rounds off the standard "eighty-four-thousandfold" collection of teachings; the latter phrase refers to a common organization of the sūtras by type, discussed in the "Shōbōgenzō bukkyō" 正法眼藏佛教. See Supplementary Notes, s.v. "Three vehicles and twelvefold teachings."

18 **fist and heel, the staff and whisk** (*kentō kyakukon, shujō hossu* 拳頭・脚跟、拄杖・拂子): Common terms of synecdoche ("fist" and "heel") and metonymy ("staff" and "whisk") for the Zen master; see Supplementary Notes, s.v. "Fist," "Staff," and "Whisk."

sūtras of being and sūtras of emptiness (*u kyō kū kyō* 有經・空經): A tentative translation; presumably, "sūtras that teach the existence of dharmas" and "sūtras that teach the emptiness of dharmas."

the buddhas true to the tail.[19] They compose a sūtra on a bodhi leaf; they compose a sūtra on the face of empty space.[20]

[47:8]
おほよそ佛祖の一動兩靜、あはせて把定・放行、おのれづから佛經の卷舒なり。窮極あらざるを、窮極の標準と參學するゆゑに、鼻孔より受經・出經す、脚尖よりも受經・出經す。父母未生前にも受經・出經あり、威音王以前にも受經・出經あり。山河大地をもて、經をうけ、經をとく、日月星辰をもて、經をうけ、經をとく。あるいは空劫以前の自己をして、經を持し、經をさづく、あるいは面目已前の身心をもて、經を持し、經をさづく。かくのごとくの經は、微塵を破して出現せしむ、法界を破していださしむるなり。

In sum, the buddhas and ancestors' one movement and two stillnesses, as well as their holding fast and letting go, are themselves the rolling up and unrolling of the sūtras of the buddhas.[21] Because they study the lack of any limit as the marker of the limit, they receive the sūtras and bring forth the sūtras through their nostrils; they receive the sūtras and bring forth the sūtras through the tips of their toes. There is receiving the sūtras and bringing forth the sūtras *before their father and mother were born*; there is receiving the sūtras and bringing forth the sūtras before King Majestic Voice.[22] They receive the sūtras and preach the sūtras by means of the mountains, rivers, and the whole earth; they receive the sūtras and preach the sūtras by means of the sun, moon, and constellations. Or they keep the sūtras and bestow the sūtras by the self before the kalpa of emptiness; or they keep the sūtras and bestow the sūtras by the body and

---

19 **sūtra of the buddhas true from the head** (*zushin ya bukkyō* 頭正也佛經); **sūtra of the buddhas true to the tail** (*bishin ya bukkyō nari* 尾正也佛經なり): From the expression, common in Dōgen's writing, "true from head to tail" (*zushin bishin* 頭正尾正).

20 **They compose a sūtra on a bodhi leaf** (*bodai yō ni kyō shi* 菩提葉に經し): Presumably playing on the palm leaf, on which the sūtras were written in India. "Compose a sūtra" renders Dōgen's use here of "sūtra" as a verb (*kyō shi* 經し), perhaps suggesting the act of composing the "warp" (*tate* 經) on a loom.

21 **one movement and two stillnesses** (*ichidō ryōjō* 一動兩靜): Presumably, meaning "any movement and rest"; an unusual expression, not occurring elsewhere in the *Shōbōgenzō*.

holding fast and letting go (*hajō hōgyō* 把定・放行): An expression, often used by Dōgen, sometimes in reverse order, alluding to the teaching methods of the Zen master; perhaps reflecting a verse by Tiantong Rujing 天童如淨 (1162-1227) (*Rujing chanshi yulu* 如淨禪師語錄, T.2002A.48:122c18):

放行把住逞風流。
Letting go and holding on, full of style.

22 **before their father and mother were born** (*bumo mishō zen* 父母未生前); **before King Majestic Voice** (*Ion'ō izen* 威音王以前): Two common fixed expressions, appearing often in the *Shōbōgenzō*, for that which precedes phenomenal existence. See Supplementary Notes, s.v. "Before your father and mother were born" and "Before King Majestic Voice."

mind before the face.²³ Such sūtras, they reveal by smashing dust motes, they bring forth by smashing dharma realms.²⁴

* * * * *

[47:9] {2:17}
第二十七祖般若多羅尊者道、貧道出息不随衆縁、入息不居蘊界、常轉如是經、百千萬億巻、非但一巻兩巻。

The Twenty-seventh Ancestor, Venerable Prajñātāra, said,²⁵

*When this humble wayfarer breathes out, he does not follow along with conditions; when he breathes in, he does not settle down in the aggregates and constituents.*²⁶ *He is perpetually turning such a sūtra, hundreds of thousands of myriads of millions of scrolls, not merely one scroll or two scrolls.*²⁷

---

23 **before the kalpa of emptiness** (*kūgō izen* 空劫以前): An expression occurring regularly in Zen texts in reference to a state before even the kalpa before the emergence of the world; see Supplementary Notes, s.v. "Before the kalpa of emptiness."

before the face (*menmoku izen* 面目已前): Likely an abbreviated form of *honrai menmoku izen* 本來面目已前 ("preceding the original face [before one's father and mother were born]").

24 **Such sūtras, they reveal by smashing dust motes** (*kaku no gotoku no kyō wa, mijin o hashite shutsugen seshimu* かくのごとくの經は、微塵を破して出現せしむ): Likely an allusion to a passage in the *Avataṃsaka-sūtra* (*Huayan jing* 華嚴經, T.279.10:273b15-22), in which the buddha wisdom within the minds of living beings is likened to a great sūtra scroll within motes of dust.

有一聰慧人、淨眼悉明見。破塵出經卷、普饒益衆生。

A sagacious person,
With pure eyes, clearly sees them all;
Smashing the dust motes, he exposes the sūtra scrolls,
And widely and abundantly benefits living beings.

25 **The Twenty-seventh Ancestor, Venerable Prajñātāra** (*dai nijūshichi so Hannyatara sonja* 第二十七祖般若多羅尊者): A saying found in several sources (see, e.g., *Hongzhi chanshi guanglu* 宏智禪師廣錄, T.2001.48:18c12-15) and cited by Dōgen in his "Shōbōgenzō kankin" 正法眼藏看經 and *Eihei kōroku* 永平廣錄 (DZZ.3:16, no. 20).

26 **aggregates and constituents** (*ungai* 蘊界): I.e., the five "heaps" (*un* 蘊; S. *skandha*) that make up the psychophysical organism, and the eighteen "elements" (*kai* 界; S. *dhātu*) of the six sense organs, their objects, and their attendant consciousnesses. See Supplementary Notes, s.v. "Four elements and five aggregates."

27 **such a sūtra** (*nyoze kyō* 如是經): The expression may be taken either as "the sūtra of breathing in and breathing out" or as "the sūtra of suchness" (or both).

[47:10]

かくのごとくの祖師道を聞取して、出息・入息のところに轉經せらるることを、參學すべし。轉經をしるがごときは、在經のところをしるべきなり。能轉・所轉、轉經・經轉なるがゆゑに、悉知悉見なるべきなり。

Hearing such words of the Ancestral Master, we should study that the sūtras are being turned where one breathes out and breathes in.[28] Those who know the turning of the sūtras must know where the sūtras are. Because it is *the turner and the turned, turning the sūtras and the sūtras turning*, it must be knowing them all and seeing them all.[29]

* * * * *

[47:11]

先師尋常道、我箇裏、不用燒香・禮拜・念佛・修懺・看經、祇管打坐、辦道功夫、身心脱落。

My former master always said, "Here, there is no need to burn incense, make bows, recollect the buddha, practice repentance, or read the sūtras; just sitting, making concentrated effort to pursue the way, body and mind are sloughed off."[30]

---

28 **where one breathes out and breathes in** (*shussoku nissoku no tokoro* 出息・入息のところ): Or "where he [i.e., the Ancestral Master] breathes out and breathes in."

29 **turning the sūtras and the sūtras turning** (*tenkyō kyōten* 轉經・經轉): Perhaps reflecting a line from a verse, quoted in "Shōbōgenzō kankin" 正法眼藏看經, attributed to the Sixth Ancestor, Huineng 慧能 (see, e.g., *Jingde chuandeng lu* 景德傳燈錄, T.2076.51:238a24):

心迷法華轉、心悟轉法華。
When the mind is deluded, the *Lotus* turns it;
When the mind is awakened, it turns the *Lotus*.

knowing them all and seeing them all (*shicchi shikken* 悉知悉見): The objects of the verbs here are uncertain: in the context, they would seem to be "the sūtras"; but the expression may reflect a passage in the *Diamond Sūtra* (*Jingang jing* 金剛經, T.235.8:750c3-6) that would make the object the person "turning" and "being turned by" the sūtras:

須菩提、當來之世若有善男子善女人、能於此經受持讀誦、則爲如來以佛智慧悉知是人、悉見是人。皆得成就無量無邊功德。

Subhūti, if in ages to come there are good men and good women who receive and keep, read and recite this sūtra, the Tathāgata, with his buddha wisdom, will know all these people, will see all these people; and they will all achieve measureless, limitless merit.

30 **My former master** (*senshi* 先師): I.e., Tiantong Rujing 天童如淨. This saying of Rujing has no known source in extant Chinese texts and is generally assumed to be the private recollection of Dōgen. A similar passage, unattributed to Rujing, appears in Dōgen's early work, the "Bendōwa" 辦道話; slightly variant versions are attributed to Rujing in "Shōbōgenzō gyōji" 正法眼藏行持 and "Shōbōgenzō zanmai ō zanmai" 正法眼藏三昧王三昧, as well as at *Hōkyō ki* 寶慶記, DZZ.7:18-20.

47. Sūtras of the Buddhas *Bukkyō* 佛經

[47:12]

かくのごとくの道取、あきらむるともがら、まれなり。ゆえはいかん。看經をよんで看經とすれば、觸す、よんで看經とせざれば、そむく。不得有語、不得無語、速道速道。この道理、參學すべし。この宗旨あるゆえに、古人云、看經須具看經眼。

Those who clarify such words are rare. Why? If we take "read the sūtras" as "read the sūtras," we violate them; if we take them not as "read the sūtras," we oppose them.[31] *"You can't say anything; you can't say nothing. Speak! Speak!"*[32] We should study this principle. Because of this essential point, *a person of old said, "To read the sūtras, you must possess the eye for reading the sūtras."*[33]

[47:13] {2:18}

まさにしるべし、古今にもし經なくば、かくのごときの道取あるべからず。脱落の看經あり。不用の看經あること、參學すべきなり。

We should realize that, if there were no sūtras in past and present, there would be no such words. We should study that there is a reading of the sūtras that is "sloughed off"; there is a reading of the sūtras that is "no need."

[47:14]

しかあればすなはち、參學の一箇半箇、かならず佛經を傳持して佛子なるべし、いたづらに外道の邪見をまなぶことなかれ。いま現成せる正法眼藏は、すなはち佛經なるがゆえに、あらゆる佛經は正法眼藏なり。一・異にあらず、自・他にあらず。しるべし、正法眼藏、そこばくおほしといへども、なんだちことごとく開明せず。しかあれども、正法眼藏を開演す、信ぜざることなし。

Thus, one or a half who studies this, surely having received transmission and kept the sūtras of the buddhas, must be a child of the Buddha. Do not learn in vain the false views of other paths. Because the treasury of the true dharma eye manifest now is the sūtras of the buddhas, all the sūtras of the buddhas are the treasury of the true dharma eye. They are neither identical nor different; they are not self or other. You should

---

31 **we violate them** (*soku su* 觸す): Taking *soku* 觸 in the sense *sokuhan* 觸犯 ("to offend"); perhaps meaning that, if we take the words at face value, we do not do them justice.

32 **"You can't say anything; you can't say nothing. Speak! Speak!"** (*futoku ugo, futoku mugo, sokudō sokudō* 不得有語、不得無語、速道速道): A passage in Chinese, perhaps reflecting the *Rujing heshang yulu* 如淨和尚語錄 (T.2002A.48:129a17). Though Dōgen would not have used this text, his full expression here occurs at *Wumen guan* 無門關 (T.2005.48:298b19).

33 **a person of old** (*kojin* 古人): I.e., Yunmen Wenyen 雲門文偃 (864-949). For the full context of his saying, see Supplementary Notes, s.v. "One great treasury of the teachings."

realize that, while the treasury of the true dharma eye may be many, you do not clarify them all.[34] Nevertheless, you expound the treasury of the true dharma eye and do not fail to believe it.

[47:15]
佛經も、しかあるべし。そこばくおほしといへども、信受奉行せんこと、一偈一句なるべし。八萬を解會すべからず、佛經の達者にあらざればとて、みだりに、佛經は佛法にあらず、といふことなかれ。なんだちが佛祖の骨髄を稱しきこゆるも、正眼をもてこれをみれば、依文の晩進なり。一句一偈を受持せるにひとしかるべし、一偈一句の受持におよばざることもあるべし。この薄解をたのんで、佛正法を謗ずることなかれ。聲色の、佛經よりも功徳なる、あるべからず。聲色の、なんぢを惑亂する、なほもとめむさぼる。佛經の、なんぢを惑亂せざる、信ぜずして謗ずることなかれ。

The sūtras of the buddhas must be the same. They may be many, but we are to accept in faith and reverently practice a single gāthā, a single line.[35] We cannot understand the eighty thousand [teachings]; but not being a master of the sūtras of the buddhas, do not rashly say that the sūtras of the buddhas are not the buddha dharma. Though you claim the bones and marrow of the buddhas and ancestors, when viewed with the true eye, you are latecomers relying on texts.[36] You must be the same as those who receive and keep a single line, a single gāthā; you may not even amount to those who receive and keep a single line, a single gāthā. Do not slander the true dharma of the buddha based on this shallow understanding. It cannot be the case that sounds and forms have more merit than the sūtras of the buddhas.[37] Sounds and forms delude and confuse

---

34 **you do not clarify them all** (*nandachi kotogotoku kaimei sezu* なんだちことごとく開明せず): The second person plural pronoun *nandachi* なんだち here has no obvious antecedent. Dōgen seems to be addressing directly those he will go on to criticize in the following sections who think that the Zen treasury of the true dharma eye obviates the need for the sūtras. The treatment of "the treasury of the true dharma eye" as plural here is unusual; presumably to be taken as "the teachings transmitted in the treasury of the true dharma eye." See Supplementary Notes, s.v. "Treasury of the true dharma eye."

35 **we are to accept in faith and reverently practice a single gāthā, a single line** (*shinju bugyō sen koto, ichige ikku naru beshi* 信受奉行せんこと、一偈一句なるべし): More literally, "our acceptance in faith and reverent practice should be one verse and one line." Both the virtue of "accepting in faith and reverently practicing" a sūtra, and of taking to heart even "a single verse, a single line" of a sūtra, are commonly encountered tropes in the Buddhist literature.

36 **bones and marrow of the buddhas and ancestors** (*busso no kotsuzui* 佛祖の骨髄): I.e., the essential teaching passed down in the Zen tradition. Dōgen's point here is that those who claim that this teaching is passed down outside of books do so on the basis of their reading of Zen books.

37 **sounds and forms** (*shōshiki* 聲色): I.e., sense objects; here, presumably the immediate sensory experience favored by Dōgen's opponents over the words of the Buddha

you; yet you seek and covet them. Do not slander the sūtras of the buddhas because you do not believe that they will not delude or confuse you.

[47:16] {2:19}
しかあるに、大宋國の一二百餘年の前後にあらゆる杜撰の臭皮袋いはく、祖師の言句、なほこころにおくべからず、いはんや經教は、ながくみるべからず、もちいるべからず、ただ身心をして枯木・死灰のごとくなるべし、破木杓・脱底桶のごとくなるべし。かくのごとくのともがら、いたづらに外道・天魔の流類となれり。もちいるべからざるをもとめてもちいる、これによりて、佛祖の法、むなしく狂顛の法となれり、あはれむべし、かなしむべし。たとひ破木杓・脱底桶も、すなはち佛祖の古經なり。この經の巻数・部帙、きはむる佛祖まれなるなり。佛經を佛法にあらずといふは、佛祖の經をもちいし時節をうかがはず、佛祖の從經出の時節を參學せず、佛祖と佛經との親疏の量をしらざなり。かくのごとくの杜撰のやから、稲麻竹葦のごとし。獅子の座にのぼり、人天の師として、天下に叢林をなせり。杜撰は杜撰に學せるがゆえに、杜撰にあらざる道理をしらず、しらざればねがはず、從冥入於冥。あはれむべし、いまだかつて佛法の身心なければ、身儀・心操、いかにあるべしとしらず。有空のむねあきらめざれば、人もし問取するとき、みだりに拳頭をたつ、しかあれども、たつる宗旨にくらし。正・邪のみちあきらめざれば、人もし問取すれば、拂子をあぐ、しかあれども、あぐる宗旨にあきらかならず。あるいは爲人の手をさづけんとするには、臨濟の四料簡・四照用、雲門の三句、洞山の三路・五位等を擧して、學道の標準とせり。

Nevertheless, in the Land of the Great Song, since about one or two hundred years ago, every illiterate stinking skin bag has been saying, "We should not take to heart even the words of the ancestral masters, let alone be forever looking at and using the sūtra teachings; we should just make our bodies and minds like *dried-up trees and dead ashes*, like a *broken wooden ladle, or a bucket missing its bottom*."[38] Such types have foolishly become followers of other paths and the Deva Māra. They seek

---

in the sūtras.

38 **illiterate stinking skin bag** (*zuzan no shū hitai* 杜撰の臭皮袋): I.e., Zen monks ignorant of the tradition. "Stinking skin bag" (*shū hitai* 臭皮袋) is a common term for the body, especially of humans; often used by Dōgen in reference especially to Zen monks; see Supplementary Notes, s.v. "Bag of skin." "Illiterate" is a loose translation for *zusan* 杜撰, more literally, "Du composition," used in pejorative reference to a literary work that, like those of Du, is ignorant of classical precedents. (Du is most often identified as the Song-dynasty poet Du Mo 杜默; for alternative theories, see M.14477.122.) Dōgen regularly uses the term to refer to those in the Zen tradition who are ignorant of the tradition.

dried-up trees and dead ashes (*koboku shikai* 枯木死灰): Or, as we might say, "dead wood and cold ashes"; a common expression in Zen texts, used in reference to a state of mind without thoughts. See Supplementary Notes, s.v. "Dried-up tree."

broken wooden ladle (*ha mokushaku* 破木杓); **bucket missing its bottom** (*datteitsū* 脱底桶): Two common expressions for something "useless," often used in Zen texts in an ironic positive sense.

and use what they should not use; and, as a result, the dharma of the buddhas and ancestors has become the worthless dharma of madmen. How pitiful. How sad. Even the "broken ladle" and the "bottomless bucket" are the old sūtras of the buddhas and ancestors. Rare are the buddhas and ancestors who have mastered the scrolls and books of these sūtras.

Those who say that the sūtras of the buddhas are not the buddha dharma are unacquainted with the occasions when the buddhas and ancestors used the sūtras, have not studied the occasions when the buddhas and ancestors emerged from the sūtras, do not know the degree to which the buddhas and ancestors are close to or distant from the sūtras of the buddhas.[39] Such illiterate types are like "*rice, hemp, bamboo, and reeds.*"[40] They have ascended the lion seat and, as the teachers of humans and devas, have established monasteries throughout the world.[41] Because the illiterates study with illiterates, they do not know the truth that is not illiterate and, not knowing it, "*they go from darkness into darkness.*"[42] How pitiful.

Never having had the body and mind of the buddha dharma, they do not know how to have physical deportment and mental constraint. Since they have not clarified the import of being and emptiness, when someone puts a question to them, they arbitrarily raise their fist, even though they are in the dark about what it means to raise it. Since they have not clarified the ways of the true and the false, when someone puts a question to them, they raise their whisk, even though they are not clear what it means to raise it. Or, in offering a hand to others, they take up as the standard for studying the way Linji's "four considerations" or "four

---

39　**emerged from the sūtras** (*jū kyō shutsu* 從經出): Perhaps reflecting a line in the *Diamond Sūtra* (*Jingang jing* 金剛經, T.235.8:749b23-24):

須菩提。一切諸佛及諸佛阿耨多羅三藐三菩提法皆從此經出。

Subhūti, all the buddhas, as well as the *anuttara-samyak-saṃbodhi* of the buddhas, have emerged from this sūtra.

40　**"rice, hemp, bamboo, and reeds"** (*tō ma chiku i* 稻麻竹葦): I.e., dense and profuse; a simile from Kumārajīva's translation of the *Lotus Sūtra*; see Supplementary Notes.

41　**ascended the lion seat** (*shishi no za ni nobori* 獅子の座にのぼり): I.e., assumed the position of abbot.

42　**"they go from darkness into darkness"** (*jū mei nyū o mei* 從冥入於冥): A phrase from the *Lotus Sūtra* (*Miaofa lianhua jing* 妙法蓮華經, T.262.9:22c24):

從冥入於冥、永不聞佛名。

They go from darkness into darkness,
Never hearing the name of the Buddha.

illuminations and applications," or Yunmen's "three phrases," or Dongshan's "three roads" or "five ranks," and so on.[43]

[47:17] {2:20}

先師天童和尚、よのつねにこれをわらふていはく、學佛、あにかくのごとくならんや。佛祖正傳する大道、おほく心にかうぶらしめ、身にかうぶらしむ。これを參學するに、參究せんと擬するにいとまあらず、なんの閑暇ありてか、晚進の言句をいれん。まことにしるべし、諸方長老無道心にして、佛法の身心を參學せざることあきらけし。

My former master, Reverend Tiantong, used to laugh at them and say,[44]

How could the study of Buddhism be like this? The great way directly transmitted by the buddhas and ancestors, we have been permitted to receive in abundance in our minds and in our bodies. In studying it, there is not enough time to try to investigate it thoroughly; what leisure time is there to include the words of latecomers? We should realize

---

43 **Linji's "four considerations"** (*Rinzai no shi ryōken* 臨濟の四料簡): Also written 四料揀. A teaching method associated with Linji Yixuan 臨濟義玄, based on a passage in the *Linji lu* 臨濟錄 (T.1985.47:497a22-23):

師晚參示眾云、有時奪人不奪境。有時奪境不奪人。有時人境俱奪。有時人境俱不奪。

At the evening convocation, the Master addressed the assembly saying, "Sometimes, I snatch away the person but don't snatch away the object; sometimes, I snatch away the object but don't snatch away the person; sometimes, I snatch away both person and object; sometimes, I don't snatch away either person or object."

The saying is quoted and its interpretation by various masters recorded in the *Rentian yanmu* 人天眼目 (T.2006.48:300b6ff).

"four illuminations and applications" (*shi shōyō* 四照用): Four methods of teaching varying the relationship between wisdom and its expression: the former precedes the latter, the latter precedes the former, the two are simultaneous, the two are not simultaneous. (See *Rentian yanmu* 人天眼目, T.2006.48:304a10ff.)

Yunmen's "three phrases" (*Unmon no sanku* 雲門の三句): A set of sayings attributed to Yunmen Wenyen 雲門文偃, of which there are two versions; see Supplementary Notes, s.v. "Yunmen's three phrases."

Dongshan's "three roads" (*Tōzan no sanro* 洞山の三路): Three phrases attributed to Dongshan Liangjie 洞山良价 (807-869); see Supplementary Notes, s.v. "Dongshan's three roads."

"five ranks" (*go i* 五位): There are several versions of the "five ranks" formula, associated especially with the Caodong 曹洞 school and attributed originally to the school's founder, Dongshan Liangjie 洞山良价; see Supplementary Notes, s.v. "Five ranks."

44 **My former master, Reverend Tiantong** (*senshi Tendō oshō* 先師天童和尚): The source of these remarks attributed to Tiantong Rujing 天童如淨 is not known; perhaps Dōgen's personal recollection. The remarks are put in Japanese, and it is possible that only the first sentence represents Rujing's words. The first sentence of the following section, however, suggests that we should read the entire passage as a quotation (or paraphrase) of Rujing.

that it is obvious *the elders in all quarters lack the mind of the way* and do not study the body and mind of the buddha dharma.[45]

[47:18]
先師の示衆、かくのごとし。まことに臨濟は、黃檗の會下に後生なり。六十拄杖をかうぶりて、つひに大愚に參ず。老婆心話のしたに、從來の行履を照顧して、さらに黃檗にかへる。このこと雷聞せるゆえに、黃檗の佛法は、臨濟ひとり相傳せりとおもへり、あまりさへ、黃檗にもすぐれたりとおもへり。またく、しかにはあらざるなり。臨濟は、わづかに黃檗の會にありて隨衆すといへども、陳尊宿すすむるとき、なにごとをとふべしとしらず、といふ。大事未明のとき、參學の玄侶として、立地聽法せんに、あに、しかのごとく茫然とあらんや。しるべし、上上の機にあらざることを。また、臨濟、かつて勝師の志氣あらず、過師の言句きこえず。黃檗は、勝師の道取あり、過師の大智あり、佛未道の道を道得せり、祖未會の法を會得せり。黃檗は、超越古今の古佛なり、百丈よりも尊長なり、馬祖よりも英俊なり。臨濟に、かくのごとくの秀氣あらざるなり。ゆえはいかん。古來未道の句、ゆめにもいまだいはず、ただ多く會して一をわすれ、一を達して多にわづらふがごとし。あに四料簡等に道味ありとして、學法の指南とせんや。

Such was my former master's address to the assembly. In truth, Linji was a junior member of the congregation of Huangbo.[46] Receiving sixty blows of the staff, eventually he visited Dayu.[47] Upon hearing him speak of the "grandmother's mind," he reflected on his previous behavior and returned to Huangbo.[48] Because this matter resounded like thunder, it was thought that Huangbo's buddha dharma was transmitted only to Linji; it was even thought that he surpassed Huangbo.[49] This is absolutely not the case. Linji was simply in Huangbo's congregation following

---

45 **elders in all quarters** (*shohō chōrō* 諸方長老): I.e., abbots of monasteries throughout the land.

46 **Linji was a junior member of the congregation of Huangbo** (*Rinzai wa, Ōbaku no eka ni goshō nari* 臨濟は、黃檗の會下に後生なり): Dōgen here recounts an abbreviated version of the famous story of Linji's study under Huangbo Xiyun 黃檗希運 (dates unknown), which appears in several sources (see, e.g., *Tiansheng guangdeng lu* 天聖廣燈錄, ZZ.135:683b3-684a18; *shinji Shōbōgenzō* 眞字正法眼藏, DZZ.5:138-142, case 27) and is repeated in "Shōbōgenzō gyōji" 正法眼藏行持, where Dōgen's treatment of Linji is much less harsh.

47 **Receiving sixty blows of the staff** (*rokujū shujō* 六十拄杖): The story has it that three times Linji sought to ask Huangbo a question, and three times he was beaten. In "Shōbōgenzō gyōji" 正法眼藏行持, Dōgen explains that each time he received twenty blows.

Dayu (*Daigu* 大愚): I.e., Gaoan Dayu 高安大愚 (dates unknown), the master to whom Linji was directed when he abandoned his practice under Huangbo.

48 **"grandmother's mind"** (*rōba shin* 老婆心): Dayu's judgment that, in beating Linji, Huangbo was behaving like a kindly grandmother.

49 **resounded like thunder** (*raimon seru* 雷聞せる): I.e., was heard everywhere.

the assembly; yet, when Venerable Chen urged him, he said that he did not know what to ask.⁵⁰ When he had yet to clarify the great matter, when, as a comrade of the dark studying the way, *he stood and listened to the dharma*, how could he be so at a loss?⁵¹ We should recognize that he was not of the highest aptitude.

Furthermore, Linji lacked the determination to surpass his master, and we do not hear from him any words that go beyond his master. Huangbo had sayings that surpassed his master; he had great wisdom that went beyond this master; he left sayings that said things the Buddha did not yet say; he understood dharmas the ancestors did not yet understand. Huangbo was an old buddha transcending past and present; he was more venerated even than Baizhang; he was more sagacious even than Mazu.⁵² Linji had no such brilliance. Why? He never said even in his dreams any line not already said long ago; he seems only to have understood the many and forgotten the one or mastered the one and been troubled by the many. How could his "four considerations" and the like be taken as having the flavor of the way and used as a guide to studying the dharma?

[47:19] {2:21}
雲門は雪峰の門人なり。人天の大師に堪爲なりとも、なほ學地といふつべし。これらをもて得本とせん、ただこれ愁末なるべし。臨濟、いまだきたらず、雲門、いまだいでざりしときは、佛祖、なにをもてか學道の標準とせし。かるがゆえにしるべし、かれらが屋裏に、佛家の道業つたはれざるなり。憑拠すべきところなきがゆえに、みだりにかくのごとく胡亂説道するなり。このともがら、みだりに佛經をさみす、人、これにしたがはざれ。もし佛經なげすつべくは、臨濟・雲門をもなげすつべし、佛經、もしもちいるべからずば、のむべき水もなし、くむべき杓もなし。

Yunmen was a follower of Xuefeng.⁵³ He had the ability to serve as a great teacher to humans and devas, but it should be said he was still at the

---

50　**when Venerable Chen urged him** (*Chin sonshuku susumuru toki* 陳尊宿すすむるとき): In some versions of the story, the head monk (*shuso* 首座) who prompted Linji to pose a question to Huangbo is identified as Muzhou Daozong 睦州道蹤 (or Daoming 道明, whose family name was Chen 陳; dates unknown).

51　**comrade of the dark studying the way** (*sangaku no genryo* 參學の玄侶): I.e., a Zen monk in training. The term *genryo* 玄侶 is interpreted as "a comrade who studies the mysteries of Zen." The only occurrence of this term in the *Shōbōgenzō*.
stood and listened to the dharma (*ricchi chōbō* 立地聽法): A fixed phrase for the practice of standing during a formal dharma talk by a teacher.

52　**Baizhang** (*Hyakujō* 百丈); **Mazu** (*Baso* 馬祖): I.e., Huangbo's master, Baizhang Huaihai 百丈懷海 (749-814), and Baizhang's master, Mazu Daoyi 馬祖道一 (709-788).

53　**Xuefeng** (*Seppō* 雪峰): I.e., Xuefeng Yicun 雪峰義存 (822-908). Dōgen here turns to Yunmen Wenyen 雲門文偃, the second of the masters he mentions at the end of section 16.

stage of a student.[54] To take these as having got the root is just to worry about the branches.[55] When Linji had not yet arrived, when Yunmen had not yet appeared, what did the buddhas and ancestors take as their standard for studying the way? For this reason, we should recognize that the work of the way of the house of the buddhas is not transmitted in their quarters.[56] It is because they lack any reliable basis that they recklessly speak such nonsense. These fellows recklessly slight the sūtras of the buddhas; let no one follow them. If we should discard the sūtras of the buddhas, we should discard Linji and Yunmen; if we should not use the sūtras of the buddhas, we will have no water to drink and no ladle with which to scoop it.

[47:20]
また、高祖の三路・五位は節目にて、杜撰のしるべき境界にあらず。宗旨正傳し、佛業直指せり、あへて餘門にひとしからざるなり。

Furthermore, the "three paths" and "five ranks" of the Eminent Ancestor are the crux, not in the realm known to illiterates.[57] Their essential point has been correctly transmitted, and the work of the buddha directly indicated; they are by no means equivalent to the other traditions.[58]

[47:21]
また、杜撰のともがらいはく、道教・儒教・釋教、ともにその極致は一揆なるべし、しばらく入門の別あるのみなり。あるいは、これを鼎の三脚にたとふ。これ、いまの大宋國の諸僧の、さかりに談ずるむねなり。もしかくのごとくいはば、これらのともがらがうへには、佛法すでに地をはらふて滅没せり、また、佛法かつて微塵のごとくばかりもきたらず、といふべし。かくのごとくのともがら、みだりに佛法の通塞を道取せんとして、あやまりて、佛經は不中用なり、祖師の門下に別傳の宗旨あり、といふ。少量の機根なり、佛道の邊際をうかがはざるゆえなり。佛經もちいるべから

---

54 **stage of a student** (*gakuchi* 學地): I.e., the stage of the student (S. *śaikṣa*) on the path prior to final awakening, the stage of the non-student (*mugaku* 無學; S. *aśaikṣa*).

55 **To take these as having got the root is just to worry about the branches** (*korera o mote tokuhon to sen, tada kore shūmatsu naru beshi* これらをもて得本とせん、ただこれ愁末なるべし): From the common Zen expression, "Just get the root and don't worry about the branches" (*tan toku hon maku shū matsu* 但得本莫愁末). The antecedents of the plural pronoun here must be Linji and Yunmen.

56 **in their quarters** (*karera ga okuri ni* かれらが屋裏に): This would appear to be a reference to the "houses" of Linji and Yunmen; yet the implied subject of the predicate "speak such nonsense" in the following sentence would seem to be those who hold up the sayings of Linji and Yunmen as "standards for studying the way."

57 **Eminent Ancestor** (*kōso* 高祖): I.e., Dongshan Liangjie 洞山良价, the third master mentioned in section 16, above.

58 **they are by no means equivalent to the other traditions** (*aete yomon ni hitoshikarazaru nari* あへて餘門にひとしからざるなり): The translation takes the implied subject to be "the three paths and five ranks"; it might also be taken as Dongshan's Caodong tradition.

47. Sūtras of the Buddhas   Bukkyō   佛經

ずといはば、祖經あらんとき、もちいるや、もちいるべからずや。祖道に
佛經のごとくなる法おほし、用・捨いかん。もし佛道のほかに祖道ありと
いはば、たれか祖道を信ぜん。祖師の、祖師とあることは、佛道を正傳す
るによりてなり、佛道を正傳せざらん祖師、たれか祖師といはん。初祖を
崇敬することは、第二十八祖なるゆえなり。佛道のほかに祖道をいはば、
十祖・二十祖たてがたからん。嫡嫡相承するによりて、祖師を恭敬する
ゆえは、佛道のおもきによりてなり。佛道を正傳せざらん祖師は、なんの
面目ありてか人天と相見せん。いはんや、ほとけをしたいしふかきこころ
ざしをひるがへして、あらたに佛道にあらざらん祖師にしたがひがたきな
り。

Again, illiterate types say that the teachings of the Daoists, the teachings of the Confucians, and the teachings of Śākya must ultimately be of one end; it is just that they have differences in their starting points.[59] Sometimes they liken them to the three legs of a tripodal pot.[60] This is a point much discussed by the monks in the Land of the Great Song nowadays. If they talk like this, we must say that, for these fellows, Buddhism has already vanished from the earth; and, what is more, not so much as a speck of the buddha dharma ever came down to them.

When such fellows recklessly try to speak of the passage and blockage of the buddha dharma, they erroneously say that the sūtras of the buddhas are useless, that there is an essential point separately transmitted among the followers of the ancestral masters. They are of small capabilities, for they have not learned of the borders of the way of the buddhas. If they say the sūtras of the buddhas ought not be used, if there were sūtras of the ancestors, should they be used or not? In the way of the ancestors, there are many teachings like those of the sūtras of the buddhas; should they be used or discarded?[61]

If we say there is a way of the ancestors apart from the way of the buddhas, who would believe in the way of the ancestors? That the ancestral masters are regarded as ancestral masters is due to their directly transmitting the way of the buddhas; who would regard as an ancestral master an ancestral master who did not directly transmit the way of the buddhas?

---

59 **the teachings of the Daoists, the teachings of the Confucians, and the teachings of Śākya must ultimately be of one end** (*Dōkyō Jukyō Shakkyō, tomo ni sono gokuchi wa ikki naru beshi* 道教・儒教・釋教、ともにその極致は一揆なるべし): The claim, popular among some Confucian and Buddhist authors in the Song period, that "the three teachings are one" (*sanjiao yizhi* 三教一致).

60 **Sometimes they liken them to the three legs of a tripodal pot** (*arui wa, kore o kanae no sankyaku ni tatou* あるいは、これを鼎の三脚にたとふ): A standard simile often associated especially with the Song monk Gushan Zhiyuan 孤山智圓 (976-1022).

61 **In the way of the ancestors** (*sodō ni* 祖道に): One is tempted to take this as "in the words of ancestors," but the subsequent discussion suggests that *dō* 道 is being used here in the broad sense of "tradition" or even "religion."

That we venerate the First Ancestor is because he is the Twenty-eighth Ancestor.[62] If we say there is a way of the ancestors apart from the way of the buddhas, it would be hard to establish ten ancestors or twenty ancestors. The reason we revere the ancestral masters for inheriting it by successor after successor is that we value the way of the buddhas. With what face would an ancestral master who did not directly transmit the way of the buddhas encounter humans and devas? Not to mention how hard it would be to abandon our deep resolve to admire the buddha and start following an ancestral master who was not on the way of the buddhas.

[47:22] {2:22}

いま杜撰の狂者、いたづらに佛道を輕忽するは、佛道所有の法を決擇することあたはざるによりてなり。しばらくかの道教・儒教をもて佛教に比するる、愚癡のかなしむべきのみにあらず、罪業の因縁なり、國土の衰弊なり、三寶の陵夷なるがゆゑに。孔・老の道、いまだ阿羅漢に同ずべからず、いはんや等覺・妙覺におよばんや。孔・老の教は、わづかに聖人の視聽を天地乾坤の大象にわきまふとも、大聖の因果を、一生・多生にあきらめがたし。わづかに身心の動靜を無爲の爲にわきまふとも、盡十方界の眞實を、無盡際斷にあきらむべからず。おほよそ孔老の教の、佛教よりも劣なること、天地懸隔の論におよばざるなり。これをみだりに一揆に論ずるは、謗佛法なり、謗孔老なり。たとひ孔・老の教に精微ありとも、近來の長老等、いかにしてかその少分をもあきらめん、いはんや萬期に大柄をとらんや。かれにも教訓あり、修練あり、いまの庸流、たやすくすべきにあらず。修し、こころむるともがら、なほあるべからず。一微塵、なほ他塵に同ずべからず。いはんや佛經の奧玄ある、いまの晩進、いかでか辦肯することあらん。兩頭ともにあきらかならざるに、いたづらに一致の胡説亂道するのみなり。

That illiterate madmen now foolishly dismiss the way of the buddhas is because they are unable to choose the dharma belonging to the way of the buddhas. First of all, to compare the teachings of the Daoists and the teachings of the Confucians to the teachings of the buddhas is not only pitifully stupid: it is also the cause of evil karma and the weakening of the country; for it represents the decline of the three treasures.[63] The ways of Confucius and Laozi are not to be equated even with the arhat; how could they approach virtual awakening or wondrous awakening?[64] The teachings of Confucius and Laozi may barely discern, in the astronomical phenomena of heaven and earth, *ken* and *kon*, what was seen

---

62 **First Ancestor** (*shoso* 初祖): I.e., Bodhidharma, the first Chinese ancestor and twenty-eighth Indian ancestor.

63 **three treasures** (*sanbō* 三寶): I.e., Buddhism, as represented by the "three treasures" (or "three jewels"; S. *tri-ratna*) of buddha, dharma, and saṃgha.

64 **virtual awakening or wondrous awakening** (*tōgaku myōgaku* 等覺・妙覺; also read *myōkaku*): I.e., the penultimate stage of the bodhisattva path, virtually equivalent to complete awakening, or the ultimate stage of buddhahood.

and heard by the sages; but they cannot clarify, in a lifetime or multiple lifetimes, the causes and effects of the Great Sage.[65] They may barely discern, in the action of non-action, the motion and rest of body and mind; but they cannot clarify, in its boundlessness cut off, the reality of all the worlds in the ten directions.[66]

In sum, the inferiority of the teachings of Confucius and Laozi to the teachings of the buddhas cannot be discussed even as the gap between heaven and earth; arbitrarily to discuss them as "the same principle" is to denigrate the buddha dharma, to slander Confucius and Laozi. The teachings of Confucius and Laozi may have their subtleties, but how could the elders of recent times clarify even a small fraction of them, let alone grasp the great handle for myriad ages?[67] They have lessons and training, but the mediocrities of today could hardly undertake them. There is simply no one who tries to practice them. Even a single speck of dust cannot be identified with another speck; how much less can the latecomers of today confirm that the sūtras of the buddhas hold inner mysteries?[68] Since they are not clear about either one, they simply talk this nonsense about "oneness."[69]

---

65 **astronomical phenomena of heaven and earth, ken and kon** (*tenchi kenkon no daizō* 天地乾坤の大象): Taking *daizō* 大象 in the sense of *tenzō* 天象 ("celestial patterns"). The compound term *kenkon* 乾坤 represents the hexagrams for heaven (yang) and earth (yin) respectively.

causes and effects of the Great Sage (*daishō no inga* 大聖の因果): I.e., the teachings on cause and effect given by Buddha Śākyamuni.

66 **action of non-action** (*mui no i* 無爲の爲): A reference to the famous Daoist teaching of "non-action" (*wuwei* 無爲), in which the sage acts without intentionally doing anything.

boundlessness cut off (*mujin saidan* 無盡際斷): A futile attempt to capture the sense of an unusual phrase, not encountered elsewhere in Dōgen's writings; perhaps expressing the ultimate emptiness of the worlds. The English loses what is presumably a play on the glyph (*jin* 盡, "exhaustive"), translated as "all" in the phrase "all the worlds in the ten directions" (*jin jippō kai* 盡十方界) and understood as "limit" in the expression "boundlessness" (*mujin* 無盡). The term *saidan* 際斷 likely reflects the fixed Buddhist expression *zengo saidan* 前後際斷 ("before and after cut off"); see Supplementary Notes, s.v. "Before and after cut off."

67 **grasp the great handle for myriad ages** (*mango ni daihei o toran* 萬期に大柄をとらん): I.e., be able to rule for ten thousand years (by following the principles of Confucianism). The "great handle" (*daihei* 大柄) is a metaphor for political rule (somewhat like English "reins of state").

68 **Even a single speck of dust cannot be identified with another speck** (*ichi mijin, nao tajin ni dōzu bekarazu* 一微塵、なほ他塵に同ずべからず): The logical relationship of this sentence to the one following would seem to be something like: "it is impossible to say even that two atoms are exactly alike; how much more difficult to identify Confucianism and Daoism with Buddhism, when the scriptures of the latter have mysteries the latecomers cannot recognize." See Supplementary Notes, s.v. "Dust."

69 **either one** (*ryōtō* 兩頭): I.e., either Confucianism and Daoism on the one hand or Buddhism on the other.

[47:23] {2:23}
大宋、いまかくのごとくのともがら、　師號に署し、師職にをり、古今に無慚なるをもて、おろかに佛道を亂辨す。佛法ありと聽許しがたし。かくのごとくの長老等、かれこれともにいはく、佛經は、佛道の本意にあらず、祖傳、これ本意なり、祖傳に奇特玄妙つたはれり。

In the Great Song nowadays, such fellows are assigned the title "master" and occupy the position of teacher; unashamed before those of past or present, they stupidly distort the way of the buddhas. It is difficult to acknowledge that they have the buddha dharma. Such elders, to a man, say that the sūtras of the buddhas are not the original intention of the way of the buddhas, that the ancestral transmission is the original intention, that the rare and profound has been passed down in the ancestral transmission.

[47:24]
かくのごとくの言句は、至愚のはなはだしきなり、狂顛のいふところなり。祖師の正傳に、またく一言半句としても、佛經に違せる奇特あらざるなり。佛經と祖道と、おなじくこれ釋迦牟尼佛より正傳流布しきたれるのみなり。ただし祖傳は、嫡嫡相承せるのみなり。しかあれども、佛經をいかでかしらざらん、いかでかあきらめざらん、いかでか讀誦せざらん。古德いはく、なんぢ、經にまどふ、經、なんぢをまよはさず。古德、看經の因縁おほし。

Such words are the ultimate of stupidity, said by the mad. In the correct transmission of the ancestral masters, there is not a single word or half a line so rare that it contradicts the sūtras of the buddhas. The sūtras of the buddhas and the way of the ancestors have both simply been directly transmitted and disseminated from Buddha Śākyamuni. It is just that the ancestral transmission has been inherited by successor after successor. Yet how could they not know the sūtras of the buddhas? How could they not be clear about them? How could they not read and recite them? An old worthy has said, "You are deluded by the sūtras; the sūtras do not delude you."[70] There are many cases of the old worthies reading the sūtras.

[47:25] {2:24}
杜撰にむかふていふべし、なんぢがいふがごとく、佛經もしなげすつべくは、佛心もなげすつべし、佛身もなげすつべし、佛身心なげすつべくは、

70　**An old worthy has said** (*kotoku iwaku* 古德いはく): The source of the saying, given here in Japanese, is not known. Commentators have suggested that the words may reflect a remark, which Dōgen quotes in his "Shōbōgenzō *Hokke* ten *Hokke*" 正法眼藏法華轉法華, by the Sixth Ancestor, Huineng 慧能, to the monk Fada 法達, a devotee of the *Lotus Sūtra* (e.g., at *Jingde chuandeng lu* 景德傳燈錄, T.2076.51:237a24):

祖曰、經意分明、汝自迷背。

The Ancestor said, "The meaning of the sūtra is clear; you yourself have deludedly gone against it."

佛子なげすつべし、佛子なげすつべくは、佛道なげすつべし、佛道なげす
つべくは、祖道なげすてざらんや、佛道・祖道ともになげすてば、　一枚
の禿子の百姓ならん、たれかなんぢを喫棒の分なしといはん、ただ王臣の
駆使のみにあらず、閻老のせめあるべし。

We should say the following to the illiterates. To discard the sūtras of
the buddhas as you say means we should also discard the mind of the
buddhas, we should discard the body of the buddhas. To discard the body
and mind of the buddhas means we should discard the children of the
buddhas. To discard the children of the buddhas means we should discard the way of the buddhas.[71] To discard the way of the buddhas means
we should discard the way of the ancestors. If we discard both the way of
the buddhas and the way of the ancestors, you will be a bald commoner.
Who would say you don't deserve to taste the rod? Not only will you be
used at will by kings and ministers, but you will be answerable to Old
Yama.[72]

[47:26]
近來の長老等、わづかに王臣の帖をたづさへて、梵利の主人といふをも
て、かくのごとくの狂言あり。是・非を辨ずるに人なし。ひとり先師の
み、このともがらをわらふ。餘山の長老等、すべてしらざるところなり。

The elders of recent times have such crazy words based simply on
the fact that they carry papers from the king or a minister and declare
themselves masters of *brahma-kṣetras*.[73] And there is no one to distinguish right from wrong. Only my former master laughed at these fellows; [their errors] are completely unrecognized by the elders of the
other mountains.[74]

[47:27]
おほよそ異域の僧侶なれば、あきらむる道かならずあるらんとおもひ、大
國の帝師なれば、達せるところさだめてあるらんとおもふべからず。異域
の衆生、かならずしも僧種にたへず、善衆生は善なり、惡衆生は惡あり。
法界のいく三界も、衆生の種品おなじかるべきなり。

As a general rule, we should not think that, because someone is a monk
from a foreign region, he will surely possess the way of understanding;
or think that, because someone is a teacher to the emperor of a great
country, he will certainly be accomplished. The living beings of foreign

---

71　**To discard the children of the buddhas** (*busshi nagesutsubeku* 佛子なげすつべ
く): Correcting Kawamura's *nazusutsubeku* なずすつべく).

72　**Old Yama** (*En Rō* 閻老): A playful epithet for King Yama, popularly seen as a
judge of the dead in the court of the underworld.

73　*brahma-kṣetras* (*bonsetsu* 梵刹): I.e., monastic establishments; the transliteration
of a Sanskrit term for "pure field," or sacred space.

74　**other mountains** (*yozan* 餘山): I.e., other monasteries.

regions do not necessarily have what it takes to be a monk: the good living beings are good; the evil living beings have evil. The types of living beings should be the same in all the three realms of the dharma realm.[75]

[47:28]
また大國の帝師となること、かならずしも有道をえらばれず、帝者また、有道をしりがたし。わづかに、臣の擧をききて、登用するのみなり。古今に、有道の帝師あり、有道にあらざる帝師おほし。にごれる代に登用せらるるは、無道の人なり。にごれる世に登用せられざるは、有道の人なり。そのゆえはいかん。知人のとき、不知人のとき、あるゆえなり。黄梅のむかし、神秀あることをわすれざるべし。神秀は帝師なり、簾前に講法す、箔前に説法す。しかのみにあらず、七百高僧の上座なり。黄梅のむかし、盧行者あること、信ずべし。樵夫より行者にうつる、搬柴をのがるとも、なほ碓米を職とす。卑賎の身うらむべしといへども、出俗越僧、得法傳衣、かつていまだむかしもきかざるところ、西天にもなし、ひとり東地にのこれる、希代の高躅なり。七百の高僧も、かたを比せず、天下の龍象、あとをたづぬる分なきがごとし。まさしく、第三十三代の祖位を嗣續して佛嫡なり。五祖、知人の知識にあらずば、いかでかかくのごとくならん。

Again, in becoming a teacher to the emperor of a great country, it is not necessarily one who possesses the way that is chosen. It is hard for the emperor to know who has the way; he simply hears the recommendation of his ministers and makes the appointment. In past and present, there have been teachers to the emperor who had the way and many teachers to the emperor who did not have the way. During corrupt reigns, those who get appointed are people without the way; during corrupt reigns, those who do not get appointed are people with the way. Why is this? Because there are times when people are recognized and times when people are not recognized.

We should not forget that long ago, at the time of Huangmei, there was Shenxiu.[76] Shenxiu was the teacher to the emperor, who lectured on the dharma before the bamboo blind, who preached the dharma before the reed screen.[77] And, in addition, he was the senior seat among seven

---

75 **all the three realms of the dharma realm** (*hokkai no iku sangai* 法界のいく三界): I.e., in any of the threefold world systems (of desire, form, and formlessness) anywhere throughout existence. Presumably, the diverse beings in these realms are "the same" in the sense that the good ones are good and the bad ones, bad.

76 **long ago, at the time of Huangmei, there was Shenxiu** (*Ōbai no mukashi, Jinshū aru* 黄梅のむかし、神秀ある): Reference to the Fifth Ancestor, Hongren of Huangmei 黄梅弘忍 (601-674), and his follower Shenxiu 神秀 (d. 706), a prominent monk who in the last years of his life served at the court of Empress Wu. In traditional Zen histories, Shenxiu is regarded as the founder of the so-called "Northern school," in contrast to the "Southern school" of the Sixth Ancestor, Huineng 慧能. The story of his defeat by Huineng in a poetry contest to determine the successor to Hongren was made famous by the *Platform Sūtra of the Sixth Ancestor* (*Liuzu tan jing* 六祖壇經, T.2007).

77 **who lectured on the dharma before the bamboo blind, who preached the dharma before the reed screen** (*renzen ni kōhō su, hakuzen ni seppō su* 簾前に講法す、箔

hundred eminent monks.[78] We should trust that long ago, at the time of Huangmei, there was the postulant Lu.[79] Having gone from woodcutter to postulant, he had escaped carrying firewood only to work pounding rice. His lowly status might be lamentable, but his leaving the laity, surpassing the monks, gaining the dharma, and receiving transmission of the robe is something previously unheard of even in antiquity; it is an outstanding trace, rare through the ages, that remains only in the Land of the East and not in Sindh in the West. It seems that even the seven hundred eminent monks were no match for him, and that even the dragon elephants of the land lacked the status to follow in his footsteps.[80] Truly, he was an heir to the Buddha, who succeeded to the position of ancestor in the thirty-third generation. How could there have been such a thing had the Fifth Ancestor not been a wise friend who could recognize the person.

[47:29] {2:25}
かくのごとくの道理、しづかに思惟すべし、卒爾にすることなかれ。知人のちからをえんことを、こひねがふべし。人をしらざるは、自・他の大患なり、天下の大患なり。廣學措大は要にあらず、知人のまなこ、知人の力量、いそぎてもとむべし。もし知人のちからなくば、曠劫に沈淪すべきなり。

We should quietly reflect on such a truth; do not be in haste about it. We should desire to get the ability to recognize the person. Failure to recognize the person is a major calamity for self and other, a major calamity for the world. Learning and skill are not essential; we should quickly seek the eye that can recognize the person, the ability to recognize the person.[81] Without the ability to recognize the person, we will remain submerged for vast kalpas.

前に説法す): I.e., taught in the presence of the emperor (who was traditionally shielded from view by blinds and screens).

78 **senior seat among seven hundred eminent monks** (*shichihyaku kōsō no jōza* 七百高僧の上座): Reference to the tradition that Shenxiu was the head monk of Hongren's community at Huangmei.

79 **postulant Lu** (*Ro anja* 盧行者): I.e., Huineng 慧能, at the time still a lay practitioner surnamed Lu 盧. Dōgen goes on here to recall the tradition that Huineng had been an illiterate woodcutter before joining Hongren's community; that, as a laymen, he had been assigned to work pounding rice for the monastery; and that he subsequently succeeded Hongren, from whom he received the robe of Bodhidharma.

80 **dragon elephants** (*ryūzō* 龍象): A term for superior religious practitioners. Although originally used in reference to great elephants (S. *mahānāga* or *hastināga*), it is often interpreted as "dragons and elephants."

81 **Learning and skill** (*kōgaku sodai* 廣學措大): A loose translation of an expression more literally rendered something like "broadly learned and in control of important matters"; akin to *hōgaku sodai* 飽學措大.

[47:30]
しかあればすなはち、佛道にさだめて佛經あることをしり、廣文深義を山海に參學して、辨道の標準とすべきなり。

Thus, realizing that the way of the buddhas definitely has the sūtras of the buddhas, we should study their extensive texts and profound meanings in the mountains and on the seas, and take them as the standard for pursuing the way.

正法眼藏佛經第四十七
Treasury of the True Dharma Eye
Sūtras of the Buddhas
Number 47

[Ryūmonji MS:]
寬元元年癸卯秋九月、庵居于越州吉田県吉峰寺而示衆
Presented to the assembly, residing in the hermitage at Kippō Monastery, Yoshida District, Esshū; ninth month of the autumn of the junior water year of the rabbit, the first year of Kangen [14 November-12 December 1243]

TREASURY OF THE TRUE DHARMA EYE

NUMBER 48

Dharma Nature
Hosshō
法性

Dharma Nature

Hosshō

Introduction

This short essay was composed at Kippōji, at the beginning of the first winter its author would spend in the snow country of Echizen. It represents number 48 in both the sixty- and seventy-five-chapter compilations of the *Shōbōgenzō* and number 54 in the Honzan edition.

The title theme concerns a common Buddhist term for ultimate reality, or what phenomena (*dharmas*) really are. Dōgen begins his essay with a warning that the dharma nature is not merely the object of Buddhist study: the study of Buddhism is itself the dharma nature; the dharma nature is itself studying Buddhism. Hence, he goes on to criticize the common view that "dharma nature" refers to a reality beyond phenomena themselves and quotes a saying of the famous Tang-dynasty Chan master Mazu Daoyi 馬祖道一 to the effect that everything we do always takes place within "the dharma nature samādhi." In his comments on the saying, Dōgen expands on this claim: the opening of blossoms in spring and the falling of leaves in autumn are the dharma nature; our mistaken belief that the opening of blossoms and falling of leaves are not the dharma nature is the dharma nature.

正法眼藏第四十八
Treasury of the True Dharma Eye
Number 48

法性
Dharma Nature

[48:1] {2:26}
あるひは經卷にしたがひ、あるひは知識にしたがひて參學するに、無師獨悟するなり。無師獨悟は、法性の施爲なり。たとひ生知なりとも、かならず尋師訪道すべし、たとひ無生知なりとも、かならず功夫辦道すべし。いづれの箇箇か生知にあらざらん、佛果菩提にいたるまでも、經卷・知識にしたがふなり。

When we study, whether following a sūtra scroll or following a wise friend, *we awaken alone without a teacher*.[1] "*Awakening alone without a teacher*" is the working of the dharma nature.[2] Even one who knows at birth must invariably *seek a teacher and inquire about the way*; even one who knows at non-birth must invariably make concentrated effort and pursue the way.[3] Which of us is not one who knows at birth? Yet until we

---

1 **whether following a sūtra scroll or following a wise friend** (*arui wa kyōkan ni shitagai, arui wa chishiki ni shitagaite* あるひは經卷にしたがひ、あるひは知識にしたがひて): A Japanese rendering (and reversal) of a fixed expression appearing several times in the *Shōbōgenzō*, "whether from a wise friend, whether from a sūtra scroll" (*waku jū chishiki waku jū kyōkan* 或從知識或從經卷); see Supplementary Notes.

2 **awakening alone without a teacher** (*mushi dokugo* 無師獨悟): An expression occurring often in Buddhist literature, especially in reference to the *pratyeka-buddha*. Synonymous with the equally common phrase "awaken by oneself without a teacher" (*mushi jigo* 無師自悟), as in the Zen expression "before [the primeval Buddha] King Majestic Voice, awaken by oneself without a teacher" (*Ion'ō izen mushi jigo* 威音王已前無師自悟); see Supplementary Notes, s.v. "Before King Majestic Voice." While of course Dōgen (like the Zen tradition more generally) emphasizes the need for a teacher, here (and in "Shōbōgenzō shisho" 正法眼藏嗣書), he uses the expression in a positive sense.

dharma nature (*hosshō* 法性): The fact or state of being dharma (S. *dharmatā*); the true nature of dharma(s) (S. *dharma-svabhāva*); etc. A standard Buddhist technical term for ultimate reality.

3 **knows at birth** (*shōchi* 生知); **knows at non-birth** (*mushō chi* 無生知): The translation of the second expression tries to retain something of Dōgen's parallel play here with two quite different terms. The expression "knowledge at birth," or "innate knowledge" (*shōchi* 生知), derives from a saying of Confucius at *Lunyu* 論語 16; see Supplementary Notes, s.v. "Knowledge at birth." The Buddhist expression *mushō chi* 無生知 is typically understood here as "knowledge of non-arising" (i.e., recognition that dharmas

reach the bodhi that is the fruit of buddhahood, we follow a sūtra scroll or a wise friend.

[48:2]

しるべし、經卷・知識にあふて法性三昧をうるを、法性三昧にあふて法性三昧をうる生知といふ。これ宿住智をうるなり、三明をうるなり、阿耨菩提を證するなり。生知にあふて、生知を習學するなり、無師智・自然智にあふて、無師智・自然智を正傳するなり。もし生知にあらざれば、經卷・知識にあふといへども、法性をきくことえず、法性を證することえざるなり。大道は、如人飲水冷暖自知の道理にはあらざるなり。一切諸佛および一切菩薩・一切衆生は、みな生知のちからにて、一切法性の大道、あきらむるなり。經卷・知識にしたがひて法性の大道をあきらむるを、みづから法性をあきらむるとす。經卷、これ法性なり、自己なり。知識、これ法性なり、自己なり。法性、これ知識なり、法性、これ自己なり。法性自己なるがゆゑに、外道・魔儻の邪計せる自己にはあらざるなり。法性には外道魔儻なし、ただ喫粥來、喫飯來、點茶來のみなり。

We should realize that attaining the samādhi of dharma nature through encountering a sūtra scroll or a wise friend is called the knowledge at birth that attains the samādhi of dharma nature through encountering the samādhi of dharma nature.[4] It is attaining the knowledge of former lives; it is attaining the three knowledges; it is verifying *anuttara-bodhi*.[5] Encountering knowledge at birth, we study knowledge at birth; encountering masterless wisdom and spontaneous wisdom, we directly transmit

---

are empty and do not arise (*mushō hō nin* 無生法忍; S. *anutpattika-dharma-kṣānti*); alternatively, it could be taken as equivalent to the common *mushō chi* 無生智 (S. *anutpāda-jñāna*), knowledge that one has achieved nirvāṇa and will not experience future rebirths. Dōgen repeats this combination in his "Shōbōgenzō shizen biku 四禪比丘."

4 **samādhi of dharma nature** (*hosshō zanmai* 法性三昧): A concentration in which one knows the nature of all dharmas. Though the name of this meditation (or the similar "samādhi of the determination of dharma nature" [*hitsu hosshō zanmai* 畢法性三昧; S. *dharma-dhātu-niyata*]) appears in lists of samādhis, it does not seem to have been a particularly popular topic in Buddhist literature and, apart from Mazu's 馬祖 reference to it quoted below, section 4, does not figure much in Chan discourse; it is not mentioned elsewhere in the *Shōbōgenzō*.

5 **knowledge of former lives** (*shukujū chi* 宿住智): Recollection of past lives (S. *pūrve-nivāsanānusmṛti-jñāna*); one of the three knowledges (*sanmyō* 三明; S. *tri-vidyā*) and six spiritual powers (*rokutsū* 六通; S. *ṣaḍ-abhijñā*); see Supplementary Notes, s.v. "Spiritual powers."

three knowledges (*sanmyō* 三明): Three spiritual knowledges (S. *tri-vidyā*) said to have been acquired by Buddha Śākyamuni during the night of his awakening, also occurring in the standard list of the six spiritual powers (*rokutsū* 六通; S. *ṣaḍ-abhijñā*) acquired by Buddhist adepts: the deva eye (*tengen* 天眼; S. *divya-cakṣus*), recollection of former lives (*shukujū* 宿住 or *shukumyō* 宿命; S. *pūrva-nivāsānusmṛti*), and knowledge of the exhaustion of the contaminants (*rojin* 漏盡; S. *āsrava-kṣaya*).

anuttara-bodhi (*anoku bodai* 阿耨菩提): The unsurpassed awakening of a buddha.

48. Dharma Nature *Hosshō* 法性

masterless wisdom and spontaneous wisdom.⁶ If we are not one with knowledge at birth, although we may encounter a sūtra scroll or a wise friend, we will not be able to hear of the dharma nature, will not be able to verify the dharma nature.

The great way is not the principle that *the person who drinks the water knows whether it is cold or hot*.⁷ All the buddhas, as well as all the bodhisattvas and all living beings, clarify the great way of the nature of all dharmas through the power of knowledge at birth. To clarify the great way of the dharma nature through following a sūtra scroll or following a wise friend is to clarify the dharma nature oneself. The sūtra scroll is the dharma nature, is the self; the wise friend is the dharma nature, is the self. The dharma nature is the wise friend; the dharma nature is the self. Because it is the self of the dharma nature, it is not the self falsely reckoned by the other paths and the minions of Māra.⁸ In the dharma nature, there are no other paths or minions of Māra; there is only *having some gruel, having some rice, making some tea*.⁹

[48:3] {2:27}

しかあるに、三二十年の久學と自稱するもの、法性の談を見聞するとき、茫然のなかに一生を蹉過す。飽叢林と自稱して、曲木の床にのぼるもの、法性の聲をきき、法性の色をみるに、身心依正、よのつねに紛然の窟坑に昇降するのみなり。そのていたらくは、いま見聞する三界十方撲落してのち、さらに法性あらはるべし、かの法性は、いまの萬象森羅にあらずと邪計するなり。法性の道理、それかくのごとくなるべからず。この森羅萬象

---

6 **masterless wisdom and spontaneous wisdom** (*mushi chi jinen chi* 無師智・自然智): Wisdom acquired without a teacher and wisdom that arises of its own accord. The juxtaposition of these two here probably reflects a fourfold list of wisdoms found in the *Lotus Sūtra* (*Miaofa lianhua jing* 妙法蓮華經, T.262.9:13b25-26): "knowledge of everything, buddha knowledge, spontaneous knowledge, and knowledge without a teacher" (*issai chi butchi jinen chi mushi chi* 一切智佛智自然智無師智).

7 **the person who drinks the water knows whether it is cold or hot** (*nyo nin on sui reidan ji chi* 如人飲水冷暖自知): A proverb used to express the subjective character of awakening by oneself. Interestingly, in his "Bendōwa" 辨道話, Dōgen uses this proverb to make what seems the opposite point of this sentence:

證の得否は、修せむものおのづからしらむこと、用水の人の、冷煖をみづからわきまふるがごとし。

Whether or not one has attained verification, those who practice know for themselves, just as people who use water can tell for themselves whether it is cold or hot.

8 **the self falsely reckoned by the other paths and the minions of Māra** (*gedō matō no jake seru jiko* 外道・魔黨の邪計せる自己): I.e., false views of the self held by members of other religions and followers of the Deva Māra, the Evil One.

9 **having some gruel, having some rice, making some tea** (*kisshuku rai, kippan rai, tencha rai* 喫粥來、喫飯來、點茶來): Breakfast, lunch, and tea; i.e., the daily routine of the monastery. Commentators have suggested various sources for these three phrases, given in Chinese, but they do not seem to quote or allude to any particular text.

と法性と、はるかに同・異の論を超越せり、離・即の談を超越せり。過・現・當來にあらず、斷・常にあらず、色・受・想・行・識にあらざるゆえに法性なり。

However, those who claim long study of twenty or thirty years waste their entire lives in bewilderment when they hear talk of the dharma nature. Those who, claiming to be surfeited with monastic life, climb into the bentwood chair — when they hear the sound of the dharma nature or see the form of the dharma nature, the secondary and primary recompense of their bodies and minds typically just go up and down in a pit of rank confusion.[10] In their condition, they falsely reckon that the dharma nature will be manifest after the three realms and ten directions we presently experience are smashed and scattered, and that that dharma nature is not the thicket of myriad forms.[11] The truth of the dharma nature is not like this. The myriad forms of the thicket and the dharma nature far transcend discussions of sameness or difference, far transcend talk of separate or identical. They are not past, present or future; they are not annihilated or permanent; they are not form, sensation, perception, formations, or consciousness.[12] Therefore, they are the dharma nature.

* * * * *

---

10 **Those who, claiming to be surfeited with monastic life, climb into the bentwood chair** (*hō sōrin to jishō shite, kyokumoku no shō ni noboru mono* 飽叢林と自稱して、曲木の床にのぼるもの): I.e., those claiming to be fully trained in the monastery, who ascend to the ceremonial chair of the abbot.

secondary and primary recompense (*eshō* 依正): A standard Buddhist term for the results of past karma, reflected respectively in the circumstances into which one is born and the mental and physical makeup of the person; see Supplementary Notes. Here, perhaps, simply the person, composed of body and mind.

11 **thicket of myriad forms** (*manzō shinra* 萬象森羅): Also read *banzō shinra* 萬象森羅; a common expression for all things in the universe, based on the image of a dense stand of trees. The following "myriad forms of the thicket" (*shinra manzō* 森羅萬象) is a common variant with the same sense. See Supplementary Notes, s.v. "Myriad forms."

12 **annihilated or permanent** (*danjō* 斷常): Two extreme views often criticized in Buddhist literature, with exact meanings varying according to context; often taken as "nihilism or eternalism." Here, perhaps, an opposition between momentary dharmas and permanent dharma nature.

form, sensation, perception, formations, or consciousness (*shiki ju sō gyō shiki* 色・受・想・行・識): I.e., the five aggregates (*goun* 五蘊; S. *pañca-skandha*) into which the person can be analyzed; see Supplementary Notes, s.v. "Four elements and five aggregates."

48. Dharma Nature Hosshō 法性

[48:4]

洪州江西馬祖大寂禪師曰、一切衆生、從無量劫來、不出法性三昧、長在法性三昧中、著衣喫飯、言談祇對、六根運用、一切施爲、盡是法性。

Chan Master Daji, Mazu of Jiangsi in Hongzhou said,[13]

All living beings, for innumerable kalpas, have not emerged from the dharma nature samādhi. Long absorbed in the dharma nature samādhi, wearing clothes and having meals, exchanging words, using the six senses, all activities — they are entirely the dharma nature.

[48:5] {2:28}

馬祖道の法性は、法性道法性なり、馬祖と同參す、法性と同參なり。すでに聞著あり、なんぞ道著なからん。法性騎馬祖なり。人喫飯、飯喫人なり。法性よりこのかた、法性三昧をいでず。法性よりのち、法性をいでず、法性よりさき、法性をいでず。法性とならび無量劫は、これ法性三昧なり。法性を無量劫といふ。

The dharma nature spoken of by Mazu is *the dharma nature spoken of by the dharma nature*. It studies together with Mazu; it studies together with the dharma nature. Since it hears, how could it not but speak?[14] It is *the dharma nature riding Mazu*.[15] It is *the person "having meals"; the meals having the person*. Ever since the dharma nature, it "has not emerged from the dharma nature samādhi"; after the dharma nature, it "has not emerged from the dharma nature"; before the dharma nature, it "has not emerged from the dharma nature."[16] "The dharma nature" together with "innumerable kalpas" — this is "the dharma nature samādhi." "Dharma nature" is called "innumerable kalpas."

---

13 **Chan Master Daji, Mazu of Jiangsi in Hongzhou** (*Kōshū Kōzei Baso Daijaku Zenji* 洪州江西馬祖大寂禪師): Mazu Daoyi 馬祖道一(709-788). His saying can be found, e.g., at *Tiansheng guangdeng lu* 天聖廣燈録, ZZ.135:652b10-12.

14 **Since it hears, how could it not but speak?** (*sude ni monjaku ari, nanzo dōjaku nakaran* すでに聞著あり、なんぞ道著なからん): Taking "the dharma nature" as the grammatical subject. Perhaps alluding to Mazu's expression "exchanging words" (*gondan shitai* 言談祇對; literally, "talking and answering") — i.e., having heard Mazu speak of it, the dharma nature naturally responds.

15 **It is the dharma nature riding Mazu** (*hosshō ki Baso nari* 法性騎馬祖なり): A pun on Mazu's sobriquet, "Ancestor Ma" (from his lay surname, Ma 馬, meaning "horse").

16 **Ever since the dharma nature, it "has not emerged from the dharma nature samādhi"** (*hosshō yori kono kata, hosshō zanmai o idezu* 法性よりこのかた、法性三昧をいでず): I.e., as long as there has been a dharma nature, it has been within the dharma nature samādhi. Here and throughout this sentence, again taking "the dharma nature" as the implied grammatical subject.

[48:6]
しかあれば、即今の遮裏は法性なり、法性は即今の遮裏なり。著衣喫飯すれば、法性三昧の著衣喫飯なり。衣法性現成なり、飯法性現成なり。喫法性現成なり、著法性現成なり。もし著衣喫飯せず、言談祇對せず、六根運用せず、一切施爲せざるは、法性三昧にあらず、不入法性なり。

 Thus, where we are just now is the dharma nature; the dharma nature is where we are just now. When we *wear clothes and have meals*, this is the dharma nature samādhi "*wearing clothes and having meals*." It is *the realization of the dharma nature of "clothes"*; it is *the realization of the dharma nature of "meals"*; it is *the realization of the dharma nature of "having"*; it is *the realization of the dharma nature of "wearing."* Not "*wearing clothes and having meals*," not "exchanging words," not "using the six senses," not engaging in "all activities," is not "the dharma nature samādhi," it is *the dharma nature of not entering*.[17]

[48:7]
即今の道現成は、諸佛相授して釋迦牟尼佛にいたり、諸祖正傳して馬祖にいたれり。佛佛祖祖、正傳授手して法性三昧に正傳せり、佛佛祖祖、不入にして法性を活鱍鱍ならしむ。文字の法師、たとひ法性の言ありとも、馬祖道の法性にはあらず。不出法性の衆生、さらに法性にあらざらんと擬するちから、たとひ得處ありとも、あらたにこれ法性の三四枚なり。法性にあらざらんと言談祇對、運用施爲する、これ法性なるべきなり。

 The present statement was handed down by the buddhas to Buddha Śākyamuni, was directly transmitted by the ancestors down to Mazu. Buddha after buddha and ancestor after ancestor, offering their hands to transmit it directly, have directly transmitted it to the dharma nature samādhi; buddha after buddha and ancestor after ancestor, not entering it, make the dharma nature brisk and lively.[18] Although the dharma masters of letters may have the term "dharma nature," it is not the dharma nature spoken of by Mazu. The strength of living beings who have "not emerged from the dharma nature" to attempt further not to be in the dharma nature, even were it to have some success, would be three or four more pieces of dharma nature.[19] The "exchange of words," the "use" and

---

17 **the dharma nature of not entering** (*funyū hosshō* 不入法性): A phrase that could also be read "not entering the dharma nature"; a play on Mazu's saying that living beings "have not emerged from the dharma nature samādhi."

18 **buddha after buddha and ancestor after ancestor, not entering it, make the dharma nature brisk and lively** (*butsubutsu soso, funyū ni shite hosshō o kappatsupatsu narashimu* 佛佛祖祖、不入にして法性を活鱍鱍ならしむ): Again, playing on Mazu's "not emerging." See Supplementary Notes, s.v. "Buddhas and ancestors" and "Brisk and lively."

19 **The strength of living beings who have "not emerged from the dharma nature" to attempt further not to be in the dharma nature** (*fushutsu hosshō no shujō, sara ni hosshō ni arazaran to gi suru chikara* 不出法性の衆生、さらに法性にあらざらんと

the "activities" that they take not to be the dharma nature — these must be the dharma nature.

[48:8]
無量劫の日月は、法性の經歷なり。現在・未來もまたかくのごとし。身心の量を身心の量として、法性にとほしと思量するこの思量、これ法性なり。身心量を身心量とせずして、法性にあらずと思量するこの思量、これ法性なり。思量・不思量、ともに法性なり。性といひぬれば、水も流通すべからず、樹も榮枯なかるべしと學するは、外道なり。

The days and months of the "innumerable kalpas" are the passage of the dharma nature; they are the same in the present and future. This thinking that takes the measure of body and mind as the measure of body and mind and thinks that they are far from the dharma nature — this is the dharma nature.[20] This thinking that does not take the measure of body and mind as the measure of body and mind and thinks that it is not the dharma nature — this is the dharma nature. Thinking and not thinking are both the dharma nature. It is followers of the other paths who study that, when we have defined them as "the nature," water ought not to flow and trees ought to have no thriving and withering.

[48:9] {2:29}
釋迦牟尼佛道、如是相、如是性。

Buddha Śākyamuni said, "Such marks, such natures."[21]

[48:10]
しかあれば、開華葉落、これ如是性なり。しかあるに、愚人おもはくは、法性界には開華葉落あるべからず。しばらく他人に疑問すべからず、なんぢが疑著を道著に依模すべし。他人の説著のごとく擧して、三復參究すべし、さきより脱出あらん向來の思量、それ邪思量なるにあらず、ただあきらめざるときの思量なり。あきらめんとき、この思量をして失せしむるにあらず。開華葉落、おのれづから開華葉落なり。法性に開華葉落あるべからずと思量せらるる思量、これ法性なり。依模脱落しきたれる思量なり、

擬するちから): Presumably, meaning something like, "whatever beings in the dharma nature may do to deny their location in the dharma nature."

20 **This thinking that takes the measure of body and mind as the measure of body and mind and thinks that they are far from the dharma nature** (*shinjin no ryō o shinjin no ryō toshite, hosshō ni tōshi to shiryō suru kono shiryō* 身心の量を身心の量として、法性にとほしと思量するこの思量): I.e., the understanding that considers the body and mind as having a measurable extent, in contrast to the "immeasurable" dharma nature. The translation loses the play on "measure" (*ryō* 量) in "thinking" (*shiryō* 思量). See Supplementary Notes, s.v. "Body and mind."

21 **Buddha Śākyamuni** (*Shakamuni butsu* 釋迦牟尼佛): From the famous passage on the "ten suchnesses" (*jū nyoze* 十如是) in the *Lotus Sūtra*; see Supplementary Notes, s.v. "Only buddhas with buddhas can exhaustively investigate the real marks of the dharmas."

このゆえに如法性の思量なり。思量法性の渾思量、かくのごとくの面目なり。

Thus, the opening of flowers and falling of leaves — this is "such natures." Still, fools think that, in the realm of the dharma nature, there should be no opening of flowers or falling of leaves. For a while, without questioning others, you should mold your doubt as a saying: you should take it up as you would the speech of another and investigate it thrice over.[22] Your previous thinking, from which you will already have escaped — that is not false thinking: it is just the thinking of a time before you have clarified [the dharma nature].[23] When you clarify it, it is not that this thinking is eliminated: the opening of flowers and falling of leaves are in themselves the opening of flowers and falling of leaves.[24] The thinking that thinks that there should be no opening of flowers and falling of leaves in the dharma nature — this is the dharma nature. It is thinking that has sloughed off the mold; for this reason, it is the thinking of such a dharma nature.[25] All thinking of the dharma nature of thinking is such a face.

---

22 **For a while, without questioning others, you should mold your doubt as a saying** (*shibaraku tanin ni gimon su bekarazu, nanji ga gijaku o dōjaku ni emo su beshi* しばらく他人に疑問すべからず、なんぢが疑著を道著に依模すべし): Directly admonishing the "fools" to question their own doubts. The verbal form *emo su* 依模す ("to model," or "to mold") is unusual and does not occur elsewhere in the *Shōbōgenzō*.

23 **Your previous thinking, from which you will already have escaped** (*saki yori dasshutsu aran kōrai no shiryō* さきより脱出あらん向來の思量): Presumably, meaning that, by investigating your doubt thrice over, you will be rid of the thinking that gave rise to it. The term *dasshutsu* 脱出 ("escape") is not found in the *Shōbōgenzō* outside its two occurrences in this chapter.

24 **the opening of flowers and falling of leaves are in themselves the opening of flowers and falling of leaves** (*kaike yōraku, onorezukara kaike yōraku nari* 開華葉落、おのれづから開華葉落なり): Presumably meaning that the opening of flowers and falling of leaves can be understood as phenomenal events in their own right, without reference to the dharma nature — hence, the fools' way of thinking also remains valid alongside the clarified view.

25 **thinking that has sloughed off the mold** (*emo datsuraku shikitareru shiryō* 依模脱落しきたれる思量): Perhaps Dōgen's variant on the expression "escape the mold" (*emo dasshutsu* 依模脱出) (see, e.g., *Biyan lu* 碧巖錄, T.2003:48:147a27). For the use of "slough off" (*datsuraku* 脱落), see Supplementary Notes.

thinking of such a dharma nature (*nyo hosshō no shiryō* 如法性の思量): Or, perhaps, "thinking of the dharma nature as such." Dōgen seems to be suggesting a threefold movement here: from "the fool's" thinking that the dharma nature is free from phenomenal change, to the higher thinking that phenomenal change is also the dharma nature, to "thinking of the dharma nature," in which the two models ("molds") have been "sloughed off."

48. Dharma Nature *Hosshō* 法性

[48:11]

馬祖道の盡是法性、まことに八九成の道なりといへども、馬祖いまだ道取せざるところおほし。いはゆる、一切法性不出法性といはず、一切法性盡是法性といはず、一切衆生不出衆生といはず、一切衆生法性之少分といはず、一切衆生一切衆生之少分といはず、一切法性是衆生之五分といはず、半箇衆生半箇法性といはず、無衆生是法性といはず、法性不是衆生といはず、法性脱出法性といはず、衆生脱落衆生といはず、ただ衆生は法性三昧をいでず、とのみきこゆ。法性は衆生三昧をいづべからずといはず、法性三昧の、衆生三昧に出入する道著なし。いはんや法性の成佛きこえず、衆生證法性きこえず、法性證法性きこえず、無情不出法性の道なし。

 Mazu's words, "they are entirely the dharma nature," are truly words of eight or nine tenths, but there is much that Mazu has not yet said. For example, he does not say, "*All dharma natures have not emerged from the dharma nature.*" He does not say, "*All dharma natures are entirely the dharma nature.*" He does not say, "*All living beings have not emerged from living beings.*" He does not say, "*All living beings are a small part of the dharma nature.*" He does not say, "*All living beings are a small part of all living beings.*" He does not say, "*All dharma natures are half of living beings.*" He does not say, "*Half a living being is half a dharma nature.*" He does not say, "*No living beings are the dharma nature.*"[26] He does not say, "T*he dharma nature is not living beings.*" He does not say, "*The dharma nature escapes from the dharma nature.*" He does not say, "*Living beings slough off living beings.*" He just informs us that living beings have not emerged from the dharma nature samādhi. He does not say that the dharma nature cannot emerge from the living being samādhi; he has no saying that the dharma nature samādhi emerges from and enters into the living being samādhi. Much less do we hear of the dharma nature attaining buddhahood, or hear of *living beings verifying the dharma nature,* or hear of *the dharma nature verifying the dharma nature.* He has no saying that *the insentient have not emerged from the dharma nature.*

---

26 **"No living beings are the dharma nature"** (*mushujō ze hosshō* 無衆生是法性): Or, perhaps, "non-living beings are the dharma nature."

[48:12] {2:30}
しばらく馬祖にとふべし、なにをよんでか衆生とする。もし法性をよんで衆生とせば、是什麼物恁麼來なり、もし衆生をよんで衆生とせば、説似一物即不中なり。速道速道。

Now, we should ask Mazu,

What are you calling "sentient beings"? If you are calling the dharma nature "sentient beings," it is, "*what thing is it that comes like this?*" If you are calling sentient beings "sentient beings," it is, "*to say it's like any thing would miss the mark.*"[27] Speak! Speak!

正法眼藏法性第四十八
The Treasury of the True Dharma Eye
Dharma Nature
Number 48

[Ryūmonji MS:]

于時日本寛元元年癸卯孟冬、在越宇吉峰精舎示衆
Presented to the assembly at Kippō Vihāra, Etsuu; at the onset of winter, the junior water year of the rabbit, the first year of Japanese Kangen [14 November-12 December 1243][28]

---

27 **"what thing is it that comes like this?"** (*ze jūmo butsu inmo rai* 是什麼物恁麼來); **"to say it's like any thing would miss the mark"** (*setsuji ichimotsu soku fuchū* 説似一物即不中): From the exchange, much quoted by Dōgen, between Nanyue Huairang 南嶽懷讓 and the Sixth Ancestor, Huineng 六祖慧能. The first sentence is the Ancestor's question; the second, is Huairang's response; see Supplementary Notes, s.v. "What thing is it that comes like this?"

28 **onset of winter** (*mōtō* 孟冬): I.e. the tenth lunar month. The sixty-chapter *Shōbōgenzō* lacks a colophon for this chapter.

Treasury of the True Dharma Eye

Number 49

Dhāraṇī
Darani
陀羅尼

Dhāraṇī

Darani

INTRODUCTION

According to its colophon, this work was produced at Kippōji, in Echizen, during the first year of the Kangen era. Since Dōgen was still living in Heiankyō until August 3 of that year, we can assume that the "Darani" essay was written sometime between August 1243 and 9 February 1244 (the last day of Kangen 1). The work represents number 49 in both the seventy-five- and sixty-chapter *Shōbōgenzō* compilations, and number 55 in the Honzan edition.

The title of the essay refers to the incantations, spells, magical formulae, and the like, common throughout the Buddhist world and especially in the esoteric Buddhism of Dōgen's world. Surprisingly, however, for an author with such profound interest in language, Dōgen virtually ignores the obvious sense of *dhāraṇī* as sacred speech and instead interprets the term as religious action — especially the actions of attending, greeting, paying obeisance, and making offerings to one's teacher. Indeed, the bulk of the essay is devoted to instruction in the proper procedure for exchanging greetings with the master. It is from the practice of this *dhāraṇī*, Dōgen concludes, that all the buddhas and ancestors have developed the aspiration for bodhi, trained themselves, attained awakening, and taught the dharma.

正法眼藏第四十九

Treasury of the True Dharma Eye
Number 49

陀羅尼

Dhāraṇī

[49:1] {2:31}
參學眼あきらかなるは、正法眼あきらかなり。正法眼あきらかなるゆえに、參學眼あきらかなることをうるなり。この關棙を正傳すること、必然として大善知識に奉覲するちからなり。これ大因緣なり、これ大陀羅尼なり。いはゆる大善知識は、佛祖なり、かならず巾瓶に勤恪すべし。

In those whose eye of study is clear, the true dharma eye is clear. Since the true dharma eye is clear, they are able to clarify the eye of study. The direct transmission of this pivot is the power that derives from attending great wise friends.[1] This is the great cause; this is the great *dhāraṇī*.[2] Great wise friends are buddhas and ancestors; we should always devotedly serve at their towel and flask.[3]

---

1 **The direct transmission of this pivot is the power that derives from attending great wise friends** (*kono kanrei o shōden suru koto, hitsunen toshite dai zenchishiki ni bugon suru chikara nari* この關棙を正傳すること、必然として大善知識に奉覲するちからなり): Probably meaning something like, "what enables this crucial clarification is one's attendance on a teacher." The term *kanrei* 關棙 (more often written *kanreisu* 關振子) refers to the fittings at the top and bottom of a door on which it swivels; used, somewhat as English uses "hinge," for a crucial point. See Supplementary Notes, s.v. "Pivot." A "wise friend" (*zenchishiki* 善知識) is a spiritual mentor.

2 **This is the great cause; this is the great *dhāraṇī*** (*kore dai innen nari, kore dai darani nari* これ大因緣なり、これ大陀羅尼なり): The antecedents of the two pronouns *kore* これ ("this") here are uncertain: they may refer to the "great wise friend" or to "the power that derives from attending" the wise friend. It may also be that the two pronouns have different antecedents: the first referring to the "wise friend"; the second, to the "power." The wise friend is sometimes called "the great cause" of spiritual development; see e.g., the *Lotus Sūtra* (*Miaofa lianhua jing* 妙法蓮華經, T.262.9:60c9-10):

善知識者是大因緣。所謂化導令得見佛、發阿耨多羅三藐三菩提心。

The wise friend is the great cause; for they guide one and enable one to see the buddha and bring forth the thought of *anuttara-samyak-saṃbodhi*.

3 **devotedly serve at their towel and flask** (*kinbyō ni gonkaku su* 巾瓶に勤恪す): I.e., "closely attend upon"; "towel and flask" (*kinbyō* 巾瓶) is a reference to the cloth and water bottle of the monk; by extension, a monk's personal attendants. Dōgen is here no doubt hinting at the stories he will allude to in the following section.

[49:2]

しかあればすなはち、擎茶來・點茶來、心要現成せり、神通現成せり。盥水來・瀉水來、不動著境なり、下面了知なり。佛祖の心要を參學するのみにあらず、心要裏の一兩位の佛祖に相逢するなり。佛祖の神通を受用するのみにあらず、神通裏の七八員の佛祖をえたるなり。これによりて、あらゆる佛祖の神通は、この一束に究盡せり、あらゆる佛祖の心要は、この一拈に究盡せり。このゆえに、佛祖を奉覲するに、天華天香をもてする、不是にあらざれども、三昧陀羅尼を拈じて奉覲供養する、これ佛祖の兒孫なり。

This being the case, *bringing the tea, making the tea* — the essence of mind appeared, the spiritual powers appeared; *bringing the basin of water and pouring the water, he did not move the object, he knew about it from down there.*[4] These are not just studying the essence of the mind

---

4 **bringing the tea, making the tea** (*kei cha rai ten cha rai* 擎茶來・點茶來): Allusion to two stories involving monks serving their masters. The first concerns the Tang-dynasty figure Longtan Chongxin 龍潭崇信 (dates unknown) and his master Tianhuang Daowu 天皇道悟 (748-807) (*Jingde chuandeng lu* 景德傳燈錄, T.2076.51:313b19-22):

一日問曰、某自到來不蒙指示心要。悟曰、自汝到來吾未嘗不指汝心要。師曰、何處指示。悟曰、汝擎茶來吾爲汝接。汝行食來吾爲汝受。汝和南時吾便低首。何處不指示心要。

One day, [Chontan] asked, "Since I arrived, I haven't been instructed on the essence of mind."
Wu said, "Since you arrived, I've never failed to show you the essence of mind."
The Master said, "Where did you instruct me?"
Wu said, "You brought me tea, and I drank it for you. You served me food, and I accepted it for you. When you paid your respects to me, I bowed my head. Where did I not instruct you on the essence of mind?"

The second story alluded to here involves Weishan Lingyu 潙山靈祐 (771-853) and his disciples Yangshan Huiji 仰山慧寂 (807-883) and Xiangyan Zhixian 香嚴智閑 (d. 898) (e.g., at *Jingde chuandeng lu* 景德傳燈錄, T.2076.51:265c16-21). Dōgen offers a Japanese translation of and commentary on the story in his "Shōbōgenzō jinzū" 正法眼藏神通; he records a Chinese version in his *shinji Shōbōgenzō* 眞字正法眼藏, DZZ.5:158, case 61:

大潙一日臥次、仰山來。師乃轉面向壁臥。仰曰、某甲是和尚弟子、不用形迹。師作起勢。仰便出。師召曰、寂子。仰廻頭。師云、聽老僧説箇夢。仰低頭作聽勢。師曰、爲我原看。仰取一盆水、一條手巾來。師遂洗面了纔坐、香嚴入來。師云、我適來與寂子作一上神通。不同小小。嚴曰、某甲在下面了了得知。師曰、子試道看。香嚴乃點一椀茶來。師歎曰、二子神通智慧、過於鶖子・目連。

One day, when Dawei [i.e., Weishan] was lying down, Yangshan came to him. The Master [Dawei] turned and lay facing the wall.
Yang said, "I'm the Reverend's disciple; no need for appearances."
The Master went to get up. As Yang was about to leave, the Master called to him, saying, "Huiji."
Yang turned his head. The Master said, "Listen while this old monk tells you of his dream."
Yang lowered his head as if to listen. The Master said, "Try interpreting it for me."
Yang brought him a basin of water and a hand towel. Dawei washed his face. As the

of the buddhas and ancestors; they are encountering one or two buddhas and ancestors within the essence of mind. They are not just enjoying the spiritual powers of the buddhas and ancestors; they are getting seven or eight buddhas and ancestors within the spiritual powers. As a result, all the spiritual powers of the buddhas and ancestors are exhaustively investigated in this one bundle; all the essence of mind of the buddhas and ancestors is exhaustively investigated in this one pinch. Therefore, when attending the buddhas and ancestors, while it is not wrong to do so with heavenly flowers and heavenly incense, those who attend and make offerings with samādhi *dhāraṇī* are the descendants of the buddhas and ancestors.[5]

[49:3] {2:32}
いはゆる大陀羅尼は、人事、これなり、人事は大陀羅尼なるがゆえに、人事の現成に相逢するなり。人事の言は、震旦の言音を依模して、世諦に流通せることひさしといふとも、梵天より相傳せず、西天より相傳せず、佛祖より正傳せり。これ聲色の境界にあらざるなり、威音王佛の前後を論ずることなかれ。

Master finished washing his face and sat down, Xiangyan came in.
The Master said, "Master Ji and I just did one surpassing spiritual power. It wasn't like the little stuff."
Yan said, "I was down there; I know all about it."
The Master said, "Try saying something."
Xiangyan went and made a bowl of tea.
The Master sighed, saying, "The spiritual power and wisdom of these two masters exceeds that of Śāriputra and Maudgalyāyana."

bringing the basin of water and pouring the water (*kan sui rai, cha sui rai* 盥水來、瀉水來): Allusion to Yangshan's act of bringing the basin for Weishan in the story above, as well as, perhaps, to a third story, involving Nanquan Puyuan 南泉普願 (748-835) and Deng Yinfeng 鄧隱峰 (dates unknown), that Dōgen quotes in the "Shōbōgenzō ō saku sendaba" 正法眼藏王索仙陀婆. Here is the version in his *shinji Shōbōgenzō* 眞字正法眼藏 (DZZ.5:160, case 64):

南泉一日見鄧隱峰來、遂指淨瓶曰、淨瓶是境、瓶中有水。不得動著境、與老僧將水來。峰遂將瓶向南泉面前瀉。南泉即休。

One day, when Nanquan saw Deng Yinfeng approaching, he pointed at a water flask and said, "The flask is an object; inside the flask, there is water. Without moving the object, bring this old monk the water."
Feng brought the bottle in front of Nanquan and poured out the water. Nanquan desisted.

5 **samādhi *dhāraṇī*** (*zanmai darani* 三昧陀羅尼): It is unclear whether Dōgen wants us to read these two terms in conjunction, or as a tatpurusha, variously interpreted as "*dhāraṇī* that is a samādhi," "*dhāraṇī* in a state of samādhi," "*dhāraṇī* for entering (or maintaining) samādhi," etc. The expression, fairly common in Buddhist literature, occurs elsewhere in the *Shōbōgenzō* only in the "Den'e" 傳衣 chapter. The virtue of offering *dhāraṇī* to the buddhas and ancestors may reflect the "Dhāraṇī" chapter of the *Lotus Sūtra* (*Miaofa lianhua jing* 妙法蓮華經, T.262.9:58b8ff), in which various beings offer *dhāraṇī* to teachers of the sūtra.

"The great *dhāraṇī*" is salutation.[6] Because salutations are the great *dhāraṇī*, one encounters it in the occurrence of salutations. Although the word *ninji*, modeled on the pronunciation of Cīnasthāna, has long been current in the secular world, it was not passed down from the heaven of Brahmā; it was not passed down from Sindh in the West: it was directly transmitted by the buddhas and ancestors.[7] It is not in the realm of sight or sound; do not discuss it as before or after Buddha King Majestic Voice.[8]

[49:4]
その人事は、燒香禮拜なり。あるいは出家の本師、あるいは傳法の本師あり。傳法の本師すなはち出家の本師なるもあり。これらの本師にかならず依止奉覲する、これ咨參の陀羅尼なり。いはゆる、時時をすごさず參侍すべし。

These salutations are burning incense and paying obeisance. There are the original masters with whom we leave home, or the original masters who transmit the dharma to us; there are also original masters who transmit the dharma to us that are themselves the original master with whom we leave home. Always to rely on and attend these original masters is the *dhāraṇī* of consulting them. In a word, we should train under them without letting a moment slip by.

[49:5]
安居のはじめ・をはり、冬年および月旦月半、さだめて燒香禮拜す。その法は、あるいは粥前、あるいは粥罷をその時節とせり。威儀を具して師の堂に參ず。威儀を具すといふは、袈裟を著し、坐具をもち、鞋襪を整理して、一片の沈・箋香等を帶して參ずるなり。師前にいたりて問訊す。侍僧、ちなみに香炉を裝し、燭をたて、師、もしさきより椅子に坐せば、すなはち燒香すべし。師、もし帳裏にあらば、すなはち燒香すべし。師、もしは臥し、もしは食し、かくのごときの時節ならば、すなはち燒香すべし。師、もし地にたちてあらば、請和尚坐、と問訊すべし、請和尚穩便、

---

6   **salutation** (*ninji* 人事): Here understood as the greetings exchanged between monks.

7   **pronunciation of Cīnasthāna** (*Shintan no gon'on* 震旦の言音): I.e., a Chinese word; Dōgen uses a transliteration of a Sanskrit name for China.
heaven of Brahmā (*bonten* 梵天); **Sindh in the West** (*Saiten* 西天): The former term refers to the heaven of the first dhyāna in the realm of form, ruled over by the god Brahmā; the translation of the latter term, used in reference to India, masks Dōgen's play here on the glyph *ten* 天 ("heaven") used in the transliteration of the Sanskrit *Sindhu* (*Tenjiku* 天竺).

8   **before or after Buddha King Majestic Voice** (*Ion'ō butsu no zengo* 威音王佛の前後): From a passage in the *Liuzu danjing* 六祖壇經, in which the necessity of having one's awakening approved by a Zen master is said to be different "before King Majestic Voice" and "after King Majestic Voice"; see Supplementary Notes, s.v. "Before King Majestic Voice."

49. Dhāraṇī *Darani* 陀羅尼

とも請す、あまた請坐の辭あり。和尚を椅子に請し坐せしめてのちに問訊す、曲躬如法なるべし。問訊しをはりて、香臺の前面にあゆみよりて、帶せる一片香を香炉にたつ。香をたつるには、香、あるいは衣襟にさしはさめることあり、あるいは懷中にもてるもあり、あるいは袖裡に帶せることもあり、おのおの人のこころにあり。問訊ののち、香を拈出して、もしかみにつつみたらば、左手へむかひて肩を轉じて、つつめる紙をさげて、兩手に香を擎げて香炉にたつるなり。すぐにたつべし、かたぶかしむることなかれ。香をたてをはりて、叉手して、右へめぐりてあゆみて、正面にいたりて、和尚にむかひて曲躬如法問訊しをはりて、展坐具禮拜するなり。拜は九拜、あるいは十二拜するなり。拜しをはりて、收坐具して問訊す。あるいは一展坐具禮三拜して、寒暄をのぶることもあり。いまの九拜は寒暄をのべず、ただ一展三拜を三度あるべきなり。その儀、はるかに七佛よりつたはれるなり。宗旨正傳しきたれり、このゆえに、この儀をもちいる。かくのごとくの禮拜、そのときをむかふるごとに廢することなし。そのほか、法益をかうぶるたびごとには禮拜す、因縁を請益せんとするにも禮拜するなり。二祖、そのかみ見處を初祖にたてまつりしとき、禮三拜するがごとき、これなり。正法眼藏の消息を開演するに、三拜す。

At the opening and close of the retreat, at winter solstice, and on the first of the month and mid-month, we invariably offer incense and pay obeisance.[9] In regard to the procedure, the time is set either before the gruel or following the gruel.[10] Properly attired, we call at the master's hall. "Properly attired" means that we call wearing the *kāṣāya*, carrying the sitting cloth, properly wearing shoes and socks, and bringing a piece of aloes wood or *jian* incense or the like.[11] Upon arriving before the master, we bow in greeting.[12]

The attendant monk then prepares the censer and places a candle. If the master is already seated in his chair, we should light the incense straightaway. If the master is behind the curtain, we should light the incense straightaway; if the master is lying down or eating, at such times

---

9 **opening and close of the retreat** (*ango no hajime owari* 安居のはじめ・をはり): Dates of the summer retreat vary; a common practice put it from the fifteenth of the fourth month through the fifteenth of the seventh month.

10 **either before the gruel or following the gruel** (*arui wa shuku zen, arui wa shuku ha* あるいは粥前、あるいは粥罷): I.e., either before or after the monks' morning meal.

11 **sitting cloth** (*zagu* 坐具): The cloth on which the monk performs his prostrations.

piece of aloes wood or *jian* incense or the like (*ippen no jin senkō tō* 一片の沈・箋香等): The exact referent of the term *senkō* 箋香 here is unclear. While in some contexts it may mean simply "stick incense," here the glyph *jian* 箋 more likely refers to a particular substance. It is identified in one Song-dynasty source (Fan Chengda's 范成大 *Guihai yuheng zhi* 桂海虞衡志, Zhi xiang 志香, KR.2k0115.001-10a) as the product of a fragrant tree of Hainan; it is often read as equivalent to *zhan* 棧 and taken as referring to a fragrant tree said in Chinese sources to grow in northern Vietnam. Dōgen uses these same terms for incense in his "Shōbōgenzō kankin" 正法眼藏看經.

12 **bow in greeting** (*monjin* 問訊): Literally, "to make inquiries"; to join the palms and lower the head in an act of greeting.

we should light the incense straightaway. If the master is standing, we should bow in greeting with the words, "*Please, Your Reverence, be seated,*" or request, "*Please, Your Reverence, make yourself comfortable.*" There are various phrases for requesting that he be seated. After having requested that the reverend take his seat, we bow in greeting, *bending the body according to form*.

After completing the bow in greeting, we walk up to the front of the incense stand and place in the censer the stick of incense we have brought. With regard to placing the incense, the incense is sometimes inserted under the lapel of the robe, sometimes carried in the breast of the robe, or sometimes kept inside the sleeves, according to the preference of the individual. After the bow of greeting, we take out the incense. If it is wrapped in paper, we turn our shoulders to the left and remove the paper in which it is wrapped. Holding up the incense with both hands, we place it in the censer. We should stand it up straight; do not let it lean to one side.

After placing the incense, we walk around to the right with hands folded [in front of the chest]; coming in front of him, we face the reverend and bow in greeting, *bending the body according to form*; after which, we spread the sitting cloth and make prostrations. The prostrations are nine prostrations or twelve prostrations. After we finish the prostrations, we gather up the sitting cloth and bow in greeting. Sometimes, we spread the sitting cloth once, do three prostrations, and offer a seasonal greeting. But for the nine prostrations here, without offering the seasonal greeting, we should just spread [the cloth] and do the three prostrations three times.[13]

These ritual procedures have been handed down from afar from the seven buddhas. Their essential point has been directly transmitted to us; for this reason, we follow these procedures. We never abandon such rituals of obeisance whenever the occasion arises. In addition, we pay obeisance whenever we receive the benefits of the dharma; and we pay obeisance when we request benefits on a case.[14] In the past, when the Second Ancestor expressed what he had seen to the First Ancestor, he

---

13 **we should just spread [the cloth] and do the three prostrations three times** (*tada itten sanpai o sando aru beki nari* ただ一展三拜を三度あるべきなり): It is not clear from this whether one is to repeat the spreading of the cloth for each of the three sets of three bows.

14 **receive the benefits of the dharma** (*hōyaku o kōburu* 法益をかうぶる); **request benefits on a case** (*innen o shineki sen to suru* 因縁を請益せんとする): I.e., when we receive a teaching and when we seek a teaching on some edifying example in the literature.

paid obeisance by three prostrations — such is [an example of] this.[15] We do three prostrations when the news of the treasury of the true dharma eye is proclaimed.[16]

[49:6] {2:33}

しるべし、禮拜は正法眼藏なり。正法眼藏は大陀羅尼なり。請益のときの拜は、近來おほく頓一拜をもちいる、古儀は三拜なり。法益の謝拜、かならずしも九拜・十二拜にあらず、あるいは三拜、あるいは觸禮一拜なり、あるいは六拜あり。ともにこれ稽首拜なり。西天にはこれらを、最上禮拜となづく。あるいは六拜あり、頭をもて地をたたく。いはく、額をもて地にあててうつなり、血のいづるまでもす。これにも展坐具せるなり。一拜・三拜・六拜、ともに額をもて地をたたくなり。あるいはこれを頓首拜となづく。世俗にもこの拜あるなり、世俗には九品の拜あり。法益のとき、また不住拜あり。いはゆる、禮拜してやまざるなり、百千拜までもいたるべし。ともにこれら、佛祖の會にもちいきたれる拜なり。

We should recognize that paying obeisance is the treasury of the true dharma eye. The treasury of the true dharma eye is the great *dhāraṇī*. For the prostrations when requesting benefits, recently many have used a single prostration with head touching the ground; the old form is three prostrations. For prostration in gratitude for the benefits of the dharma, it is not necessarily nine prostrations or twelve prostrations; it is sometimes three prostrations or a single abbreviated prostration; or there are six prostrations.[17] All of these are prostrations with head to the ground. In Sindh in the West, these are called "the highest obeisance."[18] In the six prostrations, we strike the head on the ground; that is, we hit the ground with the forehead, even drawing blood. In this case, too, we spread the

---

15　**when the Second Ancestor expressed what he had seen to the First Ancestor** (*niso, sono kami kenjo o shoso ni tatematsurishi toki* 二祖、そのかみ見處を初祖にたてまつりしとき): Reference to the famous story in which Huike 慧可 (who would become the Second Ancestor) expressed his understanding to Bodhidharma simply by bowing. Dōgen's version of the story in the "Shōbōgenzō kattō" 正法眼藏葛藤 has Huike making three prostrations, but his version in the *shinji Shōbōgenzō* 眞字正法眼藏 (DZZ.5:230, case 201), like that in the *Jingde chuandeng lu* 景德傳燈錄 (T.2076.51:219b27-c5) on which it is based, says only that he "bowed" (*raihai* 禮拜).

16　**when the news of the treasury of the true dharma eye is proclaimed** (*shōbōgenzō no shōsoku o kaien suru ni* 正法眼藏の消息を開演するに): Presumably, on the occasion of dharma talks, though it is unclear here whether the bows are to be done by the speaker, the audience, or both. See Supplementary Notes, s.v. "Treasury of the true dharma eye."

17　**abbreviated prostration** (*sokurei* 觸禮): A form of prostration in which the sitting cloth is not opened out.

18　**In Sindh in the West, these are called "the highest obeisance"** (*Saiten ni wa korera o, saijō raihai to nazuku* 西天にはこれらを、最上禮拜となづく): The expression *saijō raihai* 最上禮拜 is not attested in the Chinese canon, nor is it known what source Dōgen used for this claim.

sitting cloth. Whether in one, three, or six prostrations, we touch the ground with the forehead; this is sometimes called "prostration knocking the head." This prostration is also found in the secular world; in the secular world, there are nine grades of prostration.[19] Again, there is the continuous prostration when we receive the benefits of the dharma: that is, we pay obeisance without stopping, even up to a hundred thousand prostrations. All of these are prostrations that have been performed in the assemblies of the buddhas and ancestors.

[49:7] {2:34}
おほよそこれらの拜、ただ和尚の指揮をまぼりて、その拜を如法にすべし。おほよそ禮拜の住世せるとき、佛法住世す。禮拜、もしかくれぬれば、佛法、滅するなり。

In general, we should perform these prostrations according to form, following the guidance of the teacher. In sum, when obeisance is present in the world, the buddha dharma is present in the world; when obeisance disappears, the buddha dharma is extinguished.

[49:8]
傳法の本師を禮拜することは、時節をえらばず、處所を論せず拜するなり。あるいは臥時・食時にも拜す、行大小時にも拜す。あるいは牆壁をへだて、あるいは山川をへだてても、遥望禮拜するなり。あるいは劫波をへだてて禮拜す、あるいは生死去來をへだてて禮拜す、あるいは菩提涅槃をへだてて禮拜す。

In paying obeisance to the original masters who transmitted the dharma to us, we make prostrations without choosing the time or considering the place. We may prostrate ourselves even when they are lying down or eating; we may prostrate ourselves even when they are defecating or urinating. We may pay obeisance from a distance, separated by fences and walls, or separated by mountains and rivers. We may pay obeisance separated by kalpas; we may pay obeisance separated by birth and death, coming and going; we may pay obeisance separated by bodhi and nirvāṇa.

[49:9]
弟子小師、しかのごとく種種の拜をいたすといへども、本師和尚は答拜せず、ただ合掌するのみなり。おのづから奇拜をもちいることあれども、おぼろげの儀にはもちいず。かくのごとくの禮拜のとき、かならず北面禮拜するなり。本師和尚は、南面して端坐せり。弟子は本師和尚の面前に立地して、おもてを北にして、本師にむかひて本師を拜するなり、これ本儀な

---

19 **in the secular world, there are nine grades of prostration** (*sezoku ni wa kuhon no hai ari* 世俗には九品の拜あり): A teaching of the *Zhou li* 周禮 (Chunguan zongling 春官宗令, KR.1d0002.006.33b).

り。みづから歸依の正信おこれば、かならず北面の禮拜、そのはじめにおこなはると正傳せり。

Although disciples perform various prostrations such as these, the reverend original masters do not return the prostration but simply join their palms. While there may be times when they use the odd prostration, they do not use it in the normal forms.[20] When paying obeisance in this way, we always pay obeisance facing north; the reverend original masters are seated erect facing south. The disciple stands before the reverend original master and, facing north toward the original master, pays obeisance to the original master — this is the fundamental form. It has been directly transmitted that, when we develop the right faith to take refuge, obeisance facing north is invariably the first thing to do.

[49:10] {2:35}
このゆえに、世尊の在日に、歸佛の人衆・天衆・龍衆、ともに北面にして世尊を恭敬禮拜したてまつる。最初に、阿若憍陳如＜亦名拘隣＞・阿濕卑＜亦名阿陛＞・摩訶摩南＜亦名摩訶拘利＞・波提＜亦曰跋提＞・婆敷＜亦名十力迦葉＞、この五人のともがら、如來成道ののち、おぼえずして起立し、如來にむかひたてまつりて、北面の禮拜を供養したてまつる。外道・魔儻、すでに邪をすてて歸佛するときは、必定して自構・他構せざれども、北面禮拜するなり。

For this reason, in the days of the World-Honored One, the humans, devas, and nāgas that took refuge in the Buddha all venerated and paid obeisance to the World-Honored One while facing north. In the beginning, Ājñāta-kauṇḍinya (also called Kurin), Aśvajit (also called Ahei), Mahānāman (also called Makakuri), Bhadrika (also called Badai), and Bāṣpa (also called Jūriki Kashō) — this group of five, following the Tathāgata's attainment of the way, spontaneously rose and, facing the Tathāgata, offered him obeisance while facing north.[21] When followers of the other paths and the minions of Māra cast aside their false views and took refuge in the Buddha, though induced to do so neither by themselves nor by others, they invariably paid obeisance facing north.

---

20 **odd prostration** (*kihai* 奇拜): A single prostration done by the teacher in response to the prostrations of the disciple. The term originally occurs in the list of nine prostrations in the *Zhou li* 周禮; the word "odd" (*ki* 奇) here is said to be used in the sense "extraordinary."

21 *Ājñāta-kauṇḍinya* (*Anyakyōjinnyo* 阿若憍陳如): First member of (a slightly odd version of) the traditional list of the Buddha's first five disciples (followed in each case by a variant version of the name). While it is commonly held that, upon encountering the Buddha after his awakening, they spontaneously paid him respects, the source for Dōgen's claim that they did so while facing north is unknown.

[49:11]

それよりこのかた、西天二十八代、東土の諸代の祖師の會にきたりて正法に歸する、みなおのづから北面の禮拜するなり。これ正法の肯然なり、師弟の構意にあらず。これすなはち大陀羅尼なり、有大陀羅尼、名爲圓覺、有大陀羅尼、名爲人事、有大陀羅尼、現成禮拜なり、有大陀羅尼、其名袈裟なり、有大陀羅尼、是名正法眼藏なり。これを誦呪して盡大地を鎭護しきたる、盡方界を鎭成しきたる、盡時界を鎭現しきたる、盡佛界を鎭作しきたる、庵中・庵外を鎭通しきたる。大陀羅尼、かくのごとくなると參學究辦すべきなり。一切の陀羅尼は、この陀羅尼を字母とせり。この陀羅尼の眷屬として、一切の陀羅尼は現成せり。一切の佛祖、かならずこの陀羅尼門より發心、辦道、成道、轉法輪あるなり。

Ever since then, all who have come and taken refuge in the true dharma in the communities of the ancestral masters of the twenty-eight generations in Sindh in the West and the generations in the Land of the East have naturally paid obeisance facing north. This is their accord with the true dharma, not the plan of master or disciple. This is precisely the great *dhāraṇī*. "There is a great *dhāraṇī* called 'perfect awakening.'"[22] There is a great *dhāraṇī* called "salutations"; there is a great *dhāraṇī* that realizes obeisance. There is a great *dhāraṇī* whose name is the *kāṣāya*; there is a great *dhāraṇī* whose name is the "treasury of the true dharma eye." By their reciting this spell, all the whole earth has been pacified and protected, the realms in all directions have been pacified and formed, the realms in all times have been pacified and manifested, all the buddha realms have been pacified and created, inside the hut and outside the hut have been pacified and penetrated.[23] We should study and thoroughly examine that the great *dhāraṇī* is like this. All the *dhāraṇī* take this *dhāraṇī* as their syllabary.[24] As the retinue of this *dhāraṇī*, all the *dhāraṇī* have appeared. It is from this *dhāraṇī* gate that all the buddhas and ancestors

---

22 **"There is a great *dhāraṇī* called 'perfect awakening'"** (*u dai darani, myō i engaku* 有大陀羅尼、名爲圓覺): After the *Yuanjue jing* 圓覺經, T.842.17:913b19. The remaining members of Dōgen's list of great *dhāraṇī* here are of his own devising.

23 **By their reciting this spell, all the whole earth has been pacified and protected** (*kore o juju shite jin daichi o chingo shikitaru* これを誦呪して盡大地を鎭護しきたる): The translation takes the unexpressed agent to be "all who have come and taken refuge." Dōgen plays here with variations on the term *chingo* 鎭護 ("to pacify and protect"), commonly used in reference to the recitation of *dhāraṇī* for protection of the state.

inside the hut (*anchū* 庵中): Or "within the hermitage"; an expression with the sense "within oneself" or "within the body," as in Shitou's 石頭 "deathless one within the hut" (*anzhong busi ren* 庵中不死人) (*Caoan ge* 草庵歌, *Jingde chuandeng lu* 景德傳燈錄, T.2076.51:461c21). The contrasting "outside the hut" (*ange* 庵外) is Dōgen's variant.

24 **All the *dhāraṇī* take this *dhāraṇī* as their syllabary** (*issai no darani wa, kono darani o jimo to seri* 一切の陀羅尼は、この陀羅尼を字母とせり): I.e. this *dhāraṇī* represents the very letters (S. *mātṛkā*, of the Siddhaṃ script) with which *dhāraṇī* are composed.

invariably bring forth the mind [of bodhi], pursue the way, attain the way, and turn the wheel of dharma.

[49:12]

しかあれば、すでに佛祖の兒孫なり、この陀羅尼を審細に參究すべきなり。おほよそ爲釋迦牟尼佛衣之所覆は、爲十方一切佛祖衣之所覆なり。爲釋迦牟尼佛衣之所覆は、爲袈裟之所覆なり。袈裟は標幟の佛衆なり。この辦肯、難値難遇なり。まれに邊地の人身をうけて、愚蒙なりといへども、宿殖陀羅尼の善根力現成して、釋迦牟尼佛の法にむまれあふ。たとひ百草のほとりに自成・他成の諸佛祖を禮拜すとも、これ釋迦牟尼佛の成道なり、釋迦牟尼佛の辦道功夫なり、陀羅尼神變なり。たとひ無量億千劫に古佛・今佛を禮拜する、これ釋迦牟尼佛之所時節なり。ひとたび袈裟を身體におほふは、すでにこれ得釋迦牟尼佛之身肉手足・頭目髓腦・光明轉法輪なり。かくのごとくして袈裟を著するなり。これは現成著袈裟功德なり。これを保任し、これを好樂して、ときとともに守護し搭著して、禮拜供養釋迦牟尼佛したてまつるなり。このなかに、いく三阿僧祇劫の修行をも辦肯究盡するなり。

This being the case, since we are the descendants of the buddhas and ancestors, we should investigate this *dhāraṇī* in detail. Generally put, to be "*covered by the robe of Buddha Śākyamuni*" is to be *covered by the robe of all the buddhas and ancestors in the ten directions.*[25] To be "*covered by the robe of Buddha Śākyamuni*" is to be *covered by the kāṣāya*. The *kāṣāya* is the buddha assembly epitomized. The confirmation of this is *hard to encounter, hard to meet.*[26] It is rare that, although we are stupid and have received a human body in a peripheral land, the power of the good roots of *dhāraṇī* planted in former lives has been realized, and we have been born at the time of the dharma of Buddha Śākyamuni. Though we pay obeisance to the self-attained or other-attained buddhas and ancestors wherever the hundred grasses grow, this is the attainment of the way by Buddha Śākyamuni; it is the concentrated effort in pursuit of the way by Buddha Śākyamuni; it is the spiritual transformations of

---

25 **"covered by the robe of Buddha Śākyamuni"** (*i Shakamuni butsu e shi shofu* 爲釋迦牟尼佛衣之所覆): From the *Lotus Sūtra* (*Miaofa lianhua jing* 妙法蓮華經, T.262.9:62a2-3), in reference to one who keeps the *Lotus Sūtra*:

當知是人佛讚善哉。當知是人爲釋迦牟尼佛手摩其頭。當知是人爲釋迦牟尼佛衣之所覆。

Know that this person will be praised by the Buddha as excellent. Know that this person will be patted on the head by Buddha Śākyamuni. Know that this person will be covered by the robe of Buddha Śākyamuni.

See Supplementary Notes, s.v. "Robe of the Tathāgata." This sentence is missing from the Ryūmonji 龍門寺 and some other early MSS.

26 **hard to encounter, hard to meet** (*nanchi nangū* 難値難遇): Variant of the common *nanchigū* 難値遇 ("hard to encounter").

the *dhāraṇī*.[27] Though we pay obeisance to past buddhas and present buddhas for incalculable millions of thousands of kalpas, this is *the time of being "covered by the robe of Buddha Śākyamuni."*[28] To cover the body once with the *kāṣāya* is surely to get Buddha Śākyamuni's body and flesh, hands and feet, head and eyes, marrow and brain, radiance and turning of the wheel of the dharma. This is the way we wear the *kāṣāya*. This is *the merit of wearing the* kāṣāya *made manifest*. Maintaining it and cherishing it, protecting and wearing it over time, *we pay obeisance and make offerings to Buddha Śākyamuni*. Herein, we confirm and exhaustively investigate the practice of so many three innumerable kalpas.[29]

[49:13] {2:36}
釋迦牟尼佛を禮拜したてまつり、供養したてまつるといふは、傳法の本師を禮拜し供養し、剃髮の本師を禮拜し供養するなり。これすなはち見釋迦牟尼佛なり、以法供養釋迦牟尼佛なり、陀羅尼をもて釋迦牟尼佛を供養したてまつるなり、

To pay obeisance and to make offerings to Buddha Śākyamuni means to pay obeisance and make offerings to the original masters who transmit the dharma to us, to pay obeisance and make offerings to the original masters who tonsured us. This itself is to *see Buddha Śākyamuni, to make offerings of the dharma to Buddha Śākyamuni*, to make offerings of *dhāraṇī* to Buddha Śākyamuni.

---

27 **Though we pay obeisance to the self-attained or other-attained buddhas and ancestors wherever the hundred grasses grow** (*tatoi hyakusō no hotori ni jijō tajō no shobusso o raihai su tomo* たとひ百草のほとりに自成・他成の諸佛祖を禮拜すとも): Probably meaning something like, "no matter where we pay obeisance to any of the buddhas and ancestors." See Supplementary Notes, s.v. "Buddhas and ancestors." "The hundred grasses" (*hyakusō* 百草) is a standard metaphor for "all phenomena." The sense of the unusual expression "self-attained or other-attained" (*jijō tajō* 自成他成) is uncertain; perhaps, "attained by oneself or with the aid of another."

28 **the time of being "covered by the robe of Buddha Śākyamuni"** (*Shakamuni butsu shi sho jisetsu* 釋迦牟尼佛之所時節): Supplying the glyphs *e* 衣 and *fu* 覆 missing in the Ryūmonji 龍門寺 MS.

29 **practice of so many three innumerable kalpas** (*iku san asōgi kō no shugyō* いく三阿僧祇劫の修行): "Three innumerable kalpas" (*san asōgi kō* 三阿僧祇劫) is the standard length of time given for completion of the bodhisattva path.

49. Dhāraṇī Darani 陀羅尼

[49:14]
先師天童古佛、しめすにいはく、あるいはゆきのうへにきたりて禮拜し、あるいは糠のなかにありて禮拜する、勝躅なり、先蹤なり、大陀羅尼なり。

My former master, the Old Buddha of Tiantong, taught that coming in the snow to pay obeisance or standing amidst the husks to pay obeisance are outstanding precedents, are the traces of our predecessors, are the great *dhāraṇī*.[30]

正法眼藏陀羅尼第四十九
Treasury of the True Dharma Eye
Dhāraṇī
Number 49

[Ryūmonji MS:]

爾時寛元癸卯、在越宇吉峰精舍示衆
Presented to the assembly at Kippō Vihāra, Etsuu; in the junior water year of the rabbit, Kangen [1 January 1243 to 9 February 1244][31]

[Einō MS:][32]

同二年甲辰正月十三日書寫之、在同州吉峰庵下侍者寮。懷奘
Copied, in the acolyte's quarters, at the Kippō Hermitage, in the same province; thirteenth day, first month of the senior wood year of the dragon, the second year of the same era [22 February 1244]. Ejō

---

30 **My former master, the Old Buddha of Tiantong** (*senshi Tendō kobutsu* 先師天童古佛): I.e., Dōgen's teacher, Tiantong Rujing 天童如淨 (1162-1227). The source of his saying here is unknown.

coming in the snow to pay obeisance (*yuki no ue ni kitarite raihai shi* 雪のうへにきたりて禮拜し); **standing amidst the husks to pay obeisance** (*nuka no naka ni arite raihai suru* 糠のなかにありて禮拜する): The former phrase alludes to the story that Huike 慧可 stood through a snow storm waiting for an interview with Bodhidharma (see Supplementary Notes, s.v. "Cut off an arm"); the latter phrase recalls the story that Huineng 慧能 pounded rice at the monastery of the Fifth Ancestor, Hongren 弘忍.

31 The Tōunji 洞雲寺 MS shares an identical colophon.

32 The Einō 榮能 MS is a copy of the sixty-chapter *Shōbōgenzō*, dated 1468, owned by the Reiun'in 靈雲院 subtemple of Myōshinji 妙心寺, in Kyoto. It is the likely source of the Ejō 懷奘 colophon supplied by Kawamura's edition, which does not appear in the Tōunji 洞雲寺 MS of this chapter.

Treasury of the True Dharma Eye
Number 50

Washing the Face
Senmen
洗面

Washing the Face

Senmen

INTRODUCTION

This work represents number 50 in the seventy-five-chapter compilation of the *Shōbōgenzō* and number 56 in the Honzan edition. According to its colophon, it was presented three times at three different monasteries: first, in the tenth month of 1239, at Kōshōji, near the capital; then, in the tenth month of 1243, at Kippōji, in Echizen; and, finally, in the first month of 1250, at Eiheiji. The work is also extant in a separate, rather different version, preserved as number 50 in the sixty-chapter *Shōbōgenzō* and translated here below as Variant Text 4.

The three dates span almost the entire history of the composition of the *Shōbōgenzō*. The first corresponds exactly to the date given for the "Senjō" 洗淨 chapter, another early work on monastic hygiene, while the third date comes at the conclusion of a series of works on monastic rules that occupied Dōgen toward the end of his life.

As its title indicates, this work concerns the procedures for face-washing in the monastery. Less obvious from the title is a lengthy section on brushing the teeth and scraping the tongue with the traditional willow twig tooth stick. Interestingly, for the historian of material culture, Dōgen reports that, while the monks of Song-dynasty China retained the ritual of face-washing, his Japanese compatriots had lost it; whereas, while the Japanese monks still used the tooth stick described in the Indian vinaya, the Chinese monks had abandoned it in favor of a horsehair tooth brush. Since he sees both face-washing and use of the willow twig as "the true dharma of the old buddhas," Dōgen takes pride here in the fact that both will be practiced at his monastery.

正法眼藏第五十
Treasury of the True Dharma Eye Number 50

洗面
Washing the Face

[50:1] {2:37}

法華經云、以油塗身、澡浴塵穢、著新淨衣、內外俱淨。

In the *Lotus Sūtra*, it is said,[1]

> Anointing the body with oil,
> He bathes away the dirt;
> Donning a new clean robe,
> Both inside and out are pure.

[50:2]

いはゆるこの法は、如來、まさに法華會上にして、四安樂行の行人のために、ときましますところなり。餘會の説にひとしからず、餘經におなじかるべからず。しかあるに、身心を澡浴して香油をぬり、塵穢をのぞくは、第一の佛法なり。新淨の衣を著する、ひとつの淨法なり。塵穢を澡浴し、香油を身に塗するに、內外俱淨なるべし。內外俱淨なるとき、依報・正報、清淨なり。

The procedure spoken of here is one that was preached by the Tathāgata on the occasion of the *Lotus* assembly, for the sake of practitioners of the four practices of ease and joy.[2] It is not equivalent to the preachings of other assemblies; it is surely not the same as other sūtras. Thus, bathing body and mind, applying scented oils, and removing the dirt are the primary buddha dharma.[3] To don a new clean robe is one procedure of

---

1 ***Lotus Sūtra*** (*Hokke kyō* 法華經): From the "Sukhavihāra" chapter (*Miaofa lianhua jing* 妙法蓮華經, T.262.9:38a9-11); the grammatical subject in the sūtra passage is "the bodhisattva."

2 ***Lotus* assembly** (*hokke e* 法華會): I.e., the assembly on Vulture Peak before which Buddha Śākyamuni is said to have taught the *Lotus Sūtra*.

four practices of ease and joy (*shi anraku gyō* 四安樂行): A standard list of four types of practice based on the "Sukhavihāra" chapter of the *Lotus Sūtra*: practices of body (*shin* 身), speech (*ku* 口), mind (*i* 意), and vow (*seigan* 誓願).

3 **bathing body and mind** (*shinjin o sōyoku shite* 身心を澡浴して): Dōgen here shifts the object of the verb "to bathe" (*sōyoku* 澡浴) in the sūtra verse from the "dirt" (*jin'e* 塵穢) that is washed away; if we maintain the parallel with the sūtra, his phrase

purification. In bathing away the dirt and smearing the body with scented oil, "*both inside and out are pure.*" When "*both inside and out are pure,*" *secondary and primary recompense are pure.*[4]

[50:3]
しかあるに、佛法をきかず、佛道を參ぜざる愚人いはく、澡浴はわづかにみのはだへをすすぐといへども、身内に五臟六腑あり、かれらを一一に澡浴せざらんは、清淨なるべからず、しかあれば、あながちに身表を澡浴すべからず。かくのごとくいふともがらは、佛法いまだしらず、きかず、いまだ正師にあはず、佛祖の兒孫にあはざるなり。

Nevertheless, stupid people who have not heard the buddha dharma and have not studied the way of the buddhas say that, while bathing may wash the skin of the body a bit, within the body are the five organs and six viscera, and, if we do not bathe each of these, we will not be pure; therefore, we need not necessarily bathe the surface of the body.[5] Those who talk like this do not know, have not heard the buddha dharma; they have not met a true master and are not the descendants of the buddhas and ancestors.

[50:4] {2:38}
しばらくかくのごとくの邪見のともがらのことばをなげすてて、佛祖の正法を參學すべし。いはゆる諸法の邊際、いまだ決斷せず、諸大の内外、また不可得なり。かるがゆえに、身心の内外、また不可得なり。しかあれども、最後身の菩薩、すでにいまし道場に坐し、成道せんとするとき、まづ袈裟を洗浣し、つぎに身心を澡浴す。これ三世十方の諸佛の威儀なり。最後身の菩薩と餘類と、諸事みなおなじからず。その功德智慧、身心莊嚴、みな最尊最上なり。澡浴・洗浣の法も、またかくのごとくなるべし。いはんや諸人の身心、その邊際、ときにしたがふてことなることあり。いはゆる一坐のとき、三千界みな坐斷せらるる。このとき、かくのごとくなりといへども、自・他の測量にあらず、佛法の功德なり。その身心量、また五尺・六尺にあらず、五尺・六尺、さだまれる五尺・六尺にあらざるゆえなり。處在も、此界・他界、盡界・無量盡界等の有邊・無邊にあらず、遮裏是什麽處在、説細説麤のゆえに。心量、また思量・分別のよくしるべきにあらず、不思量・不分別のよくきはむべきにあらず。身心量かくのごとくなるがゆえに、澡浴量もかくのごとし。この量を拈得して修證する、これ佛佛祖祖の護念するところなり。計我をさきとすべからず、計我を實

---

could be read as the more thought-provoking "bathing away body and mind." See Supplementary Notes, s.v. "Body and mind."

4 **secondary and primary recompense** (*ehō shōhō* 依報・正報): Standard Buddhist terms for the two aspects of karmic consequences: respectively, the environment, or circumstances, into which one is born; and the psychophysical makeup of the person; see Supplementary Notes. Here, no doubt a gloss on the sūtra's "inside and out."

5 **five organs and six viscera** (*gozō roppu* 五臟六腑): Two categories of traditional Chinese anatomy. The former refers to the heart, lungs, liver, spleen, and kidneys; the latter, to the large and small intestines, gall bladder, bladder, stomach, and *sanjiao* 三焦 (the viscera responsible for breathing, digestion, and excretion).

50. Washing the Face　Senmen　洗面

とすべからず。しかあればすなはち、かくのごとく澡浴し、浣洗するに、身量心量を究盡して清淨ならしむるなり。たとひ四大なりとも、たとひ五蘊なりとも、たとひ不壞なりとも、澡浴するに、みな清淨なることをうるなり。これすなはち、ただ水をきたしすすぎてのち、そのあとは清淨なるとのみしるべきにあらず。水、なにとして本淨ならん、本不淨ならん。本淨・本不淨なりとも、來著のところをして淨・不淨ならしむといはず。ただ佛祖の修證を保任するとき、用水洗浣、以水澡浴等の佛法つたはれり。これによりて修證するに、淨を超越し、不淨を透脱し、非淨・非不淨を脱落するなり。

Casting aside the words of those who hold such false views, we should study for a while the true dharma of the buddhas and ancestors. That is, the limit of the dharmas has yet to be determined; the "inside and out" of the elements is also ungraspable.[6] For that reason, the "inside and out" of body and mind is also ungraspable. Nevertheless, bodhisattvas in their last bodies, when they are just about to sit at the place of awakening and attain the way, first wash their *kāṣāya* and then bathe their bodies and minds.[7] This is the deportment of all buddhas of the three times and ten directions. In all matters, bodhisattvas in their last bodies are not the same as other types: their merit and wisdom, the adornments of their bodies and minds, are all the most honored, the supreme. Their procedures for bathing and washing must also be like this. Not to mention that the limits of people's bodies and minds differ according to the time. That is, when we sit once, the three chiliocosms are all fully seated.[8] At this time, while this may be so, it is not the calculation of self or other: it is the virtue of the buddha dharma. The dimensions of that body and mind are also not five feet or six feet; for five feet or six feet is not a fixed five

---

6　**the limit of the dharmas has yet to be determined** (*shohō no henzai, imada ketsudan sezu* 諸法の邊際、いまだ決斷せず): Variation on a common claim in the Mahāyāna literature that the dharmas (taken either as phenomena or as the teachings) are inexhaustible and their limits ungraspable. The "elements" (*shodai* 諸大) refers to the four elements (earth, water, fire, and wind) from which the material world is composed; see Supplementary Notes, s.v. "Four elements and five aggregates."

7　**bodhisattvas in their last bodies** (*saigo shin no bosatsu* 最後身の菩薩): I.e., bodhisattvas at the end of their path, when they attain buddhahood. "The place of awakening" (*dōjō* 道場) refers to the *bodhi-maṇḍa*, the seat under the bodhi tree where a buddha attains supreme bodhi. The source of the claim that, before they are seated, they do their laundry and take a bath is unknown.

8　**when we sit once, the three chiliocosms are all fully seated** (*ichiza no toki, sanzen kai mina zadan seraruru* 一坐のとき、三千界みな坐斷せらるる): Likely meaning that, in seated meditation, the entire universe is sitting with the sitter; presumably given here as an example of the variation in "the limits of people's bodies and minds." "The three chiliocosms" (*sanzen kai* 三千界) is a standard expression for the world system of a buddha. "Firmly seated" is a tentative rendering of *zadan* 坐斷, a term commonly used in the sense "to hold down" or "to reject," but regularly interpreted in Sōtō writings as "to sit completely," "to sit and cut off."

feet or six feet. Its location, too, is neither the limited nor limitless [places] of this world or other worlds, all the worlds or all the incalculable worlds; for *"where are we here, that we're talking of fine and talking of coarse?"*[9] The dimensions of the mind, as well, are not something that can be known by thinking or discrimination, not something that can be investigated by not thinking or not discriminating.[10] Because the dimensions of body and mind are like this, the dimensions of bathing them are also like this. To take up these dimensions and practice and verify them — this is what buddha after buddha and ancestor after ancestor bear in mind.[11] We should not put the imputed self first; we should not take the imputed self as real.[12]

Thus, in bathing and washing in this way, we exhaustively investigate and purify the dimensions of the body and the dimensions of the mind. Whether they are the four elements, or they are the five aggregates, or they are the undestroyed, when we bathe them, any of them can achieve purity.[13] We should not think merely that this means that they are pure

---

9 **"where are we here, that we're talking of fine and talking of coarse?"** (*shari ze jinmo shozai, setsu sai setsu so* 遮裏是什麼處在、説細説麤): A fixed expression, variants of which occur several times in the *Shōbōgenzō*. There are several precedents for the expression in the Chinese Chan literature, one of which, involving Linji Yixuan 臨濟義玄 (d. 866) and Zhenzhou Puhua 鎮州普化 (dates unknown) is recorded in Dōgen's *shinji Shōbōgenzō* 眞字正法眼藏 (DZZ.5:164, case 96). The force of the question is usually something like, "Where do you think we are, that you can talk about such trivial matters?" But, here, Dōgen seems to be taking seriously the question, "where are we here?"

10 **not something that can be known by thinking or discrimination** (*mata shiryō funbetsu no yoku shiru beki ni arazu* また思量・分別のよくしるべきにあらず): A Japanese variation on a famous line from the *Lotus Sūtra* (*Miaofa lianhua jing* 妙法蓮華經, T.262.9:7a18-20):

> 我以無數方便種種因緣譬喻言辭演說諸法。是法非思量分別之所能解。
> I use innumerable techniques, and various stories, parables, and figures of speech to expound the dharmas. This dharma is not something that can be understood by thinking or discrimination.

11 **what buddha after buddha and ancestor after ancestor bear in mind** (*butsubutsu soso no gonen suru tokoro* 佛佛祖祖の護念するところ): A Japanese variation on the line, often quoted by Dōgen, from the conversation on practice and verification between the Sixth Ancestor, Huineng 慧能, and his follower Nanyue Huairang 南嶽懷讓 (677-744); see Supplementary Notes, s.v. "What thing is it that comes like this?"

12 **put the imputed self first** (*kega o saki to su* 計我をさきとす): "Imputed self" renders *kega* 計我, a technical term for the self we imagine ourselves to be; we might also read here "put caring for the self first."

13 **Whether they are the four elements, or they are the five aggregates, or they are the undestroyed** (*tatoi shidai nari tomo, tatoi goun nari tomo, tatoi fue nari tomo* たとひ四大なりとも、たとひ五蘊なりとも、たとひ不壊なりとも): Allusion to a saying on the four elements and five aggregates by the famous Tang-dynasty Chan master Zhaozhou Congshen 趙州從諗 (778-897), which Dōgen quotes in his *shinji Shōbōgenzō*

only after water has come and washed them. How could water be originally pure or originally impure? Whether it is originally pure or originally impure, we do not say that it makes the place to which it comes pure or impure. It is just that Buddhist procedures have been handed down on *using water to wash, using water to bathe, and so on*, when maintaining the practice and verification of the buddhas and ancestors. In practicing and verifying in accordance with these, we transcend purity, we pass beyond impurity, we slough off non-purity and non-impurity.

[50:5] {2:39}
しかあればすなはち、いまだ染汚せざれども澡浴し、すでに大清淨なるにも澡浴する法は、ひとり佛祖道のみに保任せり、外道のしるところにあらず。もし愚人のいふがごとくならば、五臓六腑を細塵に抹して、即空ならしめて、大海水をつくしてあらふとも、塵中なほあらはずば、いかでか清淨ならん。空中をあらはずば、いかでか内外の清淨を成就せん。愚夫また空を澡浴する法、いまだしらざるべし。空を拈來して空を澡浴し、空を拈來して身心を澡浴す。澡浴を如法に信受するもの、佛祖の修證を保任すべし。

Thus, the dharma of bathing though not yet defiled and bathing when already completely pure has been maintained only in the way of the buddhas and ancestors; it is not something known by followers of other paths. If it were as the stupid people say, then even if we were to grind down the five organs and six viscera to a fine dust, rendering them empty in themselves, and exhausted the waters of the great oceans in washing them, if we did not wash inside the dust, how could they be pure?[14] If we did not wash inside the emptiness, how could we achieve the purification of "inside and out"? The foolish commoners also surely do not know the procedure for bathing emptiness. Taking up emptiness, we bathe emptiness; taking up emptiness, we bathe body and mind. Those who believe in bathing according to proper procedure surely maintain the practice and verification of the buddhas and ancestors.

眞字正法眼藏 (DZZ.5:270, case 88) and elsewhere. See Supplementary Notes, s.v. "Four elements and five aggregates."

14 **rendering them empty in themselves** (*sokukū narashimete* 即空ならしめて): Dōgen here plays with the metaphysics of the internal organs. Even if we analyze them into their constituent dharmas and see these dharmas as empty of independent existence, according to the fools' argument, we would still need to wash inside the dharmas and inside emptiness. He then goes on to say that, in fact, we are bathing emptiness when we bathe the body.

[50:6]

いはゆる、佛佛祖祖、嫡嫡正傳する正法には、澡浴をもちいるに、身心内外、五臓六腑、依正二報、法界虚空の内外中間、たちまちに清淨なり。香華をもちいてきよむるとき、過去・現在・未來、因縁行業、たちまちに清淨なり。

That is, in the true dharma directly transmitted to successor after successor by buddha after buddha and ancestor after ancestor, when we use bathing, the inside and outside of body and mind, the five organs and six viscera, the twofold recompense of secondary and primary, and the inside, outside, and in-between of the dharma realm and empty space are instantly pure. When we purify using incense and flowers, the deeds that are causes and conditions in past, present, and future are instantly pure.[15]

[50:7] {2:40}

佛言、三沐三薰、身心清淨。

The Buddha said,[16]

Bathing three times, censing three times;
Body and mind are pure.

[50:8]

しかあれば、身をきよめ心をきよむる法は、かならず一沐しては一薰し、かくのごとくあひつらなれて、三沐三薰して、禮佛し轉經し、坐禪し經行するなり。經行、をはりて、さらに端坐坐禪せんとするには、かならず洗足するといふ。足、けがれ觸せるにあらざれども、佛祖の法、それかくのごとし。

Thus, the procedure for purifying the body and purifying the mind is always to bathe once and cense once, continuing this until, "*bathing three times, censing three times*," we worship the buddha and turn the sūtras, practice seated meditation and circumambulation. When circumambulation is finished and we are to sit upright in seated meditation, it is said that we always wash our feet. Even if our feet have not touched anything polluted, such are the procedures of the buddhas and ancestors.

---

15 **deeds that are causes and conditions in past, present, and future** (*kako genzai mirai, innen gyōgō* 過去・現在・未來、因縁行業): Perhaps variation on a phrase in the *Dazhidu lun* 大智度論 (T.1509.25:71c16-17):

知過去因縁行業、是名明。

To know the deeds that are causes and conditions in the past is called "knowledge."

16 **The Buddha** (*butsu* 佛): Source unknown. Although this phrase does occasionally occur in Zen texts, there is no evidence that the practice was ever part of the monk's bathing ritual; given the occurrence of the phrase in sermons on bathing the Buddha, it may have been part of the ritual of bathing the statue of the baby Buddha on the Buddha's birthday.

50. Washing the Face *Senmen* 洗面

[50:9]

それ三沐三薫すといふは、一沐とは一沐浴なり、通身みな沐浴す。しかうしてのち、つねのごとくして衣裳を著してのち、小爐に名香をたきて、ふところのうち、および袈裟・坐處等に薫ずるなり。しかうしてのち、また沐浴してまた薫ず。かくのごとく三番するなり。これ如法の儀なり。このとき、六根六塵あらたにきたらざれども、清淨の功徳ありて現前す、うたがふべきにあらず。三毒四倒いまだのぞこほらざれども、清淨の功徳たちまちに現前するは佛法なり。たれか凡慮をもて測度せん、なにびとか凡眼をもて覷見せん。

Regarding "bathing three times and censing three times," "bathing once" means one bath, in which the body throughout is bathed. After that, and after putting on our clothes, we light fine incense in a small censer and cense inside our robe lapels, as well as our *kāṣāya*, sitting place, and so on. After that, we bathe again and cense again, in this way repeating it three times. This is the conduct according to proper procedure. At this time, although the six sense faculties and six sense objects are not renewed, we should not doubt that they have the virtue of purity, which will appear to us. The [teaching] that, even though the three poisons and four inversions are not yet removed, the virtue of purity immediately appears to us is the buddha dharma.[17] Who could fathom this with the thought of the commoner? What person could see it with the eye of the commoner?

[50:10]

たとへば、沈香をあらひきよむるとき、片片にをりてあらふべからず、塵塵に抹してあらふべからず、ただ擧體をあらひて清淨をうるなり。佛法にかならず浣洗の法さだまれり。あるいは身をあらひ、心をあらひ、足をあらひ、面をあらひ、目をあらひ、くちをあらひ、大小二行をあらひ、手をあらひ、鉢盂をあらひ、袈裟をあらひ、頭をあらふ。これらみな、三世の諸佛諸祖の正法なり。

For example, when we wash and purify aloes wood incense, we would not break it into pieces and wash it, nor would we grind it into powder and wash it; we purify it by just washing the whole thing. In the buddha dharma, the procedures for washing have, without exception, been established. We wash the body, wash the mind, wash the feet, wash the face, wash the eyes, wash the mouth, wash the places of defecation and urination, wash the hands, wash the bowls, wash the *kāṣāya*, wash the head. All of these are the true dharma of the buddhas and ancestors of the three times.

---

17 **three poisons and four inversions** (*sandoku shitō* 三毒四倒): The former refers to a standard list of the basic defilements: greed (*ton* 貪; S. *rāga*), anger (*shin* 瞋; S. *dveṣa*), and delusion (*chi* 癡; S. *moha*); the latter, known as the *viparyāsa* (*tendō* 顛倒), refers to a standard set of false views regarding permanence (*jō* 常; S. *nitya*), pleasure (*raku* 樂; S. *sukha*), self (*ga* 我; S. *ātman*), and purity (*jō* 淨; S. *śubha*).

[50:11] {2:41}

佛・法・僧を供養したてまつらんとするには、もろもろの香をとりきたりては、まづみづからが兩手をあらひ、嗽口・洗面して、きよきころもを著し、きよき盤に淨水をうけて、この香をあらひきよめて、しかうしてのちに佛法僧の境界には供養したてまつるなり。ねがはくは、摩黎山の栴檀香を、阿那婆達池の八功德水にてあらひて、三寶に供養したてまつらんことを。

When we seek to make offerings to the buddha, dharma, and saṃgha, in bringing the various incense, we first wash our hands, rinse our mouth, wash our face, and don a clean robe; filling a clean bowl with pure water, we wash and purify the incense. After that, we respectfully offer it to the realm of the buddha, dharma, and saṃgha. We pray: "To the three treasures may we respectfully offer *candana* incense from the Malaya Mountains, washed in waters of the eight virtues from Lake Anavatapta."[18]

[50:12]

洗面は、西天竺國よりつたはれて、東震旦國に流布せり。諸部の律にあきらかなりといふとも、なほ佛祖の傳持これ正嫡なるべし。數百歲の佛佛祖祖おこなひきたれるのみにあらず、億千萬劫の前後に流通せり。ただ垢膩をのぞくのみにあらず、佛祖の命脈なり。

Washing the face was handed down from the Land of Sindhu in the West and spread in the Land of Cīnasthāna in the East.[19] While it is clearly stated in the various recensions of the vinaya, what is transmitted and kept by the buddhas and ancestors is surely the correct succession. It has not only been performed for hundreds of years by buddha after buddha and ancestor after ancestor; it has circulated before and after *koṭis* of thousands of myriads of kalpas. It is not only to remove grime and grease; it is the vital artery of the buddhas and ancestors.

---

18 **We pray** (*negawaku wa* ねがはくは): The sentence takes the form of a ritual dedication of merit in Japanese.

"***candana* incense from the Malaya Mountains**" (*Marisen no sendan kō* 摩黎山の栴檀香): Incense made from the famous sandalwood of the Western Ghats in the Malabar region of southwest India. The term *mari* 摩黎 (or 摩梨), is used for *Maraya* 摩羅耶, a transliteration of the Sanskrit *Malaya* (from which, "Malabar").

"**waters of the eight virtues from Lake Anavatapta**" (*Anabadatsu chi no hachi kudoku sui* 阿那婆達池の八功德水): Water from the lake called "unheated" (*munetsu* 無熱; S. *anavatapta*): i.e. without the torments of the dragon. Imagined to be north of the Himalayas; sometimes identified with Lake Manasarovar, in western Tibet, and traditionally thought to be the source of the four great rivers of India. The "eight virtues" (*hachi kudoku* 八功德) of water are described as sweet, cool, soft, light, pure, odorless, harmless to the throat, and harmless to the stomach.

19 **Land of Sindhu in the West** (*sai Tenjiku koku* 西天竺國); **Land of Cīnasthāna in the East** (*tō Shintan koku* 東震旦國): I.e., India and China, respectively.

50. Washing the Face *Senmen* 洗面

[50:13]

いはく、もしおもてをあらはざれば、禮をうけ他を禮する、ともに罪あり。自禮禮他、能禮所禮、性空寂なり。性脱落なり。かるがゆゑに、かならず洗面すべし。

It is said that, when one does not wash the face, there is an offense both in receiving obeisance and in offering obeisance to another.[20] One's own obeisance and the obeisance of the other — "*the one who offers obeisance and the one to whom obeisance is offered — their natures are empty and quiescent*"; their natures are sloughed off.[21] Therefore, we should always wash the face.

* * * * *

[50:14]

洗面の時節、あるひは五更、あるひは昧旦、その時節なり。先師の、天童に住せしときは、三更の三點をその時節とせり。裙・褊衫を著し、あるひは直裰を著して、手巾をたづさへて洗面架におもむく。

The time for washing the face may be either the fifth watch or at dawn.[22]

---

20 **when one does not wash the face, there is an offense both in receiving obeisance and in offering obeisance to another** (*moshi omote o arawazareba, rai o uke ta o rai suru, tomo ni tsumi ari* もしおもてをあらはざれば、禮をうけ他を禮する、ともに罪あり): Although given here as if a vinaya infraction, there is no known source for this rule. It may somehow reflect a rather different rule found the *Shisong lü* 十誦律 (T.1435.23:300a1-2):

自洗面不得作禮。亦不得向洗面者禮。

When washing one's face, do not make obeisance. Also, do not make obeisance to one who is washing his face.

21 **One's own obeisance and the obeisance of the other** (*jirai raita* 自禮禮他): The exact sense of this unusual phrase in Chinese is unclear. It might be understood as a restatement of the preceding sentence: "obeisance I receive and obeisance I do," or of the following sentence: "the self that makes obeisance and the other to whom obeisance is offered." The form of the phrase suggests a possible play on the ubiquitous expression "self-benefit and benefiting others" (*jiri rita* 自利利他).

"the one who offers obeisance and the one to whom obeisance is offered — their natures are empty and quiescent" (*nō rai sho rai, shō kūjaku* 能禮所禮、性空寂): A fixed phrase in Chinese, occurring fairly often in the Chinese Buddhist literature, from the opening line of a liturgical text known as *Wenshu pusa lifo zuoguan ji* 文殊菩薩禮佛作觀偈. (See, e.g., *Qianshouyan dabeixin zhou xingfa* 千手眼大悲心呪行法, T.1950.46:974b21-22.) Dōgen's teacher, Rujing, uses the line twice in the *Hōkyō ki* 寶慶記 (DZZ.7:14; 24). The phrase immediately following here, "their natures are sloughed off" (*shō datsuraku nari* 性脱落なり), seems to represent Dōgen's own comment on the line; see Supplementary Notes, s.v. "Slough off."

22 **fifth watch** (*gokō* 五更): The last of the traditional five, two-hour watches (*kō* 更) of the night; roughly 4:00-6:00 a.m. (though the exact times, based as they were on the sunset, varied with the season). Here begin Dōgen's concrete instructions on washing the face and brushing the teeth.

When my former master was abbot of Tiantong, he set the time as the third strike of the third watch.[23] We don the skirt and partial robe, or don the long robe, take along a hand towel, and proceed to the face-washing stands.[24]

[50:15]

手巾は一幅の布、ながさ一丈二尺なり。そのいろ、しろかるべからず、しろきは制す。

The hand towel is a single piece of cloth, one *jō* two *shaku* in length.[25] Its color must not be white; white is forbidden.

{2:42}

[50:16]

三千威儀經云、當用手巾有五事。一者當拭上下頭。二者當用一頭拭手、以一頭拭面。三者不得持拭鼻。四者以用拭膩汚、當即浣之。五者不得拭身體、若澡浴、各當自有巾。

In the *Sūtra of the Three Thousand Rules of Deportment*, it is said,[26]

> There are five points regarding use of the hand cloth. First, wipe using the top and bottom ends. Second, use one end to wipe the hands and the other end to wipe the face. Third, do not use to wipe the nose. Fourth, when soiled from wiping grease, wash immediately. Fifth, do not use to wipe the body; when bathing, each should have his own [bath] towel.

[50:17]

まさに手巾を持せんに、かくのごとく護持すべし。手巾をふたつにをりて、左のひぢにあたりて、そのうへにかく。手巾は、半分はおもてをのごひ、半分にては手をのごふ。はなをのごふべからず、とは、はなのうち、および鼻涕をのごはず。わき・せなか・はら・へそ・もも・はぎを、手巾してのごふべからず。垢膩にけがれたらんに、洗浣すべし。ぬれ、しめれらんは、火に烘じ、日にほして、かわかすべし。手巾をもて、沐浴のとき、もちいるべからず。

---

23 **third strike of the third watch** (*sankō no santen* 三更の三點): Roughly 1:30 a.m. Each two-hour watch was divided into five "strikes" (*ten* 點).

24 **skirt and partial robe** (*kun henzan* 裙・褊衫; also read *hensan*); **long robe** (*jikitotsu* 直裰): The former pair is the set of robes for the lower and upper body respectively; the latter (literally, "sewn directly") is the full robe, in which lower and upper robes are sewn together to form a single garment.

25 **one *jō* two *shaku* in length** (*nagasa ichijō nishaku* ながさ一丈二尺): Roughly twelve feet.

26 ***Sūtra of the Three Thousand Rules of Deportment*** (*Sanzen iigi kyō* 三千威儀經): A text of regulations traditionally regarded as a translation by the second-century figure An Shigao 安世高; the passage quoted here occurs at *Sanqian weiyi jing* 三千威儀經, T.1470.24:921c19-22.

50. Washing the Face Senmen 洗面

In carrying the hand cloth, we should take care of it in this way. Fold the cloth in two and hang it over the left arm by the elbow. We use half of the cloth to wipe the face and half to wipe the hands. "Do not wipe the nose" means do not wipe inside the nose or nasal mucus. Do not use the hand cloth to wipe the armpit, back, belly, navel, thighs, or calves. When soiled by grime or grease, it should be washed. When wet or damp, it should be dried out by setting near a fire or drying in the sun. We should not use the hand cloth when bathing.

[50:18]
雲堂の洗面處は後架なり。後架は照堂の西なり、その屋圖つたはれり。庵内および單寮は、便宜のところにかまふ。住持人は、方丈にて洗面す。耆年老宿居處に、便宜に洗面架をおけり。住持人、もし雲堂に宿するときは、後架にして洗面すべし。

The place for washing the face by the cloud hall is the rear washstands.[27] The rear washstands are to the west of the illuminated hall, the ground plans of which have been handed down to us.[28] In hermitages and individual quarters, it is provided wherever convenient.[29] The abbot washes his face in the abbot's quarters. Face-washing stands are provided where convenient in the residences of seniors and elders. When the abbot lodges in the cloud hall, he should wash his face at the rear washstands.

[50:19] {2:43}
洗面架にいたりて、手巾の中分をうなじにかく。ふたつのはしを左右のかたよりまへにひきこして、左右の手にて、左右のわきより手巾の左右のはしをうしろへいだして、うしろにておのおののひきちがへて、左のはしは右へきたり、右のはしは左にきたして、むねのまへにあたりてむすぶなり。かくのごとくすれば、褊衫のくびは手巾におほはれ、兩袖は手巾にゆひあげられて、ひぢよりかみにあがりぬるなり。ひぢよりしも、うで・たなごころ、あらはなり。たとへば、たすきかけたらんがごとし。そののち、もし後架ならば、面桶をとりて、かまのほとりにいたりて、一桶の湯をとりて、かへりて洗面架のうへにおく。もし餘處にては、打湯桶の湯を面桶にいる。

---

27 **cloud hall** (*undō* 雲堂): A term for the saṃgha hall (*sōdō* 僧堂), where the monks of the great assembly sleep, take their meals, sit in meditation, etc.

28 **illuminated hall** (*shōdō* 照堂): A covered corridor between the saṃgha hall and the rear washstands, which was illumined by skylights, windows, or open sides.

29 **hermitages and individual quarters** (*annai oyobi tanryō* 庵内および單寮): Separate residences within the monastic compound. The former term refers to the residences of retired abbots or other eminent monks serving at subtemples; the latter term refers to the offices of the higher-ranking monastic officers, which could also serve as their private sleeping quarters.

Upon arriving at the face-washing stand, drape the middle of the hand cloth around the nape of the neck, with the two ends pulled forward over the left and right shoulders. With the left and right hands, bring the left and right ends of the cloth under the left and right armpits to the back; cross them in the back, so that the left end comes around to the right and the right end comes around to the left; tie them together in front of the chest. In this way, the collar of the partial robe is covered by the hand cloth, and the sleeves are tied up by the cloth, so as to be raised above the elbows, while below the elbows, the forearms and hands are exposed. It is similar, for example, to wearing a sleeve cord.[30]

After that, if it is at the rear washstands, take a face bucket, go to the area of the cauldrons, get a single bucket of hot water, come back, and place it on the face-washing stand. If it is at some other place, pour the hot water from the hot water bucket into the face bucket.

[50:20]
つぎに、楊枝をつかふべし。今大宋國諸山には、嚼楊枝の法、ひさしくすたれてつたはれざれば、嚼楊枝のところなしといへども、今吉祥山永平寺、嚼楊枝のところあり。すなはち今案なり。これによれば、まづ嚼楊枝すべし。楊枝を右手にとりて、咒願すべし。

Next, we should use the willow twig. At present at the various mountains of the Land of the Great Song, since the procedure of chewing the willow twig has long been abandoned and is not handed down, there are no places where the willow twig is chewed; but now, at Eihei Monastery on Mount Kichijō, there is a place where the willow twig is chewed.[31] This is our present plan.

According to this [procedure], we should first chew the willow twig. Taking the willow twig in the left hand, we should recite the prayer.

---

30   **sleeve cord** (*tasuki* たすき): A cord used to tie back the sleeves of a robe when working or washing.

31   **various mountains** (*shozan* 諸山): Also read *shosan*. A term for the major Buddhist monasteries.

willow twig (*yōji* 楊枝): The tooth stick (S. *danta-kāṣṭha*) prescribed for monks in the vinaya; despite its name in Chinese, the stick was not necessarily fashioned from the wood of the willow. Chewing one end of the stick shredded the fibers, creating an effective tool for cleaning the teeth.

50. Washing the Face *Senmen* 洗面

[50:21]
華嚴經淨行品云、手執楊枝、當願衆生、心得正法、自然清淨。

In the *"Pure Practice"* chapter of the *Flower Garland Sūtra*, it is said,[32]
Grasping the willow twig,
Pray that living beings
Attain the true dharma in their minds
And are naturally purified.

[50:22]
この文を誦しをはりて、さらに楊枝をかまんとするに、すなはち誦すべし、

When finished chanting this text and about to chew the willow twig, we should chant:

[50:23] {2:44}
晨嚼楊枝、當願衆生、得調伏牙、噬諸煩惱。

Chewing the willow twig at daybreak,
Pray that living beings
Attain the teeth of discipline
That bite off the afflictions.[33]

[50:24]
この文を誦しをはりて、まさに嚼楊枝すべし。楊枝のながさ、あるひは四指、あるひは八指、あるひは十二指、あるひは十六指なり。

When finished chanting this text, we should chew the willow twig. The length of the willow twig may be four fingers, eight fingers, twelve fingers, or sixteen fingers.

[50:25]
摩訶僧祇律第三十四云、齒木應量用、極長十六指、極短四指。

In number 34 of the *Mahāsāṃghika Vinaya*, it is said, "For the tooth stick, use according to proper size: a maximum length of sixteen fingers; a minimum length of four fingers."[34]

---

32   **"Pure Practice" chapter of the *Flower Garland Sūtra*** (*Kegon kyō jōgyō bon* 華嚴經淨行品): *Da fangguang fo huayan jing* 大方廣佛華嚴經, T.278.9:431a25-26. Here and in the subsequent quotations from this text, the sūtra passages are not actually in the form of a prayer but, rather, occur in a long list of prescriptions for how bodhisattvas should think as they go about their daily activities.

33   **Chewing the willow twig at daybreak** (*shin shaku yōji* 晨嚼楊枝): A continuation of the *Flower Garland Sūtra* passage (T.278.9:431a26-27).

34   **number 34 of the *Mahāsāṃghika Vinaya*** (*Makasōgi ritsu dai sanjūshi* 摩訶僧祇律第三十四): Dōgen combines here two sentences of the *Mohesengqi lü* 摩訶僧祇律, fascicle 34 (T.1425.22:505b1-2, b17-18).

[50:26]

しるべし、四指よりもみじかくすべからず、十六指よりもながきは、量に應せず。ふとさは手小指大なり。しかありといへども、それよりもほそき、さまたげなし。そのかたち、手小指形なり。一端はふとく、一端ほそし。そのふときはしを、微細にかむなり。

We know from this that it should not be shorter than four fingers, and longer than sixteen fingers does not accord with proper size. The thickness is the size of the little finger, though there is nothing to prevent something thinner. Its shape is that of the little finger: one end thicker, the other end thinner. We chew the thicker end into fine strands.

[50:27]

三千威儀經云、嚼頭不得過三分。

In the *Sūtra of the Three Thousand Rules of Deportment*, it is said, "The chewed tip should not exceed three tenths of an inch."[35]

[50:28]

よくかみて、はのうへ、はのうら、みがくがごとくとぎあらふべし。たびたびとぎみがき、あらひすぐべし。はのもとのししのうへ、よくみがきあらふべし。はのあひだ、よくかきそろえ、きよくあらふべし。漱口たびたびすれば、すすぎきよめらる。しかうしてのち、したをこそぐべし。

Having chewed it well, rub and clean the front and back of the teeth as if polishing them. Rub and polish, wash and rinse them repeatedly. Polish and clean the gums at the base of the teeth. Thoroughly scrape between the teeth and wash them clean. By frequently rinsing the mouth, it will be rinsed clean. After this, scrape the tongue.

[50:29]

三千威儀經云、刮舌有五事、一者不得過三返。二者舌上血出當止。三者不得大振手汚僧伽梨衣若足。四者棄楊枝莫當人道。五者常當屏處。

In the *Sūtra of the Three Thousand Rules of Deportment*, it is said,[36]

Regarding scraping the tongue, there are five points. First, do not exceed three times. Second, stop if the surface of the tongue bleeds. Third, do not move the hand so much that the saṃghāti robe or the feet are soiled. Fourth, do not dispose of the willow twig where people walk. Fifth, always do this in a screened-off place.

---

35 *Sūtra of the Three Thousand Rules of Deportment* (*Sanzen iigi kyō* 三千威儀經): Sanqian weiyi jing 三千威儀經, T.1470.24:915b5.

36 *Sūtra of the Three Thousand Rules of Deportment* (*Sanzen iigi kyō* 三千威儀經): Sanqian weiyi jing 三千威儀經, T.1470.24:915b7-9.

50. Washing the Face Senmen 洗面

[50:30] {2:45}

いはゆる刮舌三返といふは、水を口にふくみて、舌をこそげこそげすること、三返するなり、三刮にはあらず。血いでばまさにやむべし、といふにこころうべし。よくよく刮舌すべしといふことは、三千威儀經云、淨口者、嚼楊枝・漱口・刮舌。しかあれば、楊枝は、佛祖ならびに佛祖兒孫の、護持しきたれるところなり。

The "scraping the tongue three times" mentioned here means that filling the mouth with water and scraping away at the tongue is repeated three times; it does not mean to make only three scrapes. We should heed the admonition to stop if there is bleeding. On the fact that we should thoroughly scrape the tongue, *it is said in the Sūtra of the Three Thousand Rules of Deportment, "Purifying the mouth means chewing the willow twig, rinsing the mouth, and scraping the tongue."*[37] Thus, the willow twig is something that has been upheld by the buddhas and ancestors, as well as by the descendants of the buddhas and ancestors.

[50:31]

佛在王舍城竹園之中、與千二百五十比丘倶。臘月一日、波斯匿王、是日設食。清晨躬手授佛楊枝。佛受嚼竟、擲殘、著地便生、翁鬱而起、根莖涌出、高五百由旬。枝葉雲布、周匝亦爾。漸復生華、大如車輪。遂復有菓、大如五斗瓶。根莖枝葉、純是七寶。若干種色、映殊麗妙。隨色發光、奄蔽日月。食其菓、菓者美喩甘露。香氣四塞、聞者情悦。香風來吹、更相撑角、枝葉皆出和雅之音、暢演法要、聞者無厭。一切人民、覩茲樹變、敬信之心、倍益純厚。佛乃説法、應適其意、心皆開解。志求佛者、得果生天、數甚衆多。

The Buddha was residing in the Bamboo Grove at Rājagṛha, together with one thousand two hundred fifty bhikṣus.[38] *On the first day of the twelfth month, King Prasenajit provided the meal of the day. Early that morning, he personally gave the Buddha a willow twig. After the Buddha had received and chewed it, he threw the remainder on the ground, whereupon it immediately started growing and developing luxuriant vegetation, sending out roots and stems, till it reached a height of five hundred yojana. Its branches and leaves spread out like clouds, and its circumference was comparably huge. Gradually, it also produced flowers the size of wagon wheels; and, eventually, it also produced fruit the size of a five-peck crock. Its roots, stems, branches, and leaves were entirely of the seven precious substances. Their numerous colors shone with exceptional beauty, the light from each color obscuring the*

---

37 ***Sūtra of the Three Thousand Rules of Deportment*** (*Sanzen iigi kyō* 三千威儀經): *Sanqian weiyi jing* 三千威儀經, T.1470.24:915a16-17.

38 **The Buddha was residing in the Bamboo Grove at Rājagṛha** (*butsu zai ōsha jō chikuon shi chū* 佛在王舍城竹園之中): From the *Damamūka-nidāna-sūtra* (*Xianyu jing* 賢愚經, T.202.4:362b8-19). The miracle of the willow twig described here is also recorded in the vinaya (see *Sifen lü* 四分律, T.1428.22:949a5-7).

sun and the moon. When the fruit was eaten, the flavor of the fruit was like ambrosia. Its fragrance perfumed the four quarters, and all who smelled it were pleased. When a fragrant breeze blew in and knocked them together, the branches and leaves all gave forth a harmonious and refined sound that elucidated the essentials of the dharma; and those who heard it never tired of it. The reverence and faith of all the people who observed the transformation of that tree grew increasingly pure and virtuous. When the Buddha then preached the dharma, their minds opened and understood in accord with his meaning. Those who set their minds on seeking buddhahood and attained the fruit of birth in a heaven were very great in number.

[50:32] {2:46}

佛および衆僧を供養する法は、かならず晨旦に楊枝をたてまつるなり。そののち種種の供養をまうく。ほとけに楊枝をたてまつれることおほく、ほとけ楊枝をもちゐさせたまふことおほけれども、しばらくこの波斯匿王みづからてづから供養しましす因縁、ならびにこの高樹の因縁、しるべきゆえに挙するなり。

The procedure of making offerings to the Buddha and the assembly of monks is always to offer a tooth stick early in the morning. After that, various other offerings are prepared. Although there are many cases of offering the willow twig to the Buddha, and many cases of the Buddha using the willow twig, for now, I hold up this episode of King Prasenajit himself offering one with his own hands, together with the episode of the tall tree, because we should know about them.

[50:33]

またこの日、すなはち外道六師、ともにほとけに降伏せられたてまつりて、おどろきおそりてにげはしる、つひに六師ともに投河而死。六師徒類九億人、皆來詣佛求爲弟子。佛言善來比丘、鬚髮自落、法衣在身、皆成沙門。佛爲説法、示其法要、漏盡結解、悉得羅漢。

It was also on this day that the six teachers of other paths, having all been defeated by the Buddha, ran away in shock and terror, and all six teachers eventually threw themselves into the river and died.[39]

Nine hundred million followers of the six teachers came en masse to the Buddha and asked to be his disciples. When the Buddha said, "Welcome, bhikṣus," their beards and hair fell away by themselves, dharma robes covered their bodies, and they all became śramaṇas. When the Buddha preached the dharma for them, showing them the essentials of the dharma, their contaminants were exhausted, their bonds released, and they all attained arhatship.

---

39 **six teachers of other paths** (*gedō rokushi* 外道六師): Continuing to quote from the *Damamūka-nidāna-sūtra* (*Xianyu jing* 賢愚經, T.202.4:363a7-11).

50. Washing the Face Senmen 洗面

[50:34] {2:47}
しかあればすなはち、如來すでに楊枝をもちいましますゆえに、人天これを供養したてまつるなり。あきらかにしりぬ、嚼楊枝、これ諸佛菩薩ならびに佛弟子の、かならず所持なりといふことを。もし、もちいざらんは、その法、失墜せり、かなしまざらんや。

Thus, because the Tathāgata was already using the willow twig, humans and devas made offerings of them to him. Clearly, then, we know that chewing willow twigs is something the buddhas and bodhisattvas, as well as the disciples of the buddhas, have kept without fail. If we do not use them, the procedure will be lost. How could we not lament this?

[50:35]
梵網菩薩戒經云、若佛子、常應二時頭陀、冬夏坐禪、結夏安居、常用楊枝・澡豆・三衣・瓶・鉢・坐具・錫杖・香爐・漉水嚢・手巾・刀子・火燧・鑷子・繩牀・經・律・佛像・菩薩形像。而菩薩行時、及遊方時、行來百里千里、此十八種物、常隨其身。頭陀者、從正月十五日至三月十五日、從八月十五日至十月十五日。是二時中、此十八種物、常隨其身、如鳥二翼。

In the *Brahma's Net Bodhisattva Precepts Sūtra*, it is said,[40]

> You children of the Buddha, during the *dhūta* of the two periods, the winter and summer seated meditation, and the binding of the summer retreat, you should always use willow twigs, soap, the three robes, a water flask, a bowl, a sitting cloth, a staff, an incense burner, a water filter, a hand cloth, a knife, a flintstone, tweezers, a rope chair, the sūtras, the vinaya, a buddha image, and a bodhisattva image.[41] When bodhisattvas practice the *dhūta* and when they roam about, whether they travel a hundred miles or a thousand miles, they should always have these eighteen kinds of articles close to their persons. The *dhūta* periods are from the fifteenth day of the first month until the fifteenth day of the third month, and from the fifteenth day of the eighth month until the fifteenth day of the tenth month. During these two periods, one should always keep these eighteen kinds of articles close to one's person, like the two wings of a bird.

---

40 ***Brahma's Net Bodhisattva Precepts Sūtra*** (*Bonmō bosatsu kai kyō* 梵網菩薩戒經): The Chinese *Brahmajāla-sūtra*, at *Fanwang pusa jie jing* 梵網菩薩戒經, T.1484.24:1008a13-20.

41 ***dhūta* of the two periods** (*niji zuda* 二時頭陀): The term *dhūta* (*zuda* 頭陀) refers to the practice of austerities; the "two periods" (*niji* 二時) are those defined here below.

[50:36] {2:48}

この十八種物、ひとつも虧闕すべからず。もし虧闕すれば、鳥の一翼おちたらんがごとし。一翼のこれりとも、飛行することあたはじ、鳥道の機縁にあらざらん。菩薩もまたかくのごとし、この十八種の羽翼そなはらざれば、行菩薩道あたはず。十八種のうち、楊枝すでに第一に居せり、最初に具足すべきなり。この楊枝の用・不をあきらめんともがら、すなはち佛法をあきらむる菩提薩埵なるべし。いまだかつてあきらめざらんは、佛法也未夢見在ならん。

Not a single one of these eighteen kinds of articles should be missing. If any is missing, it would be like a bird losing a wing: even if one wing remained, it could not fly and would not be an opportunity for the "path of the bird."[42] Bodhisattvas are also like this: if not equipped with these eighteen kinds of articles, they cannot follow the bodhisattva path. Among the eighteen kinds, since the willow twig occupies the first position, one should equip oneself with that first. Those who clarify whether or not the willow twig is used are surely bodhisattvas who clarify the buddha dharma. Those who have not yet clarified it must *never have seen the buddha dharma even in their dreams.*

[50:37]

しかあればすなはち、見楊枝は見佛祖なり。或有人問意旨如何。幸值永平老漢嚼楊枝。

Hence, to see the willow twig is to see the buddhas and ancestors. *If someone were to ask what this means, [I would say] "Fortunately, you've met old man Eihei chewing the willow twig."*[43]

[50:38]

この梵網菩薩戒は、過去・現在・未來の諸佛菩薩、かならず過・現・當に受持しきたれり。しかあれば、楊枝、また過・現・當に受持しきたれり。

These *Brahma's Net* bodhisattva precepts have always been received and kept in past, present, and future by the buddhas and bodhisattvas of past, present, and future. Thus, the willow twig has also been received and kept in past, present, and future.

---

42 **"path of the bird"** (*chōdō* 鳥道): A favorite expression of Dongshan Liangjie 洞山良价 (807-869) that occurs several times in Dōgen's writings; generally taken to imply "a way that follows no route and leaves no traces." See Supplementary Notes, s.v. "Dongshan's three roads."

43 **If someone were to ask what this means** (*waku u nin mon ishi ikan* 或有人問意旨如何): Dōgen shifts to Chinese for this statement and his answer. "Old man Eihei" (*Eihei rōkan* 永平老漢) is, of course, a self-reference.

50. Washing the Face *Senmen* 洗面

[50:39]

禪苑清規云、大乘梵網經、十重・四十八輕、竝須讀誦通利、善知持犯開遮。但依金口聖言、莫擅隨於庸輩。

In the *Rules of Purity for the Chan Park*, it is said,[44]

> We should recite and be well versed in all the ten grave and forty-eight lesser precepts of the Great Vehicle *Brahma's Net Sūtra*, knowing what it is to keep or break them, what is permitted and what forbidden. Rely only on the sacred words of the Golden Mouthed One; do not presume to follow the vulgar crowd.[45]

[50:40]

まさにしるべし、佛佛祖祖正傳の宗旨、それかくのごとし。これに違せんは佛道にあらず、佛法にあらず、祖道にあらず。

Truly, we should recognize that the essential point directly transmitted by buddha after buddha and ancestor after ancestor is like this. Whatever goes against this is not the word of the buddhas, not the dharma of the buddhas, not the way of the ancestors.

[50:41] {2:49}

しかあるに、大宋國いま楊枝たえてみえず。嘉定十六年癸未四月のなかに、はじめて大宋に諸山諸寺をみるに、僧侶の、楊枝をしれるなく、朝野の貴賤、おなじくしらず。僧家すべてしらざるゆえに、もし楊枝の法を問著すれば、失色して度を失す。あはれむべし、白法の失墜せることを。わづかにくちをすすぐともがらは、馬の尾を寸餘にきりたるを、牛の角の、おほきさ三分ばかりにて方につくりたるが、ながさ六七寸なる、そのはし二寸ばかりにむまのたちがみのごとくにうえて、これをもちて牙歯をあらふのみなり。僧家の器にもちいがたし。不淨の器ならん、佛法の器にあらず。俗人の祠天するにも、なほきらひぬべし。かの器、また俗人・僧家、ともにくつのちりをはらふ器にもちいる。また梳鬢のときもちいる。いささかの大小あれども、すなはちこれひとつなり。かの器をもちいるも、萬人が一人なり。

Nevertheless, in the Land of the Great Song at present, the willow twig is never seen. During the fourth month of the junior water year of the sheep, the sixteenth year of Jiading, when I first observed the various mountains and other monasteries of the Great Song, there was no cleric who knew of the willow twig, and the elites and commoners of court and countryside were likewise ignorant of it.[46] Because the monks knew

---

44 ***Rules of Purity for the Chan Park*** (*Zennen shingi* 禪苑清規): *Chanyuan qinggui* 禪苑清規, ZZ.111:877a18-b1.

45 **sacred words of the Golden Mouthed One** (*konku shōgon* 金口聖言): I.e., the teachings of the Buddha.

46 **fourth month of the junior water year of the sheep, the sixteenth year of Jiading** (*Katei jūroku nen kibi shigatsu* 嘉定十六年癸未四月): I.e., May of 1223, when Dōgen first arrived in China.

nothing of it, when I inquired about the use of the willow twig, they would pale and lose their composure. What a pity, to lose the pure dharmas. Those who at least do rinse out their mouths just clean their teeth with a thing made from horse tail, cut to a little more than an inch, that is implanted in a piece of ox horn of some three tenths of an inch across and six or seven inches long, of which the last two inches are planted with the bristles, rather like a horse's mane. This is not an implement for use by a monk: it is likely an impure implement, not an implement of the buddha dharma. Even the laity in their sacrifices to the devas would have an aversion to it. This implement is used by the laity and clerics alike as implements for brushing dust off their shoes; they also use it when brushing their hair. The size may be slightly different, but it is the same thing. Even those who use this implement are but one in ten thousand.

[50:42]
しかあれば、天下の出家・在家、ともにその口氣、はなはだくさし。二三尺をへだててものいふとき、口臭きたる、かぐものたへがたし。有道の尊宿と稱し、人天の導師と號するともがらも、漱口・刮舌・嚼楊枝の法、ありとだにもしらず。これをもて推するに、佛祖の大道、いま陵夷をみるらんこと、いくそばくといふことしらず。いまわれら、露命を萬里の蒼波にをしまず、異域の山川をわたりしのぎて、道をとぶらふとすれども、澆運かなしむべし、いくそばくの白法か、さきだちて滅没しぬらん。をしむべし、をしむべし。

Thus, the breath of renunciants and householders alike throughout the land is extremely malodorous. When they speak, even from two or three feet away, the stink coming from their mouths is difficult to bear. Even those known as venerables in possession of the way and called teachers of humans and devas do not know that the procedures for rinsing the mouth, scraping the tongue, and chewing the willow stick even exist. Judging from this, we cannot imagine to what degree we are now witnessing the deterioration of the great way of the buddhas and ancestors. Now, even as we risk our evanescent lives to the ten thousand miles of deep green waves and cross the mountains and rivers of foreign lands in search of the way, we cannot but lament our misfortune, that so many pure dharmas have already been lost. How regrettable. How regrettable.

[50:43] {2:50}
しかあるに、日本一國朝野の道俗、ともに楊枝を見聞す、佛光明を見聞するならん。しかあれども、嚼楊枝、それ如法ならず、刮舌の法、つたはれず、倉卒なるべし。しかあれども、宋人の、楊枝をしらざるにたくらぶれば、楊枝をもちいるべしとしれるは、おのづから上人の法をしれり。仙人の法にも、楊枝をもちいる。しるべし、みな出塵の器なり、清淨の調度なりといふことを。

Throughout the Land of Japan, however, the religious and laity of

50. Washing the Face Senmen 洗面

court and countryside have all likely experienced the willow twig and experienced the radiance of the Buddha. Still, our chewing of the willow twig is not in accordance with proper procedure, and the procedure of scraping the tongue has not been handed down; so, we are surely lax. Even so, in contrast to people of the Song, who do not know of the willow twig, those who have understood the necessity of using the willow twig know for themselves a procedure of the holy ones. The procedures of the immortals also make use of the willow twig.[47] We should realize that these are all utensils beyond the dusty world, implements of purity.

[50:44]

三千威儀經云、用楊枝有五事。一者斷當如度。二者破當如法。三者嚼頭不得過三分。四者疏齒當中三齧。五者當汁澡目用。

In the *Sūtra of the Three Thousand Rules of Deportment*, it is said,[48]

There are five points that pertain to using the willow twig. First, it should be cut to the proper proportions. Second, it should be broken using the proper procedure. Third, in chewing the tip, do not exceed three tenths of an inch. Fourth, in [cleaning] the gaps between teeth, it should be inserted for three bites. Fifth, the sap should be used to rinse the eyes.

[50:45]

いま嚼楊枝・漱口の水を、右手にうけてもて目をあらふこと、みな、もと三千威儀經の説なり。いま日本國の往代の庭訓なり。刮舌の法は、僧正榮西つたふ。楊枝つかひてのち、すてんとするとき、兩手をもて楊枝のかみたるかたより二片に擘破す。その破口のときかほを、よこざまに舌上にあててこそぐ。すなはち、右手に水をうけて、くちにいれて漱口し、刮舌す。漱口・刮舌たびたびし、擘楊枝の角にて、こそげこそげして、血出を度とせんとするがごとし。

Our present practice of spitting the water from chewing the willow twig and rinsing the mouth into one's right hand and using it to wash the eyes is originally entirely from the instructions of the *Sūtra of the Three Thousand Rules of Deportment*. In the Land of Japan today, it is a household rule from ages past. The procedure for scraping the tongue was transmitted by the Saṃgha Controller Eisai.[49]

---

47 **immortals** (*sennin* 仙人): I.e., Daoist sages.

48 ***Sūtra of the Three Thousand Rules of Deportment*** (*Sanzen iigi kyō* 三千威儀經): *Sanqian weiyi jing* 三千威儀經, T.1470.24:915b4-6. The fourth point here is a bit unclear; the procedure seems to be to insert the willow twig between the teeth and bite down on it three times. The fifth point recommends using the sap released into one's saliva from chewing the twig as an eye wash.

49 **Saṃgha Controller Eisai** (*sōjō Eisai* 僧正榮西): I.e., Myōan Eisai (or Yōsai) 明菴榮西 (1141-1215), founder of Kenninji 建仁寺, where Dōgen stayed for several years

After using the willow twig, when it is to be discarded, using both hands, we tear it apart into two pieces, starting at the chewed end. Take the sharp edge of the split twig, place it crosswise on the tongue and scrape. That is, putting water in the mouth with the right hand, rinse the mouth and scrape the tongue. Rinse the mouth and scrape the tongue over and over again, using the edge of the split willow twig to scrape and scrape, as if to draw blood.

[50:46] {2:51}

漱口のとき、この文を密誦すべし。

While rinsing the mouth, silently recite this text:

[50:47]

華嚴經云、澡漱口齒、當願衆生、向淨法門、究竟解脫。

In the *Flower Garland Sūtra*, it is said,
Rinsing out the mouth and teeth,
Pray that living beings
Approach the pure dharma gate
And finally attain liberation.[50]

[50:48]

たびたび漱口して、くちびるのうちと、したのした、あぎにいたるまで、右手の第一指・第二指・第三指等をもて、指のはらにてよくよくなめりたるがごとくなるごと、あらひのぞくべし。油あるもの食せらんことちかからんには、皂莢をもちいるべし。楊枝つかひおはりて、すなはち屏處にすつべし。楊枝すててのち、三彈指すべし。後架にしては、棄楊枝をうくる斗あるべし。餘處にては、屏處にすつべし。漱口の水は、面桶のほかに、はきすつべし。

Rinsing the mouth repeatedly, using the first, second, and third fingers of the right hand, we should clean out [food particles] inside the lips and under the tongue as far as the jaw, till they are thoroughly smoothed.[51] When we have recently eaten oily food, we should use black pod.[52] As

---

following his return from China in 1227. Eisai visited China twice, in 1168 and 1187-1191. He treats the use of the tooth stick and the practice of scraping the tongue in his *Shukke taikō* 出家大綱; see Fujita Takuji 藤田琢司, *Eisai zenji shū* 栄西禅師集 (2014), p. 569.

50   ***Flower Garland Sūtra*** (*Kegon kyō* 華嚴經): *Da fangguang fo huayan jing* 大方廣佛華嚴經, T.278.9:431b4-5.

51   **till they are thoroughly smoothed** (*yokuyoku nameritaru ga gotoku* よくよくなめりたるがごとく): Taking the predicate *nameri* as *katsu* 滑 ("smooth"); it might also be read as *shi* 舐 ("to lick").

52   **black pod** (*sōkyō* 皂莢): The Chinese honey locust (*Gleditsia sinensis*), the pods of which contain seeds used as a soap.

50. Washing the Face *Senmen* 洗面

soon as we are finished using the willow twig, we should discard it in an inconspicuous place. After discarding the willow twig, we should snap the fingers three times.[53] When at the rear washstand, there should be a container for receiving discarded willow twigs; when at other locations, we should discard it in an inconspicuous place. The water used to rinse the mouth should be spit out somewhere other than in the face bucket.

[50:49]
つぎに、まさしく洗面す。兩手に面桶の湯を掬して、額より兩眉毛・兩目・鼻孔・人中・顱・頬、あまねくあらふ。まづよくよく湯をすくひかけて、しかうしてのち摩沐すべし。涕唾・鼻涕を面桶の湯におとしいるることなかれ。かくのごとくあらふとき、湯を無度につひやして、面桶のほかにもらし、おとし、ちらして、はやくうしなふことなかれ。あかおち、あぶらのぞこほりぬるまで、あらふなり。耳裏あらふべし、著水不得なるがゆゑに。眼裏あらふべし、著沙不得なるがゆゑに。あるいは頭髪・頂顙までもあらふ、すなはち威儀なり。洗面、をはりて、面桶の湯をすててのちも、三彈指べし。

Next, do the face-washing proper. Using both hands, scoop up hot water from the face bucket and wash all over, from the forehead to the eyebrows, eyes, nostrils, the human center, cranium, and cheeks.[54] We should first wet them thoroughly with the hot water and then scrub them clean. Do not allow tears, saliva, or nasal mucus to drip into the hot water in the face bucket. When washing like this, do not let the hot water run out too quickly by using an immoderate amount, dripping it outside the bucket, spilling it, or splashing it about. Wash until the grime is off and the oil removed. We should wash "in the ears"; for "*water can't get in*."[55] We should wash "in the eyes"; for "*sand can't get in*." To wash to the hairline or to the crown of the head is proper deportment. Having finished washing the face, after emptying the hot water from the face bucket, we should also snap the fingers three times.

---

53 **snap the fingers three times** (*santanji* 三彈指): A common apotropaic gesture used to ward off impurities.

54 **human center** (*ninchū* 人中): I.e., the upper lip, considered as a central node in acupuncture. Some texts read *nichū* 耳中 ("within the ears") here.

55 **We should wash "in the ears"; for "water can't get in"** (*niri arau beshi, jaku sui futoku naru ga yue ni* 耳裏あらふべし、著水不得なるがゆゑに): This and the following sentence are playing on a popular saying attributed to the ninth-century figure Baishui Benren 白水本仁 (dates unknown), disciple of Dongshan Liangjie 洞山良价 (see, e.g., *Liandeng huiyao* 聯燈會要, ZZ.136:805b18):

示衆云、眼裏著沙不得。耳裏著水不得。

Addressing the assembly, he said, "Sand can't get in his eyes; water can't get in his ears."

[50:50] {2:52}

つぎに、手巾のおもてをのごふはしにて、のごひ、かわかすべし。しかうしてのち、手巾、もとのごとく脱しとりて、ふたへにして左臂にかく。雲堂の後架には、公界の拭面あり、いはゆる一疋布をまうけたり。烘櫃あり、衆家ともに拭面するに、たらざるわづらひなし。かれにも頭面のごふべし、また自己の手巾をもちいるも、ともにこれ法なり。

Next, with the end of the hand cloth used for wiping the face, we should wipe and dry. After that, we remove the hand cloth, fold it in half, and drape it over the crook of the left arm, as it was to begin with. At the rear washstands of the cloud hall, there are communal face towels — that is, cloths one bolt in length are provided.[56] There is a heating chest, so that there is no concern for a shortage [of dry towels] when members of the community all wipe their faces. We should wipe the head and face with these or use our own hand cloth; either way is proper procedure.

[50:51]

洗面のあひだ、桶・杓ならしておとをなすこと、かまびすしくすることなかれ。湯・水を狼藉にして、近邊をぬらすことなかれ。ひそかに觀想すべし、後五百歳にうまれて、邊地遠島に處すれども、宿善くちずして古佛の威儀を正傳し、染汚せず、修證する、隨喜懽喜すべし。雲堂にかへらんに、輕歩聲低なるべし。

While washing the face, do not bang the bucket and ladle, and do not be noisy. Do not get the area wet by splashing the hot and cold water about. We should reflect to ourselves that, although born in the latter five hundred years and dwelling on remote islands of a peripheral land, we should rejoice in the fact that the good accumulated in past lives has not decayed, and that we directly transmit the deportment of the old buddhas, and practice and verify it without defilement.[57] In returning to the cloud hall, step lightly to keep the sound down.

[50:52]

耆年宿德の草菴、かならず洗面架あるべし、洗面せざるは非法なり。洗面のとき、面藥をもちいる法あり。

In the thatched huts of seniors and elderly worthies, there should always be face-washing stands; to fail to wash the face is improper. When washing the face, there is a procedure using facial ointments.

56　**cloths one bolt in length** (*ichihitsu bu* 一疋布): "Bolt" translates *hiki* 疋, a length of cloth equal to two *tan* 反, or enough for a single adult robe.

57　**the latter five hundred years** (*go gohyaku sai* 後五百歳): I.e., the final, degenerate age of the dharma of Buddha Śākyamuni, as taught in the *Lotus Sūtra*.

50. Washing the Face *Senmen* 洗面

[50:53]

おほよそ嚼楊枝・洗面、これ古佛の正法なり。道心辦道のともがら、修證すべきなり。あるいは湯をえざるには、水をもちいる、舊例なり、古法なり。湯・水すべてえざらんときは、早晨よくよく拭面して、香草・末香等をぬりてのち、禮佛誦經、燒香坐禪すべし。いまだ洗面せずば、もろもろのつとめ、ともに無禮なり。

In sum, chewing the willow twig and washing the face — these are the true dharma of the old buddhas. Those who pursue the way with the mind of the way should practice and verify them. When hot water is not available, to use cold water is an ancient precedent, is an old procedure. When neither hot nor cold water is available, then in the morning, we should thoroughly rub the face, and then, after applying herbal incense, powdered incense, or the like, should pay obeisance to the buddha, recite the sūtras, burn incense, and sit in meditation. Whatever services are performed when one has not yet washed the face lack ritual propriety.

{2:53}

正法眼藏洗面第五十
Treasury of the True Dharma Eye
Washing the Face
Number 50

[Ryūmonji MS:]

延應元年己亥十月二十三日、在雍州觀音導利興聖寶林寺示衆
Presented to the assembly at Kannon Dōri Kōshō Hōrin Monastery, Yōshū; twenty-third day, tenth month of the junior earth year of the pig, the first year of En'ō [20 November 1239]

[50:54]

天竺國・震旦國は、國王・王子、大臣・百官、在家・出家、朝野男女・百姓萬民、みな洗面す。家宅の調度にも面桶あり、あるいは銀、あるひは鑞なり。天祠神廟にも、毎朝に洗面を供ず。佛祖の塔頭にも、洗面をたてまつる。在家・出家、洗面ののち、衣裳をただしくして、天をも拜し、神をも拜し、祖宗をも拜し、父母をも拜す。師匠を拜し、三寶を拜し、三界萬靈・十方眞宰を拜す。いまは農夫・田夫、漁夫・樵翁までも、洗面わするることなし。しかあれども、嚼楊枝なし。日本國は、國王・大臣、老少・朝野、在家・出家の貴賤、ともに嚼楊枝・漱口の法をわすれず、しかあれども洗面せず。一得一失なり。いま洗面・嚼楊枝、ともに護持せん、補虧闕の興隆なり、佛祖の照臨なり。

In the Land of Sindhu and the Land of Cīnasthāna, the kings and princes, great ministers and high officials, householders and renunciants, men and women of court and countryside, peasants and commoners, all practice face-washing. Among their household implements as well, there is a face bucket, whether of silver or of tin. In their temples to the devas and shrines to the gods, face-washing is offered every morning; in the stūpa sites of the buddhas and ancestors, as well, face-washing is offered.[58] Householders and renunciants, after washing their faces, don proper clothing and pay obeisance to the devas, pay obeisance to the gods, pay obeisance to the ancestors, and pay obeisance to the father and mother. We pay obeisance to our teachers, pay obeisance to the three treasures, pay obeisance to the myriad spirits of the three realms, and pay obeisance to the true lords of the ten directions.[59] Nowadays, even farmers and paddy workers, fishermen and woodsmen never neglect to wash their faces; yet they lack chewing the willow twig. In the Land of Japan, the kings and great ministers, old and young, in court and countryside, householders and renunciants of high and humble status do not neglect the practice of chewing the willow twig and rinsing the mouth; yet they do not wash the face. It is one gained, one lost. Now, our maintaining both face-washing and chewing the willow twig represents a florescence [of the dharma] that has repaired the deficiency; it is the illuminating presence of the buddhas and ancestors.

[Ryūmonji MS:]

寛元元年癸卯十月二十日、在越州吉田郡吉峰寺重示衆

Presented to the assembly again at Kippō Monastery, Yoshida District, Esshū; twentieth day, tenth month of the junior water year of the rabbit, the first year of Kangen [3 December 1243]

建長二年庚戌正月十一日、在越州吉田郡吉祥山永平寺示衆

Presented to the assembly at Eihei Monastery, Kichijōzan, Yoshida District, Esshū; eleventh day, first month of the senior metal year of the dog, the second year of Kenchō [13 February 1250]

---

58 **stūpa sites of the buddhas and ancestors** (*busso no tatchū* 佛祖の塔頭): I.e., the ancestral halls of Chan monasteries. The "face-washing" offered here and in the previous sentence may refer to the ritual washing of the icons in these shrines.

59 **true lords of the ten directions** (*jippō shinsai* 十方眞宰): Tutelary deities protective of Buddhism.

TREASURY OF THE TRUE DHARMA EYE

NUMBER 51

Face-to-Face Conferral
Menju

面授

Face-to-Face Conferral

Menju

INTRODUCTION

According to its colophon, this work was presented in the winter of 1243, at Kippōji, the monastery where Dōgen resided following his move from the capital to the province of Echizen. It represents number 51 in the seventy-five-chapter *Shōbōgenzō*, number 57 in the Honzan edition, and number 5 of fascicle 3 in the twenty-eight-text *Himitsu* collection; it is not found in the sixty-chapter *Shōbōgenzō*.

Dōgen opens the work with an account of the founding of his lineage, the famous story of Buddha Śākyamuni's transmission of the treasury of the true dharma eye to his disciple Mahākāśyapa on Vulture Peak. He then rehearses the tradition of the buddhas and ancestors, from the seven buddhas of the past, through the twenty-eight Indian ancestors to Bodhidharma and the six Chinese ancestors to Huineng 慧能, continuing down to Dōgen's own teacher, Tiantong Rujing 天童如淨. On the first day of the fifth lunar month of the first year of the Baoqing era 寶慶 (8 June 1225), Dōgen reports, Rujing accepted the Japanese disciple into the lineage, in a face-to-face conferral in the abbot's quarters of Tiantong Monastery.

Dōgen then proceeds to discuss the history and meaning of his title theme, the "face-to-face conferral," or direct, personal instruction from master to disciple. In a play on the term "face," he argues that, since every generation of the lineage receives the dharma personally transmitted from Buddha Śākyamuni and the seven buddhas, the face-to-face conferral is the transmission of the face of the buddhas from the face of the master to the face of the disciple; hence, obeisance paid to a master in the lineage is obeisance to the buddhas.

In a lengthy postscript, Dōgen takes to task the eleventh-century Chan master Jianfu Chenggu 薦福承古 for claiming that he was a successor to the famous tenth-century master Yunmen Wenyen 雲門文偃 because he had experienced an insight while reading the latter's words. Chenggu, Dōgen says, has obviously never even heard of the face-to-face confer-

51. Face-to-Face Conferral *Menju* 面授

ral. On his terms, everyone who had ever had an insight while reading a Buddhist sūtra could claim to be a direct successor to Buddha Śākyamuni himself. Instead, those who have had insight while reading a text have always sought out a teacher in the lineage to confirm their understanding face-to-face.

正法眼藏第五十一

Treasury of the True Dharma Eye
Number 51

面授

Face-to-Face Conferral

[51:1] {2:54}

爾時、釋迦牟尼佛、西天竺國靈山會上、百萬衆中、拈優曇華瞬目。於時摩訶迦葉尊者、破顏微笑。釋迦牟尼佛言、吾有正法眼藏涅槃妙心、附囑摩訶迦葉。

> At that time, Buddha Śākyamuni, in an assembly of one million at the assembly on Vulture Peak in the Land of Sindhu in the West, held up an *udumbara* flower and blinked his eyes.[1] Thereupon, Venerable Mahākāśyapa broke into a smile. Buddha Śākyamuni said, "I have a treasury of the true dharma eye, the wondrous mind of nirvāṇa; I bestow it on Mahākāśyapa."

[51:2]

これすなはち、佛佛祖祖、面授正法眼藏の道理なり。七佛の正傳して迦葉尊者にいたる。迦葉尊者より二十八授して、菩提達磨尊者にいたる。菩提達磨尊者、みづから震旦國に降儀して、正宗太祖普覺大師慧可尊者に面授す。五傳して曹溪山大鑑慧能大師にいたる。一十七授して、先師大宋國慶元府太白名山天童古佛にいたる。

> This is the principle of the treasury of the true dharma eye conferred face-to-face by buddha after buddha and ancestor after ancestor. Directly transmitted by the seven buddhas, it reached Venerable Kāśyapa.[2]

---

1 **Buddha Śākyamuni** (*Shakamuni butsu* 釋迦牟尼佛): A telling of the famous story of the transmission of Zen from Śākyamuni to the First Ancestor, Mahākāśyapa, a story of which there are several variants. Dōgen recorded other versions in his *shinji Shōbōgenzō* 眞字正法眼藏 (DZZ.5: 258, case 253), *Eihei kōroku* 永平廣錄 (DZZ.4:182, no. 1), and several *Shōbōgenzō* chapters. The passage here is given in Chinese, as if Dōgen is quoting a text, but the source is unknown.

Vulture Peak (*Ryōzen* 靈山): "Sacred Peak," denoting Gṛdhrakūṭa, the mountain in Magadha where the Buddha is supposed to have taught the *Lotus* and other sūtras.

Land of Sindhu in the West (*Sai Tenjiku koku* 西天竺國): I.e., the Indian subcontinent, the Chinese *tianzhu* 天竺 representing a transliteration of the Sanskrit *Sindhu*.

2 **seven buddhas** (*shichi butsu* 七佛): I.e., the set of seven buddhas of the past, culminating in Buddha Śākyamuni, with which the traditional history of Zen often begins; see Supplementary Notes, s.v. "Seven buddhas." Dōgen goes on here to invoke the lineage

51. Face-to-Face Conferral *Menju* 面授

Through twenty-eight conferrals from Venerable Kāśyapa, it reached Venerable Bodhidharma.[3] Venerable Bodhidharma, having personally descended to the Land of Cīnasthāna, conferred it face-to-face to Venerable Huike, Great Master Pujue, Grand Ancestor Zhengzong.[4] Through five transmissions, it reached Great Master Dajian Huineng of Mount Caoxi.[5] Through seventeen conferrals, it reached my former master, the Old Buddha of Tiantong, on Renowned Mount Taibai, in the Qingyuan Prefecture in the Land of the Great Song.[6]

[51:3]
大宋寶慶元年乙酉五月一日、道元、はじめて先師天童古佛を妙高臺に燒香禮拜す。先師古佛、はじめて道元をみる。そのとき、道元に指授面授するにいはく、

On the first day of the fifth month of the junior wood year of the rooster, the first year of Baoqing in the Great Song, I, Dōgen, first burned incense and paid obeisance at the Miaogaotai to my former master, the Old Buddha of Tiantong.[7] My former master, the Old Buddha, first saw

---

leading to his own master, Tiantong Rujing 天童如淨 (1162-1227), from the First Ancestor, Mahākāśyapa, through the Twenty-eighth Ancestor, Bodhidharma, his Chinese disciple Huike 慧可 (487–593), and the Sixth Ancestor, Huineng 慧能. Tiantong 天童 is the mountain name of Rujing's monastery, the Jingdesi 景德寺.

3 **Venerable Bodhidharma** (*Bodaidaruma sonja* 菩提達磨尊者): The famous twenty-eighth Indian ancestor, said to have brought Zen to China in the early sixth century.

4 **Land of Cīnasthāna** (*Shintan koku* 震旦國): I.e., "China," represented here by a Sanskrit name transliterated by the Chinese *Zhendan* 震旦.

Venerable Huike, Great Master Pujue, Grand Ancestor Zhengzong (*Shōshū taiso Fukaku daishi Eka sonja* 正宗太祖普覺大師慧可尊者): I.e., Bodhidharma's disciple, Huike 慧可, reckoned as the second ancestor in China; his honorific titles are more often given as Great Master Zhengzong Pujue (*Shōshū Fukaku daishi* 正宗普覺大師) and Chan Master Dazu (*Taiso zenji* 太祖禪師).

5 **Great Master Dajian Huineng of Mount Caoxi** (*Sōkeizan Daikan Enō daishi* 曹溪山大鑑慧能大師):): I.e., the famous Sixth Ancestor, Huineng 慧能; Chan Master Dajian 大鑑禪師 is a posthumous title. Mount Caoxi 曹溪山, in present-day Guangdong, is the site of his temple, the Baolinsi 寶林寺.

6 **my former master, the Old Buddha of Tiantong, on Renowned Mount Taibai, in the Qingyuan Prefecture in the Land of the Great Song** (*senshi Daisō koku Keigen fu Taihaku Myōzan Tendō Kobutsu* 先師大宋國慶元府太白名山天童古佛): I.e., Dōgen's teacher, Tiantong Rujing 天童如淨, abbot of the Jingde Monastery 景德寺 on Mount Tiantong 天童山, in present-day Zhejiang Province.

7 **On the first day of the fifth month of the junior wood year of the rooster, the first year of Baoqing in the Great Song** (*Daisō Hōkyō gannen itsuyū gogatsu ichinichi* 大宋寶慶元年乙酉五月一日): I.e., 8 June 1225.

Miaogaotai (*Myōkōdai* 妙高臺): "The Terrace of Sumeru," one of the three buildings comprising the abbot's quarters at Jingde Monastery 景德寺.

Dōgen. At that time, in giving Dōgen personal instruction and face-to-face conferral, he said,

[51:4]
佛佛祖祖面授の法門、現成せり。これすなはち靈山の拈華なり、嵩山の得髓なり、黄梅の傳衣なり、洞山の面授なり。これは佛祖の眼藏面授なり。吾屋裏のみあり、餘人は夢也未見聞在なり。

> The dharma gate conferred face-to-face by buddha after buddha and ancestor after ancestor is fulfilled. This is precisely holding up the flower on Vulture Peak; it is getting the marrow on Mount Song; it is transmitting the robe at Huangmei; it is the face-to-face conferral of Dongshan.[8] This is the face-to-face conferral of the treasury of the eye of the buddhas and ancestors. It exists only within our house; others have *never seen or heard of it even in their dreams.*

[51:5] {2:55}
この面授の道理は、釋迦牟尼佛、まのあたり迦葉佛の會下にして面授し護持しきたれるがゆえに、佛祖面なり。佛面より面授せざれば、諸佛にあらざるなり。釋迦牟尼佛まのあたり迦葉尊者をみること親附なり。阿難・羅睺羅といへども、迦葉の親附におよばず。諸大菩薩といへども、迦葉の親附におよばず、迦葉尊者の座に坐することえず。世尊と迦葉と、同座し同衣しきたるを、一代の佛儀とせり。迦葉尊者、したしく世尊の面授を面授せり、心授せり、身授せり、眼授せり。釋迦牟尼佛を供養恭敬、禮拜奉覲したてまつれり。その粉骨碎身、いく千萬變といふことをしらず、自己の面目は面目にあらず、如來の面目を面授せり。

> The principle of this face-to-face conferral is that, because Buddha Śākyamuni, in the community of Buddha Kāśyapa, personally received and maintained the face-to-face conferral, his is the face of a buddha and ancestor.[9] Had he not received the face-to-face conferral from the face of a buddha, he would not be [one of] the buddhas.[10] That Buddha Śākya-

---

8 **holding up the flower on Vulture Peak** (*Ryōzen no nenge* 靈山の拈華): Reference to the first transmission of Zen, as described in section 1, above; see Supplementary Notes, s.v. "Hold up a flower." "Getting the marrow on Mount Song" (*Sūzan no tokuzui* 嵩山の得髓) refers to Bodhidharma's transmission to Huike 慧可, of whom Bodhidharma said he had "gotten his marrow"; see Supplementary Notes, s.v. "Skin, flesh, bones, and marrow." "Transmitting the robe at Huangmei" (*Ōbai no den'e* 黄梅の傳衣) refers to the bestowal of the robe of Bodhidharma by the Fifth Ancestor, Hongren 弘忍 (688-761), to the Sixth Ancestor, Huineng 慧能. "Face-to-face conferral of Dongshan" (*Tōzan no menju* 洞山の面授) refers to the transmission of the Caodong 曹洞 lineage from its founder, Dongshan Liangjie 洞山良价 (807-869). Somewhat surprisingly, Dōgen here quotes his Chinese master in Japanese translation.

9 **Buddha Kāśyapa** (*Kashō butsu* 迦葉佛): I.e, the sixth of the seven buddhas, just prior to Buddha Śākyamuni; not to be confused with the First Ancestor, Kāśyapa, mentioned just below. See Supplementary Notes, s.v. "Seven buddhas."

10 **Had he not received the face-to-face conferral from the face of a buddha,**

muni personally saw Venerable Kāśyapa is his intimate bequest to him. Even Ānanda and Rahula did not equal his intimate bequest to Kāśyapa.[11] Even the great bodhisattvas did not equal his intimate bequest to Kāśyapa, were unable to sit in the seat of Venerable Kāśyapa. It was the practice of the Buddha during his life that the World-Honored One and Kāśyapa would share the same seat and the same robe.[12] Venerable Kāśyapa intimately got the face conferral, the mind conferral, the body conferral, the eye conferral of the World-Honored One's face-to-face conferral. He made offerings, venerated, paid obeisance, and devotedly attended Buddha Śākyamuni. No one knows how many thousands of myriads of transformations he went through, in thus *pulverizing his bones and shattering his body.*[13] His own face was not his face; he received the face-to-face conferral of the face of the Tathāgata.

[51:6]
釋迦牟尼佛、まさしく迦葉尊者をみまします、迦葉尊者、まのあたり阿難尊者をみる、阿難尊者、まのあたり迦葉尊者の佛面を禮拜す、これ面授なり。阿難尊者、この面授を住持して、商那和修を接して面授す。商那和修尊者、まさしく阿難尊者を奉覲するに、唯面與面、面授し面受す。かくのごとく、代代嫡嫡の祖師、ともに弟子は師にみえ、師は弟子をみるによりて、面授しきたれり。一祖・一師・一弟としても、あひ面授せざるは佛佛祖祖にあらず。たとへば、水を朝宗せしめて宗派を長ぜしめ、燈を續して光明つねならしむるに、億千萬法するにも本枝一如なるなり、また啐啄の迅機なるなり。

Buddha Śākyamuni truly saw Venerable Kāśyapa; Venerable Kāśyapa directly saw Venerable Ānanda; Venerable Ānanda directly paid obeisance to the buddha face of Venerable Kāśyapa: this is the face-to-face conferral.[14] Venerable Ānanda, maintaining this face-to-face conferral,

he would not be [one of] the buddhas (*butsumen yori menju sezareba, shobutsu ni arazaru nari* 佛面より面授せざれば、諸佛にあらざるなり): The translation takes the unexpressed subject to be "Buddha Śākyamuni," but the sentence might also be read as a more general claim: "those without the face-to-face conferral from the face of a buddha, are not buddhas." The expression "face of a buddha" (*butsumen* 佛面) could be read simply as "a buddha," but Dōgen is playing here and below with the "face" (*men* 面) of "face-to-face conferral" (*menju* 面授). See Supplementary Notes, s.v. "Buddha faces, ancestor faces."

11   **Ānanda and Rahula** (*Anan Ragora* 阿難羅睺羅): I.e., Śākyamuni's cousin and son, respectively.

12   **the World-Honored One and Kāśyapa would share the same seat and the same robe** (*Seson to Kashō to, dōza shi dōe shikitaru* 世尊と迦葉と、同座し同衣しきたる): Reference to the legends that Śākyamuni invited Mahākāśyapa to share his seat and entrusted his robe to Mahākāśyapa.

13   **pulverizing his bones and shattering his body** (*funkotsu saishin* 粉骨碎身): A fixed idiom for extreme ascesis.

14   **Ānanda** (*Anan* 阿難): Mahākāśyapa's disciple, the Second Ancestor.

received Śaṇavāsa and conferred it to him face-to-face.[15] When Venerable Śaṇavāsa truly attended Venerable Ānanda, only a face with a face conferred face-to-face and received face-to-face.[16] In this way, the ancestral masters of successor after successor in generation after generation, through the disciple seeing the master and the master seeing the disciple, have been conferring face-to-face. Were even one ancestor, one master, or one disciple not to confer face-to-face, it would not be buddha after buddha and ancestor after ancestor. For example, when we extend channels for water to merge into the ocean, or make light constant by continuing to light lamps, even if this covers *koṭis* of thousands of myriads of dharmas, root and branch remain one. Again, it is the simultaneous action of tapping and pecking.[17]

[51:7] {2:56}
しかあればすなはち、まのあたり釋迦牟尼佛をまぼりたてまつりて、一期の日夜をつめり、佛面に照臨せられたてまつりて、一代の日夜をつめり。これ、いく無量を往來せりとしらず、しづかにおもひやりて、隨喜すべきなり。

Therefore, they have filled their term of days and nights directly observing Buddha Śākyamuni; they have filled their lifetime of days and nights illumined by the presence of the face of the Buddha.[18] No one knows over how many incalculable [kalpas] they have come and gone like this; we should quietly reflect on it and rejoice.

[51:8]
釋迦牟尼佛の佛面を禮拜したてまつり、釋迦牟尼佛の佛眼をわがまなこにうつしたてまつり、わがまなこを佛眼にうつしたてまつりし、佛眼睛なり、佛面目なり。これをあひつたへて、いまにいたるまで一世も間斷せず面授しきたれるは、この面授なり。而今の數十代の嫡嫡は、面面なる佛面なり、本初の佛面に面受なり。この正傳面授を禮拜する、まさしく七佛釋迦牟尼佛を禮拜したてまつるなり、迦葉尊者等の二十八佛祖を禮拜供養したてまつるなり。佛祖の面目・眼睛、かくのごとし。

---

15 **Śaṇavāsa** (*Shōnawashu* 商那和修): Ānanda's disciple, the Third Ancestor.

16 **only a face with a face** (*yui men yo men* 唯面與面): A play on the expression "only a buddha with a buddha" (*yui butsu yo butsu* 唯佛與佛) in Kumārajīva's translation of the *Lotus Sūtra*; see Supplementary Notes, s.v. "Only buddhas with buddhas can exhaustively investigate the real marks of the dharmas."

17 **simultaneous action of tapping and pecking** (*sottaku no jinki* 啐啄の迅機): I.e., the combined action of master and disciple; from the image of the birth of a chick, which taps the inside of the shell while the mother pecks the outside.

18 **they have filled their term of days and nights** (*ichigo no nichiya o tsumeri* 一期の日夜をつめり): I.e., "they have spent their lives"; the translation takes the unexpressed subject to be the masters and disciples in the lineage of the face-to-face conferral.

51. Face-to-Face Conferral Menju 面授   119

They are the eye of the buddha, the face of the buddha, who have paid obeisance to the buddha face of Buddha Śākyamuni, who have reflected the buddha eye of Buddha Śākyamuni in their own eye and reflected their own eye in the buddha eye.[19] The conferral face-to-face that has handed this down to the present without interruption for even a single generation is the face-to-face conferral. Successor after successor spanning the tens of generations down to the present are face after face of buddha faces, received face-to-face from the original face of the buddha. To pay obeisance to this directly transmitted face-to-face conferral is truly to pay obeisance to Buddha Śākyamuni and the seven buddhas, to pay obeisance and make offerings to Venerable Kāśyapa and the twenty-eight buddhas and ancestors. Such are the faces and the eyes of the buddhas and ancestors.

[51:9]
この佛祖にまみゆるは、釋迦牟尼佛等の七佛にみえたてまつるなり。佛祖したしく自己を面授する正當恁麼時なり、面授佛の面授佛に面授するなり。葛藤をもて葛藤に面授して、さらに斷絶せず。眼を開して眼に眼授し、眼受す、面をあらはして面に面授し、面受す。面授は面處の受授なり。心を拈じて心に心授し、心受す、身を現じて身を身授するなり。他方・他國も、これを本祖とせり。震旦國以東、ただこの佛正傳の屋裏のみ、面授面受あり、あらたに如來をみたてまつる正眼をあひつたへきたれり。

To meet these buddhas and ancestors is to be met by Buddha Śākyamuni and the rest of the seven buddhas. It is the very moment when the buddhas and ancestors personally confer themselves face-to-face; it is the conferral face-to-face by a buddha who confers face-to-face to a buddha who confers face-to-face. They confer entanglements face-to-face to entanglements, without any interruption.[20] Opening the eye, they confer eye-to-eye to the eye and receive eye-to-eye from the eye; showing the face, they confer face-to-face to the face and receive face-to-face from the face. The face-to-face conferral is the receiving and conferring of the

---

19 **They are the eye of the buddha, the face of the buddha** (*butsu ganzei nari, butsu menmoku nari* 佛眼睛なり、佛面目なり): Again, taking the unexpressed subject to be the "masters and disciples." See Supplementary Notes, s.v. "Eye."

reflected the buddha eye of Buddha Śākyamuni in their own eye (*Shakamuni butsu no butsugen o waga manako ni utsushitatematsuri* 釋迦牟尼佛の佛眼をわがまなこにうつしたてまつり): Taking *waga manako* ("their own eye") to refer to the eyes of the masters and disciples. The verb *utsusu* うつす here and in the following clause is read as 映す; it might also be taken as 移す, which would yield, "transferred the buddha eye of Buddha Śākyamuni to their own eye."

20 **entanglements** (*kattō* 葛藤): A term usually meaning "difficulties," "complexities," etc., but regularly used by Dōgen in the sense of the "intertwining" (of master and disciple). See Supplementary Notes, s.v. "Tangled vines."

face.²¹ Taking up the mind, they confer mind-to-mind to the mind and receive mind-to-mind from the mind; revealing the body, they confer the body, body-to-body.²² In other regions and other lands as well, these are regarded as the original ancestors. From the Land of Cīnasthāna eastwards, only this house directly transmitted from the Buddha has the face-to-face conferral and face-to-face reception, and has been handing down the true eye that beholds the Tathāgata anew.

[51:10] {2:57}
釋迦牟尼佛面を禮拜するとき、五十一世ならびに七佛祖宗、ならべるにあらず、つらなるにあらざれども、俱時の面授あり。一世も師をみざれば、弟子にあらず、弟子をみざれば、師にあらず。さだまりてあひみ・あひみえて、面授しきたれり、嗣法しきたれるは、祖宗の面授處道現成なり。このゆえに、如來の面光を直拈しきたれるなり。

When we pay obeisance to the face of Buddha Śākyamuni, there is a simultaneous face-to-face conferral of the ancestors of the fifty-one generations and the seven buddhas, though they are neither ranged side by side nor lined up one after the other.²³ If we do not meet a master during our lifetime, we are not a disciple; if we do not meet a disciple, we are not a master. Definitely to see each other and be seen by each other, to have conferred face-to-face and to have inherited the dharma — this is the realization of the way on which the ancestors confer face-to-face.²⁴ Therefore, they have directly taken up the radiance of the face of the Tathāgata.

[51:11]
しかあればすなはち、千年萬年、百劫億劫といへども、この面授、これ釋迦牟尼佛の面現成授なり。この佛祖現成せるには、世尊・迦葉、五十一世、七代祖宗の影現なり、光現成なり、身現成なり、心現成なり、失脚

---

21 **receiving and conferring of the face** (*mensho no juju* 面處の受授): "The face" (*mensho* 面處) could be taken here either as the subject or the object of the verb; and the phrase might also be read, "received and conferred where there is a face."

22 **they confer the body, body-to-body** (*shin o shinju suru* 身を身授する): Here, "the body" has become the direct object that is conferred, whereas, in the preceding cases, "eye," "face," and "mind" are in the dative, and what is conferred is left unexpressed.

23 **the ancestors of the fifty-one generations and the seven buddhas** (*gojūisse narabi ni shichi butsu soshū* 五十一世ならびに七佛祖宗): I.e., the lineage of ancestors from the seven buddhas of the past through Dōgen himself, in the fifty-first generation after Buddha Śākyamuni; see Supplementary Notes, s.v. "Buddhas and ancestors."

24 **realization of the way on which the ancestors confer face-to-face** (*soshū no menju sho dō genjō* 祖宗の面授處道現成): The expression *dō genjō* 道現成 occurs elsewhere in the *Shōbōgenzō* in the sense "realization of words" — i.e., "statement," a reading that seems unlikely here (or below, section 14); the unusual use of *sho* 處 in *menju sho* 面授處 here (as in *mensho* 面處, above, section 9) may not indicate a locus but does seem to presage this sense in section 14, below.

來なり、尖鼻來なり。一言いまだ領覽せず、半句いまだ不會せずといふとも、師、すでに裏頭より弟子をみ、弟子、すでに頂顙より師を拜しきたれるは、正傳の面授なり。

Thus, even after a thousand years, ten thousand years, a hundred kalpas, or a hundred thousand kalpas, this face-to-face conferral is the conferral in which the face of Buddha Śākyamuni appears. When these buddhas and ancestors appear, it is the appearance of the form of the World-Honored One, of Kāśyapa, of the fifty-one generations and seven generations of ancestors; it is the appearance of their radiance, the appearance of their bodies, the appearance of their minds; it is their coming with feet lost, their coming with noses sharp.[25] Even though a single word may not yet have been comprehended, nor a half line not understood, the master having seen the disciple from within and the disciple having bowed to the master from the crown of his head constitute the face-to-face conferral of the direct transmission.[26]

[51:12]
かくのごとくの面授を尊重すべきなり。わづかに心跡を心田にあらはせるがごとくならん、かならずしも太尊貴生なるべからず。換面に面授し、廻頭に面授あらんは、面皮厚三寸なるべし、面皮薄一丈なるべし。すなはちの面皮、それ諸佛大圓鏡なるべし。大圓鑑を面皮とせるがゆえに、内外無瑕翳なり。大圓鑑の、大圓鑑を面授しきたれるなり。

We should respect such a face-to-face conferral. Those who merely display some trace of the mind in the field of the mind are not necessarily to be greatly honored.[27] Those who do a face-to-face conferral while changing the face, who have a face-to-face conferral while turning the head, the skin of their faces must be three inches thick, the skin of their faces must be ten feet thin.[28] The skin of the face at this point must be

---

25 **coming with feet lost** (*shikkya rai* 失脚來): The term *shikkya* 失脚 (more often read *shikkyaku*) normally means "to lose one's footing," "to stumble," hence, "to lose status"; some readers take it here to mean "coming without any feet." The sense of the parallel expression "sharp (or pointed) nose" (*senbi* 尖鼻) here is also uncertain; one MS witness reads "lost nose" (*shitsubi* 失鼻). These terms do not occur elsewhere in the *Shōbōgenzō*.

26 **nor a half line not understood** (*hanku imada fue sezu* 半句いまだ不會せず): Some readers take the negative *fue* 不會 ("not understood") as suggesting a higher state "beyond understanding"; hence, "has not yet gone beyond the understanding of a half line." A slightly less convoluted reading would be simply, "has not yet even failed to understand a half line."

27 **Those who merely display some trace of the mind in the field of the mind** (*wazuka ni shinseki o shinden ni arawaseru ga gotoku naran* わづかに心跡を心田にあらはせるがごとくならん): The exact sense is uncertain; perhaps "those merely aware of their mental state."

28 **changing the face** (*kanmen* 換面); **turning the head** (*kaitō* 廻頭): From the multivalent idiom "to turn the head and change the face" (*kaitō kanmen* 廻頭換面); here,

the "great round mirror of the buddhas"; because the great round mirror is taken as the skin of the face, it is *"without flaw or blur inside or out."*[29] The great round mirror has transmitted the great round mirror face-to-face.

[51:13] {2:58}
まのあたり釋迦牟尼佛をみたてまつる正眼を正傳しきたれるは、釋迦牟尼佛よりも親曾なり、眼尖より前後三三の釋迦牟尼佛を見出現せしむるなり。かるがゆえに、釋迦牟尼佛をおもくしたてまつり、釋迦牟尼佛を恋慕したてまつらんは、この面授正傳をおもくし尊宗し、難値難遇の敬重禮拝すべし。すなはち如來を禮拜したてまつるなり、如來に面授せられたてまつるなり。あらたに面授如來の正傳參學の宛然なるを拜見するは、自己なりとおもひきたりつる自己なりとも、他己なりとも、愛惜すべきなり、護持すべきなり。

 The direct transmission of the true eye that sees right before it Buddha Śākyamuni is more intimate than Buddha Śākyamuni himself; from the corner of the eye, it reveals a Buddha Śākyamuni of "three three before and after."[30] For this reason, those who value Buddha Śākyamuni, who love Buddha Śākyamuni, should value and revere this direct transmission of the face-to-face conferral, should venerate and pay obeisance to what is *hard to encounter, hard to meet*. This is itself to pay obeisance to the Tathāgata, to receive the face-to-face conferral from the Tathāgata. Those who behold anew that the study of the direct transmission of the

---

perhaps, expressing the identity or interdependence of master and disciple). See Supplementary Notes, s.v. "Turning the head and changing the face."

the skin of their faces must be three inches thick (*menpi kō sanzun naru beshi* 面皮厚三寸なるべし): From a fixed expression meaning to have a "thick skin," normally used in the sense to be "shameless" or "impudent." The following "ten feet thin" (*haku ichijō* 薄一丈) is Dōgen's play on the expression.

29 **"great round mirror of the buddhas"** (*shobutsu daienkyō* 諸佛大圓鏡); **"without flaw or blur inside or out"** (*naige mu kaei* 內外無瑕翳): From the story (on which Dōgen comments in his "Shōbōgenzō kokyō" 正法眼藏古鏡) of the Eighteenth Ancestor, Gayaśata, who is said to have been born accompanied by a mirror. The expressions here are a slight variant of the first two lines of Gayaśata's verse (*Jingde chuandeng lu* 景德傳燈錄, T.2076.51:212b18-19):

 諸佛大圓鑑、內外無瑕翳、兩人同得見、心眼皆相似。
 The great round mirror of the buddhas,
 Without flaw or blur inside or out.
 Both people can see the same.
 Mind and eye, all alike.

30 **a Buddha Śākyamuni of "three three before and after"** (*zengo sansan no Shakamuni butsu* 前後三三の釋迦牟尼佛): Probably meaning "multiple (or infinite) Buddhas Śākyamuni"; from a well-known but obscure saying known as "Mañjuśrī's three three before and after" (*Monju zengo sansan* 文殊前後三三), appearing several times in Dōgen's writings and commonly interpreted as indicating an incalculable number. See Supplementary Notes, s.v. "Three three in front, three three in back."

51. Face-to-Face Conferral *Menju* 面授

Tathāgata of face-to-face conferral is precisely this should cherish it, should preserve it, whether in the self they have thought was their self or in another.[31]

[51:14]
屋裏に正傳しいはく、八塔を禮拜するものは、罪障解脱し、道果感得す。これ釋迦牟尼佛の道現成處を、生處に建立し、轉法輪處に建立し、成道處に建立し、涅槃處に建立し、曲女城邊にのこり、菴羅衞林にのこれる、大地を成じ、大空を成ぜり。乃至、聲・香・味・觸・法・色處等に塔成せるを禮拜するによりて、道果現成す。この八塔を禮拜するを、西天竺國のあまねき勤修として、在家・出家・天衆・人衆、きほふて禮拜供養するなり。これすなはち一卷の經典なり。佛經はかくのごとし。いはんやまた、三十七品の法を修行して、道果を箇箇生生に成就するは、釋迦牟尼佛の亘古亘今の修行修治の蹤跡を、處處の古路に流布せしめて、古今に歷然せるがゆゑに成道す。

In the direct transmission within our house, it is said that those who pay obeisance to the eight stūpas will be liberated from their offenses and attain the fruit of the way.[32] These are places manifesting the way of Buddha Śākyamuni — erected at the place of his birth, erected at the place where he turned the wheel of dharma, erected at the place where he attained the way, erected at the place where he entered nirvāṇa, preserved in the vicinity of Kanyākubja, preserved at the Amrapālī Grove — that manifest the whole earth and manifest the whole sky.[33] And so on, down to stūpas formed from sounds, smells, tastes, tactile objects, colors, and forms, by paying obeisance to which the fruit of the way is manifest.

---

31 **the study of the direct transmission of the Tathāgata of face-to-face conferral is precisely this** (*menju nyorai no shōden sangaku no ennen naru* 面授如來の正傳參學の宛然なる): A tentative reading of a phrase difficult to parse; the translation takes it to mean that the study directly transmitted in the lineage of masters and disciples is the study of the Tathāgata present in each generation of the face-to-face conferral. On this reading, the unexpressed object of the following "cherish" (*aijaku* 愛惜) and "preserve" (*goji* 護持) might be taken either as the "study" or as the "Tathāgata."

32 **eight stūpas** (*hattō* 八塔): Reference to the tradition that stūpas were erected at eight sites associated with events in the life of Buddha Śākyamuni: typically given as Kapilavastu, where the Buddha was born; Magadha, where he achieved buddhahood; Vārāṇasī, where he first preached; Jetavana, where he revealed his spiritual powers; Kanyākubja, where he descended from Indra's heaven; Rājagṛha, where his saṃgha was purified; Vaiśālī, where he determined his lifespan; and Kuśinagara, where he entered nirvāṇa. (See, e.g., *Fo shuo ba da lingta minghao jing* 佛説八大靈塔名號經, T.1685.32:773a7-15.)

33 **Amrapālī Grove** (*Anrae rin* 菴羅衞林): Likely a reference to the Vaiśālī stūpa (see *Dasheng bensheng xindi guan jing* 大乘本生心地觀經, T.159.3:294b3-4).
manifest the whole earth and manifest the whole sky (*daichi o jō ji, daikū o jō zeri* 大地を成じ、大空を成ぜり): Or, perhaps, "form the whole earth and form the whole sky"; the sense seems to be that the stūpas represent not only the way of the buddhas but all of heaven and earth.

Paying obeisance to these eight stūpas is a wide-spread practice of the Land of Sindhu in the West, where householders and renunciants, devas and humans, vie with one another to pay obeisance and make offerings. This is none other than a role of scripture; such are the sūtras of the buddhas. Needless to say, then, those who achieve the fruit of the way in life after life by practicing the thirty-seven dharmas attain the way because the traces of Buddha Śākyamuni's practice and discipline spanning past and present have been disseminated on the old paths everywhere and are obvious in past and present.[34]

[51:15]
しるべし、かの八塔の層層なる、霜華いくばくかあらたまる。風雨しばしばをかさんとすれど、空にあとせり、色にあとせるその功德を、いまの人にをしまざること減少せず。かの根・力・覺・道、いま修行せんとするに、煩惱あり、惑障ありといへども、修證するに、そのちからなほいまあらたなり。

We should realize how many renewals of frost and flowers those eight multi-storied stūpas have witnessed.[35] Although often assailed by wind and rain, their merit has left its mark on emptiness, left its mark on form, and the generosity with which it is still shared with people today remains undiminished. And when we now try to practice those faculties, powers, awakening, and path, while there may be the afflictions and the impediment of delusions, when we practice them, their power is still fresh.[36]

[51:16] {2:59}
釋迦牟尼佛の功德、それかくのごとし。いはんやいまの面授は、かれらに比準すべからず。かの三十七品菩提分法は、この佛面・佛心・佛身・佛道・佛尖・佛舌等を根元とせり。かの八塔の功德聚、また佛面等を本基とせり。いま學佛法の漢として、透脱の活路に行履せんに、閑靜の晝夜、つらつら思量功夫すべし、歡喜隨喜すべきなり。

---

34   **thirty-seven dharmas** (*sanjūshichi hon no hō* 三十七品の法): S. *saptatriṃśad-bodhi-pakṣikā-dharmāḥ*; a venerable listing, found throughout the Buddhist canon, of seven (sometimes overlapping) sets of spiritual desiderata: (1) the four abodes of mindfulness (*shinenjū* 四念住; S. *smṛty-upasthāna*), (2) the four right abandonments (*shishōdan* 四正斷; S. *samyak-prahāṇa*), (3) the four bases of spiritual power (*shijinsoku* 四神足; S. *ṛddhi-pāda*), (4) the five faculties (*gokon* 五根; S. *indriya*), (5) the five powers (*goriki* 五力; S. *bala*), (6) the seven limbs of awakening (*shichikakushi* 七覺支; S. *bodhyaṅga*), and (7) the eightfold path (*hasshōdō* 八正道; S. *mārga*). Dōgen discusses the list in his "Shōbōgenzō sanjūshichi hon bodai bunpō" 正法眼藏三十七品菩提分法.

35   **frost and flowers** (*sōka* 霜華): I.e., "autumns and springs"; a literary expression for "years."

36   **faculties, powers, awakening, and path** (*kano kon riki kaku dō* かの根・力・覺・道): Categories of the thirty-seven dharmas mentioned in the preceding section: the five spiritual faculties (*gokon* 五根), five spiritual powers (*goriki* 五力), seven limbs of awakening (*shichi kakushi* 七覺支), and eightfold path (*hasshōdō* 八聖道).

Such is the merit of Buddha Śākyamuni. It goes without saying that the present face-to-face conferral should not be compared to those.[37] Those thirty-seven factors of bodhi have as their basis this face of the Buddha, mind of the Buddha, body of the Buddha, way of the Buddha, tip of the Buddha, tongue of the Buddha, and so on.[38] That accumulation of merit of the eight stūpas likewise has as its foundation the face of the Buddha and the rest. Now, as those who study the buddha dharma, when we seek to tread the life-saving path to liberation, in the quiet moments of our days and nights, we should think well and work hard on this, we should rejoice and be glad.

[51:17]
いはゆるわがくには、他國よりもすぐれ、わが道は、ひとり無上なり。他方には、われらがごとくならざるともがらおほかり。わがくに、わが道の無上獨尊なるといふは、靈山の衆會、あまねく十方に化導すといへども、少林の正嫡、まさしく震旦の教主なり、曹溪の兒孫、いまに面授せり。このとき、これ佛法あらたに入泥入水の好時節なり。このとき證果せずば、いづれのときか證果せん、このとき斷惑せずば、いづれのときか斷惑せん、このとき作佛ならざらんは、いづれのときか作佛ならん、このとき坐佛ならざらんは、いづれのときか行佛ならん。審細の功夫なるべし。

That is, [we should think] our land is superior to other lands, our way alone is unsurpassed; in other regions, there are many who are not our equal. The reason our land, our way, is unsurpassed and uniquely honored is that, while the assembly on Vulture Peak may have guided beings widely in the ten directions, the direct successor of Shaolin was truly the master of the teaching in Cīnasthāna, and the descendants of Caoxi conferred it face-to-face to the present.[39] Now is a good time, when the

---

37 **should not be compared to those** (*karera ni hijun su bekarazu* かれらに比準すべからず): I.e., is beyond comparison with those — the antecedents of "those" (*karera*) being the merits (*kudoku* 功德) of the "eight stūpas" and "thirty-seven factors."

38 **face of the Buddha** (*butsumen* 佛面): Taking "buddha" here to refer to Buddha Śākyamuni. See Supplementary Notes, s.v. "Buddha faces, ancestor faces."

tip of the Buddha (*bussen* 佛尖): An odd locution, perhaps recalling the "corner of the eye" (*gansen* 眼尖) in section 13, above. One manuscript witness has the less problematic "radiance of the buddha" (*bukkō* 佛光).

39 **assembly on Vulture Peak** (*Ryōzen no shue* 靈山の衆會): I.e., the teachings of Buddha Śākyamuni to his assembly on Vulture Peak.

direct successor of Shaolin (*Shōrin no shōteki* 少林の正嫡): I.e., Bodhidharma, at the Shaolinsi 少林寺.

master of the teaching in Cīnasthāna (*Shintan no kyōshu* 震旦の教主): I.e., founder of the teaching in China. The term "master of the teaching" (*kyōshu* 教主) is regularly used for a religious founder, including the Buddha.

descendants of Caoxi (*Sōkei no jison* 曹溪の兒孫): I.e., the descendants of the Sixth Ancestor, Huineng of Caoxi 曹溪慧能.

buddha dharma enters anew into the mud and into the water.[40] If we do not verify the fruit now, when will we verify the fruit? If we do not cut off the delusions now, when will we cut off the delusions? If now we are not "making a buddha," when will we make a buddha? If now we are not "a seated buddha," when will we be "a practicing buddha"?[41] We should work on this in detail.

[51:18]
釋迦牟尼佛、かたじけなく迦葉尊者に附囑面授するにいはく、吾有正法眼藏、附囑摩訶迦葉とあり。嵩山會上には、菩提達磨尊者まさしく二祖にしめしていはく、汝得吾髓。

Buddha Śākyamuni, in kindly making a face-to-face conferral of his bequest to Venerable Kāśyapa, said, "*I have a treasury of the true dharma eye; I bestow it on Mahākāśyapa*." At the assembly on Mount Song, Venerable Bodhidharma truly addressed the Second Ancestor, saying, "*You've gotten my marrow*."

[51:19] {2:60}
はかりしりぬ、正法眼藏を面授し、汝得吾髓の面授なるは、ただこの面授のみなり。この正當恁麼時、なんぢがひごろの骨髓を透脱するとき、佛祖面授あり。大悟を面授し、心印を面授するも、一隅の特地なり。傳盡にあらずといへども、いまだ欠悟の道理を參究せず。

It is obvious here that what makes the face-to-face conferral of the "treasury of the true dharma eye" and what constitutes the face-to-face conferral of "*you've gotten my marrow*" is just this face-to-face confer-

---

40 **good time, when the buddha dharma enters anew into the mud and into the water** (*buppō aratani nyūdei nissui no kō jisetsu* 佛法あらたに入泥入水の好時節): From the common image of teaching the dharma as "dragged through the mud and drenched with water" (*dadei taisui* 拖泥帶水); see Supplementary Notes, s.v. "Dragged through the mud and drenched with water." The verb tense is unmarked here; hence, it is unclear whether Dōgen is claiming that his age is a good time for Buddhism to spread or a good time in which Buddhism is spreading. In either case, the claim is in marked contrast to laments found elsewhere in the *Shōbōgenzō* that Dōgen and his readers were living in a peripheral land in a benighted age.

41 **"making a buddha"** (*sabutsu* 作佛); **"a seated buddha"** (*zabutsu* 坐佛); **"a practicing buddha"** (*gyōbutsu* 行佛): The first two expressions reflect the famous conversation on meditation, often cited by Dōgen, between Nanyue Huairang 南嶽懷讓 (677-744) and Mazu Daoyi 馬祖道一 (709-788) (*Jingde chuandeng lu* 景德傳燈錄, T.2076.51:240c18ff). When Mazu says he is practicing seated meditation (*zazen* 坐禪) in order to "make a buddha" (*zabutsu* 作佛), Nanyue asks him, "Are you studying seated meditation or are you studying seated buddha (*zabutsu* 坐佛)?" See Supplementary Notes, s.v. "Nanyue polishes a tile." Dōgen comments on this conversation at length in the "*Shōbōgenzō zazen shin*" 正法眼藏坐禪箴. The term *gyōbutsu* 行佛 here might well be read "walking buddha" (in contrast to the preceding "seated buddha"); the translation opts instead for the sense, often found in the *Shōbōgenzō*, that identifies buddhahood with Buddhist practice (as, e.g., in "*Shōbōgenzō gyōbutsu iigi*" 正法眼藏行佛威儀).

ral.[42] At this very moment, when you transcend your everyday bones and marrow, there is the face-to-face conferral of the buddhas and ancestors. To confer the great awakening face-to-face and to confer the mind seal face-to-face are also particular partial instances of this.[43] While they may not be exhaustive of transmission, they have not yet investigated the principle of lacking awakening.[44]

[51:20]
おほよそ佛祖大道は、唯面授面受、受面授面のみなり。さらに剰法あらず、虧闕あらず。この面授のあふにあへる自己の面目をも、隨喜歡喜、信受奉行すべきなり。

In sum, the great way of the buddhas and ancestors is just face-to-face conferral and face-to-face reception, receiving face-to-face and conferring face-to-face. There is nothing left over, nothing missing. And we should rejoice in, be glad about, faithfully accept, and reverently practice our own face encountered in the encounter with this face-to-face conferral.

[51:21]
道元、大宋寶慶元年乙酉五月一日、はじめて先師天童古佛を禮拜面授す。やや堂奥を聽許せらる。わづかに身心を脱落するに、面授を保任することありて、日本國に本來せり。

On the first day of the fifth month of the junior wood year of the rooster, the first year of Baoqing in the Great Song, I, Dōgen, first paid obeisance to and had a face-to-face conferral from my former master, the Old Buddha of Tiantong. I was granted a certain access to the interior of

---

42 **just this face-to-face conferral** (*tada kono menju nomi* ただこの面授のみ): The antecedent of "this" (*kono* この) is unclear; as is suggested by the following sentence, presumably, the reference is to our own participation in the tradition of conferral.

43 **to confer the great awakening face-to-face and to confer the mind seal face-to-face** (*daigo o menju shi, shin'in o menju suru* 大悟を面授し、心印を面授する): Presumably referring to accounts in Chan records in which it is said that the disciple had a "great awakening" or received the "mind seal" from the master.

particular partial instances (*ichigu no tokuchi* 一隅の特地): Or "one corner in particular"; the element *chi* 地 in *tokuchi* 特地 should be read as an adverbial marker.

44 **While they may not be exhaustive of transmission, they have not yet investigated the principle of lacking awakening** (*denjin ni arazu to iedomo, imada ketsugo no dōri o sankyū sezu* 傳盡にあらずといへども、いまだ欠悟の道理を參究せず): A sentence subject to various interpretations; perhaps meaning that [the conferrals of the great awakening and mind seal] are incomplete to the extent that they do not involve [the higher state of] "lacking awakening." The term *ketsugo* 欠悟 ("lack awakening") does not occur elsewhere in the *Shōbōgenzō*; it is typically taken here as a state "beyond" awakening.

the hall; when I somewhat sloughed off body and mind, having been entrusted with a face-to-face conferral, I came back to the Land of Japan.[45]

正法眼藏面授第五十一
Treasury of the True Dharma Eye
Face-to-Face Conferral
Number 51

[Ryūmonji MS:]
爾時寛元元年癸卯十月二十日、在越宇吉田縣吉峰精舎示衆
Presented to the assembly at Kippō Vihāra, Yoshida District, Etsuu; twentieth day, tenth month of the junior water year of the rabbit, the first year of Kangen [3 December 1243][46]

[51:22]
佛道の面授かくのごとくなる道理を、かつて見聞せず、參學なきともがらあるなかに、大宋國仁宗皇帝の御宇、景祐年中に、薦福寺の承古禪師といふものあり。

Among those who have never seen or heard of, who are without study of, the truth that the face-to-face conferral in the way of the buddhas is like this, there was, during the Jingyou years in the reign of the Emperor Renzong in the Land of the Great Song, a certain Chan Master Chenggu of the Jianfu Monastery.[47]

---

45 **I was granted a certain access to the interior of the hall** (*yaya dōō o chōko seraru* やや堂奥を聽許せらる): I.e., Dōgen was admitted to private interviews with Rujing, beginning (according to the *Hōkyō ki* 寶慶記) in the seventh month of 1225.
when I somewhat sloughed off body and mind, having been entrusted with a face-to-face conferral, I came back to the Land of Japan (*wazuka ni shinjin o datsuraku suru ni, menju o hōnin suru koto arite, nihon koku ni honrai seri* わづかに身心を脱落するに、面授を保任することありて、日本國に本來せり): The temporal sequence here is somewhat confusing, since Dōgen has earlier said (in section 3, above) and repeats here that his face-to-face conferral took place at his first meeting with Rujing, in June of 1225, not at his subsequent experience of "body and mind sloughed off" (*shinjin datsuraku* 身心脱落), thought to have occurred later that summer. (For this expression, see Supplementary Notes, s.v. "Body and mind sloughed off.") Though the exact date is uncertain, Dōgen likely returned to Japan in the second half of 1227. The English "came back" here translates the odd predicate *honrai* 本來 ("originally came"), which some readers suggest is an allusion to the first line of the transmission verse of Bodhidharma (*Jingde chuandeng lu* 景德傳燈錄, T.2076.51:219c18):

吾本來此土、傳法救迷情。
I originally came to this land
To transmit the dharma and save the deluded.

46 An identical colophon appears in the *Himitsu* MS of this chapter.

47 **Chan Master Chenggu** (*Jōko zenji* 承古禪師): Jianfu Chenggu 薦福承古 (d. 1045). The Jianfusi 薦福寺 was located in present-day Boyang 鄱陽 county in northeast

51. Face-to-Face Conferral *Menju* 面授

[51:23]

上堂云、雲門匡眞大師、如今現在、諸人還見麼。若也見得、便是山僧同
參、見麼見麼。此事直須諦當始得、不可自謾。且如往古黄檗、聞百丈和
尚舉馬大師下喝因縁、他因大省。百丈問、子向後莫嗣大師否。黄檗云、某
雖識大師、要且不見大師。若承嗣大師、恐喪我兒孫。大衆、當時馬大師遷
化、未得五年、黄檗自言不見。當知、黄檗見處不圓。要且祇具一隻眼。山
僧即不然、識得雲門大師、亦見得雲門大師、方可承嗣雲門大師。祇如雲
門、入滅已得一百餘年。如今作麼生説箇親見底道理、會麼。通人達士、方
可證明。眇劣之徒、心生疑謗。見得不在言之。未見者、如今看取不。請久
立珍重。

In a convocation, he said,

Great Master Kuangzhen of Yunmen is here now.[48] Does everyone see him? If you can see him, you're studying together with this mountain monk. Do you see him? Do you see him? This is something you only get once you clearly accede to it; do not deceive yourself.

Now, Huangbo, long ago, upon hearing Reverend Baizhang take up the episode of Great Master Ma giving a roar, had a great understanding as a result.[49] Baizhang asked, "Won't you hereafter be an heir of the Great Master?"

Huangbo said, "Although I know the Great Master, after all, I haven't seen the Great Master. If I were to succeed the Great Master, I fear I would lose my descendants."

Members of the great assembly, at the time not even five years had passed since Great Master Ma's transformation; yet Huangbo said he didn't see him. We should recognize that Huangbo's vision wasn't perfect; in fact, he had only one eye. This mountain monk is not like that: he knows Great Master Yunmen, and he sees Great Master Yunmen; he can succeed Great Master Yunmen. Yet, in the case of Yunmen, it's already more than one hundred years since his extinction.[50] How can

---

Jiangxi province. Emperor Renzong 仁宗 reigned 1022-1063; his Jingyou 景祐 era covered 1049-1054.

48 **In a convocation** (*jōdō* 上堂): A public address found at *Jianzhong Jingguo xudeng lu* 建中靖國續燈錄, ZZ.136:55a6-17.

Great Master Kuangzhen of Yunmen (*Unmon Kyōshin daishi* 雲門匡眞大師): I.e., Yunmen Wenyen 雲門文偃 (864-949). According to his biographical notice (at *Jianzhong Jingguo xudeng lu* 建中靖國續燈錄, ZZ.136:54a3), Chenggu had a sudden understanding while reading the sayings of Yunmen.

49 **Huangbo** (*Ōbaku* 黄檗); **Reverend Baizhang** (*Hyakujō oshō* 百丈和尚); **Great Master Ma** (*Ma daishi* 馬大師): Recalling a passage found in the *Jingde chuandeng lu* 景德傳燈錄 (T.2076.51:249c12-17). Huangbo Xiyun 黄檗希運 (dates unknown) was a disciple of Baizhang Huaihai 百丈懷海 (749-814), who was in turn the disciple of Mazu Daoyi 馬祖道一.

50 **already more than one hundred years since his extinction** (*nyūmetsu i toku ip-*

I talk of personally seeing him? Do you understand? People of insight and gentlemen of mastery can verify this; but the one-eyed and weak will have doubts and slander. Those who saw him will have nothing to say; those who hadn't seen him, do you see him now?

You've been standing for a long time. Take care of yourselves.

[51:24] {2:62}
いま、なんぢ、雲門大師をしり、雲門大師をみることをたとひゆるすとも、雲門大師、まのあたりなんぢをみるやいまだしや。雲門大師、なんぢをみずば、なんぢ、承嗣雲門大師不得ならん。雲門大師、いまだなんぢをゆるさざるがゆえに、なんぢもまた、雲門大師、われをみる、といはず。しりぬ、なんぢ、雲門大師といまだ相見せざりといふことを。

Now, even if we were to accept that you know Great Master Yunmen and that you see Great Master Yunmen, has Great Master Yunmen personally seen you or not? If Great Master Yunmen does not see you, you *could not "succeed Great Master Yunmen."* Since Great Master Yunmen has not acknowledged you, even you do not say, "Great Master Yunmen saw me." We know that you and Great Master Yunmen never met each other.

[51:25]
七佛諸佛の過去・現在・未來に、いづれの佛祖か師資相見せざるに嗣法せる。なんぢ、黄檗を見處不圓といふことなかれ。なんぢ、いかでか黄檗の行履をはからん、黄檗の言句をはからん。黄檗は、古佛なり、嗣法に究參なり。なんぢは、嗣法の道理、かつて夢也未見聞參學在なり。黄檗は、師に嗣法せり、祖を保任せり。黄檗は、師にまみへ、師をみる。なんぢは、すべて師をみず、祖をしらず、自己をしらず、自己をみず。なんぢをみる師なし、なんぢ、師眼いまだ參開せず。眞箇、なんぢ見處不圓なり、嗣法未圓なり。

Of the seven buddhas and all the other buddhas of past, present, and future, which buddha or ancestor inherited the dharma without master and disciple meeting each other? Do not say that Huangbo's *"vision wasn't perfect."* How can you gauge Huangbo's activities, or gauge Huangbo's words? Huangbo is an old buddha, with exhaustive examination of dharma inheritance. You have never seen, heard or studied even in your dreams the principle of dharma inheritance. Huangbo inherited the dharma from his master and maintained his ancestor.[51] Huangbo met with his master and saw his master. You have seen no master whatsoever; you do not know any ancestor; you do not know yourself; you do not

---

pyaku yo nen 入滅已得一百餘年): A slight exaggeration if our dates for the two men are correct: Yunmen is supposed to have died in 949; Chenggu, in 1045.

51 **maintained his ancestor** (*so o hōnin seri* 祖を保任せり): Probably in the sense "preserved the teachings of his dharma grandfather, Mazu (Ancestor Ma)."

see yourself.[52] There is no master that has seen you; you have not studied and opened the eye of the master.[53] In truth, you are the one whose "vision is not perfect," whose dharma inheritance is not perfect.

[51:26]
なんぢしるやいなや、雲門大師はこれ黄檗の法孫なること。なんぢいかでか百丈・黄檗の道處を測量せん。雲門大師の道處、なんぢなほ測量すべからず。百丈・黄檗の道處は、參學のちからあるもの、これを拈擧するなり。直指の落處あるもの、測量すべし。なんぢは、參學なし、落處なし、しるべからず、はかるべからざるなり。

Do you know or do you not that Great Master Yunmen is a dharma grandson of Huangbo?[54] How could you fathom what Baizhang and Huangbo say? Nor could you fathom even what Great Master Yunmen says. Those with the power of study take up what Baizhang and Huangbo say; those with the conclusion to which they point directly can fathom them.[55] But you lack the study, lack the conclusion, cannot know them, and cannot fathom them.

[51:27] {2:63}
馬大師遷化未得五年なるに、馬大師に嗣法せず、といふ。まことにわらふにもたらず。たとひ嗣法すべくは、無量劫ののちなりとも、嗣法すべし。嗣法すべからざらんは、半日なりとも須臾なりとも、嗣法すべからず。なんぢ、すべて佛道の日面月面をみざる、暗者愚蒙なり。

You say, "*not even five years had passed since Great Master Ma's transformation.*" This is really not even worth laughing at. Those who

---

52 **You have seen no master whatsoever** (*nanji wa, subete shi o mizu* なんぢは、すべて師をみず): Chenggu is said to have been studying under Fuyan Liangya 福嚴良雅 when he had his insight into Yunmen's teachings; presumably, then, we are to understand here that he had no true encounter with this teacher (or that this teacher was not a true master, or both).

53 **you have not studied and opened the eye of the master** (*nanji, shigen imada sankai sezu* なんぢ、師眼いまだ參開せず): In the context, perhaps meaning, "you have neither investigated nor opened the eye that could recognize a master." The term *shigen* 師眼 ("eye of the master") does not occur elsewhere in the *Shōbōgenzō*; the unusual *sankai* 參開 ("study and open"?) occurs several times in the *Shōbōgenzō*, always in connection with the opening of the eye.

54 **Great Master Yunmen is a dharma grandson of Huangbo** (*Unmon daishi wa kore Ōbaku no hōson naru* 雲門大師はこれ黄檗の法孫なる): Yunmen is traditionally considered the disciple of Xuefeng Yicun 雪峰義存 (822-908), in the lineage of Shitou Xiqian 石頭希遷 (700-791); but he also is said to have studied with Muzhou Daozong 睦州道蹤 (dates unknown), a follower of Huangbo 黄檗.

55 **those with the conclusion to which they point directly** (*jikishi no rakusho aru mono* 直指の落處あるもの): Probably meaning "those who get the point of what Baizhang and Huangbo are saying." "Conclusion" here renders *rakusho* 落處, a term meaning the "final point" or "destination."

should inherit the dharma should inherit the dharma even innumerable kalpas later; those who should not inherit the dharma should not inherit the dharma even after a half day, even after a moment. You are a fool and a simpleton who has seen nothing of the sun face and moon face of the way of the buddhas.[56]

[51:28]

雲門大師入滅已得一百餘年なれども雲門に承嗣す、といふ。なんぢにゆゆしきちからありて雲門に承嗣するか、三歳の孩兒よりはかなし。一千年ののち雲門に嗣法せんものは、なんぢに十倍せるちからあらん。

You say, although it is "*already more than one hundred years since the extinction*" of Great Master Yunmen, you have succeeded Yunmen. Did you succeed Yunmen because you had some awesome ability? That is less likely than a child of three. Someone inheriting the dharma of Yunmen after a thousand years would be ten times more able than you.

[51:29]

われいまなんぢをすくふ、しばらく話頭を參學すべし。百丈の道取する子向後莫承嗣大師否の道取は、馬大師に嗣法せよ、といふにはあらぬなり。しばらくなんぢ獅子奮迅話を參學すべし、烏龜倒上樹話を參學して、進歩退歩の活路を參究すべし。嗣法に恁麼の參學力あるなり。黄檗のいふ恐喪我兒孫のことば、すべてなんぢ、はかるべからず。我、の道取、および、兒孫、の人、これ、たれなりとかしれる、審細に參學すべし。かくれずあらはれて道現成せり。

Now, I shall come to your rescue. We should study the topic a bit. Baizhang's saying "*Won't you hereafter be an heir of the Great Master?*" was not saying, "inherit the dharma of Great Master Ma." You should study a bit the *talk of the lion aroused*; studying the talk of *the turtle climbing backward up the tree*, you should investigate the life-saving path on which we step forward and step back.[57] In inheriting the dharma,

---

56 **sun face and moon face of the way of the buddhas** (*butsudō no nichimen gachimen* 佛道の日面月面): I.e., the passage of time in Buddhism, playing on "sun" (day) and "moon" (month); likely an allusion to the words of Mazu himself, who, when he was unwell, described his condition as "sun-faced buddha (said to live 1800 years), moon-faced buddha (who lives for one day)"; see Supplementary Notes, s.v. "Sun face, moon face."

57 **talk of the lion aroused** (*shishi funjin wa* 獅子奮迅話): What "talk" (*wa* 話) is referred to here is uncertain and has been the subject of various speculations. Though a source has not been identified, the "lion" may represent an oblique reference to the famous "roar" (*katsu* 喝), mentioned above by Chenggu, that Mazu is supposed to have given Baizhang. The expression "the lion aroused" (*shishi funjin* 獅子奮迅; also written 師子奮迅) is a common metaphor for awesome power, especially of the buddha — as in the buddha's "samādhi of the lion aroused" (*shishi funjin zanmai* 獅子奮迅三昧).

talk of the turtle climbing backward up the tree (*uki tō jōju wa* 烏龜倒上樹話): Reference to a comment, by Xiangshan Yunliang 香山蘊良 (dates unknown), on the story that

there is such power of study.[58] You could not fathom anything of Huangbo's words, "*I fear I would lose my descendants.*" Do you know who "my" refers to, or who his "descendants" are? You should study this in detail. It has been stated clearly, with nothing hidden.[59]

[51:30]
しかあるを、佛國禪師惟白といふ、佛祖の嗣法にくらきによりて、承古を雲門の法嗣に排列せり、あやまりなるべし。晩進しらずして、承古も參學あらん、とおもふことなかれ。

However, a certain Weibo, Chan Master Foguo, in the dark as he was on the dharma inheritance of the buddhas and ancestors, listed Chenggu as a dharma heir of Yunmen — surely an error.[60] Latecomers, not knowing this, must not think that Chenggu had any study.[61]

[51:31]
なんぢがごとく文字によりて嗣法すべくは、經書をみて發明するものは、みな釋迦牟尼佛に嗣法するか、さらにしかあらざるなり。經書によれる發明、かならず正師の印可をもとむるなり。

If you could inherit the dharma through words and letters, does everyone who gains an understanding by reading sūtra texts inherit the dharma from Buddha Śākyamuni? Surely not. Those who gain an understanding based on sūtra texts always seek the seal of approval of a true master.

Baizhang once rolled up the abbot, Mazu's 馬祖, prostration mat before the latter could make bows to the Buddha on it; see Supplementary Notes, s.v. "Iron bull."

58 **In inheriting the dharma, there is such power of study** (*shihō ni inmo no sangakuriki aru nari* 嗣法に恁麼の參學力あるなり): Or, perhaps, "in those who inherit the dharma . . . ." The antecedent of "such" (*inmo* 恁麼) here is unclear; perhaps (as in section 26, above), the ability to investigate the meaning of Baizhang and Mazu's words.

59 **It has been stated clearly, with nothing hidden** (*kakurezu arawarete dō genjō seri* かくれずあらはれて道現成せり): Probably meaning that what Mazu says is obvious. Some readers take the expression *dō genjō* 道現成 as meaning "the way is realized."

60 **Weibo, Chan Master Foguo** (*Bukkoku zenji Ihaku* 佛國禪師惟白): Fayun Weibo 法雲惟白 (dates unknown), a disciple of Fayun Faxiu 法雲法秀 (1027-1090) in the Yunmen lineage, was the compiler of the *Jianzhong Jingguo xudeng lu* 建中靖國續燈錄, which includes Chenggu's biographical notice among the descendants of Yunmen (at ZZ.136:53b18).

61 **Latecomers, not knowing this, must not think that Chenggu had any study** (*banshin shirazu shite, Jōko mo sangaku aran, to omou koto nakare* 晩進しらずして、承古も參學あらん、とおもふことなかれ): The manuscript of the twenty-eight-text *Himitsu Shōbōgenzō* ends here, with the colophon given below.

[51:32] {2:64}

なんぢ承古がいふごとくには、なんぢ、雲門の語録なほいまだみざるなり。雲門の語をみしともがらのみ、雲門には嗣法せり。なんぢ、自己眼をもていまだ雲門をみず、自己眼をもて自己をみず、雲門眼をもて雲門をみず、雲門眼をもて自己をみず。かくのごとくの未參究おほし。さらに草鞋を買來買去して、正師をもとめて嗣法すべし。なんぢ、雲門大師に嗣すといふことなかれ。もしかくのごとくいはば、すなはち外道の流類なるべし。たとひ百丈なりとも、なんぢがいふがごとくいはば、おほきなるあやまりなるべし。

Chenggu, from what you say, you have not even read the words of Yunmen. Only those who have seen the words of Yunmen have inherited the dharma of Yunmen. You have not seen Yunmen with your own eyes; you have not seen yourself with your own eyes; you have not seen Yunmen with Yunmen's eyes; you have not seen yourself with Yunmen's eyes. There are many things like this you have not yet investigated. You should keep on buying straw sandals, seek out a true master, and inherit the dharma.[62] Do not say that you inherited from Great Master Yunmen. If you say it, you must be the follower of an other path. Even if Baizhang were to say it, it would be a big mistake.

[*Himitsu* MS:]

于時寬元二甲辰六月七日、在越宇吉峯精舍侍者寮書寫之。懷奘

Copied this at the acolyte's office, Kippō Monastery, Yoshida District, Etsuu; seventh day, sixth month, senior wood year of the dragon, the second year of Kangen [13 July 1244]. Ejō

---

62 **You should keep on buying straw sandals** (*sōai o mairai maiko shite* 草鞋を買來買去して): I.e., continue your travels in search of a teacher, to wear out straw sandals being a standard trope for extended pilgrimage.

TREASURY OF THE TRUE DHARMA EYE

NUMBER 52

Buddhas and Ancestors
Busso

佛祖

Buddhas and Ancestors

Busso

Introduction

This chapter was composed and presented to the assembly at Kōshōji, in the winter of 1241. It represents number 52 in the seventy-five-chapter *Shōbōgenzō*, number 15 in the Honzan edition, and number 1 of fascicle 3 in the twenty-eight-text collection; it is not found in the sixty-chapter compilation.

The "Busso" chapter is not an essay; it is merely a list of the fifty-seven names in the Buddhist lineage leading to the author. The list is divided into three sections: the seven buddhas of the past, ending with Buddha Śākyamuni; the twenty-eight Indian ancestors, ending with Bodhidharma; and the twenty-two generations of Chinese masters, ending with the author's master, Tiantong Rujing 天童如淨. The list is framed by an opening remark to the effect that these buddhas and ancestors are realized through the act of venerating them, and a closing report that, in the summer of 1225, Dōgen himself venerated the ancestor Rujing. It was, he says, two buddhas together.

正法眼藏第五十二
Treasury of the True Dharma Eye
Number 52

佛祖
Buddhas and Ancestors

[52:1] {2:65}

それ、佛祖の現成は、佛祖を舉拈して奉覲するなり。過・現・當來のみにあらず、佛向上よりも向上なるべし。まさに佛祖の面目を保任せるを拈じて、禮拜し相見す。佛祖の功德を現舉せしめて、住持しきたり、體證しきたれり。

The realization of the buddhas and ancestors is taking up the buddhas and ancestors and having an audience with them.[1] It is not only a matter of past, present, and future: it must be beyond even what is beyond the buddha.[2] Truly, taking up those who have maintained the faces of the buddhas and ancestors, we pay obeisance and encounter them. Putting the virtues of the buddhas and ancestors on display, we have been maintaining them, we have been personally verifying them.[3]

---

1 **The realization of the buddhas and ancestors is taking up the buddhas and ancestors and having an audience with them** (*sore, busso no genjō wa, busso o konen shite bugon suru nari* それ、佛祖の現成は、佛祖を舉拈して奉覲するなり): The verb *konen* 舉拈 is regularly used in the sense "to take up [a topic] for consideration"; hence, one reading of this sentence might be that the buddhas and ancestors come alive, as it were, in our study of their records. The translation leaves untranslated the first word of the Japanese sentence, *sore* それ, reading it simply as the initial particle *sore* 夫 (C. *fu*) used at the head of a discussion; however, the early MSS write this word 宗禮, in which the Chinese glyphs could be read for their sound value (as *man'yōgana* 万葉仮名) for *sore* and/or for their meaning as something like "obeisance to the ancestors." See Supplementary Notes, s.v. "Buddhas and ancestors."

2 **It is not only a matter of past, present, and future** (*ka gen tōrai nomi ni arazu* 過・現・當來のみにあらず): The grammatical subject is unexpressed; the sentence could also be read "they [i.e., the buddhas and ancestors] are not merely past, present, and future; they must be beyond even what is beyond the buddha (*butsu kōjō* 佛向上)." See Supplementary Notes, s.v. "Beyond the buddha."

3 **Putting the virtues of the buddhas and ancestors on display, we have been maintaining them, we have been personally verifying them** (*busso no kudoku o genko seshimete, jūji shikitari, taishō shikitareri* 佛祖の功德を現舉せしめて、住持しきたり、體證しきたれり): The grammatical subject is unstated and could also be taken as "they" (i.e., "the buddhas and ancestors"). The term *genko* 現舉, translated here "display" does not occur elsewhere in the *Shōbōgenzō*; it could be taken to mean either to

[52:2]

毘婆尸佛大和尚 此云廣説。
尸棄佛大和尚 此云火。
毘舍浮佛大和尚 此云一切慈。
拘留孫佛大和尚 此云金仙人。
拘那含牟尼佛大和尚 此云金色仙。
迦葉佛大和尚 此云飲光。
七佛釋迦牟尼佛大和尚 此云能忍寂默。

> The Most Reverend Buddha Vipaśyin (meaning "extensive explication")[4]
> The Most Reverend Buddha Śikhin (meaning "fire")
> The Most Reverend Buddha Viśvabhū (meaning "all-merciful")[5]
> The Most Reverend Buddha Krakucchandha (meaning "golden sage")[6]
> The Most Reverend Buddha Kanakamuni (meaning "golden-hued sage")
> The Most Reverend Buddha Kāśyapa (meaning "drinking light")[7]
> (The seventh buddha) The Most Reverend Buddha Śākyamuni (meaning "forbearance and quiescence")[8]

---

take up the virtues for study or to manifest the virtues. The latter reading is suggested by the unusual term *taishō* 體證, "personally verify," or "realize with the body."

4   **The Most Reverend Buddha Vipaśyin (meaning "extensive explication")** (*Bibashi butsu dai oshō shi un kōsetsu* 毘婆尸佛大和尚此云廣説): Here begins a list of the seven buddhas of the past with which accounts of the Zen lineage sometimes start; see Supplementary Notes, s.v. "Seven buddhas." The parenthetical remarks on the Chinese meanings of the names are likely taken from the *Lüzong xinxue mingju* 律宗新學名句 (ZZ.105:648b1), a work compiled in 1094 by the monk Weixian 惟顯. His interpretation of *vipaśyin* here as "extensive explication" (*kōsetsu* 廣説) suggests that he associated the name with the Sanskrit *vibhāṣa* (*bibasha* 毘婆沙), rather than *vipaśyin* ("insightful").

5   **"all-merciful"** (*issai ji* 一切慈): The source of this meaning is unclear; the name Viśvabhū is more commonly interpreted as "pervasive being" (*issai u* 一切有) or "pervasive arising" (*issai shō* 一切生).

6   **"golden sage"** (*kon sennin* 金仙人): Apparently, a confusion with the following, Kanakamuni.

7   **"drinking light"** (*onkō* 飲光): A common Chinese interpretation of *kāśyapa*, possibly from *kas* ("to shine") and *pa* ("to drink"). The Sanskrit name is more often associated with the tortoise (*kaśyapa*).

8   **(The seventh buddha) The Most Reverend Buddha Śākyamuni (meaning "forbearance and quiescence")** (*shichi butsu Shakamuni butsu dai oshō shi un nōnin jakumoku* 七佛釋迦牟尼佛大和尚此云能忍寂黙): The initial parenthetical can be understood, "here ends the list of the seven buddhas." The interpretation of the name Śākyamuni (normally, "sage of the Śākya") as "forbearance and quiescence" is likely derived from *saha* ("enduring") and *muni* ("silence," "silent ascetic").

52. Buddhas and Ancestors *Busso* 佛祖

[52:3] {2:66}

第一摩訶迦葉大和尚
第二阿難陀大和尚
第三商那和修大和尚
第四優婆毱多大和尚
第五提多迦大和尚
第六彌遮迦大和尚
第七婆須蜜多大和尚
第八佛陀難提大和尚
第九伏馱蜜多大和尚
第十波栗湿縛大和尚
第十一富那夜奢大和尚
第十二馬鳴大和尚
第十三迦毘摩羅大和尚
第十四那伽閼剌樹那大和尚 又龍樹、又龍勝、又龍猛。
第十五伽那提婆大和尚
第十六羅睺羅多大和尚
第十七僧伽難提大和尚
第十八伽耶舍多大和尚
第十九鳩摩羅多大和尚
第二十闍夜多大和尚
第二十一婆修盤頭大和尚
第二十二摩拏羅大和尚
第二十三鶴勒那大和尚
第二十四獅子大和尚
第二十五婆舍斯多大和尚
第二十六不如蜜多大和尚
第二十七般若多羅大和尚
西天第二十八菩提達磨大和尚

1) The Most Reverend Mahākāśyapa[9]
2) The Most Reverend Ānanda
3) The Most Reverend Śaṇavāsa
4) The Most Reverend Upagupta
5) The Most Reverend Dhītika

---

9 **1) The Most Reverend Mahākāśyapa** (*dai ichi Makakashō dai oshō* 第一摩訶迦葉大和尚): Here begins a list of the twenty-eight Indian ancestors (the numbering of which is in the original). While some of the names on the list are attested or even well-known in Indic sources, others are reconstructions, more or less tentative, from the Chinese; indeed, for a goodly number of the names, more than one such reconstruction has been proposed, but no attempt is made here to provide, or adjudicate among, the alternatives. Although the set of Indian ancestors varies in early Chan sources, by Dōgen's day the members had been largely fixed; with slight orthographic variants, Dōgen's list follows that found in the influential *Jingde chuandeng lu* 景德傳燈錄 (T.2076.51:204b28-c22, 210c27-211a9).

6) The Most Reverend Miśraka
7) The Most Reverend Vasumitra
8) The Most Reverend Buddhanandi
9) The Most Reverend Buddhamitra
10) The Most Reverend Pārśva[10]
11) The Most Reverend Puṇyayaśas[11]
12) The Most Reverend Aśvaghoṣa
13) The Most Reverend Kapimala
14) The Most Reverend Nāgārjuna (or Longshu, or Longsheng, or Longmeng)[12]
15) The Most Reverend Kāṇadeva
16) The Most Reverend Rāhulata
17) The Most Reverend Saṃghanandi
18) The Most Reverend Gayaśata
19) The Most Reverend Kumāralāta
20) The Most Reverend Jayata
21) The Most Reverend Vasubandhu
22) The Most Reverend Manorahita
23) The Most Reverend Halenayaśas
24) The Most Reverend Siṃhabhikṣu
25) The Most Reverend Vasiṣṭa
26) The Most Reverend Puṇyamitra
27) The Most Reverend Prajñātāra
(Sindh in the West 28) The Most Reverend Bodhidharma[13]

---

10 **10) The Most Reverend Pārśva** (*dai jū Harishiba dai oshō* 第十波栗湿縛大和尚): Dōgen transliterates the Sanskrit name of this famous monk, while the *Jingde chuandeng lu* 景德傳燈錄 (T.2076.51:204c20) lists him as Xie Zunzhe 脇尊者 ("Venerable Side"), a translation of *Pārśva* ("side"), a name said to derive from his ascetic practice of never letting his side touch the mat (i.e., lying down) when sleeping.

11 **11) The Most Reverend Puṇyayaśas** (*dai jūichi Funayasha dai oshō* 第十一富那夜奢大和尚): Amending Kawamura's 富那夢奢.

12 **14) The Most Reverend Nāgārjuna (or Longshu, or Longsheng, or Longmeng)** (*dai jūshi Nagaarajuna dai oshō yū Ryūju, yū Ryūshō, yū Ryūmō* 第十四那伽閼剌樹那大和尚 又龍樹、又龍勝、又龍猛): Dōgen gives a transliteration of the name of this famous figure and then provides three interpretations by Chinese translators of the etymology of the Sanskrit *nāgārjuna* (meaning roughly "dragon tree," "dragon victory," and "dragon ferocity," respectively). The *Jingde chuandeng lu* 景德傳燈錄 (T.2076.51:204c22) uses the more common Longshu 龍樹.

13 **(Sindh in the West 28) The Most Reverend Bodhidharma** (*Saiten dai nijūhachi bodai daruma* 西天第二十八菩提達磨): The parenthetical "Sindh in the West" [i.e., India] here signals the end of the list of the Indian ancestors.

52. Buddhas and Ancestors *Busso* 佛祖

[52:4] {2:67}

慧可大和尚　僧璨大和尚
道信大和尚　弘忍大和尚
慧能大和尚　行思大和尚
希遷大和尚　惟儼大和尚
曇晟大和尚　良价大和尚
道膺大和尚　道丕大和尚
觀志大和尚　緣觀大和尚
警玄大和尚　義青大和尚
道楷大和尚　子淳大和尚
清了大和尚　宗珏大和尚
智鑑大和尚　如淨大和尚　東地二十三代

The Most Reverend Huike[14]
The Most Reverend Sengcan[15]
The Most Reverend Daoxin[16]
The Most Reverend Hongren[17]
The Most Reverend Huineng[18]
The Most Reverend Xingsi[19]
The Most Reverend Xiqian[20]
The Most Reverend Weiyan[21]
The Most Reverend Tansheng[22]
The Most Reverend Liangjie[23]

14　**The Most Reverend Huike** (*Eka dai oshō* 慧可大和尚): The Second Ancestor, Shenguang Huike 神光慧可.

15　**The Most Reverend Sengcan** (*Sōsan dai oshō* 僧璨大和尚): The Third Ancestor, Jianzhi Sengcan 鑑智僧璨 (d. 606).

16　**The Most Reverend Daoxin** (*Dōshin dai oshō* 道信大和尚): The Fourth Ancestor, Dayi Daoxin 大醫道信 (580-651).

17　**The Most Reverend Hongren** (*Kōnin dai oshō* 弘忍大和尚): The Fifth Ancestor, Huangmei Hongren 黄梅弘忍 (688-761).

18　**The Most Reverend Huineng** (*Enō dai oshō* 慧能大和尚): The Sixth Ancestor, Dajian Huineng 大鑑慧能.

19　**The Most Reverend Xingsi** (*Gyōshi dai oshō* 行思大和尚): Qingyuan Xingsi 青原行思 (d. 740).

20　**The Most Reverend Xiqian** (*Kisen dai oshō* 希遷大和尚): Shitou Xiqian 石頭希遷 (700-790).

21　**The Most Reverend Weiyan** (*Igen dai oshō* 惟儼大和尚): Yaoshan Weiyan 藥山惟儼 (751-834).

22　**The Most Reverend Tansheng** (*Donjō dai oshō* 曇晟大和尚): Yunyan Tansheng 雲巖曇晟 (782-841).

23　**The Most Reverend Liangjie** (*Ryōkai dai oshō* 良价大和尚): Dongshan Liangjie 洞山良价 (807-869).

The Most Reverend Daoying[24]
The Most Reverend Daopi[25]
The Most Reverend Guanzhi[26]
The Most Reverend Yuanguan[27]
The Most Reverend Jingxuan[28]
The Most Reverend Yiqing[29]
The Most Reverend Daokai[30]
The Most Reverend Zichun[31]
The Most Reverend Qingliao[32]
The Most Reverend Zongjue[33]
The Most Reverend Zhijian[34]
The Most Reverend Rujing (Land of the East 23 generations)[35]

---

24 **The Most Reverend Daoying** (*Dōyō dai oshō* 道膺大和尚): Yunju Daoying 雲居道膺 (d. 902).

25 **The Most Reverend Daopi** (*Dōhi dai oshō* 道丕大和尚): Tongan Daopi 同安道丕 (dates unknown).

26 **The Most Reverend Guanzhi** (*Kanshi dai oshō* 觀志大和尚): Tongan Guanzhi 同安觀志 (dates unknown).

27 **The Most Reverend Yuanguan** (*Enkan dai oshō* 縁觀大和尚): Liangshan Yuanguan 梁山縁觀 (dates unknown).

28 **The Most Reverend Jingxuan** (*Kyōgen dai oshō* 警玄大和尚): Dayang Jingxuan 大陽警玄 (941-1027).

29 **The Most Reverend Yiqing** (*Gisei dai oshō* 義青大和尚): Touzi Yiqing 投子義青 (1032-1083).

30 **The Most Reverend Daokai** (*Dōkai dai oshō* 道楷大和尚): Furong Daokai 芙蓉道楷 (1043-1118).

31 **The Most Reverend Zichun** (*Shijun dai oshō* 子淳大和尚): Danxia Zichun 丹霞子淳 (1064-1117).

32 **The Most Reverend Qingliao** (*Seiryō dai oshō* 清了大和尚): Zhenxie Qingliao 眞歇清了 (1089-1151).

33 **The Most Reverend Zongjue** (*Sōkaku dai oshō* 宗珏大和尚): Tiantong Zongjue 天童宗珏 (1091-1162).

34 **The Most Reverend Zhijian** (*Chikan dai oshō* 智鑑大和尚): Xuedou Zhijian 雪竇智鑑 (1105-1192).

35 **The Most Reverend Rujing (Land of the East 23 generations)** (*Nyojō dai oshō Tōchi nijūsan dai* 如淨大和尚東地二十三代): Tiantong Rujing 天童如淨 (1162-1227). The parenthetical "Land of the East 23 generations" signals the end of the list of Dōgen's Chinese ancestors; the number 23 presumably includes the First Ancestor, Bodhidharma, listed above as the last of the Indian ancestors.

52. Buddhas and Ancestors *Busso* 佛祖

[52:5] {2:68}

道元、大宋國寶慶元年乙酉夏安居時、先師天童古佛大和尚に參侍して、この佛祖を禮拜頂戴することを究盡せり。唯佛與佛なり。

In the summer retreat of the junior wood year of the rooster, the first year of Baoqing, in the Land of the Great Song, attending my former master, the Most Reverend Old Buddha of Tiantong, I, Dōgen, exhaustively investigated the act of doing obeisance and paying respect to this buddha and ancestor.[36] It was *"only a buddha with a buddha."*[37]

正法眼藏佛祖第五十二
Treasury of the True Dharma Eye
Buddhas and Ancestors
Number 52

[*Ryūmonji* MS:]

爾時仁治二年辛丑正月三日、書于日本國雍州宇治縣觀音導利興聖寶林寺而示衆

Written and presented to the assembly at Kannon Dōri Kōshō Hōrin Monastery, Uji District, Yōshū, in the Land of Japan; third day, first month of the junior metal year of the ox, the second year of Ninji [15 February 1241][38]

[*Himitsu* MS:]

日本寬元二年甲辰五月十四日、在越州吉峰寺侍司書寫之。懷奘

Copied this at the acolyte's office, Kippō Monastery, Esshū; fourteenth day, fifth month of the senior wood year of the dragon, the second year of Kangen in Japan [20 June 1244]. Ejō

---

36 **summer retreat of the junior wood year of the rooster, the first year of Baoqing** (*Hōkyō gannen otsuyū ge ango* 寶慶元年乙酉夏安居): The first year of the Baoqing era was 1225. Dates of the summer retreat vary; a common practice put it from the fifteenth of the fourth month through the fifteenth of the seventh month. In "Shōbōgenzō menju" 正法眼藏面授, Dōgen dates his first meeting with Rujing to the first day of the fifth month — 8 June 1225.

exhaustively investigated (*gūjin seri* 究盡せり): A verb that plays on the line in the *Lotus Sūtra* evoked by Dōgen's subsequent phrase here, "only a buddha with a buddha."

37 **"only a buddha with a buddha"** (*yui butsu yo butsu* 唯佛與佛): From a line in Kumārajīva's translation of the *Lotus Sūtra*; see Supplementary Notes, s.v. "Only buddhas with buddhas can exhaustively investigate the real marks of the dharmas."

38 The *Himitsu* 秘密 MS shares an identical colophon.

TREASURY OF THE TRUE DHARMA EYE

NUMBER 53

Plum Blossoms
Baika

梅華

Plum Blossoms

Baika

Introduction

This chapter represents number 53 of the seventy-five-chapter *Shōbōgenzō* and number 59 of the Honzan edition; it does not occur in the sixty-chapter compilation. The text bears a colophon stating that it was composed in December of 1243, some months after its author had moved from the capital to mountainous Echizen province. Outside his quarters, he notes in the colophon, the snow was already three feet deep.

In the dead of winter, Dōgen writes of the Chinese plum, one of the first trees to bloom in the early spring, often while snow is still on its branches. But the "Baika" chapter is not a celebration of spring flowers; it is a study, rather, of verses on the plum found in the recorded sayings of Dōgen's Chinese master, Tiantong Rujing 天童如淨, a work he had received from China in the preceding year. Our text here comments on no less than eight such verses, emphasizing the image of the plum as the eye of the Buddha handed down in the lineage of the ancestors, and reading Rujing's verses in conversation with the images of flowers used in the Chan literature on transmission.

正法眼藏第五十三
Treasury of the True Dharma Eye
Number 53
梅華
Plum Blossoms

[53:1] {2:69}
先師天童古佛は、大宋慶元府、大白名山、天童景德寺、第三十代、堂上大和尚なり。

My former master, the Old Buddha of Tiantong, was the most reverend chief of hall, in the thirtieth generation, of the Jingde Monastery at Tiantong, renowned Mount Taibai, in the Qingyuan Prefecture of the Great Song.[1]

[53:2]
上堂示衆云、天童仲冬第一句、槎槎牙牙老梅樹、忽開華一華兩華、三四五華無數華、清不可誇、香不可誇、散作春容吹草木、衲僧箇箇頂門禿。驀劄變怪狂風暴雨、乃至交衰大地雪漫漫、老梅樹太無端、寒凍摩挲鼻孔酸。

In a convocation, he addressed the assembly, saying,[2]

Tiantong's first words of mid-winter:

    Ragged jagged old plum
    Suddenly blooms a blossom or two;
    Three, four, five blossoms, countless blossoms.[3]
    Their purity is nothing to boast of; their fragrance, nothing to boast of.
    Scattering, they make a spring scene, blowing about the grass and trees.
    Patch-robed monks, each pate bald.
    Swift strange transformations of wild winds and rough rain,

---

1 **My former master, the Old Buddha of Tiantong** (*senshi Tendō kobutsu* 先師天童古佛): I.e., Tiantong Rujing 天童如淨 (1162-1227). Tiantong is the mountain name of the Jingdesi 景德寺, located in the modern Yinzhou 鄞州 of Ningbo, Zhejiang Province. "Chief of hall" (*dōjō* 堂上) refers to the abbot.

2 **In a convocation** (*jōdō* 上堂): From the *Rujing heshang yulu* 如淨和尚語錄, T.2002A.48:128a26-b1.

3 **Tiantong's first words of mid-winter** (*Tendō chūtō dai ikku* 天童仲冬第一句): Perhaps meaning something like, "my word for the month." "Mid-winter" (*chūtō* 仲冬) refers to the second month of winter, corresponding to the eleventh month of the lunar calendar.

Till the whole earth is everywhere spread with snow.[4]
The old plum, for no reason at all,
Rubs its nose in the freezing cold, and it stings.

[53:3]

いま開演ある老梅樹、それ太無端なり、忽開華す、自結菓す。あるいは春をなし、あるいは冬をなす。あるいは狂風をなし、あるいは暴雨をなす。あるいは衲僧の頂門なり、あるいは古佛の眼睛なり。あるいは草木となれり、あるいは清香となれり。驀剗なる神變靈怪、きはむべからず。乃至大地・高天、明日・清月、これ老梅樹の樹功より樹功せり、葛藤の葛藤を結纒するなり。老梅樹の忽開華のとき、華開世界起なり。華開世界起の時節、すなはち春到なり。この時節に、開五葉の一華あり。この一華時、よく三華・四華・五華あり、百華・千華・萬華・億華あり、乃至無數華あり。これらの華開、みな老梅樹の一枝・兩枝・無數枝の不可誇なり。優曇華・優鉢羅華等、おなじく老梅樹華の一指・兩指なり。おほよそ一切の華開は、老梅樹の恩給なり。人中・天上の老梅樹あり、老梅樹中に人間・天堂を樹功せり。百千華を人天華と稱す、萬億華は佛祖華なり。恁麼の時節を、諸佛出現於世と喚作するなり、祖師本來茲土と喚作するなり。

The old plum tree expounded here is "for no reason at all": it "suddenly blooms"; it spontaneously bears fruit. Or it "makes the spring"; or it makes the winter. Or it makes the "wild winds"; or it makes the "rough rain." Or it is the "pate" of the "patch-robed monks"; or it is the eye of the Old Buddha.[5] Or it has become the "grass and trees"; or it has become the "purity" and "fragrance." Its "swift" miraculous "strange transformations" cannot be comprehended. "Till the whole earth," the high heavens, the bright sun, and clear moon — their "tree virtue" is established from the tree virtue of the old plum tree; it is tangled vines entwining tangled vines.[6] When the old plum "suddenly blooms," it is "a

---

4 **Till the whole earth is everywhere spread with snow** (*naishi kōkon daichi setsu manman* 乃至交衰大地雪漫漫): Taking *kōkon* 交衰 as equivalent to *konkon* 袞袞, in the sense "continuous," "uninterrupted."

5 **eye of the Old Buddha** (*kobutsu no ganzei* 古佛の眼睛): The translation takes this as a reference to "the Old Buddha of Tiantong" (*Tendō kobutsu* 天童古佛), but it could well be read as "eye of the old buddhas." See Supplementary Notes, s.v. "Eye."

6 **their "tree virtue" is established from the tree virtue of the old plum tree** (*kore rō baiju no jukō yori jukō seri* これ老梅樹の樹功より樹功せり): Probably meaning something like, "they are what they are by virtue of the properties of the old plum tree." The awkward English struggles to preserve a pun on the term *jukō* 樹功 ("tree virtue"), which also has the sense "establish," "accomplish," etc. The pun is repeated later in this section in the phrase, "the human realm and heavenly mansions have been established" (*ningen tendō o jukō seri* 人間天堂を樹功せり).

tangled vines entwining tangled vines (*kattō no kattō o ketten suru nari* 葛藤の葛藤を結纒するなり): Or "entanglements entwining entanglements"; probably meaning that the old plum tree, on the one hand, and the earth, heaven, sun, and moon, on the other, are completely intertwined with each other. The phrasing recalls Rujing's saying, quoted in "Shōbōgenzō kattō" 正法眼藏葛藤:

flower opens, and the world arises."⁷ The moment when "a flower opens, and the world arises" is precisely the arrival of spring. In this moment, there is the "one flower" that "opens five petals."⁸

At the time of this "one blossom," there are "three" blossoms, "four" blossoms, "five" blossoms; there are a hundred blossoms, a thousand blossoms, ten thousand blossoms, a hundred thousand blossoms; until there are "countless blossoms." All their bloomings are "nothing to boast of" on one branch, two branches, or countless branches. The *udumbara* flower, the *utpala* flower, and the like, are all one finger or two fingers of the old plum blossoms.⁹ In sum, all bloomings are gifts bestowed by the old plum tree. There is an old plum tree among humans and in the heavens above; and within the old plum tree, the human realm and heavenly mansions have been established. Hundreds of thousands of blossoms are called "human and deva blossoms"; myriads of *koṭis* of blossoms are "buddha and ancestor blossoms." Such a moment is called "the buddhas appear in this world"; it is called the Ancestral Master "originally came to this land."¹⁰

胡蘆藤種纏胡蘆。
The bottle gourd vine entwines the bottle gourd.

See Supplementary Notes, s.v. ""Tangled vines," and "The bottle gourd vine entwines the bottle gourd."

7 **"a flower opens, and the world arises"** (*ke kai sekai ki* 華開世界起): The final line of the dharma transmission verse attributed to Bodhidharma's master, Prajñātāra. See Supplementary Notes.

8 **"one flower" that "opens five petals"** (*kai goyō no ikke* 開五葉の一華): Allusion to a line in the transmission verse attributed to Bodhidharma that Dōgen will quote below, section 12 (see *Jingde chuandeng lu* 景德傳燈錄, T.2076.51:219c17-18):
 吾本來茲土、傳法救迷情、一華開五葉、結果自然成。
 I originally came to this land
 To transmit the dharma and save deluded sentient beings.
 A single flower opens five petals;
 The fruit forms, ripening naturally of itself.
See Supplementary Notes, s.v. "A single flower opens five petals."

9 **udumbara flower** (*udonge* 優曇華); **utpala flower** (*upparage* 優鉢羅華; also read *ubarage*): The former is a plant said to blossom only once every three thousand years; hence, used in Buddhism as a symbol of what is rare and precious. The latter is a flower most often taken as a blue lotus.

one finger or two fingers of the old plum blossoms (*rō baijuka no isshi ryōshi* 老梅樹華の一指・兩指): The sense of "finger" here is uncertain; perhaps an allusion to Zhuangzi's saying, "heaven and earth are one finger" (*tiandi yizhi ye* 天地一指也, KR5c0134.001.008b), typically used to suggest the equality of things. Some manuscript witnesses read the homophonous "branch" (*shi* 枝) here for "finger" (*shi* 指).

10 **"the buddhas appear in this world"** (*shobutsu shutsugen o se* 諸佛出現於世): A fixed phrase occurring often in the literature; here, perhaps, especially associated with

* * * * *

[53:4] {2:70}
先師古佛、上堂示衆云、瞿曇打失眼睛時、雪裏梅華只一枝、而今到處成荊棘、却笑春風繚亂吹。

My former master, the Old Buddha, in a convocation, addressed the assembly, saying,[11]
At the time that Gautama lost his eye,
It was just one branch of plum blossoms in the snow.
Now, it's a thicket wherever you go;
Yet we laugh as the spring wind swirls them about.

[53:5]
いまこの古佛の法輪を、盡界の最極に轉する、一切人天の得道の時節なり。乃至雲雨・風水、および草木・昆虫にいたるまでも、法益をかうぶらずといふことなし。天地・國土も、この法輪に轉ぜられて活鱍鱍地なり。未曾聞の道をきく、といふは、いまの道を聞著するをいふ。未曾有をうる、といふは、いまの法を得著するを稱するなり。おほよそおぼろげの福德にあらずば、見聞すべからざる法輪なり。

The turning here of this old buddha's dharma wheel at the extreme limits of all the worlds is the moment when all humans and devas gain the way. Even the clouds and rain, wind and water, as well as the grass, trees, and insects — there is nothing that does not receive the benefits of this dharma. Turned by this dharma wheel, even heaven and earth, countries and lands, are brisk and lively.[12] To hear words never heard before means to hear the present words; to get what has never been before is what getting the present dharma is called.[13] In short, it is a dharma wheel one could never experience without extraordinary good fortune.

---

the doctrine of the *Lotus Sūtra* that the buddhas appear in the world to teach the one, buddha vehicle (see, e.g., *Miaofa lianhua jing* 妙法蓮華經, T.262.9:8a20). See Supplementary Notes, s.v. "Buddhas, the world-honored ones, appear in the world for the reason of one great matter alone."

the Ancestral Master "originally came to this land" (*soshi hon rai shido* 祖師本來茲土): From the transmission verse of Bodhidharma alluded to above in the line "the one flower that opens five petals" and quoted below, section 12.

11 **My former master, the Old Buddha** (*senshi kobutsu* 先師古佛): From the *Rujing heshang yulu* 如淨和尚語錄, T.2002A.48:122c29-123a1. Dōgen also quotes this verse in "Shōbōgenzō ganzei" 正法眼藏眼睛 and "Shōbōgenzō udonge" 正法眼藏優曇華.

12 **brisk and lively** (*kappatsupatsuchi* 活鱍鱍地): A loose translation of a Chinese idiom expressing the quick, powerful movements of a fish; see Supplementary Notes, s.v. "Brisk and lively."

13 **never heard before** (*mizōmon* 未曾聞); **never been before** (*mizōu* 未曾有): Two expressions, common in Buddhist texts, for extraordinary revelations and miraculous events.

53. Plum Blossoms *Baika* 梅華

[53:6] {2:71}

いま現在大宋國一百八十州の内外に、山寺あり、人里の寺あり、そのかず稱計すべからず。そのなかに雲水おほし。しかあれども、先師古佛をみざるはおほく、みたるはすくなからん。いはんや、ことばを見聞するは少分なるべし。いはんや、相見問訊のともがらおほからんや。いはんや、堂奥をゆるさるる、いくばくにあらず。いかにいはんや、先師の皮肉骨髓・眼睛面目を禮拜することを聽許せられんや。

Throughout the one hundred eighty or so provinces of the Land of the Great Song today, there are mountain monasteries and village temples, their numbers beyond calculation. Within them live many monks. Yet those that have never seen my former master, the Old Buddha, are many, while those that have seen him are few. Not to mention how few there must be that have experienced his words. Not to ask whether there could be many that have met and greeted him. Not to mention that those admitted to the interior of the hall are less than a few.[14] Not to mention those permitted to pay obeisance to my former master's skin, flesh, bones, and marrow, eyes and face.

[53:7]

先師古佛、たやすく僧家の討掛搭をゆるさず。よのつねにいはく、無道心慣頭、我箇裏不可也、すなはちおいいだす。出了いはく、不一本分人、要作甚麼。かくのごときの狗子は騒人なり、掛搭不得といふ。まさしくこれをみ、まのあたりこれをきく。ひそかにおもふらくは、かれらいかなる罪根ありてか、このくにの人なりといへども、共住をゆるされざる。われなにのさいはひありてか、遠方外國の種子なりといへども、掛搭をゆるさるるのみにあらず、ほしきままに堂奥に出入して、尊儀を禮拜し、法道をきく。愚暗なりといへども、むなしかるべからざる結良縁なり。先師の、宋朝を化せしとき、なほ參得人あり、參不得人ありき。先師古佛、すでに宋朝をさりぬ、暗夜よりもくらからん。ゆえはいかん。先師古佛より前後に、先師古佛のごとくなる古佛なきがゆえに、しかいふなり。

My former master, the Old Buddha, did not lightly permit monks to request registration. He would always say, "*Those inveterately lacking the mind of the way aren't permitted at my place,*" and immediately chase them out. After they were gone, he would say, "*Not a person of the original lot — what could he do?*"[15] He would say that dogs like that bother the others and cannot register.

Actually seeing this, personally hearing this, I thought to myself, "What evil roots do they have that, though natives of this land, they are not permitted to stay with us? What good fortune do I have that, though

---

14 **those admitted to the interior of the hall** (*dōō o yurusaruru* 堂奥をゆるさるる): I.e., those granted private interviews.

15 **"Not a person of the original lot"** (*fu itsu honbun nin* 不一本分人): I.e., an inauthentic type, not in accord with his true nature.

the seed of a distant foreign land, I am not only permitted to register but, going in and out of the interior of the hall at will, I pay obeisance to his revered figure and hear his words of dharma? Dimwitted though I am, I have formed a good karmic relation that is hardly in vain."

Even when my former master was teaching in the Song, there were those able to practice and those unable to practice with him. Since my former master, the Old Buddha, has departed the Song, it is darker there than a dark night.[16] Why is this? I say this because, before and after my former master, the Old Buddha, there has not been an old buddha the likes of my former master, the Old Buddha.

[53:8] {2:72}
しかあれば、いまこれを見聞せんときの晩學おもふべし、自餘の諸方の人天も、いまのごとくの法輪を見聞すらん、參學すらん、とおもふことなかれ。雪裏の梅華は一現の曇華なり。ひごろはいくめぐりか我佛如來の正法眼睛を拜見しながら、いたづらに瞬目を蹉過して、破顔せざる。而今すでに雪裏の梅華まさしく如來眼睛なりと正傳し、承當す。これを拈じて頂門眼とし、眼中睛とす。さらに梅華裏に參到して梅華を究盡するに、さらに疑著すべき因縁いまだきたらず。これすでに天上天下、唯我獨尊の眼睛なり、法界中尊なり。

Thus, when later students now see and hear this, they should reflect on it; do not think that humans and devas in other quarters also see and hear or study a dharma wheel like the present one. The "plum blossoms in the snow" are the *udumbara* flower that appears but once.[17] How many times, day after day, while looking upon the eye of true dharma of our Buddha, the Tathāgata, have we futilely missed his blink and failed to smile?[18] Now, we receive and accede to the direct transmission that the plum blossom in the snow is truly the "eye" of the Tathāgata. We take it up as the eye on the forehead, as the pupil of the eye.[19] Further, when

---

16　**my former master, the Old Buddha, has departed the Song** (*senshi kobutsu, sude ni Sōchō o sarinu* 先師古佛、すでに宋朝をさりぬ): Rujing had died some 16 years before these words were being written.

17　***udumbara* flower that appears but once** (*ichigen no donge* 一現の曇華): From the belief that the *udumbara* blooms only once every three thousand years. Here as elsewhere, Dōgen associates the *udumbara* with the flower that Buddha Śākyamuni held up on Vulture Peak when he transmitted the treasury of the true dharma eye to Mahākāśyapa. See Supplementary Notes, s.v. "Hold up a flower."

18　**we futilely missed his blink and failed to smile** (*itazura ni shunmoku o shaka shite, hagan sezaru* いたづらに瞬目を蹉過して、破顔せざる): From the legend, in Dōgen's telling, that, when Buddha Śākyamuni held up the flower on Vulture Peak, he blinked, and Mahākāśyapa broke into a smile. See Supplementary Notes, s.v. "Break into a smile."

19　**eye on the forehead** (*chōmon gen* 頂門眼): Some readers take this as "the eye at the top of the head," though it more likely refers to the "third eye" of wisdom, at the center of the forehead.

53. Plum Blossoms *Baika* 梅華　　　　　　　　　　　153

we study within the plum blossom and exhaustively investigate the plum blossom, no occasion for doubts emerges. This is surely the eye of *"In heaven and on earth, I alone am honored"*; it is *honored throughout the dharma realm.*[20]

[53:9]
しかあればすなはち、天上の天華・人間の天華・天雨曼陀羅華・摩訶曼陀羅華・曼殊沙華・摩訶曼殊沙華、および十方無盡國土の諸華は、みな雪裏梅華の眷屬なり。梅華の恩德分をうけて華開せるがゆゑに、百億華は梅華の眷屬なり、小梅華と稱すべし。乃至空華・地華・三昧華等、ともに梅華の大少の眷屬群華なり。華裏に百億國をなす、國土に開華せる、みなこの梅華の恩分なり。梅華の恩分のほかは、さらに一恩の雨露あらざるなり。命脈、みな梅華よりなれるなり。ひとへに嵩山少林の雪漫漫地と參學することなかれ、如來の眼睛なり。頭上をてらし、脚下をてらす。ただ雪山・雪宮のゆきと參學することなかれ、老瞿曇の正法眼睛なり。五眼の眼睛、このところに究盡せり。千眼の眼睛、この眼睛に圓成すべし。

Thus, the heavenly flowers of the heavens above and the heavenly flowers among humans, *"the māndārava flowers, the mahāmāndārava flowers, the mañjūṣaka flowers, the mahāmañjūṣaka flowers that rain from the heavens,"* as well as the flowers of inexhaustible lands in the ten directions, are all the retinue of the "plum blossoms in the snow."[21] Since they have bloomed by receiving the favor of the plum blossoms, ten million flowers are the retinue of the plum blossoms and could be called *"little plum blossoms." And so on, down to the sky flowers, earth flowers, samādhi flowers, and the like,* are all larger or smaller clusters of flowers in the retinue of the plum blossoms.[22] They form ten million

---

20　"In heaven and on earth, I alone am honored" (*tenjō tenge, yui ga doku son* 天上天下、唯我獨尊): Words attributed to Buddha Śākyamuni as a newborn baby; see Supplementary Notes, s.v. "I alone am honored."

21　**heavenly flowers** (*tenge* 天華): The flowers said to fall from the heavens onto those skilled in preaching the dharma.
"the *māndārava* flowers, the *mahāmāndārava* flowers, the *mañjūṣaka* flowers, the *mahāmañjūṣaka* flowers that rain from the heavens" (*ten u mandara ge makamandara ge manjusha ge makamajusha ge* 天雨曼陀羅華・摩訶曼陀羅華・曼殊沙華・摩訶曼殊沙華): From the scene in the *Lotus Sūtra* (*Miaofa lianhua jing* 妙法蓮華經, T.262.9:2b10-11), in which these four magical flowers rain down on the buddha and his audience.

22　**sky flowers** (*kūge* 空華): "Flowers in the sky" (S. *khapuṣpa*), used for spots appearing to the diseased eye; a standard metaphor in Buddhist texts for what is mere appearance without objective reality (though Dōgen gives the term a quite different sense in his *Shōbōgenzō kūge* 正法眼藏空華). See Supplementary Notes, s.v. "Clouded eyes and sky flowers." The exact sense of "earth flowers" (*chige* 地華) here is uncertain; perhaps, "physical flowers," introduced simply in contrast to "sky flowers."
samādhi flowers (*zanmaige* 三昧華): A somewhat unusual expression, not occurring elsewhere in the *Shōbōgenzō*, the exact sense of which is uncertain; perhaps, "flowers

lands within the blossoms, and the blossoms blooming in these lands are all due to the favor of the plum blossoms. Apart from the favor of the plum blossoms, they have not the slightest benefit of rain or dew; their lifelines derive entirely from the plum blossoms.

Do not study only that Shaolin on Mount Song is the place "everywhere spread with snow": it is the "eye" of the Tathāgata, illumining above the head, illumining beneath the feet.[23] Do not study it simply as the snow of the Snowy Mountains or the Snowy Palace: it is the true dharma eye of Old Gautama.[24] The eye of the five eyes is exhaustively investigated here; the eye of the thousand eyes is perfectly realized in this "eye."[25]

[53:10] {2:73}
まことに、老瞿曇の身心光明は、究盡せざる諸法實相の一微塵あるべからず。人天の見、別ありとも、凡聖の情、隔すとも、雪漫漫は大地なり、大地は雪漫漫なり。雪漫漫にあらざれば、盡界に大地あらざるなり。この雪漫漫の表裏團圞、これ瞿曇老の眼睛なり。

Truly there cannot be a single infinitesimal dust mote of the real marks

---

occurring to one in samādhi," or "the flower that is samādhi." The image is suggestive of a verse on the "markless samādhi" (*musō zanmai* 無相三昧; S. *animitta-samādhi*) attributed to Nanyue Huairang 南嶽懷讓 (677-744) (see, e.g., *Jingde chuandeng lu* 景德傳燈錄, T.2076.51:241a6-7):

心地含諸種、遇澤悉皆萌。三昧華無相、何壞復何成。
The mind ground contains the seeds;
When they meet the moisture, they all sprout.
The flowers of the samādhi are without signs;
What decomposes; what composes?

23 **Shaolin on Mount Song is the place "everywhere spread with snow"** (*Sūzan Shōrin no setsu manman chi* 嵩山少林の雪漫漫地): Allusion to the legend that the Second Ancestor, Huike 慧可, stood throughout a snowy night at Shaolin Monastery 少林寺 on Mount Song 嵩山 waiting for an interview with Bodhidharma; see Supplementary Notes, s.v. "Cut off an arm." Mt. Song is in present-day Henan.

"eye" of the Tathāgata (*nyorai no ganzei* 如來の眼睛): Presumably, the eye lost by Gautama in Rujing's verse. For the meanings of "eye" (*ganzei* 眼睛) in Zen texts, see Supplementary Notes, s.v. "Eye."

24 **the Snowy Mountains or the Snowy Palace** (*Sessen Setsugū* 雪山・雪宮): If these are to be taken as proper nouns, the former is a reference to the Himalayas, while the latter may refer to the detached palace of the ancient state of Qi during the Warring States period.

25 **five eyes** (*gogen* 五眼): A standard set of five levels of vision, typically given as (1) the "physical eye" (*nikugen* 肉眼) of ordinary human sight, (2) the "deva eye" (*tengen* 天眼) of paranormal sight, (3) the "wisdom eye" (*egen* 慧眼) that sees emptiness, (4) the "dharma eye" (*hōgen* 法眼) of the advanced bodhisattva, and (5) the omniscient "buddha eye" (*butsugen* 佛眼).

thousand eyes (*sengen* 千眼): The eyes in the palms of each hand of the thousand-armed Bodhisattva Avalokiteśvara.

53. Plum Blossoms *Baika* 梅華

of the dharmas that is not exhaustively investigated by the body and mind and the radiance of old Gautama. Though the perceptions of humans and devas differ, and the sentience of common people and sages are separated, "everywhere spread with snow" is "the whole earth"; "the whole earth" is "everywhere spread with snow." Were it not "everywhere spread with snow," there would be no "whole earth" anywhere in all the worlds. The roundness of the surface and interior of this "everywhere spread with snow" — this is the "eye" of old man Gautama.

[53:11]
しるべし、華地悉無生なり、華無生なり。華無生なるゆえに、地無生なり。華地悉無生のゆえに、眼睛無生なり。無生といふは、無上菩提をいふ。正當恁麼時の見取は、梅華只一枝なり。正當恁麼時の道取は、雪裏梅華只一枝なり。地華生生なり。

We should realize that *blossoms and earth are both unarisen.*[26] The blossoms are unarisen; because the blossoms are unarisen, the earth is unarisen. Because *the blossoms and the earth are both unarisen*, the eye is unarisen. "Unarisen" means unsurpassed bodhi. What is seen at this very moment is *"just one branch of plum blossoms."* What is said at this very moment is *"just one branch of plum blossoms in the snow."* It is *"earth and flowers arising and arising."*[27]

[53:12]
これをさらに雪漫漫といふは、全表裏雪漫漫なり。盡界は心地なり、盡界華情なり。盡界華情なるゆえに、盡界は梅華なり。盡界梅華なるがゆえに、盡界は瞿曇の眼睛なり。而今の到處は、山河大地なり。到事到時、みな吾本來茲土、傳法救迷情、一華開五葉、結果自然成の到處現成なり。西來・東漸ありといへども、梅華、而今の到處なり。

Further to call this *"everywhere spread with snow"* means *the entire surface and interior are everywhere spread with snow.* All the worlds are

---

26 **blossoms and earth are both unarisen** (*ke chi shitsu mushō nari* 華地悉無生なり): Or "flowers and earth are both unborn." The term *mushō* 無生 ("unborn," "unarisen") is regularly used to express the "emptiness" of phenomena — i.e., that they do not really occur.

27 **"earth and flowers arising and arising"** (*chi ke shōshō nari* 地華生生なり): The clumsy translation "arising and arising" strains to retain the play here with *shōshō* 生生 ("to sprout again and again," "to increase," etc.). Dōgen seems to be recalling in this section the transmission verse of the Fourth Ancestor, Daoxin 道信 (580-651) (*Jingde chuandeng lu* 景德傳燈錄, T.2076.51:222b18-19):

華種有生性、因地華生生、大緣與信合、當生生不生。
Flowers and seeds have the nature to arise:
Dependent on the earth, flowers arise and arise.
When the great condition and faith accord,
Their very arising and arising does not arise.

the "mind ground"; *all the worlds are the "sentience of flowers."*[28] Because *all the worlds are "the sentience of flowers,"* all the worlds are the "plum blossoms." Because *all the worlds are the "plum blossoms,"* all the worlds are Gautama's "eye." The "wherever you go" of "now" is the mountains, rivers, and the whole earth.[29] Wherever the thing, wherever the time — they are all the expression of the "wherever you go" of:

> I originally came to this land
> To transmit the dharma and save deluded sentient beings.
> A single flower opens five petals;
> The fruit forms, ripening naturally of itself.[30]

While there may be coming from the west and spreading in the east, the plum blossoms are the "wherever you go" of "now."[31]

[53:13]
而今の現成かくのごとくなる、成荊棘といふ。大枝に舊枝・新枝の而今あり、小條に舊條・新條の到處あり。處は、到に參學すべし、到は、今に參學すべし。　　　三四五六華裏は、無數華裏なり。華に裏功徳の深廣なる具足せり、表功徳の高大なるを開闡せり。この表裏は、一華の華發なり。只一枝なるがゆゑに、異枝あらず、異種あらず。一枝の到處を而今と稱する、瞿曇老漢なり。只一枝のゆゑに、附嘱嫡嫡なり。

28　**All the worlds are the "mind ground"; all the worlds are the "sentience of flowers"** (*jinkai wa shinchi nari, jinkai kajō nari* 盡界は心地なり、盡界華情なり): Dōgen here alludes to a verse by the Sixth Ancestor, Huineng 慧能 (*Jingde chuandeng lu* 景德傳燈錄, T.2076.51:236b14-15):

> 心地含諸種、普雨悉皆生、頓悟華情已、菩提果自成。
> The mind ground contains the seeds;
> In the universal rain, they all sprout.
> Once you suddenly awaken to the sentience of flowers,
> The fruit of bodhi forms of itself.

29　**The "wherever you go" of "now"** (*nikon no tōsho* 而今の到處): Or, more naturally, "the present 'wherever you go,'" a phrase that could mean both "everywhere now" and "the term 'everywhere' used here." Here and below, the infelicitous English struggles to preserve Dōgen's play with Rujing's phrase, "Now, it's a thicket wherever you go" (*nikon tōsho jō keikyoku* 而今到處成荊棘).

mountains, rivers, and the whole earth (*senga daichi* 山河大地): A common expression for "the whole world"; equivalent to Rujing's "the whole earth" (*daichi* 大地).

30　**Wherever the thing, wherever the time** (*tōji tōji* 到事到時): Presumably meaning "every thing and every time"; here, again, the translation tries to preserve Dōgen's variations on Rujing's "wherever you go" (*tōsho* 到處).

I originally came to this land (*go hon rai shi do* 吾本來茲土): Bodhidharma's transmission verse; see above, Note 8.

31　**coming from the west and spreading in the east** (*seirai tōzen* 西來・東漸): Fixed expressions for Bodhidharma's arrival from India and his teachings' subsequent popularity in East Asia; see Supplementary Notes, s.v. "Coming from the west."

That the manifestation of "now" is like this, he describes as "it's a thicket." On the big branches, there is the "now" of old branches and new branches; on the little twigs, there is the "wherever you go" of old twigs and new twigs. We should study "wherever" in "you go"; we should study "you go" in "now."[32] The interior of "three, four, five" or six "blossoms" is the interior of "countless blossoms." The blossoms are endowed with an interior virtue that is deep and broad; they reveal a surface virtue that is tall and great. This "interior" and "surface" are the blooming of "a single flower." Because it is "just one branch," there is no different branch, there is no different seed.[33] The one calling the "wherever you go" of the "one branch" "now" is old man Gautama.[34] Because it is "just one branch," it is bequeathed to successor after successor.

[53:14] {2:74}
このゆえに、吾有の正法眼藏附嘱摩訶迦葉なり、汝得は吾髓なり。かくの ごとく、到處の現成、ところとしても太尊貴生にあらずといふことなきが ゆえに、開五葉なり、五葉は梅華なり。このゆえに、七佛祖あり、西天二 十八祖・東土六祖、および十九祖あり。みな只一枝の開五葉なり、五葉の 只一枝なり。一枝を參究し、五葉を參究しきたれば、雪裏梅華、の正傳附 嘱相見なり。只一枝、の語脈裏に轉身轉心しきたるに、雲月是同なり、溪 山各別なり。

For this reason, it is "*the treasury of the true dharma eye*" that "I have," "*I bequeath to Mahākāśyapa*"; it is what "you've gotten" is "my marrow."[35] In this way, because the manifestation of "wherever you go" never fails to be greatly honored everywhere, it is "opening five petals." The "five petals" are the "plum blossom." For this reason, there are the seven

---

32 **We should study "wherever" in "you go"; we should study "you go" in "now"** (*sho wa, tō ni sangaku su beshi, tō wa, kon ni sangaku su beshi* 處は、到に參學すべ し、到は、今に參學すべし): Presumably, meaning something like, "we should understand that the place [of the branches] is everywhere and everywhere is the present." Again, the awkward translation tries to preserve the language of Rujing's verse with which Dōgen is playing.

33 **different seed** (*ishu* 異種): Play with a term that normally means "different type."

34 **The one calling the "wherever you go" of the "one branch" "now" is old man Gautama** (*isshi no tōsho o nikon to shō suru, Kudon rōkan nari* 一枝の到處を而今と 稱する、瞿曇老漢なり): Presumably, meaning that Rujing and Gautama are the same "one branch."

35 **it is "the treasury of the true dharma eye" that "I have," "I bequeath to Mahākāśyapa"; it is what "you've gotten" is "my marrow"** (*go u no Shōbōgenzō fuzoku Makakashō nari, nyo toku wa go zui nari* 吾有の正法眼藏附嘱摩訶迦葉なり、 汝得は吾髓なり): Play with the syntax of the two most famous statements of transmission from master to disciple: Buddha Śākyamuni's statement, "I have a treasury of the true dharma eye; I bequeath it to Mahākāśyapa"; and Bodhidharma's saying to Huike 慧 可, "You've gotten my marrow." See Supplementary Notes, s.v. "Treasury of the True Dharma Eye," "Skin, flesh, bones, and marrow."

buddhas and ancestors, there are the twenty-eight ancestors of Sindh in the West and the six ancestors, as well as the nineteen ancestors, of the Land of the East.[36] They are all the "opening five petals" of "just one branch," the "just one branch" of the "five petals." When we have investigated the "one branch," have investigated the "five petals," it is an encounter with the bequest of the direct transmission of the "plum blossoms in the snow." When we have turned our bodies and turned our minds in the flow of the words "just one branch," it is "*clouds and moon are the same*," it is "*valleys and mountains are different*."[37]

[53:15]
しかあるを、かつて參學眼なきともがらいはく、五葉といふは、東地五代と初祖とを一華として、五世をならべて、古今前後にあらざるがゆゑに五葉といふ、と。この言は、擧して勘破するにたらざるなり。これらは參佛參祖の皮袋にあらず、あはれむべきなり。五葉一華の道、いかでか五代のみならん。六祖よりのちは道取せざるか。小兒子の説話におよばざるなり、ゆめゆめ見聞すべからず。

Nevertheless, those who have never had the eye of study say, "The 'five petals' means that the five generations of the Land of the East and the First Ancestor make 'a single flower'; because the five generations are lined up side-by-side, not past or present, earlier or later, they are called 'five petals.'"[38] These words are not worth taking up and seeing

---

36 **there are the seven buddhas and ancestors, there are the twenty-eight ancestors of Sindh in the West and the six ancestors, as well as the nineteen ancestors, of the Land of the East** (*shichi busso ari, Saiten nijūhachi so Tōdo roku so, oyobi jūkyū so ari* 七佛祖あり、西天二十八祖・東土六祖、および十九祖あり): The term *busso* 佛祖 ("buddhas and ancestors") might better be rendered here "buddha ancestors." Dōgen's lineage, from the seven buddhas of the past ending with Śākyamuni, through the twenty-eight Indian ancestors ending with Bodhidharma, and the six generations in China from Bodhidharma through the Sixth Ancestor, Huineng 慧能, to the generations following Huineng. Since there are only seventeen generations separating Dōgen from the Sixth Ancestor, he must be reckoning Huineng and himself among the "nineteen ancestors" here. See Supplementary Notes, s.v. "Seven buddhas," "Buddhas and ancestors."

37 **When we have turned our bodies and turned our minds in the flow of the words** (*gomyaku ri ni tenshin tenjin shikitaru ni* 語脈裏に轉身轉心しきたるに): Variation on a common Zen idiom, meaning to be transformed by the words.

it is "clouds and moon are the same," it is "valleys and mountains are different" (*ungetsu ze dō nari, keizan kakubetsu nari* 雲月是同なり、溪山各別なり): From a saying of Jiashan Shanhui 夾山善會 (805-881) (see, e.g., *Jingde chuandeng lu* 景德傳燈錄, T.2076.51:331a12). Perhaps meaning here, "branch" and "petals" are in one sense the same and yet remain distinct.

38 **"The 'five petals' means that the five generations of the Land of the East and the First Ancestor make 'a single flower'"** (*goyō to iu wa, Tōchi godai to shoso to o ikke toshite* 五葉といふは、東地五代と初祖とを一華として): A common interpretation, though the "five petals" of Bodhidharma's verse are also sometimes understood as

through. These are not skin bags who have studied the buddhas or studied the ancestors; they are pitiful.[39] How could the words "one flower of five petals" refer only to the five generations? Do they say nothing of those after the Sixth Ancestor? This is worth less than the talk of little children; we should never listen to it.

* * * * *

[53:16]
先師古佛、歳旦上堂曰、元正啓祚、萬物咸新、伏惟大衆、梅開早春。

> My former master, the Old Buddha, in a convocation on New Year's Day, said,[40]
> Felicitations on New Year's Day;
> The myriad things are all new.
> I submit to the great assembly
> That the plum opens early spring.[41]

[53:17] {2:75}
しづかにおもひみれば、過・現・當來の老古錐、たとひ盡十方に脱體なりとも、いまだ梅開早春の道あらずは、たれかなんぢを道盡箇といはん。ひとり先師古佛のみ、古佛中の古佛なり。

When we quietly reflect on this, while the venerable old awls of past, present, and future may cast off the body throughout the ten directions, if they lack the words, "*the plum opens early spring,*" who would call them one who has said it all?[42] My former master, the Old Buddha, alone is the old buddha among the old buddhas.

[53:18]
その宗旨は、梅開に帯せられて萬春はやし。萬春は梅裏一兩の功徳なり。一春、なほよく萬物を咸新ならしむ、萬法を元正ならしむ。啓祚は眼睛正なり。萬物といふは、過・現・來のみにあらず、威音王以前、乃至未來なり。無量無盡の過・現・來、ことごとく新なり、といふがゆえに、この新

---

predicting the development of Bodhidharma's descendants into the five houses (*goke* 五家) in the generations after the time of the Sixth Ancestor.

39 **skin bags who have studied the buddhas or studied the ancestors** (*san butsu san so no hitai* 參佛參祖の皮袋): Or "skin bags who have studied with the buddhas or studied with the ancestors." "Skin bag" (*hitai* 皮袋) is a common term in Zen literature for "person" or "human being"; see Supplementary Notes, s.v. "Bag of skin."

40 **My former master, the Old Buddha** (*senshi kobutsu* 先師古佛): Quoting the *Rujing heshang yulu* 如淨和尚語録 at T.2002A.48:123c3-4.

41 **the plum opens early spring** (*bai kai sō shun* 梅開早春): A line that plays with the verb *kai* 開, which can be read both as transitive ("to open") and as intransitive ("to bloom").

42 **venerable old awls** (*rō kosui* 老古錐): A common term for Zen masters.

は新を脱落せり。このゆえに、伏惟大衆なり、伏惟大衆は、恁麼なるがゆえに。

His point is that, borne by "the plum opening," myriad springs are early.⁴³ The myriad springs are one or two virtues within the plum. Even a single spring causes "the myriad things" to be "new," causes the myriad dharmas to be "New Year's Day." "Felicitations" means the eye is true. "The myriad things" means, not only past, present, and future, but "before King Majestic Voice" until the future.⁴⁴ Because he says that the incalculable, inexhaustible past, present, and future are all "new," the newness has sloughed off newness. Therefore, it is *"I submit to the great assembly"*; for *"submitting to the great assembly"* is like this.

* * * * *

[53:19]

先師天童古佛、上堂示衆云、一言相契、萬古不移、柳眼發新條、梅華滿舊枝。

*My former master, the Old Buddha of Tiantong, in a convocation, addressed the assembly, saying,*⁴⁵

A single word accords,
Unmoved for myriad ages.
Willow eyes sprout on new twigs;
*Plum blossoms fill the old branches.*⁴⁶

---

43 **His point is that, borne by "the plum opening," myriad springs are early** (*sono shūshi wa, baikai ni tai serarete banshun hayashi* その宗旨は、梅開に帶せられて萬春はやし): I.e., the plum's opening causes the springs to be early.

44 **"before King Majestic Voice"** (*Ion'ō izen* 威音王以前): A common expression, occurring often in Dōgen's writing and other Zen texts, used to suggest the primordial past or a state prior to any differentiation; see Supplementary Notes, s.v. "Before King Majestic Voice."

45 **My former master, the Old Buddha of Tiantong** (*senshi Tendō kobutsu* 先師天童古佛): *Rujing heshang yulu* 如淨和尚語錄 (T.2002A.48:123c27-28); a verse celebrating the installment of a new steward of the monastery. The opening line recalls words attributed to Wuxie Lingmo 五洩靈默 (747-818) upon visiting Shitou Xiqian 石頭希遷 (700-791) (There are several variants; see, e.g., *Jingde chuandeng lu* 景德傳燈錄, T.2076.51:254b8-9):

若一言相契、我即住。不然便去。

If a single word accords, I stay; if not, I go away.

46 **Willow eyes sprout on new twigs** (*ryūgen hotsu shinjō* 柳眼發新條): "Willow eyes" (*ryūgen* 柳眼) are the buds of the willow tree. Dōgen will play on these "eyes" in his comment.

53. Plum Blossoms *Baika* 梅華

[53:20]

いはく、百大劫の辦道は、終始ともに一言相契なり。一念頃の功夫は、前後おなじく萬古不移なり。新條を繁茂ならしめて眼睛を發明する、新條なりといへども眼睛なり。眼睛の他にあらざる道理なりといへども、これを新條と參究す。新は、萬物咸新に參學すべし。梅華滿舊枝といふは、梅華全舊枝なり、通舊枝なり、舊枝是梅華なり。たとへば、華枝同條參、華枝同條生、華枝同條滿なり。華枝同條滿のゆえに、吾有正法、附嘱迦葉なり。面面滿拈華、華華滿破顔なり。

    He says, pursuit of the way for a hundred great kalpas is, from start to finish, "*a single word accords*"; concentrated effort for a single moment is, before or after, "*unmoved for myriad ages.*" Causing the "new twigs" to grow in rank profusion, they open the eye; though they are "new twigs," they are the eye.[47] Although it is true that they are not other than the eye, we investigate them as "new twigs." "New," we should study in "*the myriad things are all new.*" "*Plum blossoms fill the old branches*" means *the plum blossoms are the entire old branches*, means *the old branches throughout*, means *the old branches are the plum blossoms*. For instance, *it is blossoms and branches study the same twig together; blossoms and branches grow the same twig together; blossoms and branches fill the same twig together.*[48] Because blossoms and branches fill the same twig together, it is "*I have the true dharma; I bequeath it to Kāśyapa*"; it is *face after face fills the flower held up; flower after flower fills the face that smiled.*[49]

* * * * *

---

47 **Causing the "new twigs" to grow in rank profusion, they open the eye** (*shinjō o hanmo narashimete ganzei o hatsumyō suru* 新條を繁茂ならしめて眼睛を發明する): A tentative translation, assuming the unexpressed grammatical subject should be taken as "pursuit of the way" and "concentrated effort." It is also possible to read this clause as itself the subject of the following clause: i.e., "What causes the new twigs to grow in rank profusion and opens the eye is the new twigs, is the eye."

48 **blossoms and branches study the same twig together** (*ke shi dō jō san* 華枝同條參): Here and in the following two clauses, Dōgen plays with the common expressions "study together" (*dōsan* 同參) and "born together" (*dōshō* 同生); the predicates could be read, "have the same 'twig study'; have the same 'twig birth'; have the same 'twig fill.'"

49 **face after face fills the flower held up; flower after flower fills the face that smiled** (*menmen man nenge, keke man hagan* 面面滿拈華、華華滿破顔): Perhaps, meaning that each person [in the lineage of the plum blossoms] fulfills the role of the flower held up by the Buddha on Vulture Peak; each blossom fulfills the role of Mahākāśyapa breaking into a smile upon seeing the flower.

[53:21] {2:76}

先師古佛、上堂、示大衆云、楊柳粧腰帯、梅華絡臂鞲。

My former master, the Old Buddha, in a convocation, addressed the great assembly, saying,

The willows adorn themselves with sashes,
The plum blossoms tie on armguards.[50]

[53:22]

かの臂鞲は、蜀錦・和璧にあらず、梅華開なり。梅華開は、髓吾得汝なり。

Those "armguards" are not the brocade of Shu or the jade disk of He; they are the blooming of the plum.[51] The blooming of the plum is "marrow my gotten you've."[52]

* * * * *

[53:23]

波斯匿王、請賓頭盧尊者齋次、王問、承聞尊者親見佛來、是不。尊者以手策起眉毛示之。先師古佛頌云、策起眉毛答問端、親曾見佛不相瞞、至今應供四天下、春在梅梢帯雪寒。

Once, when King Prasenajit invited Venerable Piṇḍola for a meal, the king asked, "I've heard that the Venerable One has personally seen the Buddha. Is this true?"[53]

The Venerable brushed up his eyebrows with his hand to show it.

My former master, the Old Buddha, said in a verse:

---

50 **My former master, the Old Buddha** (*senshi kobutsu* 先師古佛): Lines from a verse found at *Rujing heshang yulu* 如淨和尚語錄, T.2002A.48:126c1. Dōgen quotes the same verse in his "Shōbōgenzō kenbutsu" 正法眼藏見佛.

51 **brocade of Shu or the jade disk of He** (*shokukin kaheki* 蜀錦・和璧): I.e., rare objects: the famous brocade of the ancient state of Shu (modern Sichuan); and the jade annulus, discovered by a certain Bian He 卞和, of the ancient kingdom of Chu 楚, and presented to King Wen of Zhou 周文王.

52 **"marrow my gotten you've"** (*zui go toku nyo* 髓吾得汝): A reversal of the glyphs in Bodhidharma's saying, "You've gotten my marrow." There have been various attempts to parse this as a sentence — e.g., "I as the marrow got you," — as well as suggestions that it is meant simply to identify "the blooming of the plum" with each of the words in Bodhidharma's saying. A similar play with the saying is found in "Shōbōgenzō kattō" 正法眼藏葛藤.

53 **King Prasenajit** (*Hashinoku ō* 波斯匿王): From the *Rujing heshang yulu* 如淨和尚語錄, T.2002A.48:130c7-11. Prasenajit was king of Kośala and a devout patron of the Buddha. The same exchange is also told with King Aśoka as the interlocutor. Piṇḍola (*Binzuru* 賓頭盧) was a prominent arhat among the Buddha's followers, often depicted as having long, drooping eyebrows. Dōgen cites the exchange and Rujing's verse on it elsewhere in the *Shōbōgenzō*.

53. Plum Blossoms *Baika* 梅華   163

He brushed up his eyebrows and answered the matter;
He'd personally once seen the Buddha, and they did not deceive each other.
Worthy of offerings even now, throughout the four continents.
Spring is on the twigs of the plum, cold in their girdle of snow.

[53:24]
この因縁は、波斯匿王、ちなみに尊者の見佛・未見佛を問取するなり。見佛、といふは作佛なり、作佛、といふは策起眉毛なり。尊者、もしただ阿羅漢果を證すとも、眞阿羅漢にあらずば、見佛すべからず。見佛にあらずば、作佛すべからず。作佛にあらずば、策起眉毛佛不得ならん。

    This episode concerns King Prasenajit once asking the Venerable whether he had seen the Buddha or not seen the Buddha. To "see the Buddha" means to become a buddha; to "become a buddha" means to "brush up the eyebrows." Even though the Venerable had realized only the fruit of the arhat, had he not been a true arhat, he could not have seen the Buddha. If he had not seen the Buddha, he could not have become a buddha. If he had not become a buddha, *he could not have been a buddha who "brushed up his eyebrows."*

[53:25]
しかあればしるべし、釋迦牟尼佛の面授の弟子として、すでに四果を證して後佛の出世をまつ尊者、いかでか釋迦牟尼佛をみざらん。この見釋迦牟尼佛は、見佛にあらず、釋迦牟尼佛のごとく見釋迦牟尼佛なるを、見佛と參學しきたれり。波斯匿王、この參學眼を得開せるところに、策起眉毛の好手にあふなり。親曾見佛の道旨、しづかに參佛眼あるべし。この春は、人間にあらず、佛國にかぎらず、梅梢にあり。なにとしてかしかあるとしる、雪寒の眉毛策なり。

    Thus, we should recognize that, as a disciple who had the face-to-face conferral from Buddha Śākyamuni, and who had already verified the fourth fruit and was awaiting the appearance in the world of the subsequent buddha, how could the Venerable have failed to see Buddha Śākyamuni?[54] This seeing Buddha Śākyamuni is not "seeing the Buddha": seeing Buddha Śākyamuni as does Buddha Śākyamuni has been studied as "seeing the Buddha."[55] King Prasenajit, having opened the

---

54   **verified the fourth fruit** (*shika o shōshite* 四果を證して): I.e., achieved the state of arhat, the culmination of the four stages on the path to nirvāṇa: stream entrant, once-returner, nonreturner, and arhat.

awaiting the appearance in the world of the subsequent buddha (*gobutsu no shusse o matsu* 後佛の出世をまつ): Reference to the tradition that Piṇḍola was asked by Buddha Śākyamuni not to enter nirvāṇa but to remain in saṃsāra until the coming of the future Buddha Maitreya.

55   **seeing Buddha Śākyamuni as does Buddha Śākyamuni has been studied as "seeing the Buddha"** (*Shakamuni butsu no gotoku ken Shakamuni butsu naru o, kenbutsu to sangaku shikitareri* 釋迦牟尼佛のごとく見釋迦牟尼佛なるを、見佛と參學し

eye of this study, met a skilled hand who "brushed up his eyebrows." For the meaning of the words, *"he'd personally once seen the Buddha,"* we should have the buddha eye that quietly studies it.[56] The "spring" here is not that of humans, is not limited to the buddha lands; it is "on the twigs of the plum." How do we know this? The coldness of the snow is the eyebrows brushed up.

* * * * *

[53:26] {2:77}

先師古佛云、本來面目無生死、春在梅華入畫圖。

My former master, the Old Buddha, said,
The original face has no birth or death;
Spring in the plum blossoms enters the picture.[57]

[53:27]

春を畫圖するに、楊・梅・桃・李を畫すべからず、まさに春を畫すべし。楊・梅・桃・李を畫するは、楊・梅・桃・李を畫するなり、いまだ春を畫せるにあらず。春は畫せざるべきにあらず、しかあれども先師古佛のほかは、西天東地のあひだ、春を畫せる人いまだあらず。ひとり先師古佛のみ、春を畫する尖筆頭なり。いはゆるいまの春は、畫圖の春なり、入畫圖のゆゑに。これ餘外の力量をとぶらはず、ただ梅華をして春をつかはしむるゆゑに、畫にいれ、木にいるるなり、善巧方便なり。

When picturing spring, we should not depict willows, apricots, peaches, or plums; we should depict spring.[58] To depict willows, apricots, peaches, and plums is to depict willows, apricots, peaches, and plums; it is not yet to have depicted spring. It is not that spring cannot be depicted; yet apart from my former master, the Old Buddha, there has never

---

きたれり): I.e., Piṇḍola's seeing the Buddha has been understood here as seeing Śākyamuni as Śākyamuni sees himself.

56 **we should have the buddha eye that quietly studies it** (*shizuka ni sanbutsugen aru beshi* しづかに参佛眼あるべし): The expression *sanbutsugen* 参佛眼, here rendered "the buddha eye that studies," could also be parsed "the eye that studies (or studies with) the buddha." The translation takes the sense to be that we should calmly study [the meaning of Piṇḍola's having seen the Buddha] with the omniscient eye of a buddha (*butsugen* 佛眼). A similar usage is found in the "Shōbōgenzō kenbutsu" 正法眼藏見佛:

この見佛眼、すでに参開なる現成を見佛とす。見佛眼の活路、これ参佛眼なり。

The realization in which this eye of seeing buddha has been opened is called "seeing buddha." The life-saving path of the eye of seeing buddha — this is the buddha eye of study.

57 **My former master, the Old Buddha** (*senshi kobutsu* 先師古佛): *Rujing heshang yulu* 如淨和尚語錄, T.2002A.48:131c21-22, from a verse at a cremation.

58 **willows, apricots, peaches, or plums** (*yō bai tō ri* 楊・梅・桃・李): I.e., trees that represent springtime. Here, the translation uses "apricot" for *bai* 梅 (*ume*; *Prunus mume*, "Japanese apricot") and "plum" for *ri* 李 (*sumomo*; *Prunus salicina*, "Japanese plum").

been anyone throughout Sindh in the West and the Land of the East who has depicted it. My former master, the Old Buddha, alone is a sharp brush tip that depicts spring. What is called "spring" here is the spring of the picture; for it "enters the picture."[59] Because, without seeking after any power beyond this, he just has the plum blossoms make use of the spring, it enters the picture and enters the trees. It is a skillful device.[60]

[53:28]
先師古佛、正法眼藏あきらかなるによりて、この正法眼藏を、過去・現在・未來の十方に聚會する佛祖に正傳す。このゆえに、眼睛を究徹し、梅華を開明せり。

    Because he was clear about the treasury of the true dharma eye, my former master, the Old Buddha, correctly transmitted this treasury of the true dharma eye from the buddhas and ancestors assembled in the ten directions in past, present, and future. Therefore, he has completely mastered the eye and clarified the plum blossom.

正法眼藏梅華第五十三
Treasury of the True Dharma Eye
Plum Blossoms
Number 53

[Ryūmonji MS:]

爾時日本國寬元元年癸卯十一月六日、在越州吉田縣吉嶺寺。深雪三尺、大地漫漫

At Kippō Monastery, Yoshida District, Esshū; sixth day, eleventh month of the junior water year of the rabbit, the first year of Kangen in the Land of Japan [18 December 1243][61]
Deep snow, of three feet; the whole earth everywhere spread with it.[62]

---

59 **for it "enters the picture"** (*nyū gazu no yue ni* 入畫圖のゆえに): Following Kawamura's punctuation; it is also possible to read this as an introductory clause with the following sentence: "Since it 'enters the picture'..."

60 **Because, without seeking after any power beyond this, he just has the plum blossoms make use of the spring, it enters the picture and enters the trees** (*kore yogai no rikiryō o toburawazu, tada baika o shite haru o tsukawashimuru yue ni, ga ni ire, ki ni iruru nari* これ餘外の力量をとぶらはず、ただ梅華をして春をつかはしむるゆえに、畫にいれ、木にいるるなり): Perhaps meaning something like, "because, without using any other technique, the line evokes the spring by the plum blossoms, the spring is in the picture and in the plum trees."

61 **Kippō Monastery** 吉嶺寺: Variant orthography for Kippōji 吉峰寺, also read Yoshiminedera.

62 **Deep snow, of three feet; the whole earth everywhere spread with it** (*shinsetsu sanshaku, daichi manman* 深雪三尺、大地漫漫): Echoing the line in Rujing's verse from section 2, above:

[53:29] {2:78}

もしおのづから自魔きたりて、梅華は瞿曇の眼睛ならずとおぼえば、思量すべし、このほかに何法の、梅華よりも眼睛なりぬべきを擧しきたらんにか、眼睛とみん。そのときも、これよりほかに眼睛をもとめば、いづれのときも對面不相識なるべし、相逢未拈出なるべきがゆえに。今日はわたくしの今日にあらず、大家の今日なり。直に梅華眼睛を開明なるべし、さらにもとむることやみね。

If some personal demon happens to appear, and we think that the plum blossom is not the eye of Gautama, we should think: what could we take as the eye among the things that may have been proposed as more likely than the plum blossom to be the eye?[63] At this point, if we search for the eye elsewhere, we will always be "face-to-face without recognizing each other"; for we will be "meeting without bringing it out."[64] Today is not our own today; it is everyone's today.[65] The eye of the plum blossom should be immediately clear; do not go on searching for it.

* * * * *

乃至交衾大地雪漫漫。
Till the whole earth is everywhere spread with snow.

63   **personal demon** (*jima* 自魔): Or, perhaps, "demon of the self"; an unusual term, not appearing elsewhere in the *Shōbōgenzō*, it does occur in an eccentric list of four types of demon given in the Chinese *Dafan tianwang wen fo jueyi jing* 大梵天王問佛決疑經 (ZZ.87:663a15-17): heavenly demons (*tenma* 天魔), external demons (*gema* 外魔), other demons (*tama* 他魔), self demons (*jima* 自魔).

64   **"face-to-face without recognizing each other"** (*taimen fusōshiki* 對面不相識); **"meeting without bringing it out"** (*sōhō mi nenshutsu* 相逢未拈出): Two fixed expressions from Zen literature. The former is best known from a saying of the early figure Yang Danian 楊大年 (dates unknown) (e.g., at *Chanlin sengbao juan* 禪林僧寶傳, ZZ.137:522b2-3):

對面不相識、千里却同風。
Face-to-face without recognizing each other.
For a thousand miles, the same wind.

The latter expression is a variant of a saying attributed to Danxia Tianran 丹霞天然 (739-824) (e.g., at *Zongjing lu* 宗鏡錄, T.2016.48:419b14-15):

相逢不擎出、擧意便知有。
In meeting, they don't bring it out;
But, if one thinks about it, one knows it's there.

65   **it is everyone's today** (*taike no konnichi nari* 大家の今日なり): The term *taike* 大家 (also read *daika*) can mean (a) "great one," "maestro," etc.; (b) "great house" or "great family"; or (c) "everyone." It is sometimes taken here, by extension from (c), to mean "everything."

53. Plum Blossoms *Baika* 梅華

[53:30]

先師古佛云、明明歷歷、梅華影裏休相覓、爲雨爲雲自古今、古今寥寥有何極。

> My former master, the Old Buddha, said,[66]
> So clear, so obvious:
> Stop searching in the shapes of the plum blossoms.
> Raining down and forming clouds, themselves past and present;
> Past and present, vast and vacant — where is there any limit?

[53:31]

しかあればすなはち、くもをなし、あめをなすは、梅華の云爲なり。行雲・行雨は、梅華の千曲萬重色なり、千功萬德なり。自古今は梅華なり、梅華を古今と稱するなり。

Thus, forming clouds and making rain are the words and deeds of the plum blossom. The drifting clouds and falling rain are the shapes of the plum blossom's thousand folds and myriad layers, its thousand virtues and myriad merits. "Themselves past and present" is "the plum blossoms": the plum blossoms are called "past and present."

* * * * *

[53:32]

古來、法演禪師いはく、朔風和雪振溪林、萬物潛藏恨不深、唯有嶺梅多意氣、臘前吐出歲寒心。

> Long ago, Chan Master Fayan said,[67]
> A north wind mixed with snow shakes the valley groves;
> The myriad things are buried, without deep regret.
> But there's a plum tree on the ridge whose spirits are high;
> Even before the year's end, it vomits up all wintry thoughts.

---

66 **My former master, the Old Buddha** (*senshi kobutsu* 先師古佛): From the *Rujing heshang yulu* 如淨和尚語錄, T.2002A.48:132b19-21. Dōgen's version breaks off Rujing's seven-glyph first line, which reads *quxi quxi ming lili* 去兮去兮明歷歷 ("Gone, gone, clear and obvious").

67 **Chan Master Fayan** (*Hōen zenji* 法演禪師): I.e., Wuzu Fayan 五祖法演 (d. 1104), at *Jianzhong Jingguo xudeng lu* 建中靖國續燈錄, ZZ.136:405a11-12.

[53:33] {2:79}
しかあれば、梅華の銷息を通せざるほかは、歳寒心をしりがたし。梅華小許の功徳を、朔風に和合して雪となせり。はかりしりぬ、風をひき雪をなし、歳を序あらしめ、および溪林・萬物をあらしむる、みな梅華力なり。

Thus, without being familiar with the circumstances of the plum blossom, it is hard to understand its "wintry thoughts." A few of the virtues of the plum blossom, mixed with the "north wind," have become the "snow." It is clear that what summons the wind and makes the snow, orders the year, and gives existence to the "valley groves" and the "myriad things," is entirely the power of the plum blossom.

[53:34]
太原孚上座、頌悟道云、憶昔當初未悟時、一聲畫角一聲悲、如今枕上無閑夢、一任梅華大少吹。

Senior Seat Fu of Taiyuan said in a verse celebrating his awakening to the way,

I recall in the old days, before I understood,
The sound of the painted horn was the sound of sorrow.[68]
Now, on my pillow, no more idle dreams;
Let the plum blossoms blow it as they will.

[53:35]
孚上座は、もと講者なり、夾山の典座に開發せられて、大悟せり。これ、梅華の春風を大小吹せしむるなり。

The Senior Seat Fu was originally a lecturer; developed by the cook of Mount Jia, he had a great awakening.[69] It was the plum blossoms letting the spring winds blow as they will.

---

68 **Senior Seat Fu of Taiyuan** (*Taigen Fu jōza* 太原孚上座): Dates unknown; a disciple of Xuefeng Yicun 雪峰義存 (822-908). Dōgen's source is unknown. A (slightly variant) version of this verse is attributed to Senior Seat Fu 孚上座 in the late fourteenth-century anthology *Chanzong zaduhai* 禪宗雜毒海 (ZZ.114:131a4-5).

painted horn (*gakaku* 畫角): An ancient sonorous decorated wind instrument, used in the military to rouse the troops and in imperial processions to warn of their passing; here, likely, reveille (*kukaku* 鼓角), upon hearing which, it is said, Fu had his awakening.

69 **developed by the cook of Mount Jia** (*Kassan no tenzo ni kaihotsu serarete* 夾山の典座に開發せられて): The name of the cook is unknown; the story of his guiding Fu is told in several sources (see, e.g., case 99 of the *Biyan lu* 碧巖錄, T.2003.48:222b26-c13). The cook laughed during Fu's lecture on the *Nirvāṇa Sūtra*'s teaching on the dharma body and, when subsequently questioned about it, advised Fu to sit in meditation in order to understand the sūtra; Fu sat all night and, at the sound of the drum marking the fifth watch, suddenly had an understanding.

TREASURY OF THE TRUE DHARMA EYE

NUMBER 54

Washing and Purifying
Senjō
洗淨

Washing and Purifying

Senjō

Introduction

According its colophon, this chapter is one of the earliest texts of the *Shōbōgenzō*, composed in the autumn of 1239 at Dōgen's newly established Kōshōji. It represents number 54 in the seventy-five-chapter *Shōbōgenzō* and number 7 in the Honzan edition; it is not found in the sixty-chapter compilation.

Like the "Senmen" 洗面 ("Washing the Face") chapter, "Senjō" is a work on monastic hygiene. The title term, "washing and purifying," was a euphemism in Song-dynasty Buddhist monasteries for the procedures to be followed when using the toilet. The procedures discussed here were not original to Dōgen: as his quotations suggest, they are drawn from the *Chanyuan qinggui* 禪苑清規 (*Rules of Purity for the Chan Park*, compiled in 1103), and other works on monastic rules and regulations. Unlike such works, however, Dōgen adds commentary on the spiritual significance of the procedures as the embodied practice of the buddhas and ancestors.

正法眼藏第五十四
Treasury of the True Dharma Eye
Number 54

洗淨
Washing and Purifying

[54:1] {2:80}
佛祖の護持しきたれる修證あり、いはゆる不染汚なり。

There is a practice and verification upheld by the buddhas and ancestors: it is "not defiling."

[54:2]
南嶽山觀音院大慧禪師、因六祖問、還假修證不。大慧云、修證不無、染汚即不得。六祖云、只是不染汚、諸佛之所護念、汝亦如是、吾亦如是、乃至西天祖師亦如是、云云。

> Chan Master Dahui of Guanyin Cloister on Mount Nanyue was asked by the Sixth Ancestor, "Does it nevertheless depend on practice and verification?"[1]
>
> Dahui said, "It's not that it lacks practice and verification, but it can't be defiled by them."
>
> The Sixth Ancestor said, "Just this 'not defiled' is what the buddhas bear in mind. You're also like this, I'm also like this, down to all the ancestral masters of Sindh in the West are also like this."
>
> (End quote.)[2]

---

1 **Chan Master Dahui of Guanyin Cloister on Mount Nanyue** (*Nangakusan Kannonin Daie zenji* 南嶽山觀音院大慧禪師): I.e., Nanyue Huairang 南嶽懷讓 (677-744). The passage quoted here is found in a well-known conversation between Nanyue and his master, the Sixth Ancestor, Huineng 慧能, versions of which are found in several Chinese sources, as well as Dōgen's *shinji Shōbōgenzō* 眞字正法眼藏 (DZZ5:178, case 101), and introduced often in the *Shōbōgenzō*. See Supplementary Notes, s.v. "What thing is it that comes like this?"

"**Does it nevertheless depend on practice and verification?**" (*kan ka shushō fu* 還假修證不): The question is preceded by the following exchange. When Nanyue went to visit Huineng, the Ancestor asked him where he was coming from. Nanyue said that he was coming from the National Teacher An on Mount Song. Huineng asked, "What thing is it that comes like this?" (*ze jūmo butsu inmo rai* 是什麼物恁麼來). Nanyue answered, "To say it's like any thing wouldn't hit it." The thing that "comes like this" (*inmo rai* 恁麼來) is a play on *nyorai* 如來 (S. *tathāgata*; "thus-come one"), an epithet of the buddhas.

2 **End quote** (*unnun* 云云): Parenthetical indication in the original.

[54:3]

大比丘三千威儀經云、淨身者、洗大小便、剪十指爪。

In the *Sūtra of the Three Thousand Rules of Deportment for Great Bhikṣus*, it is said, "To 'purify the body' is to wash upon urinating and defecating, and to clip the nails of one's ten fingers."[3]

[54:4]

しかあれば、身心これ不染汚なれども、淨身の法あり、心法あり。ただ身心をきよむるのみにあらず、國土・樹下をもきよむるなり。國土いまだかつて塵穢あらざれども、きよむるは諸佛之所護念なり。佛果にいたりてなほ退せず、廢せざるなり。その宗旨、はかりつくすべきことかたし。作法、これ宗旨なり、得道、これ作法なり。

Thus, even though body and mind are "not defiled," there is a procedure for purifying the body; there is a procedure for the mind.[4] It not only purifies body and mind; it purifies the land and the bases of trees as well.[5] Even though the land has never had any dust and pollution, to purify it is *"what the buddhas bear in mind."* Having reached the fruit of buddhahood, they still do not regress, do not abandon it. The essential point of this is not something that can ever be fully calculated. Observance — this is the essential point; gaining the way — this is observance.[6]

---

3 *Sūtra of the Three Thousand Rules of Deportment for Great Bhikṣus* (*Dai biku sanzen iigi kyō* 大比丘三千威儀): *Da biqiu sanqian weiyi* 大比丘三千威儀, T.1470.24:914a16.

4 **there is a procedure for purifying the body; there is a procedure for the mind** (*jōshin no hō ari, shinbō ari* 淨身の法あり、心法あり): The term *shinbō* 心法 may evoke "the mind dharma" transmitted in the Zen lineage but should probably here be taken in parallel with the preceding clause.

5 **the land and the bases of trees** (*kokudo juge* 國土・樹下): An unusual combination. The term *kokudo* 國土 ("land") is multivalent and can refer to the nation, the earth, or a world, such as the "pure land" (*jōdo* 淨土) of Buddha Amitābha. The term *juge* 樹下 ("beneath, or at the bases of, trees") translates the Sankrit *vṛkṣa-mūla* ("tree root"), used in reference to the location of spiritual practice at the foot of trees — as in Siddhārtha's practice under the bodhi tree. Possibly, reflecting the vision of buddhas seated under jeweled trees in countless buddha lands described in the *Lotus Sūtra* (*Miaofa lianhua jing* 妙法蓮華經, T.262.9:33b15-17).

6 **Observance — this is the essential point; gaining the way — this is observance** (*sahō, kore shūshi nari, tokudō, kore sahō nari* 作法、これ宗旨なり、得道、これ作法なり): "Observance" (*sahō* 作法) refers to the rites and procedures of monastic practice; "gaining the way" (*tokudō* 得道) may refer either to the ritual entrance into the monastic order or, as more likely here, to the attainment of spiritual awakening. This line is likely the *locus classicus* for the phrase "observance is the essential point" in the later Sōtō dictum, "deportment is the buddha dharma; observance is the essential point" (*igi soku buppō, sahō kore shūshi* 威儀即佛法、作法是宗旨).

54. Washing and Purifying Senjō 洗淨

[54:5] {2:81}

華嚴經淨行品云、左右便利、當願衆生、蠲除穢汚、無婬怒癡。已而就水、當願衆生、向無上道得出世法。以水滌穢、當願衆生、具足淨忍、畢竟無垢。

> In the "Pure Practice" chapter of the *Flower Garland Sūtra*, it is said,[7]
> Doing what is needed to relieve myself,
> I pray all living beings
> May be rid of filth and pollution
> And free from lust, anger, and delusion.
> Having finished, going for water,
> I pray all living beings
> May approach the unsurpassed way
> And attain the supramundane dharma.
> Using the water to wash away filth,
> I pray all living beings
> May be endowed with pure patience
> And be in the end without impurities.

[54:6]

水、かならずしも本淨にあらず、本不淨にあらず。身、かならずしも本淨にあらず、本不淨にあらず。諸法、またかくのごとし。水、いまだ情・非情にあらず、身、いまだ情・非情にあらず、諸法、またかくのごとし。佛世尊説、それかくのごとし。しかあれども、水をもて身をきよむるにあらず、佛法によりて佛法を保任するに、この儀あり、これを洗淨と稱す。佛祖の一身心を、したしくして正傳するなり、佛祖の一句子を、ちかく見聞するなり、佛祖の一光明を、あきらかに住持するなり。おほよそ、無量無邊の功德を現成せしむるなり。身心に修行を威儀せしむる正當恁麼時、すなはち久遠の本行を具足圓成せり。このゆゑに、修行の身心、本現するなり。

Water is not necessarily intrinsically pure, nor is it intrinsically impure. The body is not necessarily intrinsically pure, nor is it intrinsically impure. All dharmas are also like this. Water is neither sentient nor insentient; the body is neither sentient nor insentient. All dharmas are also like this. The teachings of the Buddha, the World-Honored One, are also like this. However, it is not that we use water to purify the body; rather, in maintaining the buddha dharma by means of the buddha dharma, there is this rite, which is called "washing and purifying." It is to be intimate with and directly transmit the one body and mind of the buddhas and ancestors; it is to see and hear firsthand the one line of the buddhas and ancestors; it is clearly to sustain the one radiance of the buddhas and ancestors. In sum, it is to make manifest their incalculable, limitless

---

7 **"Pure Practice" chapter of the *Flower Garland Sūtra*** (*Kegonkyō jōgyōbon* 華嚴經淨行品): From the *Huayan jing* 華嚴經, at T.278.9:431a27-b2.

virtues. At the very moment that we make the practice our deportment in body and mind, we are fully endowed with and perfectly attain his original practice long ago.[8] Therefore, the body and mind of practice and verification appear in their original form.

[54:7] {2:82}
十指の爪をきるべし。十指といふは、左右の兩手の指のつめなり。足指の爪、おなじくきるべし。

One should cut the nails of one's ten fingers. "Ten fingers" means the nails on the fingers of both hands, left and right. Toenails should also be cut.

[54:8]
經にいはく、つめのながさ、もし一麥ばかりになれば、罪をうるなり。

In a sūtra, it is said, "If the length of the nails exceeds one grain of barley, that is an offense."[9]

[54:9]
しかあれば、爪をながくすべからず、爪のながきは、おのづから外道の先蹤なり、ことさらつめをきるべし。しかあるに、いま大宋國の僧家のなかに、參學眼そなはらざるともがら、おほく爪をながからしむ。あるひは一寸・兩寸、および三・四寸にながきもあり。これ、非法なり、佛法の身心にあらず。佛家の稽古あらざるによりて、かくのごとし。有道の尊宿は、しかあらざるなり。

Thus, the nails should not be long. To have long nails is itself a precendent of other paths; so it is especially important to cut the nails. Nevertheless, at present, in the monastic order of the Land of the Great Song, the types not endowed with the eye of study frequently grow their nails long. Some are one inch or two inches, or even three or four inches long. This is improper; it is not the body and mind of the buddha dharma. They

---

8 **we are fully endowed with and perfectly attain his original practice long ago** (*kuon no hongyō o gusoku enjō seri* 久遠の本行を具足圓成せり): Allusion to the career of Buddha Śākyamuni, as told in the *Lotus Sūtra*. The expression "original practice" (*hongyō* 本行), which occurs several times in the *Shōbōgenzō*, recalls a famous passage (*Miaofa lianhua jing* 妙法蓮華經, T.262.9:42c22-23):

諸善男子、我本行菩薩道所成壽命、今猶未盡、復倍上數。

Good sons, the lifespan attained by my original practice of the bodhisattva path is even now still not exhausted; it is twice the above number.

Similarly, the terms "long ago" (*kuon* 久遠) and "perfectly attain" (*enjō* 圓成) suggest the stock phrase "actually attained long ago" (*kuon jitsujō* 久遠實成), regularly used to describe Śākyamuni's ancient attainment of buddhahood (at *Miaofa lianhua jing* 妙法蓮華經, T.262.9:42b12).

9 **In a sūtra, it is said** (*kyō ni iwaku* 經にいはく): Dōgen's source for this quotation, given in Japanese, is unknown.

54. Washing and Purifying *Senjō* 洗淨

are like this because they lack investigation of the ancients in the house of the buddhas. Venerables who possess the way are not like this.

[54:10]

あるひは長髪ならしむるともがらあり、これも非法なり。大國の僧家の所作なりとして、正法ならん、とあやまることなかれ。先師古佛、ふかくいましめのことばを、天下の僧家の長髪・長爪のともがらにたまふにいはく、

Again, there are those who grow their hair long, which is also improper. Do not mistakenly think that, because it is done by monastics of a great country, it is correct practice. My former master, the Old Buddha, had severe words of admonishment for monastics throughout the land who had long hair and long nails, saying,[10]

[54:11]

不會淨髪、不是俗人、不是僧家、便是畜生。古來佛祖、誰是不淨髪者。如今不會淨髪、箇眞箇是畜生。

Those who do not keep the tonsure are not laymen and are not monastics; they are beasts. From ancient times, who among the buddhas and ancestors did not keep the tonsure? Anyone at present who does not keep the tonsure truly is a beast.

[54:12]

かくのごとく示衆するに、年來不剃頭のともがら、剃頭せるおほし。

When he instructed the assembly in this way, there were many of those who had not shaved their heads for years who shaved their heads.

[54:13]

あるひは上堂、あるいは普説のとき、彈指かまびすしくして責呵す、

Whether in convocations or in public sermons, he loudly snapped his fingers and rebuked them, [saying],[11]

---

10 **My former master, the Old Buddha** (*senshi kobutsu* 先師古佛): I.e., Tiantong Rujing 天童如淨 (1162-1227). The source of Dōgen's report of Rujing's words, given here in Chinese, is not known, but a similar passage, including the phrase, "truly is a beast" (*shinko ze chikushō* 眞箇是畜生), occurs in Dōgen's record of his conversations with Rujing; see *Hōkyō ki* 寶慶記, DZZ.7:14, number 9.

11 **he loudly snapped his fingers and rebuked them** (*danshi kamabisushiku shite shakuka su* 彈指かまびすしくして責呵す): The snapping of the fingers can, among other uses, indicate a warning; see below, section 23. What follows in the next section is offered as a report, in Japanese, of Rujing's words — though, without independent textual evidence, it is unclear to what extent Dōgen is paraphrasing his master's teachings.

[54:14] {2:83}

いかなる道理としらず、胡亂に長髪・長爪なる。あはれむべし、南浮の身心をして非道におけること。近來二三百年、祖師道、癈せるゆゑに、しかのごとくのともがらおほし。かくのごとくのやから、寺院の主人となり、師號に署して、爲衆の相をなす、人天の無福なり。いま天下の諸山に、道心箇渾無なり、得道箇久絕なり、祇管破落儻のみなり。

For whatever reason, they wantonly grow out their hair and grow out their nails. How pitiful that they would put a body and mind of Jambudvīpa on the wrong path.[12] Because the way of the ancestral masters has been abandoned over these past two or three hundred years, there are many such types. That a bunch like this has become the heads of monasteries, has been granted "master" titles, and has served as officials of the saṃgha — this is misfortune for humans and devas.[13] At the various mountains throughout the land at present, *those with the mind of the way are entirely absent, those who have gained the way are long extinct*, and all that remain are *just a gang of degenerates*.[14]

[54:15]

かくのごとく普説するに、諸方に長老の名をみだりにせるともがら、うらみず、陳説なし。しるべし、長髪は佛祖のいましむるところ、長爪は外道の所行なり。佛祖の兒孫、これらの非法をこのむべからず。身心をきよからしむべし、剪爪・剃髪すべきなり。

When he gave public sermons in this way, those from all quarters improperly named "elders" did not resent it and had nothing to say for themselves. We should know that growing out one's hair is warned against by the buddhas and ancestors, and that growing out one's nails is a practice of other paths. Descendants of the buddhas and ancestors should not be attracted to these improprieties. They should keep their bodies and minds pure and should cut their nails and shave their heads.

---

12 **put a body and mind of Jambudvīpa on the wrong path** (*Nanbu no shinjin o shite hidō ni okeru* 南浮の身心をして非道における): The term *Nanbu* 南浮 indicates "Jambudvīpa in the south": i.e., the continent to the south of Mount Sumeru in Buddhist cosmology. Of the four continents, it is the one on which a buddha appears; see Supplementary Notes, s.v. "Four Continents." "Wrong path" translates *hidō* 非道, which has a range of connotations, including "not the way of the buddhas (*butsudō* 佛道)," "not in accord with the principles (*dōri* 道理) of Buddhism," "not consistent with the way (*dō* 道) of humans," "characteristic of, or leading to, the 'evil paths' of animals, ghosts, and denizens of hell." See Supplementary Notes, s.v. "Body and mind," and "Six paths."

13 **served as officials of the saṃgha** (*ishu no sō o nasu* 爲衆の相をなす): I.e., ministers or officials appointed by the imperial court to oversee the multitude (*shu* 衆) of monks and nuns.

14 **various mountains** (*shozan* 諸山): Also read *shosan*; a term for the major Buddhist monasteries.

54. Washing and Purifying *Senjō* 洗淨

[54:16]

洗大小便おこたらしむることなかれ。舍利弗、この法をもて、外道を降伏せしむることありき。外道の本期にあらず、身子が素懷にあらざれども、佛祖の威儀現成するところに、邪法おのづから伏するなり。

Do not neglect to wash when urinating and defecating. There was an instance when Śāriputra, by means of this procedure, converted the follower of an other path.[15] It was not the prior expectation of the follower of the other path, nor was it the original intention of Śāriputra; but where the deportment of the buddhas and ancestors is manifested, the false dharma submits of its own accord.[16]

[54:16] {2:84}

樹下・露地に修習するときは、起屋なし。便宜の溪谷・河水等によりて、分土洗淨するなり。これは灰なし、ただ二七丸の土をもちいる。二七丸をもちいる法は、まづ、法衣をぬぎてたたみおきてのち、くろからず黄色なる土をとりて、一丸のおほきさ、大なる大豆許に分して、いしのうへ、あるひは便宜のところに、七丸をひとならべにおきて、二七丸をふたへにならべおく。そののち、磨石にもちいるべき石をまうく。そののち屙す。屙後、使籌、あるいは使紙。そののち、水辺にいたりて洗淨する。まづ三丸の土をたづさへて洗淨す。一丸土を掌にとりて、水すこしばかりをいれて、水に合してときて、泥よりもうすく、漿ばかりになして、まづ小便を洗淨す。つぎに一丸の土をもてさきのごとくして大便處を洗淨す。つぎに一丸の土をさきのごとくして、略して觸手をあらふ。

When engaging in practice under trees and in the open, there are no buildings.[17] One engages in purification with handfuls of earth, using a convenient valley stream or river water. For this there are no ashes, just two sets of seven balls of earth.[18] The procedure for using the two sets of seven balls is: first, remove, fold, and set aside one's dharma robe; then, taking earth that is yellowish, not black, shape it into balls that are about the size of large beans, arrange them in a single row of seven balls on a rock or some other convenient spot, and lay out a second row parallel to the first one, so that there are two sets of seven balls.[19] Next,

---

15   **Śāriputra** (*Sharihotsu* 舍利弗): The story, which occurs in several sources, tells of a brahmin who was so impressed by the toilet practices of the Buddha's disciple, Śāriputra, that he joined the Buddhist order. See, e.g., Yijing's 義淨 translation of the *Mūla-sarvāstivāda-vinaya* (*Pinaiye zashi* 毘奈耶雜事, T.1451.24:0276c29-277b4).

16   **It was not the prior expectation of the follower of the other path** (*gedō no hongo ni arazu* 外道の本期にあらず): At least in Yijing's version of the story, the brahmin seems in fact to have had a fixation on purity and had been visiting religious orders precisely to observe their toilet practices. The same passage also notes that Śāriputra was well aware that his actions were being observed.

17   **there are no buildings** (*kioku nashi* 起屋なし): I.e., fixed toilet facilities.

18   **ashes** (*hai* 灰): The use of ash as a detergent will be discussed in section 27, below.

19   **earth that is yellowish, not black** (*kurokarazu kiiro naru tsuchi* くろからず黄色

obtain a rock that is suitable for use as a scouring stone. After that, you relieve yourself. When finished relieving yourself, use a toilet stick or use paper.[20] After that, go by the water and wash and purify yourself. First, take three balls of earth and perform the washing and purifying.[21] Holding one ball of earth in the palm, pour in a little water, mix the earth and water together, make a thick fluid that is thinner than mud, and begin by washing and purifying the urine.[22] Next, take one ball of earth and, using the same procedure, wash and purify the place of defecation. Next, prepare one ball of earth as before and use it to wash the hand that has touched filth.

[54:17]
寺舍に居してよりこのかたは、その屋を起立せり、これを東司と稱す。あるときは圊といひ、廁といふときもありき。僧家の所住にかならずあるべき屋舍なり。

Ever since there has been dwelling in monastery buildings, a facility for this purpose has been built; it is called the "eastern office."[23] At times it is called the "outhouse," and there were times when it was called the

---

なる土): I.e., light brown earth that is mostly sand or clay, with little organic soil mixed in.

20 **toilet stick** (*chū* 籌): A wood or bamboo instrument, shaped like a handled scoop or spatula, used to wipe oneself after defecating; discussed below, section 24.

21 **First, take three balls of earth and perform the washing and purifying** (*mazu sangan no tsuchi o tazusaete senjō su* まづ三丸の土をたづさへて洗淨す): It is strange that Dōgen, after explaining how to prepare "two sets of seven balls" (*ni shichi gan* 二七丸), concludes this section on relieving oneself outdoors by outlining a procedure that uses only three balls of earth: one for washing after urinating, a second for washing after defecating, and a third for washing "the hand that has touched filth" (*sokushu* 觸手). Also, he says nothing about the "scouring stone" (*maseki* 磨石) that he mentions four sentences earlier.

22 **begin by washing and purifying the urine** (*mazu shōben o senjō su* まづ小便を洗淨す). Because this sentence uses the euphemism "lesser ease" (*shōben* 小便) to refer to "urine" or "urinating," and treats that noun as the object of the compound verb "to wash and purify" (*senjō* 洗淨), it is not clear what this action entails. We know from more explicit accounts of this procedure in Buddhist monastic rules that the mixture of dirt and water is used to wash the area around the urethral opening (in males, the tip of the penis). The muddy water would then be rinsed off with clean water, but the directions given by Dōgen do not make that explicit. The same ambiguity is found in Dōgen's subsequent discussion of the washing and purifying of "the place of greater ease" (*daibensho* 大便處), or "defecation."

23 **"eastern office"** (*tōsu* 東司): The name for this facility is clearly a euphemism, but its derivation is not known. In the Song monasteries that Dōgen visited, there was an eastern office (*tōsu* 東司, or "toilet," as we shall call it here) for use by the great assembly of monks who resided in the saṃgha hall, but it was located on the western side of the monastery. Major monasteries had a number of smaller toilets located in other places, as well, such as in the administrative wing and the abbot's quarters.

"toilet." It is a room or building that must always exist wherever monastics reside.

[54:18]
東司にいたる法は、かならず手巾をもつ。その法は、手巾をふたへにおりて、ひだりのひぢのうへにあたりて、衫袖のうへにかくるなり。すでに東司にいたりては、淨竿に手巾をかくべし。かくる法は、臂にかけたりつるがごとし。もし九條・七條等の袈裟を著してきたれらば、手巾にならべてかくべし。おちざらんやうに打併すべし、倉卒になげかくることなかれ。よくよく記號すべし。記號といふは、淨竿に字をかけり。白紙にかきて、月輪のごとく圓にして、淨竿につけ列せり。しかあるを、いづれの字にわが直綴はおけりとわすれず、みだらざるを、記號といふなり。衆家おほくきたらんに、自他の竿位を亂すべからず。

The procedure for going to the toilet requires that one always carry a hand cloth. The method for that is to fold the hand cloth in two and drape it over the left arm below the crook of the elbow, on top of the robe sleeve. Having arrived at the toilet, one should hang the hand cloth over the pure pole.[24] The method for hanging it is like that when draping it over the arm. If one comes wearing a nine-panel or seven-panel *kāṣāya*, or the like, one should hang that alongside the hand cloth. One should align them so they do not fall; do not toss them on the pole in haste.[25] Be very careful to take note. "Taking note" refers to the fact that there are letters written on the pure pole, called "designations"; they are written on white paper, made into a circle like the disc of the moon, and attached at intervals to the pure pole. "Taking note" means to avoid mix-ups by not forgetting by which letter one's own long robe has been left. When the community has many people in it, we should not confuse one's own pole place with those of others.

[54:19]
このあひだ、衆家きたりてたちつらなれば、叉手して揖すべし。揖するに、かならずしもあひむかひ曲躬せず、ただ叉手をむねのまへにあてて氣色ある揖なり。東司にては、直綴を著せざるにも、衆家と揖し氣色するなり。もし兩手ともにいまだ觸せず、兩手ともにものをひさげざるには、兩手を叉して揖すべし。もしすでに一手を觸せしめ、一手にものを提せらんときは、一手にて揖すべし。一手にて揖するには、手をあほげて、指頭すこしきかがめて、水を掬せんとするがごとくしてもちて、頭をいささか低頭せんとするがごとく揖するなり。他、かくのごとくせば、おのれ、かくのごとくすべし、おのれ、かくのごとくせば、他、またしかあるべし。

---

24 **pure pole** (*jōkan* 淨竿): A raised horizontal pole used for hanging clothes, etc.

25 **One should align them so they do not fall** (*ochizaran yō ni tahei su beshi* おちざらんやうに打併すべし). That is, one should make sure that the two ends of the cloth or robe that hang down on either side of the pole are lined up (*tahei* 打併) at the same height so the item is balanced and does not slip off.

During this time, if a member of the community comes and stands next to one, one should fold one's hands and then make a bow with hands clasped. In bowing with hands clasped, one does not necessarily face the other person and bend one's body: just fold one's hands, hold them up to one's chest, and give an indication of bowing with hands clasped. In the toilet, even if one is not wearing one's long robe, one gives an indication of bowing with hands clasped to a member of the community. If both of one's hands have yet to touch filth, and neither hand is holding anything, then one should fold the two hands and bow. If one hand has already touched filth, or if one hand is holding something, one should bow with a single hand. To bow with a single hand, turn the hand palm up, bend the fingers slightly, holding them as if scooping up a handful of water, and make a slight nod as if to lower one's head, thereby suggesting a bow with hands clasped. If the other person makes a particular sort of bow, we should reciprocate with that sort of bow; if we bow in a certain way, the other person should also bow in that way.

[54:20] {2:85}
褊衫および直裰を脱して、手巾のかたはらにかくる法は、直裰ぬぎとりて、ふたつのそでをうしろへあはせて、ふたつのわきのしたをとりあはせてひきあぐれば、ふたつのそでかさなれる。このときは、左手にては直裰のうなぢのうらのもとをとり、右手にてはわきをひきあぐれば、ふたつのたもとと左右の兩襟とかさなるなり。兩袖と兩襟とをかさねて、又たたざまになかよりをりて、直裰のうなぢを淨竿の那辺へなげこす。直裰の裙ならびに袖口等は、竿の遮辺にかかれり。たとへば、直裰の合腰、淨竿にかくるなり。つぎに、竿にかけたりつる手巾の遮・那兩端をひきちがへて、直裰よりひきこして、手巾のかからざりつるかたにて、又ちがへてむすびとどむ。兩三匝もちがへちがへしてむすびて、直裰を淨竿より落地せしめざらんとなり。あるひは直裰にむかひて合掌す。

The procedure for removing both partial robes and long robes and hanging them next to the hand cloth is as follows.[26] Take off the long robe, fold the two sleeves to the rear and match them up; if one aligns the two armpits and lifts them up, the two sleeves will double up. At this point, if one grasps the inside of the nape of the long robe with the left hand and holds the waist with the right hand and lifts, the two sleeves and the lapels on the left and right will fold over each other. With the two sleeves and two lapels thus doubled up, again fold in half lengthwise and throw the collar of the long robe over the far side of the pure pole. The skirt of the long robe, together with the armholes of the sleeves, etc., hang on the near side of the pole. In other words, the joined waist of the

---

26 **partial robes and long robes** (*hensan oyobi jikitotsu* 褊衫および直裰): "Partial robe" (*hensan* 褊衫; also written 偏衫 and read *henzan*) refers to the upper garment of a two-part robe, worn with a skirt (*kunsu* 裙子); "long robe" (*jikitotsu* 直裰) refers to a single-piece robe, in which the upper and lower parts have been sewn together.

54. Washing and Purifying *Senjō* 洗淨

long robe is what hangs on the pure pole. Next, take the two ends of the hand cloth that are hanging over the near and far sides of the pole, cross them, wrap them around the long robe, cross them again and tie them in a knot on the side where the hand cloth is not attached to the pole. By wrapping it two or three times around and tying it, the long robe is kept from falling on the ground from the pure pole. One may also face the long robe and bow with hands together.

[54:21]
つぎに絆子をとりて兩臂にかく。つぎに、淨架にいたりて、淨桶に水を盛りて、右手に提して淨廁にのぼる。淨桶に水をいるる法は、十分にみつることなかれ、九分を度とす。廁門のまへにして、換鞋すべし。蒲鞋をはきて、自鞋を廁門の前に脱するなり、これを換鞋といふ。

Next, take a binding cord and tie up [the sleeves of] both arms.[27] Next, go to the washstand, fill a cleaning bucket with water, carry it in the left hand and climb up to the toilet stall. The procedure for putting water into the cleaning bucket is not to fill it all the way, but to stop when it is nine-tenths full. When in front of the toilet stall door, one should change footwear. To put on the reed slippers and leave one's own footwear in front of the lavatory door is called "changing footwear."

[54:22] {2:86}
禪苑清規云、欲上東司、應須預往、勿致臨時內逼倉卒。乃疊袈裟、安寮中案上、或淨竿上。

In the *Rules of Purity for the Chan Park*, it is said,

> When one wishes to go to the toilet, one should set out in advance; do not let the onset of internal pressure compel you to rush.[28] Then, fold the *kāṣāya*, leaving it on the bench in one's quarters or on the pure pole.

---

27   **binding cord** (*bansu* 絆子): A cord to tie back the sleeves. It is tied in such a way that it forms a horizontal figure eight: the two ends of the "8" are looped over both shoulders, and the cross is in the center of the back. This effectively ties up the rectangular sleeves of a robe or undergarment, keeping them out of the way and clean when one is using the toilet or working with one's hands (preparing food, cleaning, etc.). Dōgen does not say here what garment is to be tied up, but it cannot be the "partial robe" (*hensan* 編衫) or long robe (*jikitotsu* 直裰), because those have already been removed; it must be a sleeved undershirt, worn next to the skin.

28   ***Rules of Purity for the Chan Park*** (*Zennen shingi* 禪苑清規): *Chanyuan qinggui* 禪苑清規, ZZ.111:912a4-5, from the opening lines of a section entitled "Defecating and Urinating" (*daxiao bianli* 大小便利), on which Dōgen is relying in the following account of toilet practice.

[54:23]

廁内にいたりて、左手にて門扇を掩す。つぎに、淨桶の水をすこしばかり槽裏に瀉す。つぎに淨桶を當面の淨桶位に安ず。つぎに、たちながら槽にむかひて彈指三下すべし。彈指のとき、左手は拳にして左腰につけてもつなり。つぎに袴口・衣角ををさめて、門にむかひて兩足に槽脣の兩辺をふみて、蹲居し屙す。兩辺をけがすことなかれ、前後にそましむることなかれ。このあひだ默照なるべし。隔壁と語笑し、聲をあげて吟詠することなかれ。涕唾狼藉なることなかれ、努氣卒暴なることなかれ。壁面に字をかくべからず、廁籌をもて地面を画くことなかれ。

Once inside the toilet stall, use the left hand to close the door panels. Next, pour just a little water from the cleaning bucket inside the toilet bowl.[29] Next, set the cleaning bucket down at the cleaning bucket place in front of you. Next, while still standing, face the toilet bowl and snap your fingers three times.[30] When snapping the fingers, make the left hand into a fist and hold it against the left side of the waist. Next, one gathers up the hem of one's underpants and the corners of one's robe, faces the door, straddles the toilet bowl with one foot on each of the opposite edges, squats, and relieves oneself. Do not dirty the area on either side, and do not contaminate the area in front or behind. During this time one should be in silent illumination.[31] Do not speak or titter with people on the other side of the partition wall, or raise one's voice and sing songs. Do not get "*snot and spit scattered about*"; do not grunt with exertion or act in haste.[32] We should not write words on the partition wall. Do not

29   **toilet bowl** (*sō* 槽): A pot, typically made of clay, that was set into (flush with) the floor inside each lavatory stall and served as the receptacle for human waste. Since it had to be cleaned out by hand periodically, the purpose of sprinkling water in it before use may have been to prevent feces from sticking to it.

30   **snap your fingers three times** (*danji sange* 彈指三下): According to the "Defecating and Urinating" section of the *Rules of Purity for the Chan Park*, which Dōgen is using as a reference here, the purpose of snapping the fingers is to warn away the excrement-eating ghosts (*tanfun shi ki* 噉糞之鬼) that haunt the toilet (*Chanyuan qinggui* 禪苑清規, ZZ.111:912a9-10).

31   **During this time one should be in silent illumination** (*kono aida mokushō naru beshi* このあひだ默照なるべし). "Silent illumination" (*mokushō* 默照) was a type of meditation promoted by Hongzhi Zhengjue 宏智正覺 (1091–1157), Zhenxie Qingliao 眞歇清了 (1088–1151), and other leaders of the Caodong 曹洞 lineage in Song China. The translation follows Kawamura's edition; but other textual witnesses have here, "one should maintain silence" (*mokunen* 默然), which in the context would seem the better reading. The *Rules of Purity for the Chan Park*, on which Dōgen is relying, says nothing of silent illumination in the toilet.

32   **"snot and spit scattered about"** (*tei da rōzeki* 涕唾狼藉): A set phrase, quoted from *Chanyuan qinggui* 禪苑清規, ZZ.111:912a10.

grunt with exertion or act in haste (*doki sotsubō* 努氣卒暴): The text may have been corrupted here. The compound expression "act in haste" (*sotsubō* 卒暴) seems out of context, and in fact the *Rules of Purity for the Chan Park* has at this point the more likely,

54. Washing and Purifying Senjō 洗淨   183

use the toilet stick to draw on the earthen floor.

[54:24]
厠屎退後、すべからく使籌すべし。又、かみをもちいる法あり、故紙をもちいるべからず、字をかきたらん紙、もちいるべからず。淨籌・觸籌わきまふべし。籌は、ながさ八寸につくりて三角なり、ふとさは手母指大なり。漆にてぬれるもあり、未漆なるもあり。觸は、籌斗になげをき、淨は、もとより籌架にあり。籌架は、槽のまへの板頭のほとりにおけり。

After relieving oneself of feces and stepping back, one should use the toilet stick. Also, there are rules for using paper: one must not use waste paper, and one must not use paper that has words written on it. Be sure to keep clean toilet sticks separate from soiled toilet sticks. A toilet stick is made eight inches long and is triangular. Its thickness is that of a thumb. There are some that are coated with lacquer, and some that are not lacquered. Soiled ones are to be thrown into the toilet stick receptacle. Clean ones are normally on the toilet stick stand. The toilet stick stand is placed near the plank that is in front of the toilet bowl.

[54:25] {2:87}
使籌・使紙ののち、洗淨する法は、右手に淨桶をもちて、左手をよくよくぬらしてのち、左手を掬につくりて水をうけて、まづ小便を洗淨す、三度。つぎに、大便をあらふ。洗淨、如法にして淨潔ならしむべし。このあひだ、あらく淨桶をかたぶけて、水をして手のほかにあましおとし、あぶしちらして、水をはやくうしなふことなかれ。

The procedure for washing and purifying after using toilet sticks or using paper is as follows. Carry the cleaning bucket with the left hand. After thoroughly wetting the left hand, make a cup with the left hand and scoop out some water. Begin by washing and purifying the urine three times.[33] Next, wash and purify the [place of] defecation. In washing and purifying, one must maintain propriety and keep one's thoughts pure. During this time, be careful not to run out of water too soon by roughly tipping the cleaning bucket, spilling excess water out of one's hand, or splashing it about.

"make sounds by grunting with exertion" (*nuqi zuosheng* 努氣作聲). (*Chanyuan qinggui* 禪苑清規, ZZ.111:912a10.)

33 **Begin by washing and purifying the urine** (*mazu shōben o senjō su* まづ小便を洗淨す): As above, section 16, the term *shōben* here is no doubt synonymous with "the place of urination" (*shōbensho* 小便處) — i.e., the genitals or the urethral opening.

[54:26]

洗淨しをはりて、淨桶を安桶のところにおきて、つぎに籌をとりてのごひかはかす。あるいは紙をもちいるべし。大小兩處、よくよくのごひかはかすべし。つぎに、右手にて袴口・衣角をひきつくろひて、右手に淨桶を提して廁門をいづるちなみに、蒲鞋をぬぎて自鞋をはく。つぎに淨架にかへりて、淨桶を本所に安ず。

When finished washing and purifying, one puts the cleaning bucket back in the place for resting buckets, then takes a toilet stick and wipes oneself dry. Or, one should use paper. Thoroughly wipe and dry the places of urination and defecation.[34] Next, using the right hand, one straightens up one's underpants and robes and, carrying the cleaning bucket in the right hand, goes out the toilet stall door. At that point, one takes off the reed slippers and puts on one's own footwear. Next, one returns to the washstand and sets down the cleaning bucket in its original place.

[54:27]

つぎに、洗手すべし。右手に灰匙をとりて、まづすくひて、瓦石のおもてにおきて、右手をもて滴水を點じて觸手をあらふ、瓦石にあててとぎあらふなり。たとへば、さびあるかたなを、とにあててとぐがごとし。かくのごとく、灰にて三度あらふべし。つぎに、土をおきて、水を點じてあらふこと三度すべし。つぎに、右手に皂莢をとりて、小桶の水にさしひたして、兩手あはせてもみあらふ。腕にいたらんとするまでも、よくよくあらふなり。誠心に住して、慇懃にあらふべし。灰三、土三、皂莢一なり。あはせて一七度を度とせり。つぎに、大桶にてあらふ。このときは、面藥・土灰等をもちいず、ただ水にても、ゆにてもあらふなり。一番あらひて、その水を小桶にうつして、さらにあたらしき水をいれて兩手をあらふ。

Next, we should wash our hands. One takes the ash spoon in the right hand, scoops out an initial portion [of ash], places it on the surface of the tile stone, adds an appropriate amount of water with the right hand, and washes the hand that has touched filth, rubbing it clean on the tile stone. It is, for example, like grinding a rusty sword on a whetstone. One should wash in this manner three times with ash. Next, one should place some earth, add water to it, and wash three times. Next, take some black pod in the right hand, mix it into the water in a small bucket, and wash both hands by rubbing them together.[35] Wash thoroughly, even up to the wrists. One should devote oneself to this with sincerity and wash assiduously: three times with ashes, three times with earth, and once with black pod. Altogether, one set of seven times is the rule. Next, one washes with the large bucket. At this time, one does not use a medicinal

---

34 **places of urination and defecation** (*daishō ryōsho* 大小兩處): I.e., the genitals and anus.

35 **black pod** (*saikyō* 皂莢): I.e., the powdered beans from the pods of the acacia tree (*Gleditschia sinensis*), used as a soap.

54. Washing and Purifying Senjō 洗淨

face scrub, ashes, earth, or the like, but washes only with cold water or hot water. Wash a first time, then pour that water into the small bucket, fill [the large bucket] again with fresh water, and wash both hands.

[54:28] {2:88}

華嚴經云、以水盥掌、當願衆生、得上妙手、受持佛法。

In the *Flower Garland Sūtra*, it is said,[36]

Using water to wash my palms,
I pray that all living beings
May find a most excellent hand
And receive and keep the buddha dharma.[37]

[54:29]

水杓をとらんことは、かならず右手にてすべし。このあひだ、桶杓、おとをなし、かまびすしくすることなかれ。水をちらし、皂莢をちらし、水架の辺をぬらし、おほよそ倉卒なることなかれ、狼藉なることなかれ。つぎに、公界の手巾に手をのごふ、あるいはみづからが手巾にのごふ。手をのごひをはりて、淨竿のした、直綴のまへにいたりて、絆子を脱して竿にかく。つぎに、合掌してのち、手巾をとき、直綴をとりて著す。つぎに、手巾を左臂にかけて塗香す。公界に塗香あり、香木を寶瓶形につくれり。その大は拇指大なり。ながさ、四指量につくれり。繊索の尺餘なるをもちて、香の兩端に穿貫せり。これを淨竿にかけおけり。これを兩掌をあはせてもみあはすれば、その香氣おのづから兩手に薫ず。絆を竿にかくるとき、おなじうへにかけかさねて、絆と絆とみだらしめ、亂縷せしむることなかれ。かくのごとくする、みなこれ淨佛國土なり、莊嚴佛國なり。審細にすべし、倉卒にすべからず。いそぎをはりてかへりなばやと、おもひいとなむことなかれ。ひそかに東司上不説佛法の道理を思量すべし。

When going to pick up the water ladle, one must always use the right hand. During this time, do not make noise with the bucket or ladle or otherwise raise a clamor. Do not spill water, spill black pod, let the area around the water stand get wet, or hurry in whatever one is doing, and do not leave things scattered about. Next, one wipes one's hands on a communal hand cloth, or wipes them on one's own hand cloth. When finished wiping the hands, go before the long robe at the pure pole, remove the sleeve-binding cord and hang it on the pole. Next, after bowing with palms together, untie the hand cloth, take the long robe, and put it on. Next, hang the hand cloth over the crook of the left arm and rub on incense. In the common area, there is incense for rubbing; it is incense wood, shaped like a treasure bottle.[38] Its thickness is the size of a thumb.

---

36 ***Flower Garland Sūtra*** (*Kegon kyō* 華嚴經): A continuation of the quotation above, section 5 (*Huayan jing* 華嚴經, T.278.09:431b2-3).

37 **most excellent hand** (*jōmyōshu* 上妙手): Likely meaning a skilled teacher.

38 **incense wood, shaped like a treasure bottle** (*kōboku o hōbyōgyō ni tsukureri* 香木を寶瓶形につくれり): A treasure bottle (*hōbyō* 寶瓶) is a Buddhist ritual implement

In length, it measures four fingers. A string more than a foot long is threaded through holes in both ends of the incense, and it is hung over the pure pole. When one rubs it between one's two palms, its fragrant aroma perfumes both hands. When hanging the [sleeve-binding] cord on the pole, loop it over the same place at the top; do not let it touch other cords, resulting in tangled lines. Everything done in this way is *purifying a buddha land, adorning a buddha land*; one should do them with the utmost care, never precipitately. Do not entertain the thought, "If only I can finish and get back quickly." One should think to oneself about the principle of "*not teaching the buddha dharma in the toilet.*"[39]

[54:30] {2:89}

衆家の、きたり・いる面を、しきりにまぼることなかれ。廁中の洗淨には、冷水をよろしとす、熱湯は腸風をひきおこすといふ。洗手には温湯をもちいる、さまたげなし。釜壱隻をおくことは、燒湯洗手のためなり。

When a member of the community has come in [to the toilet], do not fix your gaze in his direction. For washing and purifying within a toilet stall, cold water is good; hot water is said to bring on hemorrhoids.[40] For washing hands, use hot water; there is no impediment to that. The provision of a cauldron is for the purpose of washing the hands with heated water.

[54:31]

清規云、晚後燒湯上油。常令湯水相續、無使大衆動念。

---

used (among other functions) by monks in Song China to carry perfumed water for washing the hands. The piece of fragrant wood that Dōgen describes must have been a cylindrical spindle that had a slight narrowing at both ends, a shape that would suggest the neck and narrow area above the base of a water bottle.

39 **"not teaching the buddha dharma in the toilet"** (*tōsu jō fusetsu buppō* 東司上不説佛法). From the words of Zhaozhou Congshen 趙州從諗 (778-897) to the novice Wenyuan (*shami Wenyuan* 沙彌文遠, a disciple and frequent interlocutor of Zhaozhou in records of that master's sayings) (*Zhaozhou Zhenji chanshi yulu* 趙州眞際禪師語錄, *Guzunsu yulu* 古尊宿語錄, ZZ.118.330b10-11):

因上東司、召文遠。文遠應諾。師云、東司上不可與儞説佛法也。
Once, in the toilet, [Zhaozhou] called to Wenyuan.
Wenyuan said, "Yes?"
The Master said, "I can't teach you the buddha dharma in the toilet."

The toilet, together with the saṃgha hall (*sōdō* 僧堂) and bathhouse (*yokushitsu* 浴室), was one of the "three silent halls" (*san mokudō* 三默堂) in a monastery — i.e., places where talking was forbidden.

40 **cold water is good; hot water is said to bring on hemorrhoids** (*reisui o yoroshi to su, nettō wa chōfū o hikiokosu to iu* 冷水をよろしとす、熱湯は腸風をひきおこすといふ): Paraphrasing *Chanyuan qinggui* 禪苑清規, ZZ.111:912a12.

54. Washing and Purifying Senjō 洗淨

In the *Rules of Purity*, it is said,[41]

After the evening [convocation], [the toilet manager] heats water and tops up the oil.[42] He always insures that hot water is in continuous supply so as not to cause the monks of the great assembly to be concerned.

[54:32]

しかあればしりぬ、湯・水ともにもちいるなり。もし廁中の、觸せること あらば、門扇を掩して觸牌をかくべし。もしあやまりて落桶あらば、門扇 を掩して落桶牌をかくべし。これらの牌、かかれらん局には、のぼること なかれ。もしさきより廁上にのぼれらんに、ほかに人ありて彈指せば、し ばらくいづべし。

Thus, we know that hot water and cold water are both used. If there is anything soiled within a toilet stall, one should shut the door panels and hang up a "soiled" placard. If one has accidentally spilled a bucket, one should shut the door panels and hang up a "spilled bucket" placard. In the event that one of these placards has been hung up, do not enter [that toilet stall]. When one has already entered a toilet stall and there is a person outside who snaps his fingers, one should withdraw in due course.

[54:33]

清規云、若不洗淨、不得坐僧床、及禮三寶。亦不得受人禮拜。

In the *Rules of Purity*, it is said,[43]

If one does not do washing and purifying, one may not sit on the saṃgha platforms or make obeisance to the three treasures. Nor may one receive obeisance from others.

[54:34]

三千威儀經云、若不洗大小便、得突吉羅罪。亦不得僧淨坐具上坐、及禮三 寶。設禮無福德。

In the *Sūtra of the Three Thousand Rules of Deportment*, it is said,[44]

If one does not wash after defecating or urinating, one is guilty of a duṣkṛta offense and may not sit on the pure sitting cloth of a monk or make obeisance to the three treasures.[45] Even if one were to make obeisance, there would be no blessings or merit in it.

---

41 **Rules of Purity** (*Shingi* 清規): *Chanyuan qinggui* 禪苑清規, ZZ.111:898a18.

42 **tops up the oil** (*jōyu* 上油). I.e., adds oil to the lamps (*tō* 燈) that provide light in the toilet before dawn and after dusk.

43 **Rules of Purity** (*Shingi* 清規): *Chanyuan qinggui* 禪苑清規, ZZ.111:912a16-17.

44 **Sūtra of the Three Thousand Rules of Deportment** (*Sanzen iigi kyō* 三千威儀經): *Da biqiu sanqian weiyi* 大比丘三千威儀, T.1470.24:914a17-19.

45 **duṣkṛta offense** (*tokira zai* 突吉羅罪). A "misdeed," the least serious of five grades of offence (*gohin* 五篇) explained in the Vinaya; expiation requires confession before one other monk, or repentance by oneself.

[54:35] {2:90}
しかあればすなはち、辦道功夫の道場、この儀をさきにすべし。あに三寶を禮せざらんや、あに人の禮拜をうけざらんや、あに人を禮せざらんや。佛祖の道場、かならずこの威儀あり。佛祖道場中人、かならずこの威儀具足あり。これ自己の強爲にあらず、威儀の云爲なり、諸佛の常儀なり、諸祖の家常なり。ただ此界の諸佛のみにあらず、十方の佛儀なり、淨土・穢土の佛儀なり。小聞のともがらおもはくは、諸佛には廁屋の威儀あらず、娑婆世界の諸佛の威儀は、淨土の諸佛のごとくにあらず、とおもふ。これは學佛道にあらず。しるべし、淨穢は離人の滴血なり、あるときはあたたかなり、あるときはすさまじ。諸佛に廁屋あり、としるべし。

 We see from this that in practice places where there is concentrated effort in pursuit of the way, these observances should be of primary concern. How could one not pay obeisance to the three treasures? How could one not receive obeisance from other people? How could one not make obeisance to other people? In a practice place of the buddhas and ancestors, there is always this deportment. The people in a practice place of the buddhas and ancestors are always fully endowed with this deportment. This is not something one forces oneself to do; it is the word and deed of deportment; it is the usual practice of the buddhas; it is the everyday routine of the ancestors. These are buddha observances of the buddhas not only of this world but of the ten directions; they are the buddha observances of the pure lands and impure lands. What those of limited experience think is that buddhas have no deportment for the toilet room. They think that the deportment of the buddhas of this *sahā* world is not like that of the buddhas of the pure lands. This is not studying the way of the buddhas. We should know that pure and impure are a drop of blood from a person's body: at one point, it was warm; at the next, it is cold.[46] The buddhas have toilet rooms: we should know this.

[54:36]
十誦律第十四云、羅睺羅沙彌、宿佛廁。佛覺了、佛以右手摩羅睺羅頂、説是偈言、汝不爲貧窮、亦不失富貴、但爲求道故、出家應忍苦。

 In fascicle 14 of the *Ten Chapter Vinaya*, it is said,[47]

---

46 **pure and impure are a drop of blood from a person's body: at one point, it was warm; at the next, it is cold** (*jō e wa rinin no tekiketsu nari, aru toki wa atataka nari, aru toki wa susamaji* 淨穢は離人の滴血なり、あるときはあたたかなり、あるときはすさまじ): The term *susamaji* すさまじ ("cold") can also mean "weird," "horrible," etc. Dōgen's point here may simply be that "pure" and "impure" are not absolute categories; but it is worth remembering that, in Dōgen's cultural context, blood leaving the body (whether from menstruation or wounds) was considered a defilement (*kegare* 穢).

47 **Ten Chapter Vinaya** (*Jūju ritsu* 十誦律): From a story found at *Shisong lü* 十誦律, T.1435.23:105b19-c9. The novice Rahula, unable to find proper lodging, lies down to sleep in the Buddha's toilet room, using the toilet foot rest as his pillow. The Buddha, concerned that Rahula might be bitten by a snake that inhabited the toilet room, brings

54. Washing and Purifying *Senjō* 洗淨

The Śrāmaṇera Rahula lodged in the Buddha's toilet. When the Buddha became aware of it, the Buddha rubbed Rahula's head with his right hand and spoke this gāthā:

Not because you are poor and destitute,
Nor because you neglected your wealth and honor,
But only for the sake of seeking the way,
You have left home and had to endure hardships.

[54:37]

しかあればすなはち、佛道場に廁屋あり。佛廁屋裏の威儀は洗淨なり、祖祖相傳しきたれり。佛儀のなほのこれる、慕古の慶快なり、あひがたきにあへるなり。いはんや如來かたじけなく廁屋裏にして、羅睺羅のために説法しましす。廁屋は佛轉法輪の一會なり。この道場の進止、これ佛祖正傳せり。

We see from this that a buddha's practice place has a toilet room. The deportment inside a buddha's toilet room is washing and purifying, and that has been passed down by ancestor after ancestor. That observances of the Buddha still exist is a blessing and comfort that derives from appreciation for the ancients; it is being able to encounter that which is difficult to encounter. Not to mention that the Tathāgata was so gracious as to preach the dharma for Rahula inside the toilet room. The toilet room is one assembly where buddhas turn the wheel of dharma. What to do and what not to do in this practice place has been directly transmitted by the buddhas and ancestors.

[54:38] {2:91}

摩訶僧祇律第三十四云、廁屋不得在東在北。應在南在西。小行亦如是。

In fascicle 34 of the *Mahāsāṃghika Vinaya*, it is said,[48]

The toilet room should not be in the east or in the north; it should be in the south or in the west. The same applies to urination.[49]

---

him to his own quarters. The Buddha's rubbing Rahula's head, which had touched the toilet foot board, with his right (i.e., pure) hand is a significant detail.

48 **Mahāsāṃghika Vinaya** (*Makasōgi ritsu* 摩訶僧祇律): *Mohesengqi lü* 摩訶僧祇律, T.1425.22:504a16-18.

49 **The same applies to urination** (*shōgyō yaku nyoze* 小行亦如是): A sentence, likely referring to the placement of urinals, that does not in fact occur in the Taishō edition of the *Vinaya* text and the source of which is uncertain.

[54:39]

この方宜によるべし。これ西天竺國の諸精舎の圖なり、如來現在の建立なり。しるべし、一佛の佛儀のみにあらず、七佛の道場なり、精舎なり、諸佛の道場なり、精舎なり。はじめたるにあらず、諸佛の威儀なり。これらをあきらめざらんよりさきは、寺院を草創し、佛法を修行せん、あやまりはおほく、佛威儀そなはらず、佛菩提いまだ現前せざらん。もし道場を建立し、寺院を草創せんには、佛祖正傳の法儀によるべし。これ正嫡正傳なるがゆえに、その功徳、あつめかさなれり。佛祖正傳の嫡嗣にあらざれば、佛法の身心、いまだしらず、佛法の身心しらざれば、佛家の佛業あきらめざるなり。いま、大師釋迦牟尼佛の佛法、あまねく十方につたはれるといふは、佛身心の現成なり。佛身心現成の正當恁麼時、かくのごとし。

This standard should be followed. This was the ground plan of the vihāras in the Land of Sindhu in the West, the constructions when the Tathāgata was manifest in this world. We should recognize that it is not the buddha observance of only one buddha: it is [true of] the practice places, the vihāras, of the seven buddhas; it is the practice places, the vihāras, of all the buddhas.[50] It is not something newly started; it is the deportment of the buddhas.[51]

As long as we are not clear on these matters, when we go to found a monastery and practice the buddha dharma, we will make many mistakes, will not be endowed with the deportment of a buddha, and the bodhi of a buddha will not have appeared. If we wish to construct a practice place or found a monastery, we should follow the dharma regulations directly transmitted by the buddhas and ancestors. Because this is a direct transmission by direct descendants, its merit has accumulated and piled up. If one is not a legitimate heir to the direct transmission of the buddhas and ancestors, one still does not know the body and mind of the buddha dharma; if one does not know the body and mind of the buddha dharma, one is not clear about the buddha work of the house of the

---

50 **it is not the buddha observance of only one buddha: it is [true of] the practice places, the vihāras, of the seven buddhas** (*ichibutsu no butsugi nomi ni arazu, shichi butsu no dōjō nari, shōja nari* 一佛の佛儀のみにあらず、七佛の道場なり、精舎なり): The "seven buddhas" (*shichi butsu* 七佛), indicating Śākyamuni and six buddhas said to have preceded him, are the first figures in the Zen lineage of buddhas and ancestors as that was understood in Dōgen's day; see Supplementary Notes, s.v. "Seven buddhas." The subject of this sentence is unstated and ambiguous. The obvious candidate would be the rule for locating the toilet just mentioned, but one could understand it as all the observances for "washing and purifying" that Dōgen has described up to this point in the chapter. It is also unclear whether by describing "it" as "the practice places of the seven buddhas" Dōgen means simply that it is true of such practice places or is itself such practice places.

51 **It is not something newly started** (*hajimetaru ni arazu* はじめたるにあらず): Presumably, meaning that the procedure for toilets was not invented or first implemented by Buddha Śākyamuni.

buddhas. The fact that the buddha dharma of the Great Master, Buddha Śākyamuni, has now been transmitted widely in the ten directions means that the buddha body and mind are manifest. At the very time the buddha body and mind are manifest, this is what it is like.

正法眼藏洗淨第五十四
Treasury of the True Dharma Eye
Washing and Purifying
Number 54

[Ryūmonji MS:]

爾時延應元年己亥冬十月二十三日、在雍州宇治縣觀音導利興聖寶林寺示衆
Presented to the assembly at Kannon Dōri Kōshō Hōrin Monastery, Uji District, Yōshū; twenty-third day, tenth month, in the winter of the junior earth year of the pig, the first year of En'ō [20 November 1239]

Addenda[52]

[54:40]

三千威儀經云、若不洗大小便、得突吉羅罪、亦不得僧淨坐具上坐、及禮三寶、設禮無福德。

In the *Sūtra of the Three Thousand Rules of Deportment*, it is said,[53]

If one does not wash after defecating or urinating, one is guilty of a *duṣkṛta* offense and may not sit on the pure sitting cloth of a monk or make obeisance to the three treasures. Even if one were to make obeisance, there would be no blessings or merit in it.

---

52 In the Ryūmonji 龍門寺 and other MSS of the seventy-five chapter compilation, the colophon is followed by three quotations; they are not included in the Honzan edition and are consigned to the endnotes in Kawamura's edition. We have added them here as addenda.

53 ***Sūtra of the Three Thousand Rules of Deportment*** (*Sanzen iigi kyō* 三千威儀經): *Da biqiu sanqian weiyi* 大比丘三千威儀, T.1470.24:914a17-19. A repetition of the quotation given in section 34 above.

[54:41]

僧祇律第四十云、佛住舍衞城、爾時大愛道往至佛所、頭面禮足、卻住一面、時大愛道白佛言、世尊女人形臭、得聽洗不。佛言、得洗、時比丘尼洗外、內猶故臭、以是因縁、往曰世尊乃至當得洗內不。佛言得洗。洗法者、齊一指節、不得令過、若過洗以歇欲心者、偸蘭遮、是各説法。

In fascicle 40 of the *Mahāsāṃghika Vinaya*, it is said,[54]

The Buddha was staying at Śrāvastī. At that time, Mahāprajāpatī went to the Buddha, touched her head to his feet, and stood to one side. Then, Mahāprajāpatī addressed the Buddha, saying, "Lord, the female body stinks. Are we permitted to wash it or not?"

The Buddha said, "You may wash it."

Then, the bhikṣuṇī washed the surface of her body, but the inside still stank. Therefore, she went and inquired of the World-Honored One whether it was permitted to wash the inside or not. The Buddha instructed: "You may wash it. The rule for the washing is one finger joint and may not go beyond that. If one washes beyond that and arouses feelings of lust, it is a *sthūlātyaya* offense. These are each the rules I preach."[55]

[54:42]

大論八十三、有微細魔事者、未得跋致詊定已得文。

In fascicle 83 of the *Great Treatise* [it is said],[56]

One with subtle Māra karma, though not yet having attained *avaivartika*, falsely determines he has already attained it.[57] (End quote.)

---

54 **Mahāsāṃghika Vinaya** (*Makasōgi ritsu* 摩訶僧祇律): *Mohesengqi lü* 摩訶僧祇律, T.1425.22:545c16-21.

55 **"These are each the rules I preach"** (*ze kyaku seppō* 是各説法): The quotation seems corrupt here. The source (at T.1425.22:545c21) reads "This is called the rule for washing" (*shi ming xi fa* 是名洗法).

56 **Great Treatise** (*Dairon* 大論): The passage here is in fact a slightly corrupted quotation from the *Zhiguan fuxing zhuan hongjue* 止觀輔行傳弘決 (at T.1912.46:406b11-12), by Zhanran 湛然 (711-782), which reads:

大論八十云、有微細魔事者、未得跋致詊言已得。

In fascicle 80 of the *Great Treatise*, it is said, "One with subtle Māra karma, though not having attained *avaivartika*, falsely claims he has already attained it."

Zhanran seems here to be paraphrasing a line in fascicle 61 of the *Dazhidu lun* 大智度論 (T.1509.25:598a7-8).

57 **avaivartika** (*bachi* 跋致): I.e., the stage of non-regression (*fu taiten* 不退轉) from advancement to buddhahood, often located at the seventh stage (S. *bhūmi*) of the bodhisattva path.

TREASURY OF THE TRUE DHARMA EYE

NUMBER 55

The Ten Directions
Jippō
十方

The Ten Directions

Jippō

INTRODUCTION

This chapter was composed at Kippōji in the last days of 1243, a very productive period for Dōgen's work on the *Shōbōgenzō*. It appears as number 55 in the seventy-five-chapter compilation, number 45 in the sixty-chapter compilation, and number 60 in the ninety-five-chapter Honzan edition.

As its title indicates, the text focuses on several passages using the expression "the ten directions" (i.e., the four cardinal and four ordinal points, plus the zenith and nadir), a standard Buddhist locution for "all directions," "everywhere." The discussion opens with comments on a reference, by Buddha Śākyamuni, to "buddha lands of the ten directions." Dogen warns us not to think of the buddhas, their lands, and the ten directions as separate, much less to judge among the various buddhas — no doubt a criticism of those among his contemporaries who favored the Western Pure Land of Buddha Amitābha over our defiled Sahā realm of Buddha Śākyamuni. He goes on to identify the ten directions with the "one direction," or location, in which each thing occurs, and concludes, "the buddhas and buddha lands are not two . . . they are just the ten directions."

The text then takes up a series of sayings, by the ninth-century Chan Master Changsha Jingcen 長沙景岑, that identify "all the worlds in the ten directions" with the eye, speech, and body of the *śramaṇa*, and with the "radiance of the self." After commenting on two more Chan sayings, the work ends with the remark, "In sum, we just study that the living nose is the ten directions."

正法眼藏第五十五
Treasury of the True Dharma Eye
Number 55

十方

The Ten Directions

[55:1] {2:92}
拳頭一隻、只箇十方なり。赤心一片、玲瓏十方なり。敲出骨裏髓了也。

A single fist is just the ten directions; a single bare mind is the ten directions crystal clear.[1] *The marrow has been beaten from the bones.*[2]

[55:2]
釋迦牟尼佛、告大衆言、十方佛土中、唯有一乘法。

Buddha Śākyamuni addressed the great assembly, saying, "In the buddha lands of the ten directions, there is only the dharma of the one vehicle."[3]

[55:3]
いはゆる十方は、佛土を把來してこれをなせり。このゆえに、佛土を拈來せざれば、十方いまだあらざるなり。佛土なるゆえに、以佛爲主なり。この娑婆國土は、釋迦牟尼佛土なるがごとし。この娑婆世界を擧拈して、八兩半斤をあきらかに記して、十方佛土の七尺八尺なることを參學すべし。

These "ten directions" have been formed by grasping "the buddha lands." Therefore, if we did not take up "the buddha lands," there would be no "ten directions." Since they are "buddha lands," a buddha is their

---

1 **A single fist** (*kentō isseki* 拳頭一隻): The "fist" appears often in Zen texts, and in Dōgen's writings, as a synecdoche for the true self or a true master; see Supplementary Notes, s.v. "Fist."

a single bare mind (*sekishin ippen* 赤心一片): More literally, "a single piece of bare mind." A "bare (or 'red') mind" (*chixin* 赤心) is a common Chinese idiom for a sincere, or straightforward, mind (or heart). Zen texts often speak of "a bare mind in pieces" (*sekishin henpen* 赤心片片); see Supplementary Notes, s.v. "Bare mind in pieces."

2 **The marrow has been beaten from the bones** (*kōshutsu kotsuri zui ryō ya* 敲出骨裏髓了也): A sentence in Chinese, expressing a fairly common metaphor for divulging the truth.

3 **Buddha Śākyamuni** (*Shakamuni butsu* 釋迦牟尼佛): From the *Lotus Sūtra* (*Miaofa lianhua jing* 妙法蓮華經, T.262.9:8a17). The "one vehicle" (*ichijō* 一乘) is the form of Buddhism leading to (or in some interpretations, expressing) the complete awakening of a buddha; a central teaching of the *Lotus Sūtra*.

ruler, as this Sahā world is the buddha land of Buddha Śākyamuni. Holding up this Sahā world and noting clearly eight tael and half a catty, we should study that the buddha lands of the ten directions are seven feet or eight feet.[4]

[55:4]
この十方は、一方にいり、一佛にいる。このゆえに、現十方せり。十方・一方、是方・自方・今方なるがゆえに、眼睛方なり、拳頭方なり、露柱方なり、燈籠方なり。かくのごとくの十方佛土の十方佛、いまだ大小あらず、淨穢あらず。このゆえに、十方の唯佛與佛、あひ稱揚讚歎するなり。さらにあひ誹謗してその長短・好惡をとくを、轉法輪とし説法とせず。諸佛および佛子として、助發問訊するなり。

These ten directions enter one direction, enter one buddha. Therefore, they have manifested the ten directions.[5] Because the ten directions are one direction, this direction, one's own direction, the present direction, they are the direction of the eye, the direction of the fist, the direction of the pillar, the direction of the lantern.[6] The buddhas of the ten directions of such "buddha lands in the ten directions" are not large or small, are not pure or dirty.[7] Therefore, "only buddhas with buddhas" in the ten

---

4 **eight tael and half a catty** (*hachi ryō han kin* 八兩半斤): A tael (*ryō* 兩) is a Chinese unit of weight (varying throughout history) equal to 1/16 catty (*kin* 斤); hence the expression "eight tael, half a catty" (*hachi ryō han kin* 八兩半斤) is akin to English "six of one, a half dozen of the other." The implication here seems to be that the one buddha land of Śākyamuni is equivalent to the buddha lands of the ten directions.

seven feet or eight feet (*shichi shaku hachi shaku* 七尺八尺): Dōgen may have in mind here a conversation between Chan Masters Xuansha Shibei 玄沙師備 (835-908) and Xuefeng Yicun 雪峰義存 (822-908), which he includes in his *shinji Shōbōgenzō* 正法眼藏三白則 (DZZ.5:158, case 60) and on which he comments in "Shōbōgenzō juki" 正法眼藏授記; see Supplementary Notes, s.v. "Seven feet or eight feet."

5 **they have manifested the ten directions** (*gen jippō seri* 現十方せり): Or "they have appeared as (or in) the ten directions."

6 **Because the ten directions are one direction, this direction, one's own direction, the present direction** (*jippō ippō, zehō jihō konpō naru ga yue ni* 十方・一方、是方・自方・今方なるがゆえに): It is unclear just how to parse this passage, which offers no clues to the grammatical relationships among the five "directions" given. Taken together, the implication seems to be that "the ten directions" are this one direction where one is now.

the direction of the eye, the direction of the fist, the direction of the pillar, the direction of the lantern (*ganzei hō nari, kentō hō nari, rochū hō nari, tōrō hō nari* 眼睛方なり、拳頭方なり、露柱方なり、燈籠方なり): In this context, the former pair of "directions" may suggest the self (or Zen practitioner); the latter pair, the objective world (or the monastery). Alteratively, the former pair may suggest the Zen master; the latter pair the assembly of monks under his tutelage. See Supplementary Notes, s.v. "Eye," "Fist," "Pillars and lanterns."

7 **are not large or small, are not pure or dirty** (*daishō arazu, jōe arazu* 大小あらず、淨穢あらず): Probably indicating attributes of the buddha lands, rather than of the

55. The Ten Directions *Jippō* 十方   197

directions *praise and admire* each other.⁸ They do not take condemning each other, talking of their strengths and weaknesses, likes and dislikes, as turning the dharma wheel and preaching the dharma.⁹ As buddhas and buddhas' children, they *assist and greet* [each other].¹⁰

[55:5] {2:93}

佛祖の法を稟受するには、かくのごとく參學するなり。外道・魔黨のごとく是非毀辱することあらざるなり。いま眞丹國につたはれる佛經を披閱して、一化の始終を覷見するに、釋迦牟尼佛、いまだかつて、他方の諸佛それ劣なり、ととかず、他方の諸佛それ勝なり、ととかず、また、他方の諸佛は諸佛にあらず、ととかず。おほよそ一代の説教にすべてみえざるところは、諸佛のあひ是非する佛語なり。他方の諸佛また、釋迦牟尼佛を是非したてまつる佛語つたはれず。

In receiving the dharma of the buddhas and ancestors, one studies in this way. One does not slander and insult over rights and wrongs like followers of other paths or the minions of Māra.¹¹ When we peruse the scriptures of the Buddha transmitted to the Land of Cīnasthāna and look at the entirety of his ministry, Buddha Śākyamuni never preached that the buddhas of other directions are inferior, or preached that the buddhas of other directions are superior; nor did he preach that the buddhas of

---

buddhas themselves. The land of Buddha Amitābha is known as the "pure land" (*jōdo* 淨土) in contrast to this "defiled" Sahā (*shaba* 娑婆) world of Buddha Śākyamuni.

8 **"only buddhas with buddhas"** (*yui butsu yo butsu* 唯佛與佛): Probably, to be understood simply as "the buddhas." Dōgen uses here a phrase from the *Lotus Sūtra* often invoked in the *Shōbōgenzō*; see Supplementary Notes, s.v. "Only buddhas with buddhas can exhaustively investigate the real marks of the dharmas."

praise and admire (*shōyō santan* 稱揚讚歎): A common fixed expression in Buddhist literature; not found elsewhere in the *Shōbōgenzō*.

9 **talking of their strengths and weaknesses, likes and dislikes** (*sono chōtan kōaku o toku* その長短・好惡をとく): Probably reflecting a line in the *Lotus Sūtra* (*Miaofa lianhua jing*, T.262.9:38a3):

不説他人好惡長短。

[Those who wish to preach this sūtra] do not talk of the likes and dislikes, strengths and weaknesses of others.

10 **assist and greet** (*johotsu monjin* 助發問訊): It may be recalled that a buddha is expected to have studied under many buddhas in his career as a bodhisattva. The somewhat troubling term *johotsu* 助發, appearing several times in the *Shōbōgenzō*, seems to carry the sense "helps to develop, or promote"; in Zen usage, *monjin* 問訊 ("to inquire," "to question") typically denotes the act of bowing with palms together (*gasshō* 合掌) when greeting someone.

11 **followers of other paths or the minions of Māra** (*gedō matō* 外道・魔黨): Common pejoratives in Dōgen's writing. The former expression, the "other paths," refers to members of non-Buddhist religious traditions (S. *tīrthika*); the latter expression indicates the followers of Māra, the Evil One (S. *papīyān*), lord of the sixth heaven of the realm of desire (S. *kāma-loka*), who seeks to obstruct Buddhist awakening.

other directions are not buddhas.[12] In sum, what one does not see in all the teachings of his entire life is a word of the Buddha judging other buddhas; nor has there been transmitted any word of a buddha in which the buddhas of the other directions judge Buddha Śākyamuni.

[55:6]
このゆえに、釋迦牟尼佛、告大衆言、唯我知是相、十方佛亦然。

Therefore, *Buddha Śākyamuni addressed the great assembly saying, "I alone know its marks, as do the buddhas in the ten directions."*[13]

[55:7]
しるべし、唯我知是相の相は、打圓相なり。圓相は、遮竿得恁麼長、那竿得恁麼短なり。十方佛道は、唯我知是相、釋迦牟尼佛亦然の説著なり。唯我證是相、自方佛亦然なり。我相・知相・是相・一切相・十方相・裟婆國土相・釋迦牟尼佛相なり。

We should know that the "mark" in "*I alone know its marks*" is "*making a circular mark.*"[14] The circular mark is "*this bamboo is this long; that bamboo is that short.*"[15] In the words of the buddhas in the ten direc-

---

12 **Land of Cīnasthāna** (*Shintan koku* 眞丹國): A common Chinese transliteration, *Zhendan* 眞丹, of a Sanskrit term for China.

buddhas of other directions are not buddhas (*tahō no shobutsu wa shobutsu ni arazu* 他方の諸佛は諸佛にあらず): Supplying *wa shobutsu* は諸佛, missing in the Kawamura text — which, if unamended, would yield, "nor did he preach that [they] are not buddhas of other directions."

13 **Buddha Śākyamuni addressed the great assembly** (*Shakamuni butsu koku daishu* 釋迦牟尼佛告大衆): From the *Lotus Sūtra* (*Miaofa lianhua jing* 妙法蓮華經, T.262.9:6a18-20):

又告舍利弗、無漏不思議、甚深微妙法、我今已具得。唯我知是相、十方佛亦然。

Again I declare, Śāriputra,
The undefiled, inconceivable,
Extremely profound and subtle dharma,
I have now fully acquired.
I alone know its marks,
As do the buddhas in the ten directions.

14 "**making a circular mark**" (*da ensō* 打圓相): Or "making a full circle." The translation strains to retain Dōgen's play with the graph *sō* 相, rendered here as "mark," from the *Lotus Sūtra* passage. Zen texts regularly depict a monk's making or drawing a circle (*ichi ensō* 一圓相) with his hand or some object to express the perfect suchness of things.

15 "**this bamboo is this long; that bamboo is that short**" (*sha kan toku inmo chō, na kan toku inmo tan* 遮竿得恁麼長、那竿得恁麼短): From a saying of Cuiwei Wuxue 翠微無學 (dates unknown) included in Dōgen's *shinji Shōbōgenzō* 眞字正法眼藏 (DZZ.5:162, case 71), and treated elsewhere in his writings. Here is the version from the *Jingde chuandeng lu* 景德傳燈錄 (T.2076.51:318c4-7):

問、如何是西來的的意。翠微曰、待無人即向汝説。師良久曰。無人也請師説。翠

55. The Ten Directions *Jippō* 十方

tions, they say, "*I alone know its marks, as does Buddha Śākyamuni.*"[16] "*I alone verify its marks, as does the buddha of one's own direction.*"[17] They are *the mark of "I," the mark of "know," the mark of "its," the mark of "all," the mark of "the ten directions," the mark of "the Land of Sahā," the mark of "Buddha Śākyamuni."*[18]

[55:8]

この宗旨は、これ佛經なり。諸佛ならびに佛土は、兩頭にあらず、有情にあらず・無情にあらず、迷・悟にあらず、善・惡・無記等にあらず、淨にあらず・穢にあらず、成にあらず・住にあらず・壞にあらず・空にあらず・常にあらず・無常にあらず・有にあらず・無にあらず、自にあらず。離四句なり、絶百非なり。ただこれ十方なるのみなり、佛土なるのみなり。しかあれば、十方は有頭無尾漢なるのみなり。

This essential point — this is the sūtras of the buddhas.[19] The buddhas and the lands of the buddhas are not two; they are not sentient or insentient; not deluded or awakened; not good, bad, or neutral; not pure, not dirty; not formation, not continuation, not destruction, not emptiness; not permanent, not impermanent; not existent, not nonexistent; not themselves.[20] They are *free from the four propositions*; they have *cut off*

微下禪床引師入竹園。師又曰、無人也請和尚説。翠微指竹曰、遮竿得恁麼長、那竿得恁麼短。

> [Yunmen Wenyan 雲門文偃 (864-949)] asked, "What is the clear intention of [Bodhidharma's] coming from the west?"
> Cuiwei said, "Once no one's around, I'll tell you."
> The Master [i.e., Yunmen] waited a while and said, "No one's around; I ask the Master to tell me."
> Cuiwei got down from his meditation seat and led the Master into the bamboo garden.
> The Master said again, "No one's around; I ask the Reverend to tell me."
> Cuiwei pointed at the bamboo and said, "This bamboo is this long; that bamboo is that short."

16 **In the words of the buddhas in the ten directions** (*jippō butsu dō* 十方佛道): Dōgen is here imagining the perspective of these buddhas.

17 **"I alone verify its marks"** (*yui ga shō ze sō* 唯我證是相): The translation assumes that this sentence represents a continuation of the imagined words of the buddhas in the ten directions; it is unclear whether the following list of "marks" is also to be treated as such.

18 **the mark of "I," the mark of "know," the mark of "its"** (*gasō chisō zesō* 我相・知相・是相): Playing with the *Lotus Sūtra* line, "I alone know its marks" (*yui ga chi ze sō* 唯我知是相).

19 **This essential point — this is the sūtras of the buddhas** (*kono shūshi wa, kore bukkyō nari* この宗旨は、これ佛經なり): The antecedent of "this" (*kono* この) is unclear. Perhaps, the meaning is simply, "such is the teaching [on the ten directions] of the sūtras."

20 **not formation, not continuation, not destruction, not emptiness** (*jō ni arazu jū ni arazu e ni arazu kū ni arazu* 成にあらず・住にあらず・壞にあらず・空にあらず):

the hundred negations.²¹ They are just the ten directions; they are just the buddha lands. Hence, the ten directions are just a fellow with a head and without a tail.²²

* * * * *

[55:9] {2:94}
長沙景岑禪師、告大衆言、盡十方界、是沙門壱隻眼。

Chan Master Changsha Jingcen addressed the great assembly saying, "All the worlds in the ten directions are the single eye of the śramaṇa."²³

[55:10]
いまいふところは、瞿曇沙門眼の壱隻なり。瞿曇沙門眼は、吾有正法眼藏なり。阿誰に付属すれども、瞿曇沙門眼なり。盡十方界の角角尖尖、瞿曇の眼處なり。この盡十方界は、沙門眼のなかの壱隻なり。これより向上に如許多眼あり。

What is referred to here is one of the eyes of the Śramaṇa Gautama.²⁴ The eye of the Śramaṇa Gautama is "*I have the treasury of the true dharma eye*."²⁵ No matter to whom it is transmitted, it is the eye of the Śra-

---

Dōgen gives here a standard list of the four phases in the life of a world system, from its appearance to its disappearance in emptiness.

not themselves (*ji ni arazu* 自にあらず): Or "not the self." The Honzan 本山 edition of the text follows this with the phrase "not another" (*ta ni arazu* 他にあらず).

21 **They are free from the four propositions; they have cut off the hundred negations** (*ri shiku nari, zetsu hyappi nari* 離四句なり、絕百非なり): From the common Zen expression, "free from the four propositions and cutting off the hundred negations" (*ri shiku zetsu hyappi* 離四句絕百非). The "four propositions" (S. *catuṣkoṭi*) refers to the classical technique in Buddhist rhetoric that discusses a topic from four perspectives: true, not true, both true and not true, neither true nor not true. "The hundred negations" refers to the refutation of all an opponent's claims. Together, the two terms suggest the practice of reasoning and argumentation.

22 **a fellow with a head and without a tail** (*u tō mu bi kan* 有頭無尾漢): This expression, appearing with some frequency in Zen texts, is generally interpreted to indicate a person beyond distinctions.

23 **Chan Master Changsha Jingcen** (*Chōsha Keishin zenji* 長沙景岑禪師): Dates unknown; a disciple of Nanquan Puyuan 南泉普願 (748-835). For his saying, see Supplementary Notes, s.v. "All the worlds in the ten directions are the single eye of the *śramaṇa*." The saying and the variations that Dōgen will discuss below here appear together in his "Shōbōgenzō kōmyō" 正法眼藏光明.

24 **the Śramaṇa Gautama** (*Kudon shamon* 瞿曇沙門): A common reference to Buddha Śākyamuni. It is unclear whether Changsha had Gautama in mind in his use of *śramaṇa* ("ascetic"), and the translation will thus treat the term as a generic reference to the Buddhist monk.

25 **"I have the treasury of the true dharma eye"** (*go u shōbōgenzō* 吾有正法眼藏): The famous statement of the Buddha in the founding legend of the Zen tradition

maṇa Gautama. Each horn and each point of all the worlds in the ten directions is the eye of Gautama.[26] "All the worlds in the ten directions" here is one among the eyes of the Śramaṇa. Beyond this, he has so many eyes.[27]

[55:11]

盡十方界、是沙門家常語。

"*All the worlds in the ten directions are the everyday words of the śramaṇa.*"[28]

[55:12]

家常は尋常なり。日本國の俗のことばには、よのつね、といふ。しかあるに、沙門家のよのつねの言語は、これ盡十方界なり、言端語端なり。家常語は盡十方界なるがゆえに、盡十方界は家常語なる道理、あきらかに參學すべし。この十方、無盡なるゆえに、盡十方なり。家常にこの語をもちいるなり。かの索馬・索鹽・索水・索器のごとし、奉水・奉器・奉鹽・奉馬のごとし。たれかしらん、沒量大人、この語脈裏に轉身轉腦することを。語脈裏に轉語するなり、海口山舌、言端語直の家常なり。しかあれば、掩口し掩耳する、十方の眞箇是なり。

The "everyday" is the ordinary; in the vernacular idiom of the Land of Japan, we say "the common."[29] Thus, the common speech in the house

---

of transmission from master to disciple; see Supplementary Notes, s.v. "Treasury of the true dharma eye."

26 **Each horn and each point** (*kakukaku sensen* 角角尖尖): Usually taken to mean "each and every thing." Possibly, reflecting the Chan saying, "each leaf of the lotus is round, round, round like a mirror; each horn of the water caltrop is pointed, pointed, pointed like an awl" (*he ye tuantuan tuan si jing, ling jiao jianjian jian si zhui* 荷葉團團團似鏡、菱角尖尖尖似錐).

27 **so many eyes** (*nyo kota gen* 如許多眼): Possibly, reflecting the question, posed by Yunyan Tansheng 雲巖曇晟 (782-841), about the thousand-armed, thousand-eyed Bodhisattva Avalokiteśvara, which Dōgen discusses in his "Shōbōgenzō Kannon":

大悲菩薩、用許多手眼作麼。

How does the Bodhisattva of Great Compassion use so many hands and eyes?

28 **"everyday words of the śramaṇa"** (*shamon kajō go* 沙門家常語): This sentence also appears in Dōgen's quotation of Changsha's saying in "Shōbōgenzō kōmyō" 正法眼藏光明, but extant Chinese sources of the saying do not seem to include it. The expression "everyday words" may reflect a remark of Furong Daokai 芙蓉道楷 (1043-1118) included in Dōgen's *shinji Shōbōgenzō* 眞字正法眼藏 (DZZ.5:202, case 143) and often quoted by Dōgen; see Supplementary Notes, s.v. "Everyday tea and rice."

29 **The "everyday" is the ordinary** (*kajō wa jinjō nari* 家常は尋常なり): Dōgen is here simply explaining the Chinese idiom *jiachang* 家常 to his Japanese audience. The English "everyday" is a loose translation of a colloquial expression, meaning more literally something like "usual at home," most often associated with the daily fare of the household (what we might call "home-style" cooking); see Supplementary Notes, s.v. "Everyday tea and rice."

of the *śramaṇa* is "all the worlds in the ten directions."³⁰ It is, "*The speech is straightforward; the words are straightforward.*"³¹ Because the everyday words are "all the worlds in the ten directions," we should clearly study the principle that "all the worlds in the ten directions " are "everyday words."³² Because these "ten directions" are inexhaustible, they exhaust the ten directions.³³ We use these words in the everyday.³⁴ They are like that *requesting a horse, requesting salt, requesting water, and requesting a bowl*; like *offering water, offering a bowl, offering salt, and offering a horse.*³⁵ Who knows how the immeasurably great person

---

"**the common**" (*yonotsune* よのつね): Often written 世の常; "the way of the world," "what is commonly or usually done."

30 **the common speech in the house of the *śramaṇa*** (*shamon ke no yonotsune no gongo* 沙門家のよのつねの言語): Dōgen seems here to be playing with the term *kajō* 家常, taking the first glyph in its primary sense of "house."

31 **"The speech is straightforward; the words are straightforward"** (*gontan gotan* 言端語端): Also read *gentan gotan*. An expression perhaps best known from its use in the *Biyan lu* 碧巖錄 (T.2003.48:142a5):

至道無難、言端語端。

The supreme way isn't hard. The speech is straightforward; the words are straightforward.

32 **Because the everyday words are "all the worlds in the ten directions"** (*kajō go wa jin jippō kai naru ga yue ni* 家常語は盡十方界なるがゆえに): The translation follows the punctuation in Kawamura. This passage might also be parsed, "The speech is straightforward; the words are straightforward, because the everyday words are all the worlds in the ten directions. We should clearly study the principle that all the worlds in the ten directions are everyday words."

33 **Because these "ten directions" are inexhaustible, they exhaust the ten directions** (*kono jippō, mujin naru ga yue ni, jin jippō nari* この十方、無盡なるゆえに、盡十方なり): The translation of the expression *jin jippō kai* 盡十方界 as "all the worlds in the ten directions " has obscured the play here with the initial glyph *jin* 盡, "to exhaust," "exhaustive." Dōgen is here reading the expression as if *jin* governed "the ten directions," rather than "the worlds" — i.e., "the worlds in all the ten directions."

34 **We use these words in the everyday** (*kajō ni kono go o mochiiru nari* 家常にこの語をもちいるなり): The grammatical antecedent of "these" here is unclear; a likely sense might be, "we use words in everyday speech that are 'inexhaustible,' or 'exhaust the ten directions.'"

35 **requesting a horse, requesting salt, requesting water, and requesting a bowl** (*saku ba saku en saku sui saku ki* 索馬・索鹽・索水・索器): Allusion to a classic simile of the multivalent referents that must be discerned in the Buddha's "secret" or "cryptic words" (*mitsugo* 密語), on which Dōgen comments in his "Shōbōgenzō ō saku sendaba" 正法眼藏王索仙陀婆, from the *Nirvāṇa Sūtra* (*Da banniepan jing* 大般涅槃經, T.374.12:421a29-b8):

如來密語甚深難解。譬如大王告諸群臣先陀婆來。先陀婆者一名四實。一者鹽、二者器、三者水、四者馬。如是四法皆同此名。有智之臣善知此名。若王洗時索先陀婆即便奉水。若王食時索先陀婆即便奉鹽。若王食已將欲飲漿索先陀婆即便奉器。若王欲遊索先陀婆即便奉馬。如是智臣善解大王四種密語。是大乘經亦復如是有四無常。大乘智臣應當善知。

turns his body and turns his brain within this flow of words?[36] He turns the words within the flow of words. *The mouth of the ocean and the tongue of the mountain* — these are the "everyday" of "*speech straightforward and words direct.*"[37] Therefore, covering the mouth and covering the ears are what the ten directions truly are.[38]

[55:13]

盡十方界、沙門全身。

"All the worlds in the ten directions are the entire body of the śramaṇa."[39]

The cryptic words of the Tathāgata are extremely profound and difficult to interpret. They are, for example, like the case of the great king who calls for his ministers to bring him *saindhava* ["Sindhu-born"]. *Saindhava* is a single term with four referents: salt, a bowl, water, and a horse. These four things all have the same term. The wise minister well understands [how to interpret] this term. If the king requests *saindhava* when he is bathing, [the minister] offers him water; if the king requests *saindhava* when he is eating, he offers him salt; if the king requests *saindhava* when he will drink the broth after the food is brought, he offers him a bowl; if the kings requests *saindhava* when he will travel, he offers him a horse. In this way, the wise minister well interprets the fourfold cryptic words of the great king. The scriptures of the great vehicle similarly have four [senses of] "impermanence." The wise ministers of the great vehicle should well understand them.

36 **the immeasurably great person turns his body and turns his brain within this flow of words** (*motsuryō dainin, kono gomyaku ri ni tenshin* [or *tenjin*] *tennō suru* 没量大人、この語脈裏に轉身轉腦する): Perhaps after the saying (e.g., in the *Biyan lu* 碧巖錄, T.2003.48:169a19):

没量大人語脈裏轉却。

The immeasurably great person turns round [or is turned round] within the flow of words.

37 **the mouth of the ocean and the tongue of the mountain** (*kaiku sanzetsu* 海口山舌): I.e., the "speech" of the natural world.

38 **covering the mouth and covering the ears** (*en ku shi en ni suru* 掩口し掩耳する): I.e., stopping talk. Zen masters are often depicted covering their ears (*yan er* 掩耳) in response to a student; Master Shitou 石頭 famously covered the mouth (*yan kou* 掩口) of the Layman Pang 龐居士 (740?-808) when the latter inquired about "the one who doesn't keep company with the myriad dharmas" (*bu yu wanfa wei lü zhe* 不與萬法爲侶者) (see, e.g., *Zongmen tongyao ji* 宗門統要集, ZTS.1:70a6-7).

what the ten directions truly are (*jippō no shinko ze* 十方の眞箇是): An unusual construction, presumably derived from the common pattern "X 'truly is' (*shinko ze* 眞箇是) Y."

39 **"the entire body of the śramaṇa"** (*shamon zenshin* 沙門全身): Continuing the quotation of Changsha's saying, begun in section 9; see above, Note 23.

[55:14] {2:95}

一手指天是天、一手指地是地。雖然如是、天上天下、唯我獨尊。これ沙門全身なる十方盡界なり。頂顙・眼睛・鼻孔・皮肉・骨髓の箇箇、みな透脱盡十方の沙門身なり。盡十方を動著せず、かくのごとくなり、擬議量をまたず。盡十方界沙門身を拈來して、見盡十方界沙門身するなり。

"One hand pointing to the heavens" is heaven; "one hand pointing to the earth" is the earth.[40] Although they are such, *"in the heavens above and beneath the heavens, I alone am honored"* — this is all the worlds in the ten directions as "the entire body of the *śramaṇa*."[41] The crown of the head, the eye, the nose, the skin, flesh, bones, and marrow — each is the body of the *śramaṇa* that transcends all the ten directions.[42] It is like this without moving all the ten directions; it does not depend on considering and thinking.[43] Taking up the body of "the *śramaṇa* of all the worlds in the ten directions," we see the body of the *śramaṇa* of all the worlds in the ten directions.[44]

40 **"One hand pointing to the heavens" is heaven** (*isshu shi ten ze ten* 一手指天是天): This passage, ending "I alone am honored," is given in Chinese, as if quoting a text; in fact, it is a combination of quotation and Dōgen's interpolation. The quotation comes from the legend, popular in Zen texts, of the remarkable behavior of the Buddha at the time of his birth; see Supplementary Notes, s.v. "I alone am honored."

41 **Although they are such** (*sui nen nyo ze* 雖然如是): The subject is unexpressed; hence the antecedent of the interpolated "they" is ambiguous (most likely, "heaven and earth"). "Such" (*nyo ze* 如是) may be taken either simply as "like this" or as the more technical Buddhist term "suchness." The translation masks what seems to be play here with the *ze* 是, introduced in the last line of the preceding section, "what the ten directions truly are (*ze* 是)," and recurring in the lines "one hand pointing to the heavens is (*ze* 是) heaven" and "one hand pointing to the earth is (*ze* 是) the earth." Presumably, the repetition is intended to reinforce the identification of the buddha with heaven and earth.

42 **The crown of the head, the eye, the nose, the skin, flesh, bones and marrow** (*chōnei ganzei bikū hi niku kotsu zui* 頂顙・眼睛・鼻孔・皮肉・骨髓): All these body parts figure frequently in Zen texts as synecdoches for the (true) person. See Supplementary Notes, s.v. "Crown of the head," "Nose," "Skin, flesh, and marrow."

43 **considering and thinking** (*gigi ryō* 擬議量): Taking *ryō* 量 here as *shiryō* 思量; a somewhat unusual combination with *gigi* 擬議, a common term with the sense "to consider saying [something]," "to be on the verge of speaking." Alternatively, the three glyphs could be parsed, "the measure (i.e., "extent") of considering."

44 **Taking up the body of "the *śramaṇa* of all the worlds in the ten directions"** (*jin jippō kai shamon shin o nenrai shite* 盡十方界沙門身を拈來して): The grammatical subject being unexpressed, the agent here is ambiguous. The translation follows the punctuation in Kawamura's text, but the passage could be parsed differently: "It is like this without moving all the ten directions. Without depending on considering and thinking, taking up the body of the *śramaṇa* of all the worlds in the ten directions, we see the body of the *śramaṇa* of all the worlds in the ten directions." The expression "taking up" (*nenrai shite* 拈來して), typically meaning "to take up for consideration," harks back to the line near the beginning of our text, "if we did not take up (*nenrai sezareba* 拈來せざれば) the buddha lands, there would be no ten directions."

[55:15]
盡十方界、是自己光明。

"*All the worlds in the ten directions are the radiance of the self.*"[45]

[55:16]
自己とは、父母未生以前の鼻孔なり。鼻孔あやまりて自己の手裏にあるを、盡十方界といふ。しかあるに、自己現成して現成公案なり、開殿見佛なり。しかあれども、眼睛被別人換却木槵子了也。しかあれども、劈面來、大家相見することをうべし。さらに、呼則易、遣則難なりといへども、喚得廻頭、自廻頭堪作何用、便著者漢廻頭なり。飯待喫人、衣待著人のとき、摸索不著なるがごとくなりとも、可惜許、曾與爾三十棒。

"The self" means the nose "*before your father and mother were born.*"[46] The nose inadvertently in the hand of the self is called "all the ten directions."[47] Still, the self is realized and is the "kōan realized," is "*opening the hall and seeing the buddha.*"[48] Nevertheless, the eye has been switched by another for a soapberry seed.[49] Nevertheless, it's right in

---

45 **"the radiance of the self"** (*jiko kōmyō* 自己光明): Continuing the quotation of Changsha's saying (see above, Note 23). A somewhat unusual expression, likely derived from the more common "radiance of the buddha" (*butsu kōmyō* 佛光明), used for the nimbus surrounding a buddha's body and, by metaphorical extension, his wisdom.

46 **the nose "before your father and mother were born"** (*bumo* [also read *fubo*] *mishō izen no bikū* 父母未生以前の鼻孔): Variation on the more common Zen expression "your original face (*honrai menmoku* 本來面目) before your father and mother were born" (some would read this, "before your father and mother gave birth"). The "nose" (or "nostril"), in a similar sense, has already appeared just above, section 14. See Supplementary Notes, s.v. "Nose," "Before your father and mother were born."

47 **The nose inadvertently in the hand of the self** (*bikū ayamarite jiko no shuri ni aru* 鼻孔あやまりて自己の手裏にある): A decidedly odd expression, presumably meaning something like "the person being by nature (or finding itself) in the self." Perhaps playing with combinations of sayings in Zen texts such as "the nose is in another person's hand" (*bikū zai tanin shuri* 鼻孔在他人手裏) (*Congrong lu* 從容錄, T.2004.48:262b14), or "all the whole earth is at once in my hand" (*jin daichi ichiji zai ga shuri* 盡大地一時在我手裏) (*Biyan lu* 碧巖錄, T.2003.48:145b12). For more on the metaphorical uses of the word "nose," see Supplementary Notes, s.v. "Nose."

48 **Still, the self is realized** (*shika aru ni, jiko genjō shite* しかあるに、自己現成して): The adverbial "still" here reads *shika aru ni* しかあるに in an adversative sense; it might also be taken to mean "thus."
"opening the hall and seeing the buddha" (*kaiden kenbutsu* 開殿見佛): Likely from the *Rujing heshang yulu* 如淨和尚語錄 (T.2002A.48:121c10). A similar expression appears in the "Henzan" 遍參 chapter: "Opening the hall and seeing the buddhas and ancestors" (*shobutsu shoso o kaiden sanken suru* 諸佛諸祖を開殿參見する).

49 **the eye has been switched by another for a soapberry seed** (*ganzei hi betsunin kankyaku mokukansu ryō ya* 眼睛被別人換却木槵子了也): Generally taken to mean that one has come to see with authentically Buddhist eyes. The soapberry seed (*mokukansu* 木槵子) is used for Buddhist prayer beads (*juzu* 珠數). Dōgen has a similar line in his "Shōbōgenzō butsu kōjō ji" 正法眼藏佛向上事, probably after a saying of Chan Master

*your face; everyone should be able to see it.*⁵⁰ Furthermore, while it may be that *"summoning him is easy but sending him off is hard," "when called, he turns his head; what's the use" of turning the head ourselves? Make this fellow turn his head.*⁵¹ *When the food waits for the person to eat it, and the clothes wait for the person to wear them, though we seem to be groping for it without touching it, how sad that I've already given you the thirty blows.*⁵²

Yunmen Wenyan 雲門文偃 (*Yunmen yulu* 雲門語錄, T.1988.47:544a11-12):
若説佛説祖、佛意祖意大似將木槵子換却爾眼睛相似。
If we talk of the buddhas and talk of the ancestors, the intention of the buddhas and the intention of the ancestors resembles switching soapberry seeds for your eyes.

50   **Nevertheless, it's right in your face; everyone should be able to see it** (*hekimen* [also read *hitsumen*] *rai, daike shōken suru koto o u beshi* 劈面來、大家相見すること をうべし): A passage largely in Chinese syntax, for which no source has been identified. "Right in your face" renders the Chinese colloquialism *pimian lai* 劈面來, meaning something like "to come head on." The compound *pimian* has a literal sense "to split the face," and some interpreters, beginning with the *Shōbōgenzō shō* 正法眼藏抄 (CKZS.7:313) suggest that Dōgen has this sense in mind here.

51   **while it may be that "summoning him is easy but sending him off is hard," "when called, he turns his head; what's the use" of turning the head ourselves? Make this fellow turn his head** (*ko soku i, ken soku nan nari to iedomo, kan toku kai tō, ji kai tō kan sa ka yō, ben chaku sha kan kai tō nari* 呼則易、遣則難なりといへども、喚得廻頭、自廻頭堪作何用、便著者漢廻頭なり): A tentative translation of a passage, almost entirely in Chinese syntax, that is variously interpreted. Apart from the last sentence, the wording closely parallels the comments on case 56 of the *Biyan lu* 碧巖錄 (T.2003.48:190a18), in which the master Qinshan 欽山 calls a monk to him. The comment:

呼則易遣則難。喚得回頭。堪作什麼。
Summoning him is easy; sending him off is hard. Having been called, he turns his head. What good is that?

52   **the food waits for the person to eat it, and the clothes wait for the person to wear them** (*han tai kitsu nin, e tai jaku nin* 飯待喫人、衣待著人): Seemingly a proverb (though the source is unidentified), in Chinese syntax, meaning something like "it is the eater that makes the food and the wearer that makes the clothes." The translation masks what may be play with the predicate *chaku* 著, translated as "wears" here, as "make" in the phrase "make this fellow turn the head" in the preceding sentence, and as "touching" in the phrase just following.

groping for it without touching it (*mo saku fu jaku* 摸索不著): I.e., "being unable to find it"; a fairly common idiom in Zen texts, used as we might say one "doesn't get it." The presumed antecedent for the interpolated "it" here is "the person" who eats the food and wears the clothes.

how sad that I've already given you the thirty blows (*kashakuko, zō yo ni sanjū bō* 可惜許、曾與爾三十棒): Again, in Chinese syntax. The Chinese *kexi xu* 可惜許 ("how sad") is a common lament in Chan texts; "the thirty blows" (*sanshi bang* 三十棒) is a standard figure of speech used by the Chan master to indicate the "guilt" of the student.

[55:17] {2:96}
盡十方界、在自己光明裏。

"All the worlds in the ten directions are within the radiance of the self."[53]

[55:18]
眼皮一枚、これを自己光明とす。忽然として打綻するを在裏とす。見由在眼を盡十方界といふ。しかもかくのごとくなりといへども、同牀眠知被穿。

The eyelid is "the radiance of the self." Suddenly to open it is "are within." The dependence of seeing on what is in the eye is called "all the worlds in the ten directions."[54] Nevertheless, though this is the case, *when you sleep on the same bench, you know the holes in the quilt.*[55]

[55:19]
盡十方界、無一人不自己。

"In all the worlds in the ten directions, there is no one that is not the self."[56]

[55:20]
しかあればすなはち、箇箇の作家、箇箇の拳頭、ひとりの十方としても自己にあらざるなし。自己なるがゆえに、自自己己みなこれ十方なり。自自己己の十方、したしく十方を罣礙するなり。自自己己の命脈、ともに自己の手裏にあるがゆえに、還他本分草料なり。いまなにとしてか達磨眼睛・瞿曇鼻孔、あらたに露柱の胎裏にある。いはく、出入也十方十面一任なり。

Therefore, of every "maestro," every "fist," there is no one of the ten directions that is not the self.[57] Because they are the self, each and every

---

53 **"are within the radiance of the self"** (*zai jiko kōmyō ri* 在自己光明裏): Continuing the quotation of Changsha's saying (see above, Note 23).

54 **The dependence of seeing on what is in the eye** (*ken yu zai gen* 見由在眼): Perhaps reflecting the common Chan saying, "what's in the eye is called 'seeing'; what's in the ear is called 'hearing'" (*zai yan yue jian, zai er yue wen* 在眼曰見、在耳曰聞).

55 **when you sleep on the same bench, you know the holes in the quilt** (*dō shō min chi hi sen* 同牀眠知被穿): Generally taken to mean that one knows the reality of the self and the worlds when they are one. The same metaphor can be found in the *Biyan lu* 碧巖錄 (T.2003.48:178b21):

若不同床睡、焉知被底穿。
If they're not sleeping on the same bench,
How would he know the holes in the quilt?

56 **"there is no one that is not the self"** (*mu ichinin fu jiko* 無一人不自己): Continuing the quotation of Changsha's saying (see above, Note 23).

57 **every "maestro," every "fist"** (*ko ko no soka, ko ko no kentō* 箇箇の作家、箇箇の拳頭): "Maestro" attempts to render the Chinese *zuojia* 作家, regularly used of an author or poet and, in Zen usage, of an accomplished master; we had the "fist" used in reference to such a master in section 1, above.

self is the ten directions; the ten directions of each and every self themselves obstruct the ten directions.[58] Because the vital artery of each and every self is in the hand of the self, it is *return his original lot of feed.*[59] Why would Dharma's eye and Gautama's nose now be freshly in the womb of the pillar?[60] It is because going *in and out are left entirely to the ten directions, the ten sides.*[61]

* * * * *

[55:21]
玄沙院宗一大師云、盡十方界、是一顆明珠。

Great Master Zongyi of Xuansha Cloister said, "All the worlds in the ten directions are one bright pearl."[62]

[55:22]
あきらかにしりぬ、一顆明珠は、これ盡十方界なり。神頭鬼面、これを窟宅とせり、佛祖兒孫、これを眼睛とせり。人家男女、これを頂顋・拳頭と

---

58 **each and every self** (*ji ji ko ko* 自自己己): Loose translation of a playful expression that doubles each of the two elements in the compound term *jiko* 自己 ("self"); as if one were to say something like, "itself, itself, myself, myself."

themselves obstruct the ten directions (*shitashiku jippō o keige suru* したしく十方を罣礙する): The use of *keige su* 罣礙す ("to obstruct," "to hinder") here follows a familiar pattern in Dōgen's writings, in which the term seems to mean "to define," "to identify as."

59 **return his original lot of feed** (*gen ta honbun sōryō* 還他本分草料): Reflecting a fairly common expression in Zen texts, which treats the person as a domestic animal to be fed; see, e.g., the comment in the *Biyan lu* 碧巖錄 (T.2003.48:157c24):

何不與他本分草料。
Why doesn't he give him his original lot of feed?

60 **in the womb of the pillar** (*rōchū no tai ri* 露柱の胎裏): The question here would seem to be, in what sense is the self in the world? "Pillars pregnant" (*rochū kaitai* 露柱懷胎), commonly found in Zen texts, suggests vitality within an apparently lifeless object; see Supplementary Notes, s.v. "Pillars and lanterns."

61 **going in and out are left entirely to the ten directions, the ten sides** (*shutsu nyū ya jippō jūmen ichinin* 出入也十方十面一任): The "ten sides" are synonymous with the "ten directions." Perhaps somewhat as one might say in English, "let the four winds blow," Zen texts often speak of "leaving things to" (*yiren* 一任) the directions — as in such locutions as, "leave it entirely to the four directions and eight sides" (*yiren sifang bamian* 一任四方八面); "leave it entirely to east and west" (*yiren tongxi* 一任東西); or simply "leave it entirely to the directions" (*yiren zhufang* 一任諸方).

62 **Great Master Zongyi of Xuansha Cloister** (*Gensha in Shūitsu daishi* 玄沙院宗一大師): I.e., Chan Master Xuansha Shibei 玄沙師備. His saying, "all the worlds in the ten directions are one bright pearl," appears in Dōgen's *shinji Shōbōgenzō* 眞字正法眼藏 (DZZ.5:132, case 15) and is treated in "Shōbōgenzō ikka myōju" 正法眼藏一顆明珠. For sources of the saying, see Supplementary Notes, s.v. "One bright pearl."

せり、初心晩學、これを著衣喫飯とせり。先師、これを泥彈子として兄弟を打著す。しかもこれ單提の一著子なりといへども、祖宗の眼睛を抉出しきたれり。抉出するとき、祖宗ともに壹隻手をいだす。さらに眼睛裏放光するのみなり。

Clearly, we know that "one bright pearl" is all the worlds in the ten directions. Spirits and demons take it as their cave; the descendants of the buddhas and ancestors take it as the eye; the men and women of families take it as a head or a fist; beginners and latecomers take it as wearing clothes and having meals.[63] My former master took it as a ball of mud and hit the brothers with it.[64] Moreover, though we may say this is "one move directly presented," he has gouged out the eye of the ancestor.[65] When he gouges it out, the ancestors "each put out a hand."[66] Going further, it is just *from within their eyes shines a light.*[67]

* * * * *

---

63 **Spirits and demons** (*jinzu kimen* 神頭鬼面): More literally, perhaps, "spirit heads and demon faces"; a fixed phrase appearing in a number of Dōgen's texts.

beginners and latecomers (*shoshin bangaku* 初心晩學): A casual translation of an expression quite common in Dōgen's writings for the inexperienced practitioner; see Supplementary Notes, s.v. "Beginner's mind."

64 **My former master** (*senshi* 先師): I.e., Dōgen's late teacher, Tiantong Rujing 天童如淨 (1162-1227). For the remark to which Dōgen alludes here, see Supplementary Notes, s.v. "Gouge out Bodhidharma's eye."

65 **"one move directly presented"** (*tantei no ichi jakusu* 單提の一著子): "One move" (*ichi jakusu*) is used in reference to moving a piece in a board game; in Zen texts, often a "move" in a dialogue. "Directly presented" (*tantei* 單提) renders a term referring to a Zen master's direct teaching style. For the Chinese equivalent of this phrase, *danti yizhuo* 單提一著, see, e.g., *Rujing heshang yulu* 如淨和尚語錄, T.2002A.48:123c16.

66 **"each put out a hand"** (*tomo ni isseki shu o idasu* ともに壹隻手をいだす): Perhaps reflecting a phrase from a story recorded in Dōgen's *shinji Shōbōgenzō* 眞字正法眼藏, DZZ.5:175-176, case 97: A monk asked Luoshan Daoxian 羅山道閑 how much he should pay to have a stūpa built. Luoshan said,

若將三文錢與匠人、和尚此生決定不得塔。若將兩文錢與匠人、和尚與匠人共出一隻手。若將一文錢與匠人、帶累匠人眉鬚墮落。

If you offer the artisan three cash, the Reverend will definitely not get a stūpa in this lifetime. If you offer the artisan two cash, the Reverend and the artisan will each put out one hand. If you offer the artisan one cash, you'll so perplex him that the artisan's eyebrows and beard will fall off.

67 **"from within their eyes shines a light"** (*ganzei ri hōkō suru* 眼睛裏放光する): Probably again from the words of Rujing 如淨 (*Rujing heshang yulu* 如淨和尚語錄, T.2002A.48:123b17):

眼睛裡放光、鼻孔裡出氣。
From within the eyes shines a light;
From within the nose issues a breath.

[55:23] {2:97}
乾峰和尚、因僧問、十方薄伽梵、一路涅槃門。未審、路頭在什麼處。乾峰以拄杖畫一畫云、在遮裏。

Reverend Qianfeng was once asked by a monk, "The bhagavats in the ten directions are on one road to the gate of nirvāṇa. I don't understand, where are they on that road?"[68]

Qianfeng drew a mark with his staff and said, "They're here."

[55:24]
いはゆる在遮裏は十方なり、薄伽梵とは拄杖なり、拄杖とは在遮裏なり、一路は十方なり。しかあれども、瞿曇の鼻孔裏に、拄杖をかくすことなかれ、拄杖の鼻孔に、拄杖を撞著することなかれ。しかもかくのごとくなりとも、乾峰老漢、すでに十方薄伽梵・一路涅槃門を料理すると認ずることなかれ。ただ在遮裏と道著するのみなり。在遮裏はなきにあらず、乾峰老漢、はじめより拄杖に瞞ぜられざらん、よし。おほよそ、活鼻孔を十方と參學するのみなり。

This "they're here" is the "ten directions"; the "*bhagavats*" are the "staff"; the "staff" is "they're here"; the "one road" is the "ten directions." Nevertheless, do not hide the staff in the nose of Gautama; do not ram the staff in the nose of the staff. Nevertheless, though this is the case, do not think that old man Qianfeng has managed "*the bhagavats in the ten directions*" or "*the road to the gate of nirvāṇa*": he just says, "they're here."[69] It is not that "they're here" is not the case, and it is fine so long as old man Qianfeng is not from the start deceived by his staff. In sum, we just study the living nose as the ten directions.

正法眼藏十方第五十五
Treasury of the True Dharma Eye
The Ten Directions
Number 55

---

68   **Reverend Qianfeng** (*Kenpō oshō* 乾峰和尚): Dates unknown; a follower of Dongshan Liangjie 洞山良价 (807-869). This incident appears in Dōgen's *shinji Shōbōgenzō* 眞字正法眼藏, DZZ.5:136, case 37; see also *Zongmen tongyao ji* 宗門統要集, ZTS.1:175b7-8.

bhagavats (*bagyabon* 薄伽梵): "Revered Ones"; a common epithet of the buddhas. Rendered here in the Chinese transliteration, *bojiafan*, it is typically translated as *shizun* 世尊 ("World-Honored One").

69   **old man Qianfeng has managed "the *bhagavats* in the ten directions" or "the road to the gate of nirvāṇa"** (*Kenpō rōkan, sude ni jippō bagyabon ichiro nehan mon o ryōri suru* 乾峰老漢、すでに十方薄伽梵・一路涅槃門を料理する): The translation follows Kawamura's punctuation in taking "the *bhagavats* in the ten directions" and "the road to the gate of nirvāṇa" as two topics; the passage could also be read, "old man Qianfeng has managed the *bhagavats* in the ten directions on the road to the gate of nirvāṇa." "To manage" here translates the verb *ryōri su* 料理す, "to organize," "to arrange."

55. The Ten Directions *Jippō* 十方

[Ryūmonji MS:]

爾時寛元元年癸卯十一月十三日、在日本國越州吉峰精舍示衆
Presented to the assembly at Kippō Vihāra, Etchū, in the Land of Japan; twenty-third day, eleventh month of the junior water year of the rabbit, the first year of Kangen [25 December 1243][70]

[Tōunji MS:]

寛元三年乙巳窮冬廿四日、在越州大佛寺侍司書寫。懷奘
Copied at the acolyte's office, Daibutsu Monastery, Etchū; twenty-fourth day of winter's end, the junior wood year of the snake, the third year of Kangen [12 January 1246]. Ejō[71]

于時文明十二庚子春王正月朔日、於于越州吉田郡志比吉祥山永平寺承陽庵。比丘光周
In the Jōyō Hermitage, Eihei Monastery, Mount Kichijō, Shihi, Yoshida District, Esshū; on the first day of the first month, the King of Spring, senior metal year of the rat, the twelfth year of Bunmei [11 February 1480]. Bhikṣu Kōshū[72]

---

70 The Tōunji 洞雲寺 MS shares an identical colophon.
71 **winter's end** (*kyūtō* 窮冬): The last lunar month of the year.
72 **Jōyō Hermitage** (*Jōyōan* 承陽庵): Dōgen's memorial shrine at Eiheiji 永平寺, from his posthumous title Great Master Jōyō (*Jōyō daishi* 承陽大師).
King of Spring (*shun'ō* 春王): The first lunar month.
Bhikṣu Kōshū (*biku Kōshū* 比丘光周): Fifteenth abbot of Eiheiji (1434–1492?).

Treasury of the True Dharma Eye
Number 56

Seeing Buddha
Kenbutsu
見佛

Seeing Buddha

Kenbutsu

INTRODUCTION

This work was composed at the site known as Yamashibu 禪師峰 (or Zenji Peak) in the winter of 1243, Dōgen's first in the snow country of Echizen. It occurs as number 56 in the seventy-five-chapter compilation of the *Shōbōgenzō*, number 47 in the sixty-chapter compilation, and number 61 in the Honzan edition.

As its title indicates, the essay is devoted to the question of what it means to see a buddha. It opens with a passage from the *Diamond Sūtra*, in which the Buddha teaches that one truly sees him when one understands that all his identifying characteristics are empty of ultimate reality. While affirming this famous teaching, Dōgen proceeds in his essay to explore a richer understanding of seeing buddha that identifies it with all the acts of Buddhist piety and practice — an understanding he develops largely through a series of comments on relevant passages from his favorite scripture, the *Lotus Sūtra*. Finally, the essay closes with remarks on the famous story of the Arhat Piṇḍola's re-enactment of his seeing Buddha Śākyamuni.

正法眼藏第五十六
Treasury of the True Dharma Eye
Number 56

見佛
Seeing Buddha

[56:1] {2:98}

釋迦牟尼佛、告大衆言、若見諸相非相、即見如來。

Buddha Śākyamuni addressed the great assembly saying, "If one sees that the marks are no-marks, that is seeing the Tathāgata."[1]

[56:2]

いまの見諸相と見非相と、透脱せる體達なり、ゆゑに見如來なり。この見佛眼、すでに參開なる現成を見佛とす。見佛眼の活路、これ參佛眼なり。自佛を他方にみ、佛外に自佛をみるとき、條條の蔓枝なりといへども、見佛を參學せると、見佛を辦肯すると、見佛を脱落すると、見佛を得活すると、見佛を使得すると、日面佛見なり、月面佛見なり。恁麼の見佛、ともに無盡面・無盡身・無盡心・無盡手眼の見佛なり。而今脚尖に行履する發心發足よりこのかた、辦道功夫、および證契究徹、みな見佛裏に走入する活眼睛なり、活骨髓なり。

The "seeing marks" and seeing "no-marks" here are liberated personal realizations; hence, they are "seeing the Tathāgata."[2] The manifestation

---

1 **Buddha Śākyamuni** (*Shakamuni butsu* 釋迦牟尼佛): A well-known passage from the *Diamond Sūtra* (*Jingang bore boluomi jing* 金剛般若波羅蜜經, T.235.8:749a24-25), widely cited in Zen and other Buddhist texts. The sūtra is playing here on the technical term "mark" (*sō* 相; S. *lakṣana*), which is used in reference to both (a) the attribute by which a thing is identified as being what it is, and (b) a member of the list of thirty-two distinctive features of the body of a buddha. Here is the original context in Kumārajīva's translation of the sūtra (T.235.8:749a21-25):

須菩提、於意云何。可以身相見如來不。不也世尊。不可以身相得見如來。何以故。如來所説身相即非身相。佛告須菩提。凡所有相皆是虛妄。若見諸相非相則見如來。

"Subhūti, what do you think? Can one see the Tathāgata by his bodily marks?"
"No, World-Honored One, one cannot see the Tathāgata by his bodily marks. Why? What are called the bodily marks of the Tathāgata are no-bodily-marks."
The Buddha addressed Subhūti, "Whatever marks there are, they are all deceptive. If one sees that marks are no-marks, one sees the Tathāgata."

2 **The "seeing marks" and seeing "no-marks" here** (*ima no ken shosō to ken hisō to* いまの見諸相と見非相と): As he himself makes clear in section 3, below, Dōgen departs here from the standard understanding of the *Diamond Sūtra* line, by taking "marks"

of this eye of seeing buddha as truly studied and opened is called "seeing buddha."[3] The life-saving path of the eye of seeing buddha — this is the buddha eye of study.[4] When we see our own buddha elsewhere, or see our own buddha apart from buddha, this may be various vines and branches; but to have studied seeing buddha, to confirm seeing buddha, to slough off seeing buddha, to revive seeing buddha, and to employ seeing buddha — these are the seeing of the Sun-faced Buddha and the seeing of the Moon-faced Buddha.[5] This kind of seeing buddha is, at the same time, seeing buddha of inexhaustible faces, inexhaustible bodies,

---

(*shosō* 諸相) and "no-marks" (*hisō* 非相) as two distinct objects of the verb "to see" (*ken* 見), a reading crucial to his subsequent argument.

3   **The manifestation of this eye of seeing buddha as truly studied and opened** (*kono kenbutsu gen, sude ni sankai naru genjō* この見佛眼、すでに參開なる現成): The expression *kenbutsu gen* 見佛眼 is more naturally rendered "the eye that sees the buddha"; the translation "eye of seeing buddha" seeks to preserve the possibility that "buddha" is both the agent and the object of "seeing." The unusual *sankai* 參開 ("study and open") occurs several times in the *Shōbōgenzō*, always in connection with the opening of the eye; the translation takes *san* 參 here as *sangaku* 參學.

4   **The life-saving path of the eye of seeing buddha — this is the buddha eye of study** (*kenbutsugen no katsuro, kore sanbutsugen nari* 見佛眼の活路、これ參佛眼なり): The expression *sanbutsugen* 參佛眼 could also be parsed "the eye that studies the buddha." The translation here takes the sense to be that the spiritual practice of seeing buddha is the awakened buddha eye with which we practice. A similar usage is found in the "Shōbōgenzō baika" 正法眼藏梅華:

親曽見佛の道旨、しづかに參佛眼あるべし。

For the meaning of the words, "[Piṇḍola had] personally once seen the Buddha," we should have the buddha eye that quietly studies it.

The term *katsuro* 活路 ("life-saving path"), appearing frequently in Dōgen's writing, is often taken as "vital path," though its colloquial meaning is a "path to life" — i.e., an escape route from a deadly situation.

5   **When we see our own buddha elsewhere, or see our own buddha apart from buddha** (*jibutsu o tahō ni mi, butsugai ni jibutsu o miru toki* 自佛を他方にみ、佛外に自佛をみるとき): The exact implications are unclear; perhaps "when we see the buddha as other than ourselves, or see ourselves as other than a buddha."

vines and branches (*manshi* 蔓枝): An unusual expression, repeated below (section 10), but not found elsewhere in the *Shōbōgenzō*; suggests a dense tangle. Here, perhaps, expressing the myriad ways we may see buddha.

to have studied seeing buddha (*kenbutsu o sangaku seru* 見佛を參學せる): The series beginning with this phrase appears to represent stages on the "life-saving path" of "seeing buddha": study, understanding, transcendence, return, and application.

to revive seeing buddha (*kenbutsu o tokkatsu suru* 見佛を得活する): The expression *tokkatsu* 得活 ("to revive") here suggests the words of Dongshan Liangjie 洞山良价 (807-869), "In death, he lives" (*shichū tokkatsu* 死中得活), said in answer to the question of who it is that "talks of the mind and talks of the nature" (*sesshin sesshō* 説心説性; treated by Dōgen in the *Shōbōgenzō* chapter of that name).

inexhaustible minds, inexhaustible hands and eyes.[6] Now, ever since bringing forth the mind [of bodhi] and setting out to engage in the conduct on tiptoe, our concentrated effort in pursuit of the way, as well as our complete mastery of verification and accord, are all the living eye, the living bones and marrow, that run into seeing buddha.[7]

[56:3]
しかあれば、自盡界・他盡方、遮箇頭・那箇頭、おなじく見佛功夫なり。如來道の若見諸相非相を拈來するに、參學眼なきともがらおもはくは、諸相を相にあらずとみる、すなはち見如來、といふ。そのおもむきは、諸相は相にはあらず、如來なりとみる、といふとおもふ。まことに小量の一邊は、しかのごとくも參學すべしといへども、佛意の道成は、しかにはあらざるなり。しるべし、諸相を見取し、非相を見取する、即見如來なり。如來あり、非如來あり。

Thus, *all the worlds of self and all the directions of other, over here and over there*, are equally the concentrated effort of seeing buddha.[8] In taking up the Tathāgata's words, "*If one sees that the marks are no-marks*," those without the eye of study think that he is saying, "to see marks as

---

to employ seeing buddha (*kenbutsu o shitoku suru* 見佛を使得する): Possibly recalling the well-known Zen expression "employ the twelve times" (*shitoku jūni ji* 使得十二時) attributed to Zhaozhou 趙州; see Supplementary Notes.

seeing of the Sun-faced Buddha (*Nichimen butsu ken* 日面佛見); **seeing of the Moon-faced Buddha** (*Gachimen butsu ken* 月面佛見): From the names of two buddhas given in the *Foming jing* 佛名經; see Supplementary Notes, s.v. "Sun face, moon face." Dōgen's phrasing, like its translation here, can be read with these two buddhas as either the objects or the agents of the "seeing" (or both).

6 **seeing buddha of inexhaustible faces, inexhaustible bodies, inexhaustible minds, inexhaustible hands and eyes** (*mujin men mujin shin mujin shin mujin shugen no kenbutsu* 無盡面・無盡身・無盡心・無盡手眼の見佛): Playing off the "Sun-faced" and "Moon-faced" buddhas just above; probably to be taken as seeing all the faces, bodies, minds, hands, and eyes of the buddhas. "Inexhaustible hands and eyes" (*mujin shugen* 無盡手眼) may reflect the hands, each with an eye in the palm, of the thousand-armed Bodhisattva Avalokiteśvara (*Senju Kannon bosatsu* 千手觀音菩薩), who appears several times in the *Shōbōgenzō*.

7 **Now, ever since bringing forth the mind [of bodhi] and setting out to engage in the conduct on tiptoe** (*nikon kyakusen ni anri suru hosshin hossoku yori kono kata* 而今脚尖に行履する發心發足よりこのかた): I.e., ever since we undertook Buddhist practice; see Supplementary Notes, s.v. "Bring forth the mind." A somewhat awkward locution that plays with terms related to the foot: "tip of the foot" (*kyakusen* 脚尖), "to tread" (*anri* 行履), "to step forth" (*hossoku* 發足); to be followed by the curious image of the eye, bones, and marrow "running into" (*sōnyū* 走入) seeing buddha.

8 **all the worlds of self and all the directions of other, over here and over there** (*jijinkai tajinhō, shakotō nakotō* 自盡界・他盡方、遮箇頭・那箇頭): Unusual expressions; perhaps meaning something like, "our world and other realms, both subject and object." Taken literally, the claim seems to be that everything is engaged in the practice of "seeing buddha."

not being marks is seeing the Tathāgata."⁹ They think the point is to see that the marks are not marks but the Tathāgata. To be sure, a small one-sided [view] might well understand it like this, but the expression of the Buddha's intention is not like this.¹⁰ We should recognize that to see the marks and to see the no-marks — this is "seeing the Tathāgata." There is a Tathāgata and there is a No-Tathāgata.¹¹

* * * * *

[56:4] {2:99}
清涼院大法眼禪師云、若見諸相非相、即不見如來。

Chan Master Da Fayan of Qingliang Cloister said, "If one sees that the marks are no-marks, that is not seeing the Tathāgata."¹²

[56:5]
いまこの大法眼道は、見佛道なり。これに法眼道あり、見佛道ありて、通語するに、競頭來なり、共出手なり。法眼道は、耳處に聞著すべし、見佛道は、眼處聞聲すべし。

Here, these words of Da Fayan are the words of seeing buddha.¹³ We have in this the words of Fayan, and we have the words of seeing bud-

---

9 "**If one sees that the marks are no-marks**" (*nyaku ken shosō hisō* 若見諸相非相): Given in the original Chinese of the sūtra passage; rendered here as "those without the eye of study" would read it. According to Dōgen's preferred reading, this should be read, "If one sees the marks and the no-marks." Such a reading likely reflects the common claim that a buddha can discern all phenomena (dharmas) while at the same time seeing that they are empty of independent reality.

10 **small one-sided [view]** (*shōryō no ippen* 小量の一邊): Literally, "one side of little measure"; presumably, one shallow, partial viewpoint.

expression of the Buddha's intention (*butsui no dōjō* 佛意の道成): Taking *dōjō* 道成 as the more familiar *dō genjō* 道現成.

11 **There is a Tathāgata and there is a No-Tathāgata** (*nyorai ari, hi nyorai ari* 如來あり、非如來あり): Perhaps meaning, "there is seeing the Buddha in the marks and seeing the Buddha in the no-marks."

12 **Chan Master Da Fayan of Qingliang Cloister** (*Seiryōin Dai Hōgen zenji* 清涼院大法眼禪師): I.e., Fayan Wenyi 法眼文益 (885-958). Qingliang Cloister 清涼院 was located in the Jiangning 江寧 district of Jiangsu. This saying appears in several Chan sources; see, e.g., *Hongzhi chanshi guanglu* 宏智禪師廣錄 (T.2001.48:28c26-28; 55a10-13). The translation follows the standard (rather than Dōgen's) reading of the first clause, likely as Fayan would have parsed it.

13 **Here, these words of Da Fayan are the words of seeing buddha** (*ima kono Dai Hōgen dō wa, kenbutsu dō nari* いまこの大法眼道は、見佛道なり): The expression "words of seeing buddha" (*kenbutsu dō* 見佛道) is open to various interpretations. The most likely here is probably that, when Fayan speaks of "not seeing the Tathāgata," he is speaking of "seeing buddha." Hence, in the following sentence, the two ways of speaking contend with each other even as they both offer us something.

dha; and, put in common terms, they are competing head to head, they are mutually extending a hand.[14] The words of Fayan, we should hear with the ear; the words of seeing buddha, we should hear with the eye.[15]

[56:6]
しかあるを、この宗旨を参学する従来のおもはくは、諸相は如来相なり、一相の、如来相にあらざる、まじはれることなし。この相を、かりにも非相とすべからず。もしこれを非相とするは、捨父逃逝なり。この相すなはち如来相なるがゆえに、諸相は諸相なるべしと道取するなり、といひきたれり。まことにこれ大乗の極談なり、諸方の所証なり。しかのごとく決定一定して、信受参受すべし、さらに随風東西の軽毛なることなかれ。諸相は如来相なり、非相にあらず、と参究見佛し、決定証信して、受持すべし、諷誦通利すべし。かくのごとくして、自己の耳目に見聞ひまなからしむべし、自己の身心骨髄に脱落ならしむべし、自己の山河尽界に透脱ならしむべし、これ参学佛祖行履なり。自己の云為にあれば、自己の眼睛を発明せしむべからず、とおもふことなかれ。自己の一転語に転ぜられて、自己の一転佛祖を見脱落するなり。これ佛祖の家常なり。

Be that as it may, what has been thought by those who study the essential point of this is that the marks are marks of the Tathāgata, and there is not mixed in with them a single mark that is not the mark of the Tathāgata.[16] These marks should not, even provisionally, be considered no-marks; to consider them no-marks is *"forsaking one's father and running away."*[17] They have said that, since these marks are marks of

---

14 **We have in this the words of Fayan, and we have the words of seeing buddha** (*kore ni Hōgen dō ari, kenbutsu dō arite* これに法眼道あり、見佛道ありて): I.e., here, we have Fayan's statement on "not seeing the Tathāgata" and the Buddha's statement on "seeing the Tathāgata."

put in common terms (*tsūgo suru ni* 通語するに): A tentative translation, based on the usual sense of *tsūgo* 通語 as "common parlance," "ordinary speech"; but here the phrase is often interpreted to mean something like, "in what the two kinds of words share."

15 **we should hear with the eye** (*gensho monshō su beshi* 眼処聞声すべし): Perhaps, recalling the verse of Dongshan Liangjie 洞山良价, recorded in the *shinji Shōbōgenzō* 眞字正法眼藏 (DZZ.5:204, case 148) and discussed in "Shōbōgenzō mujō seppō" 正法眼藏無情説法:

也太奇、也太奇、無情説法不思議、若將耳聽終難會、眼處聞聲方得知。
How strange! How strange!
The insentient preaching the dharma is inconceivable.
If we use the ear to hear it, it's hard in the end to understand;
Only when the eye hears the voices do we know it.

16 **what has been thought by those who study the essential point of this** (*kono shūshi o sangaku suru jūrai no omowaku wa* この宗旨を参学する従来のおもはくは): Presumably, a reference to the opinions of those who have commented on Fayan's saying, but neither the antecedent of "this" nor the authorities Dōgen alludes to here is clear.

17 **"forsaking one's father and running away"** (*shafu tōzei* 捨父逃逝): A phrase from the parable of the prodigal son (*gūji* 窮子) that appears in the *Lotus Sūtra* (*Miaofa lianhua jing* 妙法蓮華經, T.262.9:16b26, 17c14): the son of a wealthy landowner wanders

the Tathāgata, he is saying that the marks must be marks. Truly, this is the ultimate discourse of the Great Vehicle, verified in all quarters. Determining once and for all that it is like this, we should believe and accept it, study and accept it; do not, whatever you do, be a wisp of down *following the wind east and west*.[18] Investigating it and seeing buddha, determining it and verifying our faith, we should receive and keep, recite and become well versed in [the truth that] the marks are the marks of the Tathāgata, not no-marks. In this way, we should not rest from seeing and hearing it with our own ears and eyes; we should cause it to be sloughed off from our own body and mind, bones and marrow; we should cause it to be liberated from our own mountains and rivers, and all the worlds. This is the conduct of studying the buddhas and ancestors. Do not think that, since it is our own word and deed, it should not open and illuminate our own eyes: turned by our own turning word, we see and slough off our own turning buddhas and ancestors.[19] This is the everyday life of the buddhas and ancestors.

[56:7] {2:100}
このゆえに、參取する隻條道あり。いはゆる諸相すでに非相にあらず、非相すなはち諸相なり。非相これ諸相なるゆえに、非相まことに非相なり。喚作非相の相、ならびに喚作諸相の相、ともに如來相なりと參學すべし。參學の屋裏に兩部の典釋あり、いはゆる參見典と參不見典となり。これ活眼睛の所參學なり。もしいまだこれらの典籍を著眼看の參徹せざれば、參徹眼にあらず。參徹眼にあらざれば、見佛にあらず。見佛に諸相處見・非相處見あり、吾不會佛法なり。不見佛に諸相處不見・非相處不見あり、會佛法人得なり。法眼道の八九成、それかくのごとし。

There is, therefore, a single path of inquiry: it is that the marks are definitely not no-marks, and no-marks are precisely marks. Since no-marks are marks, no-marks are truly no-marks. We should recognize that the marks we call no-marks, as well as the marks we call marks, are both

---

abroad for many years forgetting his father and his patrimony. Dōgen's reassertion of the Tathāgata's marks here may well reflect a common preference of his Japanese Buddhist contemporaries for a higher affirmation of the phenomenal world beyond insight into its emptiness.

18 **a wisp of down following the wind east and west** (*zuifū tōzai no keimō* 隨風東西の輕毛): A fixed expression, here in mixed Japanese and Chinese, for instability, "fickleness," "following fashion," etc.

19 **turned by our own turning word, we see and slough off our own turning buddhas and ancestors** (*jiko no ittengo ni ten zerarete, jiko no itten busso o ken datsuraku suru nari* 自己の一轉語に轉ぜられて、自己の一轉佛祖を見脱落するなり): I.e., we can act as our own buddha and ancestor in providing ourselves with a master's "turning word" (*ittengo* 一轉語) that will cause us to "turn around" and see things from a different perspective. For the use of "slough off" (*datsuraku* 脱落), see Supplementary Notes, s.v. "Slough off."

marks of the Tathāgata. Within the house of study are two modes of textual exegesis: texts that investigate "seeing" and texts that investigate "not seeing."[20] This is what is studied by the living eye. If we have not yet thoroughly investigated looking at these texts, it is not the eye of thorough investigation; if it is not the eye of thorough investigation, it is not seeing buddha. In seeing buddha, there is seeing marks and seeing no-marks; this is "*I don't understand the buddha dharma*"; in not seeing buddha, there is not seeing marks and not seeing no-marks; this is "*people who understand the buddha dharma have got it.*"[21] The eight or nine tenths of Fayan's words are like this.[22]

[56:8]
しかありといへども、この一大事因縁、さらにいふべし、若見諸相實相、即見如來。かくのごとくの道取、みなこれ釋迦牟尼佛之所加被力也、異面目の皮肉骨髓にあらず。

While this may be so, of the "cause of this one great matter," it should be further said, "*If one sees the real marks of the marks, that is see-*

---

20 **two modes of textual exegesis** (*ryōbu no tenjaku* 兩部の典釋): Following Kawamura's edition; some MS witnesses read here *ryōbu no tenseki* 兩部の典籍 ("two kinds of texts").

texts that investigate "seeing" and texts that investigate "not seeing" (*san ken ten to san fuken ten* 參見典と參不見典): Or, perhaps, "investigating texts of seeing and investigating texts of not seeing"; presumably, texts that speak of "seeing the Tathāgata" and of "not seeing the Tathāgata" respectively.

21 **"I don't understand the buddha dharma"** (*go fue buppō* 吾不會佛法); **"people who understand the buddha dharma have got it"** (*e buppō nin toku* 會佛法人得): The words of the Sixth Ancestor, Huineng 慧能, in a well-known dialogue recorded in Dōgen's *shinji Shōbōgenzō* 眞字正法眼藏 (DZZ.5:158, case 59):

曹溪山大鑑禪師〈嗣大滿〉因僧問、黃梅意旨何人得。師曰、會佛法人得。僧曰、和尚還得否。師曰、我不得。僧曰、和尚爲甚不得、師曰、我不會佛法。

Chan Master Dajian of Mount Caoxi (succeeded Daman) was asked by a monk: "What people have got the meaning of Huangmei [the Fifth Ancestor, Hongren]?" The Master said, "People who understand the buddha dharma have got it." The monk said, "Has the Reverend got it or not?" The Master said, "I haven't got it." The monk said, "Why has the Reverend not got it?" The Master said, "I don't understand the buddha dharma."

According to Dōgen here, Śākyamuni's "seeing the Tathāgata" corresponds to Huineng's "not understanding the buddha dharma," while Fayan's "not seeing the Tathāgata" is equivalent to people "understanding the buddha dharma."

22 **The eight or nine tenths of Fayan's words are like this** (*Hōgen dō no hakku jō, sore kaku no gotoshi* 法眼道の八九成、それかくのごとし): The term *hakku jō* 八九成 ("eight or nine tenths") is a common expression in Zen commentary used to evaluate a saying as "not bad," "almost there," sometimes as ironic high praise; see Supplementary Notes, s.v. "Eight or nine tenths complete."

ing the Tathāgata."²³ Sayings such as this are all *empowered by Buddha Śākyamuni*; they are not the skin, flesh, bones, and marrow of a different face.²⁴

* * * * *

[56:9]

爾時釋迦牟尼佛、在靈鷲山。因藥王菩薩告大衆言、若親近法師、即得菩薩道。隨順是師學、得見恆沙佛。

At that time, when Buddha Śākyamuni was on Vulture Peak, through Bodhisattva Bhaiṣajyarāja, he addressed the great assembly, saying,²⁵

If one becomes close to the dharma master,
One attains at once the bodhisattva path.
If one studies in accordance with this master,
One will be able to see buddhas numerous as the sands of the Ganges.

---

23 **"cause of this one great matter"** (*kono ichidaiji innen* この一大事因緣): A famous phrase from the *Lotus Sūtra*, in which Buddha Śākyamuni reveals that the buddhas come into this world only to lead beings to buddhahood; see Supplementary Notes, s.v. "Buddhas, the world-honored ones, appear in the world for the reason of one great matter alone."

"If one sees the real marks of the marks" (*nyaku ken shosō jissō* 若見諸相實相): A play, in Chinese, on the famous expression "the real marks of the dharmas" (*shohō jissō* 諸法實相), known especially from the *Lotus Sūtra*; see Supplementary Notes, s.v. "Only buddhas with buddhas can exhaustively investigate the real marks of the dharmas."

24 **empowered by Buddha Śākyamuni** (*Shakamuni butsu shi sho kabi riki* 釋迦牟尼佛之所加被力): Variant of a fixed expression for the power granted one by a sacred being, as, for example, when one is granted a vision.

they are not the skin, flesh, bones, and marrow of a different face (*i menmoku no hi niku kotsu zui ni arazu* 異面目の皮肉骨髓にあらず): I.e., such sayings are not the teachings of anyone but Buddha Śākyamuni. The expression "skin, flesh, bones, and marrow" (*hi niku kotsu zui* 皮肉骨髓) occurs very often throughout the *Shōbōgenzō*, indicating the essence or truth or entirety of something or someone. From the famous story, recorded in the *shinji Shōbōgenzō* 眞字正法眼藏 (DZZ.5:230, case 201), of Bodhidharma's testing of four disciples, to whom he said of each in turn that he (or, in one case, she) had gotten his skin, flesh, bones, and marrow. See Supplementary Notes, s.v. "Skin, flesh, bones, and marrow."

25 **At that time** (*ni ji* 爾時): Quoting (with slight variation) a verse from the "Dharma Master" chapter (*Hosshi bon* 法師品) of the *Lotus Sūtra* (*Miaofa lianhua jing* 妙法蓮華經, T.262.9:32b14-15). The introduction to the verse here represents Dōgen's rewriting of the opening line of the chapter (*Miaofa lianhua jing* 妙法蓮華經, T.262.9:30b29):

爾時世尊、因藥王菩薩、告八萬大士。

At that time, the World-Honored One, through the Bodhisattva Bhaiṣajyarāja, addressed the eighty thousand great persons.

56. Seeing Buddha *Kenbutsu* 見佛

[56:10] {2:101}

いはゆる親近法師といふは、二祖の八載事師のごとし。しかうしてのち、全臂得髓なり。南嶽の十五年の辨道のごとし。師の髓をうるを、親近といふ。菩薩道といふは、吾亦如是、汝亦如是なり。如許多の蔓枝行履を即得するなり。即得は、古來より現ぜるを引得するにあらず、未生を發得するにあらず、現在の漫漫を策把するにあらず、親近得を脱落するを、即得といふ。このゆゑに、一切の得は即得なり。

What is called here "*becoming close to the dharma master*" is like the Second Ancestor's eight years of serving his master; thereafter, his whole arm got the marrow.[26] It is like Nanyue's fifteen years of pursuing the way.[27] Getting the master's marrow is called "becoming close." "The bodhisattva path" is "*I'm also like this, and you're also like this*."[28] It is "attaining at once" so many observances, like vines and branch-

---

26 **the Second Ancestor's eight years of serving his master** (*niso no hassai jishi* 二祖の八載事師): Traditional biographies of the Second Ancestor, Huike 慧可 (487–593), do not typically record that he spent eight years serving his master, Bodhidharma. The influential *Jingde chuandeng lu* 景德傳燈錄 (T.2076.51:220c4-5) says rather that, before he met Bodhidharma, Huike had taken the precepts under Chan Master Baojing 寶靜 of Mount Xiang 香山 in Longmen and subsequently spent eight years there, sitting in meditation all day long. In his "Shōbōgenzō gyōji" 正法眼藏行持 (part 2, section 21), Dōgen again speaks of Huike's "eight years of attendance" (*shūji hachinen* 執侍八年), seemingly on Bodhidharma (though this is not entirely clear). He uses the same phrase elsewhere (e.g., in his *shinji Shōbōgenzō* 眞字正法眼藏, DZZ.5:178, case 101) in reference to the study of Nanyue Huairang 南嶽懷讓 (677-744) under the Sixth Ancestor, Huineng 慧能; and it may be that the legends of these two masters, mentioned together here, have somehow been conflated.

his whole arm got the marrow (*zenpi tokuzui* 全臂得髓): A tentative translation of an unusual phrase, which might otherwise be parsed, "his arm was made whole, and he got the marrow." Reference to the legends that Huike cut off his arm and presented it to Bodhidharma, and that Bodhidharma subsequently recognized Huike as having "gotten the marrow" of his teachings; see Supplementary Notes, s.v. "Cut off an arm" and "Skin, flesh, bones, and marrow." The problematic expression *zenpi* 全臂 ("whole arm") has been variously interpreted: as "the whole arm of the dharma" (*hō no zenpi* 法の全臂); as "the indestructible whole body" (*fue zenshin* 不壞全身), not scarred by the severed arm. The suggestion that Huike's arm might have been restored in some sense suggests the story, in the "Bhaiṣajyarāja" chapter of the *Lotus Sūtra*, of the Bodhisattva Priyadarśana, who sacrificed his arms to the dharma, only to have them restored.

27 **Nanyue's fifteen years of pursuing the way** (*Nangaku no jūgo nen no bendō* 南嶽の十五年の辨道): Reference to the tradition, recorded, e.g., in the *Jingde chuandeng lu* 景德傳燈錄 (T.2076.51:240c17), that Nanyue Huairang 南嶽懷讓 spent fifteen years serving under the Sixth Ancestor, Huineng 慧能.

28 **"I'm also like this, and you're also like this"** (*go yaku nyoze, nyo yaku nyoze* 吾亦如是、汝亦如是): Words of Huineng to Nanyue, said in response to Nanyue's saying that he is "not defiled" by practice and verification; from the famous dialogue recorded at *shinji Shōbōgenzō* 眞字正法眼藏 (DZZ.5:178, case 101) and cited often throughout the *Shōbōgenzō*. See Supplementary Notes, s.v. "You're also like this, I'm also like this."

es.²⁹ "Attaining at once" is not attaining by pulling in what has been apparent since ancient times; it is not attaining by producing what is not yet arisen; it is not rounding up what is presently scattered about: rather, sloughing off attaining by "becoming close" is called "attaining at once."³⁰ Therefore, all attainment is "attaining at once."

[56:11]

隨順是師學は、猶是侍者の古蹤なり、參究すべし。この正當恁麼行李時、すなはち得見の承當あり。そのところ、見恒沙佛なり。恒沙佛は、頭頭活鱍鱍聻なり。あながちに見恒沙佛をわしり、へつらふことなかれ。まづすべからく隨師學をはげむべし、隨師學得佛見なり。

"*Studying in accordance with this master*" is the old example of "*still just his acolyte*"; we should investigate it.³¹ In this *very moment of engaging in conduct*, there is accession to being "*able to see*." That juncture is "*seeing buddhas numerous as the sands of the Ganges*." "Buddhas numerous as the sands of the Ganges" is *each one brisk liveliness itself*.³² Definitely, do not go rushing to ingratiate yourself to "seeing buddhas numerous as the Ganges." First, we should exert ourselves in study fol-

---

29 **It is "attaining at once" so many observances, like vines and branches** (*nyokota no manshi anri o sokutoku suru nari* 如許多の蔓枝行履を即得するなり): From the line in the *Lotus Sūtra* verse, "One attains at once the bodhisattva path."

30 **sloughing off attaining by "becoming close" is called "attaining at once"** (*shingon toku o, datsuraku suru o sokutoku to iu* 親近得を、脱落するを即得といふ): Presumably meaning that "attaining at once the bodhisattva path" means to transcend what one has got from "becoming close to the dharma master." For the use of "slough off" (*datsuraku* 脱落), see Supplementary Notes, s.v. "Slough off."

31 **old example of "still just his acolyte"** (*yūze jisha no koshō* 猶是侍者の古蹤): Possibly reflecting a saying found in the biography of Taiyang Ming'an 太陽明安 (or Taiyang Jingxuan 太陽警玄 or Jingyan 警延, 942-1027) in the *Zongmen liandeng huiyao* 宗門聯燈會要 (ZZ.136:899a7-9):

師問僧、甚處來。云洪山。師云、先師在麼。云在。師云、在即不無。請渠出來。我要相見。僧云聻。師云、這箇猶是侍者。僧無對。師云、喫茶去。

The Master asked a monk, "Where have you come from?"
He said, "Mount Hong."
The Master said, "Is your former master there?"
He said, "He's there."
The Master said, "If he's there, he's not non-existent. Bring him out, I want to meet him."
The monk said, "Well?"
The Master said, "This is still just his acolyte."
The monk had no response.
The Master said, "Have some tea."

32 **each one brisk liveliness itself** (*zuzu kappatsupatsu nii* 頭頭活鱍鱍聻): Given in Chinese as if a quotation, but no source is known. See Supplementary Notes, s.v. "Brisk and lively."

lowing a master; study following a master is attaining the seeing of buddha.[33]

* * * * *

[56:12]

釋迦牟尼佛、告一切證菩提衆言、深入禪定、見十方佛。

Buddha Śākyamuni addressed the assembly of all who verified bodhi, saying,[34]
  Entered deeply into meditative concentration,
  Seeing the buddhas of the ten directions.

[56:13]

盡界は深なり、十方佛土中なるがゆえに。これ廣にあらず、大にあらず、小にあらず、窄にあらず。擧すれば隨他擧す、これを全收と道す。これ七尺にあらず、八尺にあらず、一丈にあらず。全收無外にして入之一字なり。この深入は禪定なり、深入禪定は見十方佛なり。深入裏許無人接渠にして得在なるがゆえに、見十方佛なり。設使將來、他亦不受のゆえに、佛十方在なり。深入は、長長出不得なり、見十方佛は、只見臥如來なり、禪定は、入來出頭不得なり。眞龍をあやしみ恐怖せずは、見佛の而今、さらに疑著を抛捨すべからず。見佛より見佛するゆえに、禪定より禪定に深入す。この禪定・見佛・深入等の道理、さきより閑功夫漢ありて造作しおきて、いまの漢に傳受するにあらず。而今の新條にあらざれども、恁麼の道理必然なり。一切の傳道受業、かくのごとし、修因得果、かくのごとし。

All the worlds are "deep"; for they are "within the buddha lands of the ten directions."[35] It is not wide, not big, not small, not narrow.[36] When

---

33 **study following a master is attaining the seeing of buddha** (*zuishi gaku toku bukken nari* 隨師學得佛見なり): Dōgen plays here in Chinese syntax with the last two lines of the *Lotus Sūtra* verse. "The seeing of buddha" (*bukken* 佛見) is ambiguous: "buddha" may be read either as the object or the agent of "seeing."

34 **Buddha Śākyamuni** (*Shakamuni butsu* 釋迦牟尼佛): A quotation (with an introduction in Chinese supplied by Dōgen) of two lines from a verse in the *Lotus Sūtra* (*Miaofa lianhua jing* 妙法蓮華經, T.262.9:39c5):

又見自身、在山林中、修習善法、證諸實相、深入禪定、見十方佛。
[Devout believers] will also see themselves,
In mountain forests,
Practicing good dharmas,
Verifying the real marks,
Entered deeply into meditative concentration,
Seeing the buddhas of the ten directions.

35 **"within the buddha lands of the ten directions"** (*jippō butsudo chū* 十方佛土中): From a verse in the *Lotus Sūtra* (*Miaofa lianhua jing* 妙法蓮華經, T.262.9:8a17):

十方佛土中、唯有一乘法。
Within the buddha lands of the ten directions,
There is only the dharma of the one vehicle.

36 **It is not wide** (*kore kō ni arazu* これ廣にあらず): Presumably, the antecedent of

we take it up, we take up "what goes along with it"; this is called completely included.[37] It is not seven feet; it is not eight feet; it is not ten feet: *completely included with nothing beyond*, it is *"the one word 'enter.'"*[38] This "entered deeply" is "meditative concentration"; "*entered deeply into meditative concentration*" is "*seeing the buddhas of the ten directions.*" Since it is "fine," "entered deeply" in there, with "no one who engages him," it is "*seeing the buddhas of the ten directions.*"[39] Since "*whatever he came up with, he wouldn't have accepted it*," the buddhas are in the ten directions.[40] "Entered deeply" is "*you can't get it out for*

---

kore これ ("it") is "deep"; perhaps meaning that this "deep" is not the "deep" of terms like "wide," etc.

37 **When we take it up, we take up "what goes along with it"** (*ko sureba zui ta ko su* 舉すれば随他舉す): Perhaps meaning something like, "when we discuss the term 'deep,' we are also discussing all it entails." The term *zui ta ko* 随他舉 (translated here "take up what goes along with it") is likely a play on the homophonous *zui ta ko* 随他去 ("goes along with it"), from a saying of Dasui Fazhen 大隋法眞 (834-919), recorded in the *shinji Shōbōgenzō* 眞字正法眼藏 (DZZ.5:138, case 24), that "this" (*shako* 這箇) "goes along with it" when the chiliocosm is destroyed at the end of the kalpa; see Supplementary Notes.

completely included (*zenshū* 全收): I.e., ["deep" is] all inclusive. Likely reflecting a common phrase in Zen literature, "the whole earth is completely included" (*daichi zenshū* 大地全收), associated especially with Yunmen Wenyan 雲門文偃 (864-949) (see, e.g., *Yunmen Kuangzheng chanshi guanglu* 雲門匡眞禪師廣錄, T.1988.47:547a23-24):

一塵纔起、大地全收。

When a single mote barely arises, the whole earth is completely included.

38 **It is not seven feet; it is not eight feet; it is not ten feet** (*kore shichi shaku ni arazu, hachi shaku ni arazu, ichi jō ni arazu* これ七尺にあらず、八尺にあらず、一丈にあらず): Perhaps recalling two stories recorded in Dōgen's *shinji Shōbōgenzō* 眞字正法眼藏, involving Chan masters Xuansha Shibei 玄沙師備 (835-908) and Xuefeng Yicun 雪峰義存 (822-908). In the first (DZZ.5:158, case 60), when Xuefeng described the height of a proposed monument stone by merely looking up and down, Xuansha preferred to measure it at "seven feet or eight feet" (*shichi shaku hachi shaku* 七尺八尺); see Supplementary Notes, s.v. "Seven or eight feet." In the second (DZZ.5:184, case 109), Xuefeng said, "If the breadth of the world is ten feet (*ichi jō* 一丈), the breadth of the old mirror is ten feet"; see Supplementary Notes, s.v. "Bare mind in pieces."

"the one word 'enter'" (*nyū shi ichiji* 入之一字): Perhaps alluding to a conversation between Yangshan Huiji 仰山慧寂 (803-887) and the magistrate Lu Xisheng 陸希聲 (d. 895) appearing as case 139 in the *shinji Shōbōgenzō* 眞字正法眼藏 (DZZ.5:200); see Supplementary Notes, s.v. "The one word 'enter.'"

39 **Since it is "fine," "entered deeply" in there, with "no one who engages him"** (*jinnyū riko mu nin sekko ni shite tokuzai naru ga yue ni* 深入裏許無人接渠にして得在なるがゆえに): Drawing on the language of a dialogue recorded in the *shinji Shōbōgenzō* 眞字正法眼藏 (DZZ.5:216, case 179); see Supplementary Notes, s.v. "Eight or nine tenths complete."

40 **"whatever he came up with, he wouldn't have accepted it"** (*shesshi shōrai, ta yaku fuju* 設使將來、他亦不受): A phrase from a dialogue between Chan Master Dongshan Liangjie 洞山良价 and an unnamed monk regarding a line in the famous poem

56. Seeing Buddha *Kenbutsu* 見佛

a long, long time"; "*seeing the buddhas of the ten directions*" is "*I only saw a recumbent tathāgata*"; "*meditative contemplation*" is *you can't come in or out.*[41] In the present time of seeing buddha, those who do not doubt or fear the real dragon need not cast off further doubts.[42] Since

---

contest between Shenxiu 神秀 (d. 706) and Huineng 慧能 to succeed the Fifth Ancestor, Hongren 弘忍 (602-675) (found, e.g., at *Hongzhi chanshi guanglu* 宏智禪師廣錄, T.2001.48:34c6-14):

舉僧問洞山、時時勤拂拭、莫使惹塵埃。爲什麼不得他衣鉢。山云、直饒道本來無一物、也未合得他衣鉢。且道、什麼人合得。僧下九十六轉語、不契。末後云、設使將來他亦不受。山深肯之。

Raised: A monk asked Dongshan, "'Always strive to polish it, and do not let the dust collect.' Why did this [line in Shenxiu's verse] not get his [Hongren's] robe and bowl?"
Shan said, "Even if he had said [the line in Huineng's verse], 'From the beginning, not one thing,' he still would not have qualified to get his robe and bowl." He added, "Who's qualified to get them?"
The monk gave ninety-six turning words, but none fit. Finally, he said, "Whatever he came up with, he wouldn't have accepted it."
Shan deeply approved it.

For Shenxiu's full verse and the context of this story, see Supplementary Notes, s.v. "Bright mirror."

41 "**you can't get it out for a long, long time**" (*chōchō shutsu futoku* 長長出不得): The words of Changsha Jingcen 長沙景岑 (dates unknown), in answer to the question, "What is the eye of the *śramaṇa*?" See Supplementary Notes, s.v. "All the worlds in the ten directions are the single eye of the *śramaṇa*." Also alluded to in "Shōbōgenzō genjō kōan" 正法眼藏現成公案.

"**I only saw a recumbent tathāgata**" (*shi ken ga nyorai* 只見臥如來): The words of Zhaozhou Congshen 趙州從諗 (778-897) in coming upon Nanquan Puyuan 南泉普願 (748-835) while the latter was taking a nap (*Jingde chuandeng lu* 景德傳燈, T.2076.51:6c9-11):

而問曰、近離什麼處。師曰、近離瑞像院。曰還見瑞像麼。師曰、不見瑞像只見臥如來。

[Nanquan] asked, "Where are you coming from?"
The Master [Zhaozhou] said, "I've just come from Ruixiang Cloister ['Cloister of the Auspicious Image']."
He said, "And did you see the auspicious image?"
The Master said, "I didn't see the auspicious image; I only saw a recumbent tathāgata."

you can't come in or out (*nyūrai shuttō futoku* 入來出頭不得): A tentative translation; some would read, "once in, you can't get out." Though given in Chinese as if quoting a text, this six-word phrase does not seem to be a fixed expression; rather, it probably combines the expressions, "admission is not possible" (*nyūrai futoku* 入來不得) and "egress (or 'appearance' or 'attendance') is not possible" (*shuttō futoku* 出頭不得).

42 **In the present time of seeing buddha, those who do not doubt or fear the real dragon need not cast off further doubts** (*shinryū o ayashimi kufu sezu wa, kenbutsu no nikon, sara ni gijaku o hōsha su bekarazu* 眞龍をあやしみ恐怖せずは、見佛の而今、さらに疑著を抛捨すべからず): A tentative translation taken to mean that, if one can accept the real thing, one will not doubt the experience of seeing buddha. "The real

one sees buddha from "seeing buddha," one enters deeply into meditative concentration from "meditative concentration."[43] The principles of "meditative concentration," "seeing buddha," "entering deeply," and the like, are not something constructed in the past by someone idly pondering them and then passed down to people now. Though they are not something new in the present, such principles are necessary. All transmission of the way and acceptance of the work is like this; practicing the cause and getting the effect are like this.

* * * * *

[56:14] {2:102}
釋迦牟尼佛、告普賢菩薩言、若有受持讀誦正憶念修習書寫是法華經者、當知、是人則見釋迦牟尼佛、如從佛口聞此經典。

Buddha Śākyamuni addressed Bodhisattva Samanthabhadra, saying,[44] *If there is anyone who receives and keeps, reads and recites, and correctly memorizes, practices, or copies this Lotus Sūtra, you should know this person thereby sees Buddha Śākyamuni and hears this scripture as if coming from the mouth of the Buddha."*

[56:15]
おほよそ一切諸佛は、見釋迦牟尼佛、成釋迦牟尼佛するを、成道作佛といふなり。かくのごとくの佛儀、もとよりこの七種の行處の條條よりうるなり。七種行人は、當知是人なり、如是當人なり。これすなはち見釋迦牟尼佛處なるがゆえに、したしくこれ如從佛口、聞此經典なり。釋迦牟尼佛は、見釋迦牟尼佛よりこのかた釋迦牟尼佛なり。これによりて、舌相あまねく三千を覆す、いづれの山海か、佛經にあらざらん。このゆえに、書寫の當人ひとり、見釋迦牟尼佛なり。佛口はよのつねに萬古に開す、いづれの時節か經典にあらざらん。このゆえに、受持の行者のみ見釋迦牟尼佛なり。乃至眼・耳・鼻等の功德も、またかくのごとくなるべきなり。および前後・左右・取捨・造次、かくのごとくなり。いまの此經典にむまれあふ、見釋迦牟尼佛をよろこばざらんや。生値釋迦牟尼佛、身心をはげまして受持・讀誦・正憶念・修習・書寫、是法華經者、則見釋迦牟尼佛なるべし。如從佛口、聞此經典、たれかこれをきほひきかざらん。いそがずつとめざるは、貧窮無福慧の衆生なり。修習するは、當知是人、則見釋迦牟尼佛なり。

---

dragon" (*shinryū* 眞龍) alludes to the well-known story of the Duke of She (*Sekkō* 葉公), who loved dragon carvings but was terrified of real dragons; a trope occurring several times in Dōgen's writing.

43 **one sees buddha from "seeing buddha"** (*kenbutsu yori kenbutsu suru* 見佛より見佛する): Perhaps meaning that the experience of seeing buddha follows (either temporally or logically) from the state (or understanding?) of "seeing buddha"; similarly, *mutatis mutandis*, the experience of meditative concentration.

44 **Buddha Śākyamuni** (*Shakamuni butsu* 釋迦牟尼佛): From the *Lotus Sūtra* (*Miaofa lianhua jing* 妙法蓮華經, T.262.9:61c22-24), with an introductory clause by Dōgen.

56. Seeing Buddha *Kenbutsu* 見佛   229

In sum, for all the buddhas, their "seeing Buddha Śākyamuni," their becoming Buddha Śākyamuni, is called "*attaining the way and becoming a buddha.*"[45] Such observances of the buddhas are from the beginning gained from each of these seven types of practice.[46] The practitioner of the seven types is "*you should know this person,*" is *the very person like this.*[47] Since this is precisely where one "sees Buddha Śākyamuni," it is intimately to "*hear this scripture as if coming from the mouth of the Buddha.*" Buddha Śākyamuni has been Buddha Śākyamuni ever since "seeing Buddha Śākyamuni."

Consequently, "his tongue covers everywhere in the trichiliocosm"; what mountain or ocean is not a sūtra of the buddhas?[48] Therefore, the very person who copies it "sees Buddha Śākyamuni." The mouth of the Buddha has always been open for ten thousand ages; what moment is not a scripture? Therefore, only the practitioner who "receives and keeps" it is "seeing Buddha Śākyamuni." Down to, the merit of eye, ear, nose, and so on, will also be like this.[49] And forward and back, left and right,

---

45   **for all the buddhas** (*issai shobutsu* 一切諸佛): The claim here that all the buddhas see and become Buddha Śākyamuni no doubt reflects Śākyamuni's revelation in the *Lotus Sūtra* that the buddhas of the ten directions are all his emanations (*bunshin* 分身; S. *ātma-bhāva-vigraha*).

46   **these seven types of practice** (*kono shichishu no gyōsho* この七種の行處): I.e., the seven practices mentioned in the quoted passage of the *Lotus Sūtra*.

47   "**you should know this person**" (*tō chi ze nin* 當知是人); **the very person like this** (*nyoze tōnin* 如是當人): Dōgen here plays with the *Lotus Sūtra* passage, "you should know this person thereby sees Buddha Śākyamuni" (*tō chi ze nin soku ken Shakamuni butsu* 當知是人則見釋迦牟尼佛). His second phrase rearranges the first, shifting the sense of the term *tō* 當 from the modal verb "should" to the adjective "the very," and replaces the two glyphs *chi ze* 知是 ("know this") with *nyoze* 如是 ("like this"), a term used for the metaphysical concept "such" or "suchness." Cf. Supplementary Notes, s.v. "Such a person."

48   "**his tongue covers everywhere in the trichiliocosm**" (*zessō amaneku sanzen o fuku su* 舌相あまねく三千を覆す): I.e., his teachings are everywhere. A Japanese reflection of a common image found throughout the Mahāyāna literature; see, e.g., the *Mahā-prajñā-pāramitā-sūtra* (*Da bore boluomiduo jing* 大般若波羅蜜多經, T.220.5:53b26-28):

爾時、世尊現廣長舌相、遍覆三千大千世界。復從舌相出無量無數種種色光、普照十方殑伽沙等諸佛世界。

At that time, the World-Honored One showed his long, broad tongue, which covered everywhere in the trichiliocosm; and, from that tongue emerged immeasurable, innumerable variably colored lights, universally illumining buddha fields in the ten directions equal to the sands of Ganges.

49   **Down to, the merit of eye, ear, nose, and so on, will also be like this** (*naishi gen ni bi tō no kudoku mo, mata kaku no gotoku naru beki nari* 乃至眼・耳・鼻等の功德も、またかくのごとくなるべきなり): Presumably, the antecedent of "like this" is "seeing Buddha Śākyamuni." The sense here of the adverbial *naishi* 乃至 ("down to"), which normally marks an elision, is unclear. Dōgen may be recalling a line in the *Lotus Sūtra*

choosing and discarding, and hasty acts are like this.⁵⁰

Having been born with "this scripture" here, how could one not be delighted to "see Buddha Śākyamuni"?⁵¹ It is *born to meet Buddha Śākyamuni.*⁵² Those who, exerting body and mind, *"receive and keep, read and recite, and correctly memorize, practice, or copy this Lotus Sūtra"* will *"thereby see Buddha Śākyamuni." "Hearing this scripture as if coming from the mouth of the Buddha,"* who would not vie to hear it? Those who do not make haste and make effort are "living beings," "impoverished and without merit or wisdom."⁵³ Those who practice, *"you should know this person thereby sees Buddha Śākyamuni."*

* * * * *

(*Miaofa lianhua jing* 妙法蓮華經, T.262.9:50b24-28):

爾時、佛告得大勢菩薩摩訶薩、汝今當知、若比丘比丘尼優婆塞優婆夷持法華經者、若有惡口罵詈誹謗、獲大罪報、如前所説。其所得功德、如向所説、眼耳鼻舌身意清淨。

At that time, the Buddha addressed the Mahāsattva-Bodhisattva Mahāsthāmaprāpta, "You should know that, if there are bhikṣus, *bhikṣuṇīs*, *upāsakas*, *upāsikās* who keep the *Lotus Sūtra*, those who insult, revile, and slander them will reap great evil retribution, as I have previously explained; while the merit that they get, as I have explained, will be the purification of eye, ear, nose, tongue, body, and mind."

50 **And forward and back, left and right, choosing and discarding, and hasty acts are like this** (*oyobi zengo sayū shusha zōji, kaku no gotoku nari* および前後・左右・取捨・造次、かくのごとくなり): A rather odd list, the exact sense of which is uncertain; if we take "forward and back, left and right" as physical movements, perhaps the point is that, all our acts, like our six senses, are cases of "seeing Buddha Śākyamuni." The term *zōji* 造次 (translated here "hasty acts") is sometimes taken as referring to an instant of time, rather than flurried activity — hence, here perhaps, "our fleeting moments."

51 **Having been born with "this scripture" here** (*ima no shi kyōten ni mumareau* いまの此經典にむまれあふ): I.e., born with the scripture mentioned here in the sūtra line, "hears this scripture as if coming from the mouth of the Buddha."

52 **born to meet Buddha Śākyamuni** (*shō chi Shakamuni butsu nari* 生値釋迦牟尼佛なり): Perhaps reflecting a line in the *Lotus Sūtra* (*Miaofa lianhua jing* 妙法蓮華經, T.262.9:60b1):

而我等宿福深厚、生値佛法。
Because the merits of our past lives are deep, we are born to meet the buddha dharma.

53 **"living beings," "impoverished and without merit or wisdom"** (*bingū mu fukue no shujō* 貧窮無福慧の衆生): From a verse in the *Lotus Sūtra* (*Miaofa lianhua jing* 妙法蓮華經, T.262.9:9b25-26):

舍利弗當知、我以佛眼觀、見六道衆生、貧窮無福慧。
Śāriputra, you should know
That, with the buddha eye, I see
Living beings of the six paths,
Impoverished and without merit or wisdom.

See Supplementary Notes, s.v. "Six paths."

56. Seeing Buddha *Kenbutsu* 見佛

[56:16]

釋迦牟尼佛、告大衆言、若善男子善女人、聞我説壽命長遠、深心信解、則爲見佛常在耆闍崛山、其大菩薩・諸聲聞衆圍遶説法。又見此娑婆世界、其地瑠璃、坦然平正。

Buddha Śākyamuni addressed the great assembly, saying,[54]

If good sons and good daughters, upon hearing me explain that my lifespan is so long, believe it with deep mind, they will thereby see the Buddha always residing on Mount Gṛdhrakūṭa, surrounded by an assembly of great bodhisattvas and *śrāvakas*, preaching the dharma. And they will see this Sahā world, its ground of *vaiḍūrya*, smooth and level.[55]

[56:17] {2:103}

この深心といふは、娑婆世界なり。信解といふは、無廻避處なり。誠諦の佛語、たれか信解せざらん。この經典にあひたてまつるるは、信解すべき機縁なり。深心信解是法華、深心信解壽命長遠のために、願生此娑婆國土しきたれり。如來の神力・慈悲力・壽命長遠力、よく心を拈じて信解せしめ、身を拈じて信解せしめ、盡界を拈じて信解せしめ、佛祖を拈じて信解せしめ、諸法を拈じて信解せしめ、實相を拈じて信解せしめ、皮肉骨髓を拈じて信解せしめ、生死去來を拈じて信解せしむるなり。これらの信解、これ見佛なり。

This "deep mind" is the "Sahā world"; "believe" is *there's nowhere to escape*.[56] The truthful words of the Buddha, who would not "believe" them?[57] That we have been granted an encounter with this scripture is an opportunity in which we should "believe." Due to "*believing with deep mind*" this *Dharma Blossom*, and "*believing with deep mind*" that

---

54 **Buddha Śākyamuni** (*Shakamuni butsu* 釋迦牟尼佛): From the *Lotus Sūtra* (*Miaofa lianhua jing* 妙法蓮華經, T.262.9:45b16-20), with an introductory clause by Dōgen. At this point in the sūtra, Śākyamuni has revealed that, though he appears to have a human lifespan, in fact he became a buddha incalculable ages ago and will continue to exist for twice that long before entering *parinirvāṇa*.

55 **And they will see this Sahā world, its ground of *vaiḍūrya*, smooth and level** (*yū ken shi shaba sekai, ki chi ruri, tannen byōshō* 又見此娑婆世界、其地瑠璃、坦然平正): I.e., they will see our world as a pure buddha land, in which the ground is level and consists of jewels. The Sanskrit *vaiḍūrya* (*ruri* 瑠璃; also written *ruri* 琉璃) is used for beryl, crystal, and other minerals; one of the seven precious substances.

56 **there's nowhere to escape** (*mu kaihi sho* 無廻避處): Or, perhaps, "a place of no escape"; also written 無迴避處. A fixed expression occurring in several Chan records, especially in works associated with Hongzhi Zhengjue 宏智正覺 (1091-1157).

57 **truthful words of the Buddha** (*jōtai no butsugo* 誠諦の佛語): Likely, variation on a line in the *Lotus Sūtra* (*Miaofa lianhua jing* 妙法蓮華經, T.262.9:42b1-2):

爾時佛告諸菩薩及一切大衆、諸善男子汝等當信解如來誠諦之語。

At that time, the Buddha declared to the bodhisattvas and the entire great assembly, "Good sons, you should trust and understand the truthful words of the Tathāgata."

"my lifespan is so long," they have been *vowing to be born in this Sahā world.*[58] The spiritual power, the power of compassion, the power of his *"lifespan so long"* — these cause us to take up mind and believe, cause us to take up body and believe, cause us to take up all the worlds and believe, cause us to take up the buddhas and ancestors and believe, cause us to take up the dharmas and believe, cause us to take up the real marks and believe, cause us to take up the skin, flesh, bones, and marrow and believe, cause us to take up birth and death, coming and going and believe.[59] Believing in these — this is "seeing buddha."[60]

[56:18] {2:104}
しかあればしりぬ、心頭眼ありて見佛す、信解眼をえて見佛す。ただ見佛のみにあらず、常在耆闍崛山をみるといふは、耆闍崛山の常在は、如來壽命と一齊なるべし。しかあれば、見佛常在耆闍崛山は、前頭來も、如來および耆闍崛山、ともに常在なり。後頭來も、如來および耆闍崛山、ともに常在なり。菩薩・聲聞もおなじく常在なるべし、説法もまた常在なるべし。娑婆世界、其地瑠璃、坦然平正、をみる。娑婆世界をみること、動著すべからず、高處高平、低處低平なり。この地は、これ瑠璃地なり。これを、坦然平正なるとみる目をいやしくすることなかれ。瑠璃爲地の地は、かくのごとし。この地を瑠璃にあらずとせば、耆闍崛山は耆闍崛山にあらず、釋迦牟尼佛は釋迦牟尼佛にあらざらん。其地瑠璃を信解する、すなはち深信解相なり、これ見佛なり。

Thus, we know that it is by having the eye of the mind that they see buddha; it is by attaining the eye of belief that they see buddha. To say that they not only see buddha but see him *"always residing on Mount Gṛdhrakūṭa"* means that his *"always residing"* on Mount Gṛdhrakūṭa

---

58 **this *Dharma Blossom*** (*ze Hokke* 是法華): I.e., "this scripture, *The Lotus Blossom of the True Dharma*."

they have been vowing to be born in this Sahā world (*gan shō shi Shaba kokudo shikitareri* 願生此娑婆國土しきたれり): Or, perhaps, "we have vowed . . . ." The grammatical subject is unstated; the translation assumes it is the "good sons and good daughters" who "believe and understand with deep mind," and who will thereby "see this Sahā world" of Buddha Śākyamuni. Though it is given in Chinese, as if quoting a scripture, there does not seem to be a clear source for this phrase; it may recall the bodhisattvas in the *Lotus Sūtra* who vow to teach the sūtra in the Sahā world after the nirvāṇa of the Buddha.

59 **cause us to take up the dharmas and believe, cause us to take up the real marks and believe** (*shohō o nenjite shinge seshime, jissō o nenjite shinge seshime* 諸法を拈じて信解せしめ、實相を拈じて信解せしめ): Based on the common fixed expression "the real marks of the dharmas" (*shohō jissō* 諸法實相), used in reference to the ultimate reality of things.

birth and death, coming and going (*shōji korai* 生死去來): I.e., rebirth in saṃsāra; a fixed expression, associated especially with a saying of Yuanwu Keqin 圜悟克勤 (1063-1135) to the effect that these are "the true human body" (*shinjitsu nintai* 眞實人體); see Supplementary Notes, s.v. "True human body."

60 **Believing in these** (*korera no shinge* これらの信解): Or "these [instances of] believing."

56. Seeing Buddha Kenbutsu 見佛

must be equivalent to the "lifespan" of the Tathāgata. This being so, "*seeing the Buddha always residing on Mount Gṛdhrakūṭa*" is the "constant residing," before, of both the Tathāgata and Mount Gṛdhrakūṭa; it is the "constant residing," after, of both the Tathāgata and Mount Gṛdhrakūṭa. Similarly, the "bodhisattvas and *śrāvakas*" must also be "constantly residing"; "preaching the dharma" must also be "constantly residing." They see the "*Sahā world, its ground of vaiḍūrya, smooth and level.*" We should not be moved by [such] seeing of the Sahā world: it is "*high places are high and level; low places are low and level.*"[61] This earth — this is a *vaiḍūrya* earth.[62] Do not scorn the eye that sees this as "smooth and level": the earth that has *vaiḍūrya* as ground is like this. If one were to maintain that this earth is not *vaiḍūrya*, Mount Gṛdhrakūṭa would not be Mount Gṛdhrakūṭa, and Buddha Śākyamuni would not be Buddha Śākyamuni. To believe in "*its ground of vaiḍūrya*" is in itself a "*mark of deep belief*"; it is seeing buddha.[63]

* * * * *

[56:19]

釋迦牟尼佛、告大衆言、一心欲見佛、不自惜身命、時我及衆僧、俱出靈鷲山。

Buddha Śākyamuni addressed the great assembly saying,[64]
If they, with single-mind, desire to see the buddha,
Without caring for their own bodies and lives,
At that time, will I and my assembly of monks,
Appear together on Vulture Peak.

---

61 "**high places are high and level; low places are low and level**" (*kōsho kōhei, teisho teihei* 高處高平、低處低平): From the response of Weishan Lingyou 潙山靈祐 (771-853) to the suggestion that an uneven rice paddy should be leveled; the anecdote is found in a number of Chan sources, as well as in Dōgen's *shinji Shōbōgenzō* 眞字正法眼藏 (DZZ.5:138, case 23); see Supplementary Notes.

62 **This earth — this is a *vaiḍūrya* earth** (*kono chi wa, kore ruri chi nari* この地は、これ瑠璃地なり): Dōgen plays here with the term *chi* 地, which can have the senses "earth," "land," "ground," "soil," etc.

63 "**mark of deep belief**" (*jinshinge sō* 深信解相): A phrase from the *Lotus Sūtra* concluding the section on which Dōgen is commenting here (*Miaofa lianhua jing* 妙法蓮華經, T.262.9:45b21-22):

若有能如是觀者、當知是爲深信解相。

If there are those who can see like this, you should know that this is a mark of their deep belief.

64 **Buddha Śākyamuni** (*Shakamuni butsu* 釋迦牟尼佛): From a verse in the *Lotus Sūtra* (*Miaofa lianhua jing* 妙法蓮華經, T.262.9:43b23-24), with an introductory clause by Dōgen.

[56:20] {2:105}

いふところの一心は、凡夫・二乗等のいふ一心にあらず、見佛の一心なり。見佛の一心といふは、靈鷲山なり、及衆僧なり。而今の箇箇、ひそかに欲見佛をもよほすは、靈鷲山心をこらして欲見佛するなり。しかあれば、一心、すでに靈鷲山なり、一身、それ心に倶出せざらんや、倶一身心ならざらんや。身心すでにかくのごとし、壽者命者、またかくのごとし。かるがゆえに、自惜を靈鷲山の但惜無上道に一任す。このゆえに、我及衆僧、靈鷲山倶出なるを見佛の一心と道取す。

The "single mind" spoken of here is not the "single mind" spoken of by common people, those of the two vehicles, and the like: it is the "single mind" of seeing buddha. "The single mind of seeing buddha" is "Vulture Peak," is "*and my assembly of monks*." Each present individual privately having the "desire to see buddha" is desiring to see buddha by concentrating the mind of Vulture Peak. Thus, the "single mind" is in itself "Vulture Peak"; and the single body, how could it not "appear together" with the mind? How could they not be a single body and mind together? Since body and mind are like this, their "lifespan and lives" are also like this.[65] Therefore, they entirely give over "caring for their own" to "caring only for the unsurpassed way" of Vulture Peak.[66] Therefore, he speaks of [the fact that] "*I and my assembly of monks*" are an "*appearance together*" on "*Vulture Peak*" as the "single mind" of "seeing buddha."[67]

* * * * *

---

65 **their "lifespan and lives" are also like this** (*jusha myōsha, mata kaku no gotoshi* 壽者命者、またかくのごとし): I.e., are also themselves "Vulture Peak." A tentative translation, taking *jusha myōsha* 壽者命者 as equivalent to *jumyōsha* 壽命者 ("lifespan"); the two terms may also be read as "those with lifespans, those with lives" (i.e., "living beings"; S. *jīva*, etc.). Dōgen seems to be playing here on the sūtra line, "without caring for their own bodies and lives" (*fu jishaku shinmyō* 不自惜身命).

66 **"caring only for the unsurpassed way"** (*tan shaku mujō dō* 但惜無上道): From a line of verse by bodhisattvas in the *Lotus Sūtra* (*Miaofa lianhua jing* 妙法蓮華經, T.262.9:36c18):

我不愛身命、但惜無上道。
We shall not love our bodies or lives,
But care only for the unsurpassed way.

67 **"I and my assembly of monks" are an "appearance together" on "Vulture Peak"** (*ga kyū shusō, Ryōjusen ku shutsu naru* 我及衆僧、靈鷲山倶出なる): A tentative translation; the phrase could also be (more interestingly) parsed, "[the fact that] 'I and my assembly of monks' and 'Vulture Peak' are an 'appearance together.'"

56. Seeing Buddha *Kenbutsu* 見佛

[56:21]

釋迦牟尼佛、告大衆言、若説此經、則爲見我、多寶如來、及諸化佛。

Buddha Śākyamuni addressed the great assembly, saying,[68]
If they preach this *sūtra*,
They will thereby see me,
Tathāgata Prabhūtaratna,
And the transformation buddhas.[69]

[56:22]

説此經は、我常住於此、以諸神通力、令顛倒衆生、雖近而不見なり。この表裏の神力如來に、則爲見我等の功德そなはる。

To "preach this *sūtra*" is,
While always residing here,
By means of my spiritual powers,
I prevent the perverse living beings
From seeing me, though I am near.[70]

The Tathāgata with these spiritual powers of surface and interior is endowed with the virtue of "they will thereby see me" and the others.[71]

* * * * *

---

68 **Buddha Śākyamuni** (*Shakamuni butsu* 釋迦牟尼佛): From a verse in the *Lotus Sūtra* (*Miaofa lianhua jing* 妙法蓮華經, T.262.9:34a14-15), with an introductory clause by Dōgen.

69 **Tathāgata Prabhūtaratna** (*Tahō nyorai* 多寶如來): The buddha who appears within his great stūpa at the scene of the preaching of the *Lotus Sūtra*; Buddha Śākyamuni joins him within the stūpa.

transformation buddhas (*kebutsu* 化佛): Buddhas appearing in human form; here, no doubt, to be taken as the "emanations of [Śākyamuni's] body" (*bunshin* 分身) mentioned below, section 23.

70 **While always residing here** (*ga jō jū o shi* 我常住於此): Quoting a verse from the *Lotus Sūtra* (*Miaofa lianhua jing* 妙法蓮華經, T.262.9:43b18-19), in which the Buddha explains his apparent disappearance into *parinirvāṇa*.

71 **The Tathāgata with these spiritual powers of surface and interior** (*kono hyōri no jinriki nyorai* この表裏の神力如來): Likely meaning the Buddha, with his paranormal powers to appear or remain invisible.

[56:23]
釋迦牟尼佛、告大衆言、能持是經者、則爲已見我、亦見多寶佛、及諸分身者。

Buddha Śākyamuni addressed the great assembly, saying,[72]
Those who can keep this sūtra
Have thereby already seen me;
And they see Prabhūtaratna
As well as the emanations of my body.

[56:24] {2:106}
この經を持することかたきゆゑに、如來、よのつねにこれをすすむ。もしおのづから持是經者あるは、すなはち見佛なり。はかりしりぬ、見佛すれば持經す。持經のもの、見佛のものなり。しかあればすなはち、乃至聞一偈一句受持するは、得見釋迦牟尼佛なり、亦見多寶佛なり、見諸分身佛なり、傳佛法藏なり、得佛正眼なり、得見佛命なり、得佛向上眼なり、得佛頂顙眼なり、得佛鼻孔なり。

Because it is difficult to keep this sūtra, the Tathāgata regularly encourages it. If perchance there are "those who can keep this sūtra," that itself is seeing buddha. It is clear that, when one sees the buddha, one keeps the sūtra. The one who keeps the sūtra is the one who sees the buddha. Thus, "to receive and keep" it, "hearing even so much as a single gāthā or a single line," is being "able to see" Buddha Śākyamuni.[73] It is "and they see Buddha Prabhūtaratna"; it is seeing the buddhas that are "emanations of my body"; it is transmitting the treasury of the buddha dharma; it is getting the true eye of the buddha; it is being able to see the lifespan of the Buddha; it is getting the eye beyond the buddha; it is getting the eye of the buddha's crown; it is getting the buddha's nose.[74]

---

72   **Buddha Śākyamuni** (*Shakamuni butsu* 釋迦牟尼佛): Quoting a verse from the *Lotus Sūtra* (*Miaofa lianhua jing* 妙法蓮華經, T.262.9:52b12-13), with an introductory clause by Dōgen.

73   **"to receive and keep" it, "hearing even so much as a single gāthā or a single line"** (*naishi mon ichige ikku juji suru* 乃至聞一偈一句受持する): Combining two phrases from a passage in the *Lotus Sūtra* (*Miaofa lianhua jing* 妙法蓮華經, T.262.9:50a18-21):

若善男子善女人、如來滅後受持是經、若讀若誦若解説若書寫、得千二百意功德。以是清淨意根、乃至聞一偈一句、通達無量無邊之義。

If, after the extinction of the Tathāgata, a good son or good daughter receives and keeps this sūtra, reads or recites it, explains or copies it, they will attain twelve hundred mental virtues. With this purified mental faculty, hearing even so much as a single gāthā or a single line, they will penetrate incalculable, limitless meanings.

74   **eye beyond the buddha** (*butsu kōjō gen* 佛向上眼): "Beyond the buddha" (*butsu kōjō* 佛向上) is a common expression in Zen texts and Dōgen's writings; see Supplementary Notes, s.v. "Beyond the buddha."

eye of the buddha's crown (*butsu chōnei gen* 佛頂顙眼): Or, perhaps, "buddha's crown

56. Seeing Buddha *Kenbutsu* 見佛

* * * * *

[56:25]

雲雷音宿王華智佛、告妙莊嚴王言、大王當知、善知識者、是大因緣。所謂化導、令得見佛發阿耨多羅三藐三菩提心。

Buddha Jaladhara-garjita-ghoṣa-susvara-nakṣatra-rāja-saṃkusumitā-bhijña addressed King Śubhavyūha, saying, "Great king, you should know that the wise friend is the great cause and condition, the guide who enables one to see buddha and bring forth the thought of *anuttara-samyak-saṃbodhi.*"[75]

[56:26]

いまこの大會は、いまだむしろをまかず。過去・現在・未來の諸佛と稱すといへども、凡夫の三世に准的すべからず。いはゆる過去は心頭なり、現在は拳頭なり、未來は腦後なり。しかあれば、雲雷音宿王華智佛は、心頭現成の見佛なり。見佛の通語、いまのごとし。化導は見佛なり、見佛は發阿耨多羅三藐三菩提心なり。發菩提心は、見佛の頭正尾正なり。

At present, in this great assembly, the sitting mats are still not rolled up.[76] Although we call them the buddhas of past, present, and future, we should not subscribe to the three times of common people: the past is the mind; the present is the fist; the future is the back of the head. Thus, Buddha Jaladhara-garjita-ghoṣa-susvara-nakṣatra-rāja-saṃkusumitābhi-jña is seeing buddha manifested by mind. The common term, "seeing buddha," is like this.[77] "The guide" is seeing buddha; seeing buddha is "*giving rise to the thought of anuttara-samyak-saṃbodhi.*" Giving rise to the thought of *bodhi* is the truth from head to tail of seeing buddha.

---

and eye." Dōgen regularly uses the term *chōnei* 頂顙 ("crown of the head"), like "eye" (*ganzei* 眼睛) and "nose" (*bikū* 鼻孔), as (a) synecdoche for the person, and (b) the "pinnacle" or best of someone (or something). In some contexts, as possibly here, *chōnei* 頂顙 may suggest a buddha's *uṣṇīṣa*, the protuberance on the top of his head that is one of his thirty-two marks, sometimes taken as symbolic of his wisdom. See Supplementary Notes, s.v. "Eye," "Crown of the head."

75   Buddha Jaladhara-garjita-ghoṣa-susvara-nakṣatra-rāja-saṃkusumitābhijña (*Unraion shukuō kechi butsu* 雲雷音宿王華智佛): From a passage of the *Lotus Sūtra* (*Miaofa lianhua jing* 妙法蓮華經, T.262.9:60c5-10). This buddha's unwieldy name might be rendered something like "Buddha Florid Wisdom of the Roar of Cloud Thunder, King of Constellations."

76   **At present, in this great assembly, the sitting mats are still not rolled up** (*ima kono daie wa, imada mushiro o makazu* いまこの大會は、いまだむしろをまかず): Presumably, meaning that the assembly in which the *Lotus Sūtra* was being taught has not ended even today.

77   **The common term, "seeing buddha," is like this** (*kenbutsu no tsūgo, ima no gotoshi* 見佛の通語、いまのごとし): Perhaps, meaning something like, "this is true in general of the term 'seeing buddha'" — i.e., that it refers to "seeing a buddha manifested by mind."

* * * * *

[56:27]

釋迦牟尼佛言、諸有修功德、柔和質直者、則皆見我身、在此而説法。

Buddha Śākyamuni said,[78]
Those who practice all the virtues
And are gentle and honest
Will all thereby see my body
Residing here and preaching the dharma.

[56:28] {2:107}

あらゆる功徳と稱するは、拖泥帶水なり、隨波逐浪なり。これを修する を、吾亦如是、汝亦如是の柔和質直者といふ。これを泥裏に見佛しきた り、波心に見佛しきたる、在此而説法にあづかる。

What is called "all the virtues" is *dragged through the mud and drenched with water*, is *chasing the waves and following the billows*.[79] Those who practice them are called, "*those who . . . are gentle and honest*," who are "*I'm also like this, and you're also like this*."[80] Having seen the buddha in the midst of the mud, having seen the buddha in the heart of the waves, they participate in his "*residing here and preaching the dharma*."[81]

[56:29]

しかあるに、近來大宋國に、禪師、と稱するともがらおほし。佛法の縱橫 をしらず、見聞いとすくなし。わづかに臨濟・雲門の兩三語を諳誦して、 佛法の全道とおもへり。佛法もし臨濟・雲門の兩三語に道盡せられば、佛 法、今日にいたるべからず。臨濟・雲門を、佛法の爲尊と稱しがたし。い かにいはんやいまのともがら、臨濟・雲門におよばず、不足言のやからな り。かれら、おのれが愚鈍にして、佛經のこころあきらめがたきをもて、

---

78 **Buddha Śākyamuni** (*Shakamuni butsu* 釋迦牟尼佛): Quoting a verse from the *Lotus Sūtra* (*Miaofa lianhua jing* 妙法蓮華經, T.262.9:43c16-17), on his continued presence post-nirvāṇa.

79 **dragged through the mud and drenched with water** (*tadei taisui* 拖泥帶水): Also read *dadei taisui* and written 拖泥滯水. A fixed expression, used in Zen especially in ironic reference to getting "sullied" by the compromises involved in teaching; see Supplementary Notes, s.v. "Dragged through the mud and drenched with water."

chasing the waves and following the billows (*zuiha chikuro* 隨波逐浪): An idiom akin to English "going with the flow" (i.e., adapting to circumstance), known in Zen literature especially as one of "the three phrases" (*sanku* 三句) of Yunmen Wenyen 雲門文偃; see Supplementary Notes, s.v. "Yunmen's three phrases."

80 **"I'm also like this, and you're also like this"** (*go yaku nyoze, nyo yaku nyoze* 吾亦如是、汝亦如是): See above, section 10.

81 **in the heart of the waves** (*hashin* 波心): Or "in the mind of the waves"; taking *hashin* 波心 in the sense "the center of the sea," in parallel with the preceding "in the midst of the mud."

56. Seeing Buddha *Kenbutsu* 見佛

みだりに佛經を謗ず、さしおきて修習せず、外道の流類といひぬべし。佛祖の兒孫にあらず、いはんや見佛の境界におよばんや。孔子・老子の宗旨に、なほいたらざるともがらなり。佛祖の屋裏兒、かの禪師と稱するやからにあひあふことなかれ、ただ見佛眼の眼睛を參究體達すべし。

Be that as it may, in the Land of the Great Song these days, there are many who are called "Chan masters."[82] They do not know the length and breadth of the buddha dharma, and they have little experience. Reciting from memory just two or three sayings of Linji or Yunmen, they think that is the entire way of the buddha dharma.[83] If the buddha dharma were exhaustively conveyed by two or three sayings of Linji or Yunmen, the buddha dharma would not have reached us today. It is hard to call Linji or Yunmen the epitome of the buddha dharma. How much less so the present types, a bunch not worth mentioning, who do not come up to Linji or Yunmen. Being themselves dull-witted and finding it difficult to clarify the heart of the Buddha's sūtras, they arbitrarily disparage the sūtras of the buddhas, disregarding them without putting them into practice; we should call them followers of other paths. They are not descendants of the buddhas and ancestors; still less do they reach the realm of seeing buddha. They are a bunch that does not even get as far as the tenets of Confucius or Laozi. Children of the house of the buddhas and ancestors, do not associate with the bunch called "Chan masters." We should just investigate and personally realize the eye of "the eye of seeing buddha."

* * * * *

---

82 **there are many who are called "Chan masters"** (*zenji, to shō suru tomogara ooshi* 禪師、と稱するともがらおほし): Or "who call themselves 'Chan masters.'" Dōgen appears here to be dismissive of those called "Chan masters." Elsewhere (e.g., in the "Shōbōgenzō butsudō" 正法眼藏佛道), he sharply criticizes the appellation "Chan school" (*zenshū* 禪宗) for the lineage of the buddhas and ancestors; but the term "Chan master" (*zenji* 禪師) has a history outside the Chan school in reference to practitioners of meditation, and of course Dōgen himself regularly uses the term in reference to members of his lineage.

83 **Linji or Yunmen** (*Rinzai Unmon* 臨濟・雲門): I.e., Linji Yixuan 臨濟義玄 (d. 866) and Yunmen Wenyen 雲門文偃. A preference for the sayings of these two famous masters over the sūtras is also criticized in "Shōbōgenzō bukkyō" 正法眼藏佛經.

[56:30]

先師天童古佛、擧、波斯匿王問賓頭盧尊者、承聞尊者親見佛來、是否。尊者以手策起眉毛示之。先師頌云、策起眉毛答問端、親曾見佛不相瞞、至今應供四天下、春在梅梢帶雪寒。

My former master, the Old Buddha of Tiantong took up [the following]:[84]

King Prasenajit asked Venerable Piṇḍola, "I've heard that the Venerable One has personally seen the Buddha.[85] Is this right?"

The Venerable brushed up his eyebrows with his hand to show it.

My former master said in a verse,

> Brushing up his eyebrows, he answered the matter.
> He once personally saw the Buddha; he doesn't deceive.
> Worthy of offerings even now, throughout the four continents.[86]
> Spring is on the twigs of the plum, cold in their girdle of snow.

[56:31] {2:108}

いはゆる見佛は、見自佛にあらず、見他佛にあらず、見佛なり。一枝梅は見一枝梅のゆゑに、開華明明なり。

"Seeing buddha" is not seeing one's own buddha, nor is it seeing another's buddha: it is seeing buddha. Because a single branch of plum is seeing a single branch of plum, *its blossoming is perfectly clear*.[87]

---

84 **My former master, the Old Buddha of Tiantong** (*senshi Tendō kobutsu* 先師天童古佛): After a record in the *Rujing heshang yulu* 如淨和尚語錄 (T.2002A.48:130c7-11); also treated in "Shōbōgenzō baika" 正法眼藏梅華.

85 **Piṇḍola** (*Binzuru* 賓頭盧): A prominent arhat among the Buddha's followers, often depicted as having long, drooping eyebrows. Prasenajit (*Hashinoku ō* 波斯匿王) was king of Kośala and a devout patron of the Buddha. The more common version of this story (as seen below, section 33) gives King Aśoka as Piṇḍola's interlocutor. Though the Zen story is quite different, it is ultimately derived from an account of Aśoka's interview with Piṇḍola in the *Ayuwang jing* 阿育王經 (T.2043.50:139c14-140a22).

"personally seen the Buddha" (*shin ken butsu rai* 親見佛來): Correcting Kawamura's *shin butsu ken rai* 親佛見來.

86 **Worthy of offerings** (*ōgu* 應供): A translation of Sanskrit *arhat* (*rakan* 羅漢). Piṇḍola was famous as the eldest of the arhats.

four continents (*shitenge* 四天下): I.e., the four great continents said to surround Mount Sumeru in Buddhist cosmology; see Supplementary Notes, s.v. "Four Continents." Humans inhabit the southern continent, Jambudvīpa.

87 **Because a single branch of plum is seeing a single branch of plum** (*isshi bai wa ken isshi bai no yue ni* 一枝梅は見一枝梅のゆゑに): Probably to be understood, "a plum branch is the seeing of a plum branch."

56. Seeing Buddha *Kenbutsu* 見佛

[56:32]

いま波斯匿王の問取する宗旨は、尊者すでに見佛なりや、作佛なりや、と問取するなり。尊者、あきらかに眉毛を策起せり、見佛の證驗なり、相瞞すべからず。至今していまだ休罷せず、應供あらはれてかくるることなし、親曾の見佛たどるべからず。かの三億家の見佛といふは、この見佛なり、見三十二相にはあらず。見三十二相は、たれか境界をへだてん。この見佛の道理をしらざる人天・聲聞・縁覺の類、おほかるべし。たとへば、拂子を豎起するおほしといへども、拂子の豎起するはおほきにあらず、といふがごとし。見佛は被佛見成なり、たとひ自己は覆藏せんことをおもふとも、見佛さきだちて漏泄せしむるなり、これ見佛の道理なり。如恒河沙數量の身心を功夫して、審細にこの策起眉毛の面目を參究すべし。たとひ百千萬劫の晝夜、つねに釋迦牟尼佛に共住せりとも、いまだ策起眉毛の力量なくば、見佛にあらず。たとひ二千餘載よりこのかた、十萬餘里の遠方にありとも、策起眉毛の力量したしく見成せば、空王以前より見釋迦牟尼佛なり。見一枝梅なり、見梅梢春なり。しかあれば、親曾見佛は、禮三拜なり、合掌問訊なり、破顔微笑なり、拳頭飛霹靂なり、跏趺坐蒲團なり。

The essential point of King Prasenajit's question was to ask whether the Venerable had seen buddha or had become buddha. The Venerable clearly brushed up his eyebrows, proof that he had seen buddha; he could not deceive. To the present day, he has never desisted; his "worthiness of offerings" has been on display and never hidden; we need not trace the seeing of buddha that he "once personally" [experienced].[88] The "seeing buddha" of those three *koṭis* of households was this seeing buddha; it was not seeing his thirty-two marks.[89] Were it seeing the thirty-two marks, who would have been blocked from the object?[90] There must be many among the classes of humans and devas, *śrāvakas*, and *pratyeka-buddhas* who do not know the principle of this seeing buddha.

---

88   **we need not trace the seeing of buddha that he "once personally" [experienced]** (*shinzō no kenbutsu tadoru bekarazu* 親曾の見佛たどるべからず): Here, as elsewhere in his writing Dōgen plays with Rujing's adverbial expression "once personally" (*shinzō* 親曾).

89   **The "seeing buddha" of those three *koṭis* of households** (*kano san oku ke no kenbutsu* かの三億家の見佛): Reference to the tradition that only one-third of the (impossibly large) population of Śrāvastī actually saw the Buddha during his residence there; see the *Dazhidu lun* 大智度論 (T.1509.25:125c5-7):

> 舍衞城中九億家。三億家眼見佛。三億家耳聞有佛而眼不見。三億家不聞不見。
> In the city of Śrāvastī, there were nine *koṭis* [90,000,000] of households. Three *koṭis* of households saw the Buddha; three *koṭis* of households heard that there was a buddha but did not see him; three *koṭis* of households neither heard of nor saw him.

90   **Were it seeing the thirty-two marks, who would have been blocked from the object** (*ken sanjūni sō wa, tare ka kyōgai o hedaten* 見三十二相は、たれか境界をへだてん): I.e., who could not have seen the thirty-two physical marks on the body of the Buddha? In fact, Buddhists have disagreed on the question of whether these marks adorn the human body visible to anyone or the "reward" body (*hōshin* 報身; S. *saṃbhogakāya*) seen only by advanced adepts.

It is like saying, for example, that, while those who stand up a whisk may be many, there are not many who stand up a whisk.[91] Seeing buddha is made manifest by buddha; even if we ourselves think to conceal it, seeing buddha is there first and leaks it out.[92] This is the principle of seeing buddha.

Exerting bodies and minds *numerous as the sands of the Ganges*, we should investigate in detail the face of this *"brushing up his eyebrows."*[93] Even were we constantly to dwell together with Buddha Śākyamuni, day and night, for hundreds of thousands of myriads of kalpas, if we still lack the strength to "brush up our eyebrows," it would not be "seeing buddha." Even though, over two thousand years later, we are in a distant quarter over a hundred thousand miles away, if we personally realize the strength to "brush up our eyebrows," it is seeing Buddha Śākyamuni from before King of Emptiness.[94] It is *seeing a single branch of plum*; it is *seeing the "spring" of "the twigs of the plum."* Thus, "*having once personally seen the Buddha*" is *paying respects with three prostrations*; it is *joining the palms and making inquiries*; it is *breaking into a smile*; it

---

91　**while those who stand up a whisk may be many, there are not many who stand up a whisk** (*hossu o juki suru ooshi to iedomo, hossu no juki suru wa ooki ni arazu* 拂子を豎起するおほしといへども、拂子の豎起するはおほきにあらず): I.e., teachers of Zen may be common enough, but authentic teachers are not. The whisk was a ritual implement held by an abbot when he ascended the high seat in a dharma hall for a formal teaching; raising this whisk as a visual display was a common gesture. See Supplementary Notes, s.v. "Whisk."

92　**Seeing buddha is made manifest by buddha** (*kenbutsu wa hi butsu genjō nari* 見佛は被佛見成なり): Taking *genjō* 見成 as equivalent to *genjō* 現成 ("realized," "obvious," "immediately available," etc.). Dōgen is playing here with the glyph *ken* 見 ("to see"), tempting us to read the phrase something like, "seeing buddha is seen (and realized?) by the buddha." Presumably, this and the immediately following clause represent an explanation of Rujing's line, "He once personally saw the Buddha; he doesn't deceive."

93　**bodies and minds numerous as the sands of the Ganges** (*nyo Goga sha sūryō no shinjin* 如恒河沙數量の身心): Presumably, referring to innumerable lifetimes.

94　**over two thousand years later** (*nisen yo sai yori kono kata* 二千餘載よりこのかた); **in a distant quarter over a hundred thousand miles away** (*jūman yo ri no enpō* 十萬餘里の遠方): I.e., far removed in time and space from Buddha Śākyamuni. The time span reflects the traditional East Asian Buddhist reckoning of the date of the *parinirvāṇa* of the Buddha as 949 BCE. The number of Chinese "miles" (*ri* 里) from the Buddha's homeland to Dōgen's Japan represents a standard expression (often given as "one hundred eight thousand miles" [*jūman hassen ri* 十萬八千里]) for a great distance. At roughly three *ri* to an English mile, the actual distance in *ri* from the Buddha's homeland to Dōgen's Japan would be closer to ten thousand.

before King of Emptiness (*Kūō izen* 空王以前): An unusual expression, likely based on the common Zen saying "before King Majestic Voice" (*Ion'ō izen* 威音王已前), used in reference to what precedes all differentiation; see Supplementary Notes, s.v. "Before King of Emptiness."

is "*a fist and flying thunder bolts*"; it is *the rush cushion for cross-legged sitting.*⁹⁵

* * * * *

[56:33] {2:109}
賓頭盧尊者、赴阿育王宮大會齋。行幸次、王作禮問尊者曰、承聞尊者親見佛來、是否。尊者以手撥開眉毛曰、會麼。王曰、不會。尊者曰、阿那婆達多龍王、請佛齋時、貧道亦預其數。

Venerable Piṇḍola attended a great maigre feast held by King Aśoka.⁹⁶ In the course of the imperial event, the king paid his respects to the Venerable and said, "I've heard that the Venerable One has personally seen the Buddha. Is this right?"

The Venerable parted his eyebrows with his hand and said, "Do you understand?"

The king said, "I don't understand."

The Venerable said, "When the Nāga King Anavatapta invited the Buddha to a maigre feast, this humble wayfarer was also included in that number."⁹⁷

[56:34]
いはゆる阿育王問の宗旨に、尊者親見佛來是否の言、これ、尊者すでに尊者なりや、と問著するなり。ときに尊者、すみやかに眉毛を撥開す。これ見佛を出現於世せしむるなり、作佛を親見せしむるなり。

The essential point of King Aśoka's question is that the words, "*The Venerable One has personally seen the Buddha. Is this right?*" are asking, "Is the Venerable One already a venerable one?" At the time, the Venerable One immediately parted his eyebrows. This causes "seeing

---

95 **joining the palms and making inquiries** (*gasshō monjin* 合掌問訊): A fixed expression for a polite greeting, with palms pressed together and head slightly lowered.

breaking into a smile (*hagan mishō* 破顏微笑): Reference to the famous story of the first transmission of the "treasury of the true dharma eye" (*shōbōgenzō* 正法眼藏) from Śākyamuni to Mahākāśyapa at an assembly on Vulture Peak; see Supplementary Notes, s.v. "Break into a smile."

"a fist and flying thunder bolts" (*kentō hi byakuryaku* 拳頭飛霹靂): Line from a verse by Dōgen's teacher, Rujing 如淨 (1162–1227); see Supplementary Notes, s.v. "Fist."

96 **Venerable Piṇḍola** (*Binzuru sonja* 賓頭盧尊者): Variant of the story raised by Rujing (above, section 30), found in several Chan texts; see, e.g., *Chanzong songgu lianzhu tongji* 禪宗頌古聯珠通集, ZZ.115:31a8-11. The famous King Aśoka is thought to have reigned c. 268-232 BCE.

97 **Nāga King Anavatapta** (*Anabadatta ryūō* 阿那婆達多龍王): The dragon king of Lake Anavatapta; see Dōgen's explanation below, section 36.

buddha" to *appear in the world*; it causes becoming a buddha to be "personally seen."[98]

[56:35]

阿那婆達多龍王請佛齋時、貧道亦預其數、といふ。しるべし、請佛の會には、唯佛與佛、稻麻竹葦すべし、四果支佛のあづかるべきにあらず。たとひ四果支佛きたれりとも、かれを擧して請佛のかずにあづかるべからず。尊者すでに自稱す、請佛齊時、貧道またそのかずなりき、と。無端にきたれる自道取なり、見佛なる道理あきらかなり。請佛といふは、請釋迦牟尼佛のみにあらず、請無量無盡三世十方一切諸佛なり。請諸佛の數にあづかる、無諱不諱の親曾見佛なり。見佛・見師・見自・見汝の指示、それかくのごとくなるべし。

He says, "*When the Nāga King Anavatapta invited the Buddha to a maigre feast, this humble wayfarer was also included in that number.*" We should recognize that, in an assembly of "invited buddhas," "*only buddhas with buddhas*" will be as "rice, hemp, bamboo, and reeds."[99] Those of the fourth fruit and *pratyeka-buddhas* would not participate.[100] Even if those of the fourth fruit and *pratyeka-buddhas* were to come, they would not be held up as numbering among the "invited buddhas." The Venerable has clearly claimed of himself, "when [King Anavatapta] invited the Buddha to a maigre feast, this humble wayfarer was in that

---

98 **This causes "seeing buddha" to appear in the world** (*kore kenbutsu o shutsugen o se seshimuru nari* これ見佛を出現於世せしむるなり): Perhaps meaning something like, "Piṇḍola's act of parting his eyebrows reveals what it means to see the buddha." The predicate "to appear in the world" (*shutsugen o se* 出現於世) is a fixed expression for the advent of a buddha; best known, perhaps, from the *Lotus Sūtra* sentence (*Miaofa lianhua jing* 妙法蓮華經, T.262.9:7a21-22) quoted above, Note 23.

it causes becoming a buddha to be "personally seen" (*sabutsu o shin ken seshimuru nari* 作佛を親見せしむるなり): Further play with the phrase from Rujing's verse, "He once personally saw the Buddha" (*shin zō ken butsu* 親曾見佛); perhaps meaning something like, "Piṇḍola's act of parting his eyebrows reveals that becoming a buddha is a matter of personally seeing." The clause might also be read, "it causes [us? King Aśoka?] to see 'becoming a buddha.'"

99 **in an assembly of "invited buddhas," "only buddhas with buddhas" will be as "rice, hemp, bamboo, and reeds"** (*shōbutsu no e ni wa, yui butsu yo butsu, tōmachikui su beshi* 請佛の會には、唯佛與佛、稻麻竹葦すべし): The introductory phrase could also be rendered, "in the assembly to which the Buddha was invited"; but Dōgen plays in this section with the expression *shō butsu* 請佛 ("invited the Buddha"), treating it as an adjective-noun construction, to make the point that the Arhat Piṇḍola was invited to a feast reserved for buddhas. "Only buddhas with buddhas" (*yui butsu yo butsu* 唯佛與佛) is a phrase from the *Lotus Sūtra*, see above, Note 23. "Rice, hemp, bamboo, and reeds" (*tōmachikui* 稻麻竹葦), a simile for great crowds, also comes from the *Lotus Sūtra*, where it is used to describe a great crowd of bodhisattvas (see Supplementary Notes); Dōgen playfully treats it as a verb here.

100 **Those of the fourth fruit** (*shika* 四果): I.e., arhats, the last of the four stages of the *śrāvaka* path leading to nirvāṇa. Piṇḍola, of course, was an arhat.

number." It is a statement about himself that came from nowhere; the truth of his seeing buddha is clear.[101] To say that [the king] "invited the Buddha" does not refer to inviting only Buddha Śākyamuni; it is inviting all the incalculable, inexhaustible buddhas of the three times and ten directions. It is the nameless, unnamed "*buddhas once personally seen*" who number among the invited buddhas.[102] Instructions about seeing buddha, seeing a teacher, seeing oneself, or seeing you should be like this.

[56:36] {2:110}
阿那婆達多龍王といふは、阿耨達池龍王なり。阿耨達池、ここには無熱惱池といふ。

"The Nāga King Anavatapta" is the nāga king of Lake Anavatapta.[103] "Lake Anavatapta" is called here "Lake without the Affliction of Heat."[104]

[56:37]
保寧仁勇禪師頌曰、我佛親見賓頭盧、眉長髮短雙眉麤。阿育王猶狐疑、唵摩尼悉哩蘇嚧。

The verse commentary of Chan Master Renyong of Baoning says,

Our Buddha personally saw Piṇḍola,
His eyebrows long, his hair short, his eyebrows rough.[105]
King Aśoka remained in doubt;
An moni xili sulu.[106]

---

101 **It is a statement about himself that came from nowhere** (*mutan ni kitareru ji dōshu nari* 無端にきたれる自道取なり): I.e., he had no reason to make this claim [other than to make clear his "seeing buddha" made him an "invited buddha"].

102 **nameless, unnamed "buddhas once personally seen"** (*mui fui no shinzō kenbutsu* 無諱不諱の親曾見佛): Further play with Rujing's line, "he once personally saw the Buddha" (*shinzō kenbutsu* 親曾見佛). The sense might be "all those unidentified buddhas ever personally seen" or, perhaps, "the buddhas personally seen, who are without name."

103 **Lake Anavatapta** (*Anokudatchi* 阿耨達池): Dōgen shifts here to a more common transliteration of the Sanskrit *anavatapta* ("unheated"). A lake, imagined to be north of the Himalayas (sometimes identified with Lake Manasarovar, in western Tibet), the name of which is said to derive from the fact that the dragons residing here are not subject to the hot sands and winds that represent one of their afflictions.

104 **is called here "Lake without the Affliction of Heat"** (*koko ni wa Munetsunō chi to iu* ここには無熱惱池といふ): I.e., the Chinese translation of the lake name, which could also be taken as "Lake without Torment."

105 **Chan Master Renyong of Baoning** (*Honei Jin'yū zenji* 保寧仁勇禪師): After the version at *Chanzong songgu lianzhu tongji* 禪宗頌古聯珠通集, ZZ.115:31a16-17.

his eyebrows rough (*sōbi so* 雙眉麤): The reading seems dubious here; the version at *Baoning Renyong chanshi yulu* 保寧仁勇禪師語錄 (ZZ.120:371a9-11) gives the more likely "his eyes rough" (*sōmoku so* 雙目麤), perhaps in the sense, "his visage fierce."

106 ***An moni xili sulu*** (*on mani shiri soro* 唵摩尼悉哩蘇嚧): A *dhāraṇī*, of unknown origin, the orthography of which varies slightly according to the text.

[56:38]
この頌は、十成の道にあらざれども、趣向の參學なるがゆえに、拈來するなり。

This verse, while it is not a saying of a hundred percent, is something to study that moves in the right direction; so, I bring it up.

* * * * *

[56:39]
趙州眞際大師、因僧問、承聞和尚親見南泉、是否。師曰、鎭州出大蘿蔔頭。

Great Master Zhenji of Zhaozhou was asked by a monk, "I've heard that Your Reverence once personally saw Nanquan.[107] Is this right?"

The Master said, "Zhenzhou produces big radishes."

[56:40]
いまの道現成は、親見南泉の證驗なり。有語にあらず、無語にあらず、下語にあらず、通語にあらず。策起眉毛にあらず、撥開眉毛にあらず、親見眉毛なり。たとひ軼才の獨歩なりとも、親見にあらずよりは、かくのごとくなるべからず。この鎭州出大蘿蔔頭の語は、眞際大師の、鎭州寶家園眞際院に住持なりしときの道なり。のちに眞際大師、の號をたてまつる。

The statement here is proof that he "personally saw Nanquan." It is not having words; it is not lacking words; it is not a comment [on another's words]; it is not a common expression. It is not "brushing up his eyebrows"; it is not "parting his eyebrows"; it is "personally seeing" the eyebrows. Even if it was the solitary step of an exceptional talent, had it not been based on "personally seeing," it would not have been as it was.[108] These words, "*Zhenzhou produces big radishes*," were said when Great Master Zhenji was abbot of Zhenji Cloister, in Doujiayuan, Zhenzhou. Later, the posthumous title Great Master Zhenji was bestowed on him.

---

107 **Great Master Zhenji of Zhaozhou** (*Jōshū Shinsai daishi* 趙州眞際大師): I.e., Zhaozhou Congshen 趙州從諗, dharma heir of the Nanquan Puyan 南泉普願 mentioned here. This dialogue appears in several Chan texts; see, e.g., *Zongmen liandeng huiyao* 宗門聯燈會要 (ZZ.136:533b17-18). The Tang district of Zhenzhou 鎭州 was in present-day Hebei, Zhaozhou's home area.

108 **the solitary step of an exceptional talent** (*issai no doppo* 軼才の獨歩): I.e., the unique expression of a genius like Zhaozhou.

56. Seeing Buddha *Kenbutsu* 見佛

[56:41]

かくのごとくなるがゆえに、見佛眼を參開するよりこのかた、佛祖正法眼藏を正傳せり。正法眼藏の正傳あるとき、佛見雍容の威儀現成し、見佛、ここに巍巍堂堂なり。

Because he was like this, ever after he opened the eye that sees buddha, he directly transmitted the treasury of the true dharma eye of the buddhas and ancestors. When there is a direct transmission of the treasury of the true dharma eye, the graceful deportment of the buddha's seeing is manifest, and seeing buddha is here solemn and imposing.

正法眼藏見佛第五十六
Treasury of the True Dharma Eye
Seeing Buddha
Number 56

[Ryūmonji MS:]

爾時寛元元年癸卯冬十一月十九日、在禪師峰山示衆
Presented to the assembly at Mount Yamashibu; nineteenth day, eleventh month, winter of the junior water year of the rabbit, the first year of Kangen [31 December 1243][109]

[Tōunji MS:]

寛元二年甲辰冬十月朔十六日、在越州吉田縣大佛寺侍者寮書寫之。懷奘
Copied in the acolyte's quarters, Daibutsu Monastery, Yoshida District, Esshū; sixteenth day, tenth month, winter of the senior wood year of the dragon, the second year of Kangen [17 November 1244]. Ejō

于時文明十二庚子年正月十日、於于越州吉祥山永平寺承陽庵。
比丘光周
In the Jōyō Hermitage, Eihei Monastery, Mount Kichijō, Esshū; on the tenth day, first month, senior metal year of the rat, the twelfth year of Bunmei [20 February 1480]. Bhikṣu Kōshū[110]

---

109 The Tōunji 洞雲寺 MS shares an identical colophon.

Yamashibu 禪師峰: Also read *Zenjibu*, the site in Echizen given in a number of colophons from this period.

110 **Jōyō Hermitage** (*Jōyōan* 承陽庵): Dōgen's memorial shrine at Eiheiji 永平寺, from his posthumous title Great Master Jōyō (*Jōyō daishi* 承陽大師).

Bhikṣu Kōshū (*biku Kōshū* 比丘光周): Fifteenth abbot of Eiheiji (1434–1492?).

TREASURY OF THE TRUE DHARMA EYE

NUMBER 57

Extensive Study

Henzan

遍參

Extensive Study

Henzan

INTRODUCTION

This chapter is extant in two versions: one, the version translated here, representing number 57 of the seventy-five-chapter compilation of the *Shōbōgenzō* and number 62 in the ninety-five-chapter Honzan edition; the other, similar but somewhat shorter, occurring as number 37 in the sixty-chapter *Shōbōgenzō* compilation (and translated below, in Volume 7). Both texts bear colophons indicating that the work was produced in the winter of 1243-44, at Yamashibu 禪師峰 (or Zenji Peak), the temple in Echizen (modern Fukui prefecture), where Dōgen delivered several *Shōbōgenzō* texts following his arrival from the capital in the summer of the same year; but it is thought that our text here represents an edited version of the draft found in the sixty-chapter compilation.

The title theme of the essay, *henzan* 遍參 (or *hensan*; also written 偏參) is the traditional Zen practice of traveling widely to study with various masters. The essay opens with a conversation between two famous Tang-dynasty monks, Xuansha Shibei 玄沙師備 and his teacher, Xuefeng Yicun 雪峰義存. Xuefeng suggests that his student undertake a trip of extensive study, but Xuansha remarks that the first Chan ancestor in China, Bodhidharma, never came to China from India and the second ancestor, Huike 慧可, never went to India from China.

In his comments on this conversation, which occupy the first half of the essay, Dōgen makes it clear that "extensive study" is not a matter of consulting widely but of penetrating the essential meaning of the buddha dharma — what he describes at one point as jumping into Bodhidharma's eye and plucking it out. Extensive study is not about traveling from place to place but about understanding that, in the words of Xuansha, "all the worlds in the ten directions are the true human body."

In the second half of the essay, Dōgen turns to an example of extensive study: the odd claim by Xuansha that he and Buddha Śākyamuni studied together under "the Xie's third boy in a fishing boat" — i.e., under Xuansha himself when he was boy who loved fishing. Here Dō-

57. Extensive Study *Henzan* 遍參

gen's comments focus on the notion that extensive study means studying together with another. He quotes a verse by his own master, Tiantong Rujing 天童如淨, celebrating an assembly of wise friends with whom Rujing had trained, and goes on to cite the examples of famous Chinese monks who spent years of study with their teachers.

Finally, Dōgen concludes the text by invoking a favorite theme of his writing and a famous centerpiece of Sōtō Zen teaching: "Extensive study," he says, "is just sitting and sloughing off body and mind."

正法眼藏第五十七

Treasury of the True Dharma Eye
Number 57

遍參

Extensive Study

[57:1] {2:112}
佛祖の大道は、究竟參徹なり、足下無絲去なり、足下雲生なり。しかもかくのごとくなりといへども、華開世界起なり、吾常於此切なり。このゆえに、甜瓜徹蒂甜なり、苦瓠連根苦なり、甜甜徹蒂甜なり。かくのごとく參學しきたれり。

The great way of the buddhas and ancestors is study and penetration of the ultimate; it is to *"go without a string at your feet"*; it is *"clouds arose underfoot."*[1] Nevertheless, though this is so, it is *"a flower opens, and the world arises"*; it is *"I'm always close to this."*[2] Therefore, it is *the sweet*

---

1 **Extensive Study** (*henzan* 遍參): Also read *hensan* and written 徧參. A term used in Zen literature for the monk's practice of traveling widely to study with various masters; it conveys the sense of something like "universal, or wide-ranging, consultation." The glyph *san* 參, here suggesting an audience with the teacher, occurs in such common compound expressions for Zen "study" or "investigation" as *sangaku* 參學, *sankyū* 參究, and *santetsu* 參徹 — all of which occur below in this text.

study and penetration of the ultimate (*kukyō santetsu* 究竟參徹): The "ultimate" is a common Buddhist expression, used for both the ultimate goal and the extreme efforts to reach it.

"go without a string at your feet" (*sokuka mu shi ko* 足下無絲去; also read *sokka mu shi ko*; also written 足下無糸去): Typically interpreted to mean untrammeled freedom; perhaps reflecting the simile that training the mind to concentrate is like training a bird to sit on your shoulder by tying a string to its foot. From a saying, also invoked in the "Shōbōgenzō zazen shin" 正法眼藏坐禪箴, attributed to the Tang-dynasty master Dongshan Liangjie 洞山良价 (807-869); see Supplementary Notes, s.v. "Dongshan's three roads."

"clouds arose underfoot" (*sokuka unshō* 足下雲生): An allusion to the power of flight, one of the standard spiritual powers of the Buddhist adept; an expression best known from an incident, told in the *Jingde chuandeng lu* 景德傳燈錄 (T.2076.51:218b2-6) and elsewhere, in which one of Bodhidharma's Indian followers flies on a cloud to rescue a fellow disciple.

2 **"a flower opens, and the world arises"** (*ke kai sekai ki* 華開世界起): The final line of the dharma transmission verse attributed to Bodhidharma's master, Prajñātāra. See Supplementary Notes, s.v. "A flower opens, and the world arises."

"I'm always close to this" (*go jō o shi setsu* 吾常於此切): A phrase also cited in

melon is sweet through to its stem; it is the bitter gourd is bitter to its root; it is the sweet sweetness is sweet through to the stem.³ This is how it has been studied.

* * * * *

[57:2]
玄沙山宗一大師、因雪峰召師云、備頭陀、何不遍參去。師云、達磨不來東土、二祖不往西天。雪峰深然之。

Great Master Zongyi of Mount Xuansha was once addressed by Xuefeng, who said, "Bei Dhūta, why don't you go off on an extensive study?"⁴

"*Shōbōgenzō jinzu*" 正法眼藏神通 and (in the variant *go jō o ze setsu* 吾常於是切) in "*Shōbōgenzō gabyō*" 正法眼藏画餅. The sense of the glyph *setsu* 切 here is subject to interpetation: the translation takes it as *sekkin* 切近 ("to be familiar with," "to be intimate with"), but it could also be, and has been, understood as *shinsetsu* 深切 ("to be ardent," "to care deeply," etc.). From a remark attributed to Dongshan Liangjie 洞山良价, in answer to a question about the three bodies of a buddha. The *Dongshan yulu* 洞山語錄 (T.1986A.47:510b24-25) gives the question as:

問、三身之中、阿那身不墮衆數。

[A monk] asked, "Among the three bodies [of the buddha], which body doesn't fall among the numbered?"

Dōgen's *shinji Shōbōgenzō* 眞字正法眼藏 (DZZ.5:152, case 55) has a variant version:

洞山因僧問、三身中那身說法。師曰、吾常於此切。僧後問曹山、洞山道吾常於此切、意旨云何。山云、要頭斫將去。僧又問雪峰。峯以拄杖劈口打曰、我也曾到洞山來。

Dongshan was asked by a monk, "Among the three bodies, which preaches the dharma?"
The Master said, "I'm always close to this."
The monk later asked Caoshan [i.e., Caoshan Benzhi 曹山本寂, 840-901], "Dongshan said, 'I'm always close to this.' What does that mean?"
Shan said, "If you want my head, cut it off and take it."
The monk again asked Xuefeng [i.e., Xuefeng Yicun 雪峰義存 (822-908)]. Feng struck him in the mouth with his staff and said, "I've been to Dongshan."

3 **the sweet melon is sweet through to its stem** (*ten ka tettai ten* 甜瓜徹蔕甜); **the bitter gourd is bitter to its root** (*ku ka ren kon ku* 苦瓠連根苦): A saying, more often in reverse order, occurring with some frequency in Chan texts; see, e.g., its use by Yunfeng Wenyue 雲峰文悅 (998-1061), *Guzunsu yulu* 故尊宿語錄, ZZ.118:688b7. The third clause here is Dōgen's variation.

4 **Great Master Zongyi of Mount Xuansha** (*Genshasan Shūitsu daishi* 玄沙山宗一大師): I.e., the Tang-dynasty Chan master Xuansha Shibei 玄沙師備 (835-905). "Xuefeng" (*Seppō* 雪峰) refers to Shibei's master, Xuefeng Yicun 雪峰義存. "Bei Dhūta" (*Bi zuda* 備頭陀; "Bei the Ascetic") is said to have been Shibei's nickname, deriving from his austere practice. Their conversation here occurs at *Jingde chuandeng lu* 景德傳燈錄, T.2076.51:344a6-7.

The Master said, "Dharma didn't come to the Land of the East; the Second Ancestor didn't go to Sindh in the West."[5]

Xuefeng deeply approved this.

[57:3]

いわく、遍参底の道理は、翻巾斗参なり、聖諦亦不爲なり、何階級之有なり。

The principle of extensive studying is *the study of a flip*; it is "*don't do even the sacred truths*"; it is "*what stages are there?*"[6]

* * * * *

[57:4]

南嶽大慧禪師、はじめて曹溪古佛に参ずるに、古佛いはく、是甚麼物恁麼來。この泥彈子を遍参すること、始終八年なり。末上に遍参する一著子を古佛に白してまうさく、懷讓會得當初來時、和尚接懷讓、是甚麼物恁麼來。ちなみに曹溪古佛道、儞作麼生會。ときに大慧まうさく、説似一物即不中。これ遍参現成なり、八年現成なり。曹溪古佛とふ、還假修證否。大慧まうさく、修證不無、染汚即不得。すなはち曹溪いはく、吾亦如是、汝亦如是、乃至西天諸佛諸祖亦如是。これより、さらに八載遍参す。頭正尾正、かぞふるに、十五白の遍参なり。

When Chan Master Dahui of Nanyue first visited the Old Buddha of Caoxi, the Old Buddha said, "What thing is it that comes like this?"[7]

---

5   **"Dharma didn't come to the Land of the East; the Second Ancestor didn't go to Sindh in the West"** (*Daruma furai Tōdo, niso fuō Saiten* 達磨不來東土、二祖不往西天): "Dharma" here refers to the First Ancestor, Bodhidharma, said to have brought the Zen lineage to China; "the Second Ancestor" is Bodhidharma's disciple Huike 慧可.

6   **study of a flip** (*honkinto san* 翻巾斗参): Or "a flip study." The "flip," or "somersault," is a common expression for Zen action.

"don't do even the sacred truths" (*shōtai yaku fui* 聖諦亦不爲); **"what stages are there?"** (*ka kaikyū shi u* 何階級之有): From a conversation between Nanyue Huairang 南嶽懷讓 (677-744) and his master, the Sixth Ancestor, Huineng 六祖慧能 (see, e.g., *Jingde chuandeng lu* 景德傳燈錄, T.2076.51:240a19-21):

後聞曹溪法席乃往參禮。問曰。當何所務即不落階級。祖曰。汝曾作什麼。師曰。聖諦亦不爲。祖曰。落何階級。曰聖諦尚不爲。何階級之有。祖深器之。

Later, upon hearing of the dharma seat at Caoxi, he [i.e., Huairang] went and paid his respects. He asked, "What business would avoid falling down the stages [of the bodhisattva path]?"
The Ancestor said, "How do you understand it?"
The Master said, "Don't do even the sacred truths."
The Ancestor said, "What stage will you fall to?"
He said, "If you don't do even the sacred truths, what stages are there?" The Ancestor deeply respected him.

7   **Chan Master Dahui of Nanyue** (*Nangaku Daie zenji* 南嶽大慧禪師): Dōgen here relates a famous dialogue between Nanyue Huairang 南嶽懷讓 and the Sixth Ancestor,

His extensive study of this ball of mud was eight years from start to finish.[8] In the end, he announced to the Old Buddha the one move of his extensive study, saying, "Huairang has understood what the Reverend put to me when I first came: 'What is it that comes like this?'"[9]

Thereupon, the Old Buddha of Caoxi said, "How do you understand it?"

At this point, Dahui said, "To say it's like any thing wouldn't hit it."

This is the realization of extensive study, the realization of eight years.[10]

The Old Buddha of Caoxi said, "Then does it depend on practice and verification?"

Dahui said, "It's not that it lacks practice and verification, but it can't be defiled by them."

Caoxi said, "You're also like this, I'm also like this, and all the ancestors of Sindh in the West are also like this."

Thereafter, he spent eight years more in extensive study.[11] True from head to tail, all told it was fifteen autumns of extensive study.

[57:5] {2:113}

恁麼來は、遍參なり。說似一物即不中、諸佛諸祖を開殿參見する、すなはち亦如是遍參なり。入畫看よりこのかた、六十五百千萬億の轉身遍參す、等閑の入一叢林、出一叢林を遍參とするにあらず、全眼睛の參見を遍參とす、打得徹を遍參とす。面皮厚多少を見徹する、すなはち遍參なり。

"Coming like this" is extensive study. "To say it's like anything wouldn't hit it": to "open the hall and see the buddhas and ancestors"

Huineng 六祖慧能, that appears regularly throughout the *Shōbōgenzō*; for the version of the story given in Dōgen's *shinji Shōbōgenzō* 眞字正法眼藏, see Supplementary Notes, s.v. "What thing is it that comes like this?" The text here mixes Chinese quotation with Japanese translation, paraphrase, and comment.

8   **His extensive study of this ball of mud was eight years from start to finish** (*kono deidansu o henzan suru koto, shiju hachinen nari* この泥彈子を遍參すること、始終八年なり): Like the *shinji Shōbōgenzō* text, some versions of the story do say that it took Nanyue eight years to come up with his answer; but the characterization of those years as "extensive study of this ball of mud" is Dōgen's comment, perhaps influenced by a saying of Tiantong Rujing 天童如淨 (1162-1227) that appears several times in the *Shōbōgenzō*; see Supplementary Notes, s.v. "Gouge out Bodhidharma's eye."

9   **one move** (*ichi jakusu* 一著子): Used in reference to moving a piece in a board game; in Zen texts, often a "move" in a dialogue.

10   **This is the realization of extensive study, the realization of eight years** (*kore henzan genjō nari, hachinen genjō nari* これ遍參現成なり、八年現成なり): This sentence represents Dōgen's comment.

11   **Thereafter** (*kore yori* これより): The final two sentences of this section represent Dōgen's comment.

is the extensive study of "also like this."[12] Ever since he "entered the picture and looked," he has extensively studied transforming the body "sixty-five hundreds of thousands of myriads of *koṭis*" of times.[13] He does not take the casual *entering a grove and leaving a grove* as extensive study; he takes seeing with the entire eye as extensive study, being able to penetrate it as extensive study.[14] Seeing through the thickness of the skin of the face — this is extensive study.[15]

[57:6]
雪峰道の遍參の宗旨、もとより出嶺をすすむるにあらず、北往南來をすむるにあらず、玄沙道の、達磨不來東土、二祖不往西天、の遍參を助發するなり。玄沙道の達磨不來東土は、來而不來の亂道にあらず、大地無寸土の道理なり。いはゆる達磨は、命脈一尖なり。たとひ東土の全土、たちまちに極涌して、參侍すとも、轉身にあらず、さらに語脈の翻身にあらず。不來東土なるゆゑに、東土に見面するなり。東土たとひ佛面祖面相見すとも、來東土にあらず、拈得佛祖失却鼻孔なり。

The essential point of the "extensive study" spoken of by Xuefeng, of course, does not recommend his leaving the peak, does not recommend his going north or coming south: it assists him in the extensive study of *"Dharma didn't come to the Land of the East; the Second Ancestor*

---

12 **"open the hall and see the buddhas and ancestors"** (*shobutsu shoso o kaiden sanken suru* 諸佛諸祖を開殿參見する): Likely reflecting the words of Dōgen's teacher, Tiantong Rujing 天童如淨 (*Rujing heshang yulu* 如淨和尚語錄, T.2002A.48:121c10). A similar expression, "opening the hall and seeing the buddha" (*kaiden kenbutsu* 開殿見佛), occurs in the "Shōbōgenzō jippō" 正法眼藏十方.

13 **"entered the picture and looked"** (*nyū ga kan* 入畫看): Again, likely reflecting Rujing (at *Rujing heshang yulu* 如淨和尚語錄, T.2002A.48:128a13); here, no doubt equivalent to the preceding "open the hall and see" (*kaiden sanken* 開殿參見). Both expressions suggest seeing from the perspective of Buddhist teachings.

"sixty-five hundreds of thousands of myriads of *koṭis*" (*rokujūgo hyaku sen man oku* 六十五百千萬億): An unusual number perhaps inspired by the twenty-seventh chapter of the *Lotus Sūtra* (*Miaofa lianhua jing* 妙法蓮華經, T.262.9:60c12), in which a buddha says of the two pious princes, Vimalagarbha and Vimalanetra:

此二子已曾供養六十五百千萬億那由多恒河沙諸佛。

These two boys have already made offerings to sixty-five hundreds of thousands of myriads of *koṭis* of *nayutas* of buddhas.

14 **entering a grove and leaving a grove** (*nyū ichi sōrin, shutsu ichi sōrin* 入一叢林、出一叢林): I.e., going from one monastery to the next.

the entire eye (*zenganzei* 全眼睛); **being able to penetrate it** (*tatokutetsu* 打得徹): Two expressions not occurring elsewhere in the *Shōbōgenzō*. The former seems to be Dōgen's invention; the latter, a fairly common phrase.

15 **thickness of the skin of the face** (*menpi kō tashō* 面皮厚多少): A fairly common expression in Zen texts, often seeming to suggest what we might call "thick skinned," but here sometimes interpreted as the "original face" (*honrai menmoku* 本來面目).

57. Extensive Study *Henzan* 遍參

didn't go to Sindh in the West" that Xuansha speaks of.[16] The "*Dharma didn't come to the Land of the East*" that Xuansha speaks of is not some confused words about coming or not coming: it is the principle that "*the whole earth lacks an inch of ground.*"[17] "Dharma" here is the tip of the vital artery.[18] Even if the entire land of the Land of the East were suddenly completely to gush up and attend upon him, this would not be transforming the body, nor would it be flipping the body in the stream of words.[19] Since he "*didn't come to the Land of the East,*" he meets the Land of the East face-to-face. Though the Land of the East encounters buddha faces and ancestor faces, this is not "coming to the Land of the East": it is *getting hold of the buddhas and ancestors and losing the nose.*[20]

---

16 **it assists him** (*johotsu suru nari* 助發するなり): The sixty-chapter *Shōbōgenzō* version of "Henzan" adds after this clause the sentence:

たとへばなんぞ遍參にあらざらんといはんがごとし。

It is, for instance, as if he were to say, "How could this not be extensive study?"

17 **"the whole earth lacks an inch of ground"** (*daichi mu sun do* 大地無寸土): A saying appearing in several Chan texts (see, e.g., *Jingde chuandeng lu* 景德傳燈錄, T.2076.51:464a26), usually attributed to Changling Shouzhou 長靈守卓 (1065-1123). The sixty-chapter *Shōbōgenzō* text has here simply:

遍參の道理を通達するなり。

It penetrates the principle of extensive study.

18 **tip of the vital artery** (*meimyaku no issen* 命脈一尖): An unusual image, perhaps suggesting that Bodhidharma here represents the ultimate meaning of the ancestral lineage.

19 **flipping the body in the stream of words** (*gomyaku no honshin* 語脈の翻身): A version of an expression appearing elsewhere in the *Shōbōgenzō* as "turning the body in the stream of words" (*gomyaku ri tenshin* [or *tenjin*] 語脈裏轉身); doubtless reflecting a fairly common Zen usage, as, e.g., in case 29 of the *Biyan lu* 碧巖錄 (T.2003.48:169a19):

没量大人語脈裏轉却。

The immeasurably great person turns round [or is turned round] within the stream of words.

The parallel passage in the sixty-chapter *Shōbōgenzō* gives:

たとひ、東土の全土、たちまちに極涌して達磨に參侍轉身する遍參ありとも、屋裏の兒孫としては、かへりてこれ遍參を參ずべし。この道は、遍參して雪峰と同參、見取せしむるなり。

Even if there were the extensive study in which the entire land of the Land of the East were suddenly to gush up, attending on Dharma and transforming the body, as the offspring within the house, [we] should still study this [as] extensive study. These words let [us] see [him] extensively studying, and studying together with Xuefeng.

20 **getting hold of the buddhas and ancestors and losing the nose** (*nentoku busso shitsukyaku bikū* 拈得佛祖失却鼻孔): Perhaps, meaning something like, "losing his identity in the lineage." "To lose the nose" (*shitsukyaku bikū* 失却鼻孔) is a fixed expression occurring with some frequency in Zen texts, in the sense to lose face or reputation; but, here, Dōgen seems to be playing with a saying found in several Chan sources (see, e.g., *Hongzhi chanshi yulu* 宏智禪師廣錄, T.2001.48:16c9):

[57:7] {2:114}

おほよそ、土は、東西にあらず、東西は土にかかはれず。二祖不往西天は、西天を遍参するには不往西天なり。二祖もし西天にゆかば、一臂落了也。しばらく二祖なにとしてか西天にゆかざる。いはゆる碧眼の眼睛裏に跳入するゆえに、不往西天なり。もし碧眼裏に跳入せずば、必定して西天にゆくべし。抉出達磨眼睛を遍参とす。西天にゆき東土にきたる、遍参にあらず。天台・南嶽にいたり、五臺・上天にゆくをもて、遍参とするにあらず。四海五湖、もし透脱せざらんは、遍参にあらず。四海五湖に往來するは、四海五湖をして遍参せしめず、路頭を滑ならしむ、脚下を滑ならしむ、ゆえに遍参を打失せしむ。

In sum, the "land" is not east or west; east and west have nothing to do with the "land." "*The Second Ancestor didn't go to Sindh in the West*" is, in extensively studying Sindh in the West, he "*didn't go to Sindh in the West.*" If the Second Ancestor had gone to Sindh in the West, *one arm would have fallen off.*[21] Now, why did the Second Ancestor not go to Sindh in the West? Because he jumped into the eye of Blue Eyes, he "didn't go to Sindh in the West."[22] If he had not jumped into Blue Eyes, he would definitely have gone to Sindh in the West. He made "*gouging out Dharma's eye*" his extensive study.[23] Going to Sindh in the West or coming to the Land of the East is not extensive study; going to Tiantai or Nanyue is not extensive study; we do not take going to Wutai or the heavens as extensive study.[24] If we have not transcended the four seas

---

拈得鼻孔失却口。
To get hold of the nose and lose the mouth.
See Supplementary Notes, s.v. "Nose."

21 **one arm would have fallen off** (*ippi rakuryō ya* 一臂落了也): No doubt playful allusion to the famous legend that Huike cut off his arm as an offering to Bodhidharma; see Supplementary Notes, s.v. "Cut off an arm." The sixty-chapter *Shōbōgenzō* text here is rather different:

二祖、もし西天にゆかば、佛法、いま東土にいたるべからず。達磨、もし東土にきたらば、佛法、いま東土に正傳すべからず。不來親曾不來なり、不往無外不往なり。これを動著せば、なにをか遍参とせん。

If the Second Ancestor had gone to Sindh in the West, the buddha dharma would not now have reached the Land of the East. If Dharma had come to the Land of the East, the buddha dharma would not now have been correctly transmitted to the Land of the East. "Not coming" is the not coming that is "personally once"; "not going" is the not going that is "without outside." If you move these, what do we take as extensive study?

22 **Blue Eyes** (*hekigan* 碧眼): A common reference to Bodhidharma.

23 **"gouging out Dharma's eye"** (*kesshutsu Daruma ganzei* 抉出達磨眼睛): No doubt recalling the remark by Rujing cited above, Note 8.

24 **Tiantai** (*Tendai* 天台); **Nanyue** (*Nangaku* 南嶽); **Wutai** (*godai* 五臺); **the heavens** (*jōten* 上天): The first three represent famous mountains of China associated with Buddhism; the referent of "the heavens" (*jōten* 上天) is somewhat ambiguous here: ordinarily, it would indicate the various heavens of Buddhist cosmology; but, given the context,

and five lakes, it is not extensive study.²⁵ Coming and going to the four seas and five lakes does not make the four seas and five lakes study extensively: it makes the road slippery; it makes the footing slippery; hence, it makes one lose extensive study.²⁶

[57:8]
おほよそ、盡十方界、是箇眞實人體、の參徹を遍參とするゆゑに、達磨不來東土、二祖不往西天、の參究あるなり。遍參は、石頭大底大、石頭小底小なり。石頭を動著せしめず、大參・小參ならしむるなり。百千萬箇を百千萬頭に參見するは、いまだ遍參にあらず、半語脈裏に百千萬轉身なるを遍參とす。たとへば、打地唯打地は遍參なり。一番打地、一番打空、一番打四方八面來は遍參にあらず。俱胝參天龍得一指頭は、遍參なり、俱胝唯豎一指は、遍參なり。

In sum, because he makes mastery of "*all the worlds in the ten directions are the true human body*" his extensive study, he has the investigation of "*Dharma didn't come to the Land of the East; the Second Ancestor didn't go to Sindh in the West.*"²⁷ Extensive study is "*the bigness of the stones is big, the smallness of the stones is small*"; it is, without moving the stones, to make them a big study, a small study.²⁸ To see

it may simply mean the "Western Heavens" (*Saiten* 西天; i.e., India).

25 **four seas and five lakes** (*shikai goko* 四海五湖): I.e., the entire realm of China; a fixed expression, sometimes in reverse order. The four seas are the oceans in the four directions; the five lakes are variously listed.

26 **it makes the road slippery** (*rotō o katsu narashimu* 路頭を滑ならしむ): Perhaps recalling the words of the Tang-dynasty Chan master Mazu Daoyi 馬祖道一 (709-788) warning of the dangers of going to study with the Chan master Shitou Xiqian 石頭希遷 (700-790): "The Shitou road is slippery" (*Shitou lu hua* 石頭路滑) (*Jingde chuandeng lu* 景德傳燈錄, T.2076.51:246b9).

27 **he makes mastery of "all the worlds in the ten directions are the true human body" his extensive study** (*jin jippō kai, ze ko shinjitsu nintai, no santetsu o henzan to suru* 盡十方界、是箇眞實人體、の參徹を遍參とする): Reference to words attributed to Xuansha Shibei 玄沙師備, recorded in the *shinji Shōbōgenzō* 眞字正法眼藏, DZZ.5:196, case 131; see Supplementary Notes, s.v. "True human body."

28 **"the bigness of the stones is big, the smallness of the stones is small"** (*sekitō daitei dai, sekitō shōtei shō* 石頭大底大、石頭小底小): A saying attributed to Guizong Daoquan 歸宗道詮 (930-985) (see, e.g., *Jingde chuandeng lu* 景德傳燈錄, T.2076.51:403b10-12):

問、九峯山中還有佛法也無。師曰、有。曰、如何是九峯山中佛法。師曰、山中石頭大底大小底小。
[A monk] asked, "Does the buddha dharma exist on Mount Jiufeng?"
The Master [Daoquan] said, "It does."
He asked, "What is the buddha dharma on Mount Jiufeng?"
The Master said, "On the mountain, the bigness of the stones is big, the smallness is small."

make them a big study, a small study (*daisan shōsan narashimuru nari* 大參・小參ならしむるなり): Or, perhaps, "to have them study the big, study the small." The terms

the hundreds of thousands of myriads in the hundreds of thousands of myriads is not yet extensive study; the turning of the body hundreds of thousands of myriad times within the flow of half a word is extensive study.[29] For example, "*Dadi just struck the ground*" is extensive study.[30] *Once striking the ground, once striking the sky, once striking the four quarters and eight sides* is not extensive study.[31] *Juzhi's studying with Tianlong and getting one finger* is extensive study; *Juzhi's just holding up one finger* is extensive study.[32]

daisan 大參 and *shōsan* 小參 can also refer to greater and lesser convocations for study in a Chan monastery.

29 **the turning of the body hundreds of thousands of myriad times within the flow of half a word** (*hangomyaku ri ni hyaku sen man tenshin* 半語脈裏に百千萬轉身): Dōgen is here playing with the Zen saying, "to be turned within the flow of words"; see above, Note 19.

30 **"Dadi just struck the ground"** (*Tachi yui ta chi* 打地唯打地): From the account of the monk called "Reverend Strike the Ground" (*Dadi heshang* 打地和尚), who just struck the ground with his staff whenever he was asked a question. (See *Jingde chuandeng lu* 景德傳燈錄, T.2076.51:261c2-3). The juxtaposition here of this expression with the following evocation of Juzhi's 俱胝 "one finger" (*ichi shi* 一指) suggests that Dōgen may be recalling the line praising the compassionate teaching techniques of the Chan masters, "like Juzhi's one finger and Dadi's just striking the ground" (*ru Juzhi yi zhi, Dadi wei da di* 如俱胝一指、打地唯打地), found in the *Yuanwu Foguo chanshi yulu* 圓悟佛果禪師語錄 (T.1997.47:784b13).

31 **striking the four quarters and eight sides** (*ta shihō hachimen rai* 打四方八面來): Seemingly recalling a well-known passage in the *Linji yulu* 臨濟語錄 (T.1985.47:503b20-22), in which Linji Yixuan's 臨濟義玄 (d. 866) eccentric follower Puhua 普化 (dates unknown), says,

明頭來、明頭打、暗頭來、暗頭打。四方八面來、旋風打、虛空來、連架打。

When the bright comes, the bright does it. When the dark comes, the dark does it. When the four quarters and eight sides come, the whirlwind does it. When empty space comes, the flail does it.

This translation treats the verb *ta* 打 simply as a generic predicate marker ("to do," "to deal with," etc.); but it is often taken in its primary sense, "to hit," "to strike," as in Dōgen's reading here, which seems to break the Chinese passage so that the verb at the end of the second clause gets attached to the head of the third clause.

32 **Juzhi's studying with Tianlong and getting one finger** (*Gutei san Tenryū toku ichi shitō* 俱胝參天龍得一指頭): Reference to the well-known story of the Tang-dynasty Chan master Juzhi of Mount Jinhua 金華山俱胝 (dates unknown), who was said to have attained awakening when his teacher Tianlong 天龍 (dates unknown) held up one finger. Thereafter, Juzhi himself always held up one finger to teach his own students. (See, e.g., *Jingde chuandeng lu* 景德傳燈錄, T.2076.51:288a23-11.) The sixty-chapter *Shōbōgenzō* has here:

俱胝唯豎一指を、遍參なりとす、更豎拳頭せば、遍參にあらざらん。爲人もかくのごとくなるべし、爲自もかくのごとくなるべし。

We take "Juzhi's just holding up one finger" as extensive study; if he then held up his fist, this would not be extensive study. "For the sake of the other" should be like this; for the sake of oneself should be like this.

57. Extensive Study *Henzan* 遍參

* * * * *

[57:9] {2:115}

玄沙示衆云、與我釋迦老子同參。時有僧出問、未審、參見甚麼人。師云、釣魚舩上謝三郎。

> Xuansha addressed the assembly, saying, "Old Master Śākya and I studied together."[33]
>
> At that time, a monk came forward and asked, "I don't understand. With whom did you study?"
>
> The Master said, "The Xie's third boy on a fishing boat."[34]

[57:10]

釋迦老子參底の頭正尾正、おのづから釋迦老子と同參なり。玄沙老漢參底の頭正尾正、おのづから玄沙老漢と同參なるゆえに、釋迦老子と玄沙老漢と同參なり。釋迦老子と玄沙老漢と、參足・參不足を究竟するを、遍參の道理とす。釋迦老子は玄沙老漢と同參するゆえに古佛なり、玄沙老漢は釋迦老子と同參なるゆえに兒孫なり。この道理、審細に遍參すべし。

The studying of Old Master Śākya that is right from head to tail is himself studying together with Old Master Śākya. The studying of Old Man Xuansha that is right from head to tail is himself studying together with Old Man Xuansha; hence, it is Old Master Śākya and Old Man Xuansha studying together. Old Master Śākya and Old Man Xuansha ultimately determining whether their study is sufficient or insufficient is the principle of extensive study. Because Old Master Śākya studies together with Old Man Xuansha, he is an old buddha; because Old Man Xuansha studies together with Old Master Śākya, he is a descendant. This principle, we should give detailed extensive study.

[57:11]

釣魚舩上謝三郡、この宗旨、あきらめ參學すべし。いはゆる釋迦老子と玄沙老漢と、同時同參の時節を遍參功夫するなり。釣魚舩上謝三郎を參見する玄沙老漢ありて同參す、玄沙山上禿頭漢を參見する謝三郎ありて同參す。同參・不同參、みづから功夫せしめ、他づから功夫ならしむべし。玄沙老漢と釋迦老子と同參す、遍參す。謝三郎と與我と參見甚麼人の道理を、遍參すべし、同參すべし。いまだ遍參の道理現在せざれば、參自不得なり、參自不足なり、參他不得なり、參他不足なり、參人不得なり、參我不得なり、參拳頭不得なり、參眼睛不得なり、自釣自上不得なり、未釣先上不得なり。

---

33 **Xuansha addressed the assembly** (*Gensha jishu* 玄沙示衆): I.e., Xuansha Shibei 玄沙師備; an anecdote found, e.g., in the *Liandeng huiyao* 聯燈會要, ZZ.136:823a14-15.

34 **"The Xie's third boy on a fishing boat"** (*chōgyo senjō Sha sanrō* 釣魚舩上謝三郎): A self reference. Xuansha's biography reports that his family name was Xie 謝, and that he loved fishing as a boy. (See *Jingde chuandeng lu* 景德傳燈錄, T.2076.51:343c24-25.)

"*The Xie's third boy on a fishing boat*": the essential point of this, we should clarify and study. This is the concentrated effort at extensive study of the moment when Old Master Śākya and Old Man Xuansha study together at the same time. They study together, as Old Man Xuansha is there studying with "*the Xie's third boy on a fishing boat*"; they study together, as the Xie's third boy is there studying with *the baldheaded fellow on Mount Xuansha*.[35] We should have ourselves concentrate, have the other concentrate, on studying together and not studying together.[36]

Old Man Xuansha and Old Master Śākya study together, study extensively. We should study extensively, study together, the principle of "with whom" the Xie's third boy and "I" studied. So long as the principle of extensive study is not immediately present to us, *study of ourselves is not possible, study of ourselves is insufficient; study of the other is not possible, study of the other is insufficient; study of the person is not possible, study of the self is not possible; study of the fist is not possible, study of the eye is not possible; fishing for oneself and rising by oneself are not possible, rising before being caught is not possible*.[37]

[57:12] {2:116}
すでに遍参究盡なるには、脱落遍参なり。海枯不見底なり、人死不留心なり。海枯といふは、全海全枯なり。しかあれども、海もし枯竭しぬれば、不見底なり。不留全留、ともに人心なり。人死のとき、心不留なり。死を拈來せるがゆえに、心不留なり。このゆえに、全人は心なり、全心は人なりとしりぬべし。かくのごとくの一方の表裏を参究するなり。

When extensive study has been exhaustively investigated, it is extensive study sloughed off. It is, "*when the ocean dries up, we cannot see the bottom*"; it is, "*when a person dies, he does not leave his mind be-*

---

35 **baldheaded fellow on Mount Xuansha** (*Genshasan jō tokutō kan* 玄沙山上禿頭漢): I.e., Xuansha as a monk; "baldhead" (*tokutō* 禿頭) is a common term for the tonsured cleric.

36 **We should have ourselves concentrate, have the other concentrate** (*mizukara kufū seshime, tazukara kufū narashimu beshi* みづから功夫せしめ、他づから功夫ならしむべし): Or perhaps, "we should have ourselves concentrate and make it the other's concentration." The "other" (*ta* 他) here is presumably the one with whom one studies together. The subject is unstated, and the sentence could still be referring to Xuansha and Śākyamuni.

37 **rising before being caught** (*michō sen jō* 未釣先上): Reminiscent of Dōgen's reference, in a passage on Xuansha's fishing in the "Shōbōgenzō ikka myōju" 正法眼藏一顆明珠, to "the golden-scaled one that rises of itself without being caught" (*fuchō jijō no kinrin* 不釣自上の金鱗). May reflect the words of Tiantong Rujing 天童如淨 (*Rujing heshang yulu* 如淨和尚語錄, T.2002A.48:127a17):

盡大地人不釣自上。
The person of all the whole earth rises of themselves without being caught.

hind."³⁸ "When the ocean dries up" means the entire ocean is entirely dried up. Nevertheless, when the ocean is entirely dried up, "*we cannot see the bottom.*" "Not leaving" and entirely leaving are both the person's mind. "When a person dies," the mind is not left behind. Since he has taken up death, the mind is not left behind. Therefore, we know that the entire person is mind, the entire mind is the person. This is the study of the surface and interior of such a single side.³⁹

* * * * *

[57:13]
先師天童古佛、あるとき、諸方の長老の道舊なる、いたりあつまりて上堂を請するに、上堂云、大道無門、諸方頂顳上跳出、虛空絕路、清涼鼻孔裏入來。恁麼相見、瞿曇賊種、臨濟禍胎。咦。大家顛倒舞春風、驚落杏華飛亂紅。

My former master, the Old Buddha of Tiantong, on one occasion when old associates among the elders from all quarters assembled and requested a convocation, *said in his convocation address,*⁴⁰

---

38 **"when the ocean dries up, we cannot see the bottom"** (*kai ko fuken tei* 海枯不見底); **"when a person dies, he does not leave his mind behind"** (*nin shi furyū shin* 人死不留心): The expression *ryūshin* 留心, translated here "leave his mind behind," normally has the sense "to pay attention," "to take heed"; hence, the second clause might also be understood, "when a person dies, he no longer cares." Variation on a saying, drawn from a verse by the poet Du Xunhe 杜荀鶴 (846-907), that occurs often in Zen literature (See, e.g., *Zongjing lu* 宗鏡錄, T.2016.48:564b12):

海枯終見底、人死不知心。
When the ocean dries up, we finally see the bottom;
When a person dies, we do not know his mind.

Dōgen's version here reflects a saying he attributes to Tiantong Rujing 天童如淨 in the *Eihei kōroku* 永平廣錄 (DZZ.4:86, no. 503). Elsewhere, he plays with other variants of the saying. In "Shōbōgenzō kokyō" 正法眼藏古鏡, he has, "Though the ocean dries up, it does not reveal the bottom" (*kai ko futō ro tei* 海枯不到露底); in "Shōbōgenzō hotsu bodai shin" 正法眼藏發菩提心, he has "When the ocean dries up, the bottom remains; though a person dies, the mind will remain" (*kai karete nao soko nokori, hito wa shi sutomo shin nokoru beki* 海かれてなほ底のこり、人は死すとも心のこるべき).

39 **surface and interior of such a single side** (*kaku no gotoku no ippō no hyōri* かくのごとくの一方の表裏): A tentative translation; perhaps, *ippō* 一方, rendered here as "a single side," refers to the unity of the person and the mind.

40 **My former master, the Old Buddha of Tiantong** (*senshi Tendō kobutsu* 先師天童古佛): Introducing a quotation of the *Rujing heshang yulu* 如淨和尚語錄 (T.2002A.48:122a16-19).

old associates (*dōkyū* 道舊): Literally, "to talk of the old"; by extension, "old friends."

> The great way has no gate;
> It springs from the crowns in all quarters.[41]
> Empty space ends the road;
> It enters the nostrils of Qingliang.[42]
> Meeting like this,
> Gautama's traitorous seed,
> Linji's disastrous embryo.[43]
> Ii![44]
> Everyone toppled over, dancing in the spring wind;[45]
> Startled, the falling apricot blossoms fly in crimson chaos.

[57:14]

而今の上堂は、先師古佛、ときに建康府の清凉寺に住持のとき、諸方の長老きたれり。これらの道舊とは、あるときは賓主とありき、あるひは隣單なりき。諸方にしてかくのごとくの舊友なり、おほからざらめやは。あつまりて上堂を請するときなり。渾無箇話の長老は交友ならず、請する、とものかずにあらず。大尊貴なるをかしづき請するなり。

This convocation address is from the time when my former master, the Old Buddha, was abbot of Qingliang Monastery, in the Prefecture of Jiankang, to which the elders from all quarters had come.[46] That these were "old associates" means they had once been guest and host or been

---

41 **It springs from the crowns in all quarters** (*shohō chōnei jō chōshutsu* 諸方頂顙上跳出): Probably to be understood to mean, "[the great way] springs from the crown of the heads of [the assembled] masters from monasteries everywhere." See Supplementary Notes, s.v. "Crown of the head."

42 **the nostrils of Qingliang** (*Seiryō bikū ri* 清凉鼻孔裏): I.e., Rujing's nostril. As Dōgen notes below, Rujing was at the time the abbot of the Qingliangsi 清凉寺. See Supplementary Notes, s.v. "Nose."

43 **Gautama's traitorous seed, Linji's disastrous embryo** (*Kudon zokushu, Rinzai katai* 瞿曇賊種、臨濟禍胎): Teasing reference to the assembled inheritors of the legacy of Buddha Śākyamuni and Chan master Linji Yixuan 臨濟義玄. The latter expression may reflect an exchange in the *Linji lu* 臨濟錄 (T.1985.47:497a2-3):

> 僧問、如何是劍刃上事。師云、禍事禍事。
> A monk asked, "What is it at the edge of the sword?"
> The Master [Linji] said, "Disaster, disaster."

44 **Ii!** (*ii* 咦): An interjection (pronounced *yi* in Mandarin), typically indicating a laugh or expression of surprise or delight.

45 **Everyone toppled over** (*taike tendō* 大家顛倒): The term *taike*, translated here as "everyone," can refer to a "great figure" or "great house"; or, as probably here, to the assembled audience. The term *tendō* 顛倒, translated as "toppled over," is regularly used for mistaken views that are "upside down" (S. *viparyasta*). Hence, the image of everyone overturned can be read as Rujing's teasing of the entire assembly as misguided.

46 **Qingliang Monastery** (*Seiryōji* 清凉寺): In modern Jiangsu Province. Rujing became abbot there in 1210.

57. Extensive Study *Henzan* 遍參

neighboring seats.⁴⁷ While from all quarters, they were thus his old friends; how could they not have been many? It was a time when they had assembled and requested a convocation. Elders completely lacking this talk were not his friends, were not numbered among those who requested [the lecture].⁴⁸ Though themselves great worthies, they attended him and requested [the lecture].

[57:15]
おほよそ先師の遍參は、諸方のきはむるところにあらず。大宋國二三百年來は、先師のごとくなる古佛あらざるなり。

In general, the extensive study of my former master was not something fulfilled by those from all quarters. In the last two or three hundred years in the Land of the Great Song, there have been no old buddhas like my former master.

[57:16] {2:117}
大道無門は、四五千條華柳巷、二三萬座管絃樓なり。しかあるを、渾身跳出するに餘外をもちいず、頂顥上に跳出するなり、鼻孔裏に入來するなり、ともにこれ參學なり。頂顥上の跳脱、いまだあらず、鼻孔裏の轉身、いまだあらざるは、參學人ならず、遍參漢にあらず。遍參の宗旨、ただ玄沙に參學すべし。

"*The great way has no gate*" is "*four or five thousand lanes of flowers and willows, twenty or thirty thousand pavilions of flutes and zithers.*"⁴⁹

---

47   **guest and host** (*hinju* 賓主); **neighboring seats** (*rintan* 隣單): The former term indicates the relationship between a visiting monk and an abbot respectively; the latter refers to assigned positions in the saṃgha hall.

48   **completely lacking this talk** (*kon mu ko wa* 渾無箇話): An unusual expression, not occurring elsewhere in Dōgen's writings; presumably, those with nothing significant to say.

49   **"four or five thousand lanes of flowers and willows, twenty or thirty thousand pavilions of flutes and zithers"** (*shigosen jō keryū kō, nisanman za kan genrō* 四五千條華柳巷、二三萬座管絃樓): "Flower and willow" (*keryū* 華柳) evoke the pleasure quarters, and the two phrases together suggest an endless entertainment district. Dōgen is here quoting (with minor variation) the verse comment by Chan master Yuantong Xian 圓通僊 on a saying of Zhaozhou Congshen 趙州從諗 (778-897) recorded in the *shinji Shōbōgenzō* 眞字正法眼藏 (DZZ.5:150, case 46):

趙州因僧問、如何是趙州。師曰、東門南門西門北門。僧曰、不問這箇。師曰、儞問趙州聻。
Zhaozhou was once asked by a monk, "What is Zhaozhou."
The Master said, "East Gate, South Gate, West Gate, North Gate."
The monk said, "I didn't ask about that."
The Master said, "You asked about Zhaozhou, right?"

Yuantong's comment (at *Chanzong songgu lianzhu tongji* 禪宗頌古聯珠通集, ZZ.115:245a18-b1):

四門開豁往來遊。脚下分明到地頭。四五百條花柳巷。二三千處管絃樓。

Still, when the whole body springs forth, without using anything else, it springs forth from "the crowns," it enters into "the nostril"; and both of these are study. One who has not sprung forth from "the crowns," has not turned the body in "the nostril," is not a person of study, is not a fellow of extensive study. We should just study with Xuansha the essential point of extensive study.

* * * * *

[57:17]
四祖かつて三祖に參學すること九載せし、すなはち遍參なり。南泉願禪師、そのかみ池陽に一住してやや三十年、やまをいでざる遍參なり。雲巖・道吾等、在藥山四十年のあひだ功夫參學する、これ遍參なり。二祖、そのかみ嵩山に參學すること八載なり、皮肉骨髓を遍參しつくす。

The Fourth Ancestor's spending nine years in study with the Third Ancestor is extensive study.[50] Chan Master Yuan of Nanquan's staying at Chiyang for some thirty years without ever leaving the mountain is extensive study.[51] Yunyan, Daowu, and others, making concentrated effort and studying during forty years at Yaoshan is extensive study.[52] The study of the Second Ancestor at Songshan was eight years; he exhausted the extensive study of skin, flesh, bones, and marrow.[53]

> The four gates are open wide, to come and go to play;
> Underfoot is clear and distinct, right to the place.
> Four or five thousand lanes of flowers and willows;
> Twenty or thirty thousand pavilions of flutes and zithers.

50 **The Fourth Ancestor's spending nine years in study with the Third Ancestor** (*shiso katsute sanso ni sangaku suru koto kusai seshi* 四祖かつて三祖に參學すること九載せし): I.e., the fourth Chinese ancestor, Daoxin 道信 (580-651), who is said to have studied with the Third Ancestor, Sengcan 僧璨 (d. 606), for nine years after his awakening at the age of fourteen (see *Jingde chuandeng lu* 景德傳燈錄, T.2076.51:221c18-21). This section is lacking in the sixty-chapter *Shōbōgenzō* text.

51 **Chan Master Yuan of Nanquan's staying at Chiyang** (*Nansen Gan zenji, sono kami chiyō ni ichijū shite* 南泉願禪師、そのかみ池陽に一住して): I.e., Nanquan Puyuan 南泉普願 (748-834), who is said to have entered Mount Nanquan, in Chiyang 池陽 (modern Anhui), in 795 and remained there for over thirty years (see *Jingde chuandeng lu* 景德傳燈錄, T.2076.51:257b25-26).

52 **Yunyan, Daowu, and others, making concentrated effort and studying during forty years at Yaoshan** (*Ungan Dōgo tō, zai Yakusan shijū nen no aida kufū sangaku suru* 雲巖・道吾等、在藥山四十年のあひだ功夫參學する): Reference to Yunyan Tancheng 雲巖曇晟 (782-841) and Daowu Yuanzhi 道吾圓智 (769-835), who studied with Yaoshan Weiyan 藥山惟儼 (751-834).

53 **The study of the Second Ancestor at Songshan was eight years** (*niso, sono kami Sūzan ni sangaku suru koto hassai nari* 二祖、そのかみ嵩山に參學すること八載なり): The second Chinese ancestor of Chan, Huike 慧可, who is held to have studied with Bodhidharma at Shaolin 少林 on Mount Song 嵩山 (in modern Henan).

he exhausted the extensive study of skin, flesh, bones, and marrow (*hi niku kotsu zui*

57. Extensive Study *Henzan* 遍參

[57:18]

遍參は、ただ祇管打坐、身心脱落なり。而今の去那邊去、來遮裏來、その間隙あらざるがごとくなる、渾體遍參なり。大道の渾體なり。毘盧頂上行は、無情三昧なり。決得恁麼は、毘盧行なり。跳出の遍參を參徹する、これ葫蘆の葫蘆を跳出する、葫蘆頂上を選佛道場とせることひさし。命如糸なり、葫蘆遍參葫蘆なり。一莖草を建立するを、遍參とせるのみなり。

Extensive study is simply "just sitting" with "body and mind sloughed off."[54] The present "going over there and coming over here," as if there were no gap between them, is extensive study with the whole body, is the whole body of the great way.[55] "*Walking atop the head of Vairocana*" is "*the insentient samādhi*"; *definitely "getting such" is the walking of Vairocana.*[56]

---

o henzan shitsukusu 皮肉骨髓を遍參しつくす): Reference to the tradition that, at the time he was to choose a successor among his four disciples, Bodhidharma said of each in turn that he (or, in one case, she) had gotten his "skin," "flesh," "bones," and, to Huike, "marrow." Dōgen regularly uses the four-character phrase to refer to the essence of Zen tradition. See Supplementary Notes, s.v. "Skin, flesh, bones, and marrow."

54 **"just sitting" with "body and mind sloughed off"** (*shikan taza, shinjin datsuraku* 祇管打坐、身心脱落): Combining two famous lines that Dōgen attributes to Tiantong Rujing 天童如淨; see Supplementary Notes, s.v. "Just sit," and "Body and mind sloughed off." This sentence is lacking in the sixty-chapter *Shōbōgenzō* text, which has at this point simply:

いままでも見一知識の風流聞一頭話の工夫みなこれよりするなり。

Even up till now, the tradition of seeing a wise friend, the concentrated effort of hearing a saying, have all derived from this.

55 **"going over there and coming over here," as if there were no gap between them** (*ko nahen ko rai shari rai, sono kenkyaku arazaru ga gotoku naru* 去那邊去來遮裏來、その間隙あらざるがごとくなる): Likely reflecting the words of Tiantong Rujing 天童如淨, in a lecture commemorating the construction of a bridge (*Rujing heshang yulu* 如淨和尚語錄, T.2002A.48:128a10-11):

去那邊去來者裡來。中間絕壑斷崖。

Going over there and coming over here; in between, a precipitous gorge, a sheer cliff.

56 **"Walking atop the head of Vairocana" is "the insentient samādhi"** (*Biru chō jō gyō wa, mujō zanmai nari* 毘盧頂上行は、無情三昧なり): The Buddha Vairocana often symbolizes the dharma, or "cosmic," body of the buddha. The translation "insentient samādhi" follows Kawamura's text, which has the unusual *mujō* 無情 ("insentient"), where other texts, including the sixty-chapter *Shōbōgenzō* version, have the more familiar *mujō* 無諍 ("unconflicted"; S. *araṇa*). The likely source for this phrase is a conversation between the Tang Emperor Suzong 肅宗 and Chan master Nanyang Huizhong 南陽慧忠 (d. 775) (*Jingde chuandeng lu* 景德傳燈錄, T.2076.51:244c15-17):

又曰、如何是無諍三昧。師曰、檀越踏毘盧頂上行。曰、此意如何。師曰、莫認自己清淨法身。

[Suzong] said again, "What is the samādhi without conflict?"
The Master said, "The *Dānapati* ['patron'; i.e., Suzong] treading atop the head of Vairocana."
[Suzong] said, "What does this mean?"

Thoroughly to study the extensive study that "springs forth" — this is the bottle gourd springing forth from the bottle gourd; for long, "atop the head" of the bottle gourd has been made the practice place where the buddha is selected.[57] It is, "*his life is like a thread*"; it is *the bottle gourd extensively studying the bottle gourd*.[58] We have merely set up "one blade of grass" and taken it as extensive study.[59]

正法眼藏徧參第五十七
Treasury of the True Dharma Eye
Extensive Study
Number 57

[Ryūmonji MS:]

爾時寬元元年癸卯十一月二十七日、在越宇禪師峰下茅庵示衆
Presented to the assembly at a thatched hermitage below Yamashibu, Etsuu; twenty-seventh day, eleventh month of the junior water year of the rabbit, the first year of Kangen [8 January 1244][60]

The Master said, "Don't acknowledge your own pure dharma body."

definitely "getting such" is the walking of Vairocana (*ketsu toku inmo wa, Biru gyō nari* 決得恁麼は、毘盧行なり): The expression *Biru gyō* 毘盧行 ("walking of Vairocana") leaves unclear whether Vairocana is walking or someone is walking on Vairocana. The sixty-chapter *Shōbōgenzō* text reads here "since you have got such" (*ki toku inmo* 既得恁麼), a phrase that suggests Dōgen may have had in mind the famous saying attributed to Yunju Daoying 雲居道膺 (d. 902); see Supplementary Notes, s.v. "Such a person."

57 **the bottle gourd springing forth from the bottle gourd** (*koro no koro o chōshutsu suru* 葫蘆の葫蘆を跳出する): Likely an allusion to the saying by Tiantong Rujing 天童如淨 much appreciated by Dōgen; see Supplementary Notes, s.v. "The bottle gourd vine entwines the bottle gourd."

practice place where the buddha is selected (*senbutsu dōjō* 選佛道場): An unusual expression, likely equivalent to the more common *senbutsu jō* 選佛場 ("site where a buddha is selected"), as given in the sixty-chapter *Shōbōgenzō* text.

58 **"life is like a thread"** (*myō nyo shi* 命如糸): Perhaps an indirect reference to the condition of having been selected as a buddha; likely an allusion to the warning of the Fifth Ancestor, Hongren 弘忍, to Huineng 慧能, upon the latter's accession to the position of sixth ancestor, that he should go into hiding to avoid conflict (*Jingde chuandeng lu* 景德傳燈錄, T.2076.51:223a22-23):

所謂授衣之人命如懸絲也。
The person to whom the robe [of Bodhidharma] is said to have been transmitted — his life is as if hanging by a thread.

59 **"one blade of grass"** (*ikkyō sō* 一莖草): Likely reflecting a well-known Zen trope, invoked elsewhere in the *Shōbōgenzō*; that equates a single blade of grass with the sixteen-foot tall body of the buddha; see Supplementary Notes, s.v. "One blade of grass." This sentence does not occur in the sixty-chapter *Shōbōgenzō* text.

60 The Tōunji 洞雲寺 MS shares an identical colophon.

57. Extensive Study *Henzan* 遍參

[Tōunji MS:]

同癸卯臘月廿七日書寫之、在同庵之侍者寮。懷奘

Copied at the acolyte's quarters of the same hermitage; twenty-seventh day, month of offerings, the same junior water year of the rabbit [7 February 1244]. Ejō[61]

---

61 **month of offerings** (*rōgetsu* 臘月): The twelfth lunar month.

TREASURY OF THE TRUE DHARMA EYE

NUMBER 58

The Eye

Ganzei

眼睛

The Eye

Ganzei

INTRODUCTION

This work bears a colophon, identical with that of the "Kajō" 家常 chapter, stating that it was produced in the winter of 1243-44, at Yamashibu 禪師峰 (or Zenji Peak), in Echizen. It represents number 58 in the seventy-five-chapter *Shōbōgenzō*, number 44 in the sixty-chapter compilation, and number 63 in the Honzan edition.

The essay proceeds by way of comments on nine sayings in the Chinese Chan literature involving the term *ganzei* 眼睛 ("eye" or "eyeball"), a word commonly used as metaphor for wisdom, as well as synecdoche for one possessed of wisdom. In his comments, Dōgen emphasizes an expanded sense of the term that includes "the mountains, rivers, and whole earth," as well as the spiritual practices of those who "beg the eye" of the teacher.

Though Chan literature is littered with talk of "the eye," in his choice of sayings on which to comment here, it is clear that Dōgen had in the mind the eye of his own teacher, Tiantong Rujing 天童如淨, whose sayings dominate the text. Thus, like the "Baika" 梅華 chapter from the previous month, this work strongly suggests the degree to which Dōgen was focused on Rujing's recorded sayings during this period.

正法眼藏第五十八
Treasury of the True Dharma Eye
Number 58

眼睛
The Eye

[58:1] {2:118}
億千萬劫の參學を拈來して、團圞せしむるは、八萬四千の眼睛なり。

When we take up the study of *koṭis* of thousands of myriads of kalpas and roll it up into a ball, it makes eighty-four thousand eyes.[1]

* * * * *

[58:2]
先師天童古佛、住瑞巖時、上堂示衆云、秋風清秋月明、大地山河露眼睛、瑞巖點瞎重相見、棒喝交馳驗衲僧。

My former master, the Old Buddha of Tiantong, when residing at the Ruiyan Monastery, in a convocation, addressed the assembly, saying,[2]

The autumn breeze is pure; the autumn moon is bright;
The mountains, rivers, and the whole earth, exposed to the eye.
Ruiyan is blinded; we meet again.[3]

---

1 **study of *koṭis* of thousands of myriads of kalpas** (*oku senman gō no sangaku* 億千萬劫の參學): I.e., the study [of Buddhism] over virtually innumerable æons; the time span here is a fixed expression for an enormous number.

eighty-four thousand eyes (*hachiman shisen no ganzei* 八萬四千の眼睛): The figure 84,000 is regularly used for the number of Buddhist teachings; hence, the implication here, "eyes that can perceive all the teachings."

2 **My former master, the Old Buddha of Tiantong** (*senshi Tendō kobutsu* 先師天童古佛): I.e., Tiantong Rujing 天童如淨 (1162-1227); served as abbot of the Ruiyansi 瑞巖寺 (in present-day Zhejiang province) before becoming abbot of Tiantongshan 天童山 (also in Zhejiang). His verse here is found at *Rujing heshang yulu* 如淨和尚語錄, T.2002A.48:126a3-4.

3 **Ruiyan is blinded; we meet again** (*Zuigan tenkatsu jō shōken* 瑞巖點瞎重相見): A tentative translation. Rujing here refers to himself as head of the monastery. "Blinded" renders the unusual *tenkatsu* 點瞎, which is variously interpreted (some, e.g., taking it to mean "to peer with one eye closed") but generally understood to indicate transcendence of normal vision; see Supplementary Notes, s.v. "Eye." The translation "we meet again" for *jūshōken* 重相見 assumes (with Dōgen's commentary, below) that the verb is reciprocal ("we see each other again"); some would take it simply as "I see anew."

Stick and shout one after another, testing the patch-robed monks.[4]

[58:3]
いま、衲僧を驗す、といふは、古佛なりや、と驗するなり。その要機は、棒喝の、交馳せしむるなり、これを點瞎とす。恁麼の見成活計は、眼睛なり。山河大地、これ眼睛露の朕兆不打なり。秋風清なり、一老なり。秋月明なり、一不老なり。秋風清なる、四大海も比すべきにあらず。秋月明なる、千日月よりもあきらかなり。清明は、眼睛なる山河大地なり。衲僧は、佛祖なり。大悟をえらばず、不悟をえらばず、朕兆前悟をえらばず、眼睛なるは、佛祖なり。驗は、眼睛露なり、瞎現成なり、活眼睛なり。相見は、相逢なり。相逢相見は、眼頭尖なり、眼睛霹靂なり。おほよそ、渾身はおほきに、渾眼はちひさかるべし、とおもふことなかれ。往往に老老大大なりとおもふも、渾身大なり、渾眼小なり、と解會せり。これ未具眼睛のゆゑなり。

"Testing the patch-robed monk" here means to test whether he is an old buddha. Its essential function is the "stick and shout" coming "one after another" — this, he takes as "blinded." A way of life like that expressed here is "the eye." "The mountains, rivers, and the whole earth" — these are the non-occurrence of any portent of "exposed to the eye."[5] "The autumn breeze is pure," "one old"; "the autumn moon is bright," "one not old."[6] "The purity of the autumn breeze" cannot be compared even to the four great oceans; "the brightness of the autumn moon" is brighter than a thousand suns and moons.[7] Their "purity" and "brightness" are the "mountains and rivers" and "the whole earth" that are "the eye." "The patch-robed monks" are the buddhas and ancestors. "The eye" that

---

4 **Stick and shout** (*bōkatsu* 棒喝): The Zen master's classic pedagogic methods of beating and shouting at the student. See Supplementary Notes, s.v. "Staff."

5 **non-occurrence of any portent of "exposed to the eye"** (*ganzei ro no chinchō futa* 眼睛露の朕兆不打): An awkward attempt to capture the phrasing of this difficult sentence; perhaps meaning something like, "[what exists] before the eye appears (or before what appears to the eye)." The unusual expression *chinchō futa* 朕兆不打 ("portent not happening") is generally taken as equivalent to the common *chinchō mibō* 朕兆未萠 ("portent not yet germinated").

6 **"one old"** (*ich irō* 一老); **"one not old"** (*ichi furō* 一不老): From the fixed phrase "one old, one not old" (*ichirō ichi furō* 一老一不老), used to express agelessness. Here, likely reflecting a verse by Dongshan Liangjie 洞山良价 (807-869) (*Dongshan Wuben chanshi yulu* 洞山悟本禪師語錄, T.1986A.47:510a19-20), quoted by Dōgen in his *Eihei kōroku* 永平廣錄 (DZZ.3:226, no. 351):

道無心合人、人無心合道。欲識箇中意、一老一不老。
When the way is without mind, it matches the person;
When the person is without mind, they match the way.
If you want to know the point in this,
It's one old, one not old.

7 **four great oceans** (*shi daikai* 四大海): Probably, the oceans on the four sides of Mount Sumeru in Buddhist cosmology.

does not choose great awakening, that does not choose non-awakening, that does not choose awakening prior to any portent — this is a buddha and ancestor. "Testing" is the "exposure" of "the eye," is the occurrence of "blinded," is the living "eye." "Meeting" is encountering each other; encountering and meeting are the eye sharp, the eye thundering.[8] Do not think that, in general, the whole body is large, while the whole eye should be small. Even those thought to be of great age often understand the whole body to be great and the whole eye to be small.[9] This is because they are not yet endowed with the eye.

* * * * *

[58:4] {2:119}

洞山悟本大師、在雲巖會時、遇雲巖作鞋次、師白雲巖曰、就和尚乞眼睛。雲巖曰、汝底與阿誰去也。師曰、某甲無。雲巖曰、有汝向什麼處著。師、無語。雲巖曰、乞眼睛底是眼睛否。師曰、非眼睛。雲巖咄之。

> When Great Master Wuben of Dongshan was in the assembly of Yunyan, he came upon Yunyan making sandals.[10] The Master said to Yunyan, "I approached your Reverence to beg the eye."
>
> Yunyan said, "To whom did you give yours?"
>
> The Master said, "I don't have it."
>
> Yunyan said, "You have it, but where did you put it?"
>
> The Master did not speak. Yunyan said, "Begging the eye is the eye, isn't it?"
>
> The Master said, "It isn't the eye."
>
> Yunyan shouted at him.

[58:5]

しかあればすなはち、全彰の參學は、乞眼睛なり。雲堂の辨道する法堂に上參し、寢堂に入室する、乞眼睛なり。おほよそ隨衆參去、隨衆參來、おのれづからの乞眼睛なり。眼睛は、自己にあらず、他己にあらざる道理、あきらかなり。

Thus, fully manifest study is "begging the eye." To pursue the way in

---

8   **the eye sharp** (*gantō sen* 眼頭尖): Here, probably not the common meaning "tip (corner) of the eye."

9   **Even those thought to be of great age** (*rōrō daidai nari to omou mo* 老老大大なりとおもふも): The expression *rōrō daidai* 老老大大 occurs often in Zen texts, in the sense "old enough to know better."

10 **Great Master Wuben of Dongshan** (*Tōzan Gohon daishi* 洞山悟本大師): I.e., Dongshan Liangjie 洞山良价, disciple of Yunyan Tansheng 雲巖曇晟 (782-841). A slightly variant version of this conversation can be found at *Jingde chuandeng lu* 景德傳燈錄, T.2076.51:315b3-6.

the cloud hall, to attend lectures in the dharma hall and enter the room in the bed chambers, are "begging the eye."[11] More generally, going along with the assembly to practice and coming along with the assembly to practice are in themselves "begging the eye." The principle is clear that "the eye" is not one's own and not another's.

[58:6]
いはく、洞山すでに、就師乞眼睛、の請益あり。はかりしりぬ、自己ならんは、人に乞請せらるべからず、他己ならんは、人に乞睛すべからず。汝底與誰去也、と指示す。汝底、の時節あり、與誰、の處分あり。某甲無、これ眼睛の自道取なり。かくのごとくの道現成、しづかに究理參學すべし。雲巖いはく、有向什麼處著。この道眼睛は、某甲無の無は、有向什麼處著なり、向什麼處著は、有なり、その恁麼道なり、と參究すべし。洞山無語、これ茫然にあらず、業識獨豎の標的なり。雲巖爲示するにいはく、乞眼睛底是眼睛否。これ點瞎眼睛の節目なり、活碎眼睛なり。いはゆる雲巖道の宗旨は、眼睛乞眼睛なり。水引水なり、山連山なり、異類中行なり、同類中生なり。洞山いはく、非眼睛。これ眼睛の自擧唱なり。非眼睛の身心・慮知・形段あらんところをば、自擧の活眼睛なりと相見すべきなり。三世諸佛は、眼睛の轉大法輪・説大法輪を立地聽しきたれり。畢竟じて參究する堂奥には、眼睛裏に跳入して、發心・修行・證大菩提するなり。この眼睛、もとよりこのかた、自己にあらず、他己にあらず。もろもろの罣礙なきがゆえに、かくのごとくの大事も罣礙あらざるなり。

It says that Dongshan has sought the benefit of approaching the teacher and begging the eye. Obviously, if it were one's own, one would not be asked for it by someone else; and if it were another's, one would not ask someone else for it. He is instructed, *"To whom did you give yours?"* There is a time that is "yours"; there is a way of dealing with it that is *"to whom did you give it"*?[12] *"I don't have it"*: this is the eye itself speaking. We should quietly study and investigate the principle behind such a statement. Yunyan says, *"You have it, but where did you put it?"* The "eye" of these words, we should investigate as a saying such that the "don't have" of *"I don't have it"* is *"you have it, where did you put it?"* and the *"where did you put it?"* is *"you have it."*[13] Dongshan "did not

---

11   **pursue the way in the cloud hall** (*undō no bendō suru* 雲堂の辦道する): I.e., practice meditation in the saṃgha hall. The translation follows the Tōunji 洞雲寺 and other MSS, which read here *undo ni bendō shi* 雲堂に辦道し.

enter the room in the bed chambers (*shindō ni nisshitsu suru* 寝堂に入室する): I.e., seek instruction at the abbot's private quarters, in the "parlor" where the abbot receives close friends and disciples.

12   **there is a way of dealing with it that is "to whom did you give it?"** (*yo sui no shobun ari* 與誰の處分あり): Or "there is a way of dealing with it that gives it to someone"; the translation tries to preserve Dōgen's use of the original phrasing of Yunyan's question.

13   **The "eye" of these words, we should investigate as a saying such that the "don't have" of "I don't have it" is "you have it, where did you put it?" and the**

speak": this is not because he was at a loss; it is a marker independently set up by his karmic consciousness.¹⁴

Yunyan instructed him, saying, *"Begging the eye is the eye, isn't it?"* This is the juncture of *"blinding"* the eye; it is *giving life to and smashing the eye*. The essential point of what Yunyan says here is *the eye "begging the eye"*; it is *water drawing water*; it is *mountains ranging across mountains*; it is *"moving among different types"*; it is *born among the same types*.¹⁵ Dongshan said, *"It isn't the eye."* This is the eye itself presenting its own song.¹⁶ Where there are the body and mind, thought and shape of what "isn't the eye," we should see it as the living eye "presenting itself." The buddhas of the three times have been standing and listening to the eye turning the great dharma wheel, preaching the great dharma wheel.¹⁷ Ultimately, in the interior of the hall of our investigation, we spring into the eye and there bring forth the mind [of bodhi],

---

"where did you put it?" is "you have it" (*kono dō ganzei wa, bōkō mu no mu wa, u kō jūmo sho chaku nari, kō jūmo sho chaku wa, u nari, sono inmo dō nari, to sankyū su beshi* この道眼睛は、某甲無の無は、有向什麼處著なり、向什麼處著は、有なり、その恁麼道なり、と參究すべし): The translation struggles to reflect Dōgen's retention of the Chinese phrases of his quotation; one possible paraphrase might be, "the eye Dongshan does not have is the very eye he put somewhere."

14 **a marker independently set up by his karmic consciousness** (*gosshiki dokuju no hyōteki* 業識獨豎の標的): A tentative translation of an unusual phrase not occurring elsewhere; perhaps meaning something like, "an expression of the working of his mind" (i.e., an intentional gesture). For the term *gosshiki* 業識 ("karmic consciousness"), see Supplementary Notes, s.v. "Karmic consciousness."

15 **"moving among different types"** (*irui chū gyō* 異類中行): An expression, occurring often in Dōgen's writings, generally taken to indicate the salvific activities of the buddhas and bodhisattvas among the various forms of living beings; especially associated with a saying of Nanchuan Puyuan 南泉普願 (748-834) found in the *shinji Shōbōgenzō* 眞字正法眼藏 (DZZ.5:154, case 57); see Supplementary Notes, s.v., "Move among different types." "Born among the same types" (*dōrui chū shō* 同類中生) is Dōgen's variant.

16 **the eye itself presenting its own song** (*ji ko shō* 自擧唱): Or "the eye itself singing its own praises."

17 **The buddhas of the three times have been standing and listening to the eye turning the great dharma wheel, preaching the great dharma wheel** (*sanze shobutsu wa, ganzei no ten dai hōrin setsu dai hōrin o ritchi chō shikitareri* 三世諸佛は、眼睛の轉大法輪・説大法輪を立地聽しきたれり): "To stand and listen" refers to the practice of the audience standing during a formal dharma talk. The sentence evokes a saying of Xuansha Shibei 玄沙師備 (835-905), on which Dōgen comments in his "Shōbōgenzō gyōbutsu iigi" 正法眼藏行佛威儀 (see *Yuanwu Foguo chanshi yulu* 圓悟佛果禪師語錄, T.1997.47:802b27-28; *shinji Shōbōgenzō* 眞字正法眼藏, DZZ.5:270, case 287):

火焔爲三世諸佛説法、三世諸佛立地聽。
The flames preach the dharma to the buddhas of the three times, and the buddhas of the three times stand and listen.

practice, and verify the great bodhi.[18] This eye is, from the beginning, not one's own, not another's. Since it is without any obstacles, a great matter such as this is also without obstacles.[19]

* * * * *

[58:7] {2:120}
このゆえに、古先いはく、奇哉十方佛、元是眼中華。

Therefore, an old forebear has said,[20]
How wonderful, the buddhas of the ten directions!
From the beginning, they are flowers in the eye.

[58:8]
いはゆる十方佛は、眼睛なり。眼中華は、十方佛なり。いまの進歩・退歩する、打坐・打睡する、しかしながら眼睛、をのづからのちからを承嗣して恁麼なり、眼睛裏の把定・放行なり。

"The buddhas of the ten directions" he speaks of are "the eye"; "flowers in the eye" are "the buddhas of the ten directions." Our present stepping forward and stepping back, sitting and sleeping, drawing on the eye's own power, are all like this, are all holding fast and letting go.[21]

* * * * *

[58:9] {2:121}
先師古佛いわく、抉出達磨眼睛、作泥彈子打人。高聲曰、著。海枯徹底過、波浪拍天高。

---

18 **in the interior of the hall of our investigation** (*sankyū suru dōō ni wa* 參究する堂奥には): I.e., "at the deepest level of study." The term *dōō* 堂奥 refers to the interior of the abbot's quarters, used metaphorically for the innermost recesses of the tradition; very common in Dōgen's writings.

19 **a great matter such as this** (*kaku no gotoku no daiji* かくのごとくの大事): Presumably, a reference to the great matter of "bringing forth the aspiration [for bodhi], practicing, and verifying the great bodhi."

20 **an old forebear** (*kosen* 古先): I.e., Langya Huijue 瑯琊慧覺 (dates unknown). His verse, cited in full in "Shōbōgenzō kūge" 正法眼藏空華, can be found at *Jianzhong Jingguo xudeng lu* 建中靖國續燈錄, ZZ.136:79a2-5.

21 **like this** (*inmo* 恁麼): The antecedent of "this" is not clear; presumably, "flowers in the eye."

holding fast and letting go (*hajō hōgyō* 把定・放行): An expression, often used by Dōgen, sometimes in reverse order, alluding to the teaching methods of the Zen master; perhaps reflecting a line by Tiantong Rujing 天童如淨 (*Rujing heshang yulu* 如淨和尚語錄, T.2002A.48:122c18):

放行把住逞風流。
Letting go and holding on, full of style.

58. The Eye *Ganzei* 眼睛

My former master, the Old Buddha said, "*I gouge out Dharma's eye, make a ball of mud, and hit people.*"[22] Raising his voice, he said, "*Look! The ocean, dried up right through to the bottom; the waves, so high they pound the heavens.*"[23]

[58:10]
これは清凉寺の方丈にして、海衆に爲示するなり。しかあれば、打人といふは、作人といはんがごとし。打のゆえに、人人は箇の面目あり。たとへば、達磨の眼睛にて、人人をつくれりといふなり、つくれるなり。その打人の道理、かくのごとし。眼睛にて打生せる人人なるがゆゑに、いま雲堂打人の拳頭、法堂打人の拄杖、方丈打人の竹篦拂子、すなはち達磨眼睛なり。達磨眼睛を挟出しきたりて泥彈子につくりて打人するは、いまの人、これを參請請益・朝上朝參・打坐功夫とらいふなり。打著什麼人、いわく、海枯徹底、浪高拍天なり。

This was instruction for the oceanic assembly, given in the abbot's quarters at the Qingliang Monastery.[24] Thus, "to hit people" is like saying "to make people." Because he hits them, each of the people has his or her own face. For instance, he is saying that he has made each of the people with Dharma's eye; they have been made. Such is the principle of his "hitting people." Because they are people born by the eye, the fist that now hits people in the cloud hall, the staff that hits people in the dharma hall, the bamboo staff and the whisk that hit people in the abbot's quarters — these are "Dharma's eye."[25] Having gouged out Dharma's eye, to make it into a ball of mud and hit people is what people today call "*making inquiries and seeking benefit,*" "*attending morning consultations,*" "*sitting and making concentrated effort.*"[26] Whom does

---

22 **My former master, the Old Buddha** (*senshi kobutsu* 先師古佛): I.e., Dōgen's teacher, Tiantong Rujing 天童如淨. Variant of remarks found in the *Rujing heshang yulu* 如淨和尚語錄 (T.2002A.48:121c12-13); see Supplementary Notes, s.v. "Gouge out Bodhidharma's eye."

23 "**Look!**" (*chaku* 著): The translation takes this verb in the sense *chakugan* 著眼 ("to look," "to set one's eye on"), a reading suggested by the *Yulu* 語錄 text (at T.2002A.48:121c13), which has *kan* 看 ("to look at," "to regard"); others interpret *chaku* 著 in the sense "to hit"; hence, here, "a hit!"

24 **oceanic assembly** (*kaishu* 海衆): Dōgen introduces here a common term for the saṃgha, seen as a pure ocean, that plays on Rujing's "ocean."

Qingliang Monastery (*Seiryōji* 清凉寺): The monastery in modern Jiangsu province, where Rujing became abbot in 1210.

25 **people born by the eye** (*ganzei nite tashō seru ninnin* 眼睛にて打生せる人人): The translation loses Dōgen's play with the element *ta* 打 ("to hit"), used as a verbal marker in *tashō* 打生 ("born"). Some texts read *taza* 打坐 ("to sit") here; a version that would yield "people who have sat by means of the eye."

26 "**attending morning consultations**" (*chōjō chōsan* 朝上朝參): An unusual expression; the meaning of *chōjō* 朝上 here is uncertain: some take it simply as "early morning"; others, as a reference to a formal convocation (*jōdō* 上堂) in the morning. By itself,

he hit? It is, "the ocean, dried up to the bottom; the waves, so high they pound the heavens."

* * * * *

[58:11]

先師古佛上堂、讚歎如來成道云、六年落草野狐精、跳出渾身是葛藤、打失眼睛無處覓、誑人剛道悟明星。

My former master, the Old Buddha, in a convocation, praised the Tathāgata's attainment of the way, saying,[27]

> For six years, a fox spirit, lurking in the grass;
> The whole body that sprang out was tangled vines.[28]
> When he lost his eye and had nothing to seek,
> He fooled people by saying he awakened to the dawn star.[29]

[58:12]

その明星にさとる、といふは、打失眼睛の正當恁麼時の傍觀人話なり。これ渾身の葛藤なり、ゆえに容易跳出なり。覓處覓は現成をも無處覓す、未現成にも無處覓なり。

"Awakened to the dawn star" is something said by a bystander at the very moment when "he lost the eye." It is the "tangled vines" of "the whole body"; therefore, they easily "sprang out." His seeking what he sought makes even its realization "nothing to seek"; and, even when not yet realized, he had "nothing to seek."[30]

* * * * *

---

the term *chōsan* 朝参 typically refers to the morning greeting in the abbot's quarters.

27 **My former master, the Old Buddha** (*senshi kobutsu* 先師古佛): From the *Rujing heshang yulu* 如淨和尚語錄 (T.2002A.48:122b14-15).

28 **six years** (*rokunen* 六年): A reference to Prince Siddhārtha's six years of ascesis prior to his attainment of buddhahood.

tangled vines (*kattō* 葛藤): More literally, "arrowroot and wisteria," commonly used figuratively for "complexities," "difficulties," etc.; see Supplementary Notes, s.v. "Tangled vines."

29 **awakened to the dawn star** (*go myōjō* 悟明星): From the tradition that the Buddha was awakened upon seeing Venus in the morning sky.

30 **His seeking what he sought makes even its realization "nothing to seek"; and, even when not yet realized, had "nothing to seek"** (*myaku shomyaku wa genjō o mo mu shomyaku su, migenjō ni mo mu shomyaku nari* 覓處覓は現成をも無處覓す、未現成にも無處覓なり): A tentative translation of a sentence variously interpreted; here, taken to mean that what the Buddha sought (i.e., awakening) is such that neither its occurrence nor its non-occurrence was anything to be sought.

[58:13] {2:122}

先師古佛上堂曰、瞿曇打失眼睛時、雪裏梅華只一枝、而今到處成荊棘、却笑春風繚亂吹。

My former master, the Old Buddha, in a convocation, said,[31]

At the time that Gautama lost his eye,
It was just one branch of plum blossoms in the snow.
Now, it's a thicket wherever you go;
Yet we laugh as the spring wind swirls them about.

[58:14]

且道すらくは、瞿曇眼睛は、ただ一二三のみにあらず。いま打失するは、いづれの眼睛なりとかせん。打失眼睛、と稱する眼睛のあるならん。さらにかくのごとくなるなかに、雪裏梅華只一枝、なる眼睛あり。はるにさきだちて、はるのこころを漏泄するなり。

Briefly put, Gautama's "eye" was not just one, two, or three. Which is the eye he lost here? Perhaps he had an eye called *"lost his eye."* Going further, given such a context, he had an eye that was *"just one branch of plum blossoms in the snow."* It precedes the spring and reveals the mind of spring.[32]

* * * * *

[58:15]

先師古佛上堂云、霖霪大雨、豁達大晴。蝦蟇啼、蚯蚓鳴、古佛不曾過去、發揮金剛眼睛。咄、葛藤葛藤。

In a convocation, my former master, the Old Buddha, said,[33]

Heavy rain for days on end,
Opening up to great clear skies.
Frogs croak,
And worms sing.[34]
The old buddhas are never past;
They show their diamond eyes.[35]

---

31 **My former master, the Old Buddha** (*senshi kobutsu* 先師古佛): From the *Rujing heshang yulu* 如淨和尚語錄 (T.2002A.48:122c29-123a1). Dōgen also quotes this verse in his "Shōbōgenzō baika" 正法眼藏梅華 and "Udonge" 優曇華.

32 **reveals the mind of spring** (*haru no kokoro o rōei suru* はるのこころを漏泄する): From the Chinese literary convention that the blossoming of the plum "divulges" (*rōei* 漏泄) the coming of spring.

33 **my former master, the Old Buddha** (*senshi kobutsu* 先師古佛): From the *Rujing heshang yulu* 如淨和尚語錄 (T.2002A.48:124a5-6).

34 **worms sing** (*kyūin mei* 蚯蚓鳴): Or "worms murmur"? Readers may supply for the verb *mei* 鳴 whatever type of sound they would like the worms to make.

35 **diamond eyes** (*kongō ganzei* 金剛眼睛): Or "vajra eyes"; a common Zen metaphor

Drat!
Tangled vines, tangled vines.

[58:16]

いはくの金剛眼睛は、霖霪大雨なり、豁達大晴なり、蝦蟆啼なり、蚯蚓鳴なり。不曾過去なるゆえに、古佛なり。古佛たとひ過去すとも、不古佛の過去に一齊なるべからず。

The "*diamond eyes*" are "*heavy rain for days on end*," are "*opening up to great clear skies*," are "*frogs croaking*," are "*worms singing.*" Because they are "*never past*," they are "*the old buddhas.*"[36] Even if the old buddhas were past, it would not be the same as the past of those who are not old buddhas.

* * * * *

[58:17]

先師古佛上堂云、日南長至、眼睛裏放光、鼻孔裏出氣。

In a convocation, my former master, the Old Buddha, said,[37]

The sun has reached its southern extreme.
From within the eyes shines a light;
From within the nose issues a breath.

[58:18] {2:123}

而今綿綿なる一陽三陽、日月長至、連底脱落なり。これ眼睛裏放光なり、日裏看山なり。このうちの消息威儀、かくのごとし。

In the present continuous one yang and three yang, the solstice is thoroughly sloughed off.[38] This is "*from within the eyes shines a light*"; it is

---

for Buddhist wisdom.

36 **Because they are "never past," they are "the old buddhas"** (*fuzō kako naru yue ni, kobutsu nari* 不曾過去なるゆえに、古佛なり): Cf. the discussion of old buddhas "never past" in "Shōbōgenzō kobutsushin" 正法眼藏古佛心.

37 **my former master, the Old Buddha** (*senshi kobutsu* 先師古佛): From the *Rujing heshang yulu* 如淨和尚語錄 (T.2002A.48:123b16-17), from a lecture given on the winter solstice.

38 **In the present continuous one yang and three yang, the solstice is thoroughly sloughed off** (*nikon menmen naru ichiyō sanyō, nichigetsu chōshi, rentei datsuraku nari* 而今綿綿なる一陽三陽、日月長至、連底脱落なり): A tentative translation of a sentence difficult to parse. "One yang and three yang" (*ichiyō sanyō* 一陽三陽) refer to the three months of winter, from the winter solstice, in the eleventh lunar month, to the start of spring, in the first month. "The solstice" loosely renders *nichigetsu chōshi* 日月長至 ("sun and moon reach their extreme"); "thoroughly" translates *rentei* 連底, which some would read here as "connectedness." For the use of "slough off" (*datsuraku* 脱落), see Supplementary Notes, s.v. "Slough off."

58. The Eye *Ganzei* 眼睛

"*seeing the mountain in the daylight.*"[39] Such are the circumstances and the deportment in this.[40]

* * * * *

[58:19]

先師古佛、ちなみに臨安府淨慈寺にして上堂するにいはく、今朝二月初一、拂子眼睛凸出、明似鏡、黒如漆。驀然踔跳、呑却乾坤一色。衲僧門下、猶是撞牆撞壁。畢竟如何。盡情拈却笑呵呵、一任春風没奈何。

My former master, the Old Buddha, once said in a convocation at the Jingci Monastery in Lin'an Prefecture,[41]

> This morning is the first of the second month.
> The eye of the whisk bulges out,
> Bright as a mirror, black as lacquer.
> Suddenly, it leaps forth,
> Swallowing the whole of heaven and earth.
> My community of patch-robed monks
> Still bumping into fences and bumping into walls.
> In the end, what is it?
> With all my might, I take it away, laughing, "Ha, ha,"
> I leave it to the spring wind — what else can I do?[42]

[58:20]

いまいふ撞牆撞壁は、渾牆撞なり、渾壁撞なり、この眼睛あり。今朝、および二月、ならびに初一、ともに條條の眼睛なり、いはゆる拂子眼睛なり。驀然として踔跳するゆえに、今朝なり、呑却乾坤いく千萬箇するゆえに、二月なり、盡情拈却のとき、初一なり。眼睛の見成活計、かくのごとし。

---

39 **"seeing the mountain in the daylight"** (*nichiri kanzan* 日裏看山): Perhaps meaning "as clear as seeing a mountain in broad daylight." Likely reflecting the words of Yunmen Wenyen 雲門文偃 (864-949); see Supplementary Notes.

40 **Such are the circumstances and the deportment in this** (*kono uchi no shōsoku iigi, kaku no gotoshi* このうちの消息威儀、かくのごとし): The antecedent of "in this" (*kono uchi* このうち) is unclear; perhaps, "the mountain" ("the circumstances") and "seeing" ("the deportment"). See Supplementary Notes, s.v. "Deportment."

41 **My former master, the Old Buddha** (*senshi kobutsu* 先師古佛): From the *Rujing heshang yulu* 如淨和尚語錄 (T.2002A.48:124a1-4). The Jingcisi 淨慈寺, where Rujing served as abbot before his move to Tiantong, was a major monastery in Hangzhou 杭州, in present-day Zhejiang province.

42 **With all my might, I take it away** (*jinjō nenkyaku* 盡情拈却): Taking *jinjō* 盡情 in the common idiomatic sense, "whole-heartedly," "completely," etc.; traditionally read here more literally, as "having exhausted feelings." The object of "take away" (*nenkyaku* 拈却) here is presumably the eye of the whisk.

The "*bumping into fences and bumping into walls*" here is the whole fence bumping, the whole wall bumping; they have this "eye."[43] "This morning" and "the second month," as well as "the first," are each individual instances of the "eye" — that is, are "the eye of the whisk." Because it suddenly "leaps forth," it is "this morning"; because it "*swallows up heaven and earth*" a thousand myriad times, it is "the second month; when he "*takes it away with all his might*" it is "the first." Such is the life realized by the eye.

正法眼藏眼睛第五十八
Treasury of the True Dharma Eye
The Eye
Number 58

[Ryūmonji MS:]

爾時寬元元年癸卯十二月十七日、在越州禪師峰下示衆
Presented to the assembly beneath Yamashibu, in Esshū; seventeenth day, twelfth month of the junior water year of the rabbit, the first year of Kangen [28 January 1244][44]

[Tōunji MS:]

同廿八日書寫之、在同峰下侍者寮。懷奘
Copied this in the acolyte's quarters beneath the same peak; on the same twenty-eighth day [8 February 1244]. Ejō

于時文明十一己亥年十二月十七日、於于越州吉田郡志比庄吉祥山永平寺承陽庵書寫之。守塔比丘光周
Copied this in the Jōyō Hermitage, Eihei Monastery, Mount Kichijō, Shihi Estate, Yoshida District, Esshū; seventeenth day, twelfth month, junior earth year of the pig, the eleventh year of Bunmei [28 January 1480]. Guardian of the Stūpa, Bhikṣu Kōshū[45]

---

43 **the whole fence bumping, the whole wall bumping** (*konshō tō nari, konheki tō nari* 渾牆撞なり、渾壁撞なり): Can be read either as "bumping into the whole fence, bumping into the whole wall" or as "the whole fence itself bumping, the whole wall itself bumping." For the use of "fences" and "walls," see Supplementary Notes, s.v. "Fences, walls, tiles, and pebbles."

they have this "eye" (*kono ganzei ari* この眼睛あり): Or simply "there is this eye" [i.e., such a way of seeing the passage]. In the former reading, the antecedent of "they" might be "the patch-robed monks" or, perhaps, the "fences" and "walls."

44 The Tōunji 洞雲寺 MS shares an identical colophon.

45 **Guardian of the Stūpa, Bhikṣu Kōshū** (*shutō biku Kōshū* 守塔比丘光周): Fifteenth abbot of Eiheiji (1434–1492?); "the stūpa" refers to Dōgen's memorial at Eiheiji.

Treasury of the True Dharma Eye
Number 59
Everyday Matters
Kajō
家常

Everyday Matters

Kajō

INTRODUCTION

This work bears a colophon, identical with that of the "Ganzei" chapter, stating that it was produced in January of 1244, at Yamashibu 禪師峰 (or Zenji Peak), in Echizen. It represents number 59 in the seventy-five-chapter *Shōbōgenzō*, number 43 in the sixty-chapter compilation, and number 64 in the Honzan edition.

The title of the essay, *kajō* 家常, rendered here "everyday matters," is more literally something like "usual at home" — i.e., the quotidian life of the household. It is often, as here, applied to the daily fare of domestic cooking, as in the common expression "everyday tea and rice" (*kajō sahan* 家常茶飯). This use is well known in Zen texts from the saying, cited several times in the *Shōbōgenzō*, of the Song-dynasty master Furong Daokai 芙蓉道楷: "The intentions and the words of the buddhas and ancestors are like everyday tea and rice." Beginning with this saying, Dōgen here takes up talk of "tea and rice" in the teachings of the Chan masters, including four examples from his own teacher, Tiantong Rujing 天童如淨. In the end, he concludes, "the everyday matters of the buddhas and ancestors are only drinking tea and eating rice."

正法眼藏第五十九

Treasury of the True Dharma Eye
Number 59

家常

Everyday Matters

[59:1] [2:124}
おほよそ佛祖の屋裏には、茶飯これ家常なり。この茶飯の義、ひさしくつたはれて、而今の現成なり。このゆえに、佛祖茶飯の活計きたれるなり。

Within the house of the buddhas and ancestors, tea and rice are everyday matters.[1] The meaning of this tea and rice has long been passed on and is realized even now.[2] Therefore, the way of life of the tea and rice of the buddhas and ancestors has come down to us.

* * * * *

[59:2]
大陽山楷和尚、問投子云、佛祖意句、如家常茶飯。離此之餘、還有爲人言句也無。投子曰、汝道、寰中天子敕、還假禹湯堯舜也無。大陽擬開口。投子拈拂子掩師口曰、汝發意來時、早有三十棒分也。大陽於此開悟、禮拜便行。投子曰、且來闍梨。大陽竟不回頭。投子曰、子、到不疑之地耶。大陽以手掩耳而去。

> Reverend Kai of Mount Dayang asked Touzi, "The intention and the words of the buddhas and ancestors are like everyday tea and rice. Apart from this, are there any other words to help people or not?"[3]

1　**tea and rice are everyday matters** (*sahan kore kajō nari* 茶飯これ家常なり): From the common expression "everyday tea and rice" (*kajō sahan* 家常茶飯), used for the "daily fare" of the home, what we might call "homestyle" cooking; see Supplementary Notes, s.v. "Everyday tea and rice."

2　**The meaning of this tea and rice** (*kono sahan no gi* この茶飯の義): The *Honzan* edition has here the homophonous *gi* 儀 ("ritual," "behavior," etc.) — hence, "the practice of [taking] this tea and rice."

3　**Reverend Kai of Mount Dayang** (*Taiyōzan Kai oshō* 大陽山楷和尚): I.e., Furong Daokai 芙蓉道楷 (1043-1118); Mount Dayang 大陽山 is located in Yingzhou 郢州 in present-day Hubei province. His exchange with Touzi Yiqing 投子義青 (1032-1083) can be found in the *Liandeng huiyao* 聯燈會要, ZZ.136:917a6-11; and Dōgen's *shinji Shōbōgenzō* 眞字正法眼藏 (DZZ.5:202, case 143). Some versions of the saying read "The words (*gonku* 言句) of the buddhas and ancestors."

Touzi said, "Tell me, when the Son of Heaven, within his realm, issues a decree, does he rely on Yu, Tang, Yao, and Shun or not?"[4]

As Dayang was about to open his mouth, Touzi took up his whisk, covered the Master's mouth, and said, "When you got the idea and came to me, you already deserved thirty blows."

With this, Dayang had an awakening and, paying obeisance, went to leave.

Touzi said, "Ācārya, come back!"

Dayang did not look back.

Touzi said, "Has the young master reached a stage without doubts?"

Dayang covered his ears with his hands and left.

[59:3] {2:125}

しかあれば、あきらかに保任すべし、佛祖意句は、佛祖家常の茶飯なり。家常の麤茶淡飯は、佛祖意句なり。佛祖は、茶飯をつくる、茶飯、佛祖を保任せしむ。しかあれども、このほかの茶飯力をからず、このうちの佛祖力をつひやさざるのみなり。還假堯舜禹湯也無、の見示を功夫參學すべきなり。離此之餘、還有爲人言句也無、この問頭の頂顙を參跳すべし。跳得也、跳不得也、と試參看すべし。

Thus, we should clearly maintain this: that "the intention and words of the buddhas and ancestors" are the everyday tea and rice of the buddhas and ancestors. The everyday fare of coarse tea and plain rice is "the intention and words of the buddhas and ancestors." The buddhas and ancestors make tea and rice; tea and rice maintain the buddhas and ancestors. Nevertheless, it is not that they draw on the power of some other tea and rice, but they do not use up the power of the buddhas and ancestors within.[5] "*Does he rely on Yu, Tang, Yao, and Shun or not?*" We should make concentrated effort and study what this tells us. "*Apart from this, are there any other words to help people or not?*" We should

---

4 **Yu, Tang, Yao, and Shun** (*U Tō Gyō Shun* 禹湯堯舜): Four legendary emperors of early China. Yu and Tang were founders of the Xia and Shang dynasties, respectively; Yao and Shun were the last of the five emperors said to precede the Xia.

5 **Nevertheless, it is not that they draw on the power of some other tea and rice, but they do not use up the power of the buddhas and ancestors within** (*shika aredomo, kono hoka no sahan riki o karazu, kono uchi no busso riki o tsuiyasazaru nomi nari* しかあれども、このほかの茶飯力をからず、このうちの佛祖力をつひやさざるのみなり): A tentative translation of a sentence variously interpreted; taking the first clause to mean that, while "tea and rice maintain the buddhas and ancestors," this does not mean that the tea and rice are other than the buddhas and ancestors; and taking the second clause to mean that, while "the buddhas and ancestors make tea and rice," this does not require any special effort on their part.

study and spring forth from the head of this question.[6] We should try studying whether we can spring forth or not spring forth from it.

* * * * *

[59:4]
南嶽山石頭庵無際大師いはく、吾結草庵無寶貝、飯了從容圖睡快。

Great Master Wuji of the Shitou Hermitage on Mount Nanyue said,[7]
I built this thatched hut that has nothing of worth;
Finished my rice, I relaxed, figuring on a quick nap.

[59:5]
道來道去、道來去する飯了は、參飯佛祖意句なり。未飯なるは未飽參なり。しかあるに、この飯了從容の道理は、飯先にも現成す、飯中にも現成す、飯後にも現成す。飯了の屋裏に喫飯ありと錯認する、四五升の參學なり。

The words "finished my rice" that he says as he comes, says as he goes, says as he comes and goes, are *"the intention and the words of a buddha and ancestor" who studies rice.*[8] One who has not yet had his rice has not yet studied his fill. Nevertheless, the principle of this *"finished my rice, I take it easy"* is present before he has the rice, while he has the rice, and after he has the rice. Mistakenly to think that there is any having rice in the house where he has "finished his rice" is a study of four or five quarts.[9]

---

6   **study and spring forth** (*sanchō* 參跳): An unusual expression not encountered elsewhere in Dōgen's writings; probably a combination of *sangaku* 參學 ("to study") and *chōshutsu* 跳出 ("to spring forth").

7   **Great Master Wuji of the Shitou Hermitage on Mount Nanyue** (*Nangakusan Sekitōan Musai daishi* 南嶽山石頭庵無際大師): I.e., Shitou Xiqian 石頭希遷 (700-790). Mount Nanyue is located in present-day Hunan province. The quoted lines appear in the *Jingde chuandeng lu* 景德傳燈錄 (T.2076.51:461c9), as the opening lines of the *Shitou heshang caoan ge* 石頭和尚草庵歌, a verse quoted elsewhere in the *Shōbōgenzō*.

8   **"intention and words of a buddha and ancestor" who studies rice** (*sanpan busso iku* 參飯佛祖意句): Some texts read here "the intention and words of a buddha and ancestor who has studied his fill" (*sanpō busso iku* 參飽佛祖意句), a version that uses a common expression for being fully trained in Buddhism in a play on "filling oneself" with rice, as seen again in the next sentence. For the sake of lexical continuity with "tea and rice," the translation uses "rice" for the glyph 飯 throughout this chapter, though the word also carries the larger senses of "food" and "meal."

9   **Mistakenly to think that there is any having rice in the house where he has "finished his rice" is a study of four or five quarts** (*hanryō no okuri ni kippan ari to shakunin suru, shigo shō no sangaku nari* 飯了の屋裏に喫飯ありと錯認する、四五升の參學なり): Probably meaning something like, "to think that the state of 'having finished my rice' concerns eating is a shallow understanding of Shitou's words here."

[59:6]

先師古佛示衆曰、記得僧問百丈、如何是奇特事。百丈云、獨坐大雄峰。大衆不得動著、且教坐殺者漢。今日忽有人問淨上座如何是奇特事、只向他道、有甚奇特事。畢竟如何。淨慈鉢盂。移過天童喫飯。

My former master, the Old Buddha, addressed the assembly, saying,[10]

We may recall that a monk asked Baizhang, "What is the extraordinary matter?"[11]

Baizhang said, "Sitting alone on Daxiong Peak."[12]

Members of the great assembly, don't be moved; just let the fellow sit there. If today someone were suddenly to ask Senior Seat Jing, "What is the extraordinary matter?" I would just say to him, "What extraordinary matter is there?"[13] In the end, what is it?[14] The Jinci pātra bowl: it has moved to Tiantong to have rice.[15]

[59:7] {2:126}

佛祖の家裏に、かならず奇特事あり、いはゆる獨坐大雄峰なり。いま坐殺者漢せしむるにあふとも、なほこれ奇特事なり。さらにかれよりも奇特なるあり、いはゆる淨慈鉢盂、移過天童喫飯なり。奇特事は、條條面面みな喫飯なり。しかあれば、獨坐大雄峰すなはちこれ喫飯なり。鉢盂は喫飯用なり、喫飯用は鉢盂なり。このゆえに、淨慈鉢盂なり、天童喫飯なり。飽了知飯あり、喫飯了飽あり、知了飽飯あり、飽了更喫飯あり。しばらく作麼生ならんかこれ鉢盂。おもはくは、祇是木頭にあらず、黒如漆にあらず、頑石ならんや、鐵漢ならんや。無底なり、無鼻孔なり。一口呑虛空、虛空合掌受なり。

"Quart" translates *shō* 升, a dry measure (of rice, etc.) equal to one-tenth peck (*to* 斗).

10 **My former master, the Old Buddha** (*senshi kobutsu* 先師古佛): I.e., Dōgen's teacher, Tiantong Rujing 天童如淨 (1162-1227); from the *Rujing heshang yulu* 如淨和尚語錄 (T.2002A.48:127b1-5). The same passage is quoted in "Shōbōgenzō hou" 正法眼藏鉢盂.

11 **Baizhang** (*Hyakujō* 百丈): I.e., Baizhang Huaihai 百丈懷海 (749-814); his conversation occurs in several sources (see, e.g., *Biyan lu* 碧巖錄, T.2003.48:166c26-27).

12 **"Daxiong Peak"** (*Daiyū hō* 大雄峰): Another name for Mount Baizhang 百丈山, in present-day Jiangxi province.

13 **Senior Seat Jing** (*Jō jōza* 淨上座): A self-reference as abbot.

14 **In the end, what is it?** (*hikkyō ikan* 畢竟如何): Though this and the following sentence are treated here as Rujing's final comment on the subject, they could as well be read as part of his answer to the question.

15 **The Jinci *pātra* bowl: it has moved to Tiantong to have rice** (*Jinzu hou. Ika Tendō kippan* 淨慈鉢盂。移過天童喫飯): A reference to Rujing's relocation from his former post at Jingcisi 淨慈寺 to Tiantongshan 天童山, where his talk is taking place. "*Pātra* bowl" (*hou* 鉢盂) refers to the Buddhist alms bowl.

59. Everyday Matters Kajō 家常

In the house of the buddhas and ancestors, there is always "the extraordinary matter": it is "*sitting alone on Daxiong Peak.*" Even to encounter here "*let this fellow sit there*" — this is also "the extraordinary matter." Going further, there is something even more extraordinary than that: it is "*The Jinci pātra bowl has moved to Tiantong to have rice.*" Each and every instance of "the extraordinary matter" is "having rice." Thus, "sitting alone on Daxiong Peak" — this is "having rice." The *pātra* bowl is used for having rice; what is used for having rice is the *pātra* bowl. Therefore, it is "*the Jinci pātra bowl*"; it is "*to Tiantong to have rice.*" There is *knowing rice after being full*; there is *being full after having rice*; there is *being full of rice after knowing it*; there is *having rice after being full*. Now, consider for the moment, what is the *pātra* bowl? I think it is not just wood; it is not black as lacquer. Is it dumb stone? Is it a man of iron?[16] It has no bottom; it has no nose. *It swallows empty space in a single gulp, and empty space receives it with palms joined.*

* * * * *

[59:8]
先師古佛、ちなみに台州瑞巖淨土禪院の方丈にして示衆するにいはく、飢來喫飯、困來打眠、爐鞴亙天。

My former master, the Old Buddha, once in the abbot's quarters of the Ruiyan Jingtu Chan Cloister, in Taizhou, addressed the assembly, saying, "'*When I get hungry, I have rice; when I get tired, I sleep.*'[17] The

---

16 **Is it dumb stone? Is it a man of iron?** (*ganseki naran ya, tekkan naran ya* 頑石ならんや、鐵漢ならんや): "Dumb stone" (*ganseki* 頑石) recalls the common expression "the dumb stones nodded" (*ganseki tentō* 頑石點頭), from the legend that, when the monk Daosheng 道生 lectured on the *Nirvāṇa Sūtra*, the stones nodded in assent. "Man of iron" (*tekkan* 鐵漢) is a common Zen term, occurring frequently in Dōgen's writings, for the solid practitioner; see Supplementary Notes, s.v. "Man of iron." Presumably, Dōgen is here simply playing with expressions including traditional materials from which the alms bowl was made: wood, lacquerware, stone, and iron.

17 **My former master, the Old Buddha** (*senshi kobutsu* 先師古佛): From the *Rujing heshang yulu* 如淨和尚語錄 (T.2002A.48:123b4). Rujing is here borrowing well-known lines from the *Nanyue Lanzan hoshang ge* 南嶽懶瓚和尚歌 (*Jingde chuandeng lu* 景德傳燈錄, T.2076.51:461b21):

饑來喫飯、困來即眠。愚人笑我、智乃知焉。
When I get hungry, I have rice;
When I get tired, I sleep.
Fools may laugh at me,
But the wise understand.

Ruiyan Jingtu Chan Cloister, in Taizhou (*Taishū Zuigan Jōdo zen'in* 台州瑞巖淨土禪院): Monastery in Huangyan District 黃巖縣, Taizhou 台州, in present-day Zhejiang province.

bellows spans the heavens."[18]

[59:9]
いはゆる飢來は、喫飯來人の活計なり。未曾喫飯人は、飢不得なり。しかあればしるべし、飢一家常ならんわれは、飯了人なりと決定すべし。困來は、困中又困なるべし、困の頂䫉上より全跳しきたれり。このゆえに、渾身の活計に都撥轉渾身せらるる而今なり。打眠は、佛眼・法眼・慧眼・祖眼・露柱燈籠眼を假借して、打眠するなり。

"When I get hungry" is the way of life of one who has "had rice"; one who has not "had rice" cannot be hungry. Thus, we should recognize that we for whom hunger is an everyday matter are definitely people who have "finished our rice." "When I get tired" is tiredness within tiredness; it has completely sprung forth from the crown of the head of tiredness. Therefore, it is the present in which the entire body is turned completely around by the way of life of the entire body. "I sleep" is to sleep by borrowing the buddha eye, the dharma eye, the wisdom eye, the ancestor eye, the pillar and lantern eye.[19]

* * * * *

[59:10] {2:127}
先師古佛、ちなみに台州瑞巖寺より臨安府淨慈寺の請におもむきて、上堂にいはく、半年喫飯坐鞍峰、坐斷煙雲千萬重、忽地一聲轟霹靂、帝郷春色杏華紅。

My former master, the Old Buddha, having been invited to move from the Ruiyan Monastery in Taizhou to the Jingci Monastery in the Lin'an Prefecture, said in a convocation,[20]

---

18 **"The bellows"** (rohai 爐鞴): Used as a metaphor for what "fans the flames" of spiritual practice.

19 **sleep by borrowing the buddha eye, the dharma eye, the wisdom eye, the ancestor eye, the pillar and lantern eye** (butsugen hōgen egen sogen rochū tōrō gen o keshaku shite, tamin suru 佛眼・法眼・慧眼・祖眼・露柱燈籠眼を假借して、打眠する): The first three eyes here belong to a standard hierarchy of "five eyes" in Buddhist literature: the physical eye of human vision, the deva eye of paranormal vision, the wisdom eye of the adept who recognizes emptiness, the dharma eye of the advanced bodhisattva, and the buddha eye of unsurpassed bodhi. See Supplementary Notes, s.v. "Eye." "Pillars and lanterns" (rochū tōrō 露柱燈籠), referring to the free-standing columns and the lanterns of monastic buildings, is an expression regularly used in Zen texts for the immediate surroundings of the phenomenal world (or of the monks' environment); see Supplementary Notes, s.v. "Pillars and lanterns."

20 **My former master, the Old Buddha** (senshi kobutsu 先師古佛): A verse found in the Rujing heshang yulu 如淨和尚語錄 (T.2002A.48:123c6-8), from an address to community on the occasion of Rujing's departure for Jingcisi.

59. Everyday Matters *Kajō* 家常

For half a year, I had rice and sat at Man Peak;
All clouds cut off — a thousand myriad layers.[21]
Suddenly, a single sound, the clap of thunder;
Spring colors of the capital — apricot blossoms of crimson.

[59:11]
佛代化儀の佛祖、その化、みなこれ坐鞭峰喫飯なり。續佛慧命の參究、これ喫飯の活計見成なり。坐鞭峰の半年、これを喫飯いふ。坐斷する煙雲いくかさなりといふことをしらず。一聲の霹靂たとひ忽地なりとも、杏華の春色くれなゐなるのみなり。帝郷、といふは、いまの赤赤條條なり。これらの恁麼は、喫飯なり。鞭峰は、瑞巖寺の峰の名なり。

The buddhas and ancestors who engage in teaching in place of the Buddha — their teachings are all "*sitting at Man Peak having rice.*"[22] The investigation that continues the Buddha's life of wisdom — this is the manifestation of the way of life of "having rice." The "half year" of "sitting at Man Peak" — this, he calls "having rice." There is no knowing how many layers of "clouds" are "cut off." The "single sound" of "thunder" may be "sudden," but the "spring colors" of "apricot blossoms" are just "crimson." "The capital" means this present nakedness.[23] Such as these is "having rice."[24] "Man Peak" is the name of the peak at Ruiyan Monastery.

* * * * *

---

21 **Man Peak** (*Banpō* 鞭峰): I.e., Ruiyansi, as Dōgen himself notes in his comment.

22 **The buddhas and ancestors who engage in teaching in place of the Buddha** (*butsu dai kegi no busso* 佛代化儀の佛祖): An odd phrase. The translation takes *dai* 代 here in the sense "to take the place of," "to substitute for"; some take it in the sense "generation," "age," and read here "at the time of the Buddha." "Engage in teaching" is a loose rendering of *kegi* 化儀, a technical term for the "manner of converting" a Buddhist audience.

23 **this present nakedness** (*ima no shakushaku jōjō* いまの赤赤條條): Variation on the colloquial *seki jōjō* 赤條條 ("stark naked"), perhaps to be interpreted here as each instance (*jōjō* 條條) of our present raw reality (*shakushaku* 赤赤).

24 **Such as these is "having rice"** (*korera no inmo wa, kippan nari* これらの恁麼は、喫飯なり): The antecedent of "these" (*korera* これら) here is not clear; it may be understood as the immediately preceding instances of "nakedness" or as the sentences of the paragraph as a whole.

[59:12]

先師古佛、ちなみに明州慶元府の瑞巖寺の佛殿にして示衆するにいはく、黄金妙相、著衣喫飯、因我禮儞。早眠晏起。咦。談玄説妙太無端、切忌拈華自熱瞞。

My former master, the Old Buddha, in the buddha hall of the Ruiyan Monstery in Qingyuan Prefecture in Mingzhou once addressed the assembly, saying,[25]

> The wondrous mark of gold —
> Getting dressed and having rice.[26]
> My obeisance to you —
> Sleeping early and waking late.
> Ii!
> Discussing the dark and talking of the wondrous, for no reason at all;
> It's strictly forbidden to deceive oneself by taking up the flower.[27]

[59:13]

たちまちに透擔來すべし。黄金妙相、といふは、著衣喫飯なり、著衣喫飯は、黄金妙相なり。さらにたれ人の、著衣喫飯すると摸索せざれ、たれ人の、黄金妙相なるといふことなかれ。かくのごとくすれば、これ道著なり、因我禮儞の、しかあるなり。我既喫飯、揖喫飯なり。切忌拈華のゆえに、しかあるなり。

We should slip our burden right now.[28] "The wondrous mark of gold" means "getting dressed and having rice"; "getting dressed and having rice" is "the wondrous mark of gold." Beyond this, do not grope for who is "getting dressed and having rice"; do not ask who is "the wondrous mark of gold." When we act like this, this is a statement.[29] "My

---

25 **My former master, the Old Buddha** (*senshi kobutsu* 先師古佛): From the *Rujing heshang yulu* 如淨和尚語錄 (T.2002A.48:125c11-12).

26 **The wondrous mark of gold** (*ōgon myōsō* 黄金妙相): Synecdoche for a buddha body, one of whose thirty-two physical marks is a golden-hued body.

Getting dressed and having rice (*jakue kippan* 著衣喫飯): Or (as rendered elsewhere in these translations) "wearing clothes and having meals," a fixed expression for everyday life.

27 **It's strictly forbidden to deceive oneself by taking up the flower** (*sekki nenge ji netsuman* 切忌拈華自熱瞞): A sentence somewhat difficult to interpret; it can be understood to mean, "do not deceive yourself with regard to the legend that Buddha Śākyamuni held up a flower on Vulture Peak and silently transmitted the dharma to Mahākāśyapa." See Supplementary Notes, s.v. "Hold up a Flower."

28 **We should slip our burden** (*tōtanrai su beshi* 透擔來すべし): An unusual expression not occurring elsewhere in Dōgen's writings; usually interpreted as "transcending the burden of our [limited] Buddhist commitments."

29 **When we act like this, this is a statement** (*kaku no gotoku sureba, kore dōjaku nari* かくのごとくすれば、これ道著なり): The sense is uncertain; perhaps, "when we

obeisance to you" is like this. It is, *I have already had my rice; bow and have your rice.* Because it is *"strictly forbidden to take up the flower,"* it is like this.

* * * * *

[59:14] {2:128}
福州長慶院圓智禪師大安和尚、上堂示衆云、大安在潙山三十來年、喫潙山飯、屙潙山屎、不學潙山禪、只看一頭水牯牛。若落路入草便牽出、若犯人苗稼即鞭撻、調伏既久、可憐生、受人言語。如今變作箇露地白牛、常在面前、終日露回回地、趁亦不去也。

Reverend Daan, Chan Master Yuanzhi of Changqing Monastery in Fuzhou, in a convocation, addressed the assembly, saying,[30]

Daan stayed at Weishan for some thirty years, eating Weishan's rice and shitting Weishan's shit. I didn't study Weishan's Chan; I just watched over a single water buffalo.[31] *If it strayed from the road into the grass, I would drag it out; if it damaged someone's crops, I would whip it. The discipline went on for a long time; how sad for it, having to take orders from someone. Now, it's changed into this white ox on open ground, always in front of me, everywhere exposed all day long; I can chase it off, and it still won't leave.*[32]

[59:15]
あきらかにこの示衆を受持すべし。佛祖の會下に功夫なる三十來年は、喫飯なり、さらに雜用心あらず。喫飯の活計現成すれば、おのづから、看一頭水牯牛、の標格なり。

Clearly, we should receive and keep this address to the assembly. "Some thirty years" of concentrated effort in a community of the bud-

---

get dressed and have rice" (or pay "my obeisance to you," or "do not ask"), we are saying something (or expressing Rujing's words?).

30 **Reverend Daan, Chan Master Yuanzhi of Changqing Monastery in Fuzhou** (*Fukushū Chōkeiin Enchi zenji Daian oshō* 福州長慶院圓智禪師大安和尚): I.e., Changqing Daan 長慶大安 (793-883). His words are found in the *Jingde chuandeng lu* 景德傳燈錄 (T.2076.51:267c6-10).

31 **Daan stayed at Weishan** (*Daian zai Isan* 大安在潙山): Daan speaks of himself in the third person. Weishan is Mount Dawei, in present-day Hunan, where Daan succeeded Weishan Lingyou 潙山靈祐 (771-853).

32 **white ox on open ground** (*roji byakugo* 露地白牛): No doubt an allusion to the scene in the *Lotus Sūtra* (*Miaofa lianhua jing* 妙法蓮華經, T.262.9:12c13-23), in which a father, having enticed his children from their burning house (of saṃsāra) and seeing them now safely seated "in the open" (*roji* 露地) presents them with carts (the buddha vehicle) pulled by great "white oxen (*byakugo* 白牛)." See Supplementary Notes, s.v. "Burning house."

dhas and ancestors was "having rice," without any extraneous concerns. When the way of life of "having rice" is realized, naturally, "*watching over a water buffalo*" is its model.

* * * * *

[59:16]

趙州眞際大師、問新到僧曰、曾到此間否。僧云、曾到。師曰、喫茶去。又問一僧、曾到此間否。僧曰、不曾到。師曰、喫茶去。院主問師、爲甚曾到此間也喫茶去、不曾到此間也喫茶去。師召院主。主應諾。師曰、喫茶去。

Great Master Zhenji of Zhaozhou asked a newly arrived monk, "Have you ever been to this place?"[33]

The monk said, "I have."

The Master said, "Go have some tea."

Again, he asked another monk, "Have you ever been to this place?"

The monk said, "I haven't."

The Master said, "Go have some tea."

The head of cloister asked the Master, "Why was it 'go have some tea' for the one who had been to this place, and 'go have some tea' for the one who hadn't been to this place?"[34]

The Master called to the head of cloister. The head answered. The Master said, "Go have some tea."

[59:17] {2:129}

いはゆる此間は、頂顈にあらず、鼻孔にあらず、趙州にあらず。此間を跳脱するゆゑに、曾到此間なり、不曾到此間なり。遮裏是甚麼處在、祇管道曾到不曾到なり。このゆゑに、先師いはく、誰在畫樓沽酒處、相邀來喫趙州茶。

"This place" is not the crown of the head; it is not the nose; it is not Zhaozhou.[35] Because it leaps free from "this place," it is "*ever been to this place*," it is "*never been to this place*." It is *Where are we here, that we're just talking of "ever been" and "never been"*?[36] Therefore, my for-

---

33 **Great Master Zhenji of Zhaozhou** (*Jōshū Shinsai daishi* 趙州眞際大師): I.e., Zhaozhou Congshen 趙州從諗 (778-897). This anecdote, occurring also in Dōgen's *shinji Shōbōgenzō* 眞字正法眼藏 (DZZ.5:248, case 233), can be found in the *Liandeng huiyao* 聯燈會要 (ZZ.136:531a1-4).

34 **head of cloister** (*inju* 院主): The chief administrator of the monastery.

35 **it is not Zhaozhou** (*Jōshū ni arazu* 趙州にあらず): Perhaps, more likely here a reference to the place, in present-day Hebei province, than to the person, Zhaozhou Congshen.

36 **Where are we here, that we're just talking of "ever been" and "never been"?** (*shari ze jinmo sho zai, shikan dō zō tō fuzō tō* 遮裏是甚麼處在、祇管道曾到不曾到): A sentence in Chinese, modeled on a fixed rhetorical question, variants of which occur

mer master said, "*Who, while sitting in a wine shop in a decorated tower, would invite someone to come and drink Zhaozhou's tea?*"[37]

[59:18]

しかあれば、佛祖の家常は喫茶喫飯のみなり。

Thus, the everyday matters of the buddhas and ancestors are only having tea and having rice.

正法眼藏家常第五十九
Treasury of the True Dharma Eye
Everyday Matters
Number 59

[Ryūmonji MS:]

爾時寛元元年癸卯十二月十七日、在越宇禪師峰下示衆
Presented to the assembly beneath Yamashibu, Etsuu; seventeenth day, twelfth month of the junior water year of the rabbit, the first year of Kangen [28 January 1244][38]

[Tōunji MS:]

同二年壬辰正月一日書寫之、在峰下侍者寮。懷奘
Copied this in the acolyte's quarters, beneath the peak; first day, first month of the senior water year of the dragon, the second year of the same [era] [10 February 1244]. Ejō

于時文明十一己亥年十二月十六日、於永平寺承陽庵書寫之。比丘光周
Copied this in the Jōyō Hermitage, Eihei Monastery; the sixteenth day, twelfth month, junior earth year of the pig, the eleventh year of Bunmei [27 January 1480]. Bhikṣu Kōshū[39]

---

several times in the *Shōbōgenzō*. The force of the question is usually something like, "Where do you think we are, that we're talking about such trivial dualities?" Perhaps best known from the retort of the monk Puhua 普化 (dates unknown), when charged with being rough by Linji Yixuan 臨濟義玄 (d. 866) (*Linji lu* 臨濟錄, T.1985.47:503b5-6; recorded also at s*hinji Shōbōgenzō* 眞字正法眼藏, DZZ.5:174, case 96):

這裏是什麼所在、説麤説細。
Where are we here, that we're talking of rough and talking of fine?

37   **my former master** (*senshi* 先師): From the *Rujing heshang yulu* 如淨和尚語錄 (T.2002A.48:123b 20-21; 129c20-21). Rujing is quoting words attributed to Fachang Yiyu 法昌倚遇 (1005-1081) (e.g., at *Xu gu cunxiu yuyao* 續古尊宿語要, ZZ.118:886b11).

38   The Tōunji 洞雲寺 MS shares an identical colophon.

39   **Jōyō Hermitage** (*Jōyōan* 承陽庵): Dōgen's memorial shrine at Eiheiji 永平寺, from his posthumous title Great Master Jōyō (*Jōyō daishi* 承陽大師).
Bhikṣu Kōshū (*biku Kōshū* 比丘光周): Fifteenth abbot of Eiheiji (1434–1492?).

TREASURY OF THE TRUE DHARMA EYE

NUMBER 60

The Thirty-seven Factors of Bodhi

Sanjūshichi hon bodai bunpō

三十七品菩提分法

The Thirty-seven Factors of Bodhi

Sanjūshichi hon bodai bunpō

INTRODUCTION

This work, one of the longer texts of the *Shōbōgenzō*, was composed in the spring of 1244, at Kippōji in Echizen. It represents number 60 in the seventy-five-chapter compilation and number 72 in the Honzan edition (or 73 in the Iwanami and Shūmuchō versions). It is not included in the sixty-chapter compilation but is found in the twenty-eight text *Himitsu* collection, where it is listed as number 11 of fascicle 1.

The essay is noteworthy on at least two grounds. The first is its title theme. The thirty-seven factors of awakening (*bodhi-pākṣika-dharma*) is a venerable set of (sometimes overlapping) lists of spiritual desiderata found throughout Buddhist literature. As such, it represents precisely the sort of conservative Buddhist teaching often dismissed by the Zen masters; and, indeed, one does not normally find the list treated in the discourse of these masters. Here, however, Dōgen takes up the individual members of the list and treats them as if they were Zen teachings, providing each factor with comments in the language of the masters.

A second noteworthy feature of the essay is its strong dismissal of lay life as a vehicle for Buddhist awakening. In his treatment of the topic of right action, Dōgen departs from his practice of providing brief Zen comments on each factor and launches into an extended argument, covering over one-third of the text, for the superiority of the renunciant life. He is adamant in his denial that any lay person — even such famous laymen as Bodhisattva Vimalakīrti or Layman Pang Yun 龐蘊居士 — ever achieved an awakening; and he is scathing in his criticism of Zen masters who deny the spiritual difference between the householder and the monastic, calling them "evil dogs" that seek only to gain favor with the laity. In this section, and in this essay as a whole, we see a fascinating combination of radical and conservative elements in Dōgen's Buddhism.

正法眼藏第六十
Treasury of the True Dharma Eye
Number 60

三十七品菩提分法
The Thirty-seven Factors of Bodhi

[60:1] {2:130}
古佛の公案あり、いはゆる三十七品菩提分法の教・行・證なり。昇降階級の葛藤する、さらに葛藤公案なり。喚作諸佛なり、喚作諸祖なり。

There is a kōan of the old buddhas: the teaching, practice, and verification of the thirty-seven factors of bodhi.[1] The entangling of the ascent and descent of their stages is a further kōan of entanglement.[2] They are called "the buddhas"; they are called "the ancestors."

* * * * *

[60:2]
四念住、四念處とも稱す。

The four abodes of mindfulness (also called the four bases of mindfulness):[3]

---

[1] **kōan of the old buddhas** (*kobutsu no kōan* 古佛の公案): Or "a kōan of the old Buddha" (i.e., Śākyamuni); the plural can refer to the seven buddhas of the past or, in Dōgen's usage, to any of those in the lineage of the buddhas and ancestors. See Supplementary Notes, s.v. "Old buddha."

thirty-seven factors of bodhi (*sanjūshichi hon bodai bunpō* 三十七品菩提分法): S. *saptatriṃśad-bodhi-pakṣikā-dharmāḥ*; a venerable listing, found throughout the Buddhist canon, of seven (sometimes overlapping) sets of spiritual desiderata: (1) the four abodes of mindfulness (*shinenjū* 四念住; S. *smṛty-upasthāna*), (2) the four right abandonments (*shishōdan* 四正斷; S. *samyak-prahāṇa*), (3) the four bases of spiritual power (*shijinsoku* 四神足; S. *ṛddhi-pāda*), (4) the five faculties (*gokon* 五根; S. *indriya*), (5) the five powers (*goriki* 五力; S. *bala*), (6) the seven limbs of awakening (*shichikakushi* 七覺支; S. *bodhyaṅga*), and (7) the eightfold path (*hasshōdō* 八正道; S. *mārga*).

[2] **The entangling of the ascent and descent of their stages** (*shōkō kaikyū no kattō suru* 昇降階級の葛藤する): "Entangling" here renders the verbal form of the term *kattō* 葛藤, for which, see Supplementary Notes, s.v. "Tangled vines." The "steps," or "stages" (*kaikyū* 階級), may refer to the members of the list of factors or to the stages of teaching, practice, and verification.

[3] **four abodes of mindfulness** (*shi nenjū* 四念住): The first set of the thirty-seven factors of bodhi. The "four bases of mindfulness" (*shi nenjo* 四念處) represents an earlier translation of the Sanskrit *smṛty-upasthāna*. (The parenthetical remark is in the original.)

[60:3]

一者、觀身不淨。二者、觀受是苦。三者、觀心無常。四者、觀法無我。

1. Observing the body as impure; 2. observing sensation as suffering; 3. observing the mind as impermanent; and 4. observing the dharmas as without self.[4]

[60:4]

觀身不淨といふは、いまの觀身の一袋皮は、盡十方界なり。これ眞實體なるがゆゑに、活路に跳躑する、觀身不淨なり。不躑ならんは、觀不得ならん、若無身ならん、行取不得ならん、説取不得ならん、觀取不得ならん。すでに觀得の現成あり、しるべし、跳躑得なり。いはゆる觀得は、毎日の行履、掃地・掃床なり。第幾月を擧して掃地し、正是第二月を擧して掃地・掃床するゆゑに、盡大地の恁麼なり。

"*Observing the body as impure*": the bag of skin of the body observed here is "*all the worlds in the ten directions*."[5] Because it is "the true body," its skipping along the life-saving path is "*observing the body as impure*."[6] Were it not skipping, it could not be observed; it would be as if there were no body: it could not be practiced; it could not be talked of; it could not be observed.[7] That it can be observed definitely occurs; so we know that it can skip along. The words "can be observed" refer to everyday conduct — sweeping the ground, sweeping the platforms. We

---

4   **1. Observing the body as impure** (*issha, kan shin fujō* 一者、觀身不淨): Dōgen gives here the standard list of four objects of mindfulness, central to some systems of *vipaśyanā* practice: body (*shin* 身; S. *kāya*), sensation (*ju* 受; S. *vedanā*), mind (*shin* 心; S. *citta*), and dharma (*hō* 法); said to overcome, respectively, the four "inverted" (*tendō* 顛倒; S. *viparyasta*) views: purity (*jō* 淨; S. *śubha*), pleasure (*raku* 樂; S. *sukha*), permanence (*jō* 常; S. *nitya*), and self (*ga* 我; S. *ātman*).

5   **"all the worlds in the ten directions"** (*jin jippō kai* 盡十方界): Given the expression "the true body" (*shinjitsu tai* 眞實體) in the following sentence, Dōgen is likely recalling here the words of Xuansha Shibei 玄沙師備 (835-908) recorded in the *shinji Shōbōgenzō* 眞字正法眼藏 (DZZ.5:196, case 131) and quoted elsewhere in the *Shōbōgenzō*; see Supplementary Notes, s.v. "True human body."

6   **its skipping along the life-saving path is "observing the body as impure"** (*katsuro ni chōchō suru, kan shin fujō nari* 活路に跳躑する、觀身不淨なり): Following Kawamura's punctuation after *suru*. The phrase could also be parsed, "it is an 'observing the body as impure' that skips along the life-saving path." The verb *chōchō* 跳躑 ("to skip"), found in several Zen texts, does not occur elsewhere in the *Shōbōgenzō*. The expression *katsuro* 活路 ("life-saving path" — i.e., "escape route") occurs quite often in Dōgen's writing; often taken as "vital path."

7   **it could not be practiced; it could not be talked of** (*gyōshu futoku naran, sesshu futoku naran* 行取不得ならん、説取不得ならん): Perhaps reflecting the words, quoted elsewhere in the *Shōbōgenzō*, of Dongshan Liangjie 洞山良价 (807-869) (see, e.g., *shinji Shōbōgenzō* 眞字正法眼藏, DZZ.5:164, case 77):

説取行不得底、行取説不得底。

I talk of what can't be practiced and practice what can't be talked of.

take up *"what number moon"* and sweep the ground; we take up *"truly, this is the second moon"* and sweep the ground, sweep the platforms.⁸ Therefore, all the whole earth is like this.⁹

[60:5]
觀身は身觀なり、身觀にて餘物觀にあらず、正當觀は卓卓來なり。身觀の現成するとき、心觀すべて摸未著なり、不現成なり。しかあるゆえに、金剛定なり、首楞嚴定なり、ともに觀身不淨なり。

"Observing the body" is the body observing; it is the body that observes, not something else observing. Precisely such observation stands out: when observation by the body occurs, observation by the mind is nowhere to be found, does not occur.¹⁰ Therefore, it is the diamond concentration, it is the *śūraṃgama* concentration; both are *"observing the body as impure."*¹¹

---

8 **"what number moon"** (*daiiku getsu* 第幾月); **"truly, this is the second moon"** (*shō ze daini getsu* 正是第二月): Reflecting a conversation between Yunyan Tansheng 雲巖曇晟 (782-841) and fellow student Daowu Yuanzhi 道吾圓智 (769-835) that is recorded in Dōgen's *shinji Shōbōgenzō* 眞字正法眼藏 (DZZ.5:166, case 83):

潭州雲巖山曇晟禪師〈嗣藥山〉一日掃地次、道吾曰、太區區生。師云、有不區區者。吾曰、恁麼則有第二月也。師堅起掃箒云、這箇是第幾月。吾休去。

Chan Master Tansheng of Mount Yunyan in Tanzhou (succeeded Yaoshan) was sweeping one day, when Daowu said, "How attentive!"
The Master said, "There's one who's not attentive."
Wu said, "If so, there's a second moon."
The Master stood up his broom and said, "What number moon is this?"
Wu desisted.

The phrase "truly, this is the second moon" (*shō ze daini getsu* 正是第二月) comes from a comment on this conversation by Xuansha Shibei 玄沙師備 (see *Jingde chuandeng lu* 景德傳燈錄, T.2076.51:315b1).

9 **all the whole earth is like this** (*jin daichi no inmo nari* 盡大地の恁麼なり): The antecedent of "like this" (*inmo* 恁麼) is unclear; and it is possible to read the phrase, "it [i.e., the 'sweeping'] is the whole earth just as it is."

10 **nowhere to be found** (*mo mijaku* 摸未著): A loose rendering of the idiom "to grope for but not touch."

11 **diamond concentration** (*kongō jō* 金剛定); ***śūraṃgama* concentration** (*shuryōgon jō* 首楞嚴定): Two widely celebrated states of samādhi, neither of which is ordinarily associated with the four abodes of mindfulness. The former, the *vajra-samādhi* (or *vajropama-samādhi*) is identified in some literature as the trance from which one enters directly into nirvāṇa (or buddhahood); the latter, "the samādhi of the heroic march," the subject of the *Śūraṃgama-samādhi sūtra*, is said to lead all beings to buddhahood.

[60:6] {2:131}

おほよそ、夜半見明星の道理を觀身不淨といふなり、淨穢の比論にあらず。有身是不淨なり、現身便不淨なり。かくのごとくの參學は、魔作佛のときは、魔を拈じて降魔し作佛す、佛作佛のときは、佛を拈じて圖佛し作佛す、人作佛のときは、人を拈じて調人し作佛するなり。まさに拈處に通路ある道理を參究すべし。

In sum, the principle of *seeing the dawn star in the middle of the night* is called *"observing the body as impure."*[12] It is not an issue of comparing purity and impurity. *Having a body is impure; manifesting a body is impure.*[13] In such study, when a demon becomes a buddha, in taking up the demonic, it subjugates the demonic and becomes a buddha; when a buddha becomes a buddha, taking up buddhahood, it figures on buddhahood and makes a buddha; when a human becomes a buddha, in taking up humanity, it tames its humanity and becomes a buddha.[14] We should investigate the principle that there is a passage in what is taken up.[15]

[60:7]

たとへば、浣衣の法のごとし。水は衣に染汚せられ、衣は水に浸却せらる。この水を用著して浣洗し、この水を換却して浣洗すといへども、なほこれ水をもちいる、なほこれ衣をあらふなり。一番洗・兩番洗に見淨ならざれば、休歇に滯累することなかれ。水盡更用水なり、衣淨更浣衣なり。水は、諸類の水、ともにもちいる、洗衣によろし。水濁知有魚の道理を參究するなり。衣は、諸類の衣、ともに浣洗あり。恁麼功夫して、浣衣公案現成なり。しかあれども、淨潔を見取するなり。この宗旨、かならずしも衣を水に浸却するを本期とせず、水の、ころもに染却するを本期とせず。染汚水をもちゐて衣を浣洗するに、浣衣の本期あり。さらに、火・風・土・水・空を用著して衣をあらひ、物をあらふ法あり、地・水・火・風・空をもちて、地・水・火・風・空をあらひきよむる法あり。

---

12 **seeing the dawn star in the middle of the night** (*yahan ken myōjō* 夜半見明星): Despite the temporal incongruity, a common expression for the moment in which Siddhārtha, upon seeing Venus in the dawn sky, became a buddha.

13 **Having a body is impure; manifesting a body is impure** (*u shin ze fujō nari, gen shin ben fujō nari* 有身是不淨なり、現身便不淨なり): I.e., "impurity" is being embodied. For some reason, Dōgen has put these phrases in Chinese, though they do not appear to be quotations.

14 **In such study** (*kaku no gotoku no sangaku wa* かくのごとくの參學は): I.e., when we understand "impurity" in this way (as the state of being embodied).

it figures on buddhahood and makes a buddha (*zubutsu shi sabutsu su* 圖佛し作佛す): Allusion to the words of Mazu Daoyi 馬祖道一 (709-788), "I'm figuring to make a buddha" (*zu sabutsu* 圖作佛), which Dōgen will evoke again below, section 24.

15 **there is a passage in what is taken up** (*nensho ni tsūro aru* 拈處に通路ある): I.e. (as in the three preceding examples), it is by taking up what one is that one becomes a buddha.

For instance, it is like the way we wash our robes. The water is dirtied by the robe, and the robe is soaked by the water. We may use this water to wash it and change this water to wash it, but we are still using the water and still washing the robe. If it does not look clean after the first or second washing, do not stop and put it off. It is, *when the water is used up, we use more water; it is, when the robe is clean, we still wash the robe.*[16] As for water, we use the water of various types, all of which are good for washing robes.[17] It is the investigation of the principle that, *when the water is muddied, you know there are fish.*[18] As for the robes, the robes of various types all get washed. With concentrated effort like this, *the kōan of washing the robe is manifest. Yet, we see cleanliness.*[19] The essential point of this is that soaking the robe in water is not necessarily what we want, and dirtying the water with the robe is not what we want; what we want in washing the robe is to wash the robe using the dirty water. Going further, there is a way of washing the robe, of washing things, using fire, wind, earth, water, and space; there is a way of washing and purifying earth, water, fire, wind, and space with earth, water, fire, wind, and space.[20]

[60:8] {2:132}
いまの觀身不淨の宗旨、またかくのごとし。これによりて蓋身・蓋觀・蓋不淨、すなはち嬢生袈裟なり。袈裟、もし嬢生袈裟にあらざれば、佛祖いまだもちいざるなり、ひとり商那和修のみならんや。この道理、よくよくこころをとめて參學究盡すべし。

The essential point of *"observing the body as impure"* here is also like this. According to this, *the entire body, the entire observation, and the*

---

16 **It is, when the water is used up, we use more water; it is, when the robe is clean, we still wash the robe** (*sui jin kō yō sui nari, e jō kō kan e nari* 水盡更用水なり、衣淨更浣衣なり): Phrases put in Chinese, though probably not a quotation.

17 **water of various types** (*shorui no mizu* 諸類の水): Perhaps reflecting the common Buddhist trope of "one water and four views" (*issui shiken* 一水四見): devas see water as jewels (or jeweled ground), humans as water, pretas ("hungry ghosts") as pus and blood, fish as a dwelling.

18 **when the water is muddied, you know there are fish** (*sui joku chi u gyo* 水濁知有魚): Another phrase in Chinese, likely reflecting the fixed saying, "when the fish moves, the water is muddied" (*yu xing shui zhuo* 魚行水濁).

19 **Yet, we see cleanliness** (*shika aredomo, jōketsu o kenshu suru nari* しかあれども、淨潔を見取するなり): The thrust of the adversative "yet" (*shika aredomo* しかあれども) here is unclear; perhaps, "despite the variety of water and robe mentioned here, we can apprehend the meaning of 'cleanliness' in the kōan of washing the robe."

20 **fire, wind, earth, water, and space** (*chi sui ka fū kū* 地・水・火・風・空): The five primary elements (*godai* 五大) of Buddhist physics; see Supplementary Notes, s.v. "Four elements and five aggregates."

entire impurity are the *kāṣāya born of mother*.²¹ If the *kāṣāya* were not the *kāṣāya born of mother*, the buddhas and ancestors would not use it. Could Śaṇavāsa be the only one? This principle, we should fix our minds on, study, and exhaustively investigate.

[60:9]
觀受是苦といふは、苦これ受なり。自受にあらず、他受にあらず、有受にあらず、無受にあらず。生身受なり、生身苦なり。甜熟苽を苦葫蘆に換却するをいふ、これ皮肉骨髓ににがきなり、有心・無心等ににがきなり、これ一上の神通修證なり、徹蔕より跳出し、連根より跳出する神通なり。このゆゑに、將謂衆生苦、更有苦衆生なり。衆生は自にあらず、衆生は他にあらず。更有苦衆生、つひに瞞他不得なり。甜苽徹蔕甜、苦匏連根苦なりといへども、苦、これたやすく摸索著すべきにあらず。自己に問著すべし、作麼生是苦。

"*Observing sensation as suffering*" means that suffering is sensation. It is not one's own sensation, not another's sensation; it is not having sensation, not lacking sensation.²² It is the sensation of a birth body; it is the suffering of a birth body.²³ It means the sweet, ripe melon is replaced by the bitter gourd: it is bitter to skin, flesh, bones, and marrow; it is bitter equally in states with mind and without mind; it is the practice and verification of "a higher spiritual power."²⁴ It is the spiritual power that

---

21 *kāṣāya born of mother* (*jō shō kesa* 孃生袈裟): Allusion to the legend, recorded in Xuanzang's 玄奘 *Datang xiyu ji* 大唐西域記 (T.2087.51:873b28-c5), that the Third Ancestor, Śaṇavāsa, was born wearing a miraculous robe, which enlarged as he grew, became a monk's habit when he left home, and a nine-panel *saṃghāṭī* robe when he took the full precepts.

22 **not having sensation, not lacking sensation** (*uju ni arazu, muju ni arazu* 有受にあらず、無受にあらず): Or, perhaps, "not an existent sensation, not a non-existent sensation."

23 **birth body** (*shōshin* 生身): i.e., the body into which one is born.

24 **the sweet, ripe melon is replaced by the bitter gourd** (*tenjuku ka o ku koro ni kankyaku suru* 甜熟苽を苦葫蘆に換却する): The translation loses the play on the word *ku* 苦, used for both "suffering" and "bitter." Dōgen alludes here to the saying he will quote just below:

甜苽徹蔕甜、苦匏連根苦。

The sweet melon is sweet through to its stem; the bitter gourd is bitter all the way to its root.

The saying, more often in reverse order, occurs with some frequency in Zen texts; it is perhaps especially associated with Yuanwu Keqin 圜悟克勤 (1063–1135) (see, e.g., *Yuanwu Foguo chanshi yulu* 圜悟佛果禪師語錄, T.1997.47:720b23-24).

bitter equally in states with mind and without mind (*ushin mushin tō ni nigaki nari* 有心・無心等ににがきなり): Taking *tō* 等 here as *hitoshiku* ("equally"), rather than *nado* ("etc."). The contrasting pair *ushin* 有心 and *mushin* 無心 can indicate respectively (a) "conscious" and "unconscious," (b) "discriminating consciousness" and "nondiscriminating consciousness," or (c) "intentional" and "unintentional."

springs forth from "through to the stem," that springs forth from "all the way to its root."[25]

Therefore, it is, "*I thought that living beings suffer; and now there are suffering living beings.*"[26] "Living beings" are not self; "living beings" are not other. "*Now there are suffering living beings*" is, in the end, "*it can't deceive anyone.*"[27] Although it may be that "*the sweet melon is sweet through to its stem, and the bitter gourd is bitter all the way to its root,*" the bitterness is not easily to be found. We should ask ourselves, "What is bitterness?"[28]

[60:10]
觀心無常は、曹溪古佛いはく、無常者即佛性也。しかあれば、諸類の所解する無常、ともに佛性なり。

"*Observing the mind as impermanent.*" The Old Buddha of Caoxi said, "*Impermanence is the buddha nature.*"[29] Thus, the impermanence understood by various types is equally buddha nature.

[60:11]
永嘉眞覺大師曰、諸行無常一切空、即是如來大圓覺。

Great Master Zhenjue of Yongjia said,

---

practice and verification of "a higher spiritual power" (*ichijō no jinzū shushō* 一上の神通修證): Likely recalling the saying of Weishan Lingyu 潙山靈祐 (771-853) that his disciple Yangshan Huiji 仰山慧寂 (803-887) had performed "a higher spiritual power" (*yishang shentong* 一上神通) by bringing him a wash basin and towel. (See, e.g., *shinji Shōbōgenzō* 眞字正法眼藏, DZZ.5:158, case 61; discussed in "Shōbōgenzō jinzū" 正法眼藏神通.)

25 **"through to the stem"** (*tettai* 徹蔕); **"all the way to its root"** (*renkon* 連根): Again, from the saying, introduced just below, on the melon and gourd.

26 **"I thought that living beings suffer; and now there are suffering living beings"** (*shōi shujō ku, kō u ku shujō* 將謂衆生苦、更有苦衆生): An expression coined by Jingqing Daofu 鏡清道怤 (864-937) (see, e.g., *Biyan lu* 碧巖錄, T.2003.48:182c3); generally taken to mean that suffering and living beings are equivalent.

27 **"it can't deceive anyone"** (*man ta futoku* 瞞他不得): Perhaps meaning "it is what it is" or "it is true to itself"; likely an allusion to the saying of Nanyue Huairang 南嶽懷讓 (677-744) about a bronze mirror recast as an image (e.g., at *shinji Shōbōgenzō* 眞字正法眼藏, DZZ.5:188-190, case 116):

雖不鑑照、瞞他一點也不得。
"Even though it doesn't reflect, it can't deceive anyone even one jot."

28 **"What is bitterness?"** (*somosan ze ku* 作麼生是苦): Or "what is suffering?"

29 **"The Old Buddha of Caoxi"** (*Sōkei kobutsu* 曹溪古佛): I.e., the Sixth Ancestor, Huineng 慧能. His saying occurs at *Jingde chuandeng lu* 景德傳燈錄, T.2076.51:239a2.

Compounded things are impermanent; all are empty.[30]
This is the great perfect awakening of the Tathāgata.

[60:12]

いまの觀心無常、すなはち如來大圓覺なり、大圓覺如來なり。心、もし不觀ならんとするにも隨他去するがゆゑに、心、もしあれば觀もあるなり。おほよそ無上菩提にいたり、無上正等覺の現成、すなはち無常なり、觀心なり。心かならずしも常にあらず、離四句、絕百非なるがゆゑに、牆壁瓦礫・石頭大小、これ心なり、これ無常なり、すなはち觀なり。

"Observing the mind as impermanent" here is "the great perfect awakening of the Tathāgata," is the Tathāgata of great perfect awakening. Even if we say the mind is not observing, since it "goes along with it," when there is mind, there is also observing.[31] In sum, reaching unsurpassed bodhi, the realization of unsurpassed, perfect awakening, is "impermanence," is "observing the mind." "The mind" is not necessarily permanent: because it is "free from the four propositions and cuts off the hundred negations," "fences, walls, tiles, and pebbles," stones big and small — these are "the mind," these are "impermanent," are "observing."[32]

---

30 **Great Master Zhenjue of Yongjia** (*Yōka Shinkaku daishi* 永嘉眞覺大師): I.e., Yongjia Xuanjue 永嘉玄覺 (665–713). His words come from the *Zhengdao ge* 證道歌, traditionally attributed to him (T.2014.48:495c19-20).

31 **"goes along with it"** (*zui ta ko* 隨他去): Likely reflecting the recommendation of Dasui Fazhen 大隋法眞 (834-919) to go along with "this" (*shako* 這箇) when it is destroyed with the chiliocosm at the end of a kalpa. (See below, section 84.)

32 **"free from the four propositions and cuts off the hundred negations"** (*ri shiku, zetsu hyappi* 離四句、絕百非): A common Zen expression. The "four propositions" (S. *catuṣkoṭi*) refers to the classical technique in Buddhist rhetoric that discusses a topic from four perspectives: true, not true, both true and not true, neither true nor not true. "The hundred negations" refers to the refutation of all of an opponent's claims. Together, the two terms suggest the practice of reasoning and argumentation.

"fences, walls, tiles, and pebbles" (*shō heki ga ryaku* 牆壁瓦礫): An expression, appearing often in Dōgen's writing, attributed to Nanyang Huizhong 南陽慧忠 (d. 775), as a definition of "the buddha mind." See Supplementary Notes, s.v. "Fences, walls, tiles, and pebbles."

stones big and small (*sekitō dai shō* 石頭大小): Likely reflecting a saying attributed to Guizong Daoquan 歸宗道詮 (930-985) (see, e.g., *Jingde chuandeng lu* 景德傳燈錄, T.2076.51:403b10-12):

問、九峯山中還有佛法也無。師曰、有。曰、如何是九峯山中佛法。師曰、山中石頭大底大小底小。

[A monk] asked, "Does the buddha dharma exist on Mount Jiufeng?"
The Master [Daoquan] said, "It does."
He asked, "What is the buddha dharma on Mount Jiufeng?"
The Master said, "The bigness of the stones on the mountain is big, the smallness is small."

60. The 37 Factors of Bodhi *Sanjūshichi hon bodai bunpō* 三十七品菩提分法

[60:13] {2:133}
觀法無我は、長者長法身、短者短法身なり。現成活計なるがゆえに無我なり。狗子佛性無なり、狗子佛性有なり、一切衆生無佛性なり、一切佛性無衆生なり、一切諸佛無衆生なり、一切諸佛無諸佛なり、一切佛性無佛性なり、一切衆生無衆生なり。かくのごとくなるがゆえに、一切法無一切法を、觀法無我と參學するなり。しるべし、跳出渾身自葛藤なり。

"Observing the dharmas as having no self" is the long one is a long dharma body; the short one is a short dharma body.³³ It is "no self" because it is the way of life actually realized.³⁴ It is the "no" of the dog's buddha nature; it is the "yes" of the dog's buddha nature.³⁵ It is "all living beings have no buddha nature"; it is all buddha nature has no living beings; it is all the buddhas have no living beings; it is all the buddhas have no buddhas; it is all buddha nature has no buddha nature; it is all living beings have no living beings.³⁶ Since it is like this, we study all dharmas have no dharmas as "observing the dharmas as having no self." We should recognize that it is "the whole body that springs forth is itself tangled vines."³⁷

---

33 **the long one is a long dharma body; the short one is a short dharma body** (*chōsha chō hosshin, tansha tan hosshin* 長者長法身、短者短法身): I.e., whether long or short, it is the dharma body of the buddha; a fixed phrase, found in a number of Zen texts, to which Dōgen also refers elsewhere in the *Shōbōgenzō*.

34 **the way of life actually realized** (*genjō kakkei* 現成活計): Or, perhaps, "the realized way of life"; an unusual expression, the reverse of which — *kakkei genjō* 活計現成 ("realization of a way of life") does occur elsewhere in the *Shōbōgenzō*.

35 **It is the "no" of the dog's buddha nature; it is the "yes" of the dog's buddha nature** (*kushi busshō mu nari, kushi busshō u nari* 狗子佛性無なり、狗子佛性有なり): The translation assumes that the unexpressed subject here and in the following is "no self" (*muga* 無我); hence, the *mu* 無 ("no") in that expression is equivalent to Zhaozhou's 趙州 famously answering both "no" (*mu* 無) and "yes" (*u* 有) to the question of whether the dog has the buddha nature — sayings discussed at length in "Shōbōgenzō busshō" 正法眼藏佛性.

36 **"all living beings have no buddha nature"** (*issai shujō mu busshō* 一切衆生無佛性): A saying attributed to Weishan Lingyou 潙山靈祐; see, e.g., *shinji Shōbōgenzō* 眞字正法眼藏 (DZZ.5:188, case 115). The variations on the saying here are Dōgen's invention.

37 **"the whole body that springs forth is itself tangled vines"** (*chōshutsu konjin ji kattō* 跳出渾身自葛藤): Variant of a verse, quoted in "Shōbōgenzō ganzei" 正法眼藏眼睛, by Dōgen's teacher, Tiantong Rujing 天童如淨 (1162-1227), in reference to Buddha Śākyamuni (*Rujing heshang yulu* 如淨和尚語錄, T.2002A.48:122b14-15):
  六年落草野狐精、跳出渾身是葛藤。
  For six years, a fox spirit, lurking in the grass;
  The whole body that sprang forth was tangled vines.
See Supplementary Notes, s.v. "Tangled vines," and "Eye."

[60:14]

釋迦牟尼佛言、一切諸佛菩薩、長安此法、爲聖胎也。

Buddha Śākyamuni said, "All the buddhas and bodhisattvas regard long repose in this teaching as the womb of the sages."[38]

[60:15]

しかあれば、諸佛菩薩、ともにこの四念住を聖胎とせり。しるべし、等覺の聖胎あり、妙覺の聖胎あり。すでに一切諸佛菩薩とあり、妙覺にあらざらん諸佛も、これを聖胎とせり。等覺よりさき、妙覺よりほかに超出せる菩薩、またこの四念住を聖胎とするなり。まことに諸佛諸祖の皮肉骨髓、ただ四念住のみなり。

Thus, the buddhas and bodhisattvas have all taken the four abodes of mindfulness as "the womb of the sages." We should recognize that there is a womb of virtual awakening, and there is a womb of wondrous awakening.[39] Since he said "all the buddhas and bodhisattvas," the buddhas who are not wondrously awakened also take them as "the womb of the sages"; and bodhisattvas who have surpassed [the path] prior to virtual awakening or outside wondrous awakening likewise take these four abodes of mindfulness as "the womb of the sages."[40] Truly, the skin, flesh, bones, and marrow of the buddhas and the ancestors is nothing but the four abodes of mindfulness.

* * * * *

---

38 **Buddha Śākyamuni** (*Shakamuni butsu* 釋迦牟尼佛): Source unknown, although possibly reflecting a passage in the *Renwang jing* 仁王經 (T.245.8:826b29-30):

一切諸佛菩薩長養十心爲聖胎也。

All the buddhas and bodhisattvas nurture the ten minds as the womb of the sages.

"The sages" (*shō* 聖; S. ārya) refers to those advanced on the Buddhist path.

39 **there is a womb of virtual awakening, and there is a womb of wondrous awakening** (*tōgaku no shōtai ari, myōgaku no shōtai ari* 等覺の聖胎あり、妙覺の聖胎あり): I.e., wombs of the two highest stages of the sages: the former is the penultimate stage of the bodhisattva path; the latter (also read *myōkaku*) is the stage of buddhahood. Some texts read *nari* なり for *ari* あり in both cases here; hence, "they (i.e., the four abodes) are the womb of virtual awakening; they are the womb of wondrous awakening."

40 **buddhas who are not wondrously awakened** (*myōgaku ni arazaran shobutsu* 妙覺にあらざらん諸佛); **bodhisattvas who have surpassed [the path] prior to virtual awakening or outside wondrous awakening** (*tōgaku yori saki, myōgaku yori hoka ni chōshutsu seru bosatsu* 等覺よりさき、妙覺よりほかに超出せる菩薩): Dōgen here introduces the unorthodox claims of Zen masters that they are beyond the traditional definitions of the path: that they are buddhas even without the unsurpassed, perfect bodhi of wondrous awakening; that they go "beyond the buddha" (*butsu kōjō* 佛向上). For the latter expression, see Supplementary Notes, s.v. "Beyond the buddha."

60. The 37 Factors of Bodhi *Sanjūshichi hon bodai bunpō* 三十七品菩提分法

[60:16]

四正斷、あるひは四正勤と稱す。

The four correct abandonments (also called the four correct efforts):[41]

[60:17]

一者、未生惡令不生。二者、已生惡令滅。三者、未生善令生。四者、已生善令增長。

1. Causing unarisen evil not to arise; 2. Causing arisen evil to cease; 3. Causing unarisen good to arise; 4. Causing arisen good to increase.

[60:18] {2:134}

未生惡令不生といふは、惡の稱、かならずしもさだまれる形段なし。ただ、地にしたがひ、界によりて立稱しきたれり。しかあれども、未生して不生ならしむるを佛法と稱し、正傳しきたれり。外道の解には、これ未萌我を根本とせり、といふ。佛法には、かくのごとくなるべからず。しばらく問取すべし、惡未生のとき、いづれのところにかある。もし未來にありといはば、ながくこれ斷滅見の外道なり。もし未來きたりて現在となるといはば、佛法の談にあらず、三世、混亂しぬべし。三世、混亂せば、諸法、混亂すべし。諸法、混亂せば、實相、混亂すべし。實相、混亂せば、唯佛與佛、混亂すべし。かるがゆえに、未來はのちに現在となる、といはざるなり。さらに問取すべし、未生惡とは、なにを稱すべきぞ。たれかこれを知取・見取せる。もし知取・見取することあらば、未生時あり、非未生時あらん。もししかあらば、未生法と稱すべからず、已滅の法と稱しつべし。外道および小乘聲聞等に學せずして、未生惡令不生の參學すべきなり。彌天の積惡、これを未生惡と稱す、不生惡なり。不生といふは、昨日説定法、今日説不定法なり。

"*Causing unarisen evil not to arise.*" What is designated "evil" does not necessarily have a fixed shape: the designation has been established according to the place and according to the realm. However, making the "unarisen" be [something that] "does not arise" is called the buddha dharma and has been directly transmitted.[42] In the opinion of other paths, it is said to have an unmanifest self as its basis; in the buddha dharma, this cannot be the case.[43] We should ask for a bit, when evil is "unarisen,"

---

41 **four correct abandonments** (*shishōdan* 四正斷): The second set of the thirty-seven factors of bodhi. "The four correct efforts" (*shishōgon* 四正勤) represents an alternative translation of *samyak-prahāṇa*. (The parenthetical remark is in the original.)

42 **making the "unarisen" be [something that] "does not arise"** (*mishō shite fushō narashimuru* 未生して不生ならしむる): An awkward attempt to capture Dōgen's diction. Judging from the sentence immediately following, his point would seem to be that orthodox Buddhist doctrine denies that what occurs comes out of a pre-existent potential.

43 **In the opinion of other paths, it is said to have an unmanifest self as its basis** (*gedō no ge ni wa, kore mihō ga o konpon to seri, to iu* 外道の解には、これ未萌我を根本とせり、といふ): "Unmanifest self" renders *mihō ga* 未萌我, an unusual expression that could mean either (a) "a self that has not yet sprouted (i.e., occurred)" or "a self before it (i.e., evil) has sprouted." The exact opinion is thus uncertain but perhaps a

where is it? If we say it is in the future, this will be forever the other path of annihilationism.⁴⁴ If we say that the future becomes the present, this is not the talk of the buddha dharma; the three times have been confused.⁴⁵ When the three times are confused, the dharmas will be confused; when the dharmas are confused, their "real mark" will be confused; when their real mark is confused, "*only buddhas with buddhas*" will be confused.⁴⁶

Therefore, we do not say that the future will later become the present. Further, we should ask, what is it that we are calling "unarisen evil? Who has known it or seen it? If it has been known or seen, there would be a time when it is unarisen and a time when it is not unarisen.⁴⁷ If so, it should not be called a dharma not yet arisen; it should be called a dharma already disappeared. We should study "*causing unarisen evil not to arise*" without learning from the other paths or the *śrāvakas* of the Small Vehicle. The accumulated evil filling the heavens — this is what is called "unarisen evil"; it is non-arising evil. "Non-arising" means "*yesterday, I preached a determinate dharma; today, I'm preaching an indeterminate dharma.*"⁴⁸

---

reference to the *satkāryavāda* position of the Sāṃkhya school of Hindu thought, which held that the effect is present in the cause (as the pot is latent in the clay from which it is fashioned).

44 this will be forever the other path of annihilationism (*nagaku kore danmetsuken no gedō nari* ながくこれ斷滅見の外道なり): Presumably, meaning that, if we hold that what has not yet happened is in the future, then it could never actually happen in the present — hence, the error of annihilationism (*danken* 斷見; S. *uccheda-dṛṣṭi*), which denies future rebirths in which the consequences of karma are experienced.

45 the three times have been confused (*sanze, konran shinu beshi* 三世、混亂しぬべし): I.e., if the future somehow turns into the present, the distinctions among past, present, and future would break down. A common argument in support of a Buddhist critique of the intelligibility of the occurrence of real dharmas.

46 the dharmas (*shohō* 諸法); **"real mark"** (*jissō* 實相); **"only buddhas with buddhas"** (*yui butsu yo butsu* 唯佛與佛): Playing on a line in Kumārajīva's translation of the *Lotus Sūtra*; see Supplementary Notes, s.v. "Only buddhas with buddhas can exhaustively investigate the real marks of the dharmas."

47 there would be a time when it is unarisen and a time when it is not unarisen (*mishō ji ari, hi mishō ji aran* 未生時あり、非未生時あらん): I.e. for someone to take it as an object of perception, it must have occurred at some point.

48 "yesterday, I preached a determinate dharma; today, I'm preaching an indeterminate dharma" (*sakujitsu setsu jōhō, konnichi setsu fujōhō* 昨日説定法、今日説不定法): After words (also cited in "Shōbōgenzō ikka myōju" 正法眼藏一顆明珠) attributed to Buddha Śākyamuni in the *Liandeng huiyao* 聯燈會要 (ZZ.136:443b9-11):

> 世尊因外道問、昨日説何法。云説定法。外道云、今日説何法、云説不定法。外道云、昨日説定法。今日何故説不定法。云昨日定。今日不定。

The World-Honored One was once asked by a non-Buddhist, "What dharma did you preach yesterday?"
He said, "I preached a determinate dharma."

60. The 37 Factors of Bodhi *Sanjūshichi hon bodai bunpō* 三十七品菩提分法

[60:19]

已生惡令滅といふは、已生は盡生なり、盡生なりとは、半生なり、半生なりとは、此生なり。此生は被生礙なり、跳出生之頂顗なり。これをして滅ならしむ、といふは、調達生身入地獄なり、調達生身得授記なり、生身入驢胎なり、生身作佛なり。かくのごとくの道理を拈來して、令滅の宗旨を、參學すべきなり。滅は、滅を跳出透脱するを滅とす。

"Causing arisen evil to cease" means "arisen" is fully arising; "it is fully arising" means it is half arising; "it is half arising" means it is this arising.[49] "This arising" is obstructed by "arising"; *it springs forth from the crown of the head of "arising."*[50] Causing this to cease is *"Devadatta, in his birth body, enters hell"*; it is *"Devadatta, in his birth body, receives the prediction."*[51] It is *the birth body enters the womb of a donkey;* it is *"the birth body becomes a buddha."*[52] It is by taking up such principles

---

The non-Buddhist said, "What dharma do you preach today?"
He said, "I'm preaching an indeterminate dharma."
The non-Buddhist said, "Yesterday, you preached a determinate dharma. Why are you preaching an indeterminate dharma today?"
He said, "Yesterday was determinate. Today is indeterminate."

49 **"arisen" is fully arising** (*ishō wa jinshō nari* 已生は盡生なり): The translation masks the play throughout this section with the glyph *shō* 生, which has the sense "to arise" but also "to live," "to be born," "life," "birth," etc. Hence, the first three sentences here could also be rendered, "'Arisen' is an entire life. 'An entire life' is half a life; 'half a life' is this life. 'This life' is obstructed by 'life'; it springs forth from the crown of the head of 'life.'"

50 **"This arising" is obstructed by "arising"** (*shishō wa hi shō ge nari* 此生は被生礙なり): I.e., this arising is defined by, is nothing but, arising; an idiosyncratic use of the verb *ge* 礙 ("to obstruct"), quite common in Dōgen's writing.

51 **"Devadatta, in his birth body, enters hell"** (*Chōdatsu shōshin nyū jigoku* 調達生身入地獄); **"Devadatta, in his birth body, receives the prediction"** (*Chōdatsu shōshin toku juki* 調達生身得授記): References to the legends of Buddha Śākyamuni's cousin Devadatta, who is widely held to have fallen directly into the *avīci* hell for his evil deeds, but whose eventual attainment of buddhahood is predicted by Śākyamuni in the *Lotus Sūtra* (*Miaofa lianhua jing* 妙法蓮華經, T.262.9:35a1-3):

告諸四衆、提婆達多却後過無量劫、當得成佛、號曰天王如來。

I declare to the fourfold assembly that, after innumerable kalpas, Devadatta will become a buddha named Tathāgata Devarāja.

52 **the birth body enters the womb of a donkey** (*shōshin nyū rotai* 生身入驢胎); **"the birth body becomes a buddha"** (*shōshin sabutsu* 生身作佛): Likely a reference to the story, related in "Shōbōgenzō kie buppōsōbō" 正法眼藏歸依佛法僧寶, in which the god Śakra, just as he was taking refuge in Buddhism, suddenly died and was reborn in the womb of a donkey. Because of his having taken refuge, he was released from the womb, returned to his former body, and attained the stage of stream entry (*yoru* 預流; S. *srotāpanna*). In his comments in that chapter, Dōgen remarks that the god went on to attain the unsurpassed bodhi of a buddha. Some commentators suggest that the second clause is an allusion to the story in the *Lotus Sūtra* of the dragon girl who became a buddha.

that we should study the essential point of "causing to cease." "Ceasing" means to spring forth and transcend ceasing.

[60:20] {2:135}

未生善令生といふは、父母未生前、面目參飽なり、朕兆已前、明擧なり、威音以前の會取なり。

"*Causing unarisen good to arise*" means studying one's fill of your face before your father and mother were born, means clearly taking up what is prior to any portent, means understanding what is before Majestic Voice.[53]

[60:21]

已生善令增長は、しるべし、已生善令生といはず、令增長するなり。自見明星訖、更教他見明星なり、眼睛作明星なり。胡亂後三十年、不曾闕鹽醋なり。たとへば、增長するゆえに已生するなり。このゆえに、溪深杓柄長なり、只爲有所以來なり。

"*Causing arisen good to increase*": we should notice that it does not say, "*causing arisen good to arise*," but "*causing it to increase*." It is, *having seen the dawn star oneself, then letting others see the dawn star*; it is *the eye becoming the dawn star.*[54] It is "*after confusion, for thirty years never lacking salt and vinegar.*"[55] For instance, it is, because it "increases," it has "arisen." Therefore, it is "*the stream is deep, the ladle handle long*"; it is "*he came only because it had it.*"[56]

---

53 **your face before your father and mother were born** (*bumo mishō zen, menmoku* 父母未生前、面目); **prior to any portent** (*chinchō izen* 朕兆已前); **before Majestic Voice** (*Ion izen* 威音以前): Three common fixed expressions, appearing often in the *Shōbōgenzō*, for that which precedes existence; presumably, to be understood here as examples of "unarisen good" (*mishō zen* 未生善). See Supplementary Notes, s.v. "Before your father and mother were born" and "Before King Majestic Voice."

54 **having seen the dawn star oneself, then letting others see the dawn star** (*ji ken myōjō kitsu, kō kyō ta ken myōjō* 自見明星訖、更教他見明星): A passage, in Chinese but without known source, referring to the awakening of Buddha Śākyamuni upon seeing Venus in the dawn sky and his subsequent teaching career.

55 **"after confusion, for thirty years never lacking salt and vinegar"** (*uron go sanjū nen, fuzō ketsu enso* 胡亂後三十年、不曾闕鹽醋): A version of the words of Mazu Daoyi 馬祖道一 (See, e.g., *Jingde chuandeng lu* 景德傳燈錄, T.2076.51:241a23-24).

56 **"the stream is deep, the ladle handle long"** (*kei shin shakuhei chō* 溪深杓柄長): Response of an anonymous hermit to the question, "What was the intention of the Ancestral Master's coming from the west?" A version of this story, cited elsewhere in the *Shōbōgenzō*, is recorded in Dōgen's *shinji Shōbōgenzō* 眞字正法眼藏 (DZZ.5:218, case 183), most likely taken from Dahui's 大慧 *Zhengfayanzang* 正法眼藏 (ZZ.118:7b12-17).

"he came only because it had it" (*shi i u shoi rai* 只爲有所以來): The words of Yaoshan Weiyan 藥山惟儼 (751-834) (*Jingde chuandeng lu* 景德傳燈錄, T.2076.51:312b3-5):

僧問、祖師未到此土、此土還有祖師意否。師曰、有。僧曰、既有祖師意、又來作什麼。師曰、只爲有所以來。

60. The 37 Factors of Bodhi *Sanjūshichi hon bodai bunpō* 三十七品菩提分法

* * * * *

[60:22]

四神足

The four bases of spiritual power:[57]

[60:23]

一者、欲神足。二者、心神足。三者、進神足。四者、思惟神足。

(1) The aspiration base of spiritual power, (2) the mind base of spiritual power, (3) the effort base of spiritual power, and (4) the thought base of spiritual power.[58]

[60:24]

欲神足は、圖作佛の身心なり、圖睡快なり、因我禮儞なり。おほよそ欲神足、さらに身心の因縁にあらざるなり。莫涯空の鳥飛なり、徹底水の魚行なり。

"*The aspiration base of spiritual power*" is the body and mind of "*figuring to make a buddha,*" is "*figuring on a quick nap,*" is "*my obeisance to you.*"[59] In sum, "*the aspiration base of spiritual power*" is not at all a

---

A monk asked, "Before the Ancestral Master [Bodhidharma] had come to this land, did this land have 'the intention of the Ancestral Master'?"
The Master [Weiyan] said, "It did."
The monk said, "Since it already had 'the intention of the Ancestral Master,' why did he come?"
The Master said, "He came only because it had it."

57 **four bases of spiritual power** (*shijinsoku* 四神足): The third set of the thirty-seven factors of bodhi; literally, "spiritual feet," a rendering of Sanskrit *ṛddhi-pāda* (as Dōgen will note below, section 28, often rendered *shinyoisoku* 四如意足). Four practices conducive to achieving spiritual powers, not to be confused with the magical powers (of flight, etc.), also called *ṛddhi-pāda*, that are the first of the five (or six) "higher knowledges" (S. *abhijñā*) of the contemplative adept.

58 **The aspiration base of spiritual power** (*yoku jinsoku* 欲神足): Dōgen's version of this list is a bit unusual and reverses the more common order of numbers 2 and 3. The four are typically seen as a progression, from (1) the "wish" (S. *chanda*) to acquire the powers, through (2) the "endeavor" (S. *vīrya*) to acquire them, and (3) the "mental focus" (S. *citta*) on them, to (4) the "meditation" (S. *mīmāṃsa*) on them.

59 "**figuring to make a buddha**" (*zu sabutsu* 圖作佛): From the famous episode, much treasured by Dōgen, involving Mazu Daoyi 馬祖道一 and his teacher, Nanyue Huairang 南嶽懷讓 (*Jingde chuandeng lu*, T.2076.51:240c20):

大德坐禪圖什麼。一日、圖作佛。

[Nanyue asked,] "Most Virtuous One, what are you figuring to do, sitting there in meditation?"
Daoyi said, "I'm figuring to make a buddha."

See Supplementary Notes, s.v. "Nanyue polishes a tile."

"**figuring on a quick nap**" (*to suikai* 圖睡快): From the opening lines of the *Caoan*

cause and condition of body and mind: it is a bird flying in a horizonless sky; it is a fish going to the bottom of the water.[60]

[60:25]

心神足は、牆壁瓦礫なり、山河大地なり、條條の三界なり、赤赤の椅子・竹木なり。盡使得なるがゆゑに、佛祖心あり、凡聖心あり、草木心あり、變化心あり。盡心は心神足なり。

"The mind base of spiritual power" is "fences, walls, tiles, and pebbles"; it is "mountains, rivers, and the whole earth"; it is the three realms in each instance; it is "chairs, bamboo, and wood" in their nakedness.[61] Since they are all usable, there is the mind of the buddhas and ancestors;

---

ge 草庵歌, by Shitou Xiqian 石頭希遷 (700-790) (*Jingde chuandeng lu* 景德傳燈錄, T.2076.51:461c9):

吾結草庵無寶貝、飯了從容圖睡快。
I built this thatched hut that has nothing of worth;
Finished my rice, I relaxed, figuring on a quick nap.

"my obeisance to you" (*in ga rai ni* 因我禮儞): From a verse by Tiantong Rujing 天童如淨, in reference to Buddha Śākyamuni (*Rujing heshang yulu* 如淨和尚語錄, T.2002A.48:125c11-12):

因我禮儞、早眠晏起。
My obeisance to you —
Sleeping early and waking late.

60 **cause and condition of body and mind** (*shinjin no innen* 身心の因緣): The exact sense is uncertain; perhaps, "something caused by the individual."

it is a bird flying in a horizonless sky; it is a fish going to the bottom of the water (*makugai kū no chō hi nari, tettei sui no gyō kō nari* 莫涯空の鳥飛なり、徹底水の魚行なり): After the final lines of the *Zuochan zhen* 坐禪箴, by Hongzhi Zhengjue 宏智正覺 (1091-1157) (on which Dōgen comments in his "Shōbōgenzō zazen shin" 正法眼藏坐禪箴; for the source, see *Hongzhi chanshi guanglu* 宏智禪師廣錄, T.2001.48:98a29-b5):

水清徹底兮、魚行遲遲。空闊莫涯兮、鳥飛杳杳。
The water is clear right through to the bottom;
A fish goes lazily along.
The sky is vast without horizon;
A bird flies far far away.

61 **"fences, walls, tiles, and pebbles"** (*shō heki ga ryaku* 牆壁瓦礫): The first of four sayings on "mind" (*shin* 心) that Dōgen lists here; this one, from the words, quoted often in Dōgen's writing, attributed to Nanyang Huizhong 南陽慧忠. See Supplementary Notes, s.v. "Fences, walls, tiles, and pebbles."

"mountains, rivers, and the whole earth" (*senga daichi* 山河大地): A common expression for the natural world; here probably reflecting a saying of Yangshan Huiji 仰山慧寂 included in the *shinji Shōbōgenzō* 眞字正法眼藏 (DZZ.5:212, case 168); see Supplementary Notes, s.v. "Sun, moon, and stars."

the three realms in each instance (*jōjō no sangai* 條條の三界): Likely reflecting the common expression, "the three realms are only mind" (*sangai yui shin* 三界唯心); see Supplementary Notes, s.v. "The three realms are only mind." "In each instance" renders *jōjō* 條條, which should probably be taken together with the parallel *shakushaku* 赤赤

60. The 37 Factors of Bodhi *Sanjūshichi hon bodai bunpō* 三十七品菩提分法

there is the mind of the common person and the sage; there is the mind of grass and trees; there is the mind of transformation.[62] The entire mind is "*the mind base of spiritual power.*"[63]

[60:26]

進神足は、百尺竿頭驀直歩なり。いづれのところかこれ百尺竿頭。いはゆる不驀直不得なり、驀直一歩は、なきにあらず。這裏是甚麼處在、説進説退。正當進神足時、盡十方界、隨神足到也、隨神足至也。

The effort base of spiritual power is "*stepping straight off the tip of a hundred-foot pole.*"[64] Where is "the tip of a hundred-foot pole"? It is, *it can't be not "straight off."* It is not that it is not *one step* "*straight off*"; but "*where are we here,*" *that we're talking about going forward or back?*[65] Precisely when there is "*the effort base of spiritual power,*"

("nakedness"), as a play with the colloquial *seki jōjō* 赤條條 ("stark naked"), seen also in "Shōbōgenzō kajō" 正法眼藏家常.

"chairs, bamboo, and wood" in their nakedness (*shakushaku no isu chikuboku* 赤赤の椅子竹木): From a discussion between Luohan Guichen 羅漢桂琛 (867-928) and Xuansha Shibei 玄沙師備 (835-908), recorded in Dōgen's *shinji Shōbōgenzō* 眞字正法眼藏 (DZZ.5:186, case 112), about whether to understand "the three realms are only one mind" (*sangai yui isshin* 三界唯一心) as a "chair" or as "bamboo and wood." See Supplementary Notes, s.v. "Chairs, bamboo, and wood."

62 **mind of the common person and the sage** (*bonshō shin* 凡聖心): I.e., the minds of ordinary humans and those advanced on the Buddhist spiritual path.

mind of grass and trees (*sōmoku shin* 草木心): The sense here is uncertain. The expression can mean "the heart, or core, of plants" (used to explain one sense of Sanskrit *hṛdaya* ["heart"]); in "Shōbōgenzō hotsu bodai shin" 正法眼藏發菩提心, Dōgen uses it in reference to spiritual practice associated with trees.

mind of transformation (*henge shin* 變化心): An expression that could refer to (a) the mind that produces magical effects, (b) the mind of an apparitional being, or (c) the mind that undergoes change.

63 **The entire mind** (*jinshin* 盡心): Could also be rendered, "all minds" or, in the colloquial sense, "with all one's heart."

64 **The effort base of spiritual power** (*shin jinsoku* 進神足): Dōgen's treatment of this topic here will play on the glyph *shin* 進 ("to advance," "to proceed," etc.), used for "effort" (*shōjin* 精進; S. *vīrya*).

"stepping straight off the top of a hundred-foot pole" (*hyakushaku kantō maku jiki ho* 百尺竿頭驀直歩): An expression variations on which occur often in Zen literature; Dōgen's source here is likely a verse by Changsha Jingcen 長沙景岑 (dates unknown) (*Jingde chuandeng lu* 景德傳燈録, T.2076.51:274b6-8):

百丈竿頭不動人、雖然得入未爲眞。百丈竿頭須進歩、十方世界是全身。

The person unmoving atop a thousand-foot pole —
Even though they've entered, it's not yet the real thing.
They should step off the top of the thousand-foot pole;
The worlds in the ten directions are their entire body.

65 **It is not that it is not one step "straight off"; but "where are we here," that**

all the realms in the ten directions arrive with the spiritual power, go off with the spiritual power.

[60:27] {2:136}

思惟神足は、一切佛祖、業識茫茫、無本可據なり。身思惟あり、心思惟あり、識思惟あり、草鞋思惟あり、空劫已前自己思惟あり。

The thought base of spiritual power is, in all the buddhas and ancestors, "the karmic consciousness is vague and confused, without a basis to rely on."[66] There is the thinking of the body; there is the thinking of the mind; there is the thinking of consciousness; there is the thinking of straw sandals; there is the thinking of the self before the kalpa of emptiness.[67]

[60:28]

これをまた四如意足といふ、無躊躇なり。

These are also called "the four wish-fulfilling bases": they are without delay.[68]

[60:29]

釋迦牟尼佛言、未運而到、名如意足。

Buddha Śākyamuni said, "To arrive before you have moved is called the 'wish-fulfilling bases.'"[69]

---

we are talking about going forward or back? (*makujiki ippo wa, naki ni arazu. shari ze jinmo sho zai, sesshin settai* 驀直一歩は、なきにあらず。這裏是甚麼處在、説進説退): The expression, "where are we here?" (*shari ze jinmo sho zai* 這裏是甚麼處在), used elsewhere in the *Shōbōgenzō*, is a fixed form appearing several times in Zen literature, in the sense, "how could we be talking about x here?" From this point to the end of the section, the text is in Chinese.

66 **in all the buddhas and ancestors, "the karmic consciousness is vague and confused, without a basis to rely on"** (*issai busso, gosshiki bōbō, mu hon ka kyo* 一切佛祖、業識茫茫、無本可據): Variation on the words of Yangshan Huiji 仰山慧寂, from a conversation with his teacher Weishan Lingyou 潙山靈祐 that is found in several Chinese sources. Dōgen records one version in his *shinji Shōbōgenzō* 眞字正法眼藏 (DZZ.5:196, case 130); see Supplementary Notes, s.v. "Karmic consciousness."

67 **straw sandals** (*sōai* 草鞋): a common metonym for Buddhist study, from their use as footwear in the monk's pilgrimage.

before the kalpa of emptiness (*kūgō izen* 空劫已前): An expression occurring regularly in Zen texts in reference to a state before even the kalpa before the emergence of the world; see Supplementary Notes, s.v. "Before the kalpa of emptiness."

68 **"the four wish-fulfilling bases"** (*shi nyoi soku* 四如意足): An alternative rendering of Sanskrit *ṛddhi-pāda*; "feet [that move] just as one wishes." The sense here is that one can arrive "without delay" (*mu chuchō* 無躊躇) wherever one wishes to go.

69 **Buddha Śākyamuni** (*Shakamuni butsu* 釋迦牟尼佛): No source has been identified.

60. The 37 Factors of Bodhi *Sanjūshichi hon bodai bunpō* 三十七品菩提分法

[60:30]

しかあればすなはち、ときこと、きりのくちのごとし。方あること、のみのはのごとし。

Thus, their sharpness is like the point of the awl; their squareness, like the blade of the chisel.[70]

* * * * *

[60:31]

五根

The five faculties:[71]

[60:32]

一者、信根。二者、精進根。三者、念根。四者、定根。五者、慧根。

(1) The faculty of faith, (2) the faculty of effort, (3) the faculty of mindfulness, (4) the faculty of concentration, and (5) the faculty of wisdom.

[60:33]

信根は、しるべし、自己にあらず、他己にあらず、自己の強爲にあらず、自己の結構にあらず、他の牽挽にあらず、自立の規矩にあらざるゆゑに、東西密相附なり、渾身似信を信と稱するなり。かならず佛果位と隨他去し、隨自去す。佛果位にあらざれば信現成あらず。このゆゑにいはく、佛法大海信爲能入なり。おほよそ信現成のところは、佛祖現成のところなり。

"The faculty of faith": we should understand that it is not our own; it is not another's; it is not something we ourselves force; it is not something we ourselves construct; it is not something induced by another; it is not a norm set up independently. Hence, it is "intimately bequeathed

---

70 **their sharpness is like the point of the awl; their squareness, like the blade of the chisel** (*toki koto, kiri no kuchi no gotoshi. hō aru koto, nomi no ha no gotoshi* ときこと、きりのくちのごとし。方あること、のみのはのごとし): An obscure remark in Japanese, likely reflecting a popular saying found in many Zen texts (see, e.g., *Dahui Pujue chanshi yulu* 大慧普覺禪師語錄, T.1998A.47:913b3-4):

俗諺所謂、只見錐頭利、不見鑿頭方。

As is said in the secular proverb, "To see only that the awl is sharp and not see that the chisel is square."

If the Chinese saying is taken to mean, "seeing one kind of sharpness but not another," Dōgen's remark might imply that both the terms "spiritual power" and "wish-fulfilling" are accurate.

71 **The five faculties** (*gokon* 五根): The fourth set of the thirty-seven factors; spiritual faculties, or "strengths" (S. *indriya*), not to be confused with the five sense faculties, or organs (also *gokon* 五根; S. *indriya*).

in east and west."[72] It is called faith when the whole body shows faith. As the stage of buddhahood, it always "goes along with it," goes along with itself.[73] If it is not the stage of buddhahood, there is no realization of faith. Therefore, it is said, "In the great ocean of the buddha dharma, faith makes it possible to enter."[74] In sum, where faith appears, there the buddhas and ancestors appear.

[60:34] {2:137}
精進根は、省來祗管打坐なり、休也休不得なり、休得更休得なり、大區區生なり、不區區者なり、大區不區、一月二月なり。

"The faculty of effort" is, *just sitting in reflection*.[75] It is *stopping but unable to stop*; it is *stopping and then stopping again*.[76] It is "*How attentive!*"; it is "*one who's not attentive*."[77] It is how attentive and not attentive, a first moon and a second moon.

---

72 **"intimately bequeathed in east and west"** (*tōzai mitsu sōfu* 東西密相附): From the opening lines of the *Cantong qi* 參同契, of Shitou Xiqian 石頭希遷 (*Jingde chuandeng lu* 景德傳燈錄, T.2076.51:459b8):

竺土大仙心、東西密相付。
The mind of the great sage of Sindhu,
Intimately bequeathed in east and west.

73 **As the stage of buddhahood, it always "goes along with it," goes along with itself** (*kanarazu bukka i to zui ta ko shi, zui ji ko su* かならず佛果位と隨他去し、隨自去す): Play with the saying of Suishan Fazhen (seen above, section 12) on "going along" with "this" at the end of the kalpa. See below, section 84, for the text.

74 **"In the great ocean of the buddha dharma, faith makes it possible to enter"** (*buppō daikai shin i nō nyū* 佛法大海信爲能入): From the *Dazhidu lun* 大智度論 (T.1509.25:63a1-2):

佛法大海、信爲能入、智爲能度。
In the great ocean of the buddha dharma, faith makes it possible to enter, and wisdom makes it possible to cross.

75 **just sitting in reflection** (*shōrai shikan taza* 省來祗管打坐): Recalling the saying Dōgen famously attributes to Tiantong Rujing 天童如淨 that studying Zen is "just sitting" (*shikan taza* 祗管打坐); possibly a variant of the line "sitting straight in reflection, totally drunk" (*shōrai tanza sui kunkun* 省來端坐醉醺醺) (*Guren shiershi ge* 古人十二時歌, *Tiansheng guangdeng lu* 天聖廣燈錄, ZZ.135:774a1).

76 **stopping but unable to stop** (*kyū ya kyū futoku* 休也休不得): Apparently a fixed phrase, appearing, for example, in the *Xutang heshang yulu* 虛堂和尚語錄 (T.2000.47:990b15); Dōgen's source is unknown.

77 **"How attentive!"** (*tai kuku sei* 大區區生): More commonly written 太區區生. This expression and the following sentence reflect the conversation on sweeping to which Dōgen alluded above, section 4.

60. The 37 Factors of Bodhi *Sanjūshichi hon bodai bunpō* 三十七品菩提分法

[60:35]

釋迦牟尼佛言、我常勤精進。是故我已得成阿耨多羅三藐三菩提。

Buddha Śākyamuni said, "I was always diligent in effort. It is for this reason, that I have already attained *anuttara-samyak-saṃbodhi*."[78]

[60:36]

いはゆる常勤は、盡過現當來、頭正尾正なり。我常勤精進を、我已得成菩提とせり。我已得成阿耨菩提のゆゑに、我常勤精進なり。しかあらずば、いかでか常勤ならん、しかあらずば、いかでか我已得ならん。論師・經師、この宗旨を見聞すべからず、いはんや參學せるあらんや。

"Always diligent" is *right from head to tail through past, present, and future*. He has taken "*I was always diligent in effort*" as "*I have already attained bodhi*": because "*I have already attained anuttara-samyak-saṃbodhi*," "*I was always diligent in effort.*" If this were not the case, how could he have been "always diligent"? If this were not the case, how could it be "I have already attained"? The treatise masters and sūtra masters cannot see or hear this essential point, much less could they have studied it.

[60:37]

念根は、枯木の赤肉團なり、赤肉團を枯木といふ、枯木は念根なり。摸索當の自己、これ念なり。有身のときの念あり、無心のときも念あり、有心の念あり、無身の念あり。盡大地人の命根、これを念根とせり、盡十方佛の命根、これは念根なり。一念に多人あり、一人に多念あり。しかあれども、有念人あり、無念人あり。人にかならずしも念あるにあらず、念かならずしも人にかかれるにあらず。しかありといへども、この念根、よく持して究盡の功徳あり。

"The faculty of mindfulness" is the lump of red meat of the dried-up tree.[79] The lump of red meat is called "a dried-up tree." A dried-up tree is "the faculty of mindfulness." The self we find through our groping — this is "mindfulness." There is the mindfulness when there is a body; there is the mindfulness when we have no mind. There is mindfulness with mind; there is mindfulness without body. The life faculty of the people of all the whole earth — this is taken as "the faculty of mindfulness"; the life faculty of the buddhas in all the ten directions — this is "the faculty of mindfulness."[80] In a single moment of mindfulness, there are many people; in a single person, there are many moments of mind-

---

78 **Buddha Śākyamuni** (*Shakamuni butsu* 釋迦牟尼佛): From the *Lotus Sūtra* (*Miaofa lianhua jing* 妙法蓮華經, T.262.9:30a4-5).

79 **lump of red meat of the dried-up tree** (*koboku no shaku nikudan* 枯木の赤肉團): Two common metaphors, mixed here to suggest the physical body in the seemingly lifeless state of meditation; see Supplementary Notes, s.v. "Dried-up tree."

80 **life faculty** (*myōkon* 命根): Dōgen plays on the glyph *kon* 根 ("faculty") here in a term used for one's allotted lifespan.

fulness.[81] Nevertheless, there are people with mindfulness, and there are people without mindfulness: people do not necessarily have mindfulness, and mindfulness does not necessarily have to do with people. Although this is the case, in maintaining this faculty of mindfulness, there are exhaustive virtues.

[60:38]

定根は、惜取眉毛なり、策起眉毛なり。このゆえに、不昧因果なり、不落因果なり。ここをもて、入驢胎、入馬胎なり。いしの、玉をつつめるがごとし、全石全玉なりといふべからず。地の、山をいただけるがごとし、盡地盡山といふべからず。しかあれども、頂顙より跳出し跳入す。

"The faculty of meditation" is *caring for his eyebrows*, is *brushing up his eyebrows*.[82] Therefore, it is, *"he isn't in the dark about cause and effect"*; it is, *"he doesn't fall into cause and effect."*[83] With this, it is *entering the womb of a donkey, entering the womb of a horse*.[84] It is like "the stone containing the gem": we cannot say it is all stone or all gem; it is like "the earth bearing the mountain": we cannot say it is all the earth or all the mountain.[85] Nevertheless, it springs forth from and springs into the crown of the head.

---

81 **In a single moment of mindfulness** (*ichi nen ni* 一念に): The translation of the term *nen* 念 as "mindfulness" masks the fact that it is also used for "moment" and for "thought"; hence, this expression could also be rendered, "in a single moment" or "in a single thought." Similarly, the sentences following could be read, "There are people with thought, and there are people with no thought: people do not necessarily have thought, and thought does not necessarily have to do with people."

82 **caring for his eyebrows** (*shakushu bimō* 惜取眉毛); **brushing up his eyebrows** (*sakuki bimō* 策起眉毛): The former phrase is a fixed expression meaning to refrain from teaching Buddhism, lest one's eyebrows fall off; the latter phrase is from the story that the arhat Piṇḍola brushed up his long, drooping eyebrows to indicate that he had personally seen the Buddha. Dōgen quotes this story from the *Rujing heshang yulu* 如淨和尚語録 (T.2002A.48:130c7-11) in "Shōbōgenzō baika" 正法眼藏梅華.

83 **"he isn't in the dark about cause and effect"** (*fumai inga* 不昧因果); **"he doesn't fall into cause and effect"** (*furaku inga* 不落因果): From the famous tale of Baizhang Huaihai 百丈懷海 (749-814) and the teacher who was reborn as a fox for saying that the person of great practice "doesn't fall into cause and effect" (*furaku inga* 不落因果). The teacher is liberated from his fox body when Baizhang tells him that such a person "isn't in the dark about cause effect" (*fumai inga* 不昧因果). The story, occurring widely in Zen sources, is recorded in the *shinji Shōbōgenzō* 眞字正法眼藏 (DZZ.5:178-80, case 102) and discussed in "Shōbōgenzō daishugyō" 正法眼藏大修行 and "Jinshin inga" 深信因果.

84 **entering the womb of a donkey, entering the womb of a horse** (*nyū rotai, nyū batai* 入驢胎、入馬胎): Variation on the more common "the womb of a donkey or the belly of a horse" (*nyū rotai bafuku* 入驢胎馬腹), a fixed expression for rebirth as an animal.

85 **"the stone containing the gem"** (*ishi no, tama o tsutsumeru* いしの、玉をつつめる); **"the earth bearing the mountain"** (*chi no, yama o itadakeru* 地の、山をいただける): A Japanese rephrasing of a Chinese saying attributed to the eighth-century figure Panshan Baoji 盤山寶積 (dates unknown) (*Jingde chuandeng lu* 景德傳燈録,

60. The 37 Factors of Bodhi *Sanjūshichi hon bodai bunpō* 三十七品菩提分法

[60:39] {2:138}

慧根は、三世諸佛不知有なり、狸奴白牯却知有なり。爲甚如此といふべからず、いはれざるなり。鼻孔有消息なり、拳頭有指尖なり。驢は驢を保任す、井は井に相見す。おほよそ根嗣根なり。

"The faculty of wisdom" is "*the buddhas of the three times, I don't know they exist*"; it is "*cats and white oxen, on the other hand, I know they exist*"[86] We should not ask, "*Why is it like this?*"; it cannot be said.[87] Nostrils have their breathing; fists have their fingertips. The donkey maintains the donkey; the well meets the well.[88] In sum, the faculties succeed the faculties.

* * * * *

[60:40]

五力

The five powers:[89]

[60:41]

一者、信力。二者、精進力。三者、念力。四者、定力。五者、慧力。

(1) The power of faith, (2) the power of effort, (3) the power of mindfulness, (4) the power of meditation, and (5) the power of wisdom.[90]

T.2076.51:253b20-21):

似地擎山不知山之孤峻。如石含玉不知玉之無瑕。

It is like the earth that bears the mountain does not know the mountain is steep; it is like the stone that contains the gem does not know the gem is flawless.

86 **"the buddhas of the three times, I don't know they exist"** (*sanze shobutsu fuchi u* 三世諸佛不知有); **"cats and white oxen, on the other hand, I know they exist"** (*rine byakuko kyaku chi u* 狸奴白牯却知有): From a saying of Nanquan Puyuan 南泉普願 (748-835), quoted in *shinji Shōbōgenzō* 眞字正法眼藏 (DZZ.5:272, case 293) and "Shōbōgenzō gyōbutsu iigi" 正法眼藏威儀. See Supplementary Notes, s.v. "Buddhas of the three times, I don't know they exist; cats and white oxen, on the other hand, I know they exist."

87 **"Why is it like this?"** (*i jin nyo shi* 爲甚如此): An idiomatic phrase often encountered in Zen talk. Presumably, the sense of the sentence is, "we can't say why the faculty of wisdom recognizes cats and cows but not the buddhas."

88 **The donkey maintains the donkey; the well meets the well** (*ro wa ro o hōnin su, i wa i ni shōken su* 驢は驢を保任す、井は井に相見す): From a dialogue, featuring Caoshan Benzhi 曹山本寂 (840-901) and Senior Seat De 德上座 (dates unknown), recorded in Dōgen's *shinji Shōbōgenzō* 眞字正法眼藏 (DZZ.5:194, case 125); see Supplementary Notes, s.v. "Like the well looking at the donkey."

89 **The five powers** (*goriki* 五力): The fifth set of the thirty-seven factors; spiritual powers (S. *bala*) derived from the cultivation of the five faculties.

90 **(1) The power of faith** (*issha, shinriki* 一者、信力): Like the five faculties, of which they are said to be the development, the five powers are regularly described as antidotes to the five hindrances (*gogai* 五蓋; S. *nīvaraṇa*) to dhyāna: faith (*shin* 信; S. śrad-

[60:42]

信力は、被自瞞無廻避處なり、被他喚必廻頭なり、從生至老、只是這箇なり、七顛也放行なり、八倒也拈來なり。このゆえに、信如水精珠なり。傳法・傳衣を信とす、傳佛・傳祖なり。

"The power of faith" is *being deceived by yourself with no place of escape.*[91] It is *being called by another and invariably turning your head*; it is *"from birth to old age, it's just this."*[92] It is *falling over seven times and letting it go*; it is *falling down eight times and taking it up.*[93] Therefore, it is *"faith is like the water-purifying gem."*[94] Transmitting the dharma and

dhā) overcomes aversion (*shin'i* 瞋恚; S. *vyāpāda*); effort (*shōjin* 精進; S. *vīrya*) overcomes torpor (*konjin* 惛沈; S. *sthāna-middha*); mindfulness (*nen* 念; S. *smṛti*) overcomes desire (*tonyoku* 貪欲; S. *kāma-cchanda*); concentration (*jō* 定; S. *samādhi*) overcomes agitation (*joke* 掉悔; S. *auddhatya-kaukṛtya*); and wisdom (*e* 慧; S. *prajñā*) overcomes doubt (*gi* 疑; S. *vicikitsā*).

91   **being deceived by yourself with no place of escape** (*hi ji man mu kaihi sho* 被自瞞無廻避處): Dōgen has put this phrase in Chinese, as if quoting a text, but no source is known.

92   **being called by another and invariably turning your head** (*hi ta kan hitsu kaitō* 被他喚必廻頭); **"from birth to old age, it's just this"** (*jū shō shi rō, shi ze shako* 從生至老、只是這箇): Perhaps, an allusion to an anecdote involving Shitou Xiqian 石頭希遷 and Wuxie Lingmo 五洩靈黙 (747-818) (*Jingde chuandeng lu* 景德傳燈錄, T.2076.51:254b10-11): Having failed to understand Shitou's teaching, Wuxie was leaving.

石頭呼之云、闍梨。師廻顧。石頭云、從生至老只是遮箇。漢更莫別求。
Shitou called to him, "Ācārya."
The Master [Wuxie] turned and looked back. Shitou said, "From birth to old age, it's just this. A man shouldn't look for anything else."

In his *shinji Shōbōgenzō* 眞字正法眼藏 (DZZ.5:126, case 4) and in the "Shōbōgenzō kokū," Dōgen records a similar anecdote, involving Mazu Daoyi 馬祖道一 and his student Prelate Liang 亮座主:

師拂袖而去。祖召曰、座主。師回首。祖曰、從生至老、只是這箇。
The Master [i.e., Liang] shook out his sleeves and withdrew. Mazu called to him, "Prelate!"
The Master turned. Mazu said, "From birth to old age, it's just this."

See Supplementary Notes, s.v. "Prelate Liang."

93   **falling over seven times and letting it go** (*shichiten ya hōgyō* 七顛也放行); **falling down eight times and taking it up** (*hattō ya nenrai* 八倒也拈來): From the idiom "fall over seven times and fall down eight times" (*shichiten hattō* 七顛八倒; also read *shitten battō*), meaning "to be utterly confused," "to make one mistake after another." The combination of "let it go" (*hōgyō* 放行) with "take it up" (*nenrai* 拈來) is unusual; the latter is typically used in reference to an object or a topic, while the former is often paired with "hold fast" (*hajō* 把定), in reference to a master's restraining and releasing a student.

94   **"faith is like the water-purifying gem"** (*shin nyo suishō ju* 信如水精珠): The expression *suishō ju* 水精珠 here is often taken as "crystal" (*suishō* 水晶); the translation reflects the occurrence of Dōgen's phrase in reference to the simile, in the *Cheng weishi lun* 成唯識論 (T.1585.31:29c4-6), of the gem that clarifies muddy water (*suishō ju* 水清珠; S. *udaka-prabhāsa-maṇi*).

60. The 37 Factors of Bodhi *Sanjūshichi hon bodai bunpō* 三十七品菩提分法

transmitting the robe constitute faith; it is transmitting the buddhas and transmitting the ancestors.

[60:43]

精進力は、説取行不得底なり、行取説不得底なり。しかあればすなはち、説得一寸、不如説得一寸なり、行得一句、不如行得一句なり、力裏得力、これ精進力なり。

"The power of effort" is "*talking of what can't be practiced*"; it is "*practicing what can't be talked of.*"[95] Thus, it is *talking of one inch is not like talking of one inch*; it is *practicing one line is not like practicing one line. To get power within power* — this is "the power of effort."

[60:44]

念力は、拽人鼻孔大殺人なり。このゆえに、鼻孔拽人なり、抛玉引玉なり、抛塼引塼なり。さらに未抛也三十棒なり、天下人用著未磷なり。

"The power of mindfulness" is *a brute pulling a person's nose.*[96] Therefore, it is *the nose pulling the person*; it is *tossing out a jade to take in a jade*; it is *tossing out a tile to take in a tile.*[97] Further, it is, *even if you have not tossed it out, thirty blows*; it is, *even if everyone in the world uses it, it won't wear down.*[98]

---

95 **"talking of what can't be practiced"** (*sesshu gyō futokutei* 説取行不得底); **"practicing what can't be talked of"** (*gyōshu setsu futokutei* 行取説不得底): From a comment of Dongshan Liangjie 洞山良价 (e.g., at *Liandeng huiyao* 聯燈會要, ZZ.136:549b14; see also *shinji Shōbōgenzō* 眞字正法眼藏, DZZ.5:164, case 77):

> 杭州大慈山性空大師〈嗣百丈、諱寰中〉示衆云、説得一丈、不如行得一尺、説得一尺、不如行取一寸。洞山曰、説取行不得底、行取説不得底。

> Great Master Xinggong of Mount Daci in Hangzhou (named Huangzhong) addressed the assembly saying, "To talk about ten feet is not like practicing one foot; to talk about one foot is not like practicing one inch."
> Dongshan said, "He talks about what can't be practiced; he practices what can't be talked about."

96 **a brute pulling a person's nose** (*ei nin bikū taisatsunin* 拽人鼻孔大殺人): Reference to the story (recorded at *shinji Shōbōgenzō* 眞字正法眼藏, DZZ.5:256, case 248) in which Shigong Huizang 石鞏慧藏 (dates unknown) demonstrated how to grasp space by pulling the nose of Xitang Zhizang 西堂智藏 (735-814); see Supplementary Notes, s.v. "Nose."

97 **tossing out a jade to take in a jade** (*hōgyoku ingyoku* 抛玉引玉): Play on the idiom "tossing out a tile and taking in a jade"; in Chinese literary usage, a polite way to ask another for a capping verse for one's poem; used in Zen for the give and take of Zen repartee (as, e.g., by Zhaozhou 趙州, at *Jingde chuandeng lu* 景德傳燈錄, T.2076.51:277a29-b2). See Supplementary Notes.

98 **even if you have not tossed it out, thirty blows** (*mihō ya sanjū bō* 未抛也三十棒); **even if everyone in the world uses it, it won't wear down** (*tenka nin yōjaku mirin* 天下人用著未磷): Two phrases put in Chinese as if quotations but without known sources. The diction of the former phrase is reminiscent of the common expression, "If you can

[60:45]

定力は、或者如子得其母なり、或者如母得其子なり。或者如子得其子なり、或者如母得其母なり。しかあれども、以頭換面にあらず、以金買金にあらず、唱而彌高なるのみなり。

"The power of concentration" is "like the child gaining its mother"; or it is like the mother gaining the child; or it is like the child gaining the child; or it is like the mother gaining the mother.[99] Nevertheless, it is not using the head to change the face; it is not using gold to buy gold: it is just the song getting higher.[100]

[60:46] {2:139}

慧力は、年代深遠なり、如船遇度なり。かるがゆえに、ふるくはいはく、如度得船。いふこころは、度必是船なり、度の度を罣礙せざるを船といふ、春氷自消氷なり。

"The power of wisdom": it is "years deep and long"; it is "like the boat meeting the ferry passenger."[101] Therefore, of old it was said, "like the ferry passenger getting a boat." That is, the "ferrying" is invariably

---

say it, thirty blows; if you can't say it, thirty blows" (*dōtoku ya sanjū bō, dōfutoku ya sanjū bō* 道得也三十棒、道不得也三十棒).

99 **"like the child gaining its mother"** (*nyo shi toku go mo* 如子得其母): Suggesting a line in the *Cantong qi* 參同契 (*Jingde chuandeng lu* 景德傳燈錄, T.2076.51:459b12-13):

四大性自復、如子得其母。

The four elements revert to their nature,
Like the child gaining its mother.

Judging from his use, immediately below, of the simile of the ferry boat, Dōgen must also have had in mind here the passage in the *Lotus Sūtra* (*Miaofa lianhua jing* 妙法蓮華經, T.262.9:54b15-16) in which the sūtra is said to satisfy all needs:

如子得母。如渡得船。

Like the child gaining its mother; like the ferry passenger getting a boat.

100 **using the head to change the face** (*i tō kan men* 以頭換面): An unusual variant of the multivalent idiom "renewing the head and changing the face" (*kai tō kan men* 改頭換面), or "turning the head and changing the face" (*kai tō kan men* 回頭換面); here, perhaps, used to indicate a merely superficial change. See Supplementary Notes, s.v. "Turning the head and changing the face." The following "using gold to buy gold" (*i kin mai kin* 以金買金) has a similar sense. The implication here is uncertain; perhaps, that the four similies of mother and child are not merely restatements of the same relationship.

the song getting higher (*shō ni mi kō* 唱而彌高): Likely a (syntactically garbled) allusion to the idiom, "the higher the song, the fewer who can match it" (*shō mi kō ni wa mi ka* 唱彌高而和彌寡).

101 **"years deep and long"** (*nendai jin'on* 年代深遠): A phrase used in reference to Linji Yixuan 臨濟義玄 (d. 866) (see *Linji lu* 臨濟錄, T.1985.47:505a11, 506a1).

like the boat meeting the ferry passenger (*nyo sen gū to* 如船遇度): Play on the *Lotus Sūtra* phrase, "like the ferry passenger getting a boat" (*nyo to toku sen* 如度得船) (see above, Note 99).

"the boat"; that the ferrying does not obstruct the ferrying is called "the boat."[102] It is *spring ice melts of its own accord*.[103]

* * * * *

[60:47]

七等覺支

The seven limbs of perfect awakening:[104]

[60:48]

一者、擇法覺支。二者、精進覺支。三者、喜覺支。四者、除覺支。五者、捨覺支。六者、定覺支。七者、念覺支。

(1) The dharma analysis limb of awakening, (2) the vigor limb of awakening, (3) the joy limb of awakening, (4) the removal limb of awakening, (5) the equanimity limb of awakening, (6) the concentration limb of awakening, (7) the mindfulness limb of awakening.

[60:49]

擇法覺支は、毫釐有差、天地懸隔なり。このゆえに、至道不難易、唯要自揀擇のみなり。

"The dharma analysis limb of awakening" is "*where there's a hair's breadth of distinction the gap is like that between heaven and earth.*"[105]

---

102 **"ferrying" is invariably "the boat"** (*to hitsu ze sen* 度必是船): A phrase in Chinese that could also be read, "the ferry passenger is invariably the boat." Perhaps more likely would be to read the term *to* 度 (translated here "ferrying") in its common Buddhist sense of spiritual "deliverance."

103 **spring ice melts of its own accord** (*shunpyō ji shōhyō* 春氷自消氷): Variant of a fixed phrase; here, likely reflecting a comment on the line of the *Cantong qi* 參同契 just following that cited above, Note 99 (see *Rentian yenmu* 人天眼目, T.2006.48:327a23-24):

四大性自復（隨所依）、如子得其母（可知也）。
火熱風動搖（春氷自消）、水濕地堅固（從旦至暮）。
The four elements revert to their nature (according to their bases),
Like the child gaining its mother (obvious).
Fire heats; wind blows (spring ice melts of itself);
Water is wet; earth, solid (from dawn to dusk).

104 **seven limbs of perfect awakening** (*shichitōkakushi* 七等覺支): The sixth set of the thirty-seven factors; S. *bodhyaṅga* (also rendered *shichikakubun* 七覺分). Dōgen regularly uses the term *tōkaku* (or *tōgaku*) 等覺 in the sense "virtual awakening," for the penultimate stage of the bodhisattva path; but here, it renders Sanskrit *saṃbodhi*. The terminology and order of the seven members differs slightly according to the source; Dōgen's list here corresponds to that found in the *Fahua cidi chumen* 法華次第初門 by Zhiyi 智顗 (538-597) (T.1925.46:682b18-c10).

105 **"dharma analysis limb of awakening"** (*jakuhō kakushi* 擇法覺支): Analytic investigation of the teachings (S. *dharma-pravicaya*).

Therefore, it is only "*the supreme way isn't hard*" or easy; *you just need to make the choice yourself.*[106]

[60:50]
精進覺支は、不曾攙奪行市なり。自買自賣ともに定價あり、知貴あり。屈己推人に相似なりといへども、通身撲不碎なり。一轉語を自賣することいまだやまざるに、一轉心を自買する商客に相逢す。驢事未了、馬事到來なり。

"The vigor limb of awakening" is *never having dominated the market.*[107] Whether buying it oneself or selling it oneself, there is a fixed price, and there is knowing its value.[108] Although it may "*look like humbling yourself and promoting another,*" it is "*thoroughly beaten but un-*

"**where there's a hair's breadth of distinction**" (*kōri u sha* 毫釐有差): From the opening lines of the *Xinxin ming* 信心銘 (T.2010.48:376b20-21), on which Dōgen will play in the next sentence:

至道無難、唯嫌揀擇。但莫憎愛、洞然明白。毫釐有差、天地懸隔。

The supreme way isn't hard:
Just dislike picking and choosing.
If we simply do not hate or love,
All will be open and clear.
Where there's a hair's breadth of distinction
The gap is like that between heaven and earth.

106 "**the supreme way isn't hard" or easy; you just need to make the choice yourself** (*shiidō bunan'i, yui yō ji kenjaku* 至道不難易、唯要自揀擇): Playing with the first two lines of the *Xinxin ming* 信心銘 (as in the preceding note).

107 "**vigor limb of awakening**" (*shōjin kakushi* 精進覺支): Diligent effort (S. *vīrya*) in spiritual training.

never having dominated the market (*fuzō zandatsu kōshi* 不曾攙奪行市): The idiom *zandatsu kōshi* 攙奪行市 ("to dominate the market") appears several times in the *Shōbōgenzō*, probably reflecting a saying of Xuansha Shibei 玄沙師備 recorded in Dōgen's *shinji Shōbōgenzō* 眞字正法眼藏 (DZZ.5:146, case 38); see Supplementary Notes, s.v. "Dominate the market."

108 **Whether buying it oneself or selling it oneself, there is a fixed price, there is knowing its value** (*ji mai ji mai tomo ni teika ari, chi ki ari* 自買自賣ともに定價あり、知貴あり): Possibly reflecting the words of Wuzu Fayan 五祖法演 (d. 1104) on his awakening (*Liandeng huiyao* 聯燈會要, ZZ.136:684a14):

幾度賣來還自買。爲憐松竹引清風。

Having sold it so many times, I bought it myself;
For pity's sake, the pine and bamboo take in the fresh breeze.

"**There is a fixed price**" (*teika ari* 定價あり) may reflect a verse by Tiantong Rujing quoted in "Shōbōgenzō shohō jissō" 正法眼藏諸法實相:

要買那堪無定價、一聲杜宇孤雲上。

If you want to buy it, how could it lack a fixed price?
The cry of a cuckoo above a single cloud.

"**Knowing its value**" (*chi ki* 知貴) may reflect the common Zen saying, "the god of the sea knows its value but doesn't know its price" (*kaishin chi ki fuchi ka* 海神知貴不知價).

broken."[109] Even while still selling a turning word oneself, one meets a merchant who buys a turning mind himself.[110] It is *"before the donkey business is over, the horse business arrives."*[111]

[60:51]
喜覺支は、老婆心切血滴滴なり。大悲千手眼、遮莫太多端、臘雪梅華先漏泄、來春消息大家寒なり。しかもかくのごとくなりといへども、活鱍鱍、笑呵呵なり。

"The joy limb of awakening" is *"grandma's mind is kind; the blood drips."*[112] *The thousand hands and eyes of the Great Compassionate One;*

---

109 **"look like humbling oneself and promoting the other"** (*kukko suinin ni sōji nari* 屈己推人に相似なり): After a saying of Touzi Datong 投子大同 (819-914) (*Jingde chuandeng lu* 景德傳燈錄, T.2076.51:320a21-22):

問、七佛是文殊弟子。文殊還有師也無。師曰、適來恁麼道也、大似屈己推人。

[Someone] asked, "The seven buddhas are the disciples of Mañjuśrī. Does Mañjuśrī have a master?"
The Master said, "To talk the way you just did looks like humbling yourself and promoting another."

"thoroughly beaten but unbroken" (*tsūshin boku fusai* 通身撲不碎): From another saying of Touzi Datong 投子大同 (*Jingde chuandeng lu* 景德傳燈錄, T.2076.51:320a15-17):

問、和尚未見先師時如何。師曰、通身不奈何。曰見先師後如何。師曰、通身撲不碎。

[Someone] asked, "Before the Reverend had met his former master, what were you like?"
The Master said, "Thoroughly hopeless."
He asked, "After you met your former master, what were you like?"
The Master said, "Thoroughly beaten but unbroken."

110 **selling a turning word oneself** (*ittengo o jimai suru* 一轉語を自賣する); **a merchant who buys a turning mind himself** (*ittenshin o jimai suru shōkyaku* 一轉心を自買する商客): Amending Kawamura, which reads "a merchant who sells a turning mind himself" (*ittenshin o jimai suru shōkyaku* 一轉心を自賣する商客). "A turning word" (*ittengo* 一轉語) is a teaching that "turns the mind" to understanding; "a turning mind" (*ittenshin* 一轉心) is Dōgen's variation. In the context here, it would seem that the seller of the turning word is himself the merchant who buys the turning mind.

111 **"before the donkey business is over, the horse business arrives"** (*roji miryō, baji tōrai* 驢事未了、馬事到來): Generally taken to mean something like, "It's just one damned thing after another." A saying first attributed to Lingyun Zhiqin 靈雲志勤 (dates unknown) (*Jingde chuandeng lu* 景德傳燈錄, T.2076.51:285b12-13):

僧問、如何是佛法大意。師曰、驢事未去馬事到來。

A monk asked, "What is the great meaning of the buddha dharma?"
The Master said, "Before the donkey business is over, the horse business arrives."

112 **"joy limb of awakening"** (*ki kakushi* 喜覺支): Taking delight (S. *prīti*) in the dharma.

"grandma's mind is kind; the blood drips" (*rōbashin setsu ketsu tekiteki* 老婆心切血滴滴): Line from a verse by Dōgen's teacher, Rujing 如淨 (1162–1227); see Supplementary Notes, s.v. "Fist," and "Karmic consciousness."

so busy even so.[113] It is

> Plum blossoms in the year-end snow first divulge it;
> Signs of the coming spring; everyone is cold.[114]

Still, be that as it may, they are *brisk and lively, laughing "ha ha."*[115]

[60:52] {2:140}
除覺支は、もしみづからがなかにありては、みづからと群せず、他のなかにありては、他と群せず。我得儞不得なり。灼然道著、異類中行なり。

"The removal limb of awakening" is, while being within oneself, uninvolved with oneself; while being with others, uninvolved with others.[116] It is *"I can do it; you can't."*[117] It is, *"clearly, if you speak," "you move among different types."*[118]

---

113 **The thousand hands and eyes of the Great Compassionate One** (*Daihi senjūgen* 大悲千手眼): Reference to the thousand-armed Bodhisattva Avalokiteśvara (*Senju Kannon* 千手觀音), who has an eye in the palm of each hand.

114 **Plum blossoms in the year-end snow** (*rōsetsu baika* 臘雪梅華): Two lines of Chinese verse, apparently of Dōgen's creation. The final phrase may reflect the saying, "When it's cold, everyone is cold" (*kanji taika kan* 寒時大家寒).

115 **they are brisk and lively, laughing "ha ha"** (*kappatsupatsu, shō kaka* 活鱍鱍、笑呵呵): Taking "everyone" as the grammatical subject, though this might also be read as a description of "joy." See Supplementary Notes, s.v. "Brisk and lively."

116 **"removal limb of awakening"** (*jo kakushi* 除覺支): Also rendered as *kyōan kakushi* 輕安覺支 ("tranquility limb of awakening"; S. *praśrabdhi*); the sense of ease from removal of mental obstacles.

117 **"I can do it; you can't"** (*ga toku ni futoku* 我得儞不得): The words of Xuansha Shibei 玄沙師備 (*Liandeng huiyao* 聯燈會要, ZZ.136:824a5-8):

> 師見鼓山來。作圓相、示之。山云、人人出這箇不得。師云、情知儞向驢胎馬腹裏、作活計。山云、和尚又作麼生。師云、人人出這箇不得。山云、和尚與麼道卻是。某甲爲甚麼不得。師云、我得、汝不得。
>
> The Master [Xuansha] saw Gushan coming; he made a circle to instruct him. Gushan said, "People can't get out of it."
> The Master said, "It's obvious to me that you're headed for a life in the donkey's womb or the horse's belly."
> Gushan said, "How about the Reverend?"
> The Master said, "People can't get out of it."
> Gushan said, "If the Reverend can say this, why can't I?"
> The Master said, "I can do it; you can't."

118 **"clearly, if you speak," "you move among different types"** (*shakunen dōjaku, irui chū gyō* 灼然道著、異類中行): Variation on the words of Nanquan Puyuan 南泉普願 (748-834) recorded in *shinji Shōbōgenzō* 眞字正法眼藏 (DZZ.5:154, case 57): "Clearly, if you speak, horns will grow on your head"; see Supplementary Notes, s.v. "Move among different types."

60. The 37 Factors of Bodhi *Sanjūshichi hon bodai bunpō* 三十七品菩提分法

[60:53]
捨覺支は、設使將來、他亦不受なり。唐人赤脚學唐歩、南海波斯求象牙なり。

"The equanimity limb of awakening" is *"whatever he came up with, he wouldn't have accepted it."*[119] It is *a person of Tang, barefoot, studying the walk of Tang; a Persian of the Southern Sea seeking the elephant tusk.*[120]

[60:54]
定覺支は、機先保護機先眼なり、自家鼻孔自家穿なり、自家把索自家牽なり。しかもかくのごとくなりといへども、さらに牧得一頭水牯牛なり。

"The concentration limb of awakening" is *"what is before the function preserves the eye before the function"*; it is *"drilling one's own nostrils oneself"*; it is *"pulling oneself with one's own rope."*[121] Nevertheless,

---

119   **"equanimity limb of awakening"** (*sha kakushi* 捨覺支): Sansrit *upekṣā*; often listed as the last of the seven limbs.
"whatever he came up with, he wouldn't have accepted it" (*shesshi shōrai, ta yaku fuju* 設使將來、他亦不受): A sentence from a dialogue between Chan Master Dongshan Liangjie 洞山良价 and an unnamed monk regarding a line in the famous poem contest between Shenxiu 神秀 and Huineng 慧能 to determine the successor of the Fifth Ancestor, Hongren 弘忍 (found, e.g., at *Hongzhi chanshi guanglu* 宏智禪師廣錄, T.2001.48:34c6-14):

舉僧問洞山、時時勤拂拭、莫使惹塵埃。爲什麼不得他衣鉢。山云、直饒道本來無一物、也未合得他衣鉢。且道、什麼人合得。僧下九十六轉語、不契。末後云、設使將來他亦不受。山深肯之。

Raised: A monk asked Dongshan, "'Always strive to polish it, and do not let the dust collect.' Why did this [line in Shenxiu's verse] not get his [Hongren's] robe and bowl?"
Shan said, "Even if he had said [the line in Huineng's verse], 'From the beginning, not one thing,' he still would not have qualified to get his robe and bowl." He added, "Who's qualified to get them?"
The monk gave ninety-six turning words, but none fit. Finally, he said, "Whatever he came up with, he wouldn't have accepted it."
Shan deeply approved it.

120   **a person of Tang, barefoot, studying the walk of Tang; a Persian of the Southern Sea seeking the elephant tusk** (*Tōjin shakukyaku gaku Tō ho, Nanka Hashi gu zōge* 唐人赤脚學唐歩、南海波斯求象牙): Two phrases in Chinese. The second is a variant of a line of verse at *Tiansheng guangdeng lu* 天聖廣燈錄 (ZZ.135:762a10); the first phrase seems to have no precedent but may represent a play on the expression "the barefoot Persian enters the Great Tang" (*shakukyaku Hashi nyū Daitō* 赤脚波斯入大唐) (see, e.g., *Jiatai pudeng lu* 嘉泰普燈錄, ZZ.137:288a6).

121   **"concentration limb of awakening"** (*jō kakushi* 定覺支): Sanskrit *samādhi*.
"what is before the function preserves the eye before the function" (*kisen hōgo kisen gen* 機先保護機先眼): Variation on a line of verse by Tiantong Rujing 天童如淨 (*Rujing heshang yulu* 如淨和尚語錄, T.2002A.48:131a22-23). "What is before the function" translates *kisen* 機先, a term occurring several times in the *Shōbōgenzō*, sometimes used

be that as it may, going further, it is *"managing to herd a single water buffalo."*[122]

[60:55]
念覺支は、露柱歩空行なり。このゆえに、口似椎眼如眉なり、といふとも、なほこれ栴檀林裏爇栴檀、師子窟中師子吼なり。

"The mindfulness limb of awakening" is *a pillar walking across the sky.*[123] Therefore, while it may be *"a mouth resembling a mallet and an eye like an eyebrow,"* it is *"burning sandalwood in a sandalwood grove, a lion roaring in a cave of lions."*[124]

* * * * *

[60:56]
八正道支、また八聖道とも稱す。

The eight-limbed correct path, also called the eightfold noble path.

[60:57]
一者、正見道支。二者、正思惟道支。三者、正語道支。四者、正業道支。五者、正命道支。六者、正精進道支。七者、正念道支。八者、正定道支。

(1) The correct view limb of the path; (2) the correct thought limb of the path; (3) the correct speech limb of the path; (4) the correct action

---

in the sense of the original state of things before they have become active; the unusual term "eye before the function" (*kisen gen* 機先眼), then, suggests a vision of matters before they occur.

"drilling one's own nostrils oneself" (*jike bikū jike sen* 自家鼻孔自家穿); **"pulling oneself with one's own rope"** (*jike ha saku jike ken* 自家把索自家牽): Two lines from a verse by Tiantong Rujing 天童如淨 (*Rujing heshang yulu* 如淨和尚語錄, T.2002A.48:132b9). See Supplementary Notes, s.v. "Nose."

122   **"managing to herd a single water buffalo"** (*bokutoku ittō suikogyū* 牧得一頭水牯牛): From a saying, quoted elsewhere in the *Shōbōgenzō* ("Gyōji jō" 行持上), of Changqing Da'an 長慶大安 (793-883); see Supplementary Notes, s.v. "Water buffalo."

123   **"mindfulness limb of awakening"** (*nen kakushi* 念覺支): Sanskrit *smṛti*; sometimes listed as the first of the seven limbs.

a pillar walking across the sky (*rochū ho kū gyō* 露柱歩空行): A phrase in Chinese but with no known source. The free-standing columns of temple buildings (*rochū* 露柱) are regularly treated as sentient in Zen texts; see Supplementary Notes, s.v. "Pillars and lanterns."

124   **"a mouth resembling a mallet and an eye like an eyebrow"** (*kū ni sui gen nyo bi* 口似椎眼如眉): After a line at *Yuanwu Foguo chanshi yulu* 圓悟佛果禪師語錄, T.1997.47:802c18-19.

"burning sandalwood in a sandalwood grove, a lion roaring in a cave of lions" (*sendan rin ri zetsu sendan, shishi kutchū shishi ku* 栴檀林裏爇栴檀、師子窟中師子吼): Again, after lines in *Yuanwu Foguo chanshi yulu* 圓悟佛果禪師語錄, T.1997.47:802c11.

limb of the path; (5) the correct livelihood limb of the path; (6) the correct effort limb of the path; (7) the correct mindfulness limb of the path; and (8) the correct concentration limb of the path.

[60:58]
正見道支は、眼睛裏藏身なり。しかあれども、身先須具身先眼なり。向前の堂堂成見なりといへども、公案見成なり、親曾見なり。おほよそ眼裏藏身せざれば、佛祖にあらざるなり。

"The correct view limb of the path" is *hiding the body inside the eye*.[125] However, it is *before the body, we must possess an eye before the body*.[126] While it may be "imposing and manifest" from the past, it is "the kōan is realized"; it is "he once personally saw."[127] In sum, those who do not "hide the body inside the eye" are not buddhas or ancestors.

---

125 **hiding the body inside the eye** (*ganzei ri zō shin* 眼睛裏藏身): Also written, as below here, *gan ri zō shin* 眼裏藏身. Dōgen uses the same expression in "Shōbōgenzō butsu kōjō ji" 正法眼藏佛向上事. "The eye" does not seem to occur often as a hiding place for the body in Zen texts; more commonly, the body is hidden in "the big dipper" (*hokuto* 北斗), in "flames" (*kaen* 火燄), etc.

126 **before the body, we must possess an eye before the body** (*shinsen shu gu shinsen gen* 身先須具身先眼): A sentence given in Chinese, for which there seems no precedent. Dōgen regularly uses the term *shinsen* 身先 (which can mean "one's future") in reference to what lies "before one has a body."

127 **"imposing and manifest" from the past** (*kyōzen no dōdō jōken* 向前の堂堂成見): The phrase *dōdō jōken* 堂堂成見 might also be taken as "an imposing fixed view"; it likely reflects a line in the *Yuanwu Foguo chanshi yulu* 圜悟佛果禪師語録, T.1997.47:799a6:

堂堂成見密密難見。
Imposing and manifest; intimate and imperceptible.

Though lost in the translation, Dōgen is playing here and below in this sentence with meanings of the glyph *ken* 見 ("to see"), used in the sense "view" (S. *dṛṣṭi*) in the phrase "correct view limb of the path."

"the kōan is realized" (*kōan genjō* 公案見成): From the famous expression *genjō kōan* 見成公案 (also written 現成公案), often rendered "the realized kōan" and regularly used in Dōgen's writing for what is manifestly so; see Supplementary Notes, s.v. "Realized kōan." Here, the term *genjō* 見成 ("realized") plays on the preceding *jōken* 成見 ("manifest") by reversing the order of its two elements.

"he once personally saw" (*shinzō ken* 親曾見): From a line of verse by Rujing alluded to several times in the *Shōbōgenzō*:

親曾見佛不相瞞。
He once personally saw the Buddha; he doesn't deceive.

In Rujing's verse (*Rujing heshang yulu* 如淨和尚語録, T.2002A.48:130c7-11), the reference is to the arhat Piṇḍola and his claim to have seen Buddha Śākyamuni.

[60:59] {2:141}

正思惟道支は、作是思惟時、十方佛皆現なり。しかあれば、十方現・諸佛現、これ作是思惟時なり。作是思惟時は、自己にあらず、他己をこえたりといへども、而今も思惟は事已、即趣波羅奈なり。思惟の處在は波羅奈なり。古佛いはく、思量箇不思量底、不思量底如何思量、非思量。これ正思量・正思惟なり。破蒲團、これ正思惟なり。

"The correct thought limb of the path" is "*When I had this thought, the buddhas of the ten directions all appeared.*"[128] Thus, the appearance of the ten directions, the appearance of the buddhas — this is "When I had this thought." "When I had this thought" was not about himself and went beyond others; yet, even now, "*After thinking this, I immediately proceeded to Vārāṇasī.*"[129] The location of thinking is Vārāṇasī. An old buddha has said, "*I'm thinking of not thinking.*"[130] "How do you think of not thinking?" "Nonthinking." This is correct thinking, "correct thought." Breaking down the rush cushion — this is "correct thought."[131]

[60:60]

正語道支は、啞子自己不啞子なり。諸人中の啞子は未道得なり、啞子界の諸人は、啞子にあらず。不慕諸聖なり、不重己靈なり。口是掛壁の參究なり、一切口掛一切壁なり。

"The correct speech limb of the path" is *the self of a mute is not a mute.*[132] It is the mute among people has not said anything; people in the

---

128 **"When I had this thought, the buddhas of the ten directions all appeared"** (*sa ze shiyui ji, jippō butsu kai gen* 作是思惟時、十方佛皆現): From a verse in the *Lotus Sūtra* (*Miaofa lianhua jing* 妙法蓮華經, T.262.9:9c19) on the Buddha's decision to teach the three vehicles; see Supplementary Notes, s.v. "Three vehicles."

129 **"After thinking this, I immediately proceeded to Vārāṇasī"** (*shiyui ze ji i, soku shu Harana* 思惟是事已、即趣波羅奈): From a later line (*Miaofa lianhua jing* 妙法蓮華經, T.262.9:10a3) in the *Lotus Sūtra* verse just quoted, on the Buddha's decision to go to the Deer Park at Vārāṇasī to give his first sermon.

130 **An old buddha** (*kobutsu* 古佛): Quoting Yaoshan Weiyan 藥山惟儼, in a dialogue included in the *shinji Shōbōgenzō* 眞字正法眼藏 (DZZ.5:196, case 129) and cited often in Dōgen's writing; see Supplementary Notes, s.v. "Yaoshan's not thinking."

131 **Breaking down the rush cushion** (*ha futon* 破蒲團): I.e., long sitting on the meditation cushion.

132 **the self of a mute is not a mute** (*ashi jiko fu ashi* 啞子自己不啞子): Perhaps reflecting a saying of Zhaozhou Congshen 趙州從諗 (778-897) cited elsewhere in the *Shōbōgenzō*:

示衆云、儞若一生不離叢林、不語十年五載、無人喚儞作啞漢、已後佛也不奈儞何。

[Zhaozhou] addressed the assembly, saying, "If for a lifetime you don't leave the grove and don't talk for ten years or five years, no one will call you a mute; after that, even the buddha won't know what to make of you."

For sources of the saying, see Supplementary Notes, s.v. "For a lifetime not leaving the grove."

60. The 37 Factors of Bodhi *Sanjūshichi hon bodai bunpō* 三十七品菩提分法

realm of the mute are not mutes. It is "*not admiring the sages*"; it is "*not valuing one's own spirit.*"[133] It is exhaustive investigation of *the mouth hanging on the wall*; it is *all mouths hanging on all walls*.[134]

[60:61]
正業道支は、出家修道なり、入山取證なり。

"The correct action limb of the path" is *leaving home and practicing the way*, is *entering the mountains and getting verification*.

[60:62]
釋迦牟尼佛言、三十七品是僧業。僧業は、大乘にあらず、小乘にあらず。僧は、佛僧・菩薩僧・聲聞僧等あり。いまだ出家せざるものの、佛法の正業を嗣續せることあらず、佛法の大道を正傳せることあらず。在家、わづかに近事男女の學道といへども、達道の先蹤なし。達道のとき、かならず出家するなり。出家に不堪ならんともがら、いかでか佛位を嗣續せん。

Buddha Śākyamuni said, "The thirty-seven factors are the action of the monk."[135] "The action of the monk" is not about the Great Vehicle or the Small Vehicle: among monks, there are buddha monks, bodhisattva monks, *śrāvaka* monks, and so on. Those who have not left home have never yet succeeded to the correct action of the buddha dharma, have never yet correctly transmitted the great way of the buddha dharma. While there may have been householders who studied the way somewhat as male and female lay followers, there is no precedent of their having mastered the way. When they master the way, they invariably

---

133 **It is "not admiring the sages"; it is "not valuing one's own spirit"** (*fubo shoshō nari, fujū korei nari* 不慕諸聖なり、不重己靈なり): From a question of Shitou Xiqian 石頭希遷 to his teacher Qingyuan Xingsi 青原行思 (d. 740) (*Jingde chuandeng lu* 景德傳燈錄, T.2076.51:240b21):

不慕諸聖不重己靈時如何。

How about when one doesn't admire the sages nor value one's own spirit?

The two clauses could also read, "They [i.e., 'people in the realm of the mute'] 'do not admire the sages; they do not value their own spirit.'"

134 **the mouth hanging on the wall** (*ku ze ka heki* 口是掛壁): Variant of an idiomatic Zen expression, most often *kō ka heki jō* 口挂壁上, for keeping silent.

135 **Buddha Śākyamuni** (*Shakamuni butsu* 釋迦牟尼佛): Quoting the *Mohe zhiguan* 摩訶止觀 of Tiantai Zhiyi 天台智顗 (T.1911.46:10a4-7):

一比丘白佛、何等比丘能受供養。佛言、若在比丘數、修僧業、得僧利者、是人能受供養。四果四向是僧數、三十七品是僧業、四果是僧利。

A bhikṣu addressed the Buddha, asking, "Which bhikṣu may receive offerings?" The Buddha said, "If they are counted as bhikṣu, practice the actions of the monk, and attain the benefits of the monk, these may receive donations. Those at the four fruits and four accesses are counted as monks; the thirty-seven factors are the actions of the monk; the four fruits are the benefits of the monk."

leave home. How could those who cannot bear to leave home succeed to the rank of a buddha?

[60:63]

しかあるに、二三百年來のあひだ、大宋國に禪宗僧と稱するともがら、おほくいはく、在家の學道と出家の學道と、これ一等なり、といふ。これ、ただ在家人の屎尿を飲食とせんがために狗子となれる類族なり。あるひは國王・大臣にむかひていはく、萬機の心はすなはち祖佛心なり、さらに別心あらず、といふ。王・臣いまだ正説・正法をわきまへず、大悦して師號等をたまふ。かくのごとくの道ある諸僧は、調達なり。啼唾をくらはんがために、かくのごとくの小兒の狂話あり、啼哭といふべし。七佛の眷属にあらず、魔儻・畜生なり。いまだ身心學道をしらず、參學せず、身心出家をしらず。王・臣の、法政にくらく、佛祖の大道をゆめにもみざるによりてかくのごとし。

Nevertheless, for the last two or three hundred years, in the Land of the Great Song, many calling themselves monks of the Chan school have said that the study of the way of householders and the study of the way of renunciants are equivalent. They are a gang that has become dogs only in order to eat the shit and drink the piss of the householders. Sometimes, they tell the king and his ministers that the mind of the myriad affairs of state is the mind of the ancestors and the buddhas, apart from which there is no other mind. The king and his ministers, not having distinguished the true teaching and true dharma, are delighted and confer on them titles of master and the like. Monks with words like this are Devadattas.[136] In order to lick up snot and spittle, they have this sort of crazy talk of little children. How lamentable. They are not followers of the seven buddhas, they are the minions of Māra and beasts. They have never known studying the way with body and mind; they have not investigated, have never known, leaving home with body and mind. Things are like this because the kings and ministers are ignorant of law and governance and have never seen the great way of the buddhas and ancestors even in their dreams.[137]

[60:64] {2:142}

維摩居士の佛出世時にあふし、道未盡の法おほし、學未到すくなからず。龐蘊居士が祖席に參歴せし、藥山の、堂奥をゆるさるず、江西におよばず。ただわづかに參學の名をぬすめりといへども、參學の實あらざるなり。自餘の李駙馬・楊文公等、おのおの參飽とおもふといへども、乳餅い

---

136 **Devadattas** (*Chōdatsu* 調達): I.e., like the evil monk who plotted against his cousin, Buddha Śākyamuni.

137 **the kings and ministers are ignorant of law and governance** (*ōshin no hōsei ni kuraku* 王臣の法政にくらく): Following Kawamura's punctuation; the sentence could also be read, "They [i.e., the self-styled monks of the Chan school] are like this because they are ignorant of the law and governance of the kings and ministers and have never seen the great way of the buddhas and ancestors even in their dreams."

まだ喫せず、いはんや畫餅を喫せんや、いはんや喫佛祖粥飯せんや、未有
鉢盂なり。あはれむべし、一生の皮袋いたづらなることを。

The layman Vimalakīrti lived at the time that the Buddha appeared
in the world; there are many teachings on which his words are not yet
exhaustive, and not a few places to which his studies do not yet reach.[138]
The layman Pang Yun studied widely at the patriarchal seats; he was
not admitted to the interior of the hall of Yaoshan and did not reach
Jiangxi.[139] He may have appropriated something of a name for study
but lacked the reality of study. Others, like the Escort Li or the Duke of
Wen Yang, may each have felt they had their fill of study, but they never
tasted dairy cakes, let alone tasted the "painted cake," not to mention
*tasted the gruel and rice of the buddhas and ancestors; they never had a
pātra bowl.*[140] What a pity that these skin bags' whole lives were wasted.

[60:65]
普勸すらくは、盡十方の天衆生・人衆生・龍衆生・諸衆生、はるかに如來
の法を慕古して、いそぎて出家修道し、佛位祖位を嗣續すべし。禪師等が
未達の道をきくことなかれ。身をしらず、心をしらざるがゆゑに、しかの
ごとくいふなり。あるひは亦、すべて衆生をあはれむこころなく、佛法を

---

138 **The layman Vimalakīrti** (*Yuima koji* 維摩居士): Protagonist of the popular
Vimalakīrti-nirdeśa-sūtra (*Yuima kyō* 維摩經), in which he appears as a wealthy lay
follower of the Buddha. Dōgen's claim that Vimalakīrti was unable to express many
teachings seems to be a sarcastic reference to his famous silence when asked to explain
the teaching of nonduality. This is not the only place in the *Shōbōgenzō* where this celebrated bodhisattva comes in for criticism.

139 **The layman Pang Yun** (*Hō Un koji* 龐蘊居士): Renowned lay Chan figure (740?-
808), said to have studied under the famed masters Mazu Daoyi 馬祖道一 and Shitou
Xiqian 石頭希遷.

he was not admitted to the interior of the hall of Yaoshan and did not reach Jiangxi
(*Yakusan no, dōō o yurusarezu, Kōzei ni oyobazu* 藥山の、堂奥をゆるされず、江西に
およばず): I.e., he did not receive the personal instruction of Yaoshan Weiyan 藥山惟
儼, successor to Shitou 石頭, nor did he reach the level of his teacher Mazu of Jiangxi
江西馬祖.

140 **the Escort Li or the Duke of Wen Yang** (*Li fuba Yō bunkō* 李駙馬・楊文公):
I.e., Li Zunxu 李遵勗 (988–1038), high-ranking military officer, student of Chan master
Guyin Yuncong 谷隱蘊聰 (965-1032) and compiler of the important collection of Chan
biographies *Tiansheng guangdeng lu* 天聖廣燈錄; and Yang Yi 楊億 (974-1020), famed
literary scholar, student of Shoushan Xingnian 首山省念 (926-993) and an editor of the
Jingde chuandeng lu 景德傳燈錄, for which he wrote a preface.

"painted cake" (*gabyō* 畫餅): Best known from the saying that "a painted cake can't
satisfy hunger" (*gabyō fujū ki* 畫餅不充飢); see Supplementary Notes, s.v. "A painted
cake can't satisfy hunger." Here, likely reflecting Dōgen's opinion, as expressed in the
"Shōbōgenzō gabyō" 正法眼藏畫餅, that our hunger is itself painted and can only be sat-
isfied by a painted cake. This entire sentence is a play on the food metaphor of "studying
one's fill" (*sanpō* 參飽).

pātra **bowl** (*hou* 鉢盂): I.e., the Buddhist monk's alms bowl.

まぼるおもひなく、ただひとすぢに在家の人の屎糞をくらはんとして、惡狗となれる人面狗・人皮狗、かくのごとくいふなり。同坐すべからず、同語すべからず、同依止すべからず。かれらはすでに生身墮畜生なり。出家人もし屎糞ゆたかならば、出家人すぐれたりといはまし。出家人の屎糞、この畜生におよぼさざるゆえに、かくのごとく道取するなり。在家心と出家心と一等なり、といふこと、證據といひ、道理といひ、五千餘軸の文にみえず、二千餘年のあとなし。五十代四十餘世の佛祖、いまだその道取なし。たとひ破戒・無戒の比丘となりて、無法・無慧なりといふとも、在家の有智・持戒にはすぐるべきなり。僧業これ智なり、悟なり、道なり、法なるがゆえに。在家たとひ隨分の善根功徳あれども、身心の善根功徳おろそかなり。一代の化儀、すべて在家得道せるものなし。これ、在家いまだ學佛道の道場ならざるゆえなり、遮障おほきゆえなり。萬機心と祖師心と一等なり、と道取するともがらの身心をさぐるに、いまだ佛法の身心にあらず、佛祖の皮肉骨髄つたはれざらん。あはれむべし、佛正法にあひながら、畜生となれることを。

We widely recommend that deva beings, human beings, dragon beings, and all the beings throughout the ten directions, longing for the distant dharma of the Tathāgata, hasten to leave home, practice the way, and succeed to the rank of a buddha and the rank of an ancestor. Do not listen to the imperfect words of the Chan masters. It is because they do not know the body and do not know the mind that they talk as they do. Or, again, lacking all feeling of compassion for living beings or thought of preserving the buddha dharma, solely to feed on the excrement of householders, they have become evil dogs, dogs with human faces, dogs with human skin, who talk as they do. We should not sit with them; we should not talk with them; we should not rely on them. They have already fallen into the state of beasts while still in this body. If renunciants had more plentiful excrement, they would say that the renunciants are superior; it is because the excrement of renunciants is not enough for these beasts that they talk like this.

The claim that the mind of the householder and the mind of the renunciant are equivalent, whether in the form of evidence or of reasoning, is not to be seen in the texts of the five thousand and more scrolls and has left no trace in the two thousand and more years.[141] The buddhas and ancestors of fifty generations or of forty and more generations have never had this saying.[142] Even becoming a bhikṣu who breaks the precepts or is without the precepts, who is without dharma and without wisdom, is

---

141 **texts of the five thousand and more scrolls** (*gosen yo jiku no mon* 五千餘軸の文); **two thousand and more years** (*nisen yo nen* 二千餘年): I.e., the entire Buddhist canon and the whole of Buddhist history since Śākyamuni.

142 **The buddhas and ancestors of fifty generations or of forty and more generations** (*gojū dai shijūyo se no busso* 五十代四十餘世の佛祖): The former figure likely reckons the lineage from Buddha Śākyamuni to Dōgen's master, Tiantong Rujing 天童如淨; the latter, from the seven buddhas to the Sixth Ancestor, Huineng 慧能.

60. The 37 Factors of Bodhi *Sanjūshichi hon bodai bunpō* 三十七品菩提分法

superior to the householder having wisdom and keeping the precepts; for the action of the monk itself is wisdom, is awakening, is the way, is the dharma. Although householders have the good roots and merit appropriate to their lot, they are poor in the good roots and merit of body and mind.[143] Over a lifetime of proselytizing, there was not a single instance of a householder gaining the way.[144] This is because the householder life is not a practice place for studying the way of the buddhas, and because it presents many obstacles. If we seek out the body and mind of those who say that the mind of the myriad affairs of state and the mind of the ancestral masters are equivalent, we will find that they are not yet the body and mind of the buddha dharma, that they have not yet received transmission of the skin, flesh, bones, and marrow of the buddhas and ancestors. What a pity that, while encountering the true dharma of the buddhas, they have become beasts.

[60:66] {2:143}
かくのごとくなるによりて、曹溪古佛、たちまちに辭親尋師す、これ正業なり。金剛經をききて發心せざりしときは、樵夫として家にあり。金剛經をききて佛法の薫力あるときは、重担を放下して出家す。しるべし、身心もし佛法あるときは、在家にとどまることあたはずといふことを。諸佛祖みなかくのごとし。出家すべからず、といふともがらは、造逆よりもおもき罪條なり、調達よりも猛惡なりといふべし。六群比丘・六群尼・十八群比丘等よりもおもしとしりて、共語すべからず。一生の壽命いくばくならず、かくのごとくの魔子・畜生等と共語すべき光陰なし。いはんやこの人身心は、先世に佛法を見聞せし種子よりうけたり、公界の調度なるがごとし。魔族となすべきにあらず、魔族とともならしむべきにあらず。佛祖の深恩をわすれず、法乳の德を保護して、惡狗の叫吹をきくことなかれ、惡狗と同坐・同食することなかれ。

This being the case, the Old Buddha of Caoxi suddenly leaving his parent and seeking a master — this is "correct action."[145] When he first heard the *Diamond Sūtra* before he had brought forth the mind [of bodhi], he was living at home as a woodcutter; when he heard the *Diamond Sūtra* suffused by the power of the buddha dharma, he cast off his heavy burden and left home. We should realize that, when body and mind have the buddha dharma, one cannot remain as a householder. All the bud-

---

143 **good roots and merit appropriate to their lot** (*zuibun no zenkon kudoku* 隨分の善根功德): I.e., the karma of their status in society (as opposed here to the karma developed in spiritual practice).

144 **Over a lifetime of proselytizing** (*ichidai no kegi* 一代の化儀): I.e., the entire teaching career of Buddha Śākyamuni.

145 **Old Buddha of Caoxi** (*Sōkei kobutsu* 曹溪古佛): I.e., the Sixth Ancestor, Huineng 慧能. Dōgen here recalls the famous account of his having been inspired to abandon his mother and go off to study with the Fifth Ancestor upon hearing a monk reciting the *Diamond Sūtra*.

dhas and ancestors are like this. We should say that those who claim we should not leave home are guilty of an offense graver than committing the heinous deeds, are more fiendishly evil than Devadatta.[146] Recognizing that [their transgressions] are graver than those of the bhikṣus of the gang of six, the bhikṣuṇīs of the gang of six, or the bhikṣus of the gang of eighteen, we should not talk with them.[147] The span of a lifetime is not much; there are not years and months to spend talking with such sons of Māra and beasts. Moreover, our human bodies and minds, received due to the seeds from our experience of the buddha dharma in a previous age, are like implements in the public realm.[148] They are not to form a gang of demons; they are not to associate with a gang of demons. Without forgetting the profound benevolence of the buddhas and ancestors, preserving and protecting the virtue of the milk of dharma, do not listen to the barking of evil dogs; do not sit with or eat with evil dogs.

[60:67] {2:144}
嵩山高祖古佛、はるかに西天の佛國をはなれて、邊邦の神丹に西來するとき、佛祖の正法、まのあたりつたはれしなり。これ出家得道にあらずば、かくのごとくなるべからず。祖師西來已前は、東地の衆生・人天、いまだかつて正法を見聞せず。しかあればしるべし、正法正傳、ただこれ出家の功德なり。

When the Old Buddha, the Eminent Ancestor of Mount Song, left the buddha land of Sindh in the West far behind and came from the west to the marginal country of Cīnasthāna, the true dharma of the buddhas and ancestors was directly transmitted.[149] Had he not left home and gained

---

146　**committing the heinous deeds** (*zōgyaku* 造逆): Reference to the five heinous crimes (*gogyaku* 五逆), the commission of which leads to rebirth in the avīci hell: patricide, matricide, killing an arhat, injuring a buddha, and damaging the saṃgha.

147　**the bhikṣus of the gang of six, the *bhikṣuṇīs* of the gang of six, or the bhikṣus of the gang of eighteen** (*rokugun biku rokugun ni jūhachigun biku* 六群比丘・六群尼・十八群比丘): A gang of six evil bhikṣus at the time of the Buddha appears frequently in Buddhist literature, with somewhat varied names; a set of (unidentified) transgressive bhikṣuṇis also appears frequently, often in conjunction with the six bhikṣus. A set of eighteen evil monks is not common in the literature (though we do find mention of a gang of seventeen [or sixteen]), and it is not clear where Dōgen got this number.

148　**implements in the public realm** (*kugai no chōdo* 公界の調度): Presumably, meaning something like "our bodies and minds are not our own but belong to the dharma." The term "public realm" (*kugai* 公界), while also used in reference to society at large, refers in a monastic setting to the common facilities in use by the saṃgha as a whole; see Supplementary Notes, s.v. "Public realm."

149　**the Old Buddha, the Eminent Ancestor of Mount Song** (*Sūzan kōso kobutsu* 嵩山高祖古佛) I.e., the First Ancestor, Bodhidharma, who resided on Mount Song 嵩山.

buddha land of Sindh in the West (*Saiten no bukkoku* 西天の佛國): I.e., India, the homeland of the Buddha.

60. The 37 Factors of Bodhi *Sanjūshichi hon bodai bunpō* 三十七品菩提分法

the way, this could not have happened. Before the Ancestral Master came from the west, beings of the Land of the East, human and deva, had never experienced the true dharma. Thus, we should recognize the direct transmission of the true dharma is due to the merit of leaving home.

[60:68]

大師釋尊、かたじけなく父王のくらい[位]をすてて嗣續せざることは、王位の、貴ならざるにあらず、佛位の、最貴なるを嗣續せんがためなり。佛位は、これ出家位なり、三界の天衆生・人衆生、ともに頂戴恭敬するくらゐなり。梵王・釋王の、同坐するところにあらず、いはんや下界の諸人王・諸龍王の、同坐するくらゐならんや、無上正等覺位なり。くらゐ、よく説法度生し、放光現瑞す。この出家位の諸業、これ正業なり、諸佛七佛の懷業なり。唯佛與佛にあらざれば、究盡せざるところなり。いまだ出家せざらんともがらは、すでに出家せるに奉覲給仕し、頭頂敬禮し、身命を抛捨して供養すべし。

The great master, Śākya, the Honored One, humbly declined to succeed to the rank of his father the king, not because the rank of king was not exalted, but in order to succeed to the highest rank of buddha. The rank of buddha is the rank of a renunciant, a rank respectfully honored by deva beings and human beings of the three realms. It is not one in which King Brahmā or King Śakra share the seat, much less is it a rank in which the human kings and dragon kings of lower realms share the seat; it is the rank of unsurpassed, perfect awakening.[150] This rank preaches the dharma and delivers living beings, radiates light and manifests auspicious signs. The action of this rank of renunciant — this is "correct action," the action cherished by the buddhas, by the seven buddhas. It is something not "exhaustively investigated" by those who are not "*only buddhas with buddhas.*"[151] Those who have not left home should attend and serve those who have left home, should prostrate and pay obeisance to them, should cast aside their very lives in offering.

---

150 **King Brahmā or King Śakra** (*Bonnō Shakuō* 梵王・釋王): King of the devas of the brahmā heaven in the first dhyāna heaven of the form realm, and king of the heaven of the thirty-three devas (S. *Trāyastriṃśa*) in the desire realm, respectively.

151 **It is something not "exhaustively investigated" by those who are not "only buddhas with buddhas"** (*yui butsu yo butsu ni arazareba, gūjin sezaru tokoro nari* 唯佛與佛にあらざれば、究盡せざるところなり): From the *Lotus Sūtra* line; see Supplementary Notes, s.v. "Only buddhas with buddhas can exhaustively investigate the real marks of the dharmas."

[60:69] {2:145}

釋迦牟尼佛言、出家受戒、是佛種子也、已得度人。

 Buddha Śākyamuni said, "*To leave home and receive the precepts is the seed of buddhahood. One has already attained deliverance.*"[152]

[60:70]

しかあればすなはちしるべし、得度といふは、出家なり。未出家は沈淪にあり、かなしむべし。おほよそ一代の佛説のなかに、出家の功徳を讚歎せること、稱計すべからず。釋尊誠説し、諸佛證明す。出家人の破戒不修なるは、得道す、在家人の得道、いまだあらず。帝者の、僧尼を禮拜するとき、僧尼、答拜せず。諸天の、出家人を拜するに、比丘・比丘尼、またく答拜せず。これ、出家の功徳すぐれたるゆえなり。もし出家の比丘・比丘尼に拜せられば、諸天の宮殿・光明・果報等、たちまちに破壞墜堕すべきがゆえに、かくのごとし。

 Thus, we should recognize that "attaining deliverance" is "leaving home"; those who have not yet left home are sunk and are to be pitied. In general, in the Buddha's preaching over a lifetime, the number of times he praised the merits of leaving home cannot be reckoned. Śākya, the Honored One, preached it with sincerity, and the buddhas attested it. Renunciants who broke the precepts and did not practice have gained the way, while there has never been a householder who gained the way. When the emperor pays obeisance to the monk or nun, the monk or nun does not bow in return. When the devas pay obeisance to the renunciant, the bhikṣu or *bhikṣuṇī* never bows in return; for the merit of the renunciant is superior. This is so because, were they to receive the bows of the bhikṣu or *bhikṣuṇī*, their palaces, radiance, karmic rewards, and the like, would immediately disintegrate and collapse.

[60:71]

おほよそ佛法東漸よりこのかた、出家人の得道は、稻麻竹葦のごとし。在家ながら得道せるもの、一人もいまだあらず。すでに佛法その眼耳におよぶときは、いそぎて出家をいとなむ。はかりしりぬ、在家は佛法の在處にあらず。しかあるに、萬機の身心すなはち佛祖の身心なり、といふやからは、いまだかつて佛法を見聞せざるなり、黒闇獄の罪人なり、おのれが言語、なほ見聞せざる愚人なり、國賊なり。萬機の心をもて佛祖の心に同ずるを詮とするは、佛法のすぐれたるによりて、しかいふを帝者よろこぶ。しるべし、佛法すぐれたりといふこと。萬機の心は、假令おのづから佛祖の心に同ずとも、佛祖の身心おのづから萬機の身心とならんとき、萬機の身心なるべからず。萬機心と佛祖心と一等なり、といふ禪師等、すべて心法のゆきかた、樣子をしらざるなり。いはんや、佛祖心をゆめにもみることあらんや。

 In general, ever since the buddha dharma's spread to the east, the renunciants who gained the way are like "rice, hemp, bamboo, and reeds,"

---

152 **Buddha Śākyamuni** (*Shakamuni butsu* 釋迦牟尼佛): Source unknown.

while there has not been a single person who gained the way as a householder.[153] As soon as the buddha dharma reaches their eyes and ears, they hasten to leave home. We should realize that the householder life is no place for the buddha dharma. Those who nevertheless claim that the body and mind of the myriad affairs of state are the body and mind of the buddhas and ancestors have never seen or heard the buddha dharma; they are evil people in a dark hell; they are ignoramuses who do not see and hear even their own words; they are traitors to the country. They assert that the mind of the myriad affairs of state is the same as the mind of the buddhas and ancestors since the emperors are delighted to hear this said, precisely because the buddha dharma is superior. We should realize that the buddha dharma is superior. Even if the mind of the myriad affairs of state happened to be the same as the mind of the buddhas and ancestors, when the body and mind of the buddhas and ancestors happens to become the body and mind of the myriad affairs of state, it will not be the body and mind of the myriad affairs of state.[154] The Chan masters who claim that the mind of the myriad affairs of state and the mind of the buddhas and ancestors are equivalent know nothing of how the mind works or what it is like; how much less have they seen the mind of the buddhas and ancestors even in their dreams.

[60:72] {2:146}
おほよそ梵王・釋王・人王・龍王・鬼神王等、おのおの三界の果報に著することなかれ。はやく出家受戒して、諸佛諸祖の道を修習すべし、曠大劫の佛因ならん。みずや、維摩老、もし出家せましかば、維摩よりもすぐれたる維摩比丘をみん。今日はわづかに空生・舍利子・文殊・彌勒等をみる、いまだ半維摩をみず。いはんや三四五の維摩をみんや。もし三四五の維摩をみず、しらざれば、一維摩いまだみず、しらず、保任せざるなり。一維摩いまだ保任せざれば、維摩佛をみず。維摩佛をみざれば、維摩文殊・維摩彌勒・維摩善現・維摩舍利子等、いまだあらざるなり。いはんや維摩山河大地、維摩草木瓦礫・風雨水火・過去現在未來等あらんや。維摩、いまだこれらの光明功徳みえざることは、不出家のゆえなり。維摩、もし出家せば、これらの功徳あるべきなり。當時、唐朝・宋朝の禪師等、これらの宗旨に達せず、みだりに維摩を擧して作得是とおもひ、道得是といふ。これらのともがら、あはれむべし、言教をしらず、佛法にくらし。

---

153 **"rice, hemp, bamboo, and reeds"** (*tō ma chiku i* 稲麻竹葦): I.e., they are dense and profuse; a simile from Kumārajīva's translation of the *Lotus Sūtra*; see Supplementary Notes.

154 **Even if the mind of the myriad affairs of state happened to be the same as the mind of the buddhas and ancestors** (*banki no shin wa, keryō onozukara busso no shin ni dōzu tomo* 萬機の心は、假令おのづから佛祖の心に同ずとも): This sentence might be understood to be saying that, even were emperors occasionally to think like Buddhist adepts, when Buddhist adepts occasionally concern themselves with affairs of state, they never think like emperors.

In sum, [we urge] King Brahmā, King Śakra, human kings, dragon kings, demon kings, and the like: do not be attached to your particular karmic consequences in the three realms. You should quickly leave home, receive the precepts, and study the way of the buddhas and ancestors, the cause of buddhahood for vast kalpas. Do you not see that, had old Vimalakīrti left home, we would see a bhikṣu Vimalakīrti superior to Vimalakīrti? Today, we see merely Subhūti, Śāriputra, Mañjuśrī, Maitreya, and the rest; we do not see even half a Vimalakīrti, let alone see three, four or five Vimalakīrtis.[155] If we do not see, do not know, three, four or five Vimalakīrtis, then we have not seen, known or maintained, a single Vimalakīrti. If we have not maintained a single Vimalakīrti, we do not see Buddha Vimalakīrti. If we do not see Buddha Vimalakīrti, then Mañjuśrī Vimalakīrti, Maitreya Vimalakīrti, Subhūti Vimalakīrti, Śāriputra Vimalakīrti, and the rest, do not yet exist. How much less could there be Vimalakīrti of mountains, rivers, and the whole earth; Vimalakīrti of grass, trees, tiles, and pebbles, of wind, rain, water, and fire, of past, present, and future, and so on? That such radiance and virtues are not seen in Vimalakīrti is because he did not leave home; had he left home, he should have these virtues. Now, the Chan masters of the Tang dynasty and Song dynasty, having failed to master these essential points, rashly hold up Vimalakīrti, thinking that what he did was right, and saying that what he said was right. These types are to be pitied: they do not know the spoken teachings and are ignorant of the buddha dharma.

[60:73]
あるいは亦あまりさへは、維摩と釋尊と、その道ひとしとおもひいへるおほし。これらまた、いまだ佛法をしらず、祖道をしらず、維摩をもしらず、はからざるなり。かれらいはく、維摩、黙然無言して諸菩薩にしめす、これ如來の無言爲人にひとし、といふ。これ、おほきに佛法をしらず、學道の力量なし、といふべし。如來の有言、すでに自餘とことなり、無言もまた諸類とひとしかるべからず。しかあれば、如來の一黙と維摩の一黙と、相似の比論にすらおよぶべからず。言説はことなりとも、黙然はひとしかるべし、と憶想せるともがらの力量をさぐるには、佛邊人とするにもおよばざるなり。かなしむべし、かれらいまだ聲色の見聞なし、いはんや跳聲色の光明あらんや。いはんや黙の黙を學すべしとだにもしらず、ありとだにもきかず。おほよそ諸類と諸類と、その動靜なほことなり、いかでか釋尊と諸類とおなじといひ、おなじからずと比論せん。これ佛祖の堂奧に參學せざるともがら、かくのごとくいふなり。

---

155 **Today, we see merely Subhūti, Śāriputra, Mañjuśrī, Maitreya, and the rest** (*konnichi wa wazuka ni Kūshō Sharishi Monju Miroku tō o miru* 今日はわづかに空生・舎利子・文殊・彌勒等をみる): Likely meaning that one finds regular mention of these famous monks in the Buddhist sūtras but not of Vimalakīrti (who, of course, is a literary creation of the *Vimalakīrti Sūtra*).

Then, on top of that, there are many who think and who say that the words of Vimalakīrti and Śākya, the Honored One, are equivalent. These also have never known the buddha dharma, never known the way of the ancestors, never known or evaluated Vimalakīrti. They say that Vimalakīrti's instructing the bodhisattvas in silence, without a word, is equivalent to the Tathāgata's being without a word for the sake of the other. This has to be called knowing nothing of the buddha dharma and having no ability to study the way. Since the words of the Tathāgata are different from those of others, his wordlessness must also not be the equivalent of other types. Thus, the silence of the Tathāgata and the silence of Vimalakīrti do not even warrant a comparison of their similarities. When we seek out the abilities of those who imagine that, while their speech is different, their silence must be equivalent, they do not amount even to those we might take to be in the vicinity of the Buddha. How sad! They have yet to see and hear the sights and sounds, let alone have the radiance springing forth from sights and sounds. Not to mention that they do not even know that we should study the silence of silence, have not even heard that it exists.[156] In general, the various types differ in their behaviors; how could we compare Śākya, the Honored One, and the various types, saying they are the same or not the same? It is those who do not study in the interior of the hall of the buddhas and ancestors who talk like this.

[60:74] {2:147}
あるいは邪人おほくおもはく、言説動容はこれ假法なり、寂默凝然はこれ眞實なり。かくのごとくいふ、また佛法にあらず。梵天・自在天等の經教を傳聞せるともがらの所計なり。佛法いかでか動靜にかかはらん。佛道に動靜ありや、動靜なしや、動靜を接すや、動靜に接せらるや、と審細に參學すべし。而今の晩學、たゆむことなかれ。

Or, again, there are many misguided people who think that speech and behavior are provisional dharmas, whereas silence and stillness are true reality. Talk like this is also not the buddha dharma; it is the thinking of those who have heard the scriptures of the deva Brahmā or the deva Īśvara, and the like.[157] How could the buddha dharma be concerned with movement and stillness? In the way of the buddhas, is there motion and stillness or is there not motion and stillness? Does it engage with motion and stillness? Is it engaged by motion and stillness? We should study this in detail. Late students of the present, do not be lax.

---

156 **we should study the silence of silence** (*moku no moku o gakusu beshi* 默の默を學すべし): This phrase might also be parsed, "silence should study silence."

157 **the scriptures of the deva Brahmā or the deva Īśvara, and the like** (*Bonten Jizaiten tō no kyōgyō* 梵天・自在天等の經教): I.e., the texts of Hinduism.

[60:75]

現在大宋國をみるに、佛祖の大道を參學せるともがら、斷絶せるがごとし、兩三箇あるにあらず。維摩は是にして一黙あり、いまは一黙せざるは維摩よりも劣なり、とおもへるともがらのみあり、さらに佛法の活路なし。あるいは亦、維摩の一黙はすなはち世尊の一黙なり、とおもふともがらのみあり、さらに分別の光明あらざるなり。かくのごとくおもひ、いふともがら、すべて、いまだかつて佛法見聞の參學なし、といふべし。大宋國人にあればとて、佛法なるらん、とおもふことなかれ。その道理、あきらめやすかるべし。

When we look at the Land of the Great Song at present, it is as if those who study the great way of the buddhas and ancestors are extinct, with not even two or three remaining. There are only those who think that Vimalakīrti was right in his silence, while now those who are not silent are inferior to Vimalakīrti; they are completely without the life-saving path of the buddha dharma. Or, again, there are only those who think that the silence of Vimalakīrti is the silence of the World-Honored One; they are completely without the light of discrimination.[158] It must be said that those who think and talk like this have no study of the experience of the buddha dharma. Do not think that, because they are people of the Land of the Great Song, [what they say] is the buddha dharma. The truth of this should be easy to understand.

[60:76] {2:148}

いはゆる、正業は僧業なり、論師・經師のしるところにあらず。僧業といふは、雲堂裏の功夫なり、佛殿裏の禮拜なり、後架裏の洗面なり。乃至、合掌・問訊・焼香・焼湯する、これ正業なり。以頭換尾するのみにあらず、以頭換頭なり、以心換心なり、以佛換佛なり、以道換道なり、これすなはち正業道支なり。あやまりて佛法の商量すれば、眉鬚堕落し、面目破顔するなり。

"Correct action" is the action of the monk, not what is known by the treatise master or sūtra master.[159] The action of the monk is concentrated effort in the cloud hall; it is paying obeisance in the buddha hall; it is washing the face at the rear stand; and so on, to joining the palms and making inquiries, burning incense and boiling water — these are "correct action."[160] They are not only *exchanging head for tail*; they are

---

158 **silence of the World-Honored One** (*seson no ichimoku* 世尊の一黙): Presumably, reference to the fourteen "indeterminate" (*muki* 無記; S. *avyākṛta*) questions on which the Buddha abstained from comment.

159 **"Correct action" is the action of the monk** (*iwayuru, shōgō wa sōgō nari* いはゆる、正業は僧業なり): This sentence could be read with the last sentence of the preceding section: "The truth of this should be easy to understand: that is, "correct action" is the action of the monk, not what is known by the treatise master or sūtra master.

160 **concentrated effort in the cloud hall** (*undō ri no kufū* 雲堂裏の功夫): I.e., meditation in the saṃgha hall.

exchanging head for head; they are exchanging mind for mind; they are exchanging buddha for buddha; they are exchanging the way for the way.¹⁶¹ This is "the correct action limb of the path." When we mistakenly deliberate about the buddha dharma, our eyebrows and beard will fall off and our face will break up.¹⁶²

[60:77]
正命道支とは、早朝粥・午時飯なり、在叢林弄精魂なり、曲木座上直指なり。老趙州の不滿二十衆、これ正命の現成なり。薬山の不滿十衆、これ正命の命脈なり。汾陽の七八衆、これ正命のかかれるところなり。もろもろの邪命をはなれたるがゆえに。

The "the correct livelihood limb of the path" is *gruel in the morning and rice at noon*; it is *staying in the grove, toying with the spirit*; it is *pointing directly from the curved wood chair*.¹⁶³ Old Zhaozhou's assembly of less than twenty; this is the realization of correct livelihood.¹⁶⁴ Yaoshan's assembly of less than ten; this is the vital artery of correct livelihood.¹⁶⁵ Fenyang's assembly of seven or eight; this is where correct livelihood rests.¹⁶⁶ For they are free from all wrong livelihood.¹⁶⁷

washing the face at the rear stand (*goka ri no senmen* 後架裏の洗面): I.e., ablutions at the sink at the rear of the saṃgha hall.

joining the palms and making inquiries (*gasshō monjin* 合掌問訊): I.e., greeting one another with a bow.

161   **exchanging head for tail** (*i tō kan bi* 以頭換尾): A Chinese colloquialism meaning "to get something backwards." The subsequent phrases are Dōgen's variations.

162   **our eyebrows and beard will fall off and our face will break up** (*bishu daraku shi, menmoku hagan suru* 眉鬚堕落し、面目破顔する): The former phrase occurs often in Zen texts as the consequence of a mistake; the latter phrase is unusual, and the likely sense of *hagan* 破顔 (normally, "break into a smile") here does not seem to occur elsewhere in the literature.

163   **gruel in the morning and rice at noon** (*sōchō shuku goji han* 早朝粥午時飯); **staying in the grove, playing with the spirit** (*zai sōrin rō zeikon* 在叢林弄精魂); **pointing directly from the curved wood chair** (*kyokumoku zajō jikishi* 曲木座上直指): Three six-character Chinese phrases on the monastic life. The "grove" (*sōrin* 叢林) is a standard expression for the monastery; "playing with the spirit" (*rō zeikon* 弄精魂) is a common sarcastic reference to meditation. The "curved wood chair" (*shukumoku za* 曲木座) is the seat from which the master teaches.

164   **Old Zhaozhou's assembly of less than twenty** (*rō Jōshū no fuman nijū shu* 老趙州の不滿二十衆): Reference to the community of Zhaozhou Congshen 趙州從諗, the small size of which is also noted in "Shōbōgenzō hakujushi" 正法眼藏柏樹子.

165   **Yaoshan's assembly of less than ten** (*Yakusan no fuman jū shu* 藥山の不滿十衆): The community of Yaoshan Weiyan 藥山惟儼.

166   **Fenyang's assembly of seven or eight** (*Funyō no shichi hachi shu* 汾陽の七八衆): The community of Fenyang Shanzhao 汾陽善昭 (947-1024).

167   **wrong livelihood** (*jamyō* 邪命): A term traditionally referring to improper ways of making a living for a bhikṣu or *bhikṣuṇī*.

[60:78]

釋迦牟尼佛言、諸聲聞人、未得正命。

Buddha Śākyamuni said, "*Śrāvakas* have not yet attained correct livelihood."[168]

[60:79] {2:149}

しかあればすなはち、聲聞の教・行・證、いまだ正命にあらざるなり。しかあるを、近日庸流いはく、聲聞・菩薩を分別すべからず、その威儀・戒律、ともにもちゐるべし、といひて、小乘聲聞の法をもて、大乘菩薩法の威儀・進止を判ず。

Thus, the teaching, practice, and verification of the *śrāvaka* are not yet "correct livelihood." Nevertheless, mediocrities in recent days, declaring that we should not distinguish between *śrāvaka* and bodhisattva, but should follow the deportment and precepts of both, use the dharma of the *śrāvaka* of the Small Vehicle to judge the deportment and behavior of the bodhisattva of the Great Vehicle.

[60:80]

釋迦牟尼佛言、聲聞持戒、菩薩破戒。

Buddha Śākyamuni said, "The *śrāvaka* keeps the precepts; the bodhisattva breaks the precepts."[169]

[60:81]

しかあれば、聲聞の持戒とおもへる、もし菩薩戒に比望するがごときは、聲聞戒みな破戒なり。自餘の定慧も、またかくのごとし。たとひ不殺生等の相、おのづから聲聞と菩薩あひにたりとも、かならず別なるべきなり、天地懸隔の論におよぶべからざるなり。いはんや佛佛祖祖正傳の宗旨と諸聲聞と、ひとしからんや。正命のみにあらず、清淨命あり。しかあればすなはち、佛祖に參學するのみ、正命なるべし。論師等の見解、もちゐるべからず、未得正命なるがゆゑに、本分命にあらず。

Thus, were we to compare what is thought of as the *śrāvaka*'s keeping the precepts with the bodhisattva precepts, the *śrāvaka* precepts are

---

168 **Buddha Śākyamuni** (Śākyamuni butsu 釋迦牟尼佛): Source unknown.

169 **Buddha Śākyamuni** (Śākyamuni butsu 釋迦牟尼佛): Perhaps based (very loosely) on a passage in the *Ratnakūṭa-sūtra* (*Da baoji jing* 大寶積經, T.310:11.516c19-22):

爾時世尊告優波離、汝今當知、聲聞菩薩學清淨戒、所發心所修行異。優波離、有聲聞乘持清淨戒、於菩薩乘名大破戒。有菩薩乘持清淨戒、於聲聞乘名大破戒。

At that time, the World-Honored One addressed Upāli, saying, "Now you should know that, while the *śrāvaka* and the bodhisattva study the pure precepts, what they aspire to and what they practice are different. Upāli, keeping the pure precepts in the *śrāvaka* vehicle is called seriously breaking the precepts in the bodhisattva vehicle; and keeping the pure precepts in the bodhisattva vehicle is called seriously breaking the precepts in the *śrāvaka* vehicle."

all "breaking the precepts." The others, concentration and wisdom, are also like this.[170] Even though the forms of not taking life and the rest happen to resemble each other for the *śrāvaka* and the bodhisattva, they are necessarily different; we cannot even discuss it in terms of the gap between heaven and earth.[171] How much less could the instruction directly transmitted by buddha after buddha and ancestor after ancestor be equivalent to that of the *śrāvakas*. It is not only correct livelihood; there is pure livelihood.[172] Thus, only studying with the buddhas and ancestors is correct livelihood. Do not use the interpretation of the treatise masters and the like; since they have not attained correct livelihood, it is not the livelihood of the original lot.[173]

[60:82]
正精進道支とは、抉出通身の行李なり、抉出通身打人面なり。倒騎佛殿打一匝、兩匝三四五匝なるがゆえに、九九算來八十二なり、重報君の千萬條なり、換頭也十字縱橫なり、換面也縱橫十字なり、入室來・上堂來なり、望州亭相見了なり、烏石嶺相見了なり。僧堂前相見了なり、佛殿裏相見了なり。兩鏡相對して三枚影あるをいふ。

"The correct effort limb of the path" means the observance of gouging out the body throughout; it means *gouging out the body throughout and hitting the person's face*.[174] Since it means *riding backwards in the buddha hall, circling it once, circling it twice, circling it three, four or five times, it is nine nines adding up to eighty-two*.[175] It means "repeatedly

170 **The others, concentration and wisdom** (*jiyo no jō e* 自餘の定慧): I.e., the other two members of the threefold discipline of precepts (*kai* 戒), meditation (*jō* 定), and wisdom (*e* 慧).

171 **the forms of not taking life and the rest** (*fusesshō tō no sō* 不殺生等の相): I.e., the form in which the precept against killing and the other precepts are given.

172 **It is not only correct livelihood; there is pure livelihood** (*shōmyō nomi ni arazu, shōjōmyō ari* 正命のみにあらず、清淨命あり): The sense is not certain; perhaps the claim is that livelihood in the tradition of the buddhas and ancestors has a purity that goes beyond the merely correct livelihood of the precepts.

173 **livelihood of the original lot** (*honbun myō* 本分命): An unusual expression, perhaps meaning something like "authentic livelihood." The term *honbun* 本分 ("original lot") is used in reference to one's fundamental nature, what one truly is.

174 **gouging out the body throughout and hitting the person's face** (*kesshutsu tsūshin ta ninmen* 抉出通身打人面): Variation on the words of Tiantong Rujing 天童如淨; see Supplementary Notes, s.v. "Gouge out Bodhidharma's eye." In his discussion of this saying in "Shōbōgenzō ganzei" 正法眼藏眼睛, Dōgen glosses the predicate *tanin* 打人 ("hit people") here as "to make people"; hence, our passage might be rendered, "gouging out the entire body and making a person's face of it." For the expression *tsūshin* 通身 ("body throughout"), see Supplementary Notes, s.v. "His body throughout is hands and eyes."

175 **riding backwards in the buddha hall** (*tōki butsuden* 倒騎佛殿): A common image in Zen literature for the untrammeled action of the adept; see, e.g., *Biyan lu* 碧巖

repaying the lord" a thousand myriad times; it means *changing the head is crisscross, vertical and horizontal*; *changing the face is "vertical and horizontal, crisscross."*[176] It is *entering the room and ascending to the hall.*[177] It is *"having met at Wangzhou pavilion"*; it is *"having met at Wushi ridge"*; it is *"having met in front of the monks' hall"*; it is *having met inside the buddha hall.*[178] It means *two mirrors facing each other and three reflections.*[179]

錄, T.2003.48:211c17:

倒騎牛兮入佛殿

Riding backwards on an ox, entering the buddha hall.

nine nines adding up to eighty-two (*kyū kyū sanrai hachijūni* 九九算來八十二): Play on a saying of Yunmen Wenyen 雲門文偃 (864-949) (*Yunmen Kuangzhen chanshi guanglu* 雲門匡眞禪師廣錄, T.1988.47:545c4):

問、如何是向上一路。師云、九九八十一。

[Someone] asked, "What is the one road beyond?"
The Master said, "Nine nines are eighty-one."

176 **"repeatedly repaying the lord"** (*jū hō kun* 重報君); **changing the head is crisscross, vertical and horizontal** (*kantō ya jūji jūō* 換頭也十字縱橫); **"changing the face is vertical and horizontal, crisscross"** (*kanmen ya jūō jūji* 換面也縱橫十字): Dōgen seems here to be reflecting capping phrases by Xuedou Zhongxian 雪竇重顯 (980-1052) on the *Cantong qi* 參同契 of Shitou Xiqian 石頭希遷 (*Mingjue chanshi yulu* 明覺禪師語錄, T.1996.47:697b6):

然於一一法(重報君)。

Thus, for each and every dharma (repeatedly repaying the lord).

And T.1996.47:697b10):

當言用及處(縱橫十字)。

Expressed according to function and place (vertical and horizontal, crisscross).

For the expressions "changing the head" (*kantō* 換頭) and "changing the face" (*kanmen* 換面), see Supplementary Notes, s.v. "Turning the head and changing the face."

177 **entering the room and ascending to the hall** (*nisshitsu rai jōdō rai* 入室來・上堂來): I.e., the student entering the abbot's quarters for personal instruction, and the master delivering a formal convocation address in the dharma hall.

178 **"having met at Wangzhou pavilion"** (*Bōshū tei shōken ryō* 望州亭相見了): This and the following clauses of this sentence reflect the words of Xuefeng Yicun 雪峰義存 (822-908), e.g., at *shinji Shōbōgenzō* 眞字正法眼藏 (DZZ.5:272, case 290):

雪峰示衆云、望州亭與諸人相見了也、烏石嶺與諸人相見了也、僧堂前與諸人相見了也。

Xuefeng addressed the assembly, saying, "I met everyone in front of the saṃgha hall. I met everyone at Wangzhou Pavilion. I met everyone at Wushi Ridge."

Wangzhou Pavilion (*Bōshū tei* 望州亭) and Wushi Ridge (*Useki rei* 烏石嶺) are spots renowned for their beauty — the former at Xuefeng 雪峰; the latter, probably the mountain of that name in Fujian.

179 **two mirrors facing each other and three reflections** (*ryōkyō sōtai shite sanmai yō aru* 兩鏡相對して三枚影ある): "Two mirrors facing each other" is a common image in Buddhist texts, though the "three reflections" here is unusual.

60. The 37 Factors of Bodhi *Sanjūshichi hon bodai bunpō* 三十七品菩提分法

[60:83]
正念道支は、被自瞞の八九成なり。念よりさらに發智すると學するは、捨父逃逝なり、念中發智と學するは、纏縛之甚なり。無念はこれ正念、といふは、外道なり。また、地水火風の精靈を念とすべからず、心意識の顛倒を念と稱せず。まさに汝得吾皮肉骨髓、すなはち正念道支なり。

"The correct mindfulness limb of the path" is eight- or nine-tenths deceived by yourself. To study that wisdom is generated after mindfulness is *"abandoning the father and running away"*; to study that wisdom is generated in the midst of mindfulness is *bondage in the extreme*.[180] To say that no thought is correct mindfulness is an other path.[181] Again, we should not take the spirits of earth, water, fire, and wind as mindfulness; we do not designate as mindfulness the inverted views of mind, mentation, and consciousness.[182] Truly, *you've gotten my skin, flesh, bones, and marrow* is "the correct mindfulness limb of the path."[183]

[60:84] {2:150}
正定道支とは、脱落佛祖なり、脱落正定なり、他是能擧なり、剖來頂顙作鼻孔なり。正法眼藏裏拈優曇華なり。優曇華裏有百千枚迦葉破顏微笑なり、活計ひさしくもちいきたりて、木杓破なり。このゆえに、落草六年、華開一夜なり、劫火洞然、大千俱壞、隨他去なり。

"The correct concentration limb of the path" means sloughing off the buddhas and ancestors; it means sloughing off correct concentration; it means *he can take it up*; it means *splitting the crown of the head to make*

---

180 **"abandoning the father and running away"** (*shafu tōzei* 捨父逃逝): From the famous parable of the prodigal son in the *Lotus Sūtra* (*Miaofa lianhua jing* 妙法蓮華經, T.262.9:16b26).

181 **To say that no thought is correct mindfulness is an other path** (*munen wa kore shōnen, to iu wa, gedō nari* 無念はこれ正念、といふは、外道なり): "Other path" renders *gedō* 外道, used in reference to non-Buddhist religions (S. *tīrthika*). The celebration of "no thought" (*munen* 無念) was a common feature of some early Chan texts, especially of the Southern School, though it is not clear whether Dōgen had a particular example in mind here. The translation masks the play here with the term *nen* 念: the passage could as well be read "no thought is correct thought" or "no mindfulness is correct mindfulness."

182 **inverted views of mind, mentation, and consciousness** (*shin i shiki no tendō* 心意識の顛倒): I.e., our ordinary deluded states of mind. "Inverted" renders *tendō* 顛倒 (S. *viparyasta*), used for views that are "upside down," or, as we might say, "just backwards."

183 **you've gotten my skin, flesh, bones, and marrow** (*nyo toku go hi niku kotsu zui* 汝得吾皮肉骨髓): From the famous story, known as *Daruma hi niku kotsu zui* 達摩皮肉骨髓, of Bodhidharma's testing of four disciples, to whom he said of each in turn that he (or, in one case, she) had gotten his skin, flesh, bones, and marrow. See *shinji Shōbōgenzō* 眞字正法眼藏, DZZ.5:230, case 201; and Supplementary Notes, s.v. "Skin, flesh, bones, and marrow."

a nostril.¹⁸⁴ It is *holding up an udumbara flower within the treasury of the true dharma eye; it is a hundred thousand Kāśyapas breaking into a smile within the udumbara flower.*¹⁸⁵ Long used in this way of life, the wooden ladle is *broken*.¹⁸⁶ Therefore, it is *lurking in the grass for six years; the flower opening in a single night.*¹⁸⁷ It is "*when the conflagration at the end of the kalpa rages, and the chiliocosm is all destroyed,*" "*go along with it.*"¹⁸⁸

* * * * *

184   **he can take it up** (*ta ze nō ko* 他是能舉): Perhaps reflecting another of Xuedou's 雪竇 capping phrases on the *Cantong qi* 參同契 (see above, Note 176) (*Mingjue chanshi yulu* 明覺禪師語錄, T.1996.47:697a27):

竺土大仙心（誰是能舉）

The mind of the great sage of Sindhu (who can take this up?).

splitting the crown of the head to make nostrils (*bōrai chōnei sa bikū* 剖來頂顙作鼻孔): This and the following two phrases are given in Chinese, as if quoting a text, but no source is known. See Supplementary Notes, s.v. "Crown of the head," "Nose."

185   **holding up an *udumbara* flower within the treasury of the true dharma eye** (*Shōbōgenzō ri nen udonge* 正法眼藏裏拈優曇華): This and the next phrase play on the famous legend of the first transmission of Zen on Vulture Peak, in which Śākyamuni held up a flower (in Dōgen's version, identified as an *udumbara* blossom) and his disciple Mahākāśyapa smiled. See Supplementary Notes, s.v. "Hold up a flower."

186   **the wooden ladle is broken** (*mokushaku ha* 木杓破): The "broken wooden ladle" (*ha mokushaku* 破木杓) is regularly used in Zen texts for something worthless (often in an ironic positive sense).

187   **lurking in the grass for six years; the flower opening in a single night** (*raku sō rokunen, ke kai ichiya* 落草六年、華開一夜): Reference to the six years Prince Siddhārtha spent in spiritual practice and the night of his awakening under the bodhi tree. The expression "lurking in the grass for six years" (*raku sō rokunen* 落草六年) likely reflects a line of verse by Tiantong Rujing 天童如淨 (*Rujing heshang yulu* 如淨和尚語錄, T.2002A.48:122b14) quoted elsewhere in the *Shōbōgenzō*:

六年落草野狐精

For six years, a fox spirit, lurking in the grass.

"The flower opening in a single night" is also reminiscent of the verse by Xuedou Zhijian 雪竇智鑑 (1105-1192) (at *Jiatai pudeng lu* 嘉泰普燈錄, ZZ.137:258a2-3) that Dōgen quotes in his "Shōbōgenzō mitsugo 密語":

The World-Honored One has secret words;
For Kāśyapa, they are not concealed.
Throughout the night, a rain of falling blossoms;
In the whole city, the streams are fragrant.

188   **"when the conflagration at the end of kalpa rages, and the chiliocosm is all destroyed," "go along with it"** (*kōka tōnen, daisen ku e, zui ta ko* 劫火洞然、大千俱壞、隨他去): From a conversation involving Dasui Fazhen 大隋法眞 (834-919) cited in Dōgen's *shinji Shōbōgenzō* 眞字正法眼藏 (DZZ.5:138, case 24); see Supplementary Notes, s.v. "Goes along with it."

60. The 37 Factors of Bodhi *Sanjūshichi hon bodai bunpō* 三十七品菩提分法

[60:85]

この三十七品菩提分法、すなはち佛祖の眼睛鼻孔・皮肉骨髓・手足面目なり。佛祖一枚、これを三十七品菩提分法と參學しきたれり。しかあれども、一千三百六十九品の公案現成なり、菩提分法なり。坐斷すべし、脱落すべし。

These thirty-seven factors of bodhi are the *eye and nose, the skin, flesh, bones, and marrow, the hands, feet, and face* of the buddhas and ancestors. The whole of the buddhas and ancestors — this is what we have been studying as the thirty-seven factors of bodhi. Nevertheless, they are one thousand three hundred sixty-nine kōans realized; they are the factors of bodhi.[189] We should cut them off; we should slough them off.[190]

正法眼藏三十七品菩提分法第六十
Treasury of the True Dharma Eye
The Thirty-seven Factors of Bodhi
Number 60[191]

[Ryūmonji MS:]

爾時寬元二年甲辰二月二十四日、在越宇吉峰精舍示衆
Presented to the assembly at the Yoshimine Vihāra, Etsuu; twenty-fourth day, second month of the senior wood year of the dragon, the second year of Kangen [3 April 1244][192]

---

189 **one thousand three hundred sixty-nine kōans realized** (*issen sanbyaku rokujūkyū bon no kōan genjō* 一千三百六十九品の公案現成): The thirty-seven factors squared, expressed as spiritual cases. See Supplementary Notes, s.v. "Realized kōan."

190 **We should cut them off; we should slough them off** (*zadan subeshi, datsuraku subeshi* 坐斷すべし、脱落すべし): The term *zadan* 坐斷, in ordinary parlance meaning "to occupy [a territory]", is used in Zen texts in the sense "to break completely," "to reject totally" (where *za* 坐 is taken as *za* 挫); it is often interpreted in Sōtō literature as "sitting completely" or "sitting and cutting off." Here, its juxtaposition with *datsuraku* 脱落 is reminiscent of the admonition Dōgen attributes to Rujing that we should "just sit" (*shikan taza* 只管打坐) and "slough off body and mind" (*shinjin datsuraku* 身心脱落). See Supplementary Notes, s.v. "Just sit" and "Body and mind sloughted off."

191 The Ryūmonji 龍門寺 and some other early MSS follow this end title with two citations, reproduced in the end notes of Kawamura's edition:

大集經云、三十七品是菩薩寶炬陀羅尼。
In the *Daji jing*, it is said, "The thirty-seven factors are the treasure torch *dhāraṇī*." (Quoting the *Mohe zhiguan* 摩訶止觀 at T.1911.46:88a8, in reference to a verse in the *Mahāsaṃnipāta-sūtra* [*Daji jing* 大集經, T397.13:25a9-26b12].)

瑜伽師地論第十八曰、修習三十七種菩提分法。
In fascicle 18 of the *Yuqie shidi lun*, it is said, "Practice the thirty-seven factors of bodhi." (Quoting the *Yogācārabhūmi-śāstra* [*Yuqie shidi lun* 瑜伽師地論, T.1579.30:375a13-14, 375a20-21].)

192 The *Himitsu* 秘密 MS shares an identical colophon.

[*Himitsu* MS:]

同三月九日、在同峰下侍司書寫之。懷奘

Copied this, in the acolyte's office, beneath the same peak; ninth day, third month of the same year [17 April 1244]. Ejō

The Sōtō Zen Text Project *Shōbōgenzō*

Volume I
The Seventy-five-Chapter Compilation, Part 1

1. The Realized Kōan *Genjō kōan* 現成公案
2. Mahā-prajñā-pāramitā *Maka hannya haramitsu* 摩訶般若波羅蜜
3. Buddha Nature *Busshō* 佛性
4. Studying the Way with Body and Mind *Shinjin gakudō* 身心學道
5. This Mind Itself Is the Buddha *Soku shin ze butsu* 即心是佛
6. Deportment of the Practicing Buddha *Gyōbutsu iigi* 行佛威儀
7. One Bright Pearl *Ikka myōju* 一顆明珠
8. The Mind Cannot Be Got *Shin fukatoku* 心不可得
9. The Old Buddha Mind *Kobutsushin* 古佛心
10. Great Awakening *Daigo* 大悟
11. Principles of Seated Meditation *Zazen gi* 坐禪儀
12. Needle of Seated Meditation *Zazen shin* 坐禪箴
13. Ocean Seal Samādhi *Kaiin zanmai* 海印三昧
14. Sky Flowers *Kūge* 空華
15. Radiance *Kōmyō* 光明

Volume II
The Seventy-five-Chapter Compilation, Part 2

16A. Sustained Practice, Part 1 *Gyōji jō* 行持上
16B. Sustained Practice, Part 2 *Gyōji ge* 行持下
17. Such *Inmo* 恁麼
18. Avalokiteśvara *Kannon* 觀音
19. The Old Mirror *Kokyō* 古鏡
20. Sometimes *Uji* 有時
21. Prediction *Juki* 授記
22. Full Function *Zenki* 全機
23. The Moon *Tsuki* 都機
24. Painted Cake *Gabyō* 畫餅
25. Sound of the Stream, Form of the Mountain *Keisei sanshoku* 谿聲山色
26. Beyond the Buddha *Butsu kōjō ji* 佛向上事
27. Talking of a Dream within a Dream *Muchū setsumu* 夢中説夢
28. Making a Bow and Getting the Marrow *Raihai tokuzui* 禮拜得髓
29. The Mountains and Waters Sūtra *Sansui kyō* 山水經
30. Sūtra Reading *Kankin* 看經

Volume III
The Seventy-five-Chapter Compilation, Part 3

31. Do No Evil *Shoaku makusa* 諸惡莫作
32. Transmitting the Robe *Den'e* 傳衣
33. Sayings *Dōtoku* 道得
34. The Teachings of the Buddhas *Bukkyō* 佛教
35. Spiritual Powers *Jinzū* 神通
36. The Arhat *Arakan* 阿羅漢

37. Spring and Autumn *Shunjū* 春秋
38. Tangled Vines *Kattō* 葛藤
39. The Inheritance Certificate *Shisho* 嗣書
40. The Cypress Tree *Hakujushi* 柏樹子
41. The Three Realms Are Only Mind *Sangai yui shin* 三界唯心
42. Talking of the Mind, Talking of the Nature *Sesshin sesshō* 説心説性
43. The Real Marks of the Dharmas *Shohō jissō* 諸法實相
44. The Way of the Buddhas *Butsudō* 佛道
45. Secret Words *Mitsugo* 密語

Volume IV
The Seventy-five-Chapter Compilation, Part 4

46. The Insentient Preach the Dharma *Mujō seppō* 無情説法
47. Sūtras of the Buddhas *Bukkyō* 佛經
48. Dharma Nature *Hosshō* 法性
49. Dhāraṇī *Darani* 陀羅尼
50. Washing the Face *Senmen* 洗面
51. Face-to-Face Conferral *Menju* 面授
52. Buddhas and Ancestors *Busso* 佛祖
53. Plum Blossoms *Baika* 梅華
54. Washing and Purifying *Senjō* 洗淨
55. The Ten Directions *Jippō* 十方
56. Seeing Buddha *Kenbutsu* 見佛
57. Extensive Study *Henzan* 遍參
58. The Eye *Ganzei* 眼睛
59. Everyday Matters *Kajō* 家常
60. The Thirty-seven Factors of Bodhi *Sanjūshichi hon bodai bunpō* 三十七品菩提分法

Volume V
The Seventy-five-Chapter Compilation, Part 5

61. Song of the Dragon *Ryūgin* 龍吟
62. The Intention of the Ancestral Master's Coming from the West
    Soshi seirai i 祖師西來意
63. Bringing Forth the Mind of Bodhi *Hotsu bodai shin* 發菩提心
64. The Udumbara Blossom *Udonge* 優曇華
65. The Entire Body of the Tathāgata *Nyorai zenshin* 如來全身
66. The King of Samādhis Samādhi *Zanmai ō zanmai* 三昧王三昧
67. Turning the Dharma Wheel *Ten hōrin* 轉法輪
68. Great Practice *Dai shugyō* 大修行
69. The Samādhi of Self Verification *Jishō zanmai* 自證三昧
70. Empty Space *Kokū* 虛空
71. The Pātra Bowl *Hou* 鉢盂
72. The Retreat *Ango* 安居
73. Reading Other Minds *Tashin tsū* 他心通
74. The King Requests Saindhava *Ō saku sendaba* 王索仙陀婆
75. Leaving Home *Shukke* 出家

Volume VI
The Twelve-Chapter Compilation

T1. The Merit of Leaving Home *Shukke kudoku* 出家功德
T2. Receiving the Precepts *Jukai* 受戒
T3. The Merit of the Kāṣāya *Kesa kudoku* 袈裟功德
T4. Bringing Forth the Mind of Bodhi *Hotsu bodai shin* 發菩提心
T5. Offerings to the Buddhas *Kuyō shobutsu* 供養諸佛
T6. Refuge in the Treasures of Buddha, Dharma, and Saṃgha
  Kie buppōsōbō 歸依佛法僧寶
T7. Deep Faith in Cause and Effect *Jinshin inga* 深信因果
T8. Karma of the Three Times *Sanjigō* 三時業
T9. Four Horses *Shime* 四馬
T10. The Bhikṣu of the Fourth Dhyāna *Shizen biku* 四禪比丘
T11. One Hundred Eight Gateways to the Illumination of the Dharma
  Ippyakuhachi hōmyōmon 一百八法明門
T12. The Eight Understandings of the Great Person *Hachi dainin gaku* 八大人覺

Volume VII
Supplementary Chapters, Variant Texts

Supplementary Chapters

S1. Talk on Pursuing the Way *Bendōwa* 辦道話
S2. Procedures for the Hall of Gathered Clouds *Jūundō shiki* 重雲堂式
S3. The *Lotus* Turns the *Lotus* *Hokke ten Hokke* 法華轉法華
S4. The Mind Cannot Be Got *Shin fukatoku* 心不可得
S5. The Four Attractions of the Bodhisattva *Bodaisatta shishōbō* 菩提薩埵四攝法
S6. Instructions to the Administration Cloister *Ji kuin mon* 示庫院文
S7. Only Buddhas with Buddhas *Yui butsu yo butsu* 唯佛與佛
S8. Birth and Death *Shōji* 生死
S9. The Way of the Buddhas *Butsudō* 佛道 (*Dōshin* 道心)

Variant Texts

V1. Talk on Pursuing the Way *Bendōwa* 辦道話
V2. The Inheritance Certificate *Shisho* 嗣書
V3. Beyond the Buddha *Butsu kōjō ji* 佛向上事
V4. Washing the Face *Senmen* 洗面
V5. Extensive Study *Henzan* 遍參
V6. Great Awakening *Daigo* 大悟
V7. Karma of the Three Times *Sanji gō* 三時業

Volume VIII

Introduction
Appendices
Supplementary Notes
Works Cited